BETWEEN CHURCH AND STATE

BETWEEN CHURCH AND STATE

The Lives of Four French Prelates in the Late Middle Ages

BERNARD GUENÉE

Translated by Arthur Goldhammer

The University of Chicago Press
Chicago and London

BERNARD GUENÉE is professor of history at the Sorbonne and director of studies at the École Pratique des Hautes Études in Paris.

Originally published as *Entre l'Église et l'État,*

The University of Chicago Press, Chicago 60637
The University of Chicago Press, Ltd., London

Printed in the United States of America

00 99 98 97 96 95 94 93 92 91 5 4 3 2 1

∞ The paper used in this publication meets the minimum requirements of the American National Standard for Information Sciences—Permanence of Paper for Printed Library Materials, ANSI Z39.48–1984.

Library of Congress Cataloging-in-Publication Data

Guenée, Bernard.
[Entre l'Eglise et l'Etat. English]
Between church and state : the lives of four French prelates in the late Middle Ages / Bernard Guenée ; translated by Arthur Goldhammer.
p. cm.
Translation of: Entre l'Eglise et l'Etat.
Includes bibliographical references.
Includes index.
ISBN 0-226-31032-9
1. Bernardus Guidonis, Bishop of Lodève, 1261 or 62–1331. 2. Le Muisit, Gilles, 1272–1353? 3. Ailly, Pierre d', 1350–1420? 4. Basin, Thomas, 1412–1491. 5. Catholic Church—France—Bishops—Biography. 6. Church and state—France—History. 7. France—Church history—Middle Ages, 987–1515. I. Title.
BX4682.G8413 1991
282'.092'244—dc20
[B] 90-35045
CIP

CONTENTS

INTRODUCTION

Biography and Biographies

The East was already devoting books to individuals well before the West adopted the practice. The Greeks began writing biographies some five centuries before the birth of Christ. By the time Jesus was born, biography was a fully independent genre. A biographer was not a historian.

Biographies multiplied rapidly. They abounded in the Hellenistic and, from the first century B.C. onward, Roman worlds. Since biography was a minor genre, however, biographies were not as likely as other works to survive the decline of the ancient world. Only a tiny fraction of the biographies written then still exist today. Yet what we have is enough to show that even among the ancients biography was already an ambiguous genre. The word was applied to a wide variety of works.

The reason for this diversity was that a biography had a specific function and was addressed to a specific audience; but there were many such functions and many such audiences. A scholar might write the life of a poet in order to help readers understand his works. A philosopher might write the life of a philosopher in order to explain his school's doctrine or to refute that of a rival school. A historian might write the life of a general, a prince, or a statesman in order to explain the wars or the political history of an age to more serious readers. Or, merely to please less serious ones, a storyteller might recount the adventures of a hero. A rhetor might eulogize a famous man after his death, in a panegyric intended to flatter a family's pride or affirm moral values or promulgate political ideas.

To perform these several functions biography assumed a variety of forms. Sometimes it was static, a simple catalogue of accomplishments or virtues. Sometimes it was chronological and traced an evolution. Sometimes it was both at once, assembling a series of fairly extensively developed chronological sequences into a static portrait. Usually, however, biography was narrative, although sometimes it was cast in the form of dialogue. In short, biography was protean.

And this Proteus, with its multifarious functions and varied forms, staked out a territory whose boundaries were ill defined. Biography was not history, but it could be close to history. Its object was different from that of history. The historian recounted noteworthy events and striking actions. The biographer looked for the trivial detail or anecdote that would illuminate a character or reveal a virtue. The childhood of a great man had no place in history, but it was essential in biography. Biography was not history, but the biographer sometimes felt quite close to the historian, whose insistent concern for the truth he might well share. The two approaches were so similar that the same man could work now as a biographer, now as a historian: Nicholas of Damascus, a contemporary of Augustus, wrote both a universal history and a life of Augustus. What is more, an author could even mix history and biography in a single work. Theopompus, who lived in the fourth century, B.C., began as a good pupil of Thucydides by writing *Hellenica.* In his *Philippica,* however, it was the life of Philip of Macedon that gave unity to the events with which it was contemporaneous. For the writer who saw himself as a historian, writing the life of a prince who, like Philip of Macedon, had dominated his times offered the best occasion for combining biography with history.

Suetonius did not succumb to that temptation, however, when he wrote the lives of the first twelve Caesars in the second century A.D. History held no attraction for him. His only goal was to write biographies. He loved the rare and unpublished document, the revealing and scabrous anecdote. And he had a passion for facts, a hunger to explore archives. He was one of many ancient biographers who left history to the historians and attempted to make biography a discipline of language and erudition.

Erudition could be oppressive, however, for both the author and his reader. Too much of the life and character of the person whose existence one hoped to recreate was left in the dark. The biographer therefore made up episodes, recreated conversations, and little by little abandoned the truth, the better to amuse and instruct his reader. Xenophon's *Cyropaedia* (fourth century B.C.) was the most fully developed of these biographical novels, but it was not the first, and it had many imitators.

One other feature also contributed to the diversity of ancient biography. Lives of isolated individuals were of course written. But very early, perhaps from the very beginning, a life was written in conjunction with other lives. These were gathered into anthologies or collections: lives of poets glorified literature: lives of philosophers glorified a particular philosophical school; lives of a family's ancestors glorified that family. The point is that it is not at all certain that the original purpose of biography was to comprehend the life of an individual. It was rather to define a particular type of man, establish a model, set an example, hold up an ideal. The collective biography allowed the reader to discern, beyond the features of a man, the characteristics of a group. In the third century B.C. Neanthes of Cyzicus wrote an anthology of lives of illustrious men, an anthology about which we know nothing except that it is evidence of a tradition that Rome would carry on and of which some traces remain. In the first century B.C. Cornelius Nepos wrote *De viris illustribus,* of which one book, dealing with great generals of foreign nations, has survived. In the second century A.D. Suetonius wrote another *De viris illustribus,* of which one book, dealing with grammarians and rhetors, has also survived. The primary purpose of these works, like that of modern biographical dictionaries, was to satisfy the curiosity of literate minds. Yet the choice of "illustrious" men is revealing. Certain groups were glorified; certain values were emphasized. The "Lives of Illustrious Men" put biography at the service of erudition that was often solid but never innocent.[1]

Biography first appeared in Western culture in the fifth century B.C., and since then it has been produced in a never-ending stream. At certain times, perhaps, that stream has run wider than at other times. Caution is in order, however. There is a danger of being misled by what happens to have survived. Nevertheless, it seems clear that from the first century B.C. to the beginning of the second century A.D., a period of some two hundred years, the Roman pagan world was particularly prolific in the field of biography, with such authors as Varro, Cornelius Nepos, Nicholas of Damascus, Tacitus, Valerius Maximus, Suetonius, and Plutarch, to mention a few of the most prominent names.

Early Christian literature was also receptive to biography. Christian writers adapted ancient forms to the new age. In 392 Saint Jerome wrote a *De viris illustribus* in order to contrast the lives of illustrious pagans with those of recent Christian authors. In 397 Sulpicius Severus wrote his *Life of Saint Martin,* which used the classical forms of ancient biography in service of the new Christian values. Countless lives of saints followed the *Vita Martini,* but for centuries hagiography answered the needs of the Christian liturgy and of Christian spirituality; the saint's life was devoted not so much to an individual as to an ideal and was concerned less with truth than with exemplary virtues. Still, not all biography was hagiography, despite the abundant hagiographic output. Ten years after the death of Charlemagne, between 820 and 830, Eginhard wrote the *Vita Karoli,* which revived the Suetonian tradition. In 1111 Sigebert of Gembloux composed a *De viris illustribus* that harked back to the erudite tradition of Saint Jerome. In 1144 Abbot Suger wrote a *Life of Louis VI,* which was actually a history of his reign. In the same period chansons de geste recounted the lives of heroes in an epic setting. In the third decade of the thirteenth century the *Life of William Marshall* was written to glorify a family. Standing midway between history and epic, it offered knights the model of a man who embodied all the virtues of their group.[2] In the thirteenth century biography was more than ever a rich, diverse, and complex genre.

We thus come to the period with which this book is concerned. Around 1255, shortly before the birth of Bernard Gui in Limousin, a young Italian Dominican by the name of Jacobus da Varagine wrote the *Golden Legend,* a remarkable collection of saints' lives that met with immediate and lasting success. Shortly before 1300, William of Nangis, the great historian of Saint-Denis, wrote a biography of Louis IX, who died in 1270, and of his son Philip III (the Bold), who died in 1285. The biography of Louis IX was one of several works that were written in order to obtain the beatification of the saintly king. In these two biographies, however, William of Nangis set out to write a work of history. Rather than attach the ambiguous title *Vita* to his two compositions, he called them *Gesta,* which clearly indicated the historical genre.

Between 1332 and 1336 in Avignon (at that time the residence of the pope and one of the leading centers of European culture), Giovanni Colonna, following the examples of Saint Jerome and Sigebert of Gembloux, composed a *De viris illustribus.* Recent advances in literacy gave him the idea of arranging his illustrious men in alphabetical order.[3] The first biographical dictionary was thus a work of secular erudition. Francesco Petrarch had met Colonna in Avignon and knew his work. In 1337 he, too, set out to write a *De viris illustribus,* on which he worked for nearly forty years, until his death. His ambition, however, was not to compile a dictionary. He wanted to be a historian. Using the tools of critical scholarship he hoped to discover the truth and then to cast it in the most beautiful Latin possible; in this way he aimed to present to his readers, as Sallust and Livy had done, examples to be emulated or avoided.[4] Petrarch was still living when Boccaccio wrote his life of Dante, which was the first literary biography, as well as *De claris mulieribus,* a collection of 104 lives of celebrated women from Eve to Queen Jeanne of Naples, who was then still alive. The latter work attested to the new place of women in society.

At the same time, in France, other biographies followed the trail blazed by the *Life of William Marshall.* These works were at once histories, epics, and "mirrors" that reflected the virtues of knighthood: among them were the *Life of Bertrand du Guesclin* (written during the reign of Charles V); the *Book of Deeds of the Good Lord Jehan le Maingre, known as Bouciquaut, Marshal of France and Governor of Jennes* (1409)[5] and *The Chronicle of the Good Duke Loys de Bourbon.* In 1404 Christine de Pisan wrote *The Book of the Deeds and Good Morals of the Sage King Charles V,* which she cast, in the manner of Suetonius, in a static form, dealing in succession with "the virtues and properties of noble courage, chivalry, and wisdom" that the king had so admirably exemplified.[6]

There is no need to multiply examples. I shall end with Thomas Basin, who in 1471 began writing histories of Charles VII and Louis XI. His aim, as he tells us himself, was to follow the example of others before him who had written lives of illustrious men (*virorum illustrium vitas*). Nevertheless, his goal was to write the history of the two kings' reigns, of their *res gestas.* Like all historians, he wanted his true narrative (*veridica narracione*) to serve as a mirror (*veluti speculum quoddam*) in which his reader might find some examples to emulate and others to avoid.[7] Thus, in these times of tradition, renaissance, and innovation, biographies proliferated, and in their abundant diversity men became heralds of faith and chivalry, subjects for history and erudition, objects of poetry and truth, and mirrors of morality.

Were I to follow the way in which biographical writing was revived and ancient forms were adapted to relatively new needs, I fear that I would tire my reader. I shall therefore proceed directly to an admittedly rather minor episode in the twenty-five-hundred-year history of biography. In France, during the romantic era of the nineteenth century, biography triumphed. Historians, scholars, and novelists all wrote biographies. Not all biographies were works of history or scholarship, but no one doubted that biography could be a historical genre. For the past 150 years biographies have enjoyed more or less uninterrupted success.[8] But the relation between history and biography has changed greatly, for at the end of the nineteenth century history began to turn its attention away from man and toward men. It began to concentrate on studying the general as opposed to the particular: institutions, structures, long-term trends.

It began to count, to weigh, and to measure.[9] Biography thereupon ceased to be of interest to history. It prospered nonetheless. The lives of exemplary men and women continued to illustrate virtues, whether republican or national or religious. Driven out of the territory of the historians, individual men and women continued to inhabit the republicans' pantheon and the Christians' paradise. Fictionalized biography, whose authors blended truth with fiction and offered their readers pleasant and cultivated entertainment, also became popular in this period. Biography, which in some ways resembled the novel and in other ways the fable, was surely a literary genre, but for historians it was a minor genre, nonhistorical and even antihistorical.[10]

Over the last ten or twenty years, however, history and biography have once again drawn closer together. History has tired of being faceless and flavorless. It is turning back to the qualitative and the singular. And biography is regaining its place among the genres of history. Yet it is not on that account renouncing the ties it has always had with the moral fable and imaginative fiction. Taking a variety of forms in order to fill different functions and reach different audiences, biography is more protean and elusive than ever. Furthermore, although history is now quite willing to strike up a relationship with biography, it remains suspicious. It asks itself which forms of biography are worthy of it. It sets a variety of conditions. It dreams of masterpieces that only a past master of all the human sciences could possibly write. Biography has become a difficult, not to say impossible, genre. It is not too misleading to say that biography, once the victim of undue scorn, is now paralyzed by unwarranted expectations.[11]

Such, at any rate, are my feelings today. The idea of writing biographies came to me in 1983. At that time it seemed quite simple. But now that I have become aware of biography's heavily freighted past and problematic present and have endured several difficult years of research and composition, I am daunted by what, upon reflection, I should have done and by how little I have in fact been able to do. And I feel obliged to justify myself, and to help my reader understand where my book fits into the larger scheme of things, by explaining how the idea came to me and precisely what I wanted to accomplish.

In 1983 I taught a one-year graduate course on the late medieval Church in which I set forth, as is customary in graduate courses, some rather large problems. I was obliged, however, to teach a second-year course on the same subject, and it occurred to me to examine the same problems by looking at the lives of a number of individuals.

Did this idea come to me because of the evolution I described a moment ago? Or was it the fruit of my own history? In any case, it was quite clear that the study of structures remained indispensable. Structuralist history illuminated the past with a wonderfully coherent light, but it also made things too simple, and biography offered one way of exploring the overwhelming complexity of things. The study of structures, it seemed to me, gives necessity more than its due. Seen from a lofty elevation and in retrospect, the history of the world may well look coherent and necessary. But "things happen only through men."[12] And the story of a life helps us to see how fragile and uncertain the destinies of these men are. Biography, it seemed to me, should make it possible to pay closer attention to chance, to events, to chronological sequence. It alone could give historians a sense of time as people actually experienced it. History and biography, I believed, are two complementary ways of getting at the same reality. The fate of a man could aid in understanding the history of a time.

Conversely, however, the only way to understand the fate of a man is by knowing the history of the times in which he lived. Biography is ill advised if it claims to be sufficient unto itself and if it aims to unfold its singularity in a vacuum. I admire those "professional" biographers who are able to jump from one "subject" and one "age" to another. But since I myself am only an amateur biographer, my only ambition is to trace the fates of individuals who lived in times, places, and milieus with which I am familiar.

The crucial question for a historian writing a biography is this: Was the life that interests me an exemplary life or an extraordinary one? Does it give a good idea of the general case, or was it an exception? A life makes sense only when compared with other lives. One way to situate the individual life is to reconstitute the lives of other members of the same social or occupational group. Collective biography of this kind goes by the name *prosopography*. Prosopography today enjoys the favor of historians, who see it as a valuable new research tool. Upon reflection, however, it is clear that prosopography has a long history. It is but the latest version of all those works entitled *De viris illustribus* compiled by such men as Giovanni Colonna, Saint Jerome, Cornelius Nepos, and Neanthes of Cyzicus. Yet this new version has some specific characteristics that make it well suited to the present day. Prosopography aims to be exhaustive. It does not focus exclusively on the illustrious but also looks at the obscure. When all possible data have been gathered, a social history can be reconstructed with the aid of computers and statistical methods, and individual lives can then be examined against that background.[13]

Naturally I have nothing against prosopography. I practiced it myself, long ago to be sure and with the crude techniques that were then still permissible.[14] Today, however, I find something frustrating about what prosopographic methods are capable of revealing, at least as far as medieval history is concerned. They tell us about careers but not about individuals. We know what people did or what they owned but not what they hoped and feared, loved and hated. My sense was that another avenue lay open, another approach that could, I hoped, bring us closer to the individuals of the past: forget about being comprehensive, about investigating the anonymous masses, and look instead at those few individuals who left enough traces of their existence that we can hope to know them better. I am well aware that this means turning our attention back to a very circumscribed elite, men who knew how to read and write. But what choice do we have? Historians may deplore the obscurity that surrounds many of our ancestors. They may attempt to dispel that obscurity. But they cannot go beyond the sources. And in any case not all who wrote, even in the Middle Ages, were illustrious men. In many respects they were ordinary men marked by their time and place. They can be good witnesses, provided they are not relied upon as the sole witnesses. Thus the idea of doing a small number of comparative biographies suggested itself.

One possibility was to examine in parallel or in conjunction several lives that unfolded in the same time and milieu. This approach was taken by Jacques Verger and Jean Jolivet, who studied the lives of Abelard and Saint Bernard in order to gain a better understanding of the problems faced by intellectuals in the first half of the twelfth century.[15] I took a similar approach in the course I taught in 1983–84. Another possibility was to juxtapose lives of men who were contemporaries of one another but who lived in different milieus. The life of a cleric such as Pierre d'Ailly had nothing in common with that of the "good lord Jehan le Maingre, known as Bouciquaut, marshal of France," except that both men lived during the reign of Charles VI. By studying two such different lives we gain two distinct yet complementary views of the period.

Ultimately I settled on a third possibility. I chose to take as my subjects several individuals—bishops—from the same milieu but who lived in different times, indeed in successive periods. By thus linking four biographies end to end, I hoped to illuminate, from one of many possible angles at any rate, that period in the history of France with which I am least unfamiliar, the period that runs from the height of Saint Louis's reign to the beginning of the Italian wars—an expanse of time that is not without a certain unity. I hoped to trace, throughout this period, the characteristics of a group of individuals who were neither especially illustrious nor especially obscure and whose lives were spent in service to church and state. And, since these prelates to one degree or another revealed themselves in their writings, I hoped that behind the facts I would discover characters.

My four biographies are therefore intimately related. They look toward a single goal and form part of a single project. Their aim is to proceed from individual cases to general questions. I therefore availed myself of everything that scholars had already said about my four prelates. At times, perhaps, I added to this body of knowledge, but I have left a great deal for other scholars to do. I do not pretend to have said all there is to say about Bernard Gui, Gilles Le Muisit, Pierre d'Ailly, or Thomas Basin. But everything that I do say I read somewhere. As ardently as I may have wished to penetrate the souls of my four prelates, I never went beyond the sources. I never filled in their silences. I believed that my readers would prefer to hear, not my intuitions and interpretations, but what my four prelates said about themselves and their times. I willingly submitted to the tyranny of the sources—and to that of chronology as well, for I do not see how a biographer who wishes to understand the truth about the evolution of an individual life can be anything other than chronological.

I do not know what a psychiatrist might say about the relations I enjoyed for several years with my four prelates. I am well aware, however, that the questions I asked and the narratives I made of them tell a great deal about myself. But very few people will know precisely what. What I can say, though, is that this book stems equally from my work and from my teaching; that it is a necessary product of my time, my age, and my character; and that I couldn't not write it—which is probably my only excuse for having written it.

Between Church and State

In 1244 Louis IX took up the cross. In 1248 he led an army to the Holy Land. In 1266 his brother, Charles I of Anjou, was crowned king of Sicily by the pope. Hundreds of French knights also joined the crusade, traversed the mountains, and helped Charles conquer his kingdom. Thousands of Frenchmen settled there. In 1270 Louis IX, having embraced the crusade once again, dispatched an army of ten thousand men by ship to Tunisia. In 1285 Philip III (the Bold), the saintly king's son and heir, took up the cross in turn and led the most powerful army ever commanded by a French king into battle with Aragon. A conquering France flaunted the cross but meanwhile asserted its worldly might.

Two centuries later the young king Charles VIII claimed to be the natural heir to the kingdom of Naples. In 1494 he crossed the mountains and set out to conquer his realm. This "journey to Naples" marked the beginning of the Italian wars as well as the return of conquering France.

In the intervening two centuries, however, France had experienced a host of misfortunes. Economic difficulties made the late thirteenth century a time of tension and uncertainty. In the early fourteenth century, after a long period of good harvests, famine returned, perhaps because the climate deteriorated, perhaps because the level of agricultural technology was no longer sufficient to meet the country's needs. In any case, France would suffer shortages for a long time to come. In the middle of the fourteenth century plague from the Orient invaded the port cities of the Mediterranean, spread throughout Europe, and killed perhaps a third of the population. Epidemic subsequently became endemic. Plague flared up now and again in various places, and for a few months ravaged a town or province. Men witnessed its return more than once in the course of a lifetime. Finally, even before the plague struck, a war had begun between France and England. Though punctuated by periods of truce and relative calm, this war, complicated by another between France and Burgundy, continued to rage for some 150 years, during which France experienced a number of disastrous "days." But even those defeats were less dreadful than the daily insecurity stemming from the enemy's raids and occupation, the damage done by armed men in both camps, and the violence of civil war. It is not hard to see why the French people in those days beseeched God to deliver them: "*A fame, bello et peste, libera nos, Domine*" (From hunger, war, and plague, deliver us, Lord).

Yet these endless sufferings were not in vain. The French came to love their imperiled country more than ever. They wished for a stronger king, one better able to protect them in their time of trial. These hard times were in fact the gestation period of the modern state. France was not simply saved at the end of the fifteenth century; it became something it had never been before. And the first thing that changed was its relation to the Church.

In the thirteenth century the Church was universal, and the state had grown up in its shadow. The state had fortified itself with the Church's cash. It had used the cross to justify its activities. It had employed clerics who naturally served both Church and state. This close alliance between the universal Church and the kingdom of France had been strengthened still further when the pope, weary of Italy's troubles, had settled at Avignon on France's border in the early fourteenth century. Soon, however, the Church, like the state, faced new difficulties. Scrupulous Christians demanded reform. Strengthened states began to resist the authority of the universal Church. Above all, tensions between the administrative center of the Church, now located in Avignon, and the spiritual center, which remained in Rome, reached intolerable levels. In 1378 a series of chance events led to what was probably an inevitable conclusion. The Church was torn by schism—the Great Schism, which would last for forty years. In 1417 the Church regained its erstwhile unity but not its former authority. It was forced to abandon some of its universal claims and to accept limits imposed by various states, limits that were more or less strict as those states were more or less proud. Soon the one great question was, Would the various national churches establish themselves in opposition to the pope or with his approval? Nearly everywhere the pope and the princes reached agreements. Concordats were signed in which the princes recognized the authority of the pope and the pope granted the princes authority over the churches in their territories. In France, however, a strong Gallican current delayed agreement between the pope and the king. But the concordat of 1472 laid the groundwork for, and the concordat of 1516 consecrated, a Gallican church subject to the king's authority. At the dawn of the sixteenth century the king of France was sovereign of a strong state and master of a loyal church. French clerics were in no doubt about which master to obey.

In the two intervening centuries, between the conquering France of the Middle Ages and the conquering France of the sixteenth century, between the universal Church and the national church, French clerics experienced difficulty and uncertainty. There were, broadly speaking, two parallel but distinct societies, the Church and the state, equally imperiled and equally demanding. To the state political loyalty was what orthodoxy was to the Church. Lèse-majesté was a heresy. The four prelates about whom I shall have something to say were alike, therefore, in that all had to live through these difficult and uncertain times in both the church and the state—or, more precisely, between church and state.

Four French Prelates

My four prelates were not contemporaries. On the contrary, they form a more or less continuous chain that covers the entire period just defined. Bernard Gui, who was born in 1261 under Saint Louis and who died in 1331 under Philip VI of Valois, knew the problems of France in the days of the last direct Capetians, Philip IV (the Fair) and Charles IV (also the Fair). Gilles Le Muisit, who was born eleven years later but who died at eighty-one in 1353, confronted the difficulties of the early 1300s and the dramas of midcentury. Pierre d'Ailly, born in 1351 and educated under Charles V, endured the trials of Charles VI's reign and then died in 1420 at sixty-nine, a short while before the demise of his ill-fated sovereign. And Thomas Basin, born in 1412, knew the desperate early years of Charles VII's reign as well as the later triumphs and the tumultuous times of Louis XI; he died in 1450 under Charles VIII, shortly before the beginning of the Italian wars.

All four of my prelates were born in the kingdom of France. But within that immense realm, which took twenty-two days to cross from north to south and sixteen days from west to east (so that people said it was twenty-two days long by sixteen days wide), in a kingdom that was diversity personified, these four men came from very different backgrounds. Their horizons were not the same. Bernard Gui was born near Limoges. Nearly all his life was spent in the south of France. He crossed the Loire only once and quickly returned to more familiar surroundings. Gilles Le Muisit was born on the very northern fringe of the kingdom, in Tournai. He lived for a time in Paris but knew nothing of the kingdom to the south. Pierre d'Ailly was born in Compiègne, not far from Paris. Although he was bishop of Le Puy, he never went there. Thomas Basin was born in Caudebec-en-Caux. A Norman, he already had a view of France different from that of Pierre d'Ailly and Gilles Le Muisit, but the time he spent in Roussillon was one of the great dramas of his life. The fact is that the one place these four prelates had in common was not France but Avignon (in the fourteenth century) and Rome (in the fifteenth). Sooner or later every bishop had to go to the pope.

My four prelates enjoyed different degrees of worldly success. Pierre d'Ailly was a man whose ambitions were gratified. He was one of the leading figures of his day and died a cardinal. Bernard Gui was a conscientious inquisitor who was belatedly rewarded with a modest bishopric. This faithful servant of God may have dreamed of a more brilliant career, but he certainly did not have one. By contrast, Gilles Le Muisit certainly did not dream of being anything more than he was, namely, abbot of Saint-Martin of Tournai and happy to be so. He lived and died near where he was born. And it is also certain that Thomas Basin dreamed of a brilliant career and that he briefly came close to power but that in the end his life was a total failure. When all is said and done, Basin played only a modest role. But as a defeated old man he wrote an invaluable memoir of his life and times. Therefore Pierre d'Ailly deserves more attention as an actor, and Thomas Basin as a witness, than my other two bishops, who were more modest as actors and more discreet as witnesses.

My prelates are thus all different from one another. But they have at least one thing in common: birth did not determine their fates.

Birth

Consider Guy of Boulogne. He was born in 1316, the son of Robert VII, count of Auvergne and Boulogne. In 1323, at seven, he became canon of Rheims; in 1340, at twenty-four, he became archbishop of Lyons; and in 1342, at twenty-six, he became a cardinal.[16] Consider next Robert of Geneva. He was born in 1342 at the château of Annecy. He was the son of Amadeus III, the count of Geneva, and the nephew of Gui of Boulogne. In 1361, at nineteen, he became bishop of Thérouanne. In 1371, at twenty-nine, he became a cardinal. And in 1378, at thirty-six, he even became pope, under the name Clement VII. Or again, consider Peter of Luxemburg. Born in 1369, he was only a scion of the cadet branch of the Luxemburgs, but still a Luxemburg, kin of emperors and kings. In 1378, at nine, he became canon of Notre-Dame of Paris; in 1384, at fifteen, he became bishop of Metz and then cardinal. In 1387, at eighteen, he died in the odor of sanctity. And finally, consider Guillaume of Estouteville. Born in 1412, he was the son of John of Estouteville, grand bouteiller of France, and of Marguerite of Harcourt. Through her he was the grandson of John VI of Harcourt, the brother-in-law of King Charles V and the nephew of Louis of Harcourt, archbishop of Rouen. In 1439, at twenty-seven, he became a bishop and cardinal.

Compare these men with my four prelates. Thomas Basin was the son of a wealthy Norman merchant. In 1447, at thirty-five, he became bishop of Lisieux. Pierre d'Ailly was the son of a wealthy bourgeois from Compiègne. In 1395, at forty-four, he became bishop of Le Puy; then, in 1411, at sixty, he was named cardinal. Gilles Le Muisit was the son of a wealthy bourgeois from Tournai. In 1331, at fifty-nine, he was abbot of Saint-Martin of Tournai. Bernard Gui was born into a modest and obscure family. In 1323, at sixty-two, he became bishop of Tuy.

Clearly we are looking at two very different career patterns. For some it was enough to be born; for others, including my four prelates, no miter lay waiting in the cradle. It is a mistake, however, to think that the first group consisted of nobles and the second of non-nobles. The real difference lay elsewhere. The first group consisted of "great lords or personages."[17] The second consisted of men who sprang from the minor nobility or the prosperous bourgeoisie or even more modest backgrounds. Their careers owed little to birth.

But the relatively modest background of this second group did not prevent their advancement. Medieval society is often thought of as static, and it is true that it liked to portray itself as one of stable hierarchy in a stable world. Philippe de Mézières said: "The government and police of a kingdom are very good when the prince maintains the inhabitants of the realm each in his degree. . . . One must not usurp the dignity and office of another."[18] Indeed, many people in this stable world did find their place marked out for them at birth. Frequently, however, one saw "the degrees of public persons perverted and altered."[19] Many continually ascended and descended the rungs of this hierarchy, carried along by the whims of fortune and carrying relatives and friends with them in their rise and fall. Medieval society was subjected to unbearable tension between the stability of which it dreamed and the mobility that reality imposed, between its proclaimed respect for a hierarchy based on birth and the obscure but constant desire to transgress that hierarchy.

My four prelates are alike in that their fates are not explained, or are explained in only very small measure, by their birth. If they rose in the social hierarchy, if they were able to compensate for their modest beginnings by acquiring the dignity of office, if they could become men of authority, it was because they had something else in them, ambition above all.

Ambition

Nicholas of Toulon was a native of the village of Toulon, to the south of Autun. Although his family was quite obscure, Nicholas was an ambitious man. One day, while still quite young, he told his mother he would be a bishop. The good woman laughed at her son and told him that on that day she would give him a white jay. But Nicholas did not lose hope. He found employment with the duke of Burgundy. In 1362 he became chaplain of Autun. In 1365 he became a canon. He served the duke so well that he became his chancellor, and finally, in 1386 (at which time he was probably more than fifty), he became bishop of Autun. Having no coat of arms, the man whose ambitions had been vindicated chose for his escutcheon a silver jay on a field of gules.[20]

Jean Balue, born in Poitou in 1421, was a man of rather lowly origins. He toiled for many years in the service of the bishop of Poitiers before going to work for the bishop of Angers. At forty Jean Balue had still not amounted to much. But he was introduced to Louis XI in 1463, after which his fortunes rose rapidly. He became bishop of Angers in 1465 at forty-four and cardinal in 1467 at forty-six. On Sunday, November 17, 1468, he received his cardinal's hat in a solemn ceremony at Notre-Dame in Paris. Jean Jouffroy, cardinal of Albi, delivered a speech full of venomous praise. The new cardinal's brilliant career proved that the pope and the king could do as they pleased. Yielding to the king's pleadings, the pope had bestowed the illustrious dignity of cardinal on an otherwise undistinguished individual, who to be sure had demonstrated talents but of a fairly common variety. Nevertheless, the orator acknowledged that the new prince of the Church possessed a flexible mind (*ingenium ad cuncta versatile*), considerable industriousness (*summam solertiam*), and an uncommon degree of ambition. The example of Jean Balue proved the truth of Appian's dictum, "Every man is the artisan of his own fortune" (*Unumquemque fabrum esse suae fortunae*), and of Quintilian's, "Those who reach the summit are those who tried" (*Qui ad summa nituntur in cacumina vadunt*).[21] Like Nicholas of Toulon, Jean Balue demonstrated that no one rose without ambition.

And Nicholas of Toulon's fourteenth century, like Jean Balue's fifteenth century, was a time when ambition triumphed. In a sense ambition became an eighth deadly sin, a new addition to the list of seven that the Church had kept for centuries but that was little known outside the monasteries until the twelfth century, when the seven deadly sins proved a handy device for preaching and confession. Within a short time this list became a key to self-understanding, which people used to account for their misdeeds and woes.

Any man could fall victim to pride, avarice, lust, wrath, gluttony, envy, or sloth. But clerics had grasped the fact that the deadly sins did not affect all groups equally and that they were not all of equal importance in society. In the twelfth century, a seigneurial and rural time, the worst sin was the pride of the powerful. As the world evolved, the clergy, on which the changes were not lost, added other sins to the most serious category. When, in the twelfth and thirteenth centuries, the West's economic advances bestowed new importance on money, poverty became a great virtue, and avarice, particularly the avarice of merchants, became a sin as grave as pride.

Then, in the late thirteenth century, a series of revolts began that continued for more than two hundred years. All this violence convinced clerics that envy was a very grave sin indeed, in particular the envy of the humble, a consequence of their impatient estate, which drove them to sedition and rebellion. It was at this time, in the fourteenth century, that ambition took its place among the most important sins.

Although ambition was not one of the seven deadly sins, it had long been denounced by the Church. Ambition was in the first place avarice,[22] but it was not just avarice or desire for wealth but also desire for honors. A cleric tempted by ambition might aspire to become a bishop.[23] The Church was thus quite familiar with ambition, but it did not declare it to be a deadly sin. Ambition was too similar to avarice and too complex. Furthermore, in a relatively stable world, its evil effects were limited.

In the fourteenth century, however, ambition, as judged by the clergy, joined pride, avarice, and envy among the major vices. One reason for this was that the conceptual framework of seven deadly sins had proved too simple to accommodate the new reality, and a more sophisticated psychology made room for more complex passions. Another was the newfound influence of Cicero, who had had a great deal to say on the subject of ambition. Third and most important, a more mobile society, in which growing governments needed to fill rapidly expanding bureaucracies, offered plenty of opportunities for ambition to spawn and triumph in the service of Church and state. Ambition, which was at once desire for wealth, desire for power, and desire for honors and which impelled the servants of Church and state to strive always for more, became the day's chief evil.

Not all ambition was wicked, however. Only the most rigorous of clerics saw it as being in all cases a sin. If a cardinal or prelate or even canon desired a higher position, was that in itself to be condemned? Certainly not. Nicholas of Toulon had dreamed all his life of becoming a bishop. When he succeeded, there is not a shred of evidence that his satisfaction was diminished by the slightest remorse. When ambitious young men dreamed of careers in the chancellery or parlement, their desire to rise was justified in their eyes by the nobility of their purpose, which was to serve. Rather ingenuously they confounded serving God, serving the prince, serving the state, and serving themselves. As one of them put it with admirable skill, they wanted, "by shunning idleness, which is the mother of all vices and the cause of sudden perdition for the young . . . to strive . . . for honor and power in order to faithfully serve God and prince and republic, to help and to profit, in accordance with God's commandments."[24] Thus not all ambition was necessarily wicked. There was good ambition and there was bad ambition.

Wicked ambition was the daughter of excess. "My heart brimmed over with excess," the poet has Pierre de la Broce say after his fall in 1278.[25] The fall of many other royal favorites in the fourteenth and fifteenth centuries was applauded by contemporaries who believed that they had been justly punished for having aimed too high or risen too fast after starting too low. Ambition in itself was not condemnable, but it was condemnable to be driven too hard by ambition, "*per ambitionem nimiam.*"[26]

Wicked ambition was the mother of pride. Ambition was to be condemned if, once the ambitious man achieved power, he succumbed to the sin that so often afflicted the powerful, namely, pride. Folk wisdom was even warier of the pride of parvenus than of the pride of princes: "When a beggar becomes a lord, there's more pride in him than in a born prince."[27]

Wicked ambition, finally, was ambition that did not follow the straight and narrow path on its rise to the top. If contemporaries judged Jean Balue's ambition condemnable, it was because they felt that he owed his cardinal's hat less to talent than to intrigue. To be legitimate, ambition had to "strive loyally and reasonably for honor and power."[28] Ambitious men were not to be condemned if they rose in consequence of "their merits and great virtues and services."[29]

My four prelates are alike in that all rose in the social hierarchy. They all strove for higher position, with more or less ardor and more or less success as the case may be. All four were ambitious men. Unlike their enemies, however, who exhibited wicked ambition, they embodied good ambition. Their talents and merits provided sufficient justification for it.

Knowledge and Talent

Among the merits that rendered ambition legitimate, the first was knowledge. That "great clerics" should be able to rise seemed normal.[30] Now, while Bernard Gui was able to obtain his education from Dominican schools exclusively, the usual way of acquiring knowledge in the late Middle Ages was the university. No one has ever doubted the value of thirteenth-century universities, but for a long time fourteenth- and fifteenth-century universities have not enjoyed a good reputation among historians, who believed that this was a period when professors were mediocre men who issued worthless degrees to the sons of the wealthy. Today this judgment stands in need of revision.

Teaching in Paris in the fourteenth century was not mediocre in either the faculty of arts or the faculty of theology. Jean Buridan, Nicolas Oresme, Pierre d'Ailly, and Jean Gerson, among others, were very great teachers and very great minds. Fourteenth-century thought was marked by nominalism. The culture of the fourteenth century was enriched by humanism. Decisive advances were made in both areas at the University of Paris. It is true that, in the first half of the fifteenth century, the civil war and later the English occupation had a severe impact on the university. These were hard times for the Sorbonne as well as for France. Like everyone else, Thomas Basin knew that the University of Paris under Louis XI was no longer what it had been under Charles VI. But the University of Paris was not the only university in France, and, taken together, French universities in the late fifteenth century turned out more graduates than they had done a century earlier.

Of course university studies in the fourteenth and fifteenth centuries were expensive. Some of the students were indeed the sons of wealthy bourgeois and did not work very hard. It can be confidently stated, however, that "the social recruitment of the universities remained quite open until the end of the Middle Ages."[31] In plain language, this means that more nobles studied in the universities than scholars for a long time thought, and that far more poor students attended than scholars were for a long time willing to believe. Although studies were costly, scholarships or subsidies awarded by princes[32] and cities[33] made it possible for poor young men to attend. Peter of Luxemburg, kin of emperors and of the kings of France, studied at the University of Paris. But so did Jean Gerson, whose parents' only wealth was children; and Nicolas de Baye, whose father was a poor tanner and a serf to boot[34] and François Villon, "of poor and modest extraction."[35]

François Villon turned out badly. But the others worked hard. They earned degrees that were not worthless and that mattered a great deal, for they were tickets to success for ambitious young men. The men who made their careers in the Church came from a wide variety of backgrounds. What they had in common was that all were good students.

The historian who studies medieval universities is thus faced with a vexing problem, which has been little investigated and remains far from solved. By now we know a great deal about the organization of universities, the teaching that went on inside them, the social background of their students, and the careers they pursued after leaving school. We know that the son of a poor man had less chance of attending university than the son of a rich man, and that family tradition was more likely to steer a lawyer's son to higher education than the son of a merchant. Yet it remains true that there were not only lawyers' sons but also merchants' sons and poor men's sons at the university. And we do not know how they got there, how they were educated.

For now I am inclined to believe that, things being as they were, the fate of each student depended, to a much greater extent than it may seem at first sight, on individual choices and personal capacities. Of the nine sons of the wealthy merchant Jean Basin, only two, Thomas and Michel the younger, attended the university. Why those two? About Michel we know nothing. But Thomas tells us about himself. He was twelve years old. He wanted to study. And his parents, who were good parents and who did not wish to stand in his way, sent him to the faculty of arts in Paris.[36]

Why did Pierre d'Ailly, Jean Gerson, Nicolas de Clamanges, and many others enjoy the good fortune of being allowed to study in that privileged enclave within the University of Paris, the Collège de Navarre? The only condition stipulated by the founder of the college was that its students should be from Champagne. But not all the students of Navarre were in fact Champenois, and not all the Champenois were students of Navarre. There was another criterion. And the proportion of gifted students at Navarre was so high that it is hard to avoid the conclusion that admission to the college was determined by an applicant's abilities.

When students ultimately received a bachelor's or master's degree, they were ranked, and this ranking had great importance. It determined, at least initially, the course of a cleric's career; those who ranked highest were the first to obtain benefices. The ranking was determined by the professors, who were no doubt susceptible to a variety of arguments. But why would they not have taken account of their students' merits? Surely it is not a coincidence that the highly ranked students usually enjoyed successful careers. In fourteenth- and fifteenth-century universities there were both good students and bad students, and success in school frequently presaged a successful career.

To excel at school a young man needed certain qualities that remained useful in later life. He needed a good memory. His memory and his enthusiasm for work presumably enabled him to acquire a broad knowledge not only of Scripture but also of theology or law or literature. He had to work quickly and to be "quite comfortable at work."[37] Thanks to his lively mind and intelligence, he no doubt excelled in the exercises required by the academic *cursus*. Since these exercises were mainly oral, and since academic life involved countless assemblies in which it was necessary to speak in order to make an impression, oratorical talent was an absolute necessity for the student who wished to shine. The leading lights of the university during the exciting and difficult times of Charles VI's reign were all great orators, men who knew how to speak well, loud, and long in both Latin and French. In the fifteenth century, when politics was less a matter of assemblies and more a matter of bureaus, eloquence was perhaps less essential for a successful career. Yet there were still many occasions when an ambitious young man was chosen because he was "clear and smart and well-spoken."[38]

Whoever needed competent clerics—whether cities for their schools[39] or princes and kings for their administrations[40]—kept an eye on the universities, which served as their hothouses. They did what they could to attract the most talented students. The universities dispensed knowledge and revealed talent. They were the training ground for the future servants of church and state.

Relatives and Friends

Powerful men needed good students. But good students needed powerful men. As brilliant as an ambitious student may have been, his career, once school was over, depended on what backing he possessed or was able to procure. There is no such thing as solitary ambition.

The surest support came from relatives. Nicholas of Besse was probably a good student. He was even a professor. But above all he was the nephew of Pope Clement VI (1342–52). The pope explained: "This is our nephew, our sister's son. We first provided for his subsistence. We sent him to Paris to study there. After which he studied in Orléans, where he was teaching when we called him to the [pontifical] court." It was not long before the Sacred College, without a single dissenting voice, asked that Nicholas be named cardinal, and Clement VI promptly acceded to the request."[41]

Historians have often criticized the nepotism of the Avignon popes. Contemporaries were sometimes scandalized by the advancement of unworthy nephews. To most clerics, however, there was nothing in itself reprehensible in the pope's elevation of one of his nephews, provided the young man was not unworthy of the honor. Such an action was even praiseworthy, for it accorded with the teaching of Scripture: "Love thy neighbor as thyself" (Matt.

19:19)—and what neighbor was closer than a nephew? The pope who aided his nephew was only doing his duty as an uncle, just as a king who supported his "cousins" was only doing what a good relative ought to do. The same was true of a bishop who made his nephews canons, or an officeholder who gave aid and assistance to "his posterity" and "his good blood relations, rich and poor alike,"[42] or the King's humblest subject, who came to the aid of his relatives in case of some dispute. It was a hard world, and at the very least one should be able to count on one's relatives. The problem is that my four prelates were men whose families may have encouraged them to study but who were obliged to make their careers on their own. They had to earn whatever support they needed through their talents.

A young cleric might seek employment with a bishop. A mere bishop was of little use, however. Jean Balue went nowhere as long as he remained in the entourage of the bishop of Poitiers and later the bishop of Angers. For a monk or brother the best patron in these times was his order; and for any cleric, regular or secular, a cardinal. The pope made cardinals, but once named a prince of the Church a man became a power unto himself, against whom even the pope was helpless. Around each cardinal, moreover, was a "family," each member of which had his own circle of assistants. And every cardinal had the means to satisfy even the most voracious appetites of those who served him well. Of the various cardinals in the Sacred College, some were more powerful, others less. Choosing the right cardinal, or, rather, attracting the attention of the right cardinal and finding a place in his circle or in the circle of one of those who served him, was the first step toward a brilliant career. When Pierre d'Ailly and Thomas Basin were just starting out, they managed to obtain the backing of a cardinal.

Church and state were so intimately intertwined, however, that the secular authorities had as much to say about the choice of bishops as did the ecclesiastical authorities. In the time of Charles VI, when the king was weak and the princes were powerful, a successful career between church and state required the support of both a cardinal and a prince. In a Church weakened by the Great Schism, the duke of Berry and the duke of Burgundy often exerted even more influence than the cardinals. These were troubled times, moreover, and the careers of servants were affected by fluctuations in the power of their masters.

Support from the high and mighty was not the only thing that influenced the fate of Charles VI's ambitious subjects. A characteristic feature of the second half of the fourteenth century was the importance of what might be called horizontal alliances, friendships between equals that superimposed themselves on hierarchical bonds. The contemporaries of Charles V and Charles VI lived in an uncertain world; readers of Cicero, they knew that in such conditions friendship could be a valuable political asset. The Order of the Necklace was one of many chivalric orders founded in the second half of the fourteenth century (in the county of Savoy in 1362, to be precise). Its members wore a silver necklace plated with gold that featured three love knots or coils as a sign of indissoluble friendship.[43] The "Marmousets" were a group that came to power when Charles VI was old enough to rid himself of his uncles (1388), and they remained in power as long as the king's health allowed him to govern (until 1392). These Marmousets were not simply individuals who enjoyed the backing of the king. They were a group bound together by close ties of kinship and friendship. It was said that they had "sworn an oath to support one another with all their might and to share, in adversity as well as prosperity, one mind, one will, and one goal."[44]

In this age of friendship, the university generally, and the University of Paris in particular, was an ideal place for the formation of close bonds between professors and students scarcely younger than themselves and between students who belonged to the same generation or attended the same faculty or college. Throughout the reign of Charles VI the University of Paris was a powerful pressure group. The careers of French clerics depended in large part on the bonds they formed while at school. In the unstable climate of Charles VI's reign, knowledge and talent alone were not enough to ensure a successful career. Success also demanded an ability to capitalize on the fluctuating power of prelates and princes and to take full advantage of relatives and friends.

Under Charles VI, in other words, a successful career required not only administrative competence but also political skill. Under Charles VII, after the king's victory, and under Louis XI, ambitious men faced an easier task. It was enough to exhibit absolute loyalty to the king, who little by little became the sole arbiter of success. In any case that was the ambition of Louis XI, who wanted to be his subjects' only master and even their father. One day the king visited the University of Poitiers, where he happened upon a certain Perreau, who "had already been studying there for three years and was a bachelor in law." The king "asked Perreau if he would serve him and told him that he must and said that he would be rewarded." Perreau "answered that his parents were keeping him at school and begged the king to leave him at his studies in order to please his parents, who would abandon him if he quit his study," to which "the king responded that, if he lost his parents, he [the king] would be his father; he would not lose."[45]

Zeal and Obedience

Ambitious men needed talent, knowledge, and patronage, but these alone were not enough. They also needed zeal and efficiency, and to know how to obey. "Obey and serve,"[46] "serve and obey":[47] these were the first duties of all subjects of the king in fifteenth-century France and still more the duties of the king's servants.

Obedience had not always been what it became in late medieval France: the mortar that held political society together. To be sure, the submission of slaves to masters,[48] of wives to husbands,[49] and of the young to the old[50] was inscribed in the nature of things, and the Church's teaching had long justified the submission of the humble to the powerful. At the height of feudal society, however, free men, vassals, and all who counted, or believed that they counted, deemed themselves to be bound to their lords only by contracts whose terms were open to discussion and which imposed rights and obligations on both parties. Feudal society was in essence a contractual society.

Alongside this contractual lay society, however, there grew up an ecclesiastical society of which obedience was the cornerstone: not submission in the sense of something determined by the natural order and beyond the power of the will, but obedience in the good and true sense, the example of which had been set by Christ, namely, voluntary consent prompted by love and freely given.

Obedience had always been a Christian virtue. It had always been a fundamental component of the monastic life. In the twelfth century Saint Bernard hoped that the Cistercian monk's obedience would be prompt, total, and joyful. When threatened by heresy, however, the Church came to rely more and more on obedience to maintain its unity. And Saint Dominic in the thirteenth century established an order in which obedience became the fundamental ingredient of the evangelical life.

Soon, the model of obedience set by the Church; the growing influence of Cicero, who advocated obedience to the law;[51] the new importance of Roman law, which required obedience to the prince; and the various dangers that threatened the kingdom's very existence from both within and without—all these things convinced the French that they must obey in order for the state to survive and retain its unity. Obedience became an essential political virtue.

No doubt obedience did not seem equally necessary, inevitable, and incontestable to everyone. Some may have read in Cicero that in the ancient world the ideal of many people was to obey no one and to live in liberty.[52] Others, confounding submission with obedience, found something servile in the latter. Still others believed that man must obey God but that to obey another man was not laudable at all.[53] And finally, other deemed themselves bound only by a conditional obedience. Subjects were bound to obey their princes only if the princes did what they were supposed to do. "Most redoubtable lord," Etienne Marcel wrote the future Charles V in 1358, "you . . . owe [the good people of Paris] protection and defense, and they owe you honor and obedience, and what they lack of the one relieves them of the obligation of the other."[54] Soon thereafter a fateful question was raised: Is obedience due a prince who sins? And in the fifteenth century, when the "Armagnacs" advocated a new kind of state based on total obedience, the "Burgundians" continued to hold that the prince ought to be obeyed but only provided that ancient French liberties were respected.

Yet in the face of all these doubts and scruples, the most authoritative voices during the reign of Charles VI affirmed that obedience to whatever was not contrary to divine precept or natural law was both necessary and beneficial. To obey the king and the laws was not a mark of servitude but a proof of liberty. Those who refused to obey were more animals than human beings, more slaves than free men.[55] Not only good princes must be obeyed but so must tyrants, because the harm that a tyrant does is more tolerable than the harm done by subjects who disobey their prince.[56] "Due subjection and proper obedience to the prince are most necessary to the realm."[57] Not just positive law but also natural law prescribed obedience.[58] Obedience was in fact a natural and necessary law of political society. It preserved the state and maintained the peace, tranquillity, and prosperity of its subjects.[59] "Royal authority and seigneurie are protected and preserved by the obedience of subjects to lords."[60]

Every subject was bound to obey the prince placed above him by birth, the prince into whose "country and obedience" he was born.[61] But beyond the natural subjection and fidelity stemming from birth, vassals and officers swore a solemn oath that subjected them to still further obedience.[62] The problem was that in those difficult times, servants of the church and state did not always know whom to obey. If Philip the Fair and Boniface VIII were in agreement, a French cleric could rest easy. But if they were at loggerheads, how was he to resolve the contradiction between two loyalties? With a powerful and respected Charles V, surrounded by lords "united among themselves and friendly to one another," obedience was easy. But with poor

Charles VI, at first too young and then too ill to govern, and with all the princes so obviously "divided, hateful, and separate,"[63] how was one to obey? "There are three kings in France," said an exasperated Olivier de Clisson in 1392, "and I do not know which to obey."[64] A few years later, in 1398, when the French government attempted to resolve the schism by "withdrawing obedience," that is, by declaring that the kingdom of France would no longer obey Benedict XIII, more than one French prelate was torn between the obedience he owed the king and that which he owed the pope. In 1420, when the Treaty of Troyes made the king of England the legitimate heir to the French throne, consciences were inevitably troubled. And in 1440, when Louis, Charles VII's young son, spurned his father and refused to obey him (or, in the formal phrase, "made withdrawal of his paternal obedience," *substraccionem . . . ab obedencia paterna*), the hearts of the king's subjects were inevitably torn between father and son.[65]

What made life dramatic in fourteenth- and fifteenth-century France was that, while everyone knew obedience was necessary, everyone was also enmeshed in a variety of allegiances, and when (as often happened) those allegiances proved contradictory, obedience, though necessary, became impossible. Caught between church and state, between pope and king, between king and princes, and between fathers and sons, French prelates in this period often led difficult lives. Their ideal was to obey and to serve. More than once, however, they were obliged to serve without knowing whom.

Success depended on zeal and obedience, efficiency and competence, but it also depended on prudence. Around the middle of the fifteenth century, in the France of Charles "the well-obeyed,"[66] the climate began to change. One of the reasons for Thomas Basin's failure was that he attempted to go on obeying in the "Burgundian" manner in a kingdom where "Armagnac" ideas now reigned supreme; he thought he could maintain a dual loyalty, to both Louis XI and his brother during the War of the Public Weal. But the king of France was less and less willing to permit the obedience that was his due to be limited or shared.

From the greatest lord to the humblest subject, everyone was now proud to obey the king. "As the dog lies at the feet of his master," Charles of Orléans told Charles VII in 1458, "I shall always remain loyally at the feet of your obedience, ready to do my loyal duty in every way that I must."[67] And in 1484 the king's "humble and most obedient subjects" were praised for "the purity of their faith in the prince and for their indefatigable obedience, in which [they] seem somehow to surpass both other nations and [their] predecessors."[68]

At the end of the fifteenth century, then, a powerful king, tamed princes, and a resigned pope made obedience easy. The ambitious young man knew that now, as in the past, he must obey and serve. But now it was enough to obey the king and serve the king. Obedience to the king became the mortar that unified France.

Dread and Fear

The Christian's love of God compelled obedience. Similarly, the subject's obedience to his prince was based on the love that, according to nature, he was supposed to feel. Every prince was supposed to be able to count on the "proper love and obedience" of his subjects.[69] The king of France knew that the love (*dilectio*) and obedience (*obedientia*) of his subjects were unparalleled anywhere.[70]

Nevertheless, the ambition of the king of France was not only to be "loved and obeyed" but also, and perhaps even more often, to be "feared and obeyed."[71] As one of his subjects told him one day, we "all, without exception" want to "serve and obey and fear and tremble . . . as we are bound to do by divine, natural, and human law."[72] Obedience was the mortar that held political society together. That mortar was a compound of love and dread (*timor*) or fear (*metus*).[73] Indeed, the proportion of dread or fear outweighed that of love. Because dread and fear played a fundamental role in medieval political society, we must pause to examine their nature.

Classical Latin possessed a number of words to denote fear. Consider three of these: *metus, timor,* and *pavor. Pavor* always meant violent fear, or panic, and it was a word so strong that it was hardly ever used by respectable writers. This crude, popular term was nevertheless the root of the modern French *peur* (by way of *paor, paour*). By contrast, *metus* and *timor* belonged to the most proper literary language. Synonyms, they originally were used to refer, in some cases, to a very powerful sentiment, like *pavor.* Gradually, however, the two words evolved. They never lost their primary meaning, but each was used in specific contexts with a different meaning.

Metus occurs infrequently in the Latin Bible, but *timeo* and *timor* occur often. Although they sometimes indicate a powerful, evil fear, they also refer to a good fear, which is not the opposite of love but, on the contrary, one of the first stages on the road leading to it. One must first fear God in order to love him (*Timor Dei initium dilectionis ejus* [Ecclus. 25:11]). The fear of God is the beginning of wisdom (*Initium sapientiae timor Domini* [Ecclus. 1:20]). He who fears God, the *timoratus,* is a wise man. That kind of fear is a virtue.

Furthermore, since all power comes from God, it is also a virtue to fear the prince. As Saint Paul said in the Epistle to the Romans 13:7: "*Reddite omnibus debita, cui tributum tributum, cui vectigal vectigal, cui timorem timorem, cui honorem honorem*" ("Render therefore to all their dues: tribute to whom tribute is due; custom to whom custom; fear to whom fear; honor to whom honor").

Although *metus* seldom appears in the Vulgate, it is the word regularly used to denote fear in legal texts, and in particular in Justianian's Code and Digest. The jurists' concern was not to denounce wicked fear but to defend or restore the rights of the weak. Hence their aim was to define those fears under the influence of which a complainant might have committed an act that he now regretted and wished the judge to nullify. Under the Code, therefore, if a man was not one of those who were fearful by nature, a *timidus* or *vanus homo*, if he was a steadfast person (*constantissimus homo*), and if, in the grip of a just dread, a justifiable fear (*non vani timoris*), this man was obliged to consent to something he later regretted, the judge could nullify that consent.[74] The lawmaker's concern was to define *timor* or, more commonly, *metus*, that is, justifiable fear, legitimate fear.

The men of the early Middle Ages knew nothing of these subtleties and confounded all the words for fear. But with the spread of learning and the revival of Roman law, and with progress in preaching and the development of canon law, the words regained their old values. The thirteenth century was quite capable of distinguishing between right fears and wrong fears. Theologians sang the praises of *timor*, or wise fear, while jurists discussed the meaning of *metus*, or just fear. For Stephen of Bourbon (died 1261), fear in general and fear of God in particular was a gift of the Holy Spirit (*De dono timoris*).[75] It marked the beginning of wisdom. Many had said the same thing before Stephen, and still others would say it after him.[76] Furthermore, in the late Middle Ages, when the king was the image of God, fear of the prince did indeed mark the beginning of political wisdom—for his subjects and still more for his servants.

Canon law, like Roman law, treated fear (*metus*) as a legitimate emotion so long as it was justifiable and so long as the person who experienced it was a steadfast man (*in virum constantem*).[77] In such violent times, when the weak as well as women and clerics had much to dread, fear became a commonplace argument in the courts. People actually went beyond the law. Anyone who wanted to explain a dubious position he had taken or who wished to repudiate an agreement he had made simply confessed that he had been compelled by force or by fear (*vi metusve causa*). Fear was thus admitted, or rather exhibited, by everyone. Did the king wish to repudiate a treaty he had signed? He had been afraid. Did a cardinal wish to reject a pope he had elected? He had been afraid. Did a great lord wish to explain his dubious conduct to the king? He had been "in great fear and great dread."[78] Did a canon wish to explain why he had not observed an interdict issued by his bishop? He had suffered from the kind of fear that can befall even the most steadfast of men (*in quemvis eciam constantissimum virum cadere potuisset*).[79] Did a wealthy widow wish to explain to the court why she had forgiven the debt of a threatening debtor? She had fallen victim to that fear "that can befall the most steadfast of persons," an understandable thing "given her sex, her age, and her widowed state."[80] In short, fear was everywhere in the late Middle Ages. And the violence of the times made it all too justifiable. But the wise fear of God and the wise fear of the prince, the legitimate fear that every steadfast man might feel, could avow, and might some day use to his advantage—these kinds of fear made fear itself into something other than a violent and reprehensible impulse of the soul. It was an ordinary emotion, a sign of wisdom, proof of sound judgment. When Thomas Basin witnessed disturbances in Utrecht and reported on what he had seen, he confessed his fear: "I was there, and I was afraid [*non sine metu*]."[81] In doing so he was not admitting a weakness but proclaiming his wisdom. To be filled with dread and to feel fear were, for the servants of church and state even more than others, very necessary virtues. They encouraged obedience and gave warning of the need for caution.

In a pressing emergency, what prudence required of one who was justifiably afraid was first of all that he hold his tongue and allow the prince's wrath to abate or the rebellious people's fury to subside. But when it became necessary to do or say something, then that thing should be done or said, but insincerely, as if spoken "with the lips" or "the mouth" but not from the heart.[82] That thing must be done or said with the firm intention of disavowing it as soon as possible. The best course was still to flee. In this world, where men were constantly threatened by plague, war, and violence, and where even the most steadfast of men was often right to be afraid, flight was generally the wisest remedy. A person must know how to make his escape. In fact, many escapes were beneficial. At Poitiers in 1356 John the Good had not fled, and the result was a misfortune for France. But Philip VI had fled at Crécy, and later, after Poitiers, that flight was deemed to have been most wise. In 1418, the dauphin Charles together with many of his supporters had fled Paris, and ultimately that flight enabled him to set France back on its feet. In difficult times, success, and more fundamentally survival, depended on knowing how to surrender at the right moment, how to flee "in the nick of time."[83]

Antiquity had exalted those who had died for the fatherland. The Church had glorified its martyrs and, later, the Crusaders who had died in defense of the Holy Land. In time, through a kind of natural transference, *"la doulce France,"* the French fatherland, took the place of the Holy Land. The influence of Horace and Cicero convinced many that it was a good thing to die for one's country. At the beginning of the fourteenth century many people said that a good citizen ought not to shrink from death if it could serve his fatherland.[84] Undeniably, a heroic current coursed through the late Middle Ages.

Nevertheless, that heroic current should not divert attention from the humble atmosphere of everyday life in the difficult times of the fourteenth and fifteenth centuries. The Church did not expect its faithful to be martyrs. Princes did not insist that their subjects be heroes. They did not ask the impossible. And the history of those times offers fewer examples of useless sacrifices than it does of reasonable capitulations, prudent retreats, and sagacious escapes. In this general climate the servants of church and state surely did at times exhibit courage. Pierre d'Ailly was often courageous in ways that his contemporaries were pleased to extol. But that courage was all the more laudable for not being futile. A brilliant career was not simply the reward of knowledge and talent, zeal and obedience, it was also the fruit of sage dreads, just fears, shrewd absences, and timely withdrawals.

Age and Experience

One final condition also had to be met if ambition was to prove successful. For those not favored by birth, success was also a matter of time. An ambitious man needed time in order to acquire experience. He needed patience. Consider John of La Goutte. Born in 1418, in 1464 John became a master in the duke of Bourbon's Chambre des Comptes at Moulins. In 1469 he was named governor general of the duke's finances at Moulins. And in 1469, at the age of fifty-one, he ordered a horoscope, or "nativity" as it was then called, from the illustrious astrologer Conrad Heingarter, who was at that time also physician to Duke John II. The astrologer did not discourage the official's ambitions. He would meet with brilliant success in his career. He would serve not only princes but also kings. Fortune would be his. But to enjoy that success he would have to wait for "the third part of [his] age." And he could afford to wait, because Conrad Heingarter declared that John of La Goutte would live to an age of eighty-five years, five months, and twenty-four days.[85] A brilliant career required a long life.

This proposition runs counter to a fundamental article of faith in the credo of present-day medievalists, who argue that medieval society was a society of youths dominated by youths.[86] And it has been demonstrated that the life expectancy in the late Middle Ages did not exceed twenty-five or thirty years.[87] The list of those who died in infancy or adolescence or youth is endless. The conclusion seems inescapable that ambition could not wait. In fifteenth-century Florence, according to David Herlihy, "the talented man played his cards early in life and soon disappeared from the scene,"[88] and no doubt this was true in Florence in the fifteenth century. But it was not true at that time everywhere else, and it was certainly not true in France.

Life expectancy was one thing, actual longevity another. The life expectancy of the men of the Middle Ages is a useful statistic calculated by historians, but the people of the time knew nothing about it. By contrast, they were well aware of how long some men lived. Nonagenarians and centenarians were not unknown. In 1305 one resident of Perigueux went so far as to declare that he was 140 years old.[89] In 1372 a Tuscan peasant claimed to be 130.[90] In 1461 one source mentioned a person from Saintonge who had lived "a hundred or six score years."[91] Such long lives did not seem implausible, but they certainly were seen as exceptional. On the other hand, the death of a young man, though a common occurrence, always seemed premature. To the men of the Middle Ages a normal lifetime was seventy or eighty years.[92]

People were well aware that in the old days, that is, just after the Creation, "people lived a long time."[93] The Bible mentioned ten patriarchs who had lived from 365 to 969 years.[94] But even at the time the Bible was written, the human life-span apparently did not exceed 120 years (Gen. 6:3) or even 100 years (Ecclus. 18:8). Psalm 90:10, which was far more widely read and commented on in the Middle Ages than the previous two passages, set an even shorter term of human life: "The days of our years are three-score years and ten; and if by reason of strength they be fourscore years, yet is their strength labor and sorrow."

When the men of the Middle Ages set the human life-span at seventy or eighty years, were they following Psalm 90 or were they reporting on their own experience? The influence of the Bible in the Middle Ages suggests the former, particularly since medieval man for a long time neither cared about age nor possessed the means to measure it. As late as the thirteenth century it was a rare person who knew his or her age. Even later, knowledge of the number of one's years hardly counted among man's foremost concerns.[95] Families did not always tell children when they had been born. People were more likely to remember the day their adult life began. Princes remembered the date of their coronation, knights the date of their dubbing,[96] clerics the date of their tonsure,[97] scholars the date they received the master of arts,[98] monks and friars the date they embarked upon the religious life.[99] Each of these dates had more emotional resonance and greater legal importance than the person's date of birth.

In the thirteenth century, however, broad cultural changes began to foster a new interest in numerical precision. Legal and governmental pressures heightened the importance of a person's age and date of birth. The growing influence of astrology made it essential for people to know exactly when they were born, knowledge without which an accurate horoscope [*nativité*] was impossible. Furthermore, a wider familiarity with writing made it easier for people to acquire that knowledge.

By the end of the Middle Ages there were still people who had no idea of their exact age, but there were also people who could give the time of their birth to the very day.[100] And many more knew their age within a year or two. Thus people knew from experience that men could live to age seventy or eighty and even beyond, but they also knew that such long lives were rare. "Hardly one man in a thousand lives seventy years," William Breda said in the fifteenth century.[101]

Recent progress in medieval demography confirms this somber impression but also leads to a rather surprising conclusion. It is true that children and youths died in incredible numbers in the Middle Ages. But once a person reached the age of twenty, the chance of living to, say, forty or fifty or sixty was roughly equal to that of suffering an imminent demise. Hence the percentage of elderly people in the society was far from negligible.[102] In one parish in Rheims in 1422, 6.5 percent of the population was over sixty.[103] And in Verona in 1425 and in Florence in 1427, 15 percent of the population was over sixty.[104] Society, in the late Middle Ages at any rate, was not a society of youths dominated by youths. It was a society in which there both young people and old people. Their respective influence remains to be seen.

Certain authors drew a more nuanced and accurate portrait of the ages of life. Isidore of Seville, a writer widely read in the Middle

Ages, defined the period from birth to age seven as *infantia;* from seven to fourteen as *pueritia;* from fourteen to twenty-eight as *adolescentia;* from twenty-eight to fifty as *juventus;* from fifty to seventy as *gravitas;* and from seventy on as *senectus,* old age, which ended in a period of senility (*senium*).[105] Around 1265 Filippo of Novara distinguished four ages that each lasted twenty years and that were like the seasons of life: childhood was springtime; youth was summer; "middle age" (or maturity) was autumn; and old age was winter.[106] In truth, however, these overly scholarly, precise, and disparate classifications had little influence on what ordinary people thought. For most people, childhood gave way to adolescence at the "age of discretion," between eleven and fourteen, after which life fell into just two parts, youth and old age. The Middle Ages all but ignored the age of maturity, the "middle age" that seems so important to us, and distinguished exclusively between youth and old age, the former ending at around forty-five or fifty. For Cicero, forty-six was the threshold of old age.[107] For Saint Thomas, old age began at fifty;[108] for Dante, at forty-five.[109] In medieval political society those who counted were necessarily either youths, that is, people under the age of fifty, or elderly, that is, people over the age of fifty; the problem lay in the relations between these two groups.

Youths generally had a terrible reputation. Their ignorance, their inexperience, their want of wisdom, and their concupiscence all counted against them. Young people were naturally guilty of follies, of youthful indiscretions (*jeunesses*), for which they had to be excused. By contrast, old age was a time of tranquillity. Cicero, whose *De senectute* was widely read in the late Middle Ages, had long ago said that the old were liberated from sensual appetite, ambition, greed, and all the other passions.[110] They were also free of fear. They still possessed the necessary memory and energy. Above all, Saint Thomas pointed out, they had acquired what only age could give, namely, true wisdom based on experience.[111] Hence old age was often considered a reward, a gift from God. Age and experience gave authority to the elderly and inspired them with good counsel. Shrewd princes chose older advisers and followed their advice. Others did as Roboam had done: they did not follow the advice of the old and instead sought the opinions of the young.[112] Such princes should know, as Cicero had warned, that "the greatest states have been ruined by young men and sustained or reestablished by old ones."[113]

The traditional image of youth and old age would therefore seem to have permitted the old to play an essential role in late medieval political society. In fact, however, things were more complex. The men of the Middle Ages had enough experience not to look upon age as an exclusive criterion. In the first place, younger men were not necessarily less wise than older ones.[114] In addition to those who were "rank youths in age and counsel,"[115] there were also those who were "young in years but mature in spirit and soul."[116] Of course the wisdom of youths was never perfect, for it always lacked experience. Jean Gerson noted that Christ at twelve was already wise, yet he lacked experience. It was in the nature of things for youths to lack experience, but they had what many of the old no longer possessed: health and energy. They were active and obedient. A shrewd prince was therefore well advised to surround himself with a select group of young people, not in order to be well counseled but in order to be well served. In 1455 Master Thibault de Caigneux, the king's quite youthful secretary, was chosen by the king's council for an embassy because he was a "young man, comfortable with work, as well as clear and smart and well-spoken."[117]

Furthermore, the period of youth lasted so long that it was quite feasible to acquire all the experience one needed before it was over. The troubled 1420s gave Guillaume Juvénal des Ursins all the experience he needed to become *conseiller* of the parlement of Poitiers at age twenty-four, in 1425. In 1445, Guillaume had been *conseiller* for twenty years, but he was still only forty-four, still a youth. Nevertheless, he possessed that "long experience," that "very wide" experience necessary to be a good chancellor to the king of France.[118] Thus the prince found reason to pause before choosing between a young quadragenarian and an old quinquagenarian.

The prince may have hesitated all the more because the quinquagenerian, no matter how well he had aged, was always vulnerable to senility. Those who kept their health while gaining age, wisdom, and experience could look upon old age as a gift from God, but others feared it as a time of sadness, melancholy, and affliction. "Remember now thy Creator in the days of thy youth, while the evil days come not, nor the years draw nigh, when thou shalt say, I have no pleasure in them" (Eccl. 12:1). For old age could mean years of weakness, infirmity, and decrepitude. The skin wrinkles, the hair turns white, the back bends, the teeth fall out, the eyes dim, the body trembles.[119] What is old age but a time of pain and affliction?[120]

For the man who wished to continue serving church and state, the crucial moment in this long decline came when he could no longer ride a horse. To serve church and state in the late Middle Ages quite concretely meant being able to ride long distances, at times quite rapidly. Exceptions did exist: an important personage who could no longer ride a horse might pay for the costly services of bearers to carry him in a sedan chair.[121] And there were relatively sedentary occupations. A conseiller in parlement did not need to be spry to go on giving the good advice expected of him. These exceptions aside, however, the rule held for civilians as well as soldiers: when a man could no longer ride, the time had come for him to retire.

Military regulations stipulated that soldiers should retire at sixty.[122] For civilians, however, there was no official age of retirement. The time varied with the individual's health and the impatience of his successor. One person was deemed to be prematurely old (*jam grandevus*) at fifty-five. Another, not yet sixty but "quite elderly and feeble and sick," was obliged to step down in favor of a rival scarcely younger than himself, already fifty-five, but "strong and hard-working."[123] Yet another remained active until sixty-seven, when he was obliged to stop work because he was "too occupied with illness" and could no longer travel "on foot, on horseback, or by wagon."[124]

The retirement imposed on the elderly by physical weakness did not necessarily spell an end to happy times, however. For many, old age was a time for reading and reflection.[125] It is rather surprising to discover that many authors awaited old age before beginning to write.[126]

Eventually, however, the time came when even that was no longer possible:

> Je voy dure vielesse
> Qui me vient tourmenter.
> Se fault que je delaisse
> L'escripre et le dicter.

[I see harsh old age coming to torment me. I shall have to give up writing and dictation.][127]

Ultimately the elderly man was "vexed and incensed by old age."[128] He lost his senses and his memory. Only death could deliver him from decrepitude.

For those not favored by birth, ambition could not succeed without long life. To put it bluntly, such men were still taking their first tentative steps at age thirty. They did not score their first major successes until forty or so, at which time they at last entered the precincts of authority. They needed fifty years to come into their own, at which time their only remaining problem was how to sustain themselves in the positions they had finally won.

Thus political society, in late medieval France at any rate, was not a society of youths dominated by youths. It cannot be fully understood unless we grasp the tensions and conflicts that arose between young and old. By young, moreover, I do not mean youths of twenty and thirty. Their only task was to obey. The real tension was between "young men" in their forties whom talent, zeal, and youthful experience had recently elevated to positions of authority, and "old men" in their fifties, who counted on their wisdom and long experience to sustain them.

Obviously those who derived their authority from their birth realized their ambitions much earlier. Such men achieved power while still truly young. Additional tensions arose between youths whom birth spared the necessity of waiting a long time in the wings and men who had needed both talent and time in order to make their mark.

All these tensions were inevitable. In a sense they were even necessary. For society in this period was a hierarchy founded on birth. Men were instinctively more willing to serve a "great lord or personage" and to recognize his authority. The great lord might not lack talent, but still he needed "two or three wise and experienced men . . . to advise him," especially if he happened to be young.[129] Birth and talent were condemned to live together. Talent served birth, but it also used birth to make its own way. French society at the end of the Middle Ages was an open society in which the weight of birth did not prevent the rise of talent. And of course talent needed to know just how high was not yet too high.

The aging man of talent, reduced to political impotence, had as his consolation the leisure to write. It is not without interest to discover that many of the works that have come down to us from the Middle Ages were written by men in their fifties, sixties, and seventies. If those works are often morose, perhaps it was because those were gloomy times. But perhaps it was also because the writers were old men worn down by life and illness.

These elderly authors were indeed witnesses to their times. But in order to evaluate their testimony properly, we must know the extent to which their ideas were shaped by their early years. Gilles Le Muisit wrote in Tournai around 1350, but he was educated in Paris before 1290. In Constance between 1415 and 1418 Pierre d'Ailly brought to fruition ideas that had sustained him in his youth, in the 1380s. It is even more important to recognize that he was born after the Black Plague. What Thomas Basin wrote between 1470 and 1490 echoed convictions he had acquired in Paris and above all in Louvain around 1430. What is more, the disaster of Agincourt (1415) and its consequences left their mark on his work.

Man cannot escape his youth, and what he says in old age can be explained only with reference to everything he thought and experienced over the course of a lifetime.

What did not happen over a period of fifty, sixty, seventy, or even eighty years? People nowadays talk of an "acceleration of history." I suspect that this cliché says more about our own ignorance than about anything else. A biography, even if it has no other merit, can at least give us the measure of one man's lifetime and make us aware of what a particular individual was able to experience. Gilles Le Muisit was born in 1272 and died in 1353. In 1272 Saint Louis had been dead only a short time. In 1353 the Black Plague that ravaged Europe was still fresh in memory. What did these two worlds have in common? Political arrangements, art, thought—all these had changed, and the first cannon had roared at Crécy in 1346. Thomas Basin was born in 1412 and died in 1490. The year 1412 shortly preceded Agincourt; in 1490 the Italian wars were just a few years away. Once again, the world had been totally transformed in eighty years, and of course the printing press had been invented.

The study of structures teaches us to understand history. The story of a life makes us feel it. The debate over whether history is a matter of structures or events is an old one, which can be traced back to at least the beginning of this century. Historians at that time began to denounce narrative history for its failure to be a science. And the advocates of narrative condemned the new history for its inability to bring the past back to life. Anatole France said, "This new history will never be anything but an autopsy."[130] And he added that statistical history, upon which scholars feasted, is to narrative history as the potato is to the rose. As for myself, my intention in writing these four lives was not to substitute roses for the potatoes that have nourished me for so long, but rather to reconcile the one with the other.

Now the time has come to allow my four prelates to testify, each in turn and in concrete detail, about themselves, their milieus, and their times.

July 14, 1986

CHAPTER

1

BERNARD GUI
(1261–1331)

Birth

In 1261 nothing remained of the Latin states of the Orient except a few fortified towns, soon to succumb to quarrels among themselves and to the assaults of the Mameluke sultan. On July 25 the Latin emperor and the patriarch fled a Constantinople that had been recaptured by the Greeks. A great dream thus came to an end. Latin Christendom was in effect reduced to the territory that stretched from Spain to Poland, from Scandinavia to Sicily—the west of Europe. The West henceforth planned crusades against the infidel and dreamed of union with the Orthodox—perennial and costly dreams and plans that in the end bore no fruit.

In this curtailed West, where pope and emperor had been at odds for centuries, the great reign of Frederick II had ended in disaster in the year 1250. The Empire was by now little more than an idea and a name. The pope had triumphed over his old rival. Countless troubles prevented him from savoring his victory, however. To be sure, the Catharist heresy, which for a time had threatened the very existence of the Church in southern France, had been all but crushed by the iron of the crusade and the firmness of the Inquisition. Local outbreaks of violence still demanded vigilance, but they were no longer a major problem. In Italy, however, the collapse of the Empire had unleashed forces that the pope could not control. Even Rome challenged his authority. Alexander IV was obliged to leave the city in 1260.

The Church, at least, remained obedient to the vicar of Christ. In reality, however, the pope found himself at the head of two churches, between which the atmosphere was at times quite tense. One was the church of curés and bishops, who naturally viewed their dioceses as corporations, loyal to the pope, in solidarity with one another, but autonomous. The discipline of this secular church was threatened, however, by institutions that were exempt from episcopal authority and that enjoyed privileged relations with the papacy. The monasteries and priories of Cluny, for example, had been unchecked by the authority of the bishops since the tenth century. An even more important exception had developed early in the thirteenth century: in response to an urgent demand for preaching and to the crying needs of the poor, Dominic had founded the Order of Preachers and Francis had risen to head the Order of Friars Minor. These mendicant orders were under the direct authority of the pope. They were disciplined, and they sought to establish close relations with the urban populace. At this they were so successful that, even though they were able to render remarkable service to the Church, their influence soon came to be seen as an intolerable threat to the discipline of the secular hierarchy. Furthermore, while the Dominicans and Franciscans both enjoyed the favor of the pope and both were the target of hostility from bishops and curés, they did not get along with each other. Which of the two orders was the more perfect? Which would enjoy the honor of burying the faithful, and therefore the money of those whom they interred? Which would be accorded the best urban sites for building monasteries? And last but not least, which would be entrusted with responsibility for the Inquisition and thus with leading the war against heresy? In a climate of mutual mistrust these issues at times erupted in violent conflict.[1]

For a time these internal tensions occupied center stage. But an even greater threat to the papacy lay in the progress of young and still deferential states. By 1261 the kindom of France had taken a major leap. King Louis IX, who had returned from the Orient a mature man in his forties blessed with an abundance of ideas, experience, and will, had in the space of just a few years transformed the institutions of France from top to bottom. Now that the abbey church of Saint-Denis had been reconstructed, he was already planning to transfer the tombs of the French kings to its choir in order to emphasize the continuity of the French royal line and strengthen the Capetians' claim to legitimacy.[2] With the Treaty of Paris (1259) he had put an end to the disputes that for more than a century had pitted the kings of France and England against each other. A powerful and respected king, a prince of peace, and the arbiter of all Europe, Louis IX reigned over France in a period that subsequent generations of Frenchmen would look back upon as a golden age.

For the time being, however, even that golden age had its problems. Among them, no doubt the most important was the danger to France created by the distance between the northern and southern halves of the kingdom. The two regions formed a single realm; they recognized the same king. Yet they were divided by almost everything else: language, custom, attitude, and of course recent history. It was the barons of the north who had crushed heresy and shaken or defeated local dynasts in the south. And in the mid-thirteenth century the north, sure of its loyalty to king and pope, enjoyed the might of its armies, the wealth of its Church, lords, and cities, and the culture of its princely lords and monasteries and of that incomparable center of learning (*clergie*), the prestigious University of Paris. The south, ruined by invasion and humiliated by defeat, had not yet accepted barons and prelates whose fathers had come from the north or who were northerners themselves. Though remote from the king and the pope, the south was on the whole loyal to both. Here and there, however, voices were raised in protest and violence occasionally broke out in opposition to either the kingdom of France or the Church of Rome. The south was uncertain.

Although the Order of Preachers was born in this south, it did not share its uncertainties. The Dominican province of Provence stretched from Bordeaux to Nice and from Limoges to Perpignan. Dominicans from the portion of this province that was also part of the kingdom of France built a solid edifice upon a threefold fidelity, to the Roman Church, to the king of France, and to their own south.

It was at the northern extreme of this Dominican province, in the diocese of Limoges, a few miles south of the city, near the village of La Roche-l'Abeille, in the tiny hamlet of Royère, whose tranquillity may well have been little troubled by rumblings of the great issues of the day, that Bernard Gui was born in 1261 or 1262.

Dominican: Pupil, Reader, Prior (1270–1307)

It was at precisely this time that surnames began to be used to distinguish between people with the same Christian name. Surnames were taken from nicknames or from a person's trade or from his birthplace or place of residence or from his father's first name. In the thirteenth century such surnames tended to become traditional and hereditary. There were thus in the north and south of France many families that bore the name Guidonis in Latin or Guidon or Gui (that is, son of Gui) in French, and obviously they were not all related. The Gui family of Royère was modest and obscure. We know nothing about Bernard Gui's father, neither his name nor what he did nor what he owned. Bernard certainly had several brothers. One was definitely named Laurent, but his name is all we know about him. It is plausible though not certain that one of the brothers bore the family's traditional first name, Gui. Of Bernard Gui's mother we know nothing either, except that she had a brother, Bertrand Auterii, who was a priest and who died in 1291, when Bernard Gui was thirty. At that time Bertrand was cantor of the church of Saint-Yrieix, a short distance south of Royère. He loved Limoges; he loved the Preachers and Minorites of Limoges, to whom he bequeathed a few sous; and above all he loved his nephew Bernard, to whom he left ten livres to be used for the purchase of books.[3] It seems clear that this maternal uncle, this avuncular curé, exerted a considerable influence on Bernard Gui's early life.

No one could tell Bernard exactly when he had been born. Knowledge of birth dates was anything but commonplace. A few families were pious enough to recall the date of a child's baptism, but such was not the case with Bernard. Although he later became fanatical about precise dating, Bernard could not even remember when he became a priest. He recalled only that he had been tonsured in the Dominican monastery at Limoges by Pierre of Saint-Astier, the bishop of Périgueux, who had retired there. Modern scholarship therefore tells us that the event occurred between 1265 and 1275. He was tonsured, like so many others, as soon as it was clear that he was roughly ten years of age. In the thirteenth and even fourteenth century a layman had no precise date from which he could measure the progress of his life. As adulthood came and memory faded, it became increasingly difficult for a person to calculate his age; he was lucky if he could come within a year or two or even five of the actual figure. But how could a monk or friar forget the precise date of his vows? That was the date of his true birth, which he celebrated regularly and which was often recorded in writing. It was a very definite milestone in the progress of a religious life. Certain of the time that had elapsed since that day, he remained unsure of only one thing, namely, how old he was at that crucial moment. When Bernard became a Dominican, he entered the world of precise memory. He never knew whether he was eighteen or nineteen years old when he took the habit, but he never forgot that on September 16, 1280, at the conclusion of the traditional one-year novitiate, he swore a solemn oath between the hands of Stephen de Salanhac in the Dominican monastery of Limoges, which he already knew so well.[4]

As children, all the young friars had no doubt studied grammar. All had had a rudimentary education; we do not know where Bernard acquired his. It was not the intention of the order that all its young wards study logic, however. It lacked the resources, and in any case such study would have been, in many cases, pointless. Of newly professed monks who appeared to possess the necessary qualities one in three was selected to study logic. The successful candidates were distinguished by their robust health (for why waste a long and costly education on a youth who seemed likely to be claimed before long by death?); by their intellectual capacities; by their facility with words (for their mission would be to teach and to preach); and by their "happy commerce," that is, their human warmth, their ability to communicate.[5] Bernard Gui must have had those qualities; he studied logic. The province of Provence had been divided since 1275 into a number of vicariates, each of which included a half-dozen monasteries.[6] The vicariate of Limoges comprised the monasteries of Limoges, Brive, Périgueux, Figeac, Bergerac, and Cahors. There was one logic class per vicariate; its pupils and teacher were housed in turn, for a period of one year, by each of the monasteries in the vicariate that deemed itself capable of bearing the financial burden. Bernard Gui thus studied logic in Limoges in 1280–81 and followed his teacher to Figeac in 1281–82.

Roughly half the students who completed two years of logic were deemed to possess the intellectual qualities necessary for the study of philosophy. There was one philosophy class for every two vicariates; its location alternated annually between the principal monasteries of each of the two vicariates. Thus at the age of twenty-one Bernard Gui found himself for the first time at some distance from Limoges. He spent the year 1282–83 in Bordeaux, where he began reading the works of Aristotle by way of the commentaries on them recently provided by Albert the Great and Thomas Aquinas. In the thirteenth century the West discovered Aristotle by way of Latin translations of his works and was enthralled by them. There was no better way of preparing minds for the truths of Christianity than by study of the Greek philosopher. Of this truth the great Dominican doctors were more convinced than anyone else. Thomas died in 1274, just before his fiftieth birthday. His older teacher, Albert the Great, outlived him, surviving until he was nearly eighty in 1280. The efforts of these two men made the study of Aristotelian philosophy an essential part of Dominican education. In 1282–83 Bernard Gui conscientiously studied the works of Aristotle in Bordeaux. He continued his studies the following year in Limoges.

At the end of that year, having concluded his study of philosophy, Bernard had his first experience as a teacher. He was assigned the task of teaching logic in his vicariate's small school, held that year in Brive. In 1285, however, he embarked on the third phase of his education; he began the study of theology. Although logic and philosophy were not taught in all monasteries, theology was. In every monastery there was a lector, whose courses all the friars, regardless of their educational background or age, were supposed to attend.[7]

For four years Bernard Gui returned to his beloved monastery in Limoges, where thanks to good teachers and a good library he was able to steep himself in the Bible and in Peter Lombard's *Sententiae,* a twelfth-century work that set forth the theology of its time so well that it was still in use as a fundamental textbook a century later.

In Montpellier the Dominican order maintained a *studium generale,* an educational center staffed by the most brilliant of its teachers, including some of the few friars from the province who had studied in Paris. Those young southern friars destined for future responsibilities were sent to Montpellier to complete their education, and Bernard Gui was one of them from 1289 to 1291. Since he turned out not to be a good enough theologian to send to Paris, his studies ended there.[8] In 1291, at age thirty, he joined the ranks of priors and lectors, the men responsible for life in the Dominican monasteries and thus for the well-being of the order.

Each monastery was headed by a prior, who was in charge of its administration. The other pillar of the Dominican community was the lector, whose only responsibility was to teach theology to the other friars. In more modest monasteries the offices of prior and lector might be filled by one person. By contrast, in larger monasteries, where both needs and resources were greater, the lector was aided by a young assistant lector. As it happens, we possess an exceptionally detailed account of what life was like for the priors and lectors of the Dominican monasteries of southern France in the thirteenth century thanks to the works that Bernard Gui himself would write on the subject somewhat later in his life.[9]

At the age of almost thirty, the young friar, having spent nearly a dozen years in the order and having completed his studies, was normally assigned to serve as an assistant lector in a large monastery or a lector in a smaller one. Then, some years later, sometimes before he had reached the age of thirty-five but more often between thirty-five and forty, the friar was deemed sufficiently mature to be assigned his first priorate. Subsequently he moved from one monastery to another, remaining in each place for from one to four years, rarely longer, and serving as prior, or lector, or both at once, according to the needs of the order.

Bernard Gui did not have only praise for his brothers. He praised those who had distinguished themselves by their virtues and those whom he had known personally and held in high esteem. His praise tells us about the order's dreams and about Bernard Gui's. The ideal Dominican was a good man, virtuous and devout, learned and wise, always active, always ready to preach the word of God, and above all always amiable and gay. For as Humbert of Romans said, the Dominican must not simply obey; he must like to obey.[10] In fact, some friars were equally enthusiastic about administration and teaching and moved from priorate to lectorate and back again with the greatest of ease. But many preferred one or the other of these activities and did everything they could to avoid the one they disliked. Some served more often and for longer periods as priors. Others served longer as lectors because someone preferred that they teach or because they themselves preferred to teach; and they did all they could, as Bernard Gui put it, not without a trace of discreet perfidy, to avoid the fatigue, the burden of the priorate.

Thus, Ytier of Compreignac's lifelong dream was to teach, indeed to teach in Limoges. He was lector in Limoges in 1288 when he was obliged to serve as prior, a position that he retained for only one year. In 1289 he was again lector in Limoges. Between 1290 and 1292 he was obliged once more to serve as prior in Limoges. But what he wanted was to teach. He was sent to Bordeaux to serve as lector. But he wanted to teach in Limoges. He did not even go to Bordeaux but remained in Limoges as lector. In 1295 he became prior of Brive. This time he actually traveled to Brive, but "he could not stand it for long . . . and once again became lector in Limoges." At Christmas 1295 he was obliged to leave Limoges and give up teaching. He became prior in Bordeaux and later in Toulouse. He must have been happy to return to teaching as lector in Cahors in 1301. He strenuously objected to resuming the "burden of the priorate." Once again, however, he found himself prior in Limoges. Selected to be prior in Périgueux in 1302, he did not even go to the monastery there. And in 1304 we find him once again prior in Limoges, where his sole joy was preaching.

Of this host of priors and lectors, few were called to fill other positions, such as provincial prior or inquisitor. Death, of course, claimed the Dominican prior or lector whenever and wherever it pleased. No doubt all friars dreamed as Bernard Gui did of dying while preaching, and such was the noble death that God granted to that dedicated teacher and preacher Ytier of Compreignac. In 1304 he had for the past two months been serving once again as prior of Limoges. Bernard Gui tells us that he had just preached, as usual, with a powerful voice. His sermon was barely over when he stopped preaching and speaking right there before the crowd. He died a few days later.[11] To die while preaching at age fifty-five: God had bestowed an extraordinary favor on the "humble," "devout," "wise" Ytier. Many others were cut down earlier, such as Peter Copelli of the diocese of Limoges, who had twice served as prior of Limoges and who, while serving as prior of Brive in 1296, asked to be relieved of his duties and returned to Limoges, where death claimed him in 1298. He was not quite fifty. In Bernard Gui's words, he was *in flore juventutis et valoris,* in the flower of his youth and valor.[12] To others, more numerous than one might think, God did not grant Ytier's noble death, but he did give the grace of long life. They died in their sixties and seventies after forty or fifty years in the Dominican habit. Peter of Fabrica died in 1312 at almost eighty years of age. He had taken the habit in 1253 and had been a Dominican for fifty-nine years.[13] Even more extraordinary, he was still active when he died, serving for the third time as prior of Morlaas. Usually older men retired, at an age that varied from sixty to seventy, to one of the monasteries of the order, where they died "in the fullness of days" (*plenus dierum*) and "in happy old age" (*in senectute bona*), as Bernard Gui put it, using expressions that would have been familiar to the assiduous Bible reader he was.

Such was the relatively circumscribed world in which Bernard Gui lived for some time. After completing his studies at Montpellier, he served as assistant lector at Limoges in 1291, then as lector at Albi from 1292 to 1294. And then, when he was not yet thirty-two or thirty-three years of age, he became prior of Albi. During the next eleven years he would serve, in the same region, as prior of Albi (1294–97), Carcassonne (1297–1301), and Castres (1301–5), before returning in 1305 to serve, also as prior, in his beloved monastery of Limoges. While prior of Albi and Carcassonne he was obliged at times to serve also as lector, but the last time that necessity arose was in 1300. Bernard Gui's work as an administrator was much appreciated, but he served as lector only when no one better was available. His brothers no more wished to hear him than he himself liked to teach. A conscientious student, he had learned his Bible and the *Sententiae* well. He could if necessary read and comment on them. But theological issues did not engage him to any great degree. He was not enamored of phrases. The ardor that Ytier of Compreignac invested in his teaching surprised him somewhat. Bernard was a man of action. An administrator, happy in his heart of hearts to be an administrator, he occasionally slipped into his reports a few words of reproach for those who preferred the quiet of the study to the heavy burdens of the priorate.

In 1303 the chapter general of the Order of Preachers divided the vast province of Provence in two. The western half, from Limoges to the Pyrenees and from Bordeaux to Carcassone, became the province of Toulouse.[14] Not much changed, however. The new administrative map simply sanctioned an already existing state of affairs. Even before 1303, the life of a Dominican born in the diocese of

Limoges or the diocese of Bayonne almost always unfolded within the limits of the new Toulouse province. Bernard Gui himself left that region only once, to go to Montpellier too study for two years in the *studium generale* there.

At the time when this inconsequential division was being made, Europe was the theater of dramatic events. Philip the Fair, king of France and grandson of Saint Louis, was then engaged in a serious conflict with Pope Boniface VIII. Such a dispute was no doubt inevitable between a pope who wished to maintain the Church's international character and to affirm, as his predecessors had done, his role as guide and judge of Christendom in all domains and a king who increasingly found it intolerable that the Church in France should be anything more than a corporation subject to his authority and contained within his realm. The quarrel quickly took a dramatic turn, however, and had extraordinary repercussions. The clash of great principles happened to coincide with specific conflicts of interest and crucial problems of money. The times were somber: on July 11, 1302, the French cavalry had been crushed at Courtrai by Flemish infantry. Meanwhile, in Italy, the pope faced, as usual, an impossible situation. There was also a conflict of characters and generations: the irascible Boniface VIII, who had become pope in 1294 at nearly sixty, was stunned by the youthful errors, which he took to be bold moves, of a king who was thirty years younger than himself and whose principal advisors and aides were only slightly older and in a few cases even younger. The crisis came to a head with the events at Anagni (September 1303), and Boniface VIII, by then a broken old man, died a few weeks later. Only muffled echoes of this great drama reached the southern part of the French kingdom, however. Toulouse was truly a long way from Paris, Courtrai, and Rome. In the controversy between the pope and the king, the prelates of northern France had every reason to support their king, but the Church in the south was deeply troubled by its inability to reconcile its two loyalties. It kept its distance, and its silence.

At the time these far-off dramas were of less importance to the prior of Castres than the serious disturbances that Albi and Carcassonne were experiencing simultaneously. The religious and political ambiguities of a region from which Catharism had yet to be entirely extirpated and Capetian power had yet to be fully accepted; the harsher aspects of royal administration; the abuses of the Dominican inquisition; the Franciscans' hatred of the Dominicans; and the doubts of the Parisian authorities, aware of the excesses of the Dominicans and little inclined to support an order so loyal to the papacy while at the same time fighting Boniface VIII—all these things explain how disorders could have erupted in 1302 and 1303 in Albi and Carcassone, disorders of which Dominicans were the first victims and of which Bernard Gui was, from Castres, an irate observer. Philip the Fair took such a dim view of the Dominicans that when Guillaume de Nogaret left for Anagni, the king himself, in a decision rare for a French monarch, chose to go to the south in person in an attempt to restore order and impose discipline on the pope's overzealous allies. When he arrived, however, southern Franciscans and bourgeois committed so many gaffes and permitted themselves so many familiarities that the king, a very reserved northerner, was deeply offended. Boniface VIII had just died, moreover, and his successor wanted a truce. Philip the Fair had no compunctions about changing sides and calling upon the Dominicans and the Inquisition to restore order. In despair a plot was hatched. Dozens of bourgeois were hanged. In 1305 Bernard Gui left Castres a satisfied man: the "rage of Carcassonne" had been crushed; justice had been done; the patience of the good had been rewarded, the pride of the wicked punished. Simple, solid, and serene, Bernard Gui could once more offer his undivided loyalties to his pope, his king, his order, and his region.

Bernard Gui lived through these dramatic events in much the same manner as other southern Dominicans, but only he recounted the story. This unenthusiastic professor, this untroubled theologian, this prior like so many others was nearly thirty-five when he first began to indulge a passion for history that would eventually become all-consuming. A Limousin who wished to become a historian in the late thirteenth century could already draw inspiration from a long tradition. Aquitaine in general had been slow to recover from Carolingian devastation. The region had few great monasteries, and what monasteries there were took little interest in history. Later Aquitaine did develop an illustrious culture, but at the beginning of the thirteenth century northerners had laid Aquitainian culture low, and what remained of intellectual life was largely secular and juridical. History was little cultivated. Still, there was Limoges. It was not just that succinct notes were recorded in annals; such notes were kept in many places, including Limoges itself, at the Saint-Etienne cathedral, at Saint-Augustin and Saint-Martin, and not far from Limoges, at Grandmont and L'Artige.[15] More important, the Saint-Martial abbey had begun to cultivate history in the first half of the eleventh century owing to its connections with Fleury (today Saint-Benoît-sur-Loire), a historiographical center of extraordinary importance, as well as to its excellent library and to the genius of Adhemar of Chabannes. And that interest in history continued uninterrupted. Bernard Itier served for twenty-five years as assistant librarian and later librarian of the abbey until his death in 1225. A passionate lover of books, he acquired many, and he bound and catalogued some 450 volumes that constituted the Saint-Martial collection. He also wrote a chronicle. After his death, history continued to be cultivated at Saint-Martial throughout the thirteenth century.

At the same time, the Dominican monastery at Limoges became a center for historical study. Gerald of Frachet was born in the diocese of Limoges. In 1225, at the age of twenty-five, he joined the Dominican order in Paris. He served as prior of Limoges from 1233 to 1245, after which other duties took him away from the city. In his fifties, however, he embarked on the study of history. He wrote the *Annales* of the Dominican order, which covered the whole history of the order up to 1254, and the *Lives of the Friars of the Order of Preachers,* which the chapter general of Strasbourg approved in 1260 and which became required reading for all Dominicans. Finally, he also composed a universal chronicle, which would be widely read for two centuries. Gerald continued work on his chronicle after his retirement in 1263, at fifty-eight, to the monastery of Limoges, where he died, "old and in the fullness of his days," in 1271.[16] He left some books and a copy of his work. In the same year, 1271, Stephen of Salanhac, also a native of the diocese of Limoges and seven years younger than Gerald, resigned the priorate of Limoges at almost sixty and retired to the same monastery. There he began writing a great historical work in honor of the Dominican order, *De Quatuor in quibus Deus Praedicatorum ordinem insignivit* (Of the Four Things Whereby God Distinguished the Order of Preachers), on which he was still at work in 1278. Stephen of Salanhac died in 1291, "old and in the fullness of his days."[17] He had spent nearly sixty years in the order (*quasi sexagenarius in ordine*). He was nearly eighty. This learned and eloquent man, this solid and prolific historian, was known throughout the country (*famosus in tota patria*).[18] However, his *De quatuor,* on which he had been unable to work for the last thirteen years of his life, remained unfinished. In Limoges Bernard Gui discovered the still-fresh memory of Gerald of Frachet. He was able to read his books.[19] He venerated Stephen of Salanhac, between whose hands he had made his vows. Shortly after the latter's death, and shortly after Bernard himself completed his studies, when he was not quite thirty-five and still the young prior of Albi, he decided that he, too, would contribute to the glory of the Dominican order by writing history, and he began to gather notes.[20] He took Stephen of Salanhac's unfinished treatise and completed it, making considerable additions to the work at the very time when the dramatic events in Albi and Carcassonne would have paralyzed many men. Word spread. At the chapter general of Toulouse, where Aimeric of Plaisance was elected master of the order on May 1, 1304, the new master encouraged Bernard. And on December 22, 1304, the prior of Castres sent Aimeric the finest historical work yet written about the Dominican order.[21]

Dominican, Inquisitor, and Historian (1307–16)

A few months later, Bernard Gui was again prior of Limoges, happy to be home again and out of the troubled region in which he had lived for thirteen years. Though a conscientious administrator, Gui was not a man for stormy times.[22] Apparently he was not very shrewd, either, for he was unable to persuade the viscount of Limoges to allow him to open the monastery wall in order to attach a much needed porch, but his successor did obtain the viscount's authorization shortly after taking office.[23] But Gui was a scholar and a lover of books, and he was admirably efficient when it came to building a library for his monastery. Large enough to hold one hundred volumes, it was completed in 1306 after less than a year's work. It was the first library to be built in any Dominican monastery in the province of Toulouse. In Toulouse itself there was no library until 1307. Bernard's construction was thus one of the earliest efforts in the West to build a room devoted especially to the preservation of books. The early, rapid construction of this library shows what kind of scholar and what kind of administrator Bernard Gui was.[24]

Gui was already embarked on his plan to build the library when the former archbishop of Bordeaux, who had a short while earlier become Pope Clement V, came to Limoges with eight cardinals. He arrived on Saturday, April 23, 1306, accepted the hospitality of the Dominican monastery, and granted a few small privileges to its prior. The next day, Sunday, the pope visited the grave of Saint Martial, blessed the assembled crowd, and left for Solignac and Bordeaux.[25]

It is not clear that this meeting altered Bernard Gui's fate. Everything that happened might have happened in spite of it. Other Dominican priors became inquisitors without being personal acquaintances of the pope. In any case, on January 16, 1307, Bernard Gui became inquisitor of Toulouse, inaugurating what was to be the most active and fruitful period of his life, during which he was simultaneously a loyal Dominican, a conscientious inquisitor, and a busy historian. On March 31, 1307, he consulted the monastery archives in Prouille. In July he was still (or again) in Prouille, copying more documents. In the same month he traveled to Condom, where he took part in the Dominican provincial chapter. Back in Toulouse on December 26, he sent the sisters of Prouille the opus on which he had worked while staying with them and which he had just completed, a history of the origins of the prestigious monastery founded by Dominic himself in 1207. Yet in the cathedral of Toulouse on March 3, 1308, he held his first major inquisitorial "sermon," a grandiose ceremony during which the inquisitor read out dozens of carefully prepared judgments.[26]

Over the next ten years we find Bernard Gui attending the chapters of his Dominican province. He wrote countless letters in connection with his inquisitorial duties, and from 1308 to 1316 he participated in nine sermons, during which he rendered judgment in 536 cases. His historical output was also considerable. He continued to add to his history of the Dominicans until 1311 but after that date made only minor additions. His interests lay elsewhere. His scholarly passion was such that, if the occasion arose, he might write his brief treatise or catalogue, much as he had written his brief history of the origins of Prouille when the opportunity had presented itself. Late in the year 1312 he completed a small treatise on the Dominican priors of L'Artige, near Limoges. Early in 1313 he wrote a chronicle of the priors of Grandmont, also near Limoges. On November 14, 1313, he presented a catalogue of the bishops of Toulouse, and on May 1, 1315, he presented another of the bishops of Limoges. He was again prior of Limoges when he conceived a new ambition, one that he shared with many other men and in particular with Gerald of Frachet, whose chronicle he obviously found in the monastery library at Limoges and followed step by step: Bernard set out to write a great universal chronicle from the time of Jesus Christ to his own day. He began gathering information in 1306, when he was forty-five. On March 26, 1311, on the second day of a new year (which for him began on the feast of the Annunciation, March 25), Bernard Gui took advantage of a moment of respite during a brief stay at the papal court, now installed in Avignon. He worked steadily at his composition while at the same time compiling and publishing separate catalogues of the popes, emperors, and kings of France, which in his mind were indispensable appendices to the larger work. And all the while he was also performing his other duties.

For years Bernard Gui's life was one of constant writing and travel. To be sure, he left the province of Toulouse only once, in 1311, when he went to Avignon. But within that province he left evidence of his visits to Prouille, Condom, Carcassonne, Agen,

Bordeaux, and Auvillars.[27] Where else he may have gone we do not know. Nevertheless, his duties normally kept him in Toulouse. We know what he was doing there on May 1; and indeed, because we know, that day may have been an exceptional one. The record nevertheless shows the kinds of activities that absorbed his time. In those days the Church felt itself threatened by the followers of Gerardo Segarelli, who had been burned in 1301, and his disciple Dolcino, who had been cut to pieces before being committed to the flames in 1301 for "pretending to lead an apostolic life and live in evangelical poverty." These men, "who claimed to belong to the order of Apostles" threatened the Church with "their apparently perfect lives" and their criticisms.[28] Previously the sect of pseudo-Apostles had infected only Lombardy, but recently it had been detected in Spain as well. On May 1, 1316, Bernard Gui therefore found the time to copy out, with long additions in his own hand, a treatise, which he had just received from Italy, on the sect's history and errors. Then he addressed to the clergy of Spain in general and the archbishop of Compostella in particular a long letter in which he explained what Dolcino's disciples were like and how to go about unmasking and punishing them.[29] At the end of this very busy day Bernard nevertheless found time to write to the master general of his order a letter offering him the gift of the now finished universal chronicle entitled *Flowers of the Chronicles.*[30] Not even on that feverish day—May 1, 1316—did the inquisitor forget that he was a historian.

It is impossible to understand Bernard Gui's production as a historian and the circulation of his works without recognizing how the Dominican and inquisitor in him were constantly aiding the scholar. He personally copied out once, perhaps even twice, the great corpus of Dominican history to which he devoted so many years. But ten other copies of the work were made during his lifetime, surely by Dominican scribes. Some of those scribes worked in Toulouse itself, alongside Bernard Gui, while others worked in a monastery to which the work was lent. Then, through the efforts of Bernard Gui himself or the zeal of his brothers, those manuscripts were distributed among the various monasteries of the province of Toulouse. Whenever the inquisitor visited, his first concern was to reread the manuscript of his corpus, correct it, and add in his own hand all the new information the historian had gathered from his incessant research. In monasteries in Toulouse, Auvillars, Rodez, Carcassonne, Prouille, Bordeaux, perhaps Limoges, and no doubt elsewhere as well, there were thus manuscripts of the corpus corrected and completed in Bernard Gui's own hand.[31] The distribution of the historian's work thus coincided with the movements of the Dominican inquisitor, so that, so far as we know, all the manuscripts were for a time to be found exclusively in the Dominican monasteries of the province of Toulouse. Thus, in 1316, Bernard, at age fifty-five at the summit of his powers, found it easy to reconcile his vows as a Dominican, his zeal as an inquisitor, and his passion as a historian. But suddenly his fate took a new turn.

Procurator General of the Dominican Order (1316–20)

In choosing a procurator general to represent the Dominican order to the pope, did master general Berenger of Landorre single out the efficient inquisitor who had been working in Toulouse for the past ten years or the distinguished historian who had just made him a gift of the *Flowers of the Chronicles*? In either case it is clear that with this selection Bernard's order demonstrated its esteem for and confidence in him. September 11, 1316, found Bernard Gui in Lyons, where the new pope and the cardinals were still assembled. He did not resign his post as inquisitor but delegated its functions.[32] And thus a man who had seldom been outside Aquitaine found himself at the pope's side, in the papal court, at the center of the Western world, at a time when very serious storm clouds were gathering.

France had no shortage of problems, but the most vexing issue of the day was Flanders. Philip the Fair, the loser at Courtrai but, two years later, the victor at Mons-en-Pévèle, had signed an advantageous peace treaty with the count of Flanders at Athis-sur-Orge in 1305, but it had taken years to win ratification of the treaty by Flemish obstructionists. And then, despite the ratification, and in spite of military expeditions virtually every year and virtually constant negotiations, the king of France had failed to enforce the treaty's terms. Philip the Fair died on November 29, 1314, without succeeding in this effort. His eldest son, Louis X, was similarly unsuccessful up to the time of his premature death on June 5, 1316. The king's early death precipitated another, far more serious problem. By his first wife Louis X had left only one daughter, still quite young and, worse still, discredited by the shadow of scandal. His second wife was pregnant. Would the child be a boy? Would it survive? For the first time in centuries the Capetian succession was in doubt. And it was still in doubt in September 1316.

At the same time, however, the crisis triggered by the death of Pope Clement V on April 20, 1314, had just been resolved after more than two years. Meeting in Lyons, the battle-weary cardinals on August 7, 1316, elected the cardinal-bishop of Porto, Jacques Duèse, who took the name John XXII. The new pope had been born in Cahors in 1245. Theology held little attraction for him, but he was a great jurist, a doctor in both civil law and canon law who had taught civil law with distinction. Subsequently he had shown himself to be an excellent administrator and had earned the favors first of Charles II, count of Provence and king of Sicily; Charles's son Robert; and finally Pope Clement V. In 1316, at seventy-two, this thin little old man, who was pale and ugly and spoke very quickly in a high-pitched voice, seemed a choice unlikely to foreclose too many future options.[33] He outwitted his electors, however, and reigned for eighteen years. To the end he retained his unshakeable health, his lively wit, and his appetite for work. The cardinals had actually given the Church the sound head and firm hand it needed.

The elderly pontiff set out to do battle against the novelties that, by his lights, threatened to destroy the Church. He was suspicious of the doctrinal uncertainties that were proliferating. In particular, he saw the dangers that the ideal of poverty posed for the Church at that moment in history. By the beginning of the fourteenth century poverty had long been a fundamental requirement of Western spirituality. Numerous voices had always arisen in opposition to the wealth of the clergy, but those voices had never contested the institution of the Church itself, and the Church, for its part, had refrained from condemning the advocates of poverty. Poverty and obedience could be harnessed together. In the early thirteenth century Saint Francis had been an obedient son of the Church, and throughout that century the mendicant orders had expanded within the framework of the Church. Pietro di Murrone, born in 1209 or 1210 in the Abruzzi, the next to youngest in a family of twelve boys, had entered a Benedictine monastery prior to 1230, had become a hermit, and had founded a small eremitic confraternity, which he skillfully organized and administered without leaving the Benedictine order. In 1286, this active leader, efficient administrator, and committed head of an order had finally given in to the weight of his years and retired from the world. He lived as a simple hermit until, on July 5, 1294, the cardinals, deadlocked and left with no alternative, had elected this eighty-five-year-old man, this living symbol of austerity and poverty, to be their pope. Pietro di Murrone became Celestine V. For a brief moment the hierarchical order and the order of perfection coincided.[34]

Nevertheless, it became increasingly difficult, even in the time of Celestine V, to reconcile obedience to the Church with evangelical poverty. The Franciscan order experienced a period of profound unrest. The "conventuals" accepted the order as it was, but the "spirituals" protested that it was no longer possible to live in the order in absolute poverty, as Francis had dreamed. In 1274, moreover, the Church, at the Council of Lyons, had abolished a large number of smaller mendicant orders that had taken poverty for their ideal. It viewed the proliferation of such orders as a possible source of disorder and heresy. In rejecting these humble orders, beloved of the Christian faithful, the Church further estranged the flock from its pastors.[35] Growing numbers of Christians despaired of being able to live a life of Christlike poverty within the bosom of the Church. Finally, the abdication of Celestine V on December 13, 1294, though legitimate under canon law, left all those who dreamed of a poor Church high and dry. The blunders of Celestine's successor, Boniface VIII, further heightened anxieties. In the early years of the fourteenth century poverty thus became the major issue facing the Church. Some people, including the followers of Segarelli and Dolcino, believed that a life of evangelical poverty was no longer possible except outside the Church. Others, including the Franciscan spirituals, wished to remain within the Church, but a Church stripped of its wealth and left, like Christ and his disciples, the owner of nothing. A Church stripped of its riches was of course a response to religious aspirations, but it also satisfied certain obvious political appetites. Some pious princes began to dream of a poor Church. The king of France felt especially devoted to the hermit of the Abruzzi, a man who was increasingly looked upon as a victim of Boniface VIII. The king bestowed favors on Celestine's order. Monasteries of "Celestines" were founded in the kingdom. And on May 5, 1313, Philip the Fair obtained from Clement V the canonization, if not of Celestine V then at least of Pietro di Murrone, who had been wise enough to remain poor even on the pontifical throne.[36] Ludwig of Bavaria, king of the Romans since 1314, found his throne contested and soon encountered the hostility of the pope; he later welcomed Franciscan spirituals in his court and also received that audacious theorist of a Church stripped of its wealth and power, Marsilius of Padua.

After his election John XXII thus found a great deal that needed to be done in the areas of administration, politics, and doctrine. He needed to resolve the still insoluble Italian question. He had to deal with the imperial problem. He had to conciliate in the dispute between France and Flanders. And above all he had to combat new and dangerous religious doctrines. He intended to do so by opposing "to the powers of destruction that power of resistance and stability, the work of Thomas Aquinas," the great Dominican thinker who had died in 1274.[37] To the pope it seemed that the best way of establishing the truth of Thomas's work was to proclaim his sainthood. Last and perhaps not least, John XXII, a remarkable administrator, set out to justify the existence of a Church now threatened by the ideal of evangelical poverty; to do this he had to prove the legitimacy not of wealth, perhaps, but at least of property. He had to show that even Christ and his disciples had had possessions, at least in common. And finally, he had to show that the essence of the matter was not poverty but charity.[38]

John XXII needed help in this mission. He could count, for example, on Bertrand de la Tour, a man born like himself in Quercy (at an unknown date) and a relative of the lords of Camboulit. Bertrand while still quite young had joined the Franciscans and become a famous doctor in theology noted for his sermons; he was a solid intellectual, conservative and orthodox, and a man of action capable of persuading and leading others. Poverty was not his problem. He obeyed the pope and backed his views. In 1320 he became a cardinal, obtained a number of benefices, and set the Franciscan order back on the proper path.[39] John XXII also relied on Guillaume de Pierre Godin. Born around 1260 to a family of wealthy Bayonne merchants, Guillaume was roughly the same age as Bernard Gui, and he too became a Dominican. The two men's paths crossed in 1282, when Guillaume was professor of philosophy in Bordeaux. But Guillaume's extraordinary intellectual and administrative abilities soon elevated him far beyond Bernard's world. From 1292 to 1296 he studied in Paris. In 1301 he served as provincial prior of Provence. In 1304 he returned to Paris to continue his studies in theology. In 1306 he became Clement V's personal theologian and carried out several embassies to the pope's satisfaction. He became a cardinal in 1312 and was a little more than fifty-five when Jacques Duèse was elected pope. He retained the confidence of the new pope. In 1318 at the pope's behest he wrote the *Tractatus de causa immediate ecclesiastice potestatis,* a skillful exposition of papal doctrine. From 1320 to 1324 he served as the pope's legate in Spain. He died, rich and powerful, in 1336, at the age of seventy-six.[40]

When Guillaume de Pierre Godin became cardinal, he selected as a member of his "house" (that is, his entourage) at Avignon an elderly Dominican of seventy-six named Bartolomeo of Lucca. Bartolomeo was born in Lucca in 1236 and joined the Dominican order. He served as auditor and confessor for Thomas Aquinas during the theologian's stay in the Naples (1272–74). Later he served as prior of several Italian monasteries. As time went by, he became more and more proud of, and was increasingly respected for, having been a pupil of Thomas's, and one of the best. Was it he who finished Thomas's *De Regimine Principum*? We do not know. But it was indeed he who, settled in Avignon with the riches of the papal library close at hand, wrote a great *Historia ecclesiastica nova,* which he completed when he was eighty, in 1316, just as John XXII became pope; Bartolomeo dedicated this work to Guillaume de Pierre Godin. Incorporated into it at points dictated by the chronology were fragments of a biography of Thomas, the first ever written, and a catalogue of his works, the first ever compiled, along with an inventory of the miracles that the illustrious Dominican had worked since his death. Taken together, these fragments took on "the obvious appearance of an application for canonization."[41]

Guglielmo of Tocco was born in 1242 into a great Neapolitan family. Though slightly younger than Bartolomeo of Lucca, he too after becoming a Dominican heard Thomas preach and teach at Naples. In 1316 he was prior of Benevento. As an old man he retained the admiration he had conceived for Thomas as a youth. Urged on by the pope, he devoted the last of his strength to the process of canonization. He made the necessary inquiries, wrote an account of Thomas's life and miracles, and twice went to Avignon to present his findings.[42] Guglielmo died before the canonization was complete, but Bartolomeo of Lucca, who shared the pope's ideas and his robust health, became bishop of Torcello on March 15, 1318. The serious problems he faced there for the next five years did not kill him. He died bishop of Torcello in 1327 at ninety-one.

These were a few of the men with whom Bernard Gui was familiar and upon whom John XXII hoped to rely. Naturally the new pope also had the opportunity to became acquainted with the new procurator general of the Dominican order. His judgment of Bernard was favorable, and on January 29, 1317, John XXII entrusted to Bertrand de la Tour and Bernard Gui the important mission of restoring peace in northern Italy and Tuscany.[43] The two ambassadors waited till spring to cross the Alps. By April 12 they had reached Turin and subsequently traveled from city to city. They spent the month of August in Bologna and then headed south. On January 27, 1318, they were in Pisa.[44] In the spring of 1318 they crossed the Alps once again and returned to Avignon. Their failure was obvious. Wherever they had visited, the two churchmen had proclaimed a truce in the pope's name to applauding crowds. But not knowing anything of the Italians and confounded by their "wily fox's tricks," they looked on helplessly as violence preceded and followed their steps.

Bernard Gui was also overwhelmed by the climate. He spent the month of August in Bologna in bed, laid low by tertian fever. When in good health it seems that he preferred long, quiet hours in the library to interminable negotiations. In Verona, Reggio, Bologna, and no doubt other cities as well the ambassador's disappointments did not prevent the historian from indulging his devouring passion. Upon his return to Avignon, Bernard gave the pope the second edition of the *Flowers of the Chronicles* on August 7, 1318, the second anniversary of the pope's election. John XXII was touched, but he was also a realist and had to concede that, as for Italy, a year's efforts had produced nothing.[45] He therefore cast about for another man, one who would be less helpless when it came to dealing with the Italian problem, and found him in the celebrated person of Bertrand du Poujet, who served a long term as papal legate in Italy.

Meanwhile, the pope found a less desperate mission for Bertrand de la Tour and Bernard Gui. On September 21, 1318, he sent them to France to attempt finally to bring peace between the king of France and the count of Flanders. The two men stopped in Paris. Gui visited some libraries and took notes.[46] Then negotiations were held in Compiègne. The talks led to a formal meeting at the priory of Royallieu, not far from Compiègne, on October 11, 1318. The results were disappointing. The pope's envoys spoke first. But Bertrand de la Tour, a Quercynois, and Bernard Gui, a Limousin, preferred to speak their southern regional dialect. Naturally few of their listeners were moved by their arguments. The bishop of Mende, Guillaume Durant, a native of the diocese of Béziers, was one of the advisers of the king of France; he may have understood them. He chose to speak Latin, which the papal envoys surely understood, but confined himself to banalities. He then yielded the floor to Henri de Sulli, bouteiller de France, who discussed Flemish affairs in detail, but in a French that the two southerners did not understand. As for the Flemish delegation, it is not at all certain that some of its Flemish-speaking members understood all or even part of this trilingual eloquence. In any case it would have taken far more than eloquence to overcome their obstinacy.[47] John XXII was obliged to find another man, who took up the matter the following year and successfully resolved it. La Tour and Gui's journey north of the Loire had been shorter and less arduous than their trip across the Alps, but their failure was just as total. Neither man was a diplomat.

Bertrand de la Tour had other talents, which John XXII used and rewarded. These embassies were just a brief interlude in his career. But Bernard Gui was not yet sixty when his career reached its summit. There is no evidence that he suffered as a result. He was probably even relieved to return to his passions and familiar surroundings. Bernard had not yet left Avignon for France when, on September 13, 1318, the pope approved the preliminary investigation into the sanctity of Thomas Aquinas and the canonization process got under way in earnest. It culminated on July 18, 1323, with an impressive ceremony in the cathedral Notre-Dame-des-Doms in Avignon, where the great theologian was proclaimed a saint. Many people had looked upon Thomas as a saint for a long time and believed that he had worked many miracles after his death. The Dominicans had been tenacious in their efforts on his behalf. They had paid for a complete collection of Thomas's works to be given to the pope, and that edition, which was placed in the pontifical library in 1317, is still there today. But the illustrious professor ultimately had been elevated to sainthood by the determination of a few men, including the pope, men in their seventies and eighties frightened by what they saw around them and eager to moor what they took to be a Church adrift to a firm doctrine, which they hoped to strengthen still more by making its author a saint. To be sure, it was possible to object, and some did object, that Thomas had not performed any miracles during his lifetime. To which John XXII might have responded that the miracle was his teaching.[48] So the gates of paradise were opened, this once at least, to a professor.

As procurator general of the Dominican order, Bernard Gui had a role to play in this process. Upon his return to France at the end of 1318, he wrote a life of Thomas based on that of Guglielmo di Tocco. He may still have been procurator general in 1320 when he compiled a new catalogue of Thomas's works.[49] He subsequently never lost interest in his hero. He was probably the eyewitness to whom we are indebted for the account of the ceremony of July 18, 1323. And in 1324 he revised and, using information gathered in the course of the canonization process, completed the life he had written in 1318. By then, however, he had for some time ceased to be procurator general of his order; his destiny had taken him farther and farther from Avignon.

At the end of 1319 he was still nominally the Dominicans' procurator general at the pontifical court. But his presence there was no longer so necessary as to prevent him from resuming his inquisitorial duties in Toulouse, where he had not been seen for three years. In September, November, and December 1319 he held three sermons and pronounced sixty-four judgments.[50] In 1320 he probably still held the title of procurator general, but he was once again in Toulouse finishing up the second edition of his catalogue of the bishops of Limoges.[51] In any case, by the end of 1320 he was no longer procurator general but simply the inquisitor of Toulouse. Although he traveled occasionally to Avignon, the tireless sexagenarian devoted most of his time to travels in his own province in the course of which he held solemn inquisitorial sermons. Between 1321 and 1323 he held six of them and pronounced 230 judgments. The sermon of June 19, 1323, was his last. In July 1323 he more than likely attended Saint Thomas's canonization ceremonies in Avignon. Did John XXII wish to reward the procurator for his contribution to this canonization? Did he wish to offer a discreet sign of his sympathy to the unlucky ambassador? Did he want to honor sixteen years of work as inquisitor? In any event, on August 26, 1323, he named Bernard Gui bishop of Tuy on the western reaches of Galice, on the Minho, almost on the shores of the Atlantic.

It is not at all obvious that Bernard Gui was enchanted by this appointment. After his transalpine travels and his journey north of the Loire, it is not clear that the prospect of living south of the Pyrenees, far from the south of France, would have elicited the slightest enthusiasm. In any case he was in no great haste to visit his diocese, and his stay there was as brief as it was discreet. The only traces of it to be found are in two charters dated February 13 and March 27, 1324.[52] During those months Bernard Gui was quite active, however, but far from Tuy. He was probably still performing duties as inquisitor of Toulouse, because his successor was not named until July 24, 1324. Bernard meanwhile drew on all his experience as inquisitor to write his *Inquisitor's Manual* (*Practica Inquisitionis Heretice Pravitatis*), the first three parts of which describe inquisitorial procedures in minute detail; the fourth part deals with the powers of the tribunal of the Inquisition, and the fifth and longest part reviews all the sects with which Bernard had occasion to become familiar, sets forth their dogmas and practices, exposes the ruses by which heretics sought to evade the inquisitors' questions, and explains how the inquisitor should proceed in order to outwit them. Yet not even the composition of this thick manual prevented Bernard Gui from working on the new book that he must have begun immediately after finishing the *Flowers of the Chronicles.*

Writing lives of saints for the faithful to read and collecting legends (from the Latin *legendus,* meaning that which is to be read) for anthologies of one sort or another had long been duties required by Christian piety and practice. In the thirteenth century the Dominicans were more apt than other orders to compile thick anthologies of hagiography. The *Speculum historiale* (*Historical Mirror*) compiled by the Frenchman Vincent of Beauvais around the middle of the century was a compendium of available historical knowledge as well as a compilation of more than five hundred hagiographies, which made it one of the most important legendaries of the Middle Ages and no doubt accounted for its tremendous success.[53] A few years later, in 1255, the young Italian Dominican Jacobus da Varagine compiled his *Legenda Sanctorum* (*Legends of the Saints*), which met with immediate and enormous success and which everyone in the West insisted on calling *The Golden Legend*. In May 1316, when the master general of the Dominican Order received the *Flores Chronicorum*, he not only strove to have Bernard Gui named procurator general of the order but also suggested that he write a new *Golden Legend*. As an obedient, erudite Dominican and a Frenchman, or more precisely a Limousin, Bernard Gui conceived a work more critical and more complete than *The Golden Legend* and also one that would devote more space to the saints of his own kingdom and province. As a preliminary to this major undertaking, he immediately compiled an anthology of the saints of the Limoges diocese, a work that was completed at the end of 1316.[54] Subsequently he had had to deal with many other concerns, and it was not until 1323 that he was able to return to work in earnest, which he did with his customary efficiency. On August 20, 1324, he was in Avignon. On that day he made John XXII a gift of the first two parts of his *Speculum Sanctorale* (*Mirror of the Saints*), and the pope transferred him from the see of Tuy to that of Lodève, which though not in the province of Toulouse was at least, in the Cévennes mountains, a bishopric in southern France, where Bernard Gui felt at home.

Portrait of Bernard Gui

In the book that Stephen of Salanhac wrote in honor of the Order of Preachers and that Bernard Gui revised and completed, various types of Dominicans were singled out: those who became popes, cardinals, and bishops; those who had been masters of theology at Paris; and other illustrious doctors and famous preachers. At sixty-three, Bernard Gui's fate was sealed: he would never be pope or cardinal. He would never be a great doctor or a great professor or a great preacher. But he numbered among those Dominicans whom the Church had chosen to make prelates.

Bernard's nomination as bishop was the Church's way of rewarding the zeal of the inquisitor and the talent of the historian. Above all, perhaps, the Church saw in Bernard a reliable servant, one of those men of unshakeable conviction so sorely needed in those troubled times. The bedrock on which Bernard Gui's certitudes rested consisted of one simple idea: in every society, and in the Church in particular, there are superiors and inferiors; there are men who derive authority from their office and other men who serve under them. In other words, every society, including the Church, is a great chain, a hierarchy of authorities. But in the thirteenth century not all laymen were yet convinced that obedience was the cardinal political virtue. For the master of the Dominicans, Humbert of Romans, however, obedience was the best cement for political and ecclesiastical societies. Every man, he said, must obey several masters: his father, his prince, his priest, his bishop, and ultimately, enthroned at the summit of this hierarchy, God. The supreme good, peace, depended on this obedience.[55] And Bernard Gui, brought up on Paul's First Epistle and steeped in the teaching of his Dominican masters, knew that the old (*seniores*) and the young (*juniores*) must vie in humility and fear of God; but if the former were supposed to lead by the example of their virtue and aim to be loved rather than feared, the paramount duty of the latter was to obey.[56] Bernard, moreover, was a mystic of obedience. On September 16, 1280, he had taken his vows between the hands of Stephen of Salanhac. Fifty years later, the bishop of Lodève still bore such "a sincere affection toward his mother, the religion that had raised him [that is, to his order], that . . . finding himself in Avignon, he renewed, with great devotion, his vows in the hands of brother Barnabas, master of the order of Preachers, uttering the usual formula and, according to the custom of the order, holding his hands between those of the master general: 'I, brother Bernard Gui, bishop of Lodève, make profession and promise obedience to God, to the blessed Mary, and to the blessed Dominic, and to you, brother Barnabas, master of the order of Friar Preachers; and I pledge to be obedient to you and your successors until death.' "[57] Throughout his long life not a flicker of doubt ever shook Bernard's robust conviction. God had granted to some men offices higher than his own; he had given them authority over him. Bernard had been satisfied to obey them. He had always known what to do and what to think. He remained, in the twilight of his life, a respectful prelate.

Some of Bernard's major works were his own idea, but he never would have undertaken or completed them without the encouragement of his superiors.[58] Other works were simply commissioned. He himself tells us that it was obedience (*obediencie meritum*) that led him to write his *Sanctoral.* He was compelled to do so by the authority of the prelate who was his superior, the master of the Dominican order (*astrinxit auctoritas superiori mei prelati, magistri ordinis Praedicatorum*).[59] What he says in his works, especially about the important and difficult cases, is what his authorities say. What challenge could have demanded greater tact than Bernard's account of the long conflict between Philip the Fair and Boniface VIII?

But the author of *Flores Chronicorum* was little troubled. He simply followed the version that the former master of the Dominicans, subsequently Benedict XI (1303–4), had elaborated in the hope of resolving the dispute.[60] When his works were finished, he offered them to his superiors with words that were often traditional but, coming from Bernard Gui, certainly were not mere formulas of courtesy. In dedicating the *Flowers of the Chronicles* to Berenger of Landorre on May 1, 1316, he wrote that he was presenting his work as an obedient son (*obediencie filius*), with due obedience (*cum obedientia debita*), to the master of the Dominicans so that the latter might examine (*examinare*), correct (*corrigere*), and approve (*probare*) it.[61] When he presented the first two parts of the *Sanctoral* to John XXII on July 20, 1324, he asked the supreme pontiff of the Holy Roman and Universal Church to correct them, to polish them, in the knowledge, he says, that "what you will have approved [*quidquid probaveritis*] will be good, and better still will be what you have corrected [*quod correxeritis*]."[62]

The certainty that obedience leads to truth sustained the historian. It gave the Christian that tranquil strength, that sober gaiety that he so appreciated in others and that so struck those who knew him. "This bishop Bernard, a man of contemplative soul and lively conversation, sometimes called his familiars to his side in the evening, after the day's fatiguing business and study were done, and asked one of them to discuss some decent, pleasant, and amusing topic, for he maintained that a good man should never go to bed without having enjoyed himself at least once during the day. As for himself, he used this time of relief with rare sobriety and always concluded with edifying words, which his devotion suggested to him with a marvelous fecundity."[63]

Coupled with real intellectual and administrative capacities, this tranquil certitude and sober gaiety made Bernard Gui an ideal subordinate, the perfect cog in a hierarchical machine. But these qualities did not prepare him to understand the lost or even the merely troubled sheep in the flock assigned to him—the souls assailed by doubt who dreamed of a purer world, of poorer prelates, and of more respectable authorities. Those who were not satisfied with the truths approved by the authorities, those for whom obedience was not enough, exhibited in Bernard Gui's eyes an incomprehensible madness, which left him dumbfounded and indignant. Consider the Albi rebels of 1302. They carried madness (*demencia*) and insanity (*insania*) to such lengths that they took down the portraits of Saints Peter and Dominic that hung over the city gate near the Dominican monastery and replaced them with the portraits of sinners of whom they approved. They thus rejected (*reprobare*) approved (*approbare*) saints and they legitimated (*authenticare*) misguided sinners. Yet truth (*veritas*) did not permit these false images (*falsas ymagines*) to remain. After a few years they were obliterated, and the authority of justice (*equitatis auctoritas*) restored the images of the saints whose names were indelibly written in the book of life.[64] Or consider the Waldenses, who were so enamored of poverty. What, in Bernard Gui's eyes, was the gravest of their errors? "Disdain for ecclesiastical power was and is the principal heresy of the Waldenses." They refused obedience (*obedire minime voluerunt*) and in their folly (*vesania*) maintained that men must obey God, not other men (*magis Deo quam hominibus obedire*).[65] And then there were the "Apostles," the followers of Gerardo Segarelli and Fra Dolcino who wished to live in evangelical poverty. "Has the habit that you are wearing been approved by the Roman Church [*ab ecclesia Romana . . . approbatus*]?" Bernard Gui asked them. And concerning all the things they did, he asked: "Why do you do these things when they have not been ordered either by the Roman Church or by ecclesiastical prelates [*cum non sint instituta fieri ab ecclesia Romana nec a prelatis ecclesie*]?"[66] Bernard could not hide his astonishment that a man like Gerardo Segarelli, whose authority was nil (*auctoritate, que nulla erat*) and who had "no notion that old paths are the safest and soundest," dared to teach the people a new doctrine (*novam doctrinam*) and a new way (*viam novam*) and dared to exhort his disciples, whom he called Apostles, "to live without obeying anyone but God [*qui viverant sub nullius obedientia nisi solius Dei*]."[67] Such novelties were a consternation and a puzzle to a man profoundly convinced that outside the Church "there is neither true penitence nor salvation."[68]

With such a premise, the inquisitor's task was simple in its principle if difficult in its practice. He did not need to plumb the depths of other people's souls. All he needed to do was to determine which suspects rejected the authority of the Church and refused to obey its priests. They were punished, and the most hardened sinners were turned over to the secular authorities. In court such people usually behaved in an evasive and slippery manner, and Bernard, as a scrupulous inquisitor, found it necessary to turn over a relatively small number, a few dozen in all.[69]

Respect for the authorities satisfied the Christian and the inquisitor; it dominated the work of the historian. Yet it was not his only guide. The historian in Bernard Gui, like all historians, was a passionate seeker of truth. And like all historians he expected his authorities to speak the truth.[70] At least he expected as much when faith was at issue. The beneficiary of a long period of progress in historical scholarship, Bernard Gui was more aware than most of the discrepancies that could be found between different texts and different accounts. Like most of his predecessors, he attributed these contradictions (*dissonancia, varietas, contrarietas, diversitas*) to "errors of the copyists."[71] He was one of the first, I believe, to say plainly that they might also be due to "the diversity of authors' opinions and positions."[72] Faced with such diversity, the man of faith and the man of science could choose to follow the most reliable authority. So it was in the case of the conflict between Philip the Fair and Boniface VIII. He could also decide to say nothing about matters concerning which opinions diverged and to stick exclusively to the naked facts. That way, at least, his brevity would not provoke boredom or doubts in his readers.[73] Finally, in cases where the authorities were equally trustworthy and the issues were minor, he could "present the contrary propositions and leave it to the reader to judge and choose."[74] Therefore the historian often bowed either to his authorities or to his readers. But Bernard Gui also knew that there was a vast realm of truth in which the faith was not at issue and which erudition could and should strive to attain by its own methods. A well-crafted argument could establish a dubious date or correct an erroneous one.[75] A new text could make it possible to fill in the gaps in a list. An optimistic historian, Bernard Gui never doubted that progress in historical knowledge was necessary and possible. To allow himself and others to make corrections and additions, he left "empty spaces here and there" in his works.[76] Respect for the authorities did not prevent him from developing independent methods of historical research and criticism. Erudition helped Bernard Gui to put himself at some distance from his authorities.

Of course the boldness of Bernard's erudition did not prevent his superiors from counting on him. His scholarly passions certainly did not prevent him from being an efficient prior and conscientious inquisitor. It was only when he was called, apparently, to a higher destiny that his qualities as a man of learning proved to be encumbering baggage. It is difficult to avoid the conclusion that the long hours spent in libraries somehow interfered with Bernard's diplomatic missions. What is more, Bernard Gui was a man who mistrusted words. In describing the November 1302 synod of Rome, at the height of the conflict between Philip the Fair and Boniface VIII, our historian cannot refrain from making this observation: "Verba quidem fuerunt et transierunt; sed nihil aliud notabile gestum apparuit in effectu" (Words there were, which passed back and forth. But in the end nothing important was done).[77] This horror of words and long-windedness helped our chronographer to produce those brief lists, catalogues, dates, facts, and notes that were the marvelous fruit of his erudition. Yet it is difficult to avoid the conclusion that the same horror paralyzed the ambassador of Pope John XXII.

Bernard Gui, moreover, really had no taste for playing a major role on the world stage. As man of action or scholar he never felt secure except in his own familiar setting. He was first of all a man of Limoges, and he loved the Limousins best of all. John XXII was from Cahors; he loved the Quercynois best of all and favored them throughout his career. Thus strictly speaking there was no regional bond between the two men, but that does not mean that their common southern origins were of no importance. John XXII did not rely solely on Quercynois, and Bernard Gui's vision was not confined to Limoges. In a broader sense his region stretched from Limoges to Bordeaux to Carcassonne and encompassed the whole Dominican province of Toulouse, whose roads, towns, and monasteries he knew intimately. He knew that this region had been the fairest part of the kingdom of Aquitaine, which had stretched from the Loire to the Pyrenees.[78] He therefore took an abstract interest in the kingdom of Aquitaine. There is no evidence that he ever explored north of Limoges. Toward the east he felt drawn to the Dominican province of Provence, from which the province of Toulouse had only recently been severed. He had studied in Montpellier. He had often traveled the road to Avignon. Because of the distance, however, he knew very little about the monasteries of Provence, a fact that he deplored.[79] A friar whom Bernard Gui knew well was named prior of Le Puy, and this appointment put him out of reach of our scholar. Bernard Gui was a loyal subject of the king of France. He possessed an admirable knowledge of the kingdom's history. Yet even after his one unfortunate venture north of the Loire, the kingdom remained for him what it had always been: a cherished but remote idea. Italy was nothing more than a nightmare that had lasted a few months, and Spain was a penance that had lasted a few weeks. Germany was such a profound mystery that he spoke of the celebrated abbey of Saint Gall as "a certain Saint Gall abbey in Germany [*in quadam abbatia Sancti Galli in Theutonia*]."[80]

This timid attitude toward geography went together with an obvious inability to locate the paths that led to the summit of power. This very simple and very righteous man, who questioned nothing but his dates and facts, respected the authorities. He himself became a man of some authority. He never understood what family and regional solidarities, what kinds of pressure, or what corridors led to the highest power. Had he been ambitious, Bernard Gui would have learned quickly that a distinguished ecclesiastical career was obtained with the support of a prince or a cardinal or, better still, with the support of a prince *and* a cardinal. He was content to dedicate his works to the master of his order and to the head of his Church. The world of powerful laymen remained totally foreign to him. He never sought the favor of one of the princes of the Church whose path happened to cross his own. Guillaume de Pierre Godin, who had been his professor of philosophy at Bordeaux in 1282, later became a cardinal and the protector of that other great historian, Bartolomeo of Lucca. Bertrand de la Tour, his fellow ambassador, became a cardinal in 1320. And Renaud de la Porte, who also became a cardinal in 1320, was a Limousin, someone whom Bernard Gui must have known well when he was bishop of Limoges.[81]

In the twilight of his life, however, Bernard Gui did show some interest in two Limousins who were decidedly out of the ordinary. Peter of Mortemart, as he was known because he was a native of Mortemart, as he was known because he was a native of Mortemart in La Marche on the border between Limousin and Poitou, possessed remarkable gifts that made up for his modest origins. He became a doctor *in utroque,* that is, in both civil and canon law. In 1314 he was a professor at the University of Toulouse. At that time or shortly thereafter, Charles, son of Philip the Fair and count of La Marche, secured the services of the most brilliant mind in his county. He was a tenacious protector of Peter of Mortemart. And when Charles de La Marche became King Charles IV of France in 1322, he compelled John XXII, whom he did not like, to make Peter first a bishop (1322) and then a cardinal (1327).[82] Shortly after settling in Avignon, Peter of Mortemart sent for Pierre Roger, whom he loved as a son. Pierre Roger had been born in 1290 in Masmonteil, near Egletons, not far from Tulle, into a family of minor nobility. The child soon entered the Benedictine monastery of La Chaise-Dieu. He grew up and revealed his gifts. In 1323 he was master of theology. The young master was quite attached to Saint Thomas's doctrine. He pleased the pope. The favor of John XXII and the affection of Peter of Mortemart enabled Pierre Roger to embark on a brilliant career, which ended on the pontifical throne under the name Clement VI (1342–52). Bernard Gui, touched by the young Limousin's devotion to Thomas, in 1325 made him a gift of his just-completed life of the saint.[83] A few years later, in 1329, he made the new cardinal Peter of Mortemart the gift of a copy of his just-completed *Sanctoral.*[84] But these homages came too late for the elderly scholar, too soon for his compatriots. They bore no fruit.

Thus Bernard Gui did not want, or did not know how, or was

unable to take advantage of solidarities that might have taken him to a higher position. Yet he did not avoid obligations imposed on him by bonds of kinship, which he found perfectly natural. He had had a good uncle, and like so many other ecclesiastics he too was a good uncle in turn. He had at least four nephews: Aimeri Hugues, Gui Gui, Pierre Gui, and Bernard Gui, who was also (since he bore the same first name) his godson. Of these, the first three were ecclesiatics. Bernard Gui encouraged their studies, gave them books, and, as soon as he was in a position to do so (that is, after 1318), obtained benefices for them. On September 21, 1318, as Bernard Gui was preparing to leave on his French mission, Aimeri Hugues at his behest received the advowson of the parish church of Thurageau in the diocese of Poitiers. On September 14, 1324, Bernard Gui had just been named bishop of Lodève and had probably not yet left Avignon when Aimeri Hugues obtained the prospect of a prebend in the Saint-Hilaire church of Poitiers. Aimeri Hugues would die in 1370 a doctor *in utroque* and bishop of Lodève.[85] On September 21, 1318, again, Gui Gui obtained a canonry in the church of Saint-Paul-de-Fenouillet. On May 14, 1324, he became, thanks to his uncle the bishop of Tuy, archdeacon of Minhor in the church of Tuy. But he lingered south of the Pyrenees no longer than his uncle and soon returned to Lodève no longer than his uncle and soon returned to Lodève as precantor and canon of the cathedral. He was present in his uncle's final moments. We lose track of him in 1339 when he was doctor *in utroque* and dean of the church of Montréal in the diocese of Carcassonne.[86] Pierre Gui, for his part, was a Dominican like his uncle, who therefore did not have to pursue benefices on his behalf. But the uncle and the nephew, who like his elder possessed intellectual talents and administrative abilities, loved each other dearly. Pierre Gui's library contained the copy once owned by Bernard Gui of the chronicle of Eusebius of Caesarea translated into Latin and continued by Saint Jerome. Prior of the Carcassonne monastery in 1335, the nephew had his uncle's *Sanctoral* copied out at the monastery's expense. Elected prior provincial of Toulouse in 1338, he apparently intended to write, but never finished, a history of Dominicans famed for their saintly qualities. An anonymous biographical note about Bernard Gui is perhaps the only surviving fragment of this vast undertaking.[87] Of all Bernard's nephews, his godson Bernard Gui was the only one not to join the ecclesiastical estate. Yet by midcentury this son of an obscure resident of Royère had become a knight and owner of a fine estate in that same town; he is the earliest known ancestor of a family of minor Limousin nobles whose fate can be traced to the end of the fifteenth century.

It is hard to believe that the bishop of Lodève's efficacious affection played no part in this rapid rise.[88] Bernard Gui was not a man of very great authority, but he had enough authority to be a very good uncle.

Bishop of Lodève (1324–31)

On October 7, 1324, when Bernard Gui made his solemn entry into Lodève, the diocese was calm; the south of France was calm. But that calm followed fresh violence that had shocked the sexagenarian bishop just as much, and made him just as uneasy, as the "rage of Carcassonne" twenty years earlier. Continuing his *Flowers of the Chronicles,* Bernard described this latest "plague" to strike the Midi in a long and admirable passage that gave vent to all his obsessions and especially to his fear of leaderless mobs. "Suddenly," in 1320, "simple folk of both sexes" assembled in groups calling themselves *pastoureaux,* as others had done seventy years before. Their ambition was to recapture the Holy Land. Yet they "had no leader or prince above them, and no ship." Nevertheless, their numbers grew, and so did their temerity. Their folly (*vesania, dementia*) met with the favor of the multitude (*favor populi, connivente et favente vulgo*). At first the authorities showed them some sympathy. Soon they were rendered powerless and struck with terror. They could not prevent the Pastoureaux from killing Jews "without any judgment" and appropriating their property. These massacres occurred throughout the kingdom of France, but especially in Bordeaux, in Gascony, in the province of Toulouse, and in the dioceses of Cahors and Albi. Then the madmen set out for Avignon and talked of seizing the wealth of both the secular and regular clergy. Finally the powers did what had to be done (*providentia et potentia majorum*). The Pastoureaux did not get past Carcassonne. That autumn some were seized and hanged, and the rest dispersed. Bernard Gui concludes his account with a sentence indicative of his surprise at such an unpredictable and incomprehensible phenomenon as well as of his satisfaction with the restoration of order: "They had sprung up in an instant, like squash (*tanquam cucurbita*). But the sun's rays had dried out their roots. They suddenly wilted and evaporated into smoke [*et tanquam fumus evanuerunt*]."[89] The diocese of Lodève therefore remained untouched by the Pastoureaux, but in the same period it had been shaken by the heresy of certain Beguines, who had "doubted and staggered." They were burned in 1322.[90] Thus all was calm in Lodève when, on October 7, 1324, the canons, clergy, and people marched out in procession to welcome their new bishop.[91]

The diocese of Lodève was a small diocese of sixty-one parishes, poor and partly mountainous.[92] Bernard Gui could have lived there in idle retirement. Instead, the bishop, in his green old age, was just as tirelessly active as the young prior and inquisitor had been. He was a good pastor, at least within the standards set by the most conscientious bishops of his day. There is no evidence that he cared much about the souls of his flock, except that he preached to them often. But there is abundant proof that he poured all of his zeal into administering his diocese well, making sure of his authority as prelate, and defending his rights as a temporal lord. A few months after his arrival he made a midwinter inspection of the entire diocese. On Sunday, March 24, 1325, he received an oath of loyalty from all 942 adult male inhabitants of Lodève. In October 1325 he published synodal statutes. He also made sure that all his vassals paid him homage, and he defended his own jurisdiction against that of the king. And he built. He ordered all the rights and dues of the bishop of Lodève to be recorded in five stout volumes. And in 1330, at the age of sixty-nine, he again made an inspection tour of his entire diocese.[93]

The writer was still as productive as the administrator was active. In 1329 he completed his lengthy *Sanctoral,* which he dedicated to John XXII. He sent one copy to the Dominicans of Toulouse and another to the new cardinal, Peter of Mortemart. And he kept track of the current events that were heard of in Lodève. He slowly completed each of his works by noting what seemed important to him: the measures taken by John XXII against the Franciscan spirituals; the ordination of ten new cardinals in December 1327; the attempt by Ludwig of Bavaria in 1328 to destroy the unity of the church by turning the Franciscan Peter of Corbière into a "pseudo-antipope"; the accession to the throne of France, in that same year, of Philip of Valois, since "no one has ever read that daughters reigned in France" and Philip was the closest male relative of the late King Charles IV; the arguments put forward, at the assembly of Vincennes in 1329, by the French king's representatives and the prelates' spokesmen in defense of their respective jurisdictions; the new king Philip VI's journey to Avignon and Marseilles in August 1330; and the abjuration that same month of Peter of Corbière.[94] On May 24, 1331, Pope John made Elie de Talleyrand, the bishop of Auxerre and brother of the count of Périgord, a cardinal. Is there any reason to believe that elderly Bishop Bernard, who had always scrupulously noted every promotion to cardinal, harbored some trace of hope or twinge of regret or tinge of bitterness when he recorded this event?[95] In any case, these were the last words he wrote. For on December 30, 1331, in "the eighth year of his episcopate . . . the worthy prelate . . . toward dawn, happily went to sleep in the Lord at the château of Lauroux, in the diocese of Lodève, in the year of Christ 1331, the seventieth or seventy-first of his life and the fifty-second since his entry into the Order of Preachers."[96]

His nephews in their piety and certain clergymen in their admiration were pleased to look upon Bernard as a saint. Perhaps they hoped that one day he, like Thomas Aquinas, would be honored at the altar. Rumors spread of certain miracles. In the summer of 1318 it was so hot in Avignon that the inquisitor of Barcelona spent three consecutive nights without sleeping. "He felt such a change come over his face and such a weakness befall his entire body that he feared . . . he might die." Encountering Bernard Gui, he begged him to pray on his behalf. "In the name of God," Bernard said, "I order sleep to weigh upon the lids of the inquisitor of Barcelona's eyes, and I command all vexation to leave him in peace." Whereupon "the father inquisitor immediately fell asleep, reposed in calm, and fully recovered his former health." In the same place and during the same week, the same stifling heat had caused another brother, from Bayonne, to suffer an attack of fever and dysentery. His life was in danger. Out of humility Bernard Gui at first refused to intervene. But "finally persuaded by the urgings of his brother, he ordered the fever and the dysentery to leave the suffering man alone after the feast of Saint Dominic [August 8], which was to be celebrated the next day or the day after." And on the appointed day the brother was delivered from his fever and dysentery. In the wake of these miracles Friar Pierre Bernard of Bayonne, who was in Avignon at the time and who later became bishop of Bayonne, in Bernard's presence and before numerous witnesses made the following remark in a jocular spirit: "Why is the Order of Preachers striving so mightily for the canonization of one of its deceased brothers when it might canonize a living saint?" Then, in December 1331, shortly after Bernard's death, the prior of the Dominicans of Limoges, who still knew nothing of Gui's demise, was praying in the choir one night after matins. Wide awake, he saw a brilliant light proceed from the prior's stall across the choir toward the main altar and then suddenly disappear.[97]

But such visions were far too commonplace. Such miracles were too minor. History was not theology, and Bernard was not Thomas. The Church had placed the angelic doctor upon its altars. It left the devout and jolly Dominican, the stalwart inquisitor, the indefatigable bishop, the prolific and scrupulous scholar where the light had disappeared, at the place to which he had wished to return in repose, next to the main altar in the choir of the Church of the Dominicans of Limoges, where "he waits with the just for the blessed resurrection."[98]

CHAPTER

2

GILLES LE MUISIT (1272–1353)

The Early Years (1272–89)

Built on the left bank of the Scheldt, the old city of Tournai found itself in the thirteenth century in a singular situation. Part of the kingdom of France, it was nevertheless on the "borders of the realm, confronting the Empire."[1] The residents spoke a variant of the Picard dialect with a strong tinge of Walloon; this dialect was difficult for a resident of Ile-de-France to understand, but it was nonetheless French, whereas people who lived a little way to the north spoke Germanic tongues to which the French speakers of the time referred as *thioises.* Yet this border town was also a capital. Rich and populous, it was an economic capital, at least by the standards of that time. And having been, since 1146, the seat of a bishop whose jurisdiction extended over most of Flanders, it was also a religious capital.[2] Clergy and laymen made it a brilliant center of French culture, so it was also an intellectual and artistic capital. And finally it was a political capital, for Tournai was surrounded by the estates of the count of Flanders, but it was not Flemish. Its burghers had received a communal charter from Philip Augustus in 1188.[3] Since that time the noble city of Tournai had been "a sort of municipal republic," proud of being itself as well as the place where two worlds met.[4] As an autonomous city, Tournai enjoyed a privileged relationship with the king of France. Situated between Flanders, which was part of the French realm, and Hainault, which was part of the Empire, it needed the king in order to survive, as much as the king needed it in order to assert his presence in Flanders and the Empire. Thus the city never wanted for the king's protection. And the bishops of Tournai always backed royal policy. What is more, the city's inhabitants were "found to be always faithful and loyal to the crown of France."[5]

Not far from the city, to the southeast, was the monastery of Saint-Martin. The monks claimed that the monastery had been founded in the distant past, but in the eleventh century the site contained only the ruins of a Church occupied by a handful of ascetics.[6] On May 2, 1092, the Church was placed under the supervision of Odo, the *scholasticus* of Tournai, who established a community that he made subject to the rule of Saint Benedict. At the time of his death in 1105 seventy monks were living at Saint-Martin of Tournai.[7] In later years the monastery knew times of glory as well as times of distress, but at the end of the thirteenth century it was a wealthy monastery. With its sixty-three monks, five lay brothers, and three novices, its complement was as large as it had been two centuries earlier. Indeed, it was one of the largest Benedictine monasteries in the West, few of which housed more than fifty monks; only Monte Cassino counted more than sixty-eight.[8] Many of Saint-Martin's sixty-eight men of religion were French speakers, and many were also natives of Tournai.[9] Their lives were closely intertwined with the life of the city. Discipline in the monastery was among the most austere anywhere, and the rule was well respected. It was here that on Allhallows' Day, November 2, 1289, Gilles Le Muisit took the habit.

Becoming a monk was the first step in a very simple career that can be summed up in a few sentences. Gilles Le Muisit possessed the qualities of an administrator. He soon began to play a part in the temporal administration of his monastery, and his responsibilities grew with time. In 1315 he had charge of the abbey's stores. Shortly before 1330 he became its prior, that is, the second in command after the abbot; his authority extended to all areas of monastic life. On April 30, 1331, more than forty years after he first took the habit, he was unanimously elected abbot. Confirmed, not without difficulties, by Pope John XXII, and blessed on October 25, 1332, he finally took possession of his abbey. His tenure as abbot was remarkable only for the care he exhibited in the administration of temporal matters and in the keeping of accounts. This conscientious but commonplace abbot's name might have vanished forever had it not been for the drama that overtook him in 1346 as he embarked on old age. But let us return to 1289.

From Youth to Old Age and Blindness (1289–1346)

In the first half of the thirteenth century the Le Muisits were a large and well-respected Tournai family. A century later they were still, apart from a few exceptional individuals, good burghers of Tournai, neither too rich nor too poor and living on the fruits of their labor. Among those who bore the name were "retail cloth merchants, wine merchants, cobblers, tailors, lace makers, bakers, dyers, surgeons and barbers, and the owners of the *Hostellerie de la Couronne* on the Grand Marché."[10] Jean Le Muisit, Gilles's father, was one of them. Of the children whom his wife Marguerite bore him, six reached adult age: four daughters, of whom we know nothing but their names, and two sons. Of the two sons Ernoul was also a man of the Church, but he was never more than a modest chaplain at Notre-Dame of Tournai and did not live long past fifty.[11] The other was our Gilles.

Jean Le Muisit was wealthy enough to give Gilles a solid education, at first in Tournai and perhaps later in Paris. It is not certain that Gilles Le Muisit lived in Paris in the ninth decade of the thirteenth century, but it is likely; Gilles himself tells us that seventy-six young men from Tournai went to the kingdom's capital at that time to continue their studies.[12] Indeed, it is more than likely if we are to take at face value certain allusions made later by the elderly abbot. In any case Gilles's stay in Paris was quite brief. For a time he studied the arts but never even obtained his master's degree. Hence he never attended the faculty of theology or the faculty of canon law. He never regretted his educational shortcomings, however. Lofty speculation was not his strong suit. He always showed respect for the great theologians, from a distance. He knew Scripture as a good monk was supposed to know it. The library of Saint-Martin was an excellent one.[13] There he was able to read the Bible, the gospels, the epistles of Peter and Paul, the works of Saint Augustine, the sermons of Saint Ambrose,[14] the homilies of Saint Gregory, and even the Venerable Bede.[15] All these were works that he was quick to cite, and they formed the basis of his simple, solid faith, which caused him neither problems nor anxieties.

Gilles Le Muisit did not have a head for either theology or canon law. He did have an open mind, however, and he shared the curiosities of the best minds of his time. He was ahead of his time in his liking for precise figures, a taste that was of course reinforced by his work as an administrator.[16] When the historians of Saint-Denis wished to say that there had been a great many Flagellants in the year 1349, they naturally resorted to the old way of expressing large quantities and put the number at "a good eight hundred thousand and more."[17] Gilles Le Muisit, who was on the scene, knew as well as the historians of Saint-Denis that the Flagellants had formed a multitude, but he gave a precise count. He reported that 160 had come to Tournai from Louvain, approximately the same number from Namur, 150 from Brugge, around 80 from Nieuport, around sixty from Dixmude, around 300 from Audenarde, approximately 450 from Valenciennes, and so on.[18]

This liking for precise figures was but one aspect of Gilles Le Muisit's consistent interest in mathematics and mathematicians. As a young monk he had seen a great deal of John of Harlebeke, a Flemish cleric well-versed in various sciences including astronomy. His knowledge of the stars was such that this "famous astrologer" could give precise "prognostications" of future conjunctions of the stars and planets. In truth, John of Harlebeke, a scientist but also a Catholic, did not publicize his prognositications. He spoke of them only to people he knew well, and Gilles Le Muisit was one of the few to hear them.[19] A half-century later, such scruples no longer hindered "the famous and learned astrologer" John of Murs. He was able to predict the course of the stars and sent his prognostications to all the schools in which astronomy was studied. In 1344 John of Murs's predictions were on everyone's lips. Gilles Le Muisit did not rest until he had procured himself a copy, which he attempted to the best of his ability to understand though not "expert in said science."[20] He knew enough, however, to realize that some of the now numerous "mathematicians" and "astrologers"[21] were wicked men, namely, those whose "prognostications and significations of figures" were so "occult and confused" that nothing could be gotten out of them and those who claimed that events ordained by the stars could not fail to occur.[22] Learned Catholic astrologers always allowed for the possibility of divine intervention.[23] What is more, their predictions were always precise and clear. As early as 1298 John of Harlebeke had predicted the troubles of which Gilles Le Muisit would be the helpless witness after 1345, and John of Murs had made a similar prediction in 1344—of this the elderly abbot was firmly convinced.

Gilles Le Muisit shared his scientific curiosities with a goodly number of his contemporaries, both clerics and laymen. His literary tastes associated him perhaps even more closely with a lay world from which the walls of his abbey scarcely separated him. To be sure, most of his reading was of the biblical sort required by his monastic estate. From his studies he never derived any knowledge of the profane Latin authors, nor did he conceive any desire to read them.[24] A man with little taste for scholarly texts, Gilles's true passion was for French poetry.

The poets whom Gilles Le Muisit read and liked were those whose language was most familiar to him and whose works were able to reach Tournai. Among them was first of all the Recluse of Molliens, who wrote in the first third of the thirteenth century. He also read the *Roman de la Rose,* which Guillaume de Lorris had begun in that same period and which Jean Clopinel of Meung-sur-

Loire had continued and greatly expanded around 1277.[25] Molliens is in Picardy. The *Roman de la Rose* was well known in Picardy as early as 1290.[26] It is not surprising that Gilles Le Muisit should have been able to feast on these works in his youth at Tournai. By contrast, the *Dit du Roi de Sicile,* in which Adam de la Halle, a *trouvère* from Arras also known as the Hunchback, recounts, in verse and in prose, the great exploits of Charles of Anjou in Italy after 1265, was written in Italy and little known in France. Gilles Le Muisit did know it, however, and he was all the more attached to the poem because his uncle Baudouin Le Muisit had followed Charles across the Alps and, after his return to Tournai, had told his young nephew stories of the campaign.[27]

Throughout his life Gilles Le Muisit remained as passionate about poetry as he had been in his youth. For geographical and circumstantial reasons he knew, and cited with equal warmth, less celebrated and more recent works. He read and appreciated the works of the Champenois Phillipe de Vitry (1291–1381). He was quick to become acquainted with the early work of the Champenois Guillaume de Machaut, who may have accompanied King John of Bohemia to Tournai in 1340 and whom Gilles may have met at that time. He also liked the poems of two modest trouvères from Hainault, Jean de la Mote and Colin Aubert. And he was one of the few to appreciate the verses of Jean Bochet, a Franciscan from Tournai.[28]

Our Benedictine liked these works not only for the aesthetic pleasure he derived from them but even more for the moral instruction they offered. He liked what was "beautifully said" (*biaus dis*),[29] but he admired Jean Bochet for being

> . . . boins trouvères
> De biaus dis et de bielles choses
> Qu'il avoit en son coer encloses.[30]

[. . . a good trouvères of beautiful words and beautiful things wrapped within his heart.]

He wished he could have read the Recluse of Molliens or the *Roman de la Rose* "every day" because they were "makers of beautiful words" from which he derived "great pleasure" but above all because one found in these works "beautiful things" and because they had "sagely dealt" with all estates and shown "how vices are reproved."[31] The beautiful things to be found in the works of the Recluse and in the *Roman de la Rose* were not simply beautiful. They had another virtue that Le Muisit greatly appreciated. They were simple and clear: "All their words are so clear that their works have no gloss."[32]

No less than the poems of the Recluse and the *Roman de la Rose,* works such as the *Dit du Roi de Sicile* offered clear moral instruction, which Gilles Le Muisit, like many of his contemporaries, was able to grasp. Above all, these works described great events. Gilles Le Muisit was no less interested in them on that account—on the contrary, for his morality was not atemporal. It was actually sustained by his passionate curiosity in everything that went on around him. Gilles Le Muisit had a taste for history.

He satisfied his taste for history with other types of reading as well. He studied, for instance, the *Liber de restauratione Sancti Martini Tornacensis,* the *Book of Restoration* in which an abbot of Saint-Martin, Hermann, in the first half of the twelfth century had recounted the monastery's origins.[33] He also read such "ancient chronicles" as were to be found in the abbey's library. And he consulted Vincent of Beauvais's *Speculum historiale,* whose huge volumes, summing up the knowledge of their day, had by the second half of the thirteenth century become an essential part of every good ecclesiastical library and which the library of Saint-Martin obviously possessed.[34] After 1296, moreover, Gilles, though busy with administrative tasks, further satisfied his taste for history by jotting down on parchment, or even on the blank folios of his account books,[35] notes in which he recorded the principal events of which he had knowledge.[36]

Except for the misfortune that befell him in 1346, Gilles Le Muisit would have left only these accounts and notes. In that year he was already quite old, but except for a few brief alerts his health was perfect and his energy undiminished. Cataracts began to threaten his eyesight, however. By 1346 he could no longer "read, write, or recognize coins," and he had to give up keeping the monastery books himself. Things then took a turn for the worse. On the feast of the Assumption of the Glorious Virgin, August 15, 1348, he celebrated mass for the last time. He was now totally blind.[37]

What a tragedy! He could no longer see "the birds fly or the beasts run."[38] He no longer experienced the "pleasure" of seeing "all human creatures, men, women, and their faces."[39] He could no longer "do any work." As the saying goes, "he is very poor who does not see." His "heart is very sad and filled with pain," and "all solace is gone."[40] Gilles Le Muisit makes no attempt to conceal his moments of sadness and discouragement because "there is no greater evil than to lose one's sight. . . . The blind man has lost all the world's charm."[41] But Gilles Le Muisit was not a man who could be kept down. For one thing, his convictions prevented it. It was God who kept people in good health or sent them afflictions.[42] Hence it was

God who had made Gilles a blind man because of his sins and misdeeds.[43] "Thus does the gentle God wish to test those whom he loves."[44] For the salvation of his soul, therefore, Gilles "will make virtue of necessity and suffer all that God may send."[45] He bore his affliction with patience. Patience! Ten times, twenty times, Gilles asked God to deliver him from his impatience, to give him patience in his adversity. He knows that, blind, "if he is not patient, he runs a risk." He knows that blind men, "if they are patient, [find] their salvation."[46] And he thinks of Tobias, whom God tested by blindness, and of Job, who "had much to suffer, [but] had great patience."[47] And Gilles, like Job, tried to be patient.

He did even better than that. The abbot of Saint-Martin's temperament was such that he was inclined not so much to admire Job's patience as to follow the prestigious example of John of Bohemia, the blind king, whom he may have seen in Tournai in 1340 and who died at Crécy on August 26, 1346. The king was only one of that battle's victims, the most illustrious. Shortly after John's death, an intimate from Hainault composed a lament for the dead of Crécy, 150 lines of which were devoted to the blind king. Gilles, condemned to everlasting darkness, found these verses to his liking and had them copied out; otherwise we might not have known about them. Though blind, John of Bohemia had continued to live as a knight. He had continued to keep "good company" and to play with dice: "Though he did not see, he played at dice for the amusement of his men and freely distributed gold and silver to his retinue, withholding nothing." He had continued to "hold great jousts and festivals." Like so many other fourteenth-century knights, he had gone to Prussia to help the Teutonic knights in battle against the pagans, and he took part in wars and suffered pain just as eagerly as "Prowess and Vigor" would have obliged him to do had he had his sight: "Had ever an unseeing man been seen to live this life?" The admirable knight's conduct proved that nature had deprived him "of the eyes of a chief but not of the heart."[48]

In his heart of hearts the abbot of Saint-Martin wished to be not another Job but a Benedictine avatar of King John. Ultimately God had robbed him of sight but had left him "patience, sense, and health."[49] Despite his great age, he retained all his faculties; he remained as "sound as an apple."[50] And he eagerly welcomed those who came to visit him, to "keep him company," to console him, with whom he laughed and gaily sampled "good wines [and] good meat" and stuffed himself with garlic and onions. With these "good companions" his "heart [was] at peace." He could seem happy and full of joy.[51]

Yet this empty joy was not enough for him, and in order to achieve patience in his affliction, "in order to avoid all vicious thoughts," in order to shun idleness and keep himself busy "with good works,"[52] he began, in 1347, to dictate, to dictate without letup, in both Latin and French, verse and prose:

> J'ay, quant je ne véoye, penet et traveillet
> A faire des registres; s'ay mainte nuit veillet:
> Moult de gens de mes fais s'en sont
> esmierveilliet.
> Mais je m'ensonnyoye pour avoir patience,
> Et nul jour n'espargoye, ne fieste, ne dimence.[53]

[When I could not see, I toiled and labored over my records. I stayed up many a night. Many people marveled at my deeds. But I taught myself to have patience, and on no day did I rest, neither on holy days nor Sundays.]

By 1349 he had finished dictating in Latin, having covered everything in his account books and notes and all that he knew about the abbey of Saint-Martin and everything that had happened in the world over the past fifty years of which he had knowledge. He then began a journal, also in Latin, of the dramatic and breathtaking events of 1349 and 1350. Subsequently he continued to keep these annals, but clearly current events were not rich enough to fill his hours of feverish activity. The amateur poet therefore decided to compose verses in French. He set about learning to "rhyme the manner." His first efforts were difficult: "At first it was hard for me, but later the work became easier."[54] Soon verses were gushing forth as from a spring, and the abbot dictated hundreds of them.

In the middle of the fourteenth century, so filled with events, a garrulous and spontaneous old abbot, his sight extinguished by a cataract, told at length what he knew and what he thought about himself and his times. All the volumes that the scribes of Saint-Martin wrote from his dictation over a period of four or five years have survived. What finer testimony could a historian ask for?

The World in Order

In order to keep himself occupied, Gilles Le Muisit, like so many moralists before him and like the Recluse of Molliens whom he so fervently admired, attempted to "think about estates."[55] He therefore dealt with popes, cardinals, prelates, deans and canons, curés and chaplains, monks, nuns, and mendicant friars; with princes, knights, and squires; with merchants; with men, women, and married couples; and so on. His review was neither well ordered nor well proportioned nor complete. It devoted more lines to important people than to modest ones. It scarcely touched on the little people of the cities. It said nothing about the peasant multitudes. Gilles Le Muisit's world was that of a man of the Church and a scion of the substantial urban bourgeoisie. Yet if his vision was, in its detail, uncertain, distorted, and incomplete, his broader views were consistent in their rigorous simplicity.

For Gilles Le Muisit, society, no matter how one looked at it, always fell into two parts. There were the good and the bad;[56] the mad (or the foolish) and the wise;[57] the men and the women;[58] the young and the old;[59] the clergy and the laity;[60] the noble and the "ignoble," that is, the "non-noble."[61] There were also the rich (or *gros*) and the poor.[62] Even more important, below the "great,"[63] the "powerful,"[64] the "potent,"[65] the "mighty,"[66] the "people of great distinction" or simply of "distinction,"[67] there were the "small,"[68] the "simple,"[69] the "ordinary,"[70] the people "of minor lineage,"[71] in a word, the "common folk," the "common people."[72] And finally there were princes and other potentates, prelates, and curés—all those who wielded a certain power—and, below them, their subjects.[73] As a scion of the solid bourgeoisie of Tournai who on occasion praised good and loyal merchants in the most glowing terms, Gilles Le Muisit was of course in a position to understand that these dichotomies were at times far too simple.[74] Sometimes the binary division was complicated and made ternary. Between the rich and the poor, the great and the small, Gilles made room for the *mediocre,* as he put it in Latin, or the *moyens* (middling) as he wrote in French.[75] But these occasional concessions to complexity did little to alter the fundamental vision that Gilles Le Muisit shared with many of his contemporaries, for whom the world was consistently and clearly bipartite.

On analysis, the multiplicity of possible points of view and terminology led to an even simpler and still more reassuring vision of society. For those who were rich were the same as those who were powerful and of great distinction, and it is those in this group that Gilles calls "authentic persons."[76] Obviously there were fewer authentic people than there were common people, but still their number was not inconsiderable. At one point Gilles tells us that in 1347, after the seizure of Calais, Edward III and a large number of Englishmen embarked and set sail for their island home. A storm struck, and many ships went down. "It is said that ten thousand people perished, and among them allegedly two thousand powerful and authentic persons [e quibus duo milia persone potentes et autentice esse dicebantur]."[77] The absolute numbers are of no importance for our purposes, but what seemed to Gilles a plausible ratio between the two is revealing. Clearly there were far more "authentic" persons than there were "prelates," whom Gilles calls "persons of authority."[78] Yet these persons of authority, these wielders of power, were of course surrounded by other authentic persons. The order of Gilles Le Muisit's world was quite simple. On one side were the persons of authority and other authentic persons; on the other side were the common people.

Gilles Le Muisit's world was ordered, but it was not static. Its order, moreover, was not disrupted but confirmed by the legitimate mobility that knowledge made possible. Gilles's own studies had not lasted long. He was not a great scholar. Nevertheless, he ascribed a fundamental importance to knowledge. "Every man has a natural desire to know," Aristotle said at the beginning of his *Metaphysics.* After Aristotle triumphed in the West, his phrase was constantly repeated in the schools, and Gilles Le Muisit, like so many others,[79] cited it frequently: "By nature everyone desires knowledge. Every man desires knowledge by nature."[80] If a pagan philosopher found knowledge natural, a Christian like Gilles found it natural and legitimate provided it was good, provided that it was joined with a good life and good habits and went with wisdom.[81] There was then "no treasure as good as the treasures of knowledge,"[82] and it was perfectly legitimate for "a good cleric to learn by staying awake night and day."[83]

Knowledge enabled good clerics to become good pastors. They could teach the people by delivering good sermons and setting good examples. They had the means to defend their flock and to govern their church. Hence patrons ought to reserve their benefices for learned clerics.[84] Monks ought to elect learned abbots, and canons ought to choose learned bishops. And in the good old days they had. In hope of being rewarded with benefices, numerous clerics studied basic sciences such as philosophy and theology and lucrative sciences such as medicine and law.[85] In the chapters there were numerous university graduates, masters, and doctors in theology, law, and medicine.[86] And the most recent popes had perpetuated this sound tradition. John XXII (1316–34) had chosen literate and wise men, both nobles and non-nobles: "He created cardinals expert in Scripture."[87] And his successor Benedict XII (1334–42) created cardinals who were "learned and expert in sacred knowledge" and "prudent men leading good lives." This was possible because the Holy Father himself "knew scripture . . . and could easily size up people's minds."[88] Nevertheless, he was less learned than his successor, Clement VI (1342–52), the present pope, who had been gaining in knowledge and virtue ever since adolescence.[89] Study thus justified the legitimate ambitions of the most modest men, to whom knowledge brought "possessions, status, honors, and praise."[90] Through knowledge the humble as well as the noble had obtained benefices. "Popes had been seen to come from modest places," thanks to knowledge.[91]

Far from disrupting the social order, this social ascension through knowledge actually reinforced it, since it ensured that the same people who were wealthy and powerful were also learned and wise. Everything was simpler when authentic persons combined power and wealth with wisdom, experience, and judgment, when they were men of sound mind and good counsel.[92] Everything was simpler when "powerful and authentic persons" were also "authentic and good."[93] Then every man's role was perfectly clear. That of prelates was to govern well. That of authentic persons was to speak, to bear witness, to say what was good and what was bad. Their words were worthy of faith,[94] and their approval was necessary.[95] As for the people, its only role was to obey, whether out of fear or love.[96] As Gilles Le Muisit saw it, God had "given all good government to all prelates, and had given [it] to all subjects truly to obey."[97] Just as women were reasonably expected to obey men,[98] and monks were reasonably expected to obey abbots,[99] so were subjects obliged to obey.[100] And if, in all humility, every person kept to their own estate, if every person wore the habit of their estate and performed the duties of their estate, then faith, hope, and charity could prevail: "Good faith, good hopes, and good charity."[101] And so, too, could peace. Peace and tranquility were the fruits of obedience, the supreme good of the ordered society of which the aged Benedictine abbot dreamed in his private darkness.[102]

Alas, the world that he had wanted to remain immutable had changed, as he was only too well aware, every day of his long life.[103] The result of these constant mutations of things and people, of these novelties,[104] of these inventions,[105] of these disorders[106] was that the world had "lost its way"[107] and "everything had changed for the worse."[108] "The world at present grows worse with every passing day."[109] The century "that is passing now" is as bad as "times past were good."[110] Thanks to his long life and excellent memory, Gilles Le Muisit retained a vivid and searing memory "of the good times people used to enjoy, of the good times of yesteryear, . . . of the good old times."[111]

The Good Old Days

Nothing could be less abstract than Gilles Le Muisit's good old days. What he knew and what he said seldom came from books. He had seen it himself or had heard it spoken of. Furthermore, for this concrete and cautious thinker, this unscholarly and unbookish man, the world was limited to very specific times and places.

Gilles Le Muisit heard almost nothing of far-off places (*de remotis partibus, de remotis regionibus*).[112] He knew virtually nothing about the geography of these parts of the world,[113] from which the only news that reached him, but for rare exceptions, consisted of rumor (*rumores*) and hearsay (*fama*). He knew nothing about the Germany that lay beyond the Rhine. He would have said nothing about Italy had it not been for the fact that one of his uncles had followed Charles of Anjou there in 1268, and had he himself not gone on pilgrimage to Rome in the jubilee year 1300 which had seen Christians throughout Europe take to the roads.[114] As it is, he makes only a brief allusion to his journey; Rome left little impression on him. Because the popes had subsequently established their court in Avignon, that name was familiar to him. How could it have been unfamiliar to a prelate? But for our Tournaisien, Avignon too lay somewhere in the depths of that remote and unknown territory that included Gascony, Poitou, Brittany, and even Normandy.[115] By contrast, Paris was closer to him, because he had probably studied there, because it was the capital of the kingdom, because many Tournaisiens were constantly involved in dealings with it, and because he himself had visited it on occasion; so was the north of France, through which he had had to travel on his way to the capital. On occasion he can also provide detailed accounts of what is going on in the county of Bar and the duchy of Lorraine, even though the latter was so foreign to him that he referred to it as a county.[116] The only regions that he really knew well and that were truly close to him were Flanders, Hainault, and Brabant.[117] Though neighbors, these territories were not friends. Hennuyers (people from Hainault) and Tournaisiens detested one another and on occasion went to war.[118] Brabanters too were warlike people.[119] Worst of all were the Flemish, wicked and perverse, rebellious, fickle, and brainless.[120] Yet Tournaisiens had always been obliged to live among them.

Gilles Le Muisit had lived in Tournai for so long, moreover, that he could—alas!—compare what it was like now with what it had been in his youth. The old abbot vividly recalled the day he first took the habit, November 2, 1289. He is much less precise about the date of his birth, never mentioning the day, the month, or the year.

At one point he even tries in some rather pretty verses to figure out his age: "Then I thought about my age. If I decided to calculate how old I am, how would I do it?" Is he being facetious? Was this perhaps a way of saying, as a person might say today, "I don't know how old I am. Let me think about it"? At one point Gilles is more precise. He states that in May 1350 he was "seventy-eight years and three months old," so that he must have been born in late January or early February 1272. Yet though he speaks often of his age and was a man given to precise figures, he is not usually so exact about his birth date. Despite the ambiguity of his expression, we can nevertheless be certain of his age within one year. Gilles was certain that when he took the habit on November 2, 1289, he was either eighteen years old or in his eighteenth year; thus he was born in either 1271 or 1272.[121]

The elderly abbot retained only a few images from his earliest years. He recalled, for instance, having seen the bishop ride through the city on horseback.[122] And he remembered certain stories he had been told.[123] Later he was told more about what went on around him, but his curiosity remained rather limited. He was only twenty-two, in 1294, when Celestine V was elected pope, but he cannot say anything definite about Celestine's brief papacy: "For in the time when he was pope, I was a youth." In those days "I was a young man and thought little about such things."[124] Two years later, in 1296, the young monk began to take note of events about which he heard news.[125] He thus entered the world of precise memories, where, thanks to his long life and excellent health, he remained for more than half a century.

With precision came pain. The first fact that Gilles Le Muisit knew, not from books but from what his elders told him, was not a happy one. It was the war between the king of France and the count of Flanders in 1214, in which Philip Augustus triumphed at Bouvines. Gilles did not know the year of the battle, but he did know that in that year "the countryside was laid waste all around, as far as Tournai." This destruction had grave consequences: "After this tempest, which destroyed wealth, the times became dissolute, people became perverted, and religion was diminished and pared down."[126] This mournful time soon came to an end, however.

The year 1247 was the first reasonably precise date that Gilles Le Muisit could cite without reference to books.[127] That year marked the approximate beginning of good times, which would endure for roughly half a century and upon which the elderly abbot could not look back without nostalgia. Celestine V was a "holy man" who led a "holy life" before, during, and after his pontificate.[128] Gilles knew almost nothing about the popes who preceded Celestine. His good times were an age not so much of good popes as of "good kings," above all "Saint Louis, the good king," and his brother, "the good Charles," who conquered Sicily, and Philip III (the Bold, 1270–85), that is, "Philippes li boins roys, li fiuls saint Loeys" (Philip, the good king, the son of Saint Louis), who went to Aragon, as well as "Edowars li boins roys d'Engletierre" (Edward, the good king of England), that is, Edward I, who, like Saint Louis, went to the Holy Land.[129] In those days of good kings, those good old days, Tournai was a tranquil and most prosperous city. Of course there had been a revolt of the weavers in 1281, which the elderly abbot sketched in a few words.[130] But for Gilles the two most important facts, complements of the city's tranquillity and prosperity, were these, upon which he expounds at length: that in 1277 construction of ramparts was begun, which made it possible to unify seigneuries and jurisdictions to the city's advantage; and that in 1283 an annual festival was instituted, together with a duty-free market, for "it was indecent that so noble a city did not yet have one."[131] At the gates of this prosperous city the abbey of Saint-Martin also prospered. Had those good old days only lasted, then all Christendom truly would have experienced the benefits:

> Se toudis eut duret depuis chis boins tempores,
> Toute crestyentés s'en sentist bien encores.[132]

Unfortunately, the troubles that may have been the instigation for the young monk's note-taking began in 1296. First came the rebellion of the count of Flanders against the king of France. Then came conflict between the king of France and the king of England. Thus began more than half a century during which "there was never a firm peace or a firm truce."[133] Constant warfare spelled repeated devastation for Tournai and the surrounding flatlands, which also suffered from the exactions of princes, fluctuations in the currency, and famine and death such as occurred in 1315–16.[134] The devastation of the territory led to the ruin of the monastery, further compounded by the abbots' mismanagement and disputes with the monks.[135] Desolation was everywhere. "Every eye that had seen the previous age was dazzled by it and felt greater admiration than I would dare say, or than I could say."[136] Things were no longer what they had been, nor were men. But the worst was yet to come. As it happens, Gilles Le Muisit's personal tragedy coincided exactly with the West's greatest time of trouble. By 1346 he could no longer see to read or write. On August 26 of that year the king of France met with disaster at Crécy, and this misfortune was followed by the surrender of Calais on August 4, 1347. By 1348 Gilles Le Muisit was totally blind. A few months later the Great Plague struck the region. It killed perhaps a third of the population and set off the greatest disorders.

It is easy to dismiss Gilles Le Muisit's complaints as the grumblings of a grouchy octogenarian. But who in the West in 1350, young or old, could have exhibited carefree optimism? Men in their fifties had known nothing but difficult times. But not Gilles Le Muisit. What the old abbot missed was not the remote time of Eden, nor was it the age of natural law, when all vices enjoyed free rein and "great, middling, and small . . . all men [and] all women . . . did just as they pleased."[137] It was a much closer time, yet one still remote from the present, a time from which countless tragedies had long since separated him: the time of his youth.

The World in Disorder

War, famine, and death were God's punishments for man's—for all men's—follies and sins.[138] Here Gilles Le Muisit's Manichaean view of society begins to break down. On the one hand there were the powerful and wealthy, and on the other hand there were the poor, and everything would be simple if the former always possessed wisdom, experience, and judgment. In fact, however, Gilles was obliged to admit that "in every estate one finds fools and wise men."[139] Virtues and vices existed everywhere.

Consider the young and the old. Gilles knew all the defects of youth, all the perils besetting the young. The young are lascivious and bold "in deed and word." Though they stand in urgent need of counsel, young people often want to act on their own, for "youths are often willful." Youth is the age of excess. "Against youth no one can defend himself." And no one can prevent young people from acting their age. Happy are those youths who, like Gilles Le Muisit, escape in time from "such wicked childhoods."[140]

Unfortunately, maturity was but a brief time of transition.[141] "When youth is all done and finished, then old age will come."[142] Although the old are sometimes wise, they have defects as well. They are lazy, selfish, and ill-tempered. And their apparent wisdom is actually impotence. They grow weak. They can no longer do anything. They dodder.[143] And when people of eighty, ninety, or a hundred tell stories about what they have seen, about what happened during their lifetime, it is pious to believe them, but it is not necessary.[144]

Equal in the face of sin, the young and the old are also equal in the face of punishment for sin and in the face of suffering and death. Gilles Le Muisit had seen too many wicked youths and too many people die young to protest against the death of the young, which was as inevitable as the death of the old. Everyone must die. "Death puts young and old alike in the bier."[145]

Since Gilles's younger days, moreover, everything had taken a turn for the worse; everyone had sinned more; and death struck even more powerful blows. At present men were dying in greater numbers and living shorter lives. For proof, consider that originally a jubilee year had been planned for every century: after 1300, 1400 was supposed to have been the next jubilee. But Pope Clement VI had been obliged to declare 1350 a jubilee year as well, because after so many wars, so much famine, and so many deaths, the survivors needed pardon sooner and above all because "human bodies today cannot live so long."[146] Was Gilles Le Muisit's sentiment justified? Today it seems reasonable to think that in the second half of the thirteenth century, which for Gilles was the good old days and which we too judge to have been a fortunate epoch, men probably lived longer and there probably were more elderly people than in the second half of the fourteenth century.[147] Unfortunately, this assertion is very difficult to prove. Consider, for example, that Gilles, who tells us so many things, says nothing that would enable us to calculate even the approximate age of the sixty-eight men of religion who lived in the abbey of Saint-Martin in 1289. On the other hand, he says enough to enable us to determine that, of the thirty-two monks and novices who lived in the monastery in 1350, twenty-nine were not yet fifty, one was in his sixties, another was more than seventy-five, and Gilles himself was seventy-eight.[148] It is impossible to say what, if any, change took place between 1250 and 1350, but it is clear what the situation was at the latter date. Few of the monks were old men, but the old men held the power. The tension between the two estates was therefore particularly high. And Gilles, torn between pride at being so old and bitterness at being so alone, had all the more reason to lament the many changes he had witnessed.

Sin and Authority

Wisdom and virtue were no longer the exclusive possession of the elderly. Nor were they any longer the exclusive province of "authentic" persons. Just as the three theological virtues had once been cultivated, so now everyone was to blame for the reign of the seven deadly sins.

There were "seven bad roots," seven "vices," "which are sins that kill the soul and consign it to flames." These were pride, envy, avarice, sloth, wrath, gluttony, and lust.[149] Gilles Le Muisit deplored the progress made "throughout the country" by lust, gluttony, wrath, and sloth.[150] But above all he deplored, frequently and at length, the progress of the three fundamental vices that caused the world "to become worse every day," that disrupted the social order and upset "all worldly estates," namely, avarice, envy, and pride.[151]

Because of "pride, envy, and covetousness," people refused to remain in their places; every man wished "to go from the bottom to the top" and "to rise high."[152] The result was total disorder. Everyone coveted the property, power, and dress of others. One could no longer trust in appearances. Even words had lost their value, "for every man possesses great glory when people call him sire."[153] Gilles Le Muisit thundered mightily against the principal source of all these disorders, namely, evil ambition:

> For those who aspire to greater honors and estates,
> for those who desire the possessions and pleasures of the world,
> Every day the times grow worse.[154]

Not all ambition was necessarily bad. It was legitimate for a man to rise because of his virtue or knowledge. But not all knowledge was good. Greed and pride made it bad. It was not good to acquire knowledge for the sole purpose of rising in the world and gaining riches, and it was not good to neglect the basic sciences in favor of the lucrative ones.[155] In the past learned men were humble and modest. Today, however, they were all too often "inflated with knowledge." Such inflation with knowledge made them "most proud" and impatient to rise. "Hope of great estates" turned their heads. And when they had risen, they were pure pride.[156]

What is more, their hope of rising was steadily diminishing. Electors in past elections had been able to agree on which men were the best, which were the most religious, the most wise, the most learned among them, among those whom they knew well and who knew them well.[157] But now,

> Envy and covetousness lurk in new forms
> . . . .
> And in elections their evils combine.
> Envy often causes great dissension
> in those colleges that hold elections.
> . . . .
> Covetousness plays its part.[158]

Out of these dissensions came debates and disorders; there were no more good pastors, and knowledge was no longer rewarded.

Things were no better when the choice was in the hands of patrons rather than electors. Among lords, both lay and ecclesiastic, who made appointments to benefices, pride, envy, and avarice had caused terrible ravages. In the past, "in the time of my childhood, good clerics and good knights could hope for reward."[159] Of course lords and prelates gave benefices to their relatives, as was only natural and as was perfectly legitimate, so long as those relatives were also good and literate clerics:

> Your relative, your cousin may have them, but only if they wish to study and love knowledge and love learning more than wealth. Boons are for the good.[160]

Gilles Le Muisit has only good things to say about the noble and literate bishop of Tournai in the middle of the thirteenth century, who gave prebends in the cathedral chapter of Tournai to a number of men of letters, among whom were four of his own nephews, men whom Gilles later came to know well and who were still living and still canons.[161] But before long this legitimate affection of one's parents and friends began to be abused. People with power offered advancement exclusively to relatives and friends.[162] Clement V (1305–14), who was born near Bordeaux, chose only close relatives and fellow Gascons to be cardinals and prelates.[163] In itself such behavior was shocking. Seen from Tournai, it was even more distressing. Later, many good men of letters, "full of learning," owed their careers to royal favor.[164] Yet patrons everywhere gave benefices to many others who were not even university graduates.

The consequences of this disorder were disastrous. Without hope that degrees would aid them in their careers, students neglected their studies.[165] Worse still, clerics no longer set good examples for laymen as they were supposed to do, and lords no longer did what they were supposed to either, that is, they no longer did those things that made them worthy of respect in the eyes of their subjects.[166] Indeed, the lords could not do what they wished to do.[167] The son of a burgher from one of the northern towns where the spirit of democracy flourished, Gilles had no notion of obedience as an essential need of all society. For him, obedience was conditional. It was to be expected only if lords did their duty. Gilles Le Muisit laid far less stress on the rights of lords than on their many duties. By heeding the counsel of "authentic" persons,[168] lords were supposed to safeguard justice, preserve ancient laws and customs, and protect their subjects' exemptions. They were not supposed to molest their subjects or permit any exaction or any new tax. Indeed, they were not even to abolish those recent usages that were considered bad.[169] Only if these conditions were met were princes loved more than feared and kings rewarded with true authority and domestic peace.[170]

> Any king who does these things will have authority,
> and his subjects will have prosperity,
> love and bountiful peace and great tranquillity.
> Where such kings are to be found, however, depends on God.[171]

Unfortunately, it had not recently been God's will that all princes and prelates should be perfect. Many were wicked. In such cases it was the subject's first duty to wait for God to punish the master. Gilles Le Muisit had read and reread the Wisdom of Solomon, and he particularly liked those verses that threatened wicked princes with the judgment and punishment of God:

> Exiguo enim conceditur misericordia,
> Potentes autem potenter tormenta patientur.
>
> (Wis. 6:6)

[For the lowliest man may be pardoned in mercy, but mighty men will be mightily tested.]

As much as Gilles exhorted subjects to obey, he even more strongly warned wicked princes of their inevitable condemnation. They would surely be punished:

> Qui male rexerint certe punientur:
> Potentates potenter poenam patientur.[172]

[The powerful powerfully will suffer great torments.][173]

Experience had shown, moreover, that wicked governments were not punished only in the other world. In the end, the abbot of Saint-Martin is full of indulgence and comprehension for the actions of men who, had their princes been good, would have had only to obey. Did the powerful set a bad example? Did they say one thing and do another? Then they ceased to be believed.[174] Did lords fail to respect ancient customs and fail to honor their subjects' exemptions? Did they impose new taxes and exactions? Then they ceased to be obeyed. Did the count of Flanders make the mistake of heeding the advice of men who were not Flemish? Did he treat his subjects harshly? Then the whole territory had begun to "murmur," and then "disturbances" had broken out and then "rebellions," and ultimately the count suffered the consequences.[175] Gilles Le Muisit was always attentive to the people's menacing but often comprehensible murmurs, which preceded their violent and all too often justifiable uprisings.

Appearances notwithstanding, the old abbot was not a man of certitudes. To be sure, he believed that things had been simple in his childhood. Power and wealth, wisdom and knowledge had all been in the hands of the same people. Those with authority and other authentic persons were good and had the ability to judge and to lead. The rest were required to believe and to obey. In Gilles's thought the views of the abbot are perfectly consistent with those of the historian. The men whom the historian deemed worthy of belief the abbot said ought to be obeyed: they were they men of authority on whom, in the final analysis, everything always rests. In a remarkable passage Gilles distinguishes three types of testimony. The first type is that which there is no compelling reason to believe. The second is that which it is pious to believe. And the third is that in which it is necessary to place credence. The first type includes the testimony of men who have visited far-off countries. They say what they saw and heard. No one can contradict them, but there is no compelling reason for those who do not wish to believe them to do so. Second, there are important men in their eighties, nineties, or hundreds who tell what has happened during their lifetime. It is pious to believe such men, but not necessary. It is, however, necessary to believe great personages who wield some kind of power. No one would dare oppose or contradict them, whether out of reverence or out of fear.[176]

Such a view made matters simple, but moral experience complicated the political theory. There were in fact wise men and madmen everywhere; there were bad princes and good subjects. Not every act of the great was necessarily good. Not every rebellion of the common people was necessarily bad. Certain principles applied to both. Above all was the fundamental idea that nothing was better than ancient customs. Nevertheless, in a world in constant flux every year brought new things. But these novelties could come from the great just as well as from the common people. The innovations of the powerful were not necessarily good, and the innovations of the common people were not necessarily bad. Both kinds of innovation might one day be approved by the authorities. In other words, Gilles Le Muisit was a man of authority who believed in authority but not fanatically. Though firm on principles, he more than once found himself perplexed by the facts.

So while the abbot of Saint-Martin was not a fanatical believer in authority, he was a believer. His misgivings could not last long. Every innovation was an occasion for debate between the great and the small in which the latter initially were not always wrong but in which ultimately authority must have the last word. If one went high enough, somewhere there was an authority that must be believed—and obeyed.

The Terrible Year—1349

Gilles Le Muisit truly needed all of his certitudes to calm the many perplexities he felt on the eve of the year 1349, all of whose terrible events he would experience and of which he was, day after day, the best available witness. By the spring of that dreadful year clouds had begun to gather in Tournai. The plague had landed on Europe's Mediterranean shores early in 1348, and for more than a year people had followed its terrifying northward progress. June 1349 was a hot month, and at last rumors of deaths in the city began to circulate. The bishop, who loved fresh air, decided to leave for Guise, where he would reside with one of the knights from his entourage. He stopped in Arras and then in Cambrai, where he celebrated mass in the cathedral, on June 11, the feast of the Blessed Sacrament. He felt extremely tired. That night, however, he dined with great pleasure. The next day he set out for Le Cateau in Cambrèsis. While riding he felt sick, but he reached Le Cateau and stopped there. On the morning of Sunday, June 13, he died. His entourage, terrified, returned the body to Tournai, where it was buried.[177]

For the next few weeks nothing happened, or, rather, nothing noteworthy happened: "No person of authority [nulla persona auctoritatis]" died. But on August 30, the day after the feast marking the beheading of John the Baptist, in the Merdenchon district (whose name suggests its insalubrious reputation), death began to mow people down. Every day five, ten, fifteen, sometimes as many as twenty or thirty bodies were carried into the churches. In each case tearful families mourned in the traditional way; curés, clerics, and gravediggers, glad of the windfall profits, observed the customary formalities. Bells rang night and day. Soon it was too much. Everyone had reached wit's end. The city authorities were obliged to intervene. They decided first that each person would receive the bells, chants, and lighting appropriate to his estate, but that all cadavers would be buried immediately, that only close relatives would wear mourning, and that there should be no banquets for more than ten persons. But it was still too much. As of September 21 it was decided that bells would no longer be rung, that not even family members would wear black, and that only two people would be invited to the burial mass. The authorities took those measures "for the good of the city [pro utilitate civitatis]." Compelled by necessity, the clergy and inhabitants accepted these innovations.[178]

The city authorities, however, thought it wise to take another step that seemed indispensable to them but that the common people refused, in spite of the circumstances, to accept. Gilles Le Muisit tells the whole story in just over a hundred verses that shed considerable light on the community's delicate relation to authority and innovation. As in all Christendom at the time, each parish in the city of Tournai had a small cemetery next to its Church. With the wave of deaths, however, the authorities soon realized that the parish cemeteries could not accommodate the influx of new corpses. They therefore decided, for the good of the city, that it would be a "pious work" to establish two new cemeteries outside the city walls, and that no new bodies could be buried in the parish cemeteries without authorization. Murmurs began in the community:

> Pro qua causa communitas
> . . . .
> Multoties murmurare
> Coeperunt atque dicere.

People asked "why the governors were making regulations regarding the cemeteries, when their predecessors had done nothing of the kind. Our fathers, our mothers, our brothers, our sisters, and our friends are buried there," people said, "and we want to be buried there too. When we pass by, we pray for the sins of the dead who lie there. But now comes this innovation [*et modo est nova via*] of having cemeteries outside the walls in which the dead from different parishes are mixed up. This is a violation of our privileges. It is contrary to reason. God does not agree." The community murmured these and other, similar things:

> Ista et his similia
> Murmurabat communia.

And wrath and agitation mounted. Faced with these rumblings, the authorities chose the right course (*capientes bonum iter*) and changed their decision. They gave up on the idea of cemeteries outside the city walls. Instead, they ordered that mass graves, large enough to hold two or three hundred bodies, be dug in the existing cemeteries. And the rumblings of the community, the disorder, came to an end:

> Sic cessavit murmur multus
> Communiae et tumultus.[179]

Things calmed down even more when the deaths ceased after the feast of All Saints. The plague had killed many people, rich, middling, and poor. Gilles noted, however, that death had spared those among the wealthiest and most powerful residents of the city who had drunk wine, who had avoided breathing foul air, and who had abstained from visiting the sick.[180]

Those two frightful months when death in Tournai was an everyday occurrence were simply the crux of a much longer drama, which began with the announcement of imminent death and took a long time to subside even after the peril was gone. So troubled were the minds of already credulous men and women in 1349 that for a time they believed as true things that turned out upon examination to be either false or doubtful. Gilles reports on four apparent miracles in order to warn his readers to be wary of appearances and not to judge things or give them names until they have run their course. The first of these took place near Tournai in the spring of 1349, prior to the bishop's death in mid-June. A young woman of fourteen, while tending her parents' cows, on several occasions saw and heard the voices of women who were dressed entirely in white. The girl related to her father, mother, brothers, and sisters what the women said. Then she began to work miracles. The lame, the blind, and the paralytic came to her in large numbers and credulously accepted what she said. The bishop was aware of this. He sent his official and the dean of the cathedral, who were good jurists, as well as other religious and learned persons, to examine and question the child. These scholars found the girl outspoken in her responses but completely ignorant. She did not even know the Paternoster or Ave Maria. It was intolerable that common folk should regard what she said and did as miracles. After receiving good advice, the bishop, after mature deliberation, ordered the parents and child to desist. The authorities, in their knowledge and wisdom, had spoken. Now the ignorant people had only to obey. Which they did. "Obedient, they ceased, and nothing more was heard of her [*Ipsique obedientes cessaverunt, et statim nullus rumor fuit de eadem*]."[181]

Nevertheless, in dealing with the two major events that accompanied the ravages of 1349—the massacre of the Jews and the penitence of the Flagellants—the authorities found it less easy to arrive at a wise and learned judgment that would quickly and triumphantly calm the situation. People asked themselves why this terrible scourge had befallen them. Moralists had one answer: because God wished to punish men for having surrendered to the seven deadly sins.[182] Scientists had another: the conjunction of the stars and planets was such that the air had been corrupted, thus triggering the epidemic.[183] But these learned explanations were overwhelmed by vulgar rumor: the Jews had poisoned the wells. Because the Jews had long since been driven out of the kingdom of France, no pogrom took place there. In the Empire, however, horrible massacres occurred as early as the end of 1348 and the first few months of 1349, that is, before the plague arrived. Gilles Le Muisit mentions this. He says nothing about far-off countries, about which he of course has no accurate information. But he knows that in Lorraine and in the county of Bar, all the Jews were burned, and his account of what happened in Cologne and Brussels is even more detailed. He recounts how the inhabitants of these places forced the authorities to wipe out the Jews, and for once this man, normally so quick to bestow praise and blame, has not a word to say, neither to condemn the weakness of the authorities nor to denounce the blindness of the people nor to pity the victims. He simply recounts the facts. He certainly does not endorse the charge of well-poisoning. In two or three places, however, he does call attention to the malice of Jews who hoped to profit from a plague that their astrologers had predicted. In any case, after All Saints day the Jews ceased to be a topic of discussion.[184] By then the only remaining threat to order was the Flagellants.

The bishop of Tournai had been dead only a few days when, at the end of June 1349, a new way of doing public penance arrived in Flanders from Germany.[185] Penitents began to wear crosses on their clothing and to carry a penitent's club in their hands. From their belts hung a kind of whip or scourge called a *scorgie* or *escorgie,* which featured three knots, each with four iron barbs. In ordered processions out of which rose numerous crucifixes and banners the penitents marched two by two, chanting in a regular fashion, with one group initiating the chant, the other responding in chorus. They sang two new canticles composed not in Latin but in their own language. Twice a day they would stop in a square, form a circle, strip to the waist, remove their shoes, and flay themselves with their scourges until they bled, singing all the while. Finally, they would prostrate themselves in prayer.

This spectacular public penance was only the visible declaration of a more profound commitment. The penitent joined a veritable society, whose members called one another brothers and obeyed superiors. He pledged to pray God to put an end to the plague, to confess all his sins, to pay his debts, and to draw up a will. He promised, moreover, to do this penance for thirty-three days, one day for each year that Christ lived, during which time he would keep silent, live on alms, and sleep wherever hospitality was offered, each night under a different roof. Beyond the thirty-three days of penance, the penitent made certain lifelong commitments: that he would always keep his penitent's garb and scourge on his bed, for example, that he would never blaspheme, and insofar as possible that he would abstain from meat and respect the holy bonds of matrimony.

Before making these profound commitments, these humble penitents sought the permission of their priests and lawful wives, and they promised to defend the rights, doctrine, and laws of Holy Church. They were thus obedient sons of the Church, who had been impelled by extraordinary events to adopt, on their own authority, new forms of penitence.

Among these penitents were there, as is sometimes said, nobles and non-nobles, rich and poor?[186] No doubt. The fact remains that initially they enjoyed the sympathy of the authorities. To persons residing in the city and castellany of Ypres who had been "moved by devotion to perform certain corporal penances," the vicars of the bishop of Thérouanne had granted the requested authorization. And on August 24 the count of Flanders had ordered his officers to receive them "benignly" and to allow them to pass "peacefully" through the county, "without hindering them or their people in any way in body or baggage."[187] But the penitents soon formed a multitude. Their passage aroused passions already heightened by the daily occurrence of death. Society's good order was threatened. The Church could no longer evade the questions of principle raised by this new form of penance.

In 1349 Gilles Van Der Hoye (*De Feno*) was a grown man. He had studied theology in Paris. Either he had been a doctor of theology for a few months, or he would soon become one. He was dean of the collegiate Church of Notre-Dame in Courtrai. He was one of the first to conceive an antipathy toward the new form of penance. These noisy scenes of flagellation, he believed, disturbed the public order and infringed upon the honors due the prince and the clergy. In these new processions, which no authorities had ordered, was there not a danger of diminishing public respect for the great princely cortèges with their flags and trumpets or for divine services, a risk of reducing the people's reverence for official ceremonies? Perhaps these penances that Christians had undertaken on their own initiative were in themselves a good thing, yet they could not be meritorious, because they inverted the normal roles of clergy and flock. It was the clergy's job to lead the faithful. The people were supposed to listen (*audire*) and obey (*obedire*).

Alard of Denterghem was far more circumspect. Alard had his talent as an administrator and the favor of the count of Flanders to thank for his position as provost of Saint Martin's in Ypres, a city whose authorities had shown much sympathy toward the new penitents. To the dean of Courtrai he replied that he would not presume to approve the new rite, which did not please him. But why condemn it so quickly? There was no inherent malice in this penance. It was done with righteous intent. Its fruits were good. Peace, harmony, and charity followed in its wake. In short, the provost of Ypres did not deny the point that all popular initiatives ought to be subject to approval by the authorities, but he did not think that all such initiatives were necessarily bad.[188] Thus in Flanders the men of learning were already at odds, and no doubt they had already begun to look to higher authority for a more reliable opinion.

While clerics argued, however, the new Flemish penitents were already invading the nearby city of Tournai. On Saturday, August 15, two hundred Brugeois entered the city, and on the following day they began their penance at the monastery of Saint-Martin. Over the next few days additional groups of penitents arrived from Ghent, Sluis, and Dordrecht. In a heavy atmosphere over which the shadow of imminent death already hovered, Tournaisiens were divided. Most approved of the novelty, but some, of "sound mind," withheld their praise.[189] Even they praised the idea of penance, however, as something quite necessary. The new penitents drew crowds and certain clerics enthusiastically joined in their activities, but the authorities still had misgivings. They did not condemn a movement that could have swept them away, but their approval was mere lip service. Mainly they attempted to interest the faithful in their own sermons and processions. While the authorities temporized, the penitents became increasingly hostile. By the end of August tensions in Tournai were running high.

On Saturday, August 29, 180 patients from Liège, led by a Dominican, arrived in town. The next day, the very day on which the plague struck Merdenchon, the Dominican, with permission from the dean of the cathedral chapter, preached a violent sermon at the Saint-Martin monastery to a mixed crowd of men and women. He argued on behalf of penitents who shed their blood, like Christ. He attacked the friars of the mendicant orders who opposed the new devotion. He even asserted that those who wished to perform the new penance had no need to ask the pope's permission or to seek a papal bull. He also said many other things that greatly pleased his audience, "and nearly all began to murmur against the mendicant orders and even against all clergy."[190] And during the first weeks of September, while death wreaked havoc in the city and hundreds of Tournaisiens, caught up in the general fervor, enlisted in the army of "red knights" for thirty-three days, the authorities preached repentance, but no one was listening.

Even in his worst moments the abbot of Saint-Martin did not share the frustrated authorities' hostility toward the new penitents. The moralist in him silenced the politician. He admired the penitents for having made possible "so great a change from evil to good." He noted with approval that many women had abandoned their indecent hairdos and clothing, that many men had stopped swearing, that people were less prone to throw dice and less apt to sing lascivious songs, that fornication and adultery were less openly flaunted, and that private wars had ceased. People were even saying that the penitents had worked miracles. Gilles Le Muisit noted this belief, but he was not convinced. On the whole, however, he had to admit that the novelties, though contrary to approved custom, had borne good fruit. The elderly abbot, caught between suspicion of innovation and satisfaction with the change in people's behavior, was more than ever gnawed by doubt and perplexity.

At first glance, everything the new penitents said and did seemed "honest and pious." There would be no cause for complaint if one could be sure that "their hearts did not give the lie to the appearance of things, if they persevered in their action, and if our holy mother the Church bestowed the approval of its authority." In the face of these innovations, Gilles Le Muisit could do no more than repeat his favorite texts: "Nescit homo utrum sit dignus amore an odio [No man knoweth whether he is worthy of either love or hatred]" (Eccles. 9:1), and "Homo videt in facie, Deus autem in corde [God sees all hearts, man sees faces]."[191] Only God can penetrate the secrets of the heart. A good Christian like Gilles Le Muisit was therefore not bound "either to approve or to disapprove." While awaiting the judgment of God and of the Holy Church, he must repeat the words of Saint Paul in 1 Corinthians 4:5: "Nolite ante tempus judicare [Judge nothing before the time]."[192]

The abbot of Saint-Martin therefore waited for the time of judgment. But that time was imminent. The new penitents' enemies had worked quickly. As was customary, they had sought the opinion of the faculty of theology in Paris. The Parisian doctors, unwilling to pronounce in so grave a case on their own authority, had deferred to the decision of the pope. But in a move that revealed their private sentiments, they had sent to Avignon to advise Clement VI one of the most celebrated theologians of the day, Jan van der Fayt, a Flemish monk from the Benedictine monastery of Saint Amand in Puelle and a fierce opponent of the Flagellants.

At Avignon, on October 5, 1349, and in the presence of the pope,

Jan van der Fayt delivered a most uncompromising speech.[193] Grave matters were best left to the judgment of the supreme authority. And it was indeed a grave matter that concerned the group to whom others referred as "Flagellants" (*Flagellatores*), who had arisen as a new sect, obeying new laws and performing new ceremonies (*nova secta, novas leges et ceremonias . . . observans*). Their behavior left bishops perplexed and uncertain how to proceed. They could not decide whether to grant the permissions requested or to resist by means of ecclesiastical censure and secular force. The pope had to take a stand, and the speaker did not hide his feelings that the new sect was wicked. It was wicked because with few exceptions its members "are men of the people, hence uneducated, ignorant, and crude" (*sunt homines populares et per consequens indocti, ignari et rude*) and "cannot distinguish between good and evil." What is more, they deceived others as "simple" as themselves and "blinded by the fog of ignorance" (*ignorantie nuvilo obfuscatus*). "*Non est populus sapiens,*" said Jan van der Fayt, citing Isaiah 17:11. Did he believe that the common people were not educated, or not intelligent, or both? In any case, one conclusion was inescapable: nothing good could come from them. The proof, according to Jan van der Fayt, was that the people believed the epidemic had been caused by the poisoning of the wells, whereas astronomers realized that the true cause was air corrupted by the position of the stars. The new sect and its new ceremonies therefore could not be good. In fact they were not good. What is more, any novelty that weakens the law is condemnable. The pope's silence could only strengthen the new sect. Jan van der Fayt therefore beseeched the pontiff to put an end to all the idle talk, to separate the wheat from the chaff, and to do away with the new sect.

And Clement VI did indeed decide. On October 20 he condemned the new penitents.[194] Now things were clear. On November 3 the faculty of theology of Paris condemned the Flagellant sect.[195] And, just as the disease had run its course in Tournai, the prelates of northern France could no longer doubt that the sect was wicked.

The denouement therefore should have been rapid, but in fact it was not. To be sure, as Gilles Le Muisit noted with some bitterness, when "the mortality ceased shortly after All Saints, the pilgrimages and services also ended" (*cessante aliquantulum mortalitate post festum Omnium Sanctorum cessavit peregrinatio et devotio*).[196] Actually, however, only the official pilgrimages ceased. The fervor of the new sect remained intact. Furthermore, the Tournai authorities did not publish the papal bull, both because they were afraid of arousing popular passions and because the king of France still had not spoken.

The king of France had not spoken because these events struck him as rather remote, and in these difficult times he had other emergencies to deal with. The moment the Flagellants attempted to enter Picardy and Champagne, however, the king reacted. In a letter dated February 15, 1350, and sent to the aldermen of Tournai, Philip VI stated that he had "heard that a sect of people, wearing the false colors of devotion and penance and calling themselves beaters and penitents" had grown up in the town. It had misled and deceived "a number of simple people, ignorant of holy scripture and of the true path of their salvation." But it had been "damned and reproved by the aforementioned Church of Rome," and the king ordered "said sect" to cease "all activities" so that "such an error should not henceforth spread through our Kingdom."[197]

On February 20 the aldermen of Tournai published the information that they had received a letter from the king in which the monarch stated that the penitents were a sect and must therefore cease their practices or face banishment. The next day the religious authorities published the papal bull they had received nearly four months earlier, but they also published the indulgences to be granted to any Christian who traveled to Rome in that jubilee year. The penitents murmured and cursed, but in the end they ceased their activities.[198] Pilgrims set out for Rome. The Christian people had once again found the proper way of doing penance, the traditional way, the way approved by the authorities, and they had done so by trusting in the supreme authority, that of the pope.

The moment the new penitents had appeared, Gilles van der Hoye, who was hostile to them, had asserted that they constituted a new sect (*haec nova secta vel confraternitas*).[199] In pleading against them to the pope, Jan van der Fayt had begged Clement VI to "separate out the chaff of this sect, or, rather, this error" (*hujus secte seu potius erroris manifestum zizania*).[200] And the pope in fact did condemn this error and this sect.[201] And the king of France did prohibit this "sect of people . . . damned and reproved by said Church of Rome."[202] From that point on, no further indecision was possible, and accounts written subsequent to the events betray no doubts that the Flagellants were indeed a "sect of people," a "new sect" (*nova secta*) acting on its own authority, a "wicked and detestable sect" (*secta mala et detestanda*), a "plague-ridden sect" (*secta pestifera gentium*). This "error" had spread, this "folly" had persisted until finally, condemned, there was no alternative but for it to disappear.

"The sect was reduced to nothing in a short time," according to the Latin continuation of William of Nangis, which was written shortly after the events. "It shrank to nothing when people saw that the popes and the kings of France were against it and hostile to it," Froissart wrote somewhat later. The more time went by, the more rapid the inevitable consequence of condemnation seemed. According to Jan van Leyden, writing in the fifteenth century, the multitude who had done penance without the authority of the pope or the Church had, after being condemned, simply evaporated (*et multitudeo illa evanuit*).[203]

Gilles Le Muisit, who lived through the events with sympathy for the participants, did not share these certainties. He knew full well that the authority of pope and king had not been established as quickly or as easily as the chroniclers said. He never used the word "folly" or even "error" or "sect" in speaking of people to whom he always referred as penitents, never as Flagellants. And after the Flagellants had been condemned and had vanished from the scene, he uttered not one word of abuse against them.

But neither did he utter one word of regret that they were gone. Since they had been condemned, and since any penance done without the authority of superiors was mere presumption and vainglory, their fate was sealed.[204] With the condemnation of the Flagellants the old abbot's doubts and perplexities vanished immediately, for there was one thing about which he was truly certain, namely, that only the authorities, and above all the pope, could say what was good and what was evil. A Christian could do nothing good without the approval of the authorities, especially that of the pope. Obedience was the only way.

The emergence of the new penitents had elicited a wide range of reactions on the part of clerks and laymen. Some had been immediately hostile; others had approved; still others had remained perplexed. In the end, however, all, except for a few errant clerics, were reunited by the conviction that the Church is a pyramid of authorities held together by obedience. The pope stood at the apex of this pyramid. He had spoken, and he had been obeyed.

One troubling fact remained, however. In the Empire the papal bull had had to stand on its own. But in the kingdom of France it had remained without effect until the king made his position known. Since Philip VI had followed Clement VI, slowly to be sure but in the end staunchly, this fact had made little impression on people's minds. When the crisis was over, a comforting certainty took hold that, powerful as murmurs and disorders might be, the peace of Christendom was not really in danger as long as an unchallenged pope occupied the Holy See. And who in 1350 could have suspected that the pope might one day be challenged?

The Final Years (1350–53)

The Flagellants had been gone for a year. The holy year was over. Life had resumed its course. Gilles Le Muisit was within a few months of eighty when a German master, Johann of Mainz, came to Tournai. He saw the old man and offered to operate on his cataract. Gilles's relatives and friends urged him to refuse, but he agreed. On Sunday, September 18, 1351, one eye was operated on, and the other operation was done on Thursday, September 22. The operations were quick and did not cause terrible pain, and they were successful. "I recovered my sight," Gilles wrote, "and I saw, not as a young man, but within the limits imposed by my age, for I was close to eighty years old. I saw the sky, the sun, the moon, and the stars again." Of course he still could not see to read or write, but he recognized people fairly well and was able to celebrate mass. Once again he devoted himself to the duties of his office and abandoned verse and prose.

And we know nothing more about Gilles Le Muisit, except that he died at age eighty-one on October 15, 1353. He was buried in the choir of the abbey Church, to the right of the altar.[205]

CHAPTER

3

PIERRE D'AILLY (1351–1420)

The Early Years (1351–64)

Gilles Le Muisit was not yet dead, and the Black Plague had just passed, when Pierre d'Ailly was born in Compiègne. There is no proof that he ever came to know the precise date of his birth. In his abundant works he never mentions the date of his birth nor does he ever allude to his age. Once and only once, and long after the event, in 1414, in discussing the relation between the movements of the stars and historical events, he refers to a famous conjunction of Saturn, Jupiter, and Mars, about which scholars had been talking for more than half a century; he explained that it had been the cause of a subsiding of the waters, which had led to a shortage of food followed by a plague that had caused many deaths throughout the world. In discussing this disastrous conjunction, which had been responsible for "many other ills whose effects are still felt today," Pierre d'Ailly remarked in passing that he had been "born approximately five years later." Since Pierre himself gives the precise date of the conjunction as March 14, 1345 (1346 by our calendar), he at least knew that he had been born in 1351.[1]

Compiègne in those days was already a city with a long past. As early as the sixth century there had been, in the midst of thick forests, a royal palace in the town that had been one of the favorite residences of the Carolingians. After Charles the Bald lost Aix-la-Chapelle, he had even hoped to make Compiègne a new Aix. In 877 he ordered that a chapel be consecrated near the palace, a chapel that was supposed to have been staffed by one hundred clerics and in which lay the remains of Saint Cornelius. After various episodes in the twelfth century this chapel became a great Benedictine abbey. In the shadow of the palace and monastery prospered a small city, blessed with a rich market, nearby forests, and a port where cargoes that had traveled this far up the Oise were unloaded before continuing their journey northward by land. This small but wealthy city grew into a strong commune protected by walls. In the thirteenth century, however, the commune of Compiègne, like many others, experienced financial difficulties. It vanished in 1319. But the prosperous city survived, and it not only served as home to the king but attracted the concern of Paris merchants, because the capital's wood supply and communications with northern France depended in part on Compiègne. And it was in the richest parish of this prosperous city, not far from the Saint-Antoine Church, in the rue des Domeliers, in a family house that adjoined the walls of the Franciscan monastery on one side and the house of Colart the Butcher on the other, that Pierre d'Ailly was born.[2]

Pierre's family name was Marguerite (which means daisy), and on his commoner-parents' coat of arms there were six daisies. In those days, however, individuals and families often identified themselves not by their surname but by the name of the place from which they sprang. The Marguerites, as it happens, were natives of Ailly. Did they hail from the Ailly that lies close to Abbeville or the Ailly on the Noye south of Amiens and closer to Compiègne? In any case, the Marguerites were Picards who still had property and interests in Picardy, and even though they had lived in Compiègne for a long time, they still thought of themselves as being from Ailly—whence the name d'Ailly.[3]

We do not know precisely what line of business the Marguerites of Ailly were in that might account for their prosperity in Compiègne, but there is no doubt that they formed a very prosperous burgher clan. Our Pierre's great-grandfather Thomas and his wife Jeanne Harelle had endowed in Saint-Antoine Church a chaplaincy attached to the altar of Saint-Liénard, or Saint Leonard, next to which lay their common tomb. In 1344 Thomas's son, Pierre's grandfather, who was also called Pierre, was able to add to the endowment of this family chaplaincy thirteen and a half *journaux* of land he owned in the region of Nesle.[4] And Colard d'Ailly and his wife Pétronille, Pierre's father and mother, owned in addition to their house in the rue des Domeliers other houses and other estates.[5]

Several of the children of Colard and Pétronille lived to adulthood. There was a son about whom we know little more than his first name, François, which in the middle of the fourteenth century was not yet a very common first name.[6] But the d'Aillys lived close to the Franciscan monastery. And there were also two daughters, whose names we do not know. Both would marry Compiègne burghers. The first wed a man by the name of J. le Tenneur (the Bookkeeper), by whom she had at least six children. The other daughter married a certain le Prestre, by whom she had at least three sons.[7] Colard and Pétronille also had another son, Pierre, whom his friends would call "the incomparable light of the church" (*lux unica cleri*),[8] "the light of our times" (*lumen nostri aevi*),[9] and who for forty years did indeed dominate his age. Of course there was no particular reason why this scion of prosperous small-town burghers should enjoy such a remarkable fate—no particular reason, that is, apart from his gifts.

In 1356 King John the Good of France was defeated and taken prisoner at Poitiers. In Paris grave events followed this defeat, events accompanied by violence that compelled John's son, the dauphin Charles, who though not yet twenty bravely confronted the situation, to abandon his capital. On May 4, 1358, the dauphin held estates at Compiègne and secured important financial backing from his loyal supporters. Three weeks later the great peasant revolt known as the Jacquerie broke out in the valleys of the Oise and the Thérain, not far from Compiègne; the disturbances, of which nobles were the principal victims, spread rapidly. Many nobles took refuge in Compiègne. The Jacques, or rebellious peasants, came to the city gates and demanded that the refugees be handed over, but the city refused. As these tragic events unfolded in the spring of 1358, little Pierre was seven years old. There is no evidence that he was marked by what took place. He never spoke of the events. In any case, Pierre d'Ailly was not a man to dwell on his past. A voluble talker and facile writer, he never recounted his childhood, neither this period nor the ensuing years during which the kingdom slowly made its way out of the abyss. By August 1358 the dauphin had returned to Paris. In 1360 the disastrous treaty of Calais ceded numerous fair provinces of the French realm to the king of England, in return for which France received if nothing else at least the gift of peace. On April 8, 1364, John the Good died. Shortly thereafter, on May 16, at Cocherel in Normandy, Bertrand Du Guesclin crushed the armies of Charles, king of Navarre, troops that had long plagued the Valois kings. And on May 19 the son of King John was anointed at Rheims. Thus the glorious reign of the wise king Charles V began in peace and victory. It was at around this time, in 1363, 1364, or at the latest in 1365, that young Pierre d'Ailly, with no more baggage than the elementary education he may have received from some modest cleric in Compiègne, and obviously tonsured, was sent to Paris to study.[10]

The University of Paris and the College of Navarre

Much later, in 1410, describing the world in his *Imago Mundi,* Pierre d'Ailly would express his astonishment that neither Orosius nor Isidore of Seville nor the other cosmographers of antiquity had said anything about the kingdom of France, "which is now the greatest of all the kingdoms of Europe." Nor had they said anything about its capital, Paris, the site of "the greatest center for the study of the divine sciences and human letters." One possible reason for this silence was that the kingdom and its capital might "not have been as populous and as famous then as [they are] now."[11] In any case, things had changed a great deal since antiquity. And when young Pierre d'Ailly went to study in the capital of France, the University of Paris had been famous for a long time.[12]

The learned men of the time praised Charlemagne for having "sown on a vast scale in France [and] in the city of Paris."[13] In truth he did nothing of the kind. But by the twelfth century schools were flourishing in Paris in the shadow of Notre-Dame and on the Left Bank, under the authority of the bishop and under the control of a dignitary of the cathedral chapter whom he appointed, the chancellor of the church of Paris. In the thirteenth century the masters of Paris turned to the pope and king in order to limit the chancellor's excessive powers, obtain autonomy, and win recognition as a "university." By the fourteenth century the masters of the university formed a powerful corporation, which called itself "the very humble and very devout daughter" of the pope[14] as well as the "very humble and very devout daughter . . . of the king."[15] The masters and their students loudly and repeatedly proclaimed that they were the grateful daughters of this "mother"[16] to whom they owed everything[17] and that the University of Paris was "the light of the world,"[18] the "light of [the] holy church,"[19] the "beautiful, clear light of [the] all holy church and [of] Christendom,"[20] the "light of the faith,"[21] the "light of science,"[22] the "mother of studies and defender of the faith,"[23] the "mistress of truth,"[24] and the "fountain of knowledge."[25]

From this fountain of knowledge flowed, as Gerson, using a metaphorical language dear to the men of the Middle Ages, put it later on, four rivers that irrigated the entire earth.[26] In other words, the academic corporation was in fact an aggregate of four quasi-autonomous corporations comprising the four faculties of arts, medicine, law, and theology. The faculty of arts took children of twelve to fourteen and turned them out five or six years later at age seventeen to twenty after initiation in the seven liberal arts, which included the three literary arts of the *trivium* (grammar, rhetoric, and dialectics, or philosophy) and the four scientific arts of the *quadrivium* (arithmetic, geometry, astronomy, music). Upon completing his studies in the arts and graduating from the faculty, the young master of arts might very well end his studies altogether. Or he might go to Orléans to study Roman law, for Paris offered no instruction in Roman law and Orléans was the closest available center. In Paris, the young master of arts could choose between the faculty of medicine, which had few members, the faculty of law, which offered instruction in the canon law that governed the life of the Church, or the faculty of theology.

Paris was not the place to go in the West for the best education in medicine or canon law, but the university had no equal when it came to the arts and, even more, to theology. Now, theology was the queen of sciences. To be sure, each discipline contributed its portion of truth. Philosophers discussed "subtle things." Mathematicians examined "difficult things." Jurists weighed the "things of the city." But only theologians delved into profound, unfathomable, and impenetrable truths.[27] And if the University of Paris was called the light of the world, the light of the faith, it was because "the throne that sustains the faith," "the throne of the faith, namely, knowledge of holy scripture and divine science, which is called theology," was "more abundantly and more truly found" in Paris than "in all other universities."[28] The University of Paris was famous because its faculty of theology was "in a sense the seat of catholic truth."[29]

The Paris masters could not say enough in praise of their university. This praise was not merely the fruit of corporate self-satisfaction. It also expressed sincere admiration and gratitude to an institution that, through continuous progress, had reached a pinnacle of perfection. For two centuries the University of Paris had fostered technical advances from which intellectual life had greatly benefited. Among these was silent reading, in which the eye was the only intermediary between the text and the reader's mind, a practice that had gradually supplanted an older form of reading in which the lips pronounced every word. Silent reading was of course more rapid, and it became still more efficient as texts acquired tables of contents and indexes that facilitated access, as chapters grew shorter, as paragraphs were more clearly marked, as punctuation was improved and extended, as more intelligent use was made of capital letters, and as separations between words were more clearly indicated.[30] In order to meet the needs of ever more numerous students capable of reading faster and faster, several technical innovations were introduced to aid in the rapid reproduction of books. Each section (*pecia*) of the work to be copied (*exemplar*) was given to a different scribe, allowing the entire work to be reproduced in the time it took to copy one section. Working for a readership of academics, the scribes could make use of traditional abbreviations that were well known to professional scholars and did not impede rapid reading. Around 1300, moreover, scribes finally gave up a technique of writing in which the quill had to be lifted frequently from the parchment and adopted a new technique in which the quill remained in contact with the text and was lifted only at the ends of words in order to mark a clear separation. This "Gothic cursive" was not only more legible but also more rapid than the old style of writing. Finally, construction work had begun on new libraries in which books, carefully arranged and well catalogued, could be consulted by master and students, now, thanks to silent reading, able to work side by side without interfering with one another.

Outside the productive silence of the libraries, however, the spoken word reigned supreme. It was an efficient form of communication, all the more so because orators were trained from the beginning of their studies to employ a method of argument and exposition in which parts, subparts, paragraphs, and arguments were not only clearly marked (first, second, third, and so on) but also logically related and couched in a Latin which, though obviously not Ciceronian, was nevertheless a living, functional tongue well suited to its purpose and comprehensible to clerics from many different countries. By the time Pierre d'Ailly entered the university as a young lad, these wonderful technical advances had made of the scholastic method an incomparable educational instrument.

There were of course some dark spots. Thoughtful scholars complained of the shortage of good copyists capable of producing accurate texts.[31] They also deplored misuses of scholasticism. They regretted that some mistook obscurity for subtlety[32] or went to ridiculous lengths in subdividing texts into chapters and paragraphs.[33] Nothing could prevent mediocre minds from abusing a fine instrument. But there was no dearth of great doctors, whose training had equipped them well to engage in debates on fundamental issues.

Parisian intellectuals were concerned with any number of problems, yet all were in some way related to the central debate that stemmed from Aristotle's conquest of the West. During the twelfth and thirteenth centuries Latin translations of Aristotle's works had gained authority. Faith and reason had clashed head-on. Many had thought about the question, and each thinker had proposed his solution. Later in his life Pierre d'Ailly would take an interest, for instance, in the work of William of Auvergne, who was born in Aurillac in 1180 and became first a professor of theology in Paris, then bishop of Paris in 1228, and who died in 1249. William is a good example of the reaction of an Augustinian, Platonizing theologian to this new world of thought.[34] Thomas Aquinas was only one of many great thirteenth-century theologians, but it was his good fortune to have been born late, in 1225. By the time he died in 1274, his genius had enabled him to create out of the works of his predecessors an admirable synthesis, whose primary feature was a clear distinction between reason and faith, whose necessary accord he also stressed. Although reason and faith, he insisted, follow different paths, both lead to the truth. It is therefore legitimate to proceed by way of reason, as far as it is possible to go, toward revelation. A theologian may legitimately ask of a natural theology based on reason that it carry him to the threshold of the theology revealed by Scripture.[35] The second fundamental feature of the Thomist synthesis is that, in treating the problem of being, Thomas, guided by Aristotle and concerned to give a better proof of the existence of God, saw more reality in the general idea than in its particular realizations. A particular man was less real than the notion of man. Thomas was a "realist."[36]

Thomas's construction left many of his contemporaries unconvinced. He placed entirely too much faith in reason. And in 1277, when the bishop of Paris, Etienne Tempier, condemned 219 propositions from Aristotle and his recent commentators as contrary to Christian dogma, some of the condemned assertions accurately reflected Thomist thought.[37] But the Dominican order worked tirelessly to establish the authority of its most illustrious friar's work over the entire Church. When John XXII canonized Thomas in 1323, the order believed that it had achieved its goal. Unfortunately, many theologians were already out to demonstrate the vanity of Thomas's efforts. The most radical of the critics was William of Ockham, a Franciscan born at Ockham in Surrey some years prior to 1300. He had studied theology at Oxford, where in commenting on the *Sententiae* in 1318–20 he had taken positions that Thomists in Avignon immediately found worrisome.[38] In these and later commentaries William proved rigorously that it was impossible through reason alone to achieve the slightest theological certainty. Reason had its own, ultimately rather limited domain, that of philosophy. The theologian who made use of reason outside that domain could not hope to go beyond the probable. In addition, William of Ockham was a radical "nominalist." For him, that is, a word was only a word;

an idea possessed nothing more than a name. Only the particular was real.[39]

At first, in 1340, William's ideas were condemned in Paris.[40] Within a generation, however, they had caught on. When young Pierre d'Ailly arrived at the university, Dominican masters were still teaching their illustrious forebear's doctrine to and against all comers, but other scholars, aware of the "discordances" in the Thomist construction pointed out by Ockham's works,[41] had abandoned what would soon be called the *via antiqua,* which trusted in reason and believed in the reality of the universal, in favor of what soon came to be known as the *via moderna.*[42] The "modern way" opened up broad new perspectives. By rejecting natural theology it justified more intensive study of Scripture and encouraged attempts to approach God not by reason but by other means. It also bestowed fully autonomous reality on the visible world and thus gave grounds to believe that one might come to know that world by empirical means; hence the progress of nominalism led, in the fourteenth century, to spectacular development of the sciences. Finally, since the modern way attached great importance to the individual, it had important political implications. Thus the debates that raged among Parisian masters early in the reign of Charles V were anything but idle word games and intellectual jousts. The best scholars brought a profound culture and a proven method to these debates on the fundamental issues of the day.

Jean Buridan was undoubtedly the most outstanding of the leading Parisian scholars of the mid-fourteenth century. His teaching at the faculty of arts surely played a not insignificant part in the triumph of nominalism in Paris and encouraged physicists to explore the new and ultimately fruitful avenue of experimentation. The best of Jean Buridan's many students was Nicolas Oresme. In the history of Western thought, Nicolas Oresme is a name to conjure with, a thinker of the stature of Descartes. Prior to his death in 1382 at about sixty, Oresme was first of all a great commentator and translator of Aristotle. He had produced a commentary on the Stagirite's *Physics* and, at a time when scientists and philosophers were still using only Latin, he translated Aristotle's *Ethics and Politics* into admirable French and provided useful glosses. Oresme revealed his thought even more fully in his own works, not only those on physics and astronomy but also his famous treatise *On the Origin, Nature, and Mutation of Money,* which in effect founded the discipline of political economy in France. This great mind attracted a remarkable array of friends, including Philippe de Mézières, the great mathematician John of Murs, and Philippe de Vitry, the Champenois poet and musician whom Petrarch, though no lover of French authors, ranked so high.[43] After 1362 the favor of King John and later of King Charles enticed Oresme away from the College of Navarre. Before that, however, his presence had dominated the school for nearly fifteen years. He studied theology and taught arts at the school as early as 1348, and from 1356 to 1361 he had even been its head.[44] It was to this same College of Navarre, still marked by the very recent presence of so illustrious a mind, that Pierre d'Ailly came in 1363, 1364, or 1365 to pursue his studies.

Neither the young student who came to study in the faculty of arts nor, for that matter, the more advanced student was left to his own devices in the big city. Students were generally received by one of the many colleges that had been founded in the thirteenth and fourteenth centuries, and it was from the colleges that they received room, board, and instruction. The student's fundamental allegiance, his decisive milieu, was the college. Pierre d'Ailly's fate owed much to the fact that he was accepted by the College of Navarre.

The College of Navarre had been endowed by Jeanne de Navarre, the wife of Philip the Fair, in a will drawn up prior to her death in 1305. Being countess of Champagne, she had wanted the students of the college to be Champenois. Being also queen of France, she had endowed it handsomely. The college was to admit seventy scholars, fifty of whom were to study the arts and twenty to study theology. In all colleges it was customary—and it was this custom that made the colleges such tightly knit communities—for recent masters in arts who had gone on to study theology to teach the arts to younger students. The College of Navarre quickly became one of the leading colleges in Paris. Within a few decades of its foundation two characteristics designated this particular college as an institution of note. First, it was of exceptionally high intellectual caliber, as Oresme's presence attests. Second, in a university that liked to think of itself as the king's eldest daughter, this royally endowed college was an object of special royal favor. The king's confessor chose its scholars, and the king's scholars felt a particular attachment to the king. Every August 25, the feast of Saint Louis, the college celebrated its annual festival, and often the king took part. Mass was celebrated according to a liturgy appropriate to the day. Sermons were delivered by the finest orators among the college's former students. Later, in the fifteenth century, it became customary for colleges to stage theatrical performances, and the students performed a mystery of Saint Louis, the text of which was preserved in the library.[45]

Compiègne, to be sure, was not exactly in Champagne, but many exceptions to the rule governing the scholars' geographic origins were tolerated. And Pierre d'Ailly's parents were not poor, but, then, not all the parents of the "poor scholars" admitted to the college were actually living in misery. And so it was that Pierre d'Ailly came to the College of Navarre, a hotbed of royal and intellectual fervor, some time around 1364.

Forty years later, in 1406, the grown man was still acutely aware of his good fortune as a youth: "I was originally your boarder," he told the king, "in your College of Navarre."[46]

Parisian Studies (1364–78)

Pierre d'Ailly began at the College of Navarre by studying grammar and completed his study of the arts in 1368.[47] He was then seventeen, perhaps slightly younger than his fellow masters of arts, who were typically eighteen to twenty. The brilliant young master naturally remained at the College of Navarre to study theology, and the academic year 1368–69 was in fact his first year of theological study.[48] In 1368 he was required, like all masters of arts pursuing higher studies, to join what was called a "nation," a sort of mutual aid society in which Parisian masters of arts joined with others according to their geographic origins. Recognized as early as the first half of the thirteenth century, independent, and powerful, the nations, four in number, played an important part in the lives of Parisian masters. The "Norman" nation included both Normans and Bretons. The "Picard" included Picards, Flemish, and Walloons. The "English" included masters from England, of course, as well as those who came from central and northern Europe. And the "French," the largest of the four nations, included those who hailed from southern Europe as well as from the ecclesiastical provinces of Tours, Bourges, Sens, and Rheims.[49] Compiègne was located in the diocese of Soissons and the province of Rheims. Pierre d'Ailly therefore joined the French nation, which in addition enjoyed particularly close relations with the College of Navarre since its members met at the college and its seal and archives were kept there.[50]

For the first five to seven years of theological study, students were content to listen to a master. Thus in the years after 1368 Pierre d'Ailly was an attentive and silent student of theology. But he was also a brilliant professor of the arts, because, as was customary, he taught arts students at the College of Navarre, where he held the position of master regent. Then, in 1374, after a lengthy initiation, he became a bachelor of theology. Thereafter he followed the standard course of all bachelors in theology, which was to comment on the two fundamental texts of all theological instruction, first the Bible and then the *Sententiae* in which Peter Lombard, in the middle of the twelfth century, had been the first scholar to set forth in methodical fashion all the central questions of faith and dogma.[51] Thus from 1374 to 1376 Pierre d'Ailly was a "biblical" bachelor, and in 1376 and 1377 he was a "sententiary" bachelor. By 1377 he was a "trained" bachelor, ready to begin the final phase of the interminable theological curriculum that would end four years later with the award of licentiate and doctorate.

There was nothing out of the ordinary in the duration of Pierre d'Ailly's studies. What is unusual is that notes of so many of the courses he gave have survived to this day. The principal courses given by the most famous masters had for some time been preserved in writing, either in lecture notes written by the masters themselves or in notes taken by their students. To this custom we owe, in particular, countless "Commentaries on the Sententiae," which give a good picture of Parisian debates. In Pierre d'Ailly's case, however, we possess an exceptional collection of lecture notes. As professor of arts from 1368 to 1374 he commented on Boethius and Aristotle, expounded on the soul, and taught astronomy. All his lectures have survived.[52] We also possess the solemn eulogies on the Bible that he delivered at the beginning (*Principium in cursum Bibliae*) and end of his biblical instruction of 1375–76;[53] his commentaries on the *Sententiae* for 1376–77; and the texts of numerous exercises required of the trained bachelor.[54]

Pierre d'Ailly himself took the greatest care to preserve all these scholastic exercises. Throughout his life he reread, corrected, and reused them—evidence of a rare fidelity to his own views and to an early consciousness of self. These texts enable us to understand more fully how this impassioned orator, who spoke with such clarity, reasoned with such assurance, and wielded such powerful images, achieved such influence over his audience and was carried so far so quickly. On October 21, 1372, at the age of twenty-one, he was elected procurator of the nation of France.[55] He thus became for a period of a few months the principal official of the most important nation in Paris. Actually there was nothing unusual about the procurator's youth. Young masters were not afraid of being represented by a young procurator. Still, the chosen official needed a commanding personality, and Pierre d'Ailly quickly impressed his fellow students, who must have sensed in him the future man of action and who surely succumbed to his gifts as an orator.

His elders, too, were aware of Pierre's eloquence. In 1375 he was still just twenty-four and only a subdeacon when he was chosen by the bishop of Amiens to deliver the traditional sermon to the priests of the diocese gathered in synod.[56] The bishop was a man by the name of Jean de la Grange. He was already an important personage and soon to become one of the most powerful prelates, not just in the realm, but in all Christendom.

To judge the satisfaction the young theology student must have felt upon receiving the invitation of the bishop of Amiens, one must recall that in the fourteenth-century church no stronger pressure group was imaginable than that of a cardinal and his house. The cardinal had his protégés, who in turn had protégés of their own. It was very difficult to have an illustrious career in the church without first attracting, directly or indirectly, the attention of a cardinal. Now, the most powerful of all these potent princes of the church in the mid-fourteenth century was Gui of Boulogne. Born in 1316 to a great family with roots in both central and northern France, in Auvergne and Boulogne, Gui had an exceptional career. He became archbishop of Lyons in 1340, at twenty-four, and cardinal two years later, at twenty-six. What were the young cardinal's ideas about religion? What were his pious concerns? What were his Christian virtues? We do not know. For him, obviously, the essence of the business lay elsewhere. In 1350 he went to Rome to do his devotions during the jubilee year. On the way back he met Petrarch. "How beautiful Italy is," he remarked to the poet in conversation. "But," he hastened to add, "France is better governed." Gui of Boulogne was indeed a great administrator, a great diplomat, and a great statesman. Thanks to these eminent qualities he played a considerable role in both the church and the kingdom and controlled the most powerful network of solidarities to be found in the mid-fourteenth-century church.[57]

Gui's principal protégé was his nephew, Robert of Geneva, who actually was born in the château d'Annecy in 1342. He was the son of Amadeus III, count of Geneva, and through his mother, Mahaut of Boulogne, was Gui's nephew. Young Robert was destined for a career in the church and in 1350, at just eight years of age, was entrusted to his uncle. In 1361, at nineteen and with a special dispensation for his youth, he became bishop of Thérouanne. In 1368, at twenty-six, he became bishop of Cambrai. And in 1371 he was named cardinal. Like his uncle Gui of Boulogne, he was then twenty-nine. At that same age Pierre d'Ailly, with all his gifts, was just a "trained bachelor" in the faculty of theology at Paris. Robert of Geneva obviously owed his rapid rise to his illustrious birth and to the support of his uncle, though he lacked even the administrative and political talents of the latter. As for Christian virtues, his contemporaries credited him with as many as they could: he cut an imposing figure, although he limped a bit; he had a handsome face, although he squinted a bit; and he had a beautiful, strong voice and chanted mass quite elegantly (*cantavit seu celebravit divina officia multum eleganter*).[58]

After his nephew, the man whom Gui of Boulogne backed most strongly was none other than Jean de la Grange. Jean had been born some time between 1325 and 1330, the son of a modest notary from Ambierle. It is not certain that he pursued advanced studies of any kind. But Ambierle was in that region of central France from which the Boulogne-Auvergne dynasty drew many of its servants, and Jean de la Grange's admirable talents as administrator, financier, and diplomat made him Gui of Boulogne's right-hand man. Gui died in 1373, whereupon Jean de la Grange passed without a hitch from the cardinal's service to that of the king. At last he could spread his own wings, and he already enjoyed considerable influence. He became bishop of Amiens in 1375 and in the following year was named cardinal. A mature man, in his fifties, a prince of the church and trusted counselor of Charles V, he began to play a leading role and would continue to do so until his death in 1402. He left behind his numerous bastards, an immense fortune, an edifying will, and an admirable tomb that he had had constructed in the choir of Saint-Martial in Avignon.[59] He was a powerful cardinal, close to the king of France, and Pierre d'Ailly knew that he could choose no better patron if he wished to have an illustrious career. How could he have failed to rejoice when he attracted the notice of Jean de la Grange?

Pierre d'Ailly was also known to another intimate adviser of Charles V, Philippe de Mézières. Did this acquaintance come about through Jean de la Grange, or was it through Philippe's friend Nicolas Oresme? In any case, Philippe was a most extraordinary personage.[60] In the first place, his career was astonishing. Philippe was a Picard, born in 1327 to a family of minor rural nobility that counted among its holdings the château de Mézières in Santerre. He was baptized in the cathedral of Amiens, and it was also in Amiens that he studied grammar. Then he began his training in arms. He went to fight in the East. By 1361 at the latest he was chancellor to the king of Cyprus. That position brought him into contact with Charles V, whose adviser he became in 1373. Along with this brilliant career Philippe followed an unusual spiritual itinerary. The first decisive event occurred at age twenty while he was still in the East: he saw Jerusalem. After returning from the East, he set aside his arms for a time and from 1349 to 1354 studied at the University of Paris. After returning to the East as chancellor to the king of Cyprus, he was profoundly influenced by a meeting with the papal legate, a Carmelite who initiated him into the spirituality of his order. A few years later, while in Venice on his way to Avignon, he moved in circles with close ties to the Carthusians and was attracted to their brand of spirituality. Back in Paris, he began reading Saint Bernard and took him for his master. In the course of this spiritual ascent Philippe de Mézières had developed certain fundamental spiritual intuitions and commitments. He ardently desired reform of the Church, and he wanted Christians to renew the Crusade and liberate Jerusalem, where Christ had suffered his passion. Philippe's commitment to the Crusade was rooted in, and derived its power from, the cult of the passion, and to liberate the holy places he wanted to found a new knightly order, the Order of the Passion. He was more successful in a related commitment, his devotion to the cult of the Virgin. Although the presentation of the Virgin in the Temple, the holy day celebrating the purification of the Virgin on February 2, was not based on any authentic biblical text, it was nevertheless observed by the Eastern church, and Philippe worked passionately to secure its observance in the West. The holy day was in fact celebrated for the first time in Avignon, while he was there. By 1373 Charles V was also working to establish the holy day. Philippe's astonishing personality, his temporal and spiritual battles, his love of Holy Scripture, and the ardor of his faith must have been deeply attractive to the young theologian.[61] By a lucky coincidence Philippe de Mézières was also a trusted advisor of the king. Pierre d'Ailly was scarcely twenty-five and already he was known to two powerful men, men seated on the stairs to the throne, one a cardinal and the more political of the two, the other a knight and the more mystical. The young cleric had a future.

For the time being, Pierre d'Ailly continued to hold audiences spellbound with his teaching and preaching. He preached to the synod of Paris in 1374.[62] He delivered the sermon of Saint Louis at the College of Navarre in 1377.[63] The authorities were all the more disposed to call on him because he was a brilliant orator who, whether in the capacity of professor or that of preacher, expressed the most traditional ideas with the greatest of passion. To be sure, he thundered against wicked clerics, both those devoid of all learning and those who, though learned and well-spoken, preached evil through their example. He vividly described, in order to condemn, the habits of those who sowed disorder in the clerical order.[64] These brilliant if commonplace fulminations no doubt delighted his audience without provoking the sinners. In any case there was nothing subversive about Pierre's attacks. The existence of wicked clerics did not call the existence of the clergy into question. Pierre d'Ailly had moral concerns but no political or doctrinal problems. This brilliant, solid mind trusted in the authorities.

He trusted the authority of Nicolas Oresme, for example, when he expressed admiration for true mathematicians while condemning false ones, the magi and sorcerers. Pierre d'Ailly followed Oresme in condemning as human pride the will to penetrate the secrets of God and of the future. He reminded his listeners of Acts 1:7: "It is not for you to know the times or the seasons, which the Father hath put in his own power."[65] Having grown up in a nominalist climate, Pierre d'Ailly showed himself to be a faithful disciple of William of Ockham in conceding that the number of certitudes to which man could aspire through reason alone was severely limited. Beyond these, reason yielded only probabilities. Man, left to his own devices, remained limited to probabilities;[66] happily there were authorities who allowed him to rise above the probable to attain the certain. Pierre d'Ailly thus enlarged the realm of the probable for no other reason than to exalt the benefits of authority. And the *Letter to the New Hebrews* (*Epistola ad novos Hebraeos*) that the young trained bachelor addressed to Philippe de Mézières in 1378 was not so much a dissertation on the authorities as a hymn to the authority of the church.

Roger Bacon was an exceptional thirteenth-century figure. Born around 1210, Bacon, a Franciscan monk, died sometimes after 1292. Over the course of a long life his audacious ideas caused him many ups and downs. He had dared to distrust the authorities and place his faith more in reason and experience. His bold thinking and encyclopedic knowledge had led him to conclusions that frightened his contemporaries. He professed, for instance, the most profound respect for Saint Jerome, but he gave numerous proofs that in Jerome's Latin translation of the Bible, the Vulgate, which the Church had adopted as its official version of Holy Scripture, the illustrious doctor had made mistakes or had not said everything or had added to the text. In order to recover the truth of the Hebrew text, Roger Bacon proposed that the Vulgate be corrected.[67] Such an audacious proposal had met with no response in Bacon's time. But now, at the end of the reign of Charles V, in Paris, Roger Bacon's views concerning the Bible began to be adopted by others. Philippe de Mézières was troubled by this development. And Pierre d'Ailly, in his *Letter to the New Hebrews*, crushed the shade of the unfortunate Franciscan beneath the weight of the authorities.

Authorities exist, the young theologian said, and they must be believed. Jerome was a learned man of very great authority. One therefore must trust in the translation he gave. Nevertheless, the obligation to believe a human authority is not absolute. Salvation does not hinge on such belief: "Nulla auctoritas humana firmiter est credenda de necessitate salutis." All human authority is of course liable to error. By himself Jerome was an authority whom one was obliged to believe not *firmiter* but simply *probabiliter.* Not to believe him would be evidence of audacity and presumption but not of heresy. But Jerome was not alone. His translation had been approved by the authority of the Church. While it was not absolutely necessary to believe a human authority, it was absolutely necessary, in order to be saved, to believe in the authority of Holy Scripture (*auctoritas sacrae seu canonicae scripturae a quolibet firmiter est credenda de necessitate salutis*). It was absolutely necessary, in order to be saved, to believe in the authority of the Christian Church (*auctoritas ecclesiae christianae a quolibet firmiter credenda est de necessitate salutis*). What is more, the Bible owed its authority exclusively to the approval of the Church. Saint Augustine said: "I would not believe the Gospel if the authority of the Church did not compel me to do so" (*Ego Evangelio non crederem nisi me ecclesiae catholicae commoveret auctoritas*).[68] Pierre d'Ailly perhaps did not go as far as Augustine. Nevertheless, he is forced to recognize that we consider the Old and New Testaments canonical or divine because we believe in the authority of the Church that approves them (*propter auctoritatem ecclesiae catholicae quae eas ita recepit et approbat*). Now, the Church had also approved Jerome's translation. It would not have done so had there been some error. Not to trust in Jerome's translation would make it possible to doubt any other text approved by the Church. It would simply be presumptuous to doubt Jerome if he were alone, for there is no obligation to believe any human authority in any manner other than *probabiliter.* It was a far graver matter to call into question a translation by Jerome approved by the authority of the Church, in which it was necessary to believe *firmiter, de necessitate salutis.* Who in the Church possessed authority? Pierre d'Ailly did not concern himself with this question at this time. But he never for a moment doubted that the authorities must be believed, and first and foremost the authority of the Church.[69]

Believe, yes. And obey. In a world in which all authority comes from God, it is well that those to whom God has given some measure of authority should make themselves loved more than feared. But the most important thing is that others obey. Order and peace depend on it. Some years later, in April 1381, Pierre d'Ailly would deliver a sermon on the text of Matthew 16:18: "Upon this rock I will build my church." That rock, that unshakeable granite, was the Bible. And on that rock was built the house of which Christians were the stones and of which the mortar was faith and obedience. Pierre d'Ailly then reminded his listeners of Augustine's praise of the Bible on which the Church based its teaching. The Bible exhorts each individual in this world to do well what his or her estate requires: "It makes women subject to their husbands in chaste and faithful obedience . . . and it teaches men to govern their wives according to the laws of a sincere love. It makes children subject to their parents in docility freely accepted, and in tender affection it bestows upon parents responsibility for their children. It compels servants to obey their masters not so much from necessity of their condition as from love of their duties, and it renders masters benevolent toward their servants in consideration of God Most High, their common master. . . . It teaches kings to serve their peoples; it admonishes peoples to submit to the laws. . . . It teaches to whom honor is due and to whom reverence and to whom . . . obedience."[70]

Thus Pierre d'Ailly lived happily in certainty. He respected the authorities. He knew whom to believe. He knew whom to obey. But then, suddenly, in 1378, came the drama. The church now had two popes.

The Beginnings of the Schism (1378–84)

In the early fourteenth century, in response to the wishes of two French popes, Clement V and John XXII, Avignon little by little became the seat of the papacy. In itself there was nothing unreasonable about this development. The pope was perfectly at home in Avignon, because the Comtat Venaissin was a possession of the Church. Close to the kingdom of France but not part of it, the city enjoyed a peace that contrasted favorably with the chronic insecurity afflicting Italy and Rome. Finally, Avignon was more centrally located than Rome with respect to the rest of Latin Christendom. Over time, given the succession of French popes, the growing numbers of French cardinals, and the many curialists who had grown accustomed to Avignon, the city had become the normal residence of the papacy and the capital of Christendom.[71] If policy justified the choice of Avignon, however, mystique condemned it. The blood of martyrs had never flowed in Avignon. The tomb of Peter was in Rome. The pope was bishop of Rome. In Rome were the many churches to which pilgrims traveled in search of indulgences. It was to Rome that the faithful went by the thousands in the jubilee years

1300 and 1350. As time passed and the pope and cardinals became more and more settled in Avignon, Christians, especially Italian Christians, became more and more indignant that they had abandoned Rome. Ultimately mystique triumphed over policy. On October 16, 1367, Urban V entered Rome. But the political situation was decidedly untenable. In 1370 he and the entire curia returned to Avignon, where he died on December 19. His successor, Gregory XI, felt compelled to return to Rome. He entered the city on January 17, 1377. In the months that followed everything hung in the balance. Part of the curia was still in Avignon, the other part in Rome. And the atmosphere in Rome was still threatening. Anything was possible. Everything was to be feared. And then, on March 27, Gregory XI died.

The cardinals met in conclave at the Vatican on April 7. Jean de la Grange, the leader of the French party, was not present, however. And Robert of Geneva, Gui of Boulogne's nephew and the most likely of the French cardinals to become pope, was only thirty-six years old. Outside the Vatican the mob was clamoring for a Roman pope, or at least an Italian. Of the four Italian cardinals present at the conclave, however, one was definitely too old and another definitely too young. A third was from Florence, and how could the Romans be forced to accept a Florentine? And the fourth was from Milan, and how could the Romans be forced to accept a Milanese? The cardinals therefore turned outside the conclave and chose a Neapolitan of modest origins, a man in his sixties, a brilliant jurist, a doctor of canon law who had once been professor at the University of Naples but who for nearly twenty years had occupied an important post in the curia and who, in addition, was known by all the cardinals: Bartolomeo Prignano. He accepted and took the name Urban VI. He was crowned on April 18. The conditions under which he was chosen were truly dreadful, but the election was perfectly regular.

To be sure, the new pope did nothing to win the sympathy of those who had elected him. But the most important new element in the situation was that Jean de la Grange was now in Rome. Things began to take a different course. The French cardinals suddenly felt scruples at having cast their votes in fear. They left Rome and declared the election of Urban VI null and void. On September 20, 1378, they elected Robert of Geneva pope, and he took the name Clement VII. Naturally Urban VI did not give in. In Rome he even remained master of the field. Defeated in Italy, Clement VII left the country and settled in Avignon, which he entered on January 20, 1379. Thus the Church had two popes, one in Rome, the other in Avignon.

The emperor, the count of Flanders, and the king of England remained loyal to Urban VI, whose election they deemed it scandalous to challenge. Charles V was different. Jean de la Grange could not have operated for long without his approval, and it was Jean himself who informed the king. It therefore comes as no surprise to discover that a few weeks later, on November 16, 1378, Charles V recognized Clement VII. The king was quickly followed by his princes, his clergy, and his subjects. Soon all of France was "Clementine"—all of France, that is, except the University of Paris. Naturally the king would have liked the university to back Clement VII. But the university was an international body. Its masters came from all over Europe. And the decision had to be taken not by the university as a whole but by each faculty and each nation. Divided and paralyzed, the university asked the king for time, and the king acceded to the request.[72] Then the faculties of medicine and canon law, which were smaller than the other faculties and which recruited students more locally, recognized Clement VII. The nations of France and Normandy had no trouble recognizing Clement VII, either. But the Picard and English nations leaned toward Urban VI. And the masters of the prestigious faculty of theology, diverse in origin and in many cases from distant lands, anxious to take the long view, and also bound by benefices in their native countries, did not wish to sequester themselves in Clementine Christendom. Instead of recognizing the pope of Avignon, they took advantage of the king's patience and for many long months, in 1379 and 1380, ardently sought a path that would enable the church to recover its unity. It soon became clear to several of the masters that the only possible way out was to hold a general council. In May or June 1379 a German master, Heinrich von Langenstein, said as much in his *Epistola pacis*. In May 1380 another German master, Conrad von Gelnhausen, developed the point further in his *Epistola concordiae*. Charles V, worried by the continuing division within the church, was willing to listen.[73] In this troubled climate Pierre d'Ailly, still young and perplexed, kept a low profile. On the feast of Saint Dominic, August 8, 1379, he celebrated the saint before an audience of powerful men. His eloquent sermon recommended nothing other than pious patience.[74]

But Charles V, though only forty-two, died on September 16, 1380. The ensuing months were a feverish time for the university, and for the first time Pierre d'Ailly would play a leading role. On September 16 the bishops, barons, and representatives of the capital gathered in the chamber of the dying king at the château de Beauté, a few leagues from Paris. Charles V still had sufficient strength to make a long speech. He declared his firm belief that Clement VII was the true pastor of the church, but in any event he wished "to obey on this point the general council or any other competent council that may pass judgment on the issue."[75] A few hours later he died. The Paris masters were able to congratulate themselves that, thanks to their efforts, the unity of the church would soon be restored, and they set to work on the details of the council.

While the fate of the church was being decided, however, the attention of the masters and students of the University of Paris was partly diverted to another drama of the most serious sort. On September 24 the king's body had been solemnly transported from Beauté to Notre-Dame in Paris. When the procession reached the abbey of Saint-Antoine, the canons of Notre-Dame and the canons of the Sainte-Chapelle attempted to join in just after the king's body, the latter on the right, the former on the left, with the bishop. But the rector of the university and the masters and students of the four faculties claimed that it was their right to follow immediately behind the royal body. A ruckus ensued. The provost of Paris and his sergeants waded in against the academics, many of whom were trampled by horses. Some, including the venerable master Jean Rousse, a doctor of theology, were seriously injured. The strongest of the lot hurled themselves into the Seine and swam to safety on the Left Bank. The weakest were stripped of their belongings and tossed into prison. The sergeants even confiscated two large silver maces that the vergers customarily carried ahead of the rector.[76]

The event was grave in itself. It was even more grave because of the personality of the provost of Paris. Hugues Aubriot was the son of a wealthy merchant from Dijon. He had made a rich marriage. His fortune was considerable. He had made a career in government and since 1367 had served as provost of Paris; the late king had trusted him implicitly. Like his predecessors, Hugues Aubriot was also judge-ordinary of the Jews, guardian of numerous churches, and conservator of the privileges of the university, but the energetic provost believed that his primary role was to maintain order in the city, to keep a tight rein on that perennial source of disorder, the clergy and students, and to show as little respect as possible for the privileges of members of the university and for the jurisdictional rights of the bishop and churches. For thirteen years the provost and the bishop had clashed constantly, and so had the provost and the university. Now that the king, who had protected the provost, was gone, the dispute that erupted at his funeral between canons and academics provided the bishop and the university with an opportunity to join forces in an attempt to depose the provost.

A suit was brought before the Parlement, but cases in Parlement had a way of dragging on interminably. Hugues Aubriot soon gave his adversaries another opportunity to act, this time in more rapid and decisive fashion. On November 15, 1380, rioters attacked the Jewish quarter, pillaged property, destroyed homes, and plucked babies from their mothers' arms in order to baptize them. The victims complained to the provost, who ordered the criers to announce that stolen property was to be returned to its owners and kidnapped children were to be returned to their mothers.[77] Widespread outrage greeted this order. Charges were filed against the heretic in the church tribunals. In a campaign of extraordinary violence he was accused of numerous "horrible and abominable deeds." Not only had he returned Jewish children to their mothers, but he was accustomed "to live with women bestially."[78] He confessed infrequently and did not go often to communion. He showed disrespect for the mass by striding about inside churches during the elevation. One day, for example, the bishop of Coutances was celebrating mass in a chapel. He had reached the elevation. Hugues Aubriot, together with sergeants from the Châtelet, entered the church (perhaps in search of one of the many criminals who sought refuge in the churches—legal places of asylum—after committing their crimes). A monk asked the provost to kneel down, whereupon the official made a long speech, no doubt punctuated with the phrase "I deny God" that was said to come so easily to his lips, in which he explained that the mass was pointless, that he did not believe in this God the bishop was adoring, and that in any case the bishop, to his shame, was at the king's court when he should have been in his diocese. The whole Latin Quarter wanted to see the infamous provost, no longer protected by the king, hanged or burned.[79] Pierre d'Ailly was among those most ardent in seeking his downfall.[80]

The year 1381 was thus a feverish time in Paris, during which the problem of the schism, the Aubriot affair, and Pierre d'Ailly's destiny were all intertwined. On January 21 Hugues Aubriot, summoned before the inquisitor, failed to appear. He was immediately excommunicated. On February 1 the provost chose to surrender to the bishop, who put him in prison.[81] The university pressed its suit before Parlement with renewed ardor. It spent the month of February gathering the documents and the cash it needed to proceed. The master most involved in this activity was Dominique Petit.[82] Petit was three or four years younger than Pierre d'Ailly. He was a native of Varennes in Argonne, thus from the diocese of Rheims.[83] He had been a student at the College of Navarre, where Pierre d'Ailly had been his professor of arts.[84] After receiving his master of arts in 1373, he in turn began teaching arts while studying theology. His personality was such that he was soon elected rector of the faculty of arts, and for a time he was also head of the university.[85] The faculty of arts designated the former rector to act on its behalf in the Aubriot affair, so Dominique Petit devoted most of February 1381 to the university's case in Parlement against Hugues Aubriot. In the meantime the licentiate in theology was conferred on Pierre d'Ailly.

On April 6, 1381, the case took a small step forward. The presidents of the court compiled a list of sergeants of the Châtelet who were to be summoned to appear at the same time as the provost.[86] A few days later, on April 10 and 11, Pierre d'Ailly surmounted the remaining hurdles between him and the prestigious decree of doctor in theology.[87] He had either just turned or was about to turn thirty, very young for a doctor. He was young, brilliant, orthodox, and already much changed by the events that had recently shaken the church. In one of the sermons he was obliged to deliver in this period, he still exhorted his audience to obedience, which remained the supreme virtue. But who was one now to obey? Pierre d'Ailly hoped to preserve the unity of the church by not saying that one must obey Peter, and above all by not saying which Peter. The rock on which Christ had built his church was not Peter: "Who therefore would claim to establish the firmness of the church on the feebleness of Peter?" The unshakeable rock on which the church of Christ was built was the Bible.[88]

Furthermore, the supreme authority by which the church was to be guided was not Peter but the general council. Having achieved the pinnacle of academic honor and having overcome his former misgivings, Pierre d'Ailly became one of the most ardent defenders of the general council idea among the Paris masters. Probably during these same weeks, in an admirable diatribe couched in the form of a letter written by the devil Leviathan (*Epistola diaboli Leviathan*), he attacked those powerful men, prelates and jurists, who opposed the council.[89] Once upon a time, he has the devil say, I was powerful, tranquil, and prosperous in my city of Babylon. Then Jesus of Nazareth, the son of a carpenter, poor and humble though he was, began building Jerusalem. The city prospered and erected walls, which were patrolled night and day by guards who watched and prayed under the command of an uneducated fisherman named Peter. "My arms were powerless against Jerusalem. Fortunately, dissension developed within the city. Within some said, I am for Urban; others, I am for Clement; still others, I am for a general council; I favor arbitration; I think both should resign. And some said, I obey such and such a prince, while others said, I obey such and such a king, and still others said, I want such and such a benefice. Meanwhile, the city was destroyed, and its defenders fled in every direction. I was overjoyed! What more faithful servants, what more courageous soldiers could I ask for than the prelates of this Church? But now a few individuals, contemptible and vile, dare to oppose my ministers. These frogs would make their way out of the swamp. And they endlessly croak, 'We need a general council. We need a general council.' *Venite igitur, et opprimamus eos.* Come then, let us oppress them. Do not allow them to stand on the Scripture they call canonical. Do not allow them to preach poverty and humility. Do not allow them to call blessed the wretched and afflicted. Let us follow the laws of this world, the Code of Justinian and the Decretum of Gratian. Let us battle against the general council out of which might come a new leader respected by all and capable of restoring unity and peace to Jerusalem. Love the best places at table and the best seats in the church. Let none of you utter the hateful words that the woman spoke to Solomon [1 Kings 3:25–26]: " 'Give her the living child.' And they all said, 'Let it be neither mine nor thine, but divide it.' "

Meanwhile, Hugues Aubriot, though in prison, was still nominally provost of Paris. But the inquisitorial proceedings were drawing to a close. On May 17, 1381, the deposed provost was dragged onto the parvis of Notre-Dame. Bareheaded, on his knees, a candle in his hand, and facing a podium upon which sat enthroned the bishop and the inquisitor on one side, the rector of the university on the other, and in the presence of thousands of spectators, most of them students, he heard himself sentenced to life in prison. For the university it was a day of triumph.[90]

Before the inquisitor pronounced sentence, however, the bishop spoke at length. He branded Hugues Aubriot as a man guilty of heresy and Judaic perfidy, a despiser of the sacraments of the church and of pontifical authority. Then he attacked, more generally, all the heretics and schismatics who had not rallied to the side of Clement VII.[91] The university, triumphant but also troubled, sensed that it had better act quickly.

On May 20 the four faculties met in plenary assembly and reached agreement that the best way to end the schism was to hold a general council.[92] Pierre d'Ailly was chosen to apprise the court of the university's opinion. The court, certain members of which were sympathetic to the young and eloquent doctor, allowed him to speak.[93] The university may, accordingly, have believed itself on the verge of a second triumph.

In fact it was on the brink of disaster. Unwittingly it had already leaped into the void. After the death of Charles V, his eldest son had been anointed at Rheims on November 4, 1380, but Charles VI was not yet twelve, and his uncles, the deceased king's three brothers—Louis, duke of Anjou, Jean, duke of Berry, and Philip, duke of Burgundy—had ended a period of paralyzing uncertainty by agreeing among themselves to share power. Louis of Anjou was an ardent champion of Clement VII. Like Clement, he wanted to end the schism by taking action, by resorting to arms. He hoped that an expedition to Italy would force Urban VI to flee Rome and provide himself, Louis, with an ultramontane kingdom. The decision taken by the university on May 20 irritated him. The duke of Burgundy, for his part, was not pleased with the humiliation suffered by the Burgundian Hugues Aubriot.[94] And several of the sergeants of the Châtelet who had been summoned before Parlement on April 6 also happened to be servants of the duke of Anjou.[95] The three brothers, so often divided, agreed to oppose the university. And no sooner had the bishop, with the support of the university, triumphed over the provost that he found himself on the side of the dukes in their effort to subdue his former ally.

During his visit to the court, Pierre d'Ailly had no doubt quickly grasped where things stood. The young and brilliant doctor, suddenly prudent, vanished from the scene, and when the university sent another delegation to court in mid-June, Pierre d'Ailly was not part of it. It was headed by the venerable master Jean Rousse, doctor of theology, the very same man who had suffered such rude blows on the day of the royal funeral. Jean Rousse was not even allowed to speak before the duke of Anjou, and the following night the king's men broke down the door of the room in which he lay sleeping, pulled him out of bed, led him away without allowing him to dress, and locked him up in the darkest dungeon of the Châtelet.[96] A few days later news reached Paris of letters of Clement VII ordering the bishop of Paris to remove from their benefices any clerics suspected of being Urbanists and to replace any masters of the university thus punished with others who were Clementines.[97] On July 15, some months after the death of the preceding chancellor, Clement VII named as chancellor of Notre-Dame and head of the university one of his most loyal servants, a man who had for some years been his chaplain, Jean Blanchard.

Jean Blanchard was almost sixty. He was born around 1322 in the diocese of Tournai.[98] His career had been brilliant in the usual way. He had studied in Paris first arts and then theology. Before reaching forty he was a doctor in theology and had accumulated numerous benefices. His birthplace had naturally steered him toward a powerful lay patron, Louis de Male, the count of Flanders, whom he served as chaplain. He was also the chaplain and dining companion of a powerful cardinal, a cousin of the count of Flanders: the very same Gui of Boulogne in whose shadow we have already seen so many clerics prosper. In 1363, at the age of forty, Jean Blanchard was already dean of the church in Liège. It was then, unfortunately for him, that his true nature began to reveal itself. The man seemed greedy and tactless. A violent conflict with the canons of Liège forced him to leave town. A diplomatic mission he made on behalf of the count of Flanders proved so disastrous that Louis de Male wanted never to see him again. Gui of Boulogne, still his protector, died in 1373. Jean Blanchard was fifty, and he was finished—or would have been, had not Robert of Geneva taken his uncle's old servant into his household. Then Robert of Geneva became pope, and Pope Clement VII, to compensate Jean Blanchard for the rich benefices he had lost in Urbanist territory and to assure himself of a possibly tactless but certainly loyal partisan in Paris, appointed him chancellor of Notre-Dame on July 15, 1381. The chancellor no longer played much of a role in the university, but he was still the person who officially granted degrees. Clement VII could count on Jean Blanchard to license no scholars who were not Clementines.[99]

Shortly thereafter, poor Jean Rousse was released from the Châtelet, but only after pledging to speak no more about a general council and to remain loyal to Clement VII.[100] His colleagues realized that the game was over. The great international tribunal was reduced to silence. Christendom accustomed itself to schism. For three years the masters of the university had lived in tumultuous times, which had left their mark. But now they knew that they had been defeated. The majority gave in. Many others left Paris without hope of return. Some, including Jean Rousse, went to Rome to join Urban VI. Others returned to their native lands, now Urbanist, or joined the faculties of recently established universities in the Empire. Still others, out of prudence, simply disappeared for a time. Among this group was Pierre d'Ailly, who had been one of the university's leading spokesmen during the events of May. Yet he still had contacts at court powerful enough to make sure that nothing dreadful happened to him and able to obtain for him a prebend as canon of the cathedral chapter of Noyon. On September 14, 1381, Pierre was accepted as canon by the chapter.[101] For the next three years he quietly bided his time in Noyon, awaiting better days.

The young canon had so little severed his ties with society, with Paris, and with the court that in 1384 he was appointed head of the College of Navarre by the king's confessor.[102] At age thirty-three, in full possession of his powers, Pierre d'Ailly returned to Paris. He was now a personage of some repute. For the next thirty-five years he would play a leading role in the dramatic events that overtook Christendom and France.

The End of the World?

I shall relate only the gist of a complicated story. In 1388 Charles VI was twenty years old. He felt mature enough to govern himself and his kingdom. Unfortunately, in 1392, he suffered the first bout of a madness that would plague him for life and that would leave him fewer and fewer moments of lucidity; he therefore relinquished power once more to his uncles. Not to the duke of Anjou, who had died in 1384, but to Jean, duke of Berry, who would die in 1416 at the age of seventy-six, and to Philip, duke of Burgundy, whose courage in the battle of Poitiers had earned him the surname "the Bold" and who would die in 1404 at the age of sixty-two. As the years went by, those who had been center stage in 1392 were gradually replaced, or supplanted, by the men of a new generation. The duke of Berry had no son, but the duke of Burgundy had one, Jean, who would one day be known as Jean sans Peur, John the Fearless. Born in 1371, John was at this point scarcely more than twenty. He had inherited his father's boldness but was never to acquire his wisdom. As for the king's brother, Louis, two years younger than his cousin John, Charles VI before succumbing to madness had made him a gift of the duchy of Orléans, and the young duke of Orléans lusted after pleasure and power with equal ardor.

Of the leading actors of the previous generation, the first to disappear was the pope. Clement VII died in 1394 at fifty-two. By then it had long been apparent that the pope of Avignon would never rule all of Christendom and, further, that the schism was becoming increasingly intolerable to Christian consciences. Nevertheless, the personal ties that existed between the pope and the French court still paralyzed the latter. When Clement VII died, however, he was replaced by Cardinal Pedro de Luna, who took the name Benedict XIII. The new pope was then sixty-seven. Though not short of virtues, he was not French but Catalan. The court of France began to persuade itself that the unity of the church required, as a first step, the disappearance of the pope of Avignon. In this respect it seconded public opinion. But it met an obstacle in the obstinacy of Benedict XIII, who in his own mind had no intention of repeating Celestine V's mistake of removing the tiara from his own head. Surrender being out of the question, France followed a long, difficult, and cautious course marked by a series of tense assemblies of the clergy toward what was called, in the consecrated expression of the day, *soustraction d'obédience,* withdrawal of obedience.

At this point a new drama made unity of the church even more imperative. The Turks were threatening Byzantium. Christendom raised an army, and John of Burgundy led the French contingent. The army got as far as Bulgaria when on September 25, 1396, it met with disaster at Nicopolis. France continued to distance itself from the pope. In May 1398 another assembly of the clergy was held. A minority, supported by the duke of Orléans, favored further delay. But the majority, backed by the king's uncles, had decided on withdrawal of obedience. On July 27, 1398, the *ordonnance de soustraction* was dispatched. But France's withdrawal of obedience was but one step on the road to church unity. An attempt now had to be made to persuade Benedict XIII to give up his office; the "Clementine" territories had to be wooed away from allegiance to Avignon, and the "Urbanist" territories had to be convinced to abandon the pope of Rome; then a council could be held to elect a new and unchallenged pope. All these hopes were disappointed. A new epidemic of plague ravaged France in 1400, and in the meantime Benedict XIII refused to give in; neither his supporters nor his adversaries would lay down their arms. The situation stood at a total impasse. France was exhausted. In May 1403 Louis d'Orléans was able to win restoration of obedience.

While the duke of Orléans was thus consolidating his authority, Philip the Bold died in 1404, leaving the two young cousins, Louis d'Orléans and John the Fearless, to confront each other. Neither the poor mad king nor the aging duke of Berry could control these two, whose rivalry would plunge France into civil war. By now the schism was merely part of a larger and more bitter conflict in France. The restoration of obedience had satisfied no one. In 1406 another and particularly stormy assembly of the clergy again raised the question whether it was necessary to continue to obey the pope or to cease to obey him; no answer was immediately forthcoming. In this tense and ambiguous situation the unimaginable happened. On November 23, 1407, the duke of Orléans was assassinated. Not only did John the Fearless admit having given the order; he went so far as to attempt to justify the act by calling it tyrannicide. The death of the duke of Orléans had all sorts of consequences. It left Benedict XIII's supporters without troops. It cleared the way for a second withdrawal of obedience (May 1408) and for the Council of Pisa (1409), which culminated in the selection of a new pope. The Council of Pisa thus marked the triumph of a policy that had been pursued stubbornly through a thousand twists and turns over the past ten years. Unfortunately that triumph was fleeting because neither of the two popes would surrender. Meanwhile, the duke's assassination led to a long civil war, which was interrupted by apparent reconciliations and bloodied by violence such as the riots that took place in Paris in 1413 and which ultimately brought on a foreign invasion, resulting in yet another disaster for the French army at Agincourt on October 25, 1415.

In the meantime another council met at Constance in October 1414 in one more attempt to restore the unity of the church. Martin V was elected in November 1417 and recognized by all Christendom. The Church began to bind up its wounds at the very moment when France was sinking into a long period of misery. In 1418 John the Fearless took control of Paris, where a mob massacred many of his adversaries. In 1419 John was murdered on the Montereau bridge by servants of the dauphin, Charles, who was present at the scene. In 1420 the Treaty of Troyes disinherited Charles. Charles VI gave his daughter and thus the hope of his kingdom to the victor at Agincourt, King Henry V of England, while his deposed son held on as best he could south of the Loire. Then, on October 21, 1422, Charles VI died after a long reign not short on difficulties and dramas in which so many men had been caught up, buffeted, or crushed.

All these dramas could of course be portrayed as consequences of two accidents, the madness of Charles VI on the one hand and, on the other, the "peculiarities" of Urban VI, which had forced the cardinals to elect Clement VII. There can be no doubt, even today, that Charles VI's madness was an unforeseeable and unfortunate accident and that a wise king might have spared France all these trials. But the "peculiarities" of Urban VI so casually cited by the cardinals who abandoned him were surely not responsible for the Great Schism. Some of Urban VI's electors may have voted under the influence of fear. The pope may have shown himself quite soon to be tactless and imperious. Nevertheless, he was canonically elected. He was the legitimate, incontestable pope, whom many refused to challenge. The election of Clement VII, the origins of the schism, and its long duration therefore had other causes, which modern scholarship has sought to clarify.

Today it seems clear that the direct cause of the election of Clement VII and of the schism was not so much Urban VI's character as it was the vigorous action of the cardinal of Amiens, Jean de la Grange, combined with the power of the pressure group composed of creatures of the late Cardinal Gui of Boulogne.[103] But Jean de la Grange would not have been as successful as he was if the cardinals had not believed, rightly or wrongly, that their position was threatened by Urban VI. In a secular state in the fourteenth century power was divided between the king and his council; similarly, power in the church was divided between the pope and the Sacred College. Urban VI wanted, or seemed to want, to alter this unstable balance. For the cardinals in 1378 that wish was probably the crux of the matter. Clement VII and his electors truly hoped to govern Christendom from Rome. Things turned out otherwise. They were obliged to leave Italy. They resigned themselves fairly easily to their enforced residence in Avignon because in Italy they felt they were on foreign soil. The schism did not arise out of the debate between Avignon and Rome, but that debate allowed the schism to take root. In order to understand why various states so easily accommodated themselves to the division of the Church, however, we have to delve a little more deeply. The young and increasingly vigorous states of the fourteenth century found it more and more difficult to tolerate an international institution like the Church. The schism weakened whatever authority the pope possessed. His demands for cash became less urgent. Princes increased their domination over their local churches. Indeed, the schism gave new vigor to national churches.[104] In the cold analyses of today's historians it is clear that the schism was not incompatible with aims that can be described as political.

The schism was, however, incompatible with those aspects of religion that can be described as mystical. The Christians of the time did not like to see the fabric of their Church rent. To them this sad spectacle had only one meaning: it presaged the end of the world. The coming of the Antichrist and the end of the world, described in the Book of Revelation and in many other passages of the Bible, had always been an obsession of the Christian spirit. By the time Charles V came to the throne, these were standard and important themes. Prior to 1377 Louis d'Anjou borrowed from the library of his brother the king the manuscript that his artists most likely copied before making the magnificent tapestry of the Apocalypse that can still be seen in Angers today.[105] With the schism of 1378, however, the idea that the world was nearing its end became more urgent and more oppressive than ever. Dates were given. People remembered the words of Arnaud de Villeneuve. A Catalan, Arnaud was a great physician who died in 1311. Among other things he was the author of a *Treatise on the Time of the Coming of the Antichrist* (*Tractatus de tempore adventus Antichristi*), in which, on the basis of prophecies in Daniel and the commentaries of Saint Augustine, he had predicted that the Antichrist would arrive in 1375 or 1376 or 1377.[106] People also remembered what the angel had said to Joachim of Floris. Joachim, who died in 1202, was a Calabrian abbot who had derived from the Bible, of which he was a remarkable exegete, a number of doctrines and prophecies that the Church had condemned but that many people had received with fervor. For two centuries Joachim's prestige had grown steadily. He was credited with more than he actually wrote. According to four Latin verses in circulation at the time, an angel had said to Joachim: "When fourteen hundred years will have passed since the Virgin gave birth, then will the Antichrist reign."[107] Treatises on the Antichrist proliferated, and preachers heralded the coming of the Antichrist and the end of the world. People in fact talked so much about the Antichrist that had he appeared, one contemporary said, the children would have recognized him and would not have been surprised.[108]

In December 1385,[109] as he preached an Advent sermon,[110] Pierre d'Ailly also spoke of Christ's four comings and in particular of the last, at the end of the world (*De Adventu Domini sermo tertius*). He showed easily that Arnaud de Villeneuve's prophecy was false, because if one read Daniel, Matthew 24, and Saint Augustine (*City of God* 20.14) properly, the persecution of the Antichrist was supposed to last three years and six months and the end of the world was to follow immediately. But eight years had already elapsed since the persecution of the present schism began.[111] Should one believe instead in what the angel told Joachim, namely, that the Antichrist would arrive in fifteen years? How dare one fix a date? Pierre d'Ailly was well aware of the words of Christ (Mark 13:32; cf. Matt. 24:36): "But of that day and that hour knoweth no man, no, not the angels which are in heaven, neither the Son, but the Father." And he also said (Acts 1:7): "*Non est vestrum nosse* . . . It is not for you to know the times or the seasons, which the Father hath put in his own power."[112] Accordingly, Pierre d'Ailly argued, it is in vain that we strive to calculate the number of years that the world has left to live, since the voice of truth tells us that it is not for us to know.[113] Note, however, that Christ is speaking in the present. He says to his disciples: "It is not for you, *Non est vestrum.*" He does not say that man will never know. (*Non dicit non erit sed non est*).[114] And if Pierre d'Ailly nevertheless forbids himself to set a date, he has no doubt that the date is near, for Christ has already said: "The hour is near." Pierre continues: "Since a long time has passed since he said that, it follows that only a very short time remains until the end of the world."[115] Furthermore, to announce that the end of the world is imminent is useful only to sinners, to dissuade them from sin.[116]

Finally, Christ clearly stated what signs would herald the end of the world: "The sun [shall] be darkened, and the moon shall not give her light, and the stars shall fall from heaven" (Matt. 24:29). "What does this mean," Pierre d'Ailly concluded, "but that the lights of the church shall be darkened? And is this not, alas! the painful spectacle that we now have before our eyes? For if by sun we are to understand the radiance of prelates, by moon the light of princes, and by stars the luminosity of subjects, then it is certain that darkness has spread everywhere, since we are witnessing the extinction among prelates of the torch of wisdom, among princes of the sparkle of justice, and among subjects and almost universally of the splendor of grace." To be sure, we cannot set a date, but when we see the cruel division of the present schism we must fear that soon the Antichrist will be here.[117] The last days had come. Saint Paul (2 Tim. 3:1–5) said: "This know also, that in the last days perilous times shall come. For men shall be lovers of their own selves, covetous [*cupidi*], boasters [*elatii*], proud [*superbi*], blasphemers, disobedient to parents, unthankful, unholy, without natural affection, trucebreakers, false accusers, incontinent [*tumidi*], fierce, despisers of those that are good, traitors, heady, highminded, lovers of pleasures more than lovers of God."[118] Pierre d'Ailly's contemporaries may have been in doubt about when the world would end, but they were in no doubt that the time of the schism was a time of sin.

In truth, clerics had always hammered away at men's sins. Evagrius Ponticus was born in the Hellespont but lived for a long time first in Alexandria and then in the Egyptian desert. He was a contemporary of Augustine and Jerome, a great mind who, because of his commitment to Origen's teachings, had been condemned and subsequently forgotten. Sometime around the year 400 he compiled a list of the principal sins, cleverly combining already ancient traditions brought to light by Alexandrian scholars.[119] Evagrius's list and others that derived from it were transmitted from the East to the West. Pope Gregory the Great (died 604) used it to establish his own list of capital sins. With slight revisions this Roman list passed down through the centuries, although it was little known outside the monasteries. Monks used it to facilitate their examinations of conscience. Then, in the middle of the twelfth century, when the church began truly to concern itself with laymen, Peter Lombard took note of the list of seven deadly sins in his *Sententiae*. Subsequently the seven deadly sins proved a convenient instrument for pastoral and confessional purposes. The clergy made everyone familiar with the list through sermons and "exempla," which helped to shape the mentality of the age. Even the simplest people knew the sins by name. More learned men used them to explain history, making the deadly sins the cause of God's wrath and man's tribulations.[120]

Peter Lombard had listed, in order, *superbia* (pride), *ira* (wrath), *invidia* (envy), *avaritia* (avarice), *accidia* (sloth), *gula* (gluttony), and *luxuria* (lust). As an aid to memory, Peter Lombard's readers took the first letter of each sin and formed the acronym *siiaagl,* from which they could easily reconstruct, albeit with several possibilities for inversion, the list of seven deadly sins. After Peter Lombard the identity of the seven sins remained constant, and the order in which he gave them remained the most common down to the end of the Middle Ages. There were other orders, however. During the thirteenth century, in particular, the following order appeared: *superbia, avaritia, luxuria, ira, gula, invidia, accidia.* This yielded the acronym *saligia.*[121] That the sins were listed in various orders probably meant that for many people the precise hierarchy was of little importance. The fact that *saligia* is much more like an ordinary word than *siiaagl* most likely encouraged a shift. But the different orders also attest to a deep need to list the seven deadly sins so as to reflect their relative importance. In a rather crude way the lists may thus reflect the weight ascribed to each sin in a particular period.

Initium peccati omnis superbia, said Ecclesiasticus 10:13: "Pride is the first of all sins." It was pride that led the fallen angel to perdition. Gregory the Great had made pride the father of all sins. In later years pride would always remain the greatest sin. But Saint Paul (1 Tim. 6:10) also said: *Radix omnium malorum est cupiditas* ("The love of money is the root of all evil"). And in the twelfth and thirteenth centuries, when economic progress in the West attached new significance to money, poverty became a supreme virtue, and avarice, or love of money, in some instances became the father of sins.[122] Although avarice rarely dethroned pride, it did stake an incontestable claim to second place. After this accursed pair, lust soon claimed the third position. Envy in the thirteenth century was still one of the least of the deadly sins, but in the fourteenth century it gradually took its place alongside the "monstrous trinity"[123] as one of the great causes of the day's woes. If pride was the sin of the great, envy was the sin of the small, for it caused them to suffer "impatience with [their] estate," made them desire "riches and exalted things" that they had no business wanting, and drove them to "murmurs" and rebellion.[124]

By 1378, therefore, the seven deadly sins had had a lengthy history. Pride, avarice, lust, and envy had frequently been blamed for man's woes. Many considered the Great Plague to have been their work. And now that the Great Schism heralded the imminent end of the world, no one doubted their triumph. When Pierre d'Ailly addressed the audience of powerful men on Saint Dominic's feast, August 8, 1379, he was still unsure how the schism might be overcome, but he knew for certain that in the city of the devil the lot of the common man was envy; of nobles, pride; of courtiers, deceit; of priests, craftiness; of soldiers, lust; and of all, avarice (*vulgaribus invidia, nobilibus superbia, fraus curialibus, scelus sacerdotibus, voluptas militibus, denique cupiditas omnibus*).[125]

In his sermon Pierre d'Ailly conceded that the seven deadly sins outweighed all others. Yet he also observed that the framework laid out by monks several centuries earlier was no longer adequate for comprehending the distressing present-day reality. Other sins clamored for attention. Among them was one sin that Charles VI's subjects mentioned more often than any other and frequently placed on a par with the seven deadly sins, namely, ambition. To be sure, ambition had plagued the world for centuries, but now it ranked as one of its greatest scourges. In 1416 Jean Courtecuisse depicted the world as "marvelously" troubled by four winds, which stirred up "great tempests": one was "pride, another ambition, a third lust, and a fourth envy."[126]

The wind of ambition, to put it in a nutshell, "strives upward."[127] Ambition is first of all appetite for power. And since pride itself is the *libido dominandi*[128] and "the prideful . . . have placed their desires in temporal domination and long to have others subject to them,"[129] and since "the prideful" are those "who above all others seek to rise too high,"[130] and since "pride is born on high and raises him who acquires it most high indeed,"[131] it is evident that the wind of ambition "is rather close to pride"[132] and that ambition is the auxiliary of pride[133] and is born of pride.[134] At the same time, however, ambition is *ambitio possidendi,* the desire for wealth.[135] Hence it is nothing other than *cupiditas, avaritia.*[136] It is the "covetousness" that drives men toward "the profits and riches of this world"[137] and that impels clerics, in particular, toward benefices.[138] Benefices, however, do not simply fill the purses of the clergy. They enable clerics "to achieve great honor."[139] And ambition is not simply a will to power or a desire for riches but also the pursuit of honors. For clerics in particular it is *cupiditas dignitatum.*[140] It is, more generally, "lust after honor,"[141] the avid quest for honor, renown, and glory.[142] "Covetous ambition" wishes to "acquire honor" and "rise to glory."[143] "The hunger of ambition is . . . lust after honor and praise."[144] Charles VI's more cultivated subjects were fervent admirers of Cicero. Cicero in *De officiis* defined ambition as the quest for honors (*honorum contentio*), and he distinguished between the desire for honors (*cupiditas honorum*) and the desire for power (*cupiditas potentiae*), for money (*cupiditas pecuniae*), or for glory (*cupiditas gloriae*).[145] It is therefore quite conceivable that reading Cicero helped our clerics to grasp the multifarious sin of ambition in all its complexity. Nevertheless, ambition, regardless of its object, by nature always "strove upward."

To laymen, moreover, at least in the time of Charles VI, the desire to rise seemed quite natural. Lay servants of the state were scarcely reproached for their ambition. They really did not even see themselves as ambitious. In any case they did not suffer from ambition of the wicked sort. By contrast, ambition obsessed clerical consciences, because it diverted clerics for the humility and poverty appropriate to their state and because it called the status quo into question. It threatened the stability of society. It posed a danger to the order willed by God. Hence it was the first of all evils. And the woes of the day stemmed from the fact that instead of frugal mediocrity insatiable ambition reigned (*et, quod omnium malorum caput est, pro frugi mediocritate inexplebilis ambitio*).[146]

Now Pierre d'Ailly's friends may have deplored his ambition,[147] and his enemies may have been outraged by it;[148] but no one ever doubted that it devoured him.

Portrait of Pierre d'Ailly

At least he had talent equal to his ambition. About Pierre d'Ailly's appearance we know very little. A stone that is supposed to portray him shows him with a "round, regular, beardless" face.[149] His friend Nicolas de Clamanges, who in praising him should have preceded his moral description with a physical one, according to the rules of good rhetoric, chose to praise the man rather than his envelope.[150] Hence we know nothing certain about Pierre's body except that he enjoyed that one primary good without which no ambition can succeed: he had his health. The only illnesses from which we know he suffered were a cold in 1406 and a number of indispositions that were too opportune not to be suspect.[151] And this sound body was the faithful servant of a superior mind.

Pierre d'Ailly was superior first of all by dint of his knowledge. In the church there was a long tradition of hostility to knowledge. Many centuries earlier Saint Gregory had praised *sanctas simplicitas, docta ignorantia.* Saint Francis proclaimed: *Ignorans sum et idiota,* "I am an ignorant man, nothing more."[152] Early in the fifteenth century Boniface Ferrer followed countless others in reminding his listeners of the words of the apostle Paul (1 Cor: 8:1): *Scientia inflat,* "Knowledge puffeth up." He further remarked that knowledge was in sum the root of all evil, that learned men were blinded by pride (*elatio, superbia*), avarice and ambition (*ambitio vel cupiditas, ambitio ad dignitates*), and that the Antichrist and his disciples would try to seduce men with power and riches (*potentiam et divitias*), knowledge, wisdom, and eloquence (*scientiam et eloquentiam, sapientiam et facundiam*) and would convince them with innumerable proofs, arguments, treatises, and books.[153] At about the same time Jean Gerson was, to be sure, not hostile to culture or even to its diffusion. It was only tyrants, he said, who "impede studies to prevent the acquisition of knowledge" and who "want their subjects to have little ability, little knowledge, and little love for one another," whereas good royal government requires subjects that have "ability, knowledge, and friendship."[154] Nevertheless, Gerson was also wary of the pride (*superbia*) that caused men to exhibit too much curiosity (*curiositas*) about secondary matters and that drove them to read and write too many books when there was only one eternal book.[155] Nothing was more alien to Pierre d'Ailly than such hostility toward or even mere suspicion of knowledge. Of course he preached, as the church had been doing for a long time, that knowledge was nothing without a good life,[156] but like most clerics he did not doubt that study could lead to wisdom,[157] that knowledge and wisdom were one and the same,[158] and that God was first and foremost knowledge and wisdom, and that learned and wise men, especially doctors, and most especially doctors of theology, ought to have the primary claim on the benefices, authority, and power of the Church.[159] Far from being an instrument of evil ambition, knowledge in Pierre d'Ailly's view enjoyed a clear conscience. Thus he could without remorse surrender to the fervent love of study that possessed him, for he did not see it as a danger to either religion or morality.

As early as the 1380s the young doctor of theology possessed a broad culture. It was nevertheless still limited to those subjects, works, and points of view that the university believed a young doctor of theology ought to know or share. Pierre d'Ailly knew very little history, geography, or astronomy, but he possessed an astonishing knowledge of the Vulgate. It is true that his exegesis of the text was allegorical, in the most traditional spirit. He had no desire to give any other interpretation, because he had no intention of contesting a Latin text that the Church had approved with its authority. And in any case he had no capacity to give any other interpretation, since he knew only Latin and French. Literal exegesis would have required linguistic knowledge he did not possess.[160] He was of course familiar with the Church Fathers, especially Augustine.[161] Established on these firm foundations, Pierre's culture was also nourished by the many great works that had enriched Christian spirituality since the twelfth century. Saint Bernard died in 1153. More than two centuries later he was still one of the favorite authors of Parisian clerics, who admired his learning and his eloquence.[162] Pierre d'Ailly was one of Bernard's great admirers. He also took a particular interest in Joachim of Floris (died 1202); the theologian William of Auvergne (died 1249), over whose works he labored as a veritable editor;[163] and many other authors, including William of Ockham, whose thought dominated the University of Paris in his day. In fact, the young doctor's culture faithfully reflected the prevailing culture of the university. It was astonishing only for its breadth.

In the teeming cultural milieu of the University of Paris, however, a new element appeared just as the schism befell Christianity and divided the university. The Middle Ages were not unaware of antiquity. Indeed, antiquity was close and familiar to the medieval men who carried on its traditions. But the Middle Ages had embraced only a part of antiquity's rich legacy, and more to devour it than truly to know it. The rediscovery of antiquity was one of the great developments of the fourteenth century. In Paris that rediscovery had made some little progress after mid-century under kings John the Good and Charles V, but nothing compared to the progress made in Italy, which had achieved a considerable lead thanks to the long, scholarly labors of a man of genius, Francesco Petrarca (Petrarch). The passionate search for new works; the determination to establish correct texts; disgust with the Latin spoken by contemporaries; a desire to return to the beautiful Latin of old; and the importance attached to form, language, and rhetoric—all these were characteristic features of the humanism of Petrarch and his disciples. Petrarch died in 1374 at the age of seventy. Manuscripts of his works circulated in France, perhaps during his lifetime but in any case immediately after his death, not only in Franco-Italian circles at the curia of Avignon but also in Paris, particularly at the university and more particularly at the College of Navarre, where the literary arts were enthusiastically studied.[164] The College of Navarre thus became the "cradle of French humanism," but by then Pierre d'Ailly was thirty years old and, having long since completed his work in the humanities, was pursuing studies in theology. Students who came to the College of Navarre just ten years after Pierre d'Ailly were caught up in the humanist renaissance.[165] Despite subsequent efforts, Pierre d'Ailly remained a man whose time preceded that renaissance. His Latin would never be "Ciceronian."[166] His knowledge of classical antiquity would always remain surprisingly weak.[167] Curious as he was and capable of improvement, Pierre d'Ailly was as much as any other man a prisoner of his youth. He remained a superior intellect trained in Paris under the reign of Charles V.

"I am a man of brief memory," Pierre d'Ailly complained one day in 1406.[168] Perhaps he had noticed that at age fifty-five his memory was no longer as good as it had been at thirty. Yet all signs are that it was excellent. It permitted him to acquire a vast culture, and it was among the qualities that enabled him to work with exceptional rapidity. In 1385, at thirty-four, he was capable of writing in one night a treatise that today occupies forty printed octavo pages.[169] And twenty years later, in 1406, his work was scarcely less rapid.[170] His labor, moreover, was made even more efficient by a fine personal library, many of whose books he had written himself.[171] While still a student he had already begun collecting his own compositions. Subsequently he never strayed far from the volumes that contained his works. He reread and annotated them frequently.[172] On occasion he was able to reuse passages written long before. In 1417, for example, he delivered a sermon containing phrases written in 1382.[173] It should come as no surprise, then, that Pierre d'Ailly was a prolific author or that his works were preserved. Some two hundred of his titles survive, ranging from substantial treatises to long sermons to relatively brief pamphlets.

A fertile penman, Pierre d'Ailly wrote (in the Gothic cursive hand that first came into use in the fourteenth century and that allowed the authors of that time to write, without dictation, quickly and abundantly on their own)[174] on all subjects, in all genres, numerous works, intended to be read, whose qualities of form and content inevitably attracted the attention of his contemporaries. But Pierre did not think of himself, and his contemporaries did not see him, primarily as an author to be read. The best evidence for this is that only a few of his letters have survived.[175] Friends of Pierre d'Ailly such as Jean de Montreuil, Nicolas de Clamanges, and Jean Gerson left admirable collections of letters that throw an exceptional light on the climate of the times. These men may have wished to imitate the great Latin writers or Petrarch, or they may have attempted to set an example of fine style, of *ars dictaminis,* for the secretaries who would one day put their talents to work in chancelleries all over Europe. It is therefore worthy of note that Pierre d'Ailly, who was so careful about preserving his other works, did not keep copies of his letters and that his correspondents did not keep the letters they received. For Pierre d'Ailly a letter must have been a fugitive exercise in writing. And his Latin was certainly not of a sort to impress men who were to one degree or another disciples of Petrarch. In short, Pierre d'Ailly was not viewed primarily as a writer either by himself or by his contemporaries. He was above all an orator.

Seldom has the spoken word exerted greater power or possessed greater efficacy than in the second half of the fourteenth century. It was used for teaching in the universities. Wisdom may have had other servants besides eloquence but none that she needed quite so much.[176] To teach was good; to preach was better still. The first duty of every cleric was to preach—to the people, to be sure, but the most eloquent would sooner or later be called to speak before the court, the king, or the pope. They would be obliged to deliver one of the lengthy, formal harangues that were an essential part of every embassy. Sometimes their assignment was to try to convince Parlement.[177] Above all they were obliged to make speeches and to participate in debate in the various assemblies, cabinets, and councils—some calm, some stormy and impassioned—in which the day's policies were made and unmade. Everywhere eloquence triumphed. If a cleric displayed the qualities of an orator, he immediately became famous. He was asked to speak, and people came to hear him. His sermons and speeches were written down and copied and anthologized as models. Now, of the handful of celebrated orators who dominated the age, there was only one who, before he was twenty-five, was invited to speak before the bishop of Amiens, only one whom the powerful of this world for forty years never tired of hearing, and only one who, at the age of sixty-five, still held the Council of Constance in thrall as one of the most eloquent men in Christendom: that man was Pierre d'Ailly.

The orator in the time of Cicero needed powerful lungs and a strong voice above all.[178] In the time of Charles VI he needed even more powerful lungs and an even stronger voice to hold audiences through lengthy sermons and interminable speeches. No doubt Pierre d'Ailly possessed the necessary equipment. And like all the great orators in this bilingual society he preached in both Latin and French. Froissart said that he was "above all well-spoken [*bien enlangagié*] in Latin and in French."[179] In either language Pierre's speeches were notable first of all for their admirable composition. He never felt anything but scorn for speeches that were "disorderly horror and horrible confusion" (*inordinatus horror horrendaque confusio*).[180] Without composition there was no order (*si . . . compositio dici posset ubi non est ordo*).[181] And Pierre d'Ailly always began his sermons, as was proper, with a phrase from the Old or the New Testament. Then, after a brief prologue, he delivered the body of the text, clearly divided into three parts. Within each part, three principal topics were clearly delineated ("I therefore said first. . . . I said second. . . . I said third. . . ."). And within each topic three points were clearly indicated ("First, then. . . . Second. . . . Third. . . .").[182] Pierre d'Ailly's eloquence was thus solidly scholastic. It was forged prior to the revival of classical rhetoric of which, in France, Nicolas de Clamanges would later pride himself on having been the artisan.[183]

But Pierre d'Ailly was too great an orator to confine himself to the curt clarity of scholastic architectonics. One day in 1381 he said that he wanted to "renounce the rhythms of the divisions [that is, of scholastic logic] and adopt as far as possible the style of the Fathers."[184] Although he never actually renounced those rhythms, he knew how to infuse life into them. He engaged his listeners in the movement of his repetitions. Should he, for example, sing the praises of divine Scripture or hold his tongue? "Torn every which way by the diverse and contrary pulls of perplexity," he said, "sometimes I find myself unable to speak and sometimes I cannot keep silent." Then he sets out a first argument. "And that is why I find myself unable to speak." Then a second argument: "And that is why I cannot keep silent." And then a third argument: "And that is why I find myself unable to speak." And a fourth: "And that is why I cannot keep silent." And so on, four more times.[185] This example is taken from the first course taught by the young biblical bachelor in the academic year 1375–76. No doubt it enthralled audiences used to more arid lessons, particularly since within this overarching architecture of repetition the pace of argument was accelerated by an accumulation of questions, a massing of words, an alliteration of syllables that cannot be captured in translation: "Here, in a few words, is the innumerable host of saints: Apostles evangelize, disciples proclaim the word, martyrs triumph, confessors exult, doctors preach, priests pray, monks psalmodize, virgins chant, and all the choirs of saints echo the words of the psalmist: 'Exalt ye the Lord our God and worship at his footstool' (Psalm 99:5)."[186]

These lyrical flights alternate with citations, familiar proverbs ("Quant la maison sera arse, l'en fera provision d'eaue"),[187] striking images, concrete examples, and simple parables. In short, Pierre d'Ailly could speak to the intelligence, the heart, and the imagination. The careful composition of his speeches never interfered with the breathless rhythm of his sentences or the teeming flow of images. How could he have failed to captivate his audience on that Ash Wednesday when, in the hope of exhorting them to do penance, he concisely evoked the brevity of human life with its three stages and sad end:

> Tu vas morir tost sans mesure
> Tu seras cendre et pourreture
> Tu aras paine longue et dure.
>
> [You will die sooner than you think.
> You will be ashes and decay.
> You will suffer long and harsh torment.]

And then he continued:

> Alas! Pitiful song! Alas! Horrible dance! Yet sing who will and dance who will. Dance, dance, little girls, dance to this song. Sing, sing, maidens, this gay whirl.
>
> Alas! There is, I believe, no man, be his heart ever so jolly or gay, who, if he pondered these words, would find in himself the talent or wish to laugh or sing or kick up his heels or dance. No, he would forget all such mad pleasures and do penance instead.
>
> Ponder, therefore, your beginning, your middle, and your end.
>
> Consider your birth the beginning, your life the middle, and your death the culmination.
>
> If you are handsome, if you are strong, if you are young, wait a little; ponder the end and draw the conclusion.
>
> Alas! Comes a little fever and your beauty pales. Comes a little illness and your strength drains away. Comes old age and your youth is gone forever.
>
> It will submerge your life, diminish your joy, rob your health. It will flay you face, rot your mouth, make your breath stink. It will turn your heart melancholy, your wit mad, and your body weak. And finally it will bring on death and separate body from soul.
>
> Alas! Hard farewell! Painful end! Pitiful conclusion!
>
> Your soul will go to hell, or at least to the fire of purgatory, to receive pain and punishment for its sins.[188]

Pierre d'Ailly used his effective eloquence on behalf of simple and clear ideas. Like his student Jean Gerson, he had no liking for those intellectuals who mistook obscurity for subtlety (*quibus obscuritas subtilitas est*).[189] These clear ideas were also stable ideas. Not that Pierre d'Ailly was incapable, over the course of his long life, of changing in small ways or of developing new interests. It is striking, however, that in all essential respects the old man's ideas about ethics, philosophy, theology, and politics were the same as the youth's. What Pierre d'Ailly said and wrote at Constance was the faithful echo of what he had said and written in Paris forty years earlier.[190] Pierre brought his youth with him to Constance. He was not the only one to do so. The ideas that reigned in Paris in the 1370s and 1380s and the events that marked the city during that period still cast a shadow over the council more than thirty years later.

In the end, what was most remarkable, most surprising, and most unexpected about Pierre d'Ailly's ideas was their moderation. There was a striking contrast between his flaming words, his audacious speech, and his fundamentally measured thoughts. Pierre d'Ailly allowed himself to be carried away by words but was able to restrain his ideas. The seething orator was a judicious thinker, hostile to all excess. With all his ardor, for example, he exhorted his audience to fast. Every Christian must fast, but without ostentation: "He who wishes to fast well must do so secretly in order to preserve himself from the wind of vainglory and the noise of hypocrisy."[191] He encouraged penitence but condemned the excess of the Flagellants, some of whom still remained in northern France a half century after the Black Plague.[192] Although he thundered against the sins of wicked priests, when he saw other Christians condemn fornicating priests and refuse to attend masses celebrated by men deemed unworthy because of their sin, he attacked the reluctant parishioners for excess of scruple. To be sure, under the old law masses celebrated by fornicating priests were invalid. But present times were so wicked, and wicked ways were so incorrigible, that the authorities were obliged to overlook the strict letter of the law and accommodate to what the times allowed.[193] Christians, as "true sons of obedience,"[194] were obliged to follow the authorities' lead and not move faster or farther than the authorities allowed. Pierre d'Ailly stated moderate ideas with great passion. Though his words were flamboyant, he never lost his sense of what was possible or his respect for the authorities. He was an orator capable of pleasing the humble without displeasing the powerful.

Thinker, writer, speaker of exceptional talent, eminent intellectual, Pierre d'Ailly was a man well aware of his worth and determined to preserve and publicize his works.[195] He wanted, and possessed the requisite ability, to be still more. He burned to become a man of action, a man of power, a man of authority, and he was blessed with the necessary qualities. As the young procurator of the French nation, he had already demonstrated the administrative efficiency that would later lead to other responsibilities. He also possessed the decisiveness, firmness, and stamina needed for a great political career. After the age of fifty, for example, he was still capable of those long or rapid rides on horseback without which not even the finest mind could have aspired to continue in a leading role on the great world stage in the time of Charles VI.[196] Those political and administrative virtues were necessary, and Pierre d'Ailly had them. But they were not sufficient, and in fact Pierre possessed other qualities as well.

He possessed the ambition to rise, the determined will to forge ahead, to put himself in the limelight, and to downgrade others. Even his friends deplored his competitiveness. Twenty-five years later, Jean Gerson, speaking as an admiring and lucid disciple, expressed the hope that one day his old master would shed these traits as well as overcome that hideous capital sin, wrath.[197] Wrath (*ira*), passion (*furor*), and zeal may at times have induced Pierre d'Ailly to go too far. But Pierre had one saving virtue: he knew just how far he could let himself go. He was a prudent hothead. Consider what happened in 1381. Though still early in his career, he had already enjoyed long experience in a prominent position. But when shrewd observers realized that the court's patience was at an end, it was Jean Rousse who found himself at the head of the university delegation, and soon in prison. During the agitated reign of Charles VI Pierre d'Ailly was not the only person who knew just when to keep quiet, when to avoid a meeting, even when to leave town. For clerics it was especially easy to beat a prudent retreat, because they could always go to a city in which they held a benefice. Pierre d'Ailly was not the only prudent man of his day. But his success no doubt owed a great deal to his superior skill in practicing the audacity of the possible.

Friends and Enemies

In any case, neither Pierre d'Ailly's defects nor his qualities by themselves account for his success. There is no such thing as solitary ambition, and Pierre d'Ailly was no exception. Like others, indeed more than most, he was supported by "friends, helpers, allies, and consorts"[198] against the large numbers of the "hateful and malevolent" that his character inevitably attracted.[199] Social and political life, everyone knew, required allegiances, yet in the Middle Ages the relative importance ascribed to different kinds of allegiance varied from time to time. Above all other forms of solidarity Charles VI's subjects stressed friendship as the indispensable mortar of all political relations. They stated repeatedly that nothing is more beautiful than having friends[200] and nothing more dreadful than the crime of *lèse-amitié,* doing harm to one's friends.[201] In a world as menacing as theirs, friendship no doubt seemed more necessary than ever. But an even more important reason for their emphasis on friendship was that they had read Aristotle and Cicero.

Cicero wrote his *De amicitia* at the very end of his life, in 44 B.C. The work was read and copied throughout the Middle Ages.[202] During the reign of Charles VI, however, Cicero was especially beloved in Paris, and this particular work was more widely read than ever.[203] Laurent de Premierfait provided the first French translation in 1410. It is not clear, however, that Cicero's work was as influential as the work that inspired it, Aristotle's *Nicomachean Ethics,* which dates from the fourth century B.C. The *Nicomachean Ethics* shared the fate of Aristotle's other works. These became known in the West by way of twelfth- and thirteenth-century Latin translations. The *Ethics* was translated into Latin in the first half of the thirteenth century by an Oxford master with the rare virtue of knowing Greek: Robert Grosseteste. His translation achieved wide currency, and Parisian clerics in the second half of the fourteenth century could read it without difficulty. Under Charles VI, however, they could also read Nicolas Oresme's recent French translation. And as it happens, Aristotle devoted books eight and nine of the *Nicomachean Ethics* to friendship.

Friendship, he said, is necessary to the city, for if the city's unity is maintained by justice, it is also maintained by concord, which is the fruit of friendship.[204] Men also need friendship: "Friendship helps young people avoid mistakes," Aristotle wrote in Greek.[205] But Nicolas Oresme's French translation emended: "Friends are necessary to young people to preserve them from sin."[206] In a gloss he explains: "For at such an age they are commonly too inclined toward concupiscence." The text then continues: "And older people need friends to do them services and to make up for the deficiencies in their action and operation [and] for the purpose of giving aid and comfort to their debility and weakness. And those of sovereign age, that is, median [that is, in midlife] and perfect, need friends to accomplish their actions." Friendship is therefore necessary, and Aristotle continued his analysis by distinguishing three types of friendship between equals. The object of friendship can be that which is "good, pleasant, [or] useful."[207] The only true friendship is that whose object is the good. Usually, however, friendship is less perfect: its object is that which is either useful or pleasant. "Useful friendship" is found above all "in old men and seniors. For they do not seek or pursue pleasant things, but they do seek useful things." Oresme adds this gloss: "Old people do not much savor corporeal delights, for which nature in them has cooled. And they do seek useful things for the sustenance of their nature, which is feeble." To be sure, the text continues, "some young people feel such friendship, and they are those who seek and pursue gain. . . . But the friendship of youths seems to be more for pleasure, for they live according to the passions of concupiscence and similarly seek and pursue that which is pleasant to them according to the present time."[208]

These are the types of friendship between equals. There is, however, "another kind of friendship, that which involves an inequality between the parties, such as that of father to son and in general of elder to younger, man to wife, ruler to subject. These friendships also differ from one another, for the friendship between parents and children is not the same as that between rulers and subjects, nor is the friendship of father to son the same as that of son to father or that of husband to wife the same as that of wife to husband."[209]

Pierre d'Ailly was among those youths aware of the useful aspects of such unequal friendships. The friendship of Jean de la Grange and Philippe de Mézières guided him in the early stages of his career. But Pierre d'Ailly was no vulgar man of ambition. His attachment to Philippe de Mézières was more profound than that; it was based on shared ideas, aspirations, and tastes. It survived Charles V's death and Philippe de Mézières's retirement. More than that, this durable friendship was for a long time one of the sources that sustained Pierre d'Ailly's spiritual life, because after Charles V's death Philippe de Mézières retired to the monastery that the Celestines maintained in Paris. He did not die until 1405, when he was nearly eighty. For a quarter of a century the old man continued in retirement to follow events in this world with passion and anguish. Pierre d'Ailly remained loyal to him and close to the Celestines.

The Celestines were a Benedictine congregation founded by Pietro di Murrone. They were already thriving in Italy when, in 1294, their founder became pope under the name Celestine V. The saintly Celestine for a time buoyed the hopes of those who favored a poorer, purer church. Crushed by the weight of the world and of his years (he was eighty-five), however, Celestine soon abdicated and was replaced by Boniface VIII. The Celestine order benefited from its founder's prestige and from the dispute between his successor and the king of France. Partly out of sincere motives but also in order to thwart his adversary, Philip the Fair worked for the canonization of Pietro di Murrone and brought his Celestine order to France. Philip's successors also displayed a particular fondness for the disciples of Pope Celestine. And the Celestines prospered. The order marked an important milestone in 1352 with the foundation of a convent in Paris in an old Carmelite monastery on the right bank of the Seine near the hôtel de Sens and not far from the royal hôtel of Saint-Paul.[210] The Celestines' Parisian convent immediately enjoyed a privileged relationship with the king, the royal family, and the monarchy. The confraternity of royal notaries and secretaries, whose membership was drawn from the ranks of highly qualified clerks who staffed the royal chancellery, set itself up in the church of the Celestines in December 1352.[211] Later, members of the royal family were buried there. The schism confronted the French Celestines with a dilemma, which Clement VII quickly resolved. In 1380 they were declared to constitute a province exempt from the jurisdiction of the abbot, who was in Italy, and the Paris convent became the headquarters of this autonomous French province. It was to this convent, some months later, that Philippe de Mézières retired after the death of Charles V.

The Celestines, faithful to the spirit of their founder, were at times quite close to the Franciscan spirituals. They ardently hoped to see the church reformed and returned to poverty and to the evangelical spirit. And they saw the Donation of Constantine as a source of great evils for the church.[212] The Donation was the deed (which we now know to have been an eighth-century forgery but whose authenticity neither the Celestines nor any of their contemporaries doubted) by which the emperor Constantine supposedly ceded sovereignty over Italy and the West to Pope Sylvester I and therefore to the Roman Church. The Celestines believed, and bitterly regretted, that the Donation had made the Church a temporal power. And like the Celestines, Philippe de Mézières, Pierre d'Ailly, and Pierre's students Jean Gerson and Nicolas de Clamanges deplored the Donation's sad consequences.[213] But Philippe de Mézières and the Celestines shared with Pierre d'Ailly and his friends more than an ardent desire for ecclesiastical reform. They were also united by their love of the king and of the French kingdom. In that, of course, they were not alone. Many other subjects of Charles VI felt the same way. But patriotic feelings were particularly intense in the Celestine monastery and in the College of Navarre, both closely tied to the crown. Thus the friendship between Philippe de Mézières and Pierre d'Ailly was strengthened by the fact that the Celestine convent, in which Philippe lived, and the College of Navarre, to which Pierre had such strong ties, were both places of intense religious fervor and patriotic ardor. Saint Jerome said: "Sola Gallia monstra caruit"—only Gaul did not nurture that monster, heresy. It was no accident that Pierre d'Ailly and his friends repeated these words so often when their souls were troubled during the time of schism.[214] They expressed their pride at being both Christians and Frenchmen.

It was Peter of Luxemburg's singular destiny to draw even closer together the College of Navarre and the convent of Celestines, Pierre d'Ailly and Philippe de Mézières, the France of Charles VI and the Church of Clement VII. Peter was born on July 20, 1369, at the château of Ligny-en-Barrois. His father, Guy of Luxemburg, was nothing more than lord of Ligny in the Barrois, which was not part of France but on the border of the kingdom between Champagne and Lorraine. A good captain, he served under Charles V. But he was also a member of the cadet branch of the illustrious Luxemburg family, whose senior branch in the fourteenth century held the duchy of Luxemburg, the kingdom of Bohemia, and the Empire and whose daughters often married the sons of France. Peter of Luxemburg was thus the son of a modest Barrois lord, but he was also kin to Emperor Charles IV, King Charles V of France, the count of Geneva, and many other powerful men.[215] It was therefore no ordinary child that the College of Navarre admitted as a day student when eight-year-old Peter came to study there in 1377.[216] Within the Church Peter would have advanced easily in any case, but when Clement VII became pope he wished to secure the loyalty of the Luxemburgs, to whom he was related and who were in a position to help him subdue the western marches of the Empire. Peter's rise was therefore meteoric. In 1378, at the age of nine, he was canon of Notre-Dame of Paris. In 1384 he was named bishop of Metz and soon thereafter was named cardinal. He was not yet fifteen. For a time he went to Lorraine, but neither the soldiers nor the prelates employed there on the mission of winning recognition of Clement VII needed him. He returned to Paris in 1386. He left the city in the spring of 1387 to settle, like so many other cardinals, at Villeneuve-lès-Avignon, located on the right bank of the Rhône and thus in the kingdom of France, but close to the pope. It was there that he died on July 2, 1387.

Thus the child who lived in Paris for several periods of time between 1377 and 1386, when he was between eight and seventeen, enjoyed an extraordinary career. But his life was still more extraordinary. Not that he was an exceptional student at the College of Navarre. At times he studied, according to one witness, but moderately.[217] What was exceptional was the ardor and precocity of his faith. That faith was guided and strengthened by frequent visits to the Carthusians and Celestines and by long conversations with Philippe de Mézières. The old man and the child together read lives of saints and other books.[218] Like the old man, the child felt a particular devotion to Christ on the Cross and to the Virgin. He aspired to poverty and had taken a vow of chastity. He also prayed as much as he could.[219] He confessed several times a week. And he fasted and mortified his flesh. Lice covered his body, which he refused to clean.[220] His confessor became alarmed. His entourage was dumbfounded by this manner of life, which was so ill suited to Peter's youth, nobility, and rank of cardinal. One day, Pierre Dallovargue, his secretary, a man of around forty and canon of Saint-Pierre of Lille, joined other intimates and confronted Peter. They told him: "Lord, you are young, and there is no doubt that you must study. . . . With this knowledge and your nobility you will be in a position to be useful to the Church. That is why you were made cardinal. You could do what you are doing if you were a Preacher or Minorite. If you wanted to engage in such forms of devotion, you should have entered an order, not accepted the estate of cardinal." To which the cardinal replied: "You are mistaken. Rest assured that we at the curia are not doing what we should be doing. Know for a fact that the Holy Church of God will not be restored by learning, nobility, power, and arms but by faith, prayer, and charity."[221] So spoke Peter of Luxemburg one day at Avignon during a meal in his chamber.

When he died a short while later, on July 2, 1387, no one doubted that a saint had passed away. He performed miracles even during his funeral ceremony. People flocked to his tomb. Jean Froissart, on his way home from the county of Foix in the spring of 1389, detoured through Avignon in order to visit the grave.[222] Clement VII dreamed of building his church upon this latter-day Peter. Peter's brothers, his sister Jeanne, the Celestines, the University of Paris, and the king of France all cherished his memory. Soon Philippe de Mézières and Pierre d'Ailly would work together on behalf of canonization of the "cardinal saint" whom both had known and loved and "whom in his youth, God" had called "to his company."[223]

Thus friendship often brought Pierre d'Ailly to the convent of Celestines, but he found most of his friends at the university, especially at the College of Navarre where he had long labored first as student and later as professor. Many of his friends are today forgotten. Others played only a fleeting part in his life. But a few played such important roles under Charles VI, their lives were so closely linked to Pierre d'Ailly's, and their names will come up so often in what follows that it is worth pausing here to say a few words about the circle of friends of which Pierre d'Ailly was the center.

Jean Courtecuisse had been a classmate of young Pierre d'Ailly at the College of Navarre. He came originally from the diocese of Le Mans, where he was born into a very well-to-do family some time between 1353 and 1355.[224] He entered the College of Navarre around 1367, a few years after Pierre d'Ailly, and took the same courses. He received his licentiate in arts in 1373, his baccalaureate in theology in 1382, his licentiate in theology probably in 1389, and shortly thereafter his doctorate in theology. He was a highly cultivated man, who at the end of his life apparently possessed a library of more than eighty volumes, including numerous works by Cicero, of whom he was a fervent reader.[225] He was above all a great orator. Jean de Montreuil would later say that Jean Gerson and Jean Courtecuisse were the two stars whose eloquence illuminated the Church of Paris.[226] Despite his verbal brilliance, however, Jean possessed a judicious, not to say hesitant, mind; although he left little mark on events, events nevertheless propelled him in the same direction as Pierre d'Ailly. When he died in 1423 at around seventy years of age, he was bishop of Geneva.

Pierre d'Ailly met the second of his friends when they were fellow students at the faculty of theology. Gilles Des Champs was the same age as Pierre d'Ailly. He was born between 1350 and 1353 in the diocese of Rouen. His family belonged to the minor Norman nobility. Although not a student at the College of Navarre, he began his study of theology in 1371, at which time he became a friend of Pierre d'Ailly.[227] Gilles was well versed in theology and had an interest in law.[228] He was not, however, a scholar by nature. Apparently he left no body of work. He was an excellent orator and above all a man of action, who relied not on firmness but on flexibility and compromise to attain his ends.[229] For a time Gilles Des Champs and Pierre d'Ailly were very close. Later their lives took different paths. When Gilles died in 1413 at approximately sixty years of age, he was cardinal.

Although Dominique Petit was not much younger than Jean Courtecuisse or Gilles Des Champs, he was young enough to have been Pierre d'Ailly's student rather than classmate at the College of Navarre.[230] In fact he was born around 1355.[231] He hailed from Varennes-en-Argonne, thus from the diocese of Rheims, and therefore studied arts and theology at the College of Navarre. He received his master of arts in 1373 and his master of theology in 1388. As a doctor of theology his destiny would unfold entirely within the walls of the University of Paris. He saw a great deal of Pierre d'Ailly and his friends and held them in high esteem.[232] His sympathies, however, were more Burgundian than French. And all things considered, Dominique Petit was a rather run-of-the-mill scholar. He occupied the highest positions but did not play a leading role. When he was scarcely more than sixty he vanished from the scene, although he did not die until 1427, when he was nearly seventy-five. For Pierre d'Ailly Dominique Petit was simply a colorless and rather obscure disciple.

Jean Charlin, known as Jean de Montreuil, was born in 1353 or 1354.[233] He came to Paris from a relatively great distance, since he was a native of Monthureux-le-Sec (then called Monstereul le Sec) in the diocese of Toul, a tiny French enclave in the midst of imperial territory, which was administratively linked to the Champenois *bailliage* of Langres.[234] He was no doubt somewhat older than the others when he came to Paris from Montreuil, because he was still a student at the College of Navarre in 1374 and did not receive his licentiate in arts until then or perhaps even later.[235] Thus Jean de Montreuil was only two or three years younger than Pierre d'Ailly, yet he was his pupil. Subsequently Jean often expressed the respect and gratitude he felt for his master, but he was not Pierre's most intimate disciple.[236] He was of course a priest. And he loved France as fiercely as Pierre d'Ailly. His political and religious choices often paralleled those of his teacher. Nevertheless, this priest apparently did not study theology. He chose, moreover, a career as secretary in the secular chancelleries. Before long he had been named royal notary and secretary, a position he held until his death in 1418 at about sixty-five. Jean de Montreuil and Pierre d'Ailly were thus good friends but never really close, because their professional activities scarcely overlapped and also because Jean, though highly cultivated, was much more of a "humanist" than Pierre. Professionally Jean was well aware of the advantage of fine Latin in political propaganda. He knew that one letter from Florence's chancellor Coluccio Salutati was worth a thousand men-at-arms, or so said the chancellor's enemies.[237] Jean put himself to school with the Italian humanists,[238] who found his neophyte's ardor rather pedantic.[239] Nevertheless, Jean found himself at the center of a small group of French humanists, all, or almost all, graduates of Navarre and close friends. Pierre d'Ailly knew them all but was not really a member of the group. Master and pupil liked and respected each other, but they were not close friends.

Jean de Montreuil was particularly close to another of Pierre d'Ailly's students, Nicolas de Clamanges.[240] Nicolas Poilevillain was born in 1363.[241] We know nothing about his family except that it was from Clamanges, not far from Châlons-sur-Marne. As a cleric in the diocese of Châlons and a native Champenois, Nicolas de Clamanges naturally entered the College of Navarre at age eleven in 1375.[242] Later he recalled the years he spent there as the best years of his life. He made lasting friendships and rapid and brilliant progress in his study of the arts. In April 1380, before his seventeenth birthday, he was awarded the licentiate.[243] A short while later, in the eventful month of May 1381, he gave his *inceptio*, or inaugural lecture, as a young master of arts. Then, like so many others, including Pierre d'Ailly, he began teaching arts even as he studied theology. A brilliant teacher of the arts, he was nevertheless a lackluster student of theology. His studies dragged on through the 1380s until he received his baccalaureate in theology.[244] But that was as far as he went. This was one priest not destined to become a theologian. He had little appreciation of his professors' scholastic methods, and in any case theology held little attraction for him, whereas the arts fulfilled a deep need. Nicolas de Clamanges was no orator. His fragile health and timidity kept him away from crowds. He thrived on silence and books, however, and was a wonderful writer and man of letters. He liked Cicero, Pliny, and Quintilian. He was one of those who made the College of Navarre a center of humanist studies in the 1380s. Before he was thirty he was regarded as the university's finest writer. His destiny was to serve as a secretary. He prided himself on the letters he wrote, of which he carefully preserved copies. It comes as no surprise to discover that this secretary and humanist was a close friend of Jean de Montreuil, nor that his friendship with Pierre d'Ailly, at one time quite profound, did not endure. The student no doubt admired and was grateful to his former teacher, and as men of the church their ideas were similar. The vices of the clergy and abuses of the church scandalized both, and they hoped that the church would rediscover its primitive virtues. But the student before long was only too keenly aware of having surpassed the teacher, at least in the field of "eloquence" (that is, in the art of writing beautiful Latin). There were too many differences between Pierre d'Ailly, the theologian, and Nicolas de Clamanges, the devotee of belles-lettres, between the orator and the writer, between the public speaker and the private scholar, between the man of action and the man of study, between the anxious man of ambition and the timid but proud humanist. Life, not death, separated them. At the end of the 1420s Nicolas de Clamanges was still at work. Nicolas did not die until 1437, when he was seventy-four. He bequeathed his books to the College of Navarre, where he was buried.

Pierre d'Ailly thus had many students at the College of Navarre whose fates would, for the next thirty years, be intertwined with his own. But the student to whom he was closest has yet to be mentioned: Jean Gerson.[245] Jean Charlier was born in the same year as Nicolas de Clamanges, 1363. He was baptized on the day he was born, the feast day of Saint Nicasius and his sister Eutropia, December 14. He was born to a family residing in Gerson-lès-Barby not far from Rethel and Sorbon. The city of Rethel was dominated by its Benedictine priory, which was under the authority of Saint-Remi of Rheims. It was located in the diocese of Rheims. The Rethelois was one of Champagne's seven county-peerages. Jean's father, Arnoul le

Charlier, and his mother, Elisabeth la Chardenière, were not very rich although they did possess some property. They had little education. Elisabeth could not even write.[246] But they were very pious. Jean was their eldest son. In the twenty-two years from 1363 to 1385 God blessed the couple with eleven more children, nine of whom, three boys and six girls, lived to adulthood. Of the six daughters only one, Marion, married. The three younger sons, like Jean, who was the eldest, entered the service of the church. Jean the younger, born in 1367, became a Benedictine and naturally entered the monastery of Saint-Remi of Rheims. Nor is it surprising that the two younger brothers, Nicolas, born in 1382, and still another Jean, born in 1385, both became Celestines. No doubt the family's piety greatly influenced this outcome, but even more important was the eldest son's exceptional personality, which soon overshadowed parents and children alike.

Jean Gerson learned the rudiments of grammar from the Benedictines of Saint-Remi, either in their priory at Rethel or their monastery at Rheims. He was tonsured at age twelve or thirteen by the archbishop of Rheims. And in 1377, when he was not quite fourteen, he was accepted like so many other Champenois youths by the College of Navarre. His masters were Pierre d'Ailly and Gilles Des Champs. He received his master of arts in 1381, the same year as Nicolas de Clamanges. And, also like Nicolas de Clamanges, he began his study of theology in that same year, but he proved to be a brilliant theologian and completed his work in 1392. He achieved celebrity in Parisian academic circles well before becoming a doctor, however, for like Pierre d'Ailly he was a remarkable professor and an extraordinary preacher. Like his master, moreover, this deeply religious spirit felt close to the Celestines; he cursed the Donation of Constantine and ardently hoped that the Church would return to poverty and reform itself.[247] Master and pupil had so much in common that a deep friendship formed between them. Nevertheless, they were separated by differences of age and character. Twelve years younger, Jean Gerson acquired at the College of Navarre a humanist culture that Pierre d'Ailly lacked. Furthermore, although Jean Gerson's spirit soared higher and his works reached farther than the spirit and works of his master, so that today his name somewhat eclipses that of Pierre d'Ailly, it must be conceded that this noble-minded man had little love of responsibilities. This eminent intellectual did not like to act or take sides. By conviction and temperament he was a man of peace and concord. Opposition of any kind disarmed him, and hostility paralyzed him. As one who lived in troubled times, Jean Gerson was tempted on a hundred occasions to retire. His great voice often remained silent in times of turmoil and decision. From our vantage point, Gerson's thought and works place him far above his contemporaries. But ours is an optical illusion born of distance, which causes us to forget all the others, whether friends or enemies, whose temperaments, convictions, and actions marked the reign of Charles VI as much as, or more than, Gerson did.

Around Pierre d'Ailly, then, formed a group of fairly close friends, all of whom were associated in one way or another with the University of Paris and, in most cases, with the College of Navarre. Many had ties to both the College of Navarre and the Celestine convent. A few were exact contemporaries of Pierre d'Ailly. A greater number were his students, and it was to them that Pierre was closest. To be sure, generational differences existed between Pierre d'Ailly and these younger men. At the College of Navarre they had been steeped in the new humanist culture. But the friendship between pupil and master was the strongest of bonds. Some of these former pupils, skilled with the pen, had chosen careers as secretaries. They were close to their former master but not as close as those who, like him, were theologians and saw the age from the same angle he did. In the fabric of friendships that was woven around Pierre d'Ailly, each person had his proper place, his specific distance. But that distance varied, for life sometimes separated men who had once been quite close. Nevertheless, friends expected tokens of esteem and even admiration from one another; they expected words of encouragement and praise, good advice, consolation, and effective support in difficult times. Most of all they expected firm backing in making their way up the rungs of the hierarchy. The noble sentiment of friendship was the efficient lever of legitimate ambition. In this difficult world friendship was necessary for anyone who wished to confront and overcome those evil ambitions, hateful envies, intrigues, favors, and "friendships" for which Pierre d'Ailly and his friends could find no words harsh enough and by means of which their enemies rose and threatened them.[248] And, God knows, Pierre d'Ailly and his friends had more than the usual share of enemies.

Among those enemies were occasionally theologians, but for Pierre d'Ailly the theologians were just that: mere occasional enemies. His nearly constant bêtes noires, whom experience had taught him were almost always evil, were the jurists. He reserved his hatred for those who had studied civil law, of course, but even more for those who had studied canon law, for they were men of the Church and their conduct was therefore all the more despicable. For canon law itself Pierre d'Ailly had nothing but respect. He also knew a great deal about it. He frequently cited the Decretum, decretals, and decretalists.[249] Everything would have been fine if only the canonists had recognized the preeminence of theology, if only they had used their knowledge on behalf of truth and justice, if only they had pleaded "for the widow and the orphan, for the good of the public, and for the liberty of the Church."[250] Alas, such jurists were rare. And the wicked jurists, which is to say, most jurists, believed that the science of law was the queen of sciences.[251] They venerated "their decretal epistles as Holy Writ."[252] They believed that God was bound by laws that men had made.[253] They saw no point in arguing about the Trinity.[254] Armed with the lucrative science acquired in the faculty of litigation (*facultas litium*),[255] their love of gain drove them to prostitute their tongues, to poke the ashes of smoldering disputes, to violate contracts, to hide adulteries, to defame marriage, to destroy equity, and to sabotage peace. Even worse, these ambitious men lusted after and received benefices that should have gone not to lawyers but to doctors of Holy Scripture.[256]

Differences of training and outlook and persistent rivalry are grounds enough to account for the nearly perpetual animosity between theologians and jurists. Pierre d'Ailly counted few jurists among his friends. One such was Guillaume Fillastre. Fillastre, born in 1347 or 1348, was slightly older than Pierre d'Ailly. An Angevin from Durtal, he came from an apparently modest family.[257] In 1385 he received the licentiate *in utroque,* that is, in both civil law and canon law. There is no evidence that he knew Pierre d'Ailly at that time, but their paths would later cross. Both men were good orators. They held similar political positions and shared common tastes. Guillaume Fillastre did not neglect theology; in old age he evinced the same interest in science and cosmography as did Pierre d'Ailly. Finally, the fates of Guillaume and Pierre were parallel. Both became cardinals in 1411. But Guillaume lived slightly longer than Pierre. He did not die until 1428, at seventy-nine or eighty.

A very different sort of jurist, the epitome of the detestable lawyer and adversary that Pierre d'Ailly would encounter at every step of his career, was Simon de Cramaud.[258] Cramaud was a small hamlet on the border of Poitou and Limousin, where a few families lived in the shadow of the Château de Rochechouart. Born there in 1345, Simon was the second son of a squire with a small property. War ruined his father, leaving Simon at twenty-five the son of a minor and penniless noble. All he possessed was his talent, but that was considerable. He was first of all a gifted student. He excelled in the study of civil law at Orléans and later in the study of canon law at Paris. In 1376 he was a doctor *in utroque* and master regent of the

Paris faculty of law.[259] A brilliant academic, Simon had a clear, practical mind. Theological speculations and moral meditations were not his forte. On occasion he might write an incisive brief in connection with a case, but he was no scholar.[260] He was, however, a great and effective orator, whose speeches, brief, clear, and to the point, caused a sensation. He was also a man of action, without parallel as an administrator, an ambassador, or leader of an assembly. In truth Simon de Cramaud had only one fault: he was too fond of women. Boniface Ferrer would later point out that Simon had devoted little time to meditating on the Book of Job and subsequent books of the Bible because he had rushed straight to the Song of Songs, which had absorbed all his attention. His experience, Boniface said, enabled him to give a literal commentary on that book, something not even Saint Gregory had been able to do.[261] Naive modern scholars have scoured the libraries in search of Simon de Cramaud's commentary on the Song of Songs—obviously in vain. Boniface Ferrer was of course making a joke, and his readers at the time knew perfectly well what he meant. Simon de Cramaud had been too fond of women. But that mild fault had not hampered the career of this exceptionally gifted cleric, whose "sense of his person and self-confidence" was such as to enable him to amass "honors, estates, benefices, and profits."[262] Simon was still studying law when the duke of Berry took him into his service and quickly came to appreciate his competence. Similarly, Clement VII "knew and liked him well."[263] With this double patronage Simon's success was assured; increasingly indispensable to his protectors, he went a long way in just a few years. In 1385 he was the duke of Berry's chancellor as well as the bishop of Poitiers. This efficient, lucid careerist, this prelate little touched by God, this high-liver was the epitome of everything that outraged Pierre d'Ailly and his friends. Still, at forty this son of an impoverished and ruined noble was a powerful man. He was also wealthy. And he was already dreaming of a cardinal's hat. Eventually he got one, but not for more than thirty years, in 1413, two years after Pierre d'Ailly received his, and after many setbacks. Simon de Cramaud was destined to survive Pierre d'Ailly. He died on January 19, 1423, "very old and suffering greatly from gravel" and "so debilitated that he had neither sense nor discretion."[264] He was approximately seventy-eight years old.

Such was Pierre d'Ailly's world, such were his friends and enemies, and such was Pierre d'Ailly himself in that fall of 1384, when the young and brilliant doctor of theology returned to Paris to fill the first of his many roles.

The Jean Blanchard Affair (1384–86)

In the autumn of 1384 tensions between the university and its chancellor were running high. The Blanchard affair had begun. Recall that on July 15, 1381, at the height of the crisis that had struck the university in that year, Clement VII had named Jean Blanchard chancellor of Notre-Dame. As vice-chancellor Blanchard immediately chose Pierre Plaoul or Playoul, a cleric of modest origins who was born in the diocese of Liège in 1353, became master of arts in 1371, and at that time also began the study of theology. His study must have proceeded slowly, since he did not obtain his doctorate until 1394, but by 1381 he was the dining companion of Pierre Ameilh, who had been the loyal servant of Gui of Boulogne before entering the service of Robert of Geneva, and Robert, shortly after becoming pope on December 16, 1378, named his loyal servant Pierre a cardinal.[265] The cardinal's protégé, Pierre Plaoul, survived the affair that brought down the pope's protégé, Jean Blanchard. Pierre Plaoul was a great and tireless orator who, before he died as bishop of Senlis in 1415 at the age of sixty-two, would play an important role in the Council of Pisa in 1409. For the time being, however, the vice-chancellor's behavior was not above reproach.[266] Nevertheless, Jean Blanchard's personality was such that the university concentrated its fire on him.

No sooner was he named chancellor, apparently, than Jean Blanchard began to display the same tactlessness and greed that had served him so poorly in Liège. No doubt chancellors had always asked those to whom they awarded university degrees to pay a small sum to defray the costs of the chancellery. Jean Blanchard, however, attempted to abuse the practice and enrich himself. In order to make his point to the candidates, he dragged out what should have been brief formalities. Recalcitrant candidates were greeted with vague suspicions of being Urbanists. The chancellor was supposed to accept without objection the order of merit established by the masters, upon which depended the award of benefices to university graduates, but instead Blanchard took the liberty of advancing the names of those who had shown themselves generous toward him. It was also observed that his own students progressed more rapidly and easily than did those of other masters. Many other complaints were raised. The chancellor's ingenuity was inexhaustible. In 1381 it had cost only a few sous to obtain a license. In 1384 a licentiate in arts required the payment of several francs and a licentiate in theology at least twenty francs, sometimes much more.

Blanchard also combined cynicism with greed. One day, an Augustinian to whom he had, on some pretext, refused to grant a licentiate in theology tired of the endless battle and came to see him with twenty-one francs in his purse. The monk first handed the chancellor twelve francs, but Blanchard remained stony-faced. The monk then emptied his purse into his hand, took eight of the remaining nine francs, and gave them to the chancellor, who then approved the degree. But upon seeing the coin that the monk had kept for himself, Blanchard shouted, "That one too! That one too!" The Augustinian complied, sighing that he had nothing left. Jean Blanchard took the coin and said, "But anyway a franc is so very little."[267] Everyone paid, some more willingly, others less. In 1383, for example, Jean Blanchard indicated to Gilles Des Champs that his suspected Urbanist sympathies might hamper his studies. Gilles got the message. He abandoned his master, registered as a student of the chancellor, and paid Blanchard twenty-four francs for expenses and twenty-four francs for clothing. Having demonstrated his adaptability and wealth, Gilles Des Champs graduated first in his class.[268]

The students paid, but their anger mounted. In June 1384 their cup ran over. On that day a new master of theology gave the traditional dinner, and Jean Blanchard had the audacity to occupy the place of honor, which normally went to the rector. That was the last straw. A few days later, the chancellor was summoned to a general assembly, and there, in the midst of a hostile crowd, he was compelled to listen to a violent speech in which a recent licentiate in law explained that anyone who disobeyed his superior was considered a heretic under canon law and therefore liable to punishment by forfeit of his benefices and decapitation.[269] With passions unleashed, the affair began. At the behest of the Augustinian prior general the pope on June 28, 1384, ordered an investigation into the conditions under which degrees were granted in the university.[270]

At that moment Pierre d'Ailly returned to Paris. In the ensuing proceedings between university and chancellor before the pope, the new master of Navarre immediately assumed a key role. He acted forcefully and spoke with a vehemence that did not win universal sympathy and admiration, even among the academics. In the spring of 1385 a remarkable incident occurred. In an insignificant assembly and on an insignificant pretext Pierre d'Ailly launched a violent attack on one Jean de Trélon, a master of arts and theology. Jean de Trélon then remarked out loud that it was not surprising that Pierre d'Ailly insulted him, since he did not hesitate to heap obloquy on the great of this world (*quia de majoribus mundi obloquutus est*). What did Jean mean by the great of this world? Did not these words refer to the pope and the king? The accusation was ambiguous and dangerous, and Pierre d'Ailly did not like anyone to stand up to him. He liked even less being suspected of lacking respect for the great of this world. He made his case so well that on June 6, 1385, before an assembly of nearly 120 masters, foremost among whom sat Gilles Des Champs, Jean de Trélon was obliged to apologize and to state that by the "great of this world" he had meant not the pope or the king but simply the dean of the faculty of theology, Raoul Glachard, and the chancellor of Paris, Jean Blanchard, whom he believed Pierre d'Ailly had insulted. Indeed, Jean de Trélon went on, in words sure to please the irascible Pierre d'Ailly, the function of the theologian, namely, to foster faith in men's hearts and defend it wherever it existed, was so important that it was proper to refer to theologians as the great of this world even though they were neither men of authority nor men of power (*quamvis non essent majores mundi auctoritative vel potestative*).[271] Jean de Trélon was humiliated. Pierre d'Ailly was appeased. By making a drama of a few words, he had shown himself to be excessively concerned with his reputation, thin-skinned, vindictive, tenacious, pitiless, and willing to press his advantage to crush his adversary.

Pierre d'Ailly proved to be an equally redoubtable and effective enemy of Jean Blanchard. In autumn 1385 he went to Avignon to plead the university's case to Clement VII.[272] At his prompting the university screwed up its courage and appealed to Parlement. And his frenetic labor supplied the university with arguments in the form of a long treatise entitled *Radix omnium malorum cupiditas* (Greed is the root of all evil). Rising above the mediocrity of the case, he was able to identify important principles, asserting that if need be the body must defend itself against its own head.

Pierre d'Ailly gave unstintingly of himself. Within a short time the university triumphed. Parlement rendered no judgment. The pope did not condemn Jean Blanchard, but he did offer his discredited old servant an honorable way out. On September 28, 1386, Jean Blanchard "freely" resigned his chancellorship, and the pope made him archdeacon of Ghent, which yielded him no income because Ghent was in Urbanist territory. But the pope also made him treasurer of the Rheims chapter, and fortunately Rheims was Clementine. Thus the chancellor enjoyed several happy years of retirement. The pope's solicitude toward him never wavered until his death in 1391 at the age of nearly seventy.[273]

A few years later, Pierre d'Ailly's young disciple Jean Gerson celebrated the university's triumph over the *superbes*, that is, the provost Aubriot and the chancellor Jean Blanchard. He gave due prominence to the importance of his master's writings and actions in the case.[274] Today we can see that Pierre d'Ailly's genius did more than win a fleeting political victory for the university. It elevated a debate that had originated in a rather paltry affair. In order to depose a greedy chancellor, Pierre d'Ailly had called for reform of the Church. The recourse to Parlement heralded the coming of Gallicanism. The right of a body to defend itself against its head presaged the conciliar movement. To be sure, these ideas were not altogether new in 1385–86. In his attack on Jean Blanchard Pierre d'Ailly forged no new weapons. He was, however, able to apply existing ideas to a common situation. Soon to play an important part in the great controversies of the day, those ideas thus became widely available.

The Juan of Monzon Affair (1387–89)

Jean Blanchard had not been gone from Paris for a year when Juan of Monzon, a young Dominican from Aragon, completed his studies in theology. In May 1387 Juan gave the series of lectures required of doctoral candidates, and in the course of those lectures he argued, as he was expected to do, in favor of various propositions. Among other things he asserted that Mary, the mother of God, had not, at the moment of conception, been preserved from all taint of original sin. In taking this position the young theologian merely echoed the traditional opinion of the great Doctors of the Church.[275] Saint Bernard had rejected the idea of the immaculate conception, and so had Saint Thomas. The most learned theologians of the twelfth and thirteenth centuries taught that any conception, even that of the Virgin, involved defilement; that, had the Virgin not been defiled, Christ would not truly be the universal redeemer; and that without original sin the life of the Virgin, which followed the life of Eve, would be drained of part of its significance: "Eve was conceived without sin, but she conceived in sin; Mary was conceived in sin, but she conceived without sin." Despite this scholarly repudiation, however, growing numbers of the faithful throughout the West celebrated the day of her conception on December 8, nine months before her birth on September 8. Their celebration was not intended to imply that Mary's conception was immaculate, but it made no sense to celebrate it unless it was free of all taint. Certain scholars responded quickly to the yearning of the faithful. Being close to ordinary Christians, the Franciscans approved the celebration of Mary's conception in 1263. One of them, Duns Scotus (1266–1308), was the first great Doctor to proclaim the immaculate conception. Despite continued misgivings within the order, the Minorites soon became ardent defenders of the immaculate conception. While the authorities remained silent, battle raged between proponents and adversaries of the new belief. And the number of proponents in Charles V's France had already grown quite large. The general climate there was one of fervent devotion to the Virgin, and to many who experienced this fervor the thought that her conception had not been immaculate was intolerable. In the thirteenth century only the Dominicans remained faithful to the traditional view. Indeed, the Dominicans in general clung obstinately to tradition. They were hostile to humanism. They rejected nominalism. The remained realists and Thomists. And they invoked the authority of Saint Thomas as grounds for their continued rejection of the immaculate conception. Threatened by the growing popularity of the new belief, they insisted with increasing frequency that the immaculate conception was an error. Their obstinate faith became more and more scandalous. As early as 1362 two Dominicans in Châlons-sur-Marne had stated from the pulpit that the immaculate conception was a false and heretical opinion; the affair had caused quite a stir.[276] And when, in May 1387, faithful to tradition and to his order, Juan of Monzon invoked the authority of Saint Thomas and denied the immaculate conception in the presence of the assembled faculty; when he went even further and asserted that to maintain that the Virgin, mother of God, was untouched by original sin was expressly, even quite expressly, contrary to faith (*expresse, immo expressisime contra fidem*); the outcry was tremendous.[277] To proponents of the immaculate conception it seemed that the moment had come to vanquish their adversaries by forcing the authorities to declare themselves.

The Minorites naturally were among Juan of Monzon's fiercest opponents.[278] Fiercest of all, however, were Pierre d'Ailly and his friends. In his youth Pierre had been fond of Saint Dominic. In 1379, in one of his earliest sermons, he had delivered a ringing eulogy of the saint, who was "better even than I know how to say, more saintly, more perfect."[279] In later years Pierre's devotion to the founder of the Dominicans did not diminish, but the order's positions were impossibly contrary to those of Pierre d'Ailly and his friends at the College of Navarre and among the Celestines. Clashes were inevitable. In particular, the Dominicans' refusal to accept the immaculate conception was bound to offend men like Philippe de Mézières, so devoted to the Virgin that he had introduced a new holy day to the West, the presentation of the Virgin in the Temple, and Pierre d'Ailly, so devoted to the Virgin that he had only recently written a eulogy of Saint Joseph.[280] Juan of Monzon encountered a hostile climate at the faculty of theology, but his strongest adversaries were Pierre d'Ailly and his friends.

Nevertheless, Juan was not alone. Behind him were the Dominicans and probably other supporters as well. And within the university there were some clerics who, like the authorities, remained silent. The unfortunate Dominican's words unleashed violent passions, however. His adversaries were not men of moderation and compromise. They obliterated or ridiculed anyone who did not loudly proclaim his support of the immaculate conception. Since all our evidence concerning the affair comes from the victors, it is hard to penetrate their silences and sarcasms to reconstruct the features of the vanquished. No sooner had Pierre d'Ailly and his friends triumphed than the victor's faithful disciple Jean Gerson recounted the story of Juan of Monzon's famous lecture. The orator is portrayed as stout and rotund, morally as well as physically, a man with a loud, screechy voice and an obscure, conceited, aggressive style. To be sure, not all the audience was hostile. Some actually liked obscurity. But in the end the audience tired and gave unequivocal signs of impatience. Finally murmurs forced him to descend from the podium, Gerson tells us, rather like a still-hungry bear forced to abandon a half-eaten carcass.[281]

That very night the dean of the faculty of theology was informed. Many who had witnessed the scene stayed up late discussing what had happened. Unanimous, they agreed that another assembly must be held as soon as the speaker had recovered his composure. On the following day, in fact, the masters of the faculty of theology did assemble, and the dean, Master Raoul Glachard, delivered the opening speech. Glachard found himself in a very uncomfortable position, for he was, although Gerson does not say so, a Dominican. Nor does Gerson reveal that, even before this affair, relations between Glachard and the friends of Pierre d'Ailly could not have been worse. As all the faculty knew, and as Jean de Trélon to his misfortune had dared to say out loud in 1385, Pierre d'Ailly had long been heaping sarcasm on the unfortunate dean.[282] Gerson, who was not yet thirty, heavily stressed the fact that the dean was an extremely old man (*extreme senectute vir*). Raoul Glachard had in fact been born in the same year as Anagni, in 1303. In the year of Crécy, 1346, he was already master of arts and bachelor of theology. Just after the Black Plague, in the year of Pierre d'Ailly's birth, 1351, he became a doctor of theology, and at forty-eight the new doctor was not really young. Yet thirty-six years later, in 1387, he was still there, dean of the faculty of theology. His great age had of course sapped his strength (*propter senium quasi viribus corporalibus destituto*), yet the young were unrelenting in their attack.[283]

Despite the charged atmosphere and impatient crowd, however, the old man was still capable of embarking on an interminable speech. Gerson relates the words he addressed to the orthodox doctors of theology. Your authority in matters of faith, he is alleged to have said, has long been recognized by bishops and by the pope. There are many examples. My great age has permitted me to witness several of them (*Et enim michi plura videre vetustas dedit*). The first was during the reign of John XXII (who had died more than fifty years earlier, in 1334). Fortunately the dean did not go into detail about that instance (*pretereo tempora Johannis pape XXII*), but he did detail examples from "our own time" (*nostra etate*), which demonstrated the weight given to the opinions of the faculty by Pope Urban V (1362–70), by Jean de Craonne, the archbishop of Rheims (1355–73), and by the bishops of Paris. I do not wish, the dean continued, to tire you with my garrulousness, which is an old man's vice (*vicio senectutis multiloquio*). Here are the facts. Some young men (*quidam juvenes*) came to see me last night. They vented their indignation. Today my office obliges me to attack not a man but a doctrine. And the poor old dean, embarrassed, trembling, and pitiful in the face of youth's rampant passions, added, I hope no one will hold this against me. I am afraid of nothing, he persuaded himself. No one can deprive me of anything more than tedium and satiety (*vite tedium atque sacietas*). Old age, the attentive reader of Cicero's *De senectute* adds, has vanquished the tyranny of fear (*vincere tirannicum timorem senectute*). The young—both partisans and adversaries of the immaculate conception—had already had enough when the dean picked up a paper and began to read the incriminated propositions. He had not finished two sentences when Juan of Monzon rose: "I have no need to hide," he said. "I am the one who said all that. Such a long speech was unnecessary. It was indeed from this head"—and he touched his forehead with his finger—"that all these propositions emerged." He then warned the masters to be prudent and to proceed in full awareness of the consequences, because he would sooner see his order and monastery collapse than retract what he had said.[284]

Did people actually speak the words and exhibit the attitudes that Gerson imputes to them? Nothing is less certain. But it is certain that a duel was under way with the proponents of the immaculate conception—not just Juan of Monzon but the entire Dominican order. For weeks a committee of twenty-eight masters sifted through Juan's propositions and reread Saint Thomas. Juan himself was summoned to appear, but he chose to absent himself and remain silent. The Jews were awaiting the Messiah and the Bretons were awaiting King Arthur, while the faculty of theology, Gerson triumphantly concluded, awaited Juan of Monzon in vain.[285] In the end the committee singled out fourteen condemnable propositions from the Dominican doctor's statements and writings. And four days after the cardinal of Luxemburg gave up the ghost at Avignon on July 6, 1387, the faculty of theology formally condemned Juan's fourteen propositions, and in particular the four that dealt with the immaculate conception, as false, scandalous, presumptuously affirmed, and offensive to pious ears.[286]

That same day the faculty sent copies of the condemnation to the bishop of Paris so that he might take appropriate measures.[287] The bishop summoned Juan of Monzon and asked the inquisitor to intervene. But the inquisitor was a Dominican. He did nothing.[288] And Juan of Monzon stayed out of sight. The bishop, meanwhile, hesitated. He was in no rush to take action in a matter on which the authorities had not yet taken a position. In order to force him to act, a crowd of academics (*in multitudine capiosa*) led by the young Turks of the immaculate conception demonstrated in front of his palace. On August 23 the fourteen propositions were prohibited; Juan of Monzon was to be incarcerated pending judgment and punishment.[289] But Juan fled Paris for Avignon and appealed to the pope, while the Dominicans canvassed their monasteries for the 1,050 florins needed to take their case to the papal tribunal.[290]

Juan's appeal placed Clement VII in a difficult situation. On one side was Saint Thomas, whom Urban V had proclaimed a Doctor of the church, who rejected the immaculate conception, and whom Juan of Monzon invoked as his authority. On the other side was the pious pressure of the University of Paris, which Clement VII was in no position to antagonize.[291] Throughout the academic year 1387–88, and despite a deadly disease that forced students to leave Paris for a time,[292] the fervor of the immaculate conception's proponents did not diminish.

The cleric Jean Petit was born in the Caux region of Normandy in 1365. Pierre Plaoul had awarded him a licentiate in arts, probably in 1384, after which he had studied law in Orléans for two years. Subsequently he gave up the study of law and returned to Paris, where he began teaching the arts and studying theology. He was a student of theology in July 1387 when the faculty of theology condemned the fourteen propositions of Juan of Monzon. A man of violent character and brutal speech, this young cleric was not destined to pass unnoticed. A scholarship student at the Treasurer's College and a protégé of the duke of Burgundy, he had nothing in common with Pierre d'Ailly and his friends.[293] Nevertheless, he believed with equal fervor in the immaculate conception of the Virgin. He wrote a hymn to the conception of the Virgin and a poem of 1,856 lines entitled the *Disputoison des Pastourelles,* in which "an amorous company of nine virgins of noble birth" engages in dispute with "nine ugly and wrinkled old women." The nine old women include the Suspected Heretic, the Litigious, Superfluity, False Bargain, Deception, and Presumption. The young virgins include Holy Theology, Reason the Wise, Authority, Canon Law, Civil Law, and Faith. The virgins defend the doctrine of the immaculate conception, and of course victory goes to youth. A few months later Jean Petit wrote another long poem in which Juan Monzon appears in a digression. The two men engage in argument, and the novice theologian easily refutes the doctor.[294]

Like Jean Petit, Simon de Plumetot was also a Norman, a native of Plumetot between Caen and Bayeux. He knew that he had been born on the eve of Saint Agatha's day, that is, on February 4, 1371, in the middle of the night. A scholarship student in arts at Saint-Victor, he was sixteen years old when the Monzon Affair erupted. He, too, attacked the Dominicans. He, too, was stirred in his soul to celebrate *Marion nette,* the Virgin conceived without sin, in poetry:

> Marie, tu es la plus amee,
> Quar en Dieu as grant grace trouvee.
> Je dis premierement en ma chansonnette
> Que toutes seurmonte Marion neste.
>
> [Marie, you are the most beloved,
> for you have found great grace in God.
> In my little song I say first of all
> that immaculate Mary is the best of all women.]

Furthermore, all the birds

> Le cucu et la cardineite,
> Le rosiniol et l'alouette,
> Le corbiau et la turterele,
> . . . .
> M'ont aprins ceste chansonnette:
> Dieu concevit Marion neste.
>
> [The cuckoo and the cardinal,
> the nightingale and the lark,
> the crow and the turtledove,
> . . . .

> have taught me this little song:
> God conceived Mary immaculate.]

Later Simon de Plumetot would study law, and having chosen the side of Henry VI, would die, chancellor and canon of Bayeux, curé of Saint-Pierre of Caen, and counselor to the king in his parlement at Rouen, on July 9, 1443, *"in senectute bona,"* at the age of seventy-two. Among his papers was found the *chansonnette* of his youth.[295]

In the same year, 1388, Jean de Rouvroy was a very young cleric at the College of Navarre. Subsequently he would study theology, rally to the side of Charles VII, and become canon of Bourges. In 1435, when he was almost sixty, the old canon, remembering the fervor of his youth, rose as an ardent champion of the immaculate conception at the Council of Basel.[296]

That fervor prevailed in Paris, but meanwhile the case before the papal tribunal moved forward. In May 1388 the university sent a delegation to Avignon to defend its position. Members of the delegation included four doctors and a few other academics. The group was led by one of the doctors, Pierre d'Ailly. Next in rank was Pierre's inevitable alter ego, Gilles Des Champs. The other two doctors were a Cistercian and a Benedictine. With them were Pierre d'Ailly's cherished disciple Jean Gerson, and Pierre Plaoul, the former vice-chancellor, who thus found himself in the company of the men who had brought down Jean Blanchard.[297] Because Pierre d'Ailly and his friends were not the only academic proponents of the immaculate conception, the university delegation included others as well, but it was dominated by d'Ailly's group.

Surely Pierre d'Ailly had a powerful personality. Yet it seems odd that the university, to defend its cause, did not choose to send older scholars, whose age would have given them greater authority. In 1388 Pierre d'Ailly was thirty-seven. Gilles Des Champs was no older. Pierre Plaoul was thirty-five. Jean Gerson was twenty-five. Glachard, the elderly dean, had felt attacked by younger men, according to Gerson. To Jean Petit, who was around twenty-three, the cause of the immaculate conception was championed by the young. Of course it was common at the time to represent vice and error in the shape of ugly old women and to embody virtue and truth in beautiful and graceful young damsels.[298] But nothing indicates that this opposition of youth and old age was not meaningful in itself. And there is every reason to believe that it was meaningful in a very specific way to Jean Petit, a man who throughout his life was very sensitive to differences of age. Clearly the debate over the immaculate conception was not simply a debate between the Dominicans and everyone else. Acceptance of the immaculate conception was a demand of youth. The Monzon affair did not erupt as it did because of provocative statements made by the Dominican doctor, who said nothing that was not traditional. It erupted because a fervent new generation found those traditional ideas impossible.

After spending several weeks of July 1388 at Avignon in the presence of the pope and cardinals, Pierre d'Ailly spoke. His companions followed suit. According to Michel Pintoin, a monk of Saint-Denis, they defended the cause of the Virgin so ably that all present concluded: "Blessed be the University, a most excellent vine to have produced such offshoots. In truth, if dignities were always given to those who deserved them, all these men would be made cardinals."[299]

Pierre d'Ailly's argument was striking, all the more so because his case was not an easy one to make. Compelled to justify an innovation, he began by distinguishing the various ways in which the Church might approve a written document. Sometimes the Church asserted that a document was correct on every point and contained no errors contrary to the faith. Such approval was granted to very few texts, such as the Bible or an occasional doctrine of the universal Church. More often the Church in approving a document simply meant to indicate that it was useful and capable of serving the faith and that it could therefore be propagated in the schools. It did not assert that such a document contained no errors. Saint Thomas's doctrine was approved by the Church, but it did not follow that it contained no errors. And in fact there were contradictions in the work of Saint Thomas. Pierre d'Ailly had no difficulty enumerating some of these contradictions because collections of them had been in circulation since the end of the thirteenth century, and like any other theologian he had been able to consult them. Hence, Pierre concluded, all that Saint Thomas could claim was what Saint Augustine had already said: I may be mistaken—I may be mistaken, but I will not be a heretic, because I will not persist in error. Heresy is defined not by error but by stubborn persistence in error once authority has spoken. Who in the Church had the authority to decide? It was up to theologians to define doctrine (*doctrinaliter*), to reprove errors, and to approve universal truths. The doctors had no jurisdiction, however. Bishops had the right to pronounce judgment and to define the faith *judicialiter*. But their authority was inferior and subordinate (*auctoritate inferiori et subordinata*). Only the pope possessed the supreme authority (*auctoritate judiciali suprema*) to define the faith by means of decrees (*judicialiter*) binding on all Catholics.[300] Granted, Saint Thomas had rejected the immaculate conception. But Saint Thomas could have been wrong. Now that the doctors of the faculty had spoken *doctrinaliter* and the bishop of Paris had spoken *judicialiter,* it was up to the pope to render judgment and state the truth.

Pierre d'Ailly was able to justify innovation only by exalting the present authorities in the Church. He did not merely invoke the usual pyramid of authorities. He gave that pyramid greater weight than he gave to the authority of yesterday's doctors. The pope was of course the supreme authority. All that remained for Pierre d'Ailly was to convince Clement VII that the fourteen propositions condemned by the faculty on July 6, 1387, were in fact condemnable. By now the outcome was so predictable that Juan of Monzon waited no longer. On August 3, 1388, he left Avignon for Aragon, his homeland, and then sailed to Sicily to join the camp of Urban VI.[301] In France an entire generation, and Pierre d'Ailly in particular, neared its moment of triumph.

In November 1388 the young king, Charles VI, decided to govern himself and dismissed his uncles with thanks. On January 23, 1389, Pierre d'Ailly delivered the Septuagesima Sunday sermon at the university. His theme was the parable of the man who sends laborers to toil in his vineyard (Matt. 20:1–16). In language more dazzling than ever, he denounced those poor workers who now toiled in the Lord's vineyard, who worked in the Church, it seemed, not so much by the will of God as by the audacity of the devil, those clerics who, driven by ambition (*ambitio*), pride (*elatio*), and presumption (*praesumptio*), had reached the summit of power (*culmen regiminis*) and the glory of honors (*gloriam honoris*). In the past men had earned ecclesiastical dignities through virtue. What was happening now in the Christian Church was the same thing that Sallust had complained of in the Roman state: the triumph of lust, avarice, and ambition. Nothing remained to distinguish the bad from the good. Worse still, the wicked held the dignities, and the good were subject to the power of the unworthy.[302] In other circumstances Pierre d'Ailly's audience might have seen nothing in these words but harsh yet commonplace strictures on the current state of the Church. Everyone knew, however, that the pope's decision was imminent and that the triumph of the immaculate conception's supporters was at hand. And everyone knew Pierre d'Ailly too well to ignore the implicit threat to the undeserving workers in the Lord's vineyard, to the unworthy dignitaries of the Church—in other words, to Pierre d'Ailly's enemies on the eve of their defeat.

On January 27, 1389, the pope condemned Juan of Monzon's fourteen propositions.[303] On March 17, at the behest of the university, the officiality of Paris promulgated the papal judgment. Immediately the university decided to expel anyone who would not take an oath accepting the condemnation of Juan of Monzon and in the future not to admit anyone who would not preach the immaculate conception. Many who had contested the immaculate conception capitulated, recanted, and took the oath. The Dominican masters did not. They left the university, which took joy in its impoverishment. The most moderate academics, such as Gerson, later regretted this extreme measure.[304] But the most zealous of the victors (Pierre d'Ailly among them) became irreconcilable enemies of the Dominicans, and vice versa.

The university wished to complete its triumph. The king's chaplain was a Dominican who had supported Juan of Monzon. Pierre d'Ailly was dispatched to the king. On March 21, 1389, he preached in the presence of Charles VI. The young man was convinced. He spurned his chaplain and decreed that no Dominican would ever again hold the post; to fill it he chose Pierre d'Ailly.[305] From now on it was Pierre d'Ailly who would distribute the king's largesse, no small responsibility and one that gave him the right to appoint and supervise the administrators of all the *maisons-Dieu* and hospitals of which the king was patron.[306] The power of the king's chaplain actually far exceeded his legal responsibilities. The chaplain saw the king daily. In the spring of 1389 Pierre d'Ailly therefore named his loyal ally Gilles Des Champs to head the College of Navarre and installed himself in the royal palace.[307]

The new royal chaplain's first thought was for his former student, Peter of Luxemburg. The young cardinal had been dead for nearly two years. Miracles proliferated around his grave, to which the faithful came in droves. Pierre's efforts were so strenuous that in May 1389 both the king and the university wrote the pope asking that Peter be beatified, and Pierre d'Ailly was chosen to carry both letters to Clement VII. He arrived in Avignon on June 14 and two days later delivered a speech to the papal court celebrating the virtues and miracles of his former pupil.[308]

Pierre d'Ailly now had the king's ear. The pope, having followed Pierre's activities for a long time and having seen him twice at Avignon, was well aware of this. Clement VII was familiar with the virtues of the king's new chaplain. He also knew that Pierre d'Ailly was one of those men it was better to have with you than against you. In 1386 he had chosen a lackluster successor for Jean Blanchard. On October 7, 1389, he appointed Pierre d'Ailly chancellor of the university, certain that in doing so he would please the king, the university, and the candidate himself.[309]

On that same day the king, accompanied by his chaplain and a large retinue, set out from Paris for a visit to southern France. Charles VI's new advisers judged that it was high time that the young king and his brother show themselves in the southern reaches of the kingdom.[310] On October 14 the king made his entrance to Lyons. A few days later he was in Avignon. And on November 1, 1389, Pierre d'Ailly preached to the pope, the king, and an audience of cardinals and great lords and solemnly beseeched the pope to beatify Peter of Luxemburg.[311]

What a triumph for this child of modest Compiègne burghers! He now moved among the mighty of this world. He was powerful. He was also rich. Not only had Pierre d'Ailly used all his talents to get ahead; he had also, very early in the game, begun collecting benefices. Almost all clerics in those days sought benefices, but few were able to acquire so many so quickly. In 1376, at the age of twenty-four, he had acquired a canonry in Soissons.[312] In 1381 he had obtained another in Noyon, which had proved most useful.[313] In 1389 he also became canon of Meaux and Amiens. Four canonries in four cathedral chapters! When he became chancellor, he gave up the canonries in Meaux and Amiens to the man he replaced. In subsequent years, however, he loudly repeated what poor Jean Blanchard had earlier alleged in his own defense: that the chancellorship of Paris yielded very little income. And in order to resist what Canon Salembier in 1392 called "vulgar temptations," the very same temptations to which Jean Blanchard had yielded, Pierre obtained benefices in Cambrai, Compiègne, Rouen, and Paris; on October 29, 1392, Clement VII was obliged to grant official authorization of what Pierre had managed to do.[314] But return for a moment to 1389. At the age of thirty-eight and in the space of a few months Pierre d'Ailly reaped the fruit of years of hard work. He was now a powerful figure both at court and in the university.

From Chancellor to Bishop (1389–95)

After the triumphs of 1389 Pierre d'Ailly enjoyed two or three years of calm routine. At court the Marmousets (advisers of Charles V who stayed on under Charles VI), who had come to power in 1388, continued to govern. At the university professors taught and students studied. Nothing happened. In the spring of 1392, however, a new fever gripped the university. The cause was nothing out of the ordinary. The government had been looking for ways to curtail the legal and fiscal privileges of academics. In particular, Jean le Mercier, seigneur de Nouvion, adviser and maître d'hôtel to the king and a specialist in financial matters, was accused of seeking to impose a tax on them. The conflict was commonplace, but the arguments that grew out of it were not. Opponents of academic privileges did not argue that such privileges were abuses that the secular government ought to correct; instead they questioned the whole relation of church to state. "Several doctors of theology, from the order of mendicants," asserted "that the punishment of all criminals was up to kings and princes and not to men of the church." They maintained "that Emperor Constantine had illegally ceded temporal justice to the blessed Sylvester and that his successors had the right to revoke that concession." This extreme position, a product of the heated debate over poverty stemming from the much earlier Franciscan challenge to the church establishment, was now taken up by men of the court (*nonnulli decuriones*). For the Church it was a position fraught with peril.[315]

Although the sympathies of Pierre d'Ailly and his friends were with the Franciscans, they did not approve the excesses of the Minorites' "spiritual" faction. They wanted to see the church purified, not stripped naked. Abuses were to be corrected, but privileges also were to be defended, particularly the privileges of the university. When those privileges appeared to be threatened and the university decided to go on strike, it was able to count on the sympathy of the chancellor, even if his position at court obliged him to maintain a certain reserve. There is no doubt that it was one of his most gifted students (Jean Gerson, perhaps, or Nicolas de Clamanges) who composed an elegant pamphlet in Latin verse exalting the university and appealing, over the head of Le Mercier, to the king:

> From where will you receive your light, if the light that
> has always illuminated the world goes out?
> Will Le Mercier or some other minister
> Give you lasting glory?
> . . . .
> Be not the cause of your own ruin,
> Do not allow this stain to besmirch your renown.

Numerous copies of these verses were posted at the gates of public places.[316] Tension ran high. But the government, which had other concerns, suddenly gave in. In July 1392 the king received a delegation from the university and confirmed its privileges. The delegates promised to resume their courses and went away feeling quite satisfied.[317]

This brief flare-up had been over for just a few weeks when the king, in August 1392, succumbed for the first time to the madness that would hold him in its grip, with fewer and fewer intervals of lucidity, until his death. The consequences were immediate. The king's brother, Louis of Orléans, was only nineteen, too young to assume leadership on his own. The king's uncles returned, and the Marmousets were out. The university probably applauded the imprisonment of its persecutor, Jean Le Mercier. But soon the victors had to face the problem of the schism, now fourteen years old. People had made their accommodation with the division in the church, and for a time it had seemed possible to live with it. But it had come to be unbearable to Christian consciences. Politicians saw clearly that the schism was the one remaining obstacle to a much-desired rapprochement between Clementine France and Urbanist England, and for twenty-five years this would be the obsession of both churchmen and statesmen.

Clement VII and his supporters had envisioned only one solution to the schism: the reconquest of Italy by force of arms. But now even the Avignon pope's most loyal supporters believed that any new attempt at armed conquest was doomed to failure like the previous one. It became increasingly difficult to finance a military expedition.[318] The use of force was out of the question. Yet the schism had to be ended without renunciation, disavowal, or self-denial. What was to be done?

The first thing to do was something that, according to Gerson, virtually no one had thought of until then: pray. In early 1393 prayers, processions, and sermons throughout France called for union. For Gilles Des Champs soon declared to the university that to content oneself with prayers was to test God; the Church demanded action. The university burned to act, to find remedies for the schism. And after twelve years the royal government rescinded the ban it had imposed in 1381. It allowed the university to discuss the situation. In January 1394 a university delegation was received by the king in the presence of the dukes of Berry, Burgundy, and Orléans. The duke of Berry answered the academics' speech in these terms: "This execrable schism has lasted far too long. It is a shame for the king and the royal family. Everyone is tired of it. Examine the possible courses of action. If one appears good to the council, it will be followed."[319] With the authorization of the government, the university would once again play a leading role.

Immediately thereafter, a chest in which written suggestions could be left was placed in the cloister of the Mathurins. Fifty-four masters examined the ten thousand submissions.[320] Pierre d'Ailly and Gilles Des Champs then summarized the results and prepared a letter to the king. Without the king, they argued, nothing was possible. During his childhood and adolescence it had been possible for wicked men to prolong the schism. The Church, moreover, had been stripped of its liberties. Its former virtues had disappeared. Simony reigned. The highest dignities went to the least worthy and most ignorant men. Faith wavered. Heretics pursued in one place could go to another and avoid punishment. Lest anyone mistake their allusion, the implacable vanquishers of Juan of Monzon, five years after their victory, recalled the case: "In this there is nothing implausible, as experience has shown. It happened in the case of the perfidious Dominican who blasphemed divine majesty and offended the glorious Virgin Mary."[321] Therefore the schism in the Church must be ended. The king was now a mature man. He could act. He should act. Three solutions were open to him. The first was surrender: both popes would renounce, clearing the way for the election of a new pontiff. That solution would be the best and most rapid. If, however, the popes refused, perhaps they would agree to designate arbiters, who might reach a compromise. This solution would avoid the difficulties of the third possibility, a general council, which would take longer than the other two and which was also more dangerous.

Such was the synthesis that Pierre d'Ailly and Gilles Des Champs constructed from the ten thousand suggestions. It exhibited their usual clarity and precision, as well as their persistent obsessions and hostilities. For one very good reason they did not themselves draft the letter to the king. Fine Latin was now de rigueur, and the two men were sadly aware of what their styles lacked in grace. At roughly this time, in fact, Pierre d'Ailly borrowed from Jean de Montreuil an anthology of letters that the royal notary-secretary had either composed himself or copied in Italy from a collection of letters by the master of the genre, the Florentine chancellor Coluccio Salutati. At age forty-three Pierre d'Ailly studied the works of these famous humanists as lessons in style. He copied their letters.[322] Sadly, however, he was forced to admit that he could not write as well. Gilles Des Champs and he therefore agreed to entrust the drafting of so formal a document to a man younger than themselves, their friend Nicolas de Clamanges, whose Ciceronian style was admired by all and who clothed his elders' arguments in the finest rhetorical trappings.[323]

The handsomely crafted letter received the unanimous assent of all the faculties and nations of the university at a general assembly held on June 6, "on the eve of Pentecost, the day when the Holy Spirit descended into the souls of Christ's disciples."[324] It did not meet with the anticipated success, however. The Dominicans, who had lost all authority outside the university, attacked it violently.

One of them in particular lashed out at the work of these "inexperienced little youths" (*juvenculi, inexperti*), which he described as not only presumptuous in form and composed in an inflated poetic style but also blasphemous, defamatory, seditious, and scandalous in substance. It proposed three unacceptable ways of ending the schism, and in addition its authors supported a heresy by asserting that the Virgin had not been conceived in original sin and of the seed of man but had been born of the Holy Spirit.[325] These Dominican attacks on youth, humanism, and the immaculate conception were really beside the point, however. The crucial impediment to progress was that the princes were reluctant to submit the proposals to Clement VII.

Although the pope was only fifty-two, his time had run out. In August 1394 the stubborn pontiff was still making preparations for a military expedition to Italy.[326] On September 16 he who had almost never been sick suffered a stroke. It happened around ten in the morning. The pope was placed on his bed. He had only a few minutes to live. In his final agony his only thoughts were for his soul and for the young saint who had justified his Church. He joined his hands, raised his eyes to heaven, and said: "Good Lord God, ah, Good Lord God, I beg you to have mercy on my soul and forgive me my sins. And I beg you, sweet mother of God, to help me find your blessed son, our Lord." He then rested a little before adding: "All the blessed of Paradise, I beg you to help my soul today." And then: "Ah, ah, Luxemburg, I beg you to help me." All present prayed for the health of the pope's body and urged the pope to do the same. But the pope loudly shouted: "For the soul, for the soul, for the soul." And then he closed his eyes and gave up his soul to God.[327] So ended the life of Clement VII, whom Nicolas de Clamanges would one day accuse of having been "the servant of the servants of the princes of France."[328]

Was the pope bound to the princes? Were the princes bound to the pope? In any case, Clement VII's death changed everything, or at any rate accelerated an evolution that the events of the past few months had shown to be inevitable. News of the pope's death reached Paris on September 22, 1394.[329] In the interest of unity the king and the university again expressed the common hope that no new pope would be elected. If there had to be a pope, many surely shared Nicolas de Clamanges's hope that he would be both French and a graduate of the University of Paris.[330] But on September 28 the cardinals assembled in Avignon hastened to elect a pope who turned out to be neither.

Pedro de Luna, who took the name Benedict XIII, was an Aragonese of good family, probably born in 1327. In any case he knew that when elected pope in 1394 he was sixty-six years old.[331] The new pope, who died in 1423 at the ripe old age of ninety-six, was an exceptional man. An eminent specialist in canon law, he had studied and taught the subject at Montpellier. A man of action and skilled diplomat, he nevertheless held humanism in high regard. Most important of all, this man of the Church, a cardinal since 1375, was a pious Christian who wanted the Church reformed, who ardently hoped for an end to the schism, and who declared himself ready if need be to lay down the tiara in emulation of his predecessor Celestine V, whose humility, lack of ambition, and willingness to abdicate the papacy were an example and a reproach to all men of authority in the period of the Great Schism.[332] Of course Celestine V's resignation had disastrous consequences. It had cleared the way for Boniface VIII. Perfection and hierarchy had ceased to coincide. Piety might prompt a man of authority to resign, but it might also compel him to remain in office. And the new pope was soon convinced that for the good of the Church he had best remain.

From the first there was a distance between the Aragonese pope on the one hand and French opinion and the French government on the other. That distance quickly increased. The new pope was more deeply religious than his predecessor; the princes' concerns still were primarily political. The new pope wanted unity, but for him the key issue remained the place of the papacy in the church. The princes wanted unity, but this pope, indeed the papacy in general, mattered to them less and less. The progress of the conciliar movement made it possible to envision a universal church in which the pope's authority would be diminished. The progress of Gallicanism made it possible to envision a Church of France whose ties to the pope would be loosened. On the whole, therefore, France distanced itself from the pope of Avignon. Within France, however, some in government and one current of public opinion opposed this change. So that, while for sixteen years all France had more or less staunchly supported Clement VII, the accession of Benedict XIII marked the beginning of dissension and division. The elderly dukes of Berry and Burgundy became redoubtable adversaries of the new pope, while the young duke of Orléans would tie his fate to Benedict's. At the university, men who had long been friends were now forced to make a choice. They were constrained by divisions between the pope and the princes and among the princes themselves. They were compelled by their convictions. Their ambition did the rest—along with the shrewdness of Benedict XIII. In 1393 and 1394, Pedro de Luna had served as Clement VII's legate in Paris.[333] He was remarkably familiar with the Parisian milieu and knew precisely which men's loyalty he needed to secure.

At this point the destinies of men who had long lived together at the university and in the College of Navarre began to diverge. Of the three authors of the June 6, 1394, letter, Gilles Des Champs, who for nearly twenty years had been Pierre d'Ailly's alter ego, chose to ally himself with the duke of Berry. Soon he would become the right-hand man of Simon de Cramaud, the man who epitomized all that Pierre d'Ailly and his friends had previously detested. Of the other two authors, both Pierre d'Ailly, the older, and Nicolas de Clamanges, the younger, turned toward Benedict XIII, who did all he could to win their loyalty.

At this crucial juncture friendships turned out to be of decisive importance. In October or November 1394, Nicolas de Clamanges employed his finest Latin in a letter to the new pope. He set forth the state of the Church and offered all sorts of advice about how to end the schism. He also suggested a man for the occasion. His words were more or less as follows: "Among so many remarkable men, is not the most commendable by reason of his faith, wisdom, loyalty, and zeal, and the most ardent in wanting to restore the unity of the Church, Pierre, chancellor of the Church of Paris and chaplain to the king? To put it in a nutshell, here is a man worthy of you. His virtue is unique. To be sure, wicked men, out of jealousy, have often attacked him. The accursed tongue of the wicked has frequently sullied his name. But I have no hesitation in saying that after you he is the other light of our age. Make him your counselor, an auxiliary in your labors. Welcome him, love him, honor him. Trust in him totally. You will not regret choosing such a servant."[334] Has friendship ever prompted eloquence to write a handsomer letter of recommendation?

An anonymous mutual friend of Nicolas de Clamanges and Pierre d'Ailly felt that the disciple actually had gone a bit far in his praise of the master. Nicolas lost no time justifying himself in the same style: "Such men are rare in our time, and rare are the stars whose light penetrates the fogs of the age. If you do not wish me to praise this remarkable man, I do not see anyone on this earth worthy of my praise. I see no one superior to him in culture, singular wisdom, or admirable industry or in the decency of his life, the gravity of his behavior, the solidity of his faith, and the measured moderation of his actions and words. Finally, I know of no one else who has shown greater love of his country and Church or greater zeal for the public good" (*in charitate denique patriae, amore ecclesiae, zelo reipublicae, quem sibi praelatum putem*).[335]

The pupil had aided his master. The master returned the favor. The name of Nicolas de Clamanges figured on the *rotulus*, or roll, that Pierre d'Ailly presented to the pope on December 13, 1394.[336] It was customary for corporations such as the university and for powerful personages to submit to the pope lists of clerics wishing to receive benefices in particular chapters or parishes. If the pope agreed, the person did not necessarily receive the hoped-for benefice, for there were always more candidates than there were benefices available. But the fortunate individual was at least in a better position to obtain the benefice if a vacancy should occur. For a cleric's name to appear on a *rotulus* therefore marked an important stage in his career. It meant that he could one day hope to earn enough to live on or, if already provided with a living, to live better. To be in a position to submit a *rotulus* to the pope was even better; it was an obvious sign of power, which enabled a man to make sure of advancement for his relatives, servants, and friends.

In any case Benedict XIII had not needed Nicolas de Clamanges's letter to persuade him of the wisdom of securing the loyalty of the king's chaplain, whose awesome effectiveness he had witnessed personally in Paris. By a happy coincidence Pierre found himself in Avignon just a few weeks after the pope's election, for the king immediately chose to send his chaplain to pay a call on the new pope. Pierre arrived in Avignon in October.[337] He stayed for three months, during which time Benedict XIII bestowed favors on many people but above all on Pierre d'Ailly. He and Pierre saw each other frequently and took meals together. The pope conferred a canonry in Bayeux on the royal chaplain. He allowed him to hold all the benefices he had already obtained and any others that he might secure in the future.[338] And he approved three *rotuli* that Pierre submitted. No sooner had the royal chaplain arrived in Avignon that he submitted a list containing the names of six close associates; Benedict XIII granted his approval on October 21. Next, on December 13, he approved a second list that included the names of sixty clerics of Pierre's acquaintance. Finally, before leaving Avignon, the chaplain presented a third list mentioning three of his relatives, and the pope granted his approval on February 9, 1395, three days after Pierre's departure.[339] The titles of the three lists are not particularly significant; relatives of Pierre figure on all three. Taken together, the three lists tell us a great deal about the group of people whose hopes were invested in the king's chaplain.

First were Pierre d'Ailly's relatives, foremost among whom were those who bore the same name as Pierre himself, Pierre and Henri d'Ailly, both clerics in the diocese of Soissons and certainly, like our

Pierre d'Ailly, natives of Compiègne. Pierre d'Ailly the younger was surely the godson of the elder Pierre. In 1394 he was a student in Paris and already chaplain of the Saint-Léonard chapel that Thomas d'Ailly had founded at the beginning of the fourteenth century in the Saint-Antoine church at Compiègne. He hoped to add another benefice to this modest chaplaincy. Henri d'Ailly apparently was still awaiting his first benefice. We hear nothing more about these two nephews of Pierre d'Ailly, both of whom must have died young. But there were also the Le Prestres, sons of a sister of Pierre d'Ailly's who married in Compiègne. Among them was Raoul Le Prestre, a cleric in the diocese of Soissons and in 1394 the holder of several prebends in the dioceses of Soissons, Laon, and Noyon. His uncle would soon make him a canon of Cambrai and later one of the executors of his will.[340] Of all the nephews of Pierre d'Ailly, none was closer to him, and none owed him more, than Raoul Le Prestre. Another of Pierre's sisters married a Compiègne hosier by the name of Le Tenneur. She had six children, but apparently none of them had entered the Church or needed their uncle.[341] By contrast, in the diocese of Amiens there was a whole tribe of Le Maires who were all clerics and who gravitated toward their prestigious relative: Firmin Le Maire, priest, master of arts, and already canon of Amiens; Pierre Le Maire, subdeacon and bachelor of civil and canon law; and Hugues and Jean Le Maire, both of whom were still simple clerics.

Apart from these eight nephews and relatives, Pierre d'Ailly extended his favors to a few close acquaintances: Pierre Sansonnet, a cleric in the diocese of Troyes and probably the brother of Gilles Sansonnet, who had studied arts and who had died suddenly in Compiègne in 1391 while on a mission entrusted to him by Pierre d'Ailly;[342] Gilles de Doullens, a cleric in the diocese of Amiens and a master of arts and medicine; Thomas Hourdel, a priest in the diocese of Amiens; Alfred Quiquebelle, a priest in the diocese of Paris; and Jean Le Moine, a cleric in the diocese of Chartres.

In addition to these relatives and close acquaintances, Pierre d'Ailly took an interest in the careers of some sixty other clerics. Some were clearly close neighbors, such as Michel Le Charon, a member of a large Compiègne family, master of arts, and curé of Saint-Antoine in Compiègne.[343] Others were obviously former students of whom he had a favorable opinion and whose careers he wished to promote. It was in this way that the name of Nicolas de Clamanges, who had just written two fine letters speaking well of his master and friend, came to figure on the list that the king's chaplain submitted to Pope Benedict XIII in December 1394.

The king's chaplain, having become in his heart a supporter of the pope, had hardly returned to Paris when an assembly of the clergy organized by the government in honor of the purification of the Virgin (February 2, 1395) held its first session. One hundred fifty prelates had been invited. "Many excused themselves on grounds of old age, infirmity, or insufficient resources" (*antiquitatis vel infirmitatis causa aut occasione penurie rei familiaris*).[344] Nevertheless, on the appointed day roughly one hundred ten appeared at the palace,[345] among them archbishops and bishops from all over France, abbots, masters and doctors of the University of Paris such as Pierre d'Ailly, Gilles Des Champs, and Jean Courtecuisse, and many others.[346]

In accordance with the princes' wishes, Simon de Cramaud was elected president of the assembly on the first day. The duke of Berry's counselor, who was now patriarch of Alexandria but not yet cardinal, because the duke of Berry had been unable to persuade Clement VII in the face of vigorous opposition from Pedro de Luna, had no reason at all to mollify Benedict XIII. In Simon's view, the only way to achieve unity was for both popes to abdicate, and for fifteen years he would remain a stubborn proponent of this course of action. For now his goal was to make sure that of the three solutions to the problem of the schism envisioned in Paris in 1394, only the first—abdication—would receive the unequivocal endorsement of the assembly. There was some resistance, however, and some of the participants in the assembly felt misgivings. Some prelates felt that the pope ought to be shown greater consideration. In particular, Pierre d'Ailly, who did not forget that he was the king's chaplain but who was also responsive to the secret wishes of the pope, did not reject the idea of abdication; nevertheless, he thought it only decent to allow the pope to choose the manner of it. Perhaps compromise was the best way after all. Compromise could even lead to abdication if the arbiters chosen by the two popes agreed on their simultaneous abdication.

Pierre's position was subtle and complex. It must have surprised those of his listeners who had been accustomed to clear and simple ideas from him. It betrayed the embarrassment of a man who, though still closely tied to the king and the university, now felt closer to the pope. Pierre's speech persuaded few in the audience. By an irony of fate, or more likely a skillful maneuver by that superb tactician Simon de Cramaud, it was Gilles Des Champs, Pierre d'Ailly's erstwhile loyal friend, who refuted Pierre's position point by point. He demonstrated that abdication was the simple, rapid solution and that the assembly ought to recommend it to the king forthwith. After fifteen days of clever speeches and shrewd maneuvers, Simon de Cramaud's text received eighty-seven votes, against only twenty-two votes in favor of mollifying the pope. The patriarch then completed his master stroke by consigning his opponents to oblivion,[347] and the court learned with satisfaction that the assembly had chosen abdication "as if by inspiration of the Holy Spirit" and recommended that the king send "a solemn embassy to Monseigneur Benedict" to inform him of this decision.[348] In Paris Simon de Cramaud and Gilles Des Champs reigned triumphant. And Pierre d'Ailly, who only a few months before had enjoyed uncontested authority in the academy and who even now was still a trusted adviser of the king, had begun to lose ground both at court and in the university.

The embassy suggested by the assembly departed from Paris on April 14, 1395.[349] It was indeed a solemn mission. Besides the diplomatic personnel it included the duke of Berry, attended by a retinue of thirteen, the duke of Burgundy, with a retinue of nine, the duke of Orléans, with a retinue of twelve, seven royal councillors, and ten delegates of the University of Paris—fifty-four persons in all.[350] This large entourage arrived in Avignon on May 21.[351] During the negotiations, Gilles Des Champs, acting not as a representative of the university but as a royal councillor, served as spokesman, arguing in favor of abdication. From the first Benedict XIII responded that, in order to end the schism, the two popes must first meet and reach an agreement. And from that position he did not budge. The affair dragged on until June 26. On that day the "first stone was laid in the newly built church of Saint Peter Celestine in which Saint Peter of Luxemburg lay buried. A large crowd heard a fine sermon delivered by Master Gilles Des Champs."[352] Gilles "strongly commended that cardinal's life" and then proposed that two petitions containing the "choice and opinion" of each party be placed next to the body of the saint. He had no doubt "that the saintly cardinal, upon whose heart this matter had weighed so heavily during his lifetime, would by some miracle show which opinion and choice would be the best and most advantageous for the holy Church."[353] And so "two petitions were drawn up, one containing the view of the pope, the other that of the king. Then the coffin containing the body was raised and the two petitions were placed on it, while prayers were offered to the cardinal, who had felt such great desire and affection for the Church, that he might show the hearts of men which choice was better."[354] Alas, no miracle occurred. The young saint inspired nothing in men's hearts. Everyone clung to his original position. And on July 8 the French took leave of the pope. They were "very angry" and determined to pursue the course of abdication despite the pope's opposition.

Pierre d'Ailly did not take part in the great embassy. He was not chosen as a delegate by either the king or the university, because on April 2, 1395, Benedict XIII had named him bishop of Le Puy.[355] A few days later, on the eve of the embassy's departure from Paris on April 13, the new bishop had resigned his chancellorship. To be sure, Pierre d'Ailly was just as anxious in 1395 as he had been in 1389 to turn the post over to a close ally. In 1389 he had made Gilles Des Champs head of the College of Navarre. To succeed him as chancellor on April 13, 1395, he chose his faithful disciple Jean Gerson.[356] Nevertheless, the link between Pierre d'Ailly and the university had been broken. He no longer meant much to the university he had entered more than thirty years earlier and which he had dominated for nearly fifteen years. In theory his position vis-à-vis the king had not changed. But caught between the pope and the princes, the man who once had been so energetic and decisive became cautious and moderate.

Much later, after the Council of Pisa in 1411, when most of Benedict XIII's supporters had abandoned him, Boniface Ferrer wrote a treatise in defense of the elderly pontiff. Born, like the pope, in Aragon, Boniface was the brother of Saint Vincent Ferrier, or Ferrer. And he himself was prior of the Great Charterhouse. When the pious and vehement Carthusian saw his compatriot forsaken by so many in authority, he drafted a violent polemic that lashed out in many directions. Pierre d'Ailly was one of his targets. In one passage Pierre is not mentioned by name, and the facts are not strictly accurate, either because after fifteen years Boniface's memory was playing tricks on him or, more likely, because the author did not wish to compromise Benedict XIII by involving him in what was not a very glorious affair. There is no doubt, however, that it was Pierre d'Ailly that Boniface Ferrer had in mind.[357] In Paris in the time of Clement VII, he tells us, there was a great master, one of the greatest of all. In his courses and sermons and before assemblies he constantly spoke in a loud and clear voice about the unity of the Church and the abdication of the two popes. He seemed to be animated by a great zeal. He spread his fire in all directions. One day, someone asked the pope for a rich benefice. And the pope replied: "No, I won't give it to you. I want to shut the mouth of a dragon who is always spitting fire." And he gave it to the great master, who, once it was stuck in his throat, immediately became hoarse (*et statim effectus est raucus, habens illud in gutture*). Later the great master received a bishopric, whereupon he fell more silent than Zachariah, for he never regained his voice. The anecdote cast Pierre d'Ailly in a cruel light. But really the attack menaced not just one bishop but the entire Church, because Boniface Ferrer concluded by asking how, if prelates became prelates through intrigue (*ambitiones*) and were ready to abandon the straight and narrow in order to hold on to status and wealth, they could be honored and believed. Such men were not worthy of being pastors of souls. One day Boniface Ferrer would invoke the example of Pierre d'Ailly in order to deny all authority. But for now what interests us in this attack is the implication that in the eyes of many who had previously listened to and admired him, Pierre d'Ailly had joined the herd of the fat and mute.

The Conquest of Cambrai (1396–98)

Le Puy was one of the most popular pilgrimage sites in France. It was also a fine bishopric, whose bishop enjoyed the archiepiscopal privilege of wearing the pallium; as an immediate suffragan of the pope, he also enjoyed the distinction of standing in the hierarchy directly beneath the Holy See. Yet Le Puy, located south of the Loire, had the immense drawback of its distance from Paris. Pierre d'Ailly never set foot in the town. For the Podots, as the inhabitants of Le Puy were known, Pierre was the very epitome of the bad bishop, or so we are told by Elie de Lestrange. Elie was born in 1340. Nothing in his background disposed him to think well of Pierre d'Ailly. The scion of good Limousin noble stock, Elie de Lestrange was related to Gregory XI.[358] His brother, Guillaume de Lestrange, died archbishop of Rouen in 1389 and had been a trusted adviser of Charles V. Elie himself had studied law and was a doctor *in utroque*. He had been bishop of Saintes since 1381. In 1396 he achieved national prominence as one of Benedict XIII's staunchest supporters among French bishops. Owing to his unwavering allegiance to Benedict he suffered many setbacks in his long and irascible later years. (Elie died in 1418 at nearly eighty years of age.)

Now, it happens that Elie de Lestrange succeeded Pierre d'Ailly as bishop of Le Puy, and he found matters there in such a state that he filed charges against his predecessor. Pierre d'Ailly claimed that he had been bishop of Le Puy for only seventeen or eighteen months, but Elie de Lestrange insisted that he had held the post for twenty-eight months and had received three years' worth of revenues. Yet he had done nothing good in Le Puy (*et tamen ibi nihil fecit de bono*). He had contented himself with extracting as much profit as he could through his agents. He had refused to pay a roofer five livres to put a new roof on the official's hearing room. He had paid out no more than twenty sous and six denarii for repairs to the cathedral. He had never lived in Le Puy, never said mass in its church, and never defended its rights.[359] What Elie de Lestrange says is no doubt true, except in one particular: Pierre d'Ailly did not serve as bishop of Le Puy for twenty-eight months. The critic's strictures lose some of their force, moreover, when one realizes that Elie de Lestrange himself, although transferred from Saintes to Le Puy on May 20, 1397, did not set foot in his new diocese until June 25, 1399, some twenty-five months later.[360] It is therefore just to say that Pierre d'Ailly was a little show to visit his diocese while bishop of Le Puy, but no slower than other bishops. The principal reason he never visited the diocese at all was that on November 15, 1396 (nineteen months after his nomination to Le Puy, thus approximately confirming Pierre's own estimate), Benedict XIII made him bishop of Noyon; then, a few months later, the pope named him bishop of Cambrai.

The diocese of Cambrai was enormous, consisting of more than a thousand parishes on the right bank of the Scheldt.[361] It also included the cities of Le Cateau, Valenciennes, Brussels, and Antwerp. The bishop of Cambrai also held the title of count of Cambrésis. The count-bishop was powerful and rich. In fact, however, his position was not an easy one. Although tensions between the bishop and the city's inhabitants had lessened some time earlier, peace in the county was still threatened by the daily violence and plunder of an unruly nobility. But even this violence was overshadowed by a still greater problem: the city, county, and diocese of Cambrai lay on the border between two worlds. The bishop of Cambrai was suffragan of the archbishop of Rheims. But the diocese, county, and city stood on the right bank of the Scheldt, hence in the territory of the Empire. In roughly six hundred of the diocese's parishes the faithful spoke French, but in some four hundred others they spoke only Flemish. In this diocese, where wavering loyalties stood in open confrontation, the schism's consequences proved particularly disastrous. Finally, the count-bishop was surrounded by powerful princes. To the south was the king of France. Close by were the count of Hainault and the duke of Brabant, part of whose lands lay in the diocese of Cambrai. Of most immediate concern was the count of Flanders, whose territory, on the other bank of the Scheldt, "was contiguous with the territory of Cambresis" and who, "as count of Flanders," was "guardian of the chapter and churches of Cambrai and Cambresis."[362] In 1396 the powerful count of Flanders was none other than Philip the Bold, the duke of Burgundy and uncle of King Charles VI. For the time being, at least, the king of France, the count of Hainault, and the duke of Brabant posed no threat, but Philip the Bold was obviously bent on subduing Cambrai.

In 1390 Andrew of Luxemburg, the brother of Peter of Luxemburg, became bishop of Cambrai. Clement VII named the brother of his own personal saint to the diocese of which he himself had once been bishop. When Andrew died on October 31, 1396, Philip the Bold sought to capitalize on the situation by putting a man he could count on in Cambrai. To the canons of Cambrai he strongly recommended Louis de la Trémoille, his former counselor and presently bishop of Tournai. On December 1 the canons in fact elected Louis de la Trémoille and requested the pope's approval. But Benedict XIII cared nothing about the duke of Burgundy's desires, and on November 15 he made up his mind to transfer the bishop of Noyon to Cambrai and Pierre d'Ailly from Le Puy to Noyon. Pierre thus returned to familiar haunts. But the bishop of Noyon, unwilling to take on the duke of Burgundy, withdrew, and on March 19, 1397, Benedict XIII assigned Pierre d'Ailly to the bishopric of Cambrai.[363] Pierre d'Ailly accepted the challenge. He accepted from the pope of Avignon a half-Clementine, half-Urbanist diocese, and he stood his ground in the face of a powerful and hostile Clementine prince, Philip the Bold.

A canon of Cambrai, Pierre d'Ailly was well aware of the situation in the diocese.[364] With full knowledge he placed himself in an impossible position, something the bishop of Noyon had been unwilling to do. Many others would have refused. Still others who might have accepted would have been destroyed. Pierre accepted. He lived through some intense and harrowing moments. But after "many perils, anxieties, terrors, and labors," he triumphed.[365] At the height of his powers, at forty-six, this great intellectual proved, more than at any other time of his life, that he possessed, even outside the familiar milieu of the university, the precise mixture of courage and audacity, shrewdness (not to say duplicity), prudence, and luck needed to make a formidable man of action. It is worth pausing a moment to trace step by step his conquest of Cambrai.

On March 19, 1397, Benedict XIII assigned Pierre d'Ailly to the bishopric of Cambrai. On May 4 he named Michel de Creney, bishop of Auxerre and former confessor of King Charles VI, a man whom Pierre had known well at the College of Navarre and at court, and Simon de Bussy, bishop of Soissons, to receive the oath of loyalty of the new bishop of Cambrai.[366] Pierre d'Ailly, it must be said, exhibited greater eagerness to reach his new diocese than he had ever shown about going to Le Puy. On June 2 his loyal nephew Raoul Le Prestre (who claimed to be a bachelor of law at the University of Angers), acting in Pierre's name and in the presence of Guy Marcoul and others, took possession of Pierre's see at Cambrai.[367] At that point Pierre d'Ailly himself was in Soissons, and on June 5, in the chapel of the bishopric, Simon de Bussy and Michel de Creney received his oath.[368] On May 13 the duke of Burgundy established his summer residence at Beauté near Nogent-sur-Marne.[369] On June 8 he wrote Pierre d'Ailly a threatening letter, indicating that Pierre would be wise "to relieve himself of the aforementioned acceptance and reception."[370] Pierre received the letter in Soissons. At once he began hasty preparations to leave the kingdom and take up residence in his diocese. He avoided Cambrai, however, and settled in Cateau, which was in both his diocese and the county of Hainault, whose count was on his side. From there on June 21 he wrote to the duke of Burgundy.

"Most noble and excellent prince and my most feared lord," he began, "I commend myself to you as humbly as I can."[371] Pierre's old friend Philippe de Mézières did not like the expression "most feared" (*metuentissimo*). "This phrase and manner of address, 'most feared,' which clerics have once again seized upon for the purpose of flattery, is highly displeasing to God and to his honest subjects . . . for 'feared' implies tyranny. Quite contrary in meaning are *serenissimo* and *metuentissimo,* that is, most serene and most feared. Great flatterers, notaries and chancellors, bishops and counselors, in order to acquire the grace and benevolence of kings and emperors, and ultimately to achieve great estates, have for reasons of subtle flattery chosen to employ the sweet harmony of 'most feared,' in order to give to kings, who usually are proud men, cause to be feared rather than loved." Charlemagne did not call himself "most feared," nor did Saint Louis. "This hollow and flattering and inflated offering" was first served up to Philip the Fair and later spread throughout the kingdom. There were now, Philippe de Mézières continued, many princes who "govern their subjects as tyrants and for that reason, by divine permission, they are called 'most feared.' But if they governed their subjects naturally in equity, in true love, and in humanity, they would be called *serenissimi* like their blessed and much beloved predecessors."[372] Philippe de Mézières most certainly did not like the expression "most feared," and Pierre d'Ailly had surely read or heard these handsome variations on the theme of the beloved good prince and the proud, feared tyrant. But this was not the moment to heed such advice, and Pierre d'Ailly for the time being had no interest in flouting a well-established custom.

"And may it please you to know, my most feared lord, that by the same rider who brought me your letters in Soissons, where I lay gravely ill, I send you this brief letter." This grave illness excused

Pierre's failure to respond immediately to his most feared lord. Yet it was not so grave that it prevented him from leaving Soissons and the kingdom at once, with the duke's rider following in his train. Pierre d'Ailly suffered many such opportune bouts with fever in his lifetime; they did little damage to his health.

Pierre d'Ailly then defended himself. He had done nothing but obey the pope: "I wished to obey him as I must and did not wish to incur his wrath, which would be perilous to me, and not only to my body but above all to my soul." Furthermore, he did not accept the bishopric of Cambrai "out of hostility or contempt for the king or for you, whom I wish to obey and serve with all my power as I must," because at that time he had had no indication that either the king or the duke was unhappy with his nomination.

After giving this respectful explanation, Pierre cannot refrain, however, from dealing the duke a stinging reproach. In his letter the duke had written that Pierre already had enough from having served the king. In reply Pierre asked: What about the bishop of Tournai? Did not he too have enough? "As for what you wrote concerning the value and estate of my person and the time I served the king, I was certainly well provided for elsewhere, my most feared lord, I confess that that is true, and more than was my due, and may it please God that monseigneur de Tournai and all other clerics according to their deserts and merits should be as content with their estates as I was with mine, for by God I very much wished that not a word had ever been spoken concerning my translation."

"As for what you wrote concerning the wisdom of relieving myself of the aforementioned acceptance and reception," it was already too late. I "had already taken an oath of fealty to the pope of said bishopric prior to receiving your letters." Through a proxy "I have been received by the clergy to the delight and joy of the people." And I "have hastened there to recognize their good wishes and obedience, and I have administered several sacraments and performed several episcopal services. . . . And for that reason I cannot relinquish said bishopric without special license and authority from our Holy Father the Pope, as is clear and obvious to all who know the laws."

At this point only one solution remained. "May it please you to have me not only excused but also recommended, so that by God's and your grace I may spiritually and temporally do some good in this bishopric, which sorely needs it, and which you have always loved, comforted, and aided, for otherwise I know that I shall be able to do nothing advantageous there." Pierre d'Ailly then concludes with one of those flights of vaguely menacing eloquence that were his specialty: "And if by this compulsion I were to fail in my duty, as of this moment and before God I beg forgiveness and leave responsibility to you, for which you may one day be called to explain yourself in the great chambers of accounts. And for God's sake, for God's sake, my most feared lord, know and remember that we all are mortal and hasten toward our end, which is uncertain." One last time he protests that the duke is "the lord of the world after the king whom I would most like to serve and obey." The letter ends: "Written at Castel en Cambresis on the day of the Holy Sacrament. Your very humble chaplain and orator, P., bishop of Cambrai, unworthy." Humble chaplain of the duke and unworthy bishop of Cambrai—but still bishop.[373]

At around the same time as this admirable letter—humble and dignified, lucid and closely reasoned, ironic and threatening—Pierre also wrote dozens of other, shorter letters to alert friends to the situation and gather support. He wrote to the duke of Orléans, the duke of Bourbon, the powerful count of Saint-Pol (who in this region was the duke of Burgundy's right arm and who was none other than Waleran of Luxemburg, the elder brother of Peter, the young and sainted cardinal, and of Andrew, the recently deceased bishop of Cambrai). He also wrote to the abbot of Saint-Denis, the prior of the Carthusians, and the provincial of the Celestines, as well as to Michel de Creney, who had just received his oath at Soissons, and even, in desperation, to Simon de Cramaud.[374]

On June 30 he rewrote his letter to the duke of Burgundy. He had not yet given the first version to the duke's messenger, who was still awaiting Pierre's reply. He pointed out that the duke's letter was dated June 8, that is, after Pierre's oath. He begged pardon for not going to Beauté in person: "The state of my person is presently not such that I can go to you and inform you and beg your pardon concerning what you have written and tell you in full everything that is involved; I have been and remain so oppressed by illness and weakness that I am unfit for a lengthy journey by horseback." Pierre shortened his argument. He eliminated the ironic paragraph and the threatening rhetoric. And he made one other change to avoid provoking the duke of Orléans should that prince happen to read the letter: "You are," he wrote the duke of Burgundy, "one of the lords of the world after the king whom I would most like to serve and obey."[375]

In any case, this letter did not alter the position of the church of Cambrai's protector, who ordered the chapter in writing to deny the bishop entry into his episcopal city.[376] Nevertheless, August 18 found Pierre d'Ailly in the abbey of Cantimpré at the gates of Cambrai.[377] The climate was unusually tense. Burgundian men-at-arms, having delivered the duke's letter, patrolled the town.[378] A delegation of canons and burghers begged the bishop to postpone his entry, but he declined.[379] He spent that night in a nearby castle and then, on Sunday morning, August 19, arrived at Saint-Ladre gate "disguised as a squire" (*in habitu dissimulatio scutiferi*), according to an account written in 1411 by the pious Carthusian Boniface Ferrer, who claimed to have seen and heard everything that happened.[380] He then went to a modest house (*in tuguriis*), donned the episcopal insignia, and waited. When the hour came, a small procession made its way through a hostile crowd gathered along the customary route and at length reached the cathedral. Not a canon was to be found. The bishop, assisted only by chaplains and vicars, celebrated mass despite insults from the servants of the dukes of Berry and Burgundy.[381] After mass the bishop presided over the traditional meal, which was particularly hushed owing to the large number of empty seats. The day ended with one final incident. One of the bells in the cathedral's bell tower, the "Glorious" (*Gloriosa*), was supposed to be sounded on any evening when the bishop was present; if the bishop so wished, he could ring the bell himself. But the canons refused to allow Pierre d'Ailly to ring the Gloriosa.[382]

A few days later, on August 24 or 25, Pierre was still in Cambrai when he received a letter from the pope, who exhorted him, somewhat belatedly, to make his solemn entry into the city and not to accept any offer of translation.[383] With this letter in hand, Pierre waited a little longer. Then, on September 3, he summoned the canons. In substance he told them this: During my solemn entry you failed to receive me as you were supposed to do. But here is the pope's letter. You see it, and you touch it (*quas vidistis et palpastis*). You must obey it. Allow me, therefore, to ring the bell. Otherwise it will mean excommunication for each of you and interdiction for the church of Cambrai.[384] On September 5, after two days of reflection, the canons answered: "We never refused to do what we were supposed to do for you. It may be true that we failed to perform certain minor rites during the ceremony. We did not do so, however, out of contempt for the apostolic see or for you personally. Rather, the prince's wrath confronted us with certain dangers, as you well know. We were afraid, and fear may afflict even steadfast men [*metum . . . qui cadere potuit in viros constantes*]. And now, in order that we may avoid the punishments with which we are threatened by apostolic authority, and as much as we fear the wrath of which we have spoken, you may as of tonight ring the bell as you requested." Whereupon the canon who was to ring the bell went to the bell tower with the bishop and offered him the rope. The bishop took the rope and rang the Glorious three times. Then an affidavit was prepared in the presence of, among others, Guy Marcoul, licentiate in law, Gilles de Doullens, master of arts and medicine, and Raoul Le Prestre, canon of Noyon, all allies of the bishop.[385]

This apparent triumph did not settle everything, however. Countless enemies still dogged the bishop's every step and monitored his every word in hope of discovering the slightest pretext that might be used to remove him from the diocese.[386] Pierre d'Ailly chose to retreat to Cateau, and it was probably from there that he dispatched, in November, numerous letters whose optimism did little to conceal his difficulties.[387] Everywhere in the diocese, he wrote the pope, I find a tolerable obedience, but not without extraordinary trouble and effort. I trust that God will support me through these tribulations and adversities. I hope that the situation will improve with each passing day. You must, however, put an end to my adversaries' hopes of yet another translation, and you must silence my successor in Le Puy by obliging him to end his unjust accusations.[388]

Pierre d'Ailly's position was still shaky. At the very least he needed to obtain investiture of his temporal authority from the king of the Romans. In March 1398 King Wenceslas went to Rheims to discuss the unity of the Church with King Charles VI of France. The journey was the idea of the duke of Orléans, who informed Pierre d'Ailly. The two kings met on March 22, 1398. Their discussions lasted several days. They failed to produce the desired results, however, because Wenceslas was constantly drunk and because Charles, after another attack of madness, hastily left the city.[389] Wenceslas then headed back toward imperial territory. Pierre d'Ailly had not wished to incur the wrath of the duke of Burgundy by going to Rheims. He decided, however, to overtake Wenceslas the moment he set foot on imperial soil. The duke of Burgundy knew of these plans and gave orders that the bishop be arrested the minute he ventured beyond the limits of his diocese and entered the Rethel region—and if the bishop resisted, he was to be killed. One of the duke's officers actually arrested Pierre d'Ailly, but it happens that this officer had been a student of the bishop of Cambrai's at the University of Paris. His love for his master was stronger than his fear of the duke, and he let Pierre go.[390] Wenceslas had stopped at Yvoix or Ivoy (today Carignan), a few miles east of Mouzon, the first way station in imperial territory on the road from Rheims to Trier and a traditional site of meetings between French and German princes.[391] And there, on April 3, 1398, Pierre d'Ailly overtook the king of the Romans. The political circumstances were so favorable, Wenceslas so earnestly hoped to please the duke of Orléans, and Pierre d'Ailly was so convincing that the bishop appointed by Benedict XIII immediately obtained the desired investiture, even though Wenceslas was nominally a prince of Roman obedience.[392] Pierre returned to Cambrai, of which he was now the uncontested pastor. His adversaries were resigned. He had triumphed over all adversity.

The First Withdrawal of Obedience (1398–1403)

Pierre's triumph, however, proved a bitter one. Antwerp, in the northern reaches of the diocese, close to territory under Roman obedience, and under little compulsion from the civil authorities, delayed for four years before agreeing to receive its new bishop.[393] In Cambrai itself the count-bishop continued to suffer affronts stemming from the duke of Burgundy's rancor. In particular, murder and plunder by the lords of Esnes had long disturbed the county's peace. The city's chapter had long opposed these attacks, but in vain. One day, both sides, weary of the struggle, asked the duke of Burgundy to arbitrate their dispute. The duke agreed. On May 28, 1399, however, the duke's loyal ally Waleran of Luxemburg made his conditions known: the city chapter and council would have to pledge to refuse obedience to the bishop in the event he failed to honor the agreement. The next day, the canons, the provost, and the aldermen of Cambrai explained to Pierre d'Ailly that they had "always been reputed loyal and faithful, obedient as required," and that they "did not wish to sign an obligation such as that contained in the aforementioned article without his seal and consent." They therefore asked their bishop if it pleased him "that the men of the chapter and the provost and aldermen contract an obligation and promise" to do as they were asked. And Pierre d'Ailly agreed. To "the reverend fathers" he responded "that he held them as a group to be wiser than himself alone."[394] What an astonishing thought to come from the likes of Pierre d'Ailly, a man always so respectful of hierarchy, so conscious of the importance of obedience in both church and state! Now that he was count-bishop of Cambrai and a prince of the Empire, however, he was obliged to reckon with powerful "democratic" ideas then current in northern France and the Low Countries, ideas according to which the prince was obliged to respect his subjects' "liberties" and wishes. No doubt those ideas were particularly disturbing to a bishop who surely was aware of the increasingly influential notion that the authority of the general council outweighs that of the pope. And his uneasiness can only have been accentuated by the extraordinary events to which contemporary Europe was witness.

In 1398 the French government finally took the extreme step that it had been preparing to take for several years. An assembly of the clergy was held in Paris in May and June, with Simon de Cramaud presiding. Gilles Des Champs, Pierre Plaoul, and others had argued vigorously in favor of withdrawal of obedience. Simon de Cramaud once again overcame the scruples of some of the clerics in attendance. Then, on July 27, 1398, the kingdom of France withdrew its obedience from the pope of Avignon; in other words, France decided that it would no longer recognize the pope's authority and no longer obey his orders. This was a truly extraordinary step: a body was going to attempt to live without its head. Contrast this with the English revolt of the following year; it, at least, did not challenge the notion that a king is necessary. But the rebels did dare to change monarchs. In September 1399 Richard II was forced to abdicate; Henry IV became king.

The English revolt and the French withdrawal of obedience were events of the same order. Both were refusals to obey, which sowed disorder in church and state. Many people were aware of this, Pierre d'Ailly foremost among them. In condemning the 1398 withdrawal of obedience a few years after the fact, he pointed out that it had provoked mirth among those partisans of the pope of Rome, the English: "The English *hoc deridebant a nobis.* And when they were told that they had stripped their king, they said that we had done worse, and that we had stripped our pope."[395] Pierre could thus denounce the English and the French in one breath, but the Germans could not, because on August 20, 1400, the electors deposed Wenceslas. To be sure, they had plenty of good reasons for deposing the drunkard king of the Romans. Nevertheless, the decision had not been an easy one. Indeed, obedience was so deeply ingrained in the minds of the French that they never even considered challenging the authority of their poor mad king. Certain of the most lucid Frenchmen had a clear idea of the connection between withdrawal of obedience and deposition of kings; they saw clearly the threat that withdrawal of obedience posed for the king of France. The University of Toulouse remained loyal to Benedict XIII and hostile to the withdrawal of obedience, even though it had been forced to go along with that withdrawal in 1398. Late in 1401 it dared to draft a letter in which it showed, among other things, how the principle of withdrawal of obedience could be turned against the king.[396]

The English surely were right. The refusal to obey the pope was of the same order as—it was even worse than—the deposition of a king. The 1398 decision saddened the hearts of many clerics, whose lives were temporarily or permanently changed. Vincent Ferrier, Boniface's brother, was born in Valence in 1350. He was a Dominican. In 1398 he was serving as Benedict XIII's confessor. A few weeks after the withdrawal of obedience, he found himself in Avignon, gravely ill. Christ appeared to him, touched him, healed him, and ordered him to go out and preach to the world. Benedict XIII wanted him to stay. But Vincent Ferrier had no doubt that the coming of the Antichrist and the end of the world were closer than ever. Better to obey God than to obey the pope. On November 22, 1398, he left Avignon and began his itinerant preaching, which continued until his death at Vannes in 1419 at the age of sixty-nine.[397]

Nicolas de Clamanges made a major decision late in 1397. He accepted a position as *scriptor* in the papal chancellery and left Paris for Avignon.[398] His decision caused a furor in the small Parisian circle in which he had lived. It was seen as treasonous; the leading French humanist had abandoned his colleagues.[399] Nicolas, who immediately found Avignon to his liking, flourished in the exceptional cultural milieu. Alas, in June 1398 the plague struck Avignon. Nicolas was given up for dead and escaped only by a miracle.[400] He had hardly recovered when the bad news arrived from Paris. On June 22 Benedict XIII gave him the treasury of Langres. Shortly after the withdrawal of obedience was proclaimed, Nicolas therefore left Avignon. He refused, however, to return to Paris, which he now detested and where turmoil and confusion now reigned, where neither the tongue nor the mind was free, and where insatiable ambition wreaked havoc.[401] His fragile health, his timidity, and his bitterness conspired to isolate him in haughty retirement. He settled in Langres. From there he wrote to Pierre d'Ailly, and he could not find words adequate to deplore the lamentable state of the Church. The Church was collapsing, the apostolic see was collapsing, the authority of the sovereign pontiff was collapsing (*ruit . . . ruit . . . ruit*). Obedience, fear, order, religion were no more (*perit obediencia. . . , perit metus. . . , perit ordo. . . , perit sacra religio . . .*). The ecclesiastical orders were overturned, worldly estates were confounded, everything was topsy-turvy.[402] A short while later, in 1400 or 1401, he drafted and once more sent to Pierre d'Ailly his *De Ruina et Raparacione Ecclesie,* in which he defended Benedict XIII and prolixly deplored the ruin of the Church, caused by the sins of its clerics. He strongly condemned the abuses but refrained from criticizing the structure of the Church.[403]

In 1396 Jean Gerson personally took possession of the deaconate of Bruges, which he had obtained through the favor of Benedict XIII and the duke of Burgundy.[404] During the dramatic events of 1398 the chancellor remained aloof. Things were happening in Paris, but he was in Bruges. He did not attend the assembly of the clergy in May and June. A short while later he did return to Paris, but in the spring of 1399 he again left for Bruges. He was still there in February 1400, so depressed that he considered giving up the chancellorship of the university and leaving Paris for good. He explained his thinking in a letter addressed to an unknown person, possibly Pierre d'Ailly.[405] The post of chancellor, he said, is definitely more than I can bear. I am forced (*cogor enim*) to please great lords who are enemies of one another. In such a case it is folly not to flee. The wrath of the prince means death (Prov. 16:14), and no man can serve two masters (Matt. 6:24). And I am also forced (*cogor*) to favor my friends, yet they do not protect me against my enemies. I am forced to resist the importunate or else to commit sin. I am forced, by accepting the advice of others or the customs of the day, to promote ignorant and dissolute men, at times in preference to other, better candidates. I am forced to frequent the importunate. I am forced to listen to endless rumors and gossip, which sully the soul. I am forced to write pointless speeches. I am forced to swim in the troubled waters of the court. I am forced to miss masses and prayers. When dangerous ideas are put forward, I am forced either to stifle conscience by holding my tongue or to court great danger by correcting the errors. No, truly, I can leave and I must leave. I cannot change my nature, and my nature is not suited to action. It is fearful and troubled by trifles, as I have proved a thousand times. Nobody is irreplaceable. Every man has received his own gift from God. Why do violence to my nature?

There is no better testimony to the disarray into which so many clerics were plunged after 1398 than this moving confession, this lucid analysis of the difficulties of a chancellor.

Pierre d'Ailly himself had had no difficulty with the post of chancellor that so overwhelmed his disciple. He had just demonstrated how well suited for action his nature was. He shared neither Nicolas de Clamanges's timidity nor Jean Gerson's fears. Yet in the wake of his triumph in Cambrai, events forced him to lie low. For him as for so many others, this difficult time was a time of retreat. For a variety of reasons Pierre was no longer the king's chaplain. The post was incompatible with episcopal office. Hence the bishop of Cambrai no longer carried any weight at court. Had he had any weight, the hostility of the duke of Burgundy would in any case have prevented him from using it. To be sure, that hostility had gained him the support of the duke of Orléans, to which he was indebted for the ease with which he had obtained investiture from Wenceslas.[406] By 1398, however, the duke of Orléans was no longer calling the tune in Paris; now it was the duke of Berry and the duke of Burgundy who were in charge. For the past three years, moreover, Pierre had been moving closer to Benedict XIII but had not become one of Benedict's unconditional supporters. The hostility of the duke of Burgundy had thrown him into the arms of the duke of Orléans. His own decision had thus conspired with circumstances to place him in the camp of Benedict XIII and Louis of Orléans, aligning him with one of the main forces in contention in the frightful years to come.

But the conflict was not confined to the great. The opinion of other people also mattered. And the fact that the changes in Pierre d'Ailly's allegiances had coincided with his episcopal promotions had earned him the scorn of many, particularly among academics, his former colleagues, of whom he had once been the admired spokesman. Recall that Boniface Ferrer would one day remark that the pope's boons had first turned Pierre's voice hoarse and finally silenced it altogether. As early as June 1398, during the assembly of the clergy in Paris, Pierre Plaoul made a transparent and not very flattering allusion to Pierre d'Ailly in open session where no one could miss it. Plaoul was speaking in favor of a resolution whose effect would have been to deny Benedict XIII the right to nominate prelates. If the pope's right was maintained, he argued, the cause of unity would be compromised, because Benedict XIII would continue to promote his supporters, and "out of the natural affection that everyone feels upon being promoted, many will change their correct and holy opinion, as some have done already, who were of the aforementioned opinion and who, owing to the promotion they received, changed their view to the contrary."[407] For many people Pierre d'Ailly became the very epitome of ambition.

The bishop of Cambrai accordingly avoided a Paris that had become hostile to him. He did not attend the assembly of 1398.[408] Until the end of 1402 he vanished from the ecclesiastical and political scene, in which he had played a leading role.[409] We do not know when he composed the remarkable French poem entitled *Les contredits de Franc Gontier* (The Antithesis of Franc Gontier), but it would be pleasant if it was indeed written during this depressing period. The character Franc Gontier was invented by one of the greatest poets of the fourteenth century, Philippe de Vitry, who was born, to his own knowledge, on October 31, 1291.[410] He died bishop of Meaux on June 9, 1362. During his long life he served several kings of France as notary and secretary. He was a remarkable poet, one of the few French poets Petrarch respected. Among other things he wrote a thirty-two-line poem entitled *Dit de Franc Gontier* (The Story of Franc Gontier).[411]

Soubs feuille verd, sur herbe delictable,
Sur ruy bruyant et sur claire fontaine,

[Beneath green leaf, on delightful grass,
on a babbling stream by a clear spring]

the poet envisioned a hut in which Gontier and his wife sampled

des doux mets de nature.
Là sus mangeoient Gontier et dame Heleine
Fromage frais, laict, beurre, fromagée
Cresme, maton, prune, noix, pomme, poire,
Cibor, oignon, escalogne froyée
Sur crouste grise au gros sel pour mieux boire.

[nature's succulent dishes.
There Gontier and his lady Helen ate
fresh cheese, milk, butter,
thick cream, cottage cheese, plums, nuts, apples, pears,
White and yellow onions, and shallots
rubbed on a salty gray crust to stimulate thirst.]

Then, his meal finished, Gontier went to cut down a tree, and the poet heard him

en abattant son arbre
Dieu mercier de sa vie très sure.
Ne scai, dit il, que sont piliers de marbre,
Pommeaux luisans, murs vestus de paincture.
Je n'ay paour de trahison tissue
Soubs beau samblant, ne qui empoisonné soye
En vaisseau d'or. Je n'ay la teste nue
Devant tyran, ne genoil qui se ploye.

[while cutting down his tree he
thanked God for his very secure life.
I know nothing, said he, of marble pillars,
Dazzling pommels, or walls covered with painting.
I have no fear of treason plotted
beneath a fine exterior or of poison
secreted in golden vessels. I do not go bareheaded
before tyrants, and I have not knees that bend.]

Nor does Gontier suffer from "lust, ambition, or gluttony."

Labour me plait en joyeuse franchise.
J'aim' Dame Heleine, et elle moi sans faille,
Et c'est assez. . . .

[It pleases me to work in joyful freedom.
I love Lady Helen, and she loves me, without blemish.
And that is enough.]

With a sigh the poet concludes: "Alas, the court serf is worthless, but Franc Gontier is a pure gem, worth his weight in gold."

This pastoral quickly became a classic. Eustache Deschamps imitated it. And Pierre d'Ailly, in the thirty-two lines of his *Contredits de Franc Gontier*, parodied the original by describing not Gontier and his hut but the tyrant and his court:

Ung chasteau sçay, sur roche espouvantable,
En lieu venteux, sur rive perilleuse.
Là vis tyran, séant à haute table,
En grand palais, en sale plantureuse,
Environné de famille nombreuse,
Pleine de fraud', d'envie et de murmure,
Vuide de foi, d'amour, de paix joyeuse,
Serve subjecte, en convoiteuse ardure.

[There was a castle on a frightful cliff,
in a windy place on a perilous shore.
There lived a tyrant, who dined at high table
in a great palace in a luxurious hall,
surrounded by a large retinue,
Filled with deceit, envy, and rumor,
Devoid of faith, love, and joyful peace,
In thrall, abject, in covetous ardor.

Pierre then describes the tyrant's gluttonous predilections and concludes the account of his sad life with these lines:

Acquirer veult ou royaume ou empire,
Par avarice sent douloureux martyre.
Trahison doute, en nul il ne se fye,
Coeur a felon, enflé d'orgueil et d'ire,
Triste, pensif, plein de melancolie.
Las! trop mieulx vaut de Franc Gontier la vie,
Sobre liesse et nette povreté,
Que poursuivir, par orde gloutonnie,
Cour de tyran, riche malheureté.

[Who would acquire kingdom or empire
becomes a doleful martyr to greed.
Fearing treason, he trusts no one,
With a treacherous heart, he is swollen with pride and wrath,
sad, pensive, and filled with melancholy.
Enough! Far better lead Franc Gontier's life

of sober gaiety and decent poverty
than pursue sumptuous unhappiness in the insatiable
gluttony of the tyrant's court.][412]

Literary considerations are not without significance in the composition of these lines, which precisely echo the *Dit* of Philippe de Vitry. Moral didacticism also has a part, in the preaching against the seven deadly sins. Still, one cannot help thinking that painful experience also left its mark on the poem. Pierre d'Ailly had personal knowledge of the court "filled with deceit, envy, and rumor" and of the tyrant "swollen with pride and wrath." He described these things much as Nicolas de Clamanges at the same time spoke of Paris from Langres and as Jean Gerson spoke of the university from Bruges. The poem reflected the three scattered friends' state of mind so well that Nicolas de Clamanges paraphrased it in Latin.[413] Estranged from Paris and condemning his former home, Pierre d'Ailly was very likely the least sincere of the three men. For him the bitter joy of liberation from the "serfdom of the court" no doubt held little pleasure.

At this important moment in his life, having lost his position in Paris but having gained, as count-bishop of Cambrai, the status of imperial prince, Pierre d'Ailly, nearly fifty, began to think of death and to prepare for his end. His preparations were made easier by the fact that he now controlled an enormous fortune. His annual income, according to Boniface Ferrer, amounted to more than the capital of the city of Compiègne where he was born.[414] In 1399 he ordered a tomb built for himself beneath the so-called Requiem Altar in the cathedral of Cambrai.[415] In 1402 he gave the Saint-Antoine church in Compiègne, where he was baptized, a clock that had cost ten gold *écus*, each worth eighteen *sous parisis*; an illuminated Soissons-style missal in two volumes, which cost sixty gold francs; and the sum of fifty gold francs to endow a living for the curé, on condition that the collect *Omnipotens sempiterne Deus, qui vivorum simul et mortuorum* be said prior to all masses celebrated at the main altar (where several collects might be said).[416] In 1402 he gave seven hundred livres to the Cambrai chapter to celebrate an annual solemn mass in honor of the Holy Trinity; upon his death this was to be transformed into an obit.[417] In 1402 or early 1403 he endowed, at the College of Navarre and for the salvation of soul and the souls of his benefactors, particularly the king and his brother Louis, duke of Orléans, a perpetual mass to be celebrated daily and four solemn obits to be celebrated each year on the Ember Days. In return he bequeathed the college several sources of income, from which the surplus, if any, was to be used for the two college libraries and the chapel. The masters and pupils of the College of Navarre accepted this will on June 20, 1403.[418] At the same time Pierre also drew up another will concerning his funeral rites and endowing several obits. He was to live for twenty more years, however, and this second will was superseded by a third.[419] Generally we hear of wills only in connection with the hour of death, when a person's last wishes are carried out. But it makes more sense to examine wills in relation to the moment when they were drafted, when for the first time a person saw fit to have a will drawn up, for this tells us how the testator viewed his or her life at that moment. Surely it was no accident that Pierre d'Ailly took the steps he did at a time when he had lost all influence in Paris, had just been installed as count-bishop of Cambrai, and was about to turn fifty.

Pierre d'Ailly thought about death during these years of political retirement. But his appetite for life was so strong, his need to know and think, to speak and act, so urgent, that he could not halt his ceaseless activity. The only difference now was that the nature of that activity changed. And the man also changed. With insatiable curiosity he explored many sources, some familiar, others new. The bishop of Cambrai did not turn up his nose at opportunities made available by residence in his diocese. At the home of his friend Jean Le Tartier, the abbot of Cantimpré,[420] for example, he met another of the abbot's friends, Jean Froissart, then in his sixties and soon to die.[421] He also remained in touch with Nicolas de Clamanges, who wrote him from Langres, and with Jean de Montreuil, who in 1401 wrote him an important letter from Paris. Early in that year, the king's notary-secretary returned home from an embassy to Germany. In Paris he found himself with time on his hands. He read, or reread, the *Roman de la Rose,* which Guillaume de Lorris and Jean de Meun had written in the thirteenth century and which had enjoyed uninterrupted success ever since. Jean de Meun's work filled him with enthusiasm. In it he found a blunt style, praise of natural love, and a misogyny that pleased his robust temperament and flattered his clerical prejudices.[422] He immediately wrote a brief treatise in praise of the *Roman*[423] and in March or April sent it to both Christine de Pisan and his master Pierre d'Ailly.[424] Jean de Montreuil was right to send his treatise to two people familiar with the work of Jean de Meun, but he was wrong to expect them to approve. Christine de Pisan became incensed, and in June or July responded with a defense of women's honor and the rights of courtly love. Thus began a celebrated dispute that would agitate Parisian literary circles for the next two years. The dispute also touched a broader audience, for the issue was one of the utmost importance: love, marriage, and women. Pierre d'Ailly for his part never answered Jean de Montreuil directly. He remained aloof from the controversy. He did, however, make an indirect response that must have been quite disappointing to the royal notary-secretary. It revealed how close the bishop of Cambrai was at this point to his disciple Jean Gerson.

Jean Gerson quickly overcame the discouragement that had caused him briefly to consider resigning his position as chancellor. By the fall of 1400 he was back in Paris. He had resumed his teaching duties and was preaching and writing. But Gerson's instruction and preaching had taken a new turn. As he grew older and gained familiarity with the works of Jan van Ruysbroeck, who had died in 1381 at the age of eighty-seven after demonstrating a mystical technique for submerging the self in divine beatitude,[425] the chancellor had turned away from scholastic theology and toward mystical theology. At the university he taught a course on the spiritual life of the soul (*De vita spirituali animae*). He had also become more and more preoccupied with the Christian education of "simple folk." He was increasingly anxious to preach, and to preach in French.[426] Nevertheless, it was in a Latin sermon delivered at the College of Navarre for the festival of Saint Louis (August 25, 1401) that Jean Gerson for the first time took a position in the controversy over the *Roman de la Rose.* "The preceptor," he said, "often must take the side of decency and goodness against those who not only dare out of patent immodesty to name the shameful parts of the body and the most abominable sins but, out of still more indecent audacity, defend themselves by saying that the personage Reason exhorted them to do so, oblivious of the fact that in so doing they fall into the error of the Beghards and Turlupins, who believed that one ought not to be ashamed of anything given by nature."[427] Gerson's allusion proves that his audience in that summer of 1401 was stirred up by the debate over the *Roman.* It also indicates which side Gerson was on. Along with Christine de Pisan he was one of those who condemned the *Roman de la Rose,* but not for the same reasons as she did. Gerson attacked the exaltation of natural love and the mockery of marriage and chastity. A few months later, in 1402, he made two more substantial contributions to the debate in the form of a treatise and a letter. He attacked the defenders of a poem that encouraged illegitimate love and unrestrained lust.[428] The series of sermons entitled *Poenitemini,* which Gerson delivered in French to the parishioners of Saint-Germain-l'Auxerrois and Saint-Jean-en-Grève between December 1402 and March 1403, examined the seven deadly sins and dealt at length with lust and chastity; it was a last, ringing response to what was more than a mere literary controversy.[429]

Pierre d'Ailly closely followed his illustrious disciple's evolution. One day he attended one of Gerson's lectures on the spiritual life of the soul. Later, in 1402, Gerson sent his former master the text of the full year's course of lectures, in which he had attempted to lay the theological foundation for a doctrine of contemplation. He told Pierre d'Ailly how moved he and his students had been to see his former teacher in the hall. The whole faculty had been struck dumb. The theology faculty's leading light, the learned doctor, the illustrious prelate had deigned to lower himself. It was as if the sun had gone begging light from a star, as if the ocean had gone begging water from a river. But the bishop of Cambrai took an active interest in his pupil's lectures,[430] particularly since Ruysbroeck had been abbot of Groenendael near Brussels, a monastery located in his diocese.[431]

Thus when Pierre d'Ailly received Jean de Montreuil's letter in the spring of 1401, he was well versed, as were all clerics, in the Song of Songs, and he was also familiar with the *Roman de la Rose* and initiated into the mystical currents that had begun to course through the age. He did not answer Jean directly. But a few weeks after receiving his letters, and a short while before Gerson made his own first allusion to the affair, Pierre d'Ailly wrote in French *Le jardin amoureux de l'âme dévote* (The Devout Soul's Garden of Love). In a tone reminiscent of the *Song of Songs* Pierre d'Ailly followed the structure of the *Roman de la Rose* but transformed the fountain of Narcissus into a fountain of grace, the orchard of love into a garden of Christ, and carnal love into love of God. He even quoted the *Roman de la Rose* to the effect that "amorous law or the art of love is herein contained in full" but exhorted "law-abiding lovers" to shun "the perilous school" and call upon "true students of love" to love God.[432] Thus Pierre d'Ailly did not intervene in the dispute; rather, by a discreet but effective inversion of the *Roman,* he was able to speak of the one true love, the love of God.

A sincere Christian, Pierre d'Ailly was also a conscientious prelate. He preached often in his diocese, just as Jean Gerson did in Paris. He spoke in Latin to his clerics in synods. He spoke in French to laymen, and in Cambrai pious hands copied out the texts of his sermons.[433] Pierre exhorted his flock, and especially his clerics, not to sin. It was a simple fact that a sinful cleric could not count on the layman's respect and obedience.[434] Pierre d'Ailly was therefore an ardent proponent of a moral reform of the clergy. Suppose, however, that the man in authority continued to sin; was disobedience justified for that reason alone? That was the question that Pierre d'Ailly had long been asking himself, and it was more than ever the question of the day, following the withdrawal of obedience and the deposition of the English monarch.

As it happens, Pierre d'Ailly was one of the first men on the Continent to discover Richard Fitz Ralph, whose works he had initially encountered in the 1370s.[435] Fitz Ralph had been vice-chancellor of the University of Oxford and had died archbishop of Armagh in Ireland in 1360.[436] His fundamental theory was that a man in a state of mortal sin could not exercise just authority (*Peccans mortaliter est . . . indignus dominio*).[437] This, Pierre d'Ailly repeatedly affirmed, was an absurd position, for any man was capable of sin. God in his "sovereign mastery" had willed that even the greatest men should sometimes sin: "He made a poor fisherman the sovereign pastor of his holy Church (Peter). He made a public sinner his evangelist and authentic doctor of his holy Scripture (Matthew). He made his greatest persecutor the greatest preacher of his holy doctrine (Paul)."[438] Hence any authority could be challenged. Pierre d'Ailly was simply invoking the most authentic Christian tradition when he said that all authority comes from God and that it is not based on the worthiness or unworthiness of the person who exercises it. Therefore one can exhort men of authority not to sin, but if they persist in error one must exhort their subjects to demonstrate obedience. Like Philippe de Mézières, Nicolas de Clamanges, and Jean Gerson, Pierre d'Ailly was a devoted follower of "Dame Obedience."[439] The first duty of all Christians was to "be true sons of obedience."[440] Hence it was inevitable that the withdrawal of obedience would signal hard times for the bishop of Cambrai and his friends. Late in 1402 or early in 1403 Pierre d'Ailly wrote his *Tractatus de materia concilii generalis.* To help resolve the schism he was willing to tolerate the idea of a council. But he did not see this council as anything more than a council of the Church of Avignon, and it was to be convoked only after Benedict XIII had been restored as head of that church.[441]

The withdrawal of obedience had in fact proved disappointing. Benedict XIII remained intransigent. There seemed no way out of the impasse. Thanks to the determination of the duke of Orléans, the assent of the king in a moment of lucidity, and the resignation of the other principals in the affair, France reinstated its obedience to the pope. Letters ordering the restitution of obedience were dispatched on May 28, 1403. On May 30 high mass was celebrated at Notre-Dame in the presence of the king and the dukes. Pierre d'Ailly, back in Paris, commented in French on the royal decision. On June 4, during the great procession for the Monday of Pentecost,

Jean Gerson also spoke out. In this atmosphere of concord, the chancellor felt comfortable celebrating the end of dissension in the Church of France, the rapprochement of the dukes of Berry, Burgundy, and Orléans, the imminent restoration of unity, and, last but not least, the dawn of reform.[442] In this enthusiastic climate of reconciliation, the university could make no more generous gesture than to restore the rights of those unwaveringly loyal partisans of Benedict XIII, the Dominicans. The chancellor declared that he had always deplored the excessive measures of 1389. The Dominicans resumed their teaching.[443] In the summer of 1403 Nicolas de Clamanges returned from Avignon.[444] In September Pierre d'Ailly served as the king's ambassador to Benedict XIII. Rather than exhort the pope on behalf of the king, he offered warm words of congratulation.[445] It was as though a bad dream had ended. Once again French clerics could obey both the pope and the king. With this dual obedience they regained their confidence.

The Assembly of 1406

The moment was fleeting, however. Benedict XIII did so little of what was expected of him, so little of what the duke of Orléans had thought he would do, that in the eyes of the clergy, the duke's uncles, and even the king the duke seemed to have been duped. The reinstatement of apostolic taxes came as a painful surprise to the clergy. With the levy of a new *décime,* or special tithe on the clergy, and the determination that all clerics, even those such as academics who were usually exempt, should be obliged to pay it, the pope alienated an already hostile University of Paris. Growing numbers of clerics with troubled consciences began to ask whether the restitution of obedience in 1403 had been strictly legal.[446] In another development, Philip the Bold, the duke of Burgundy, died on April 27, 1404, at the age of sixty-two. The accession of his thirty-three-year-old son, the young and ebullient John the Fearless, augured trouble ahead for France. The storm came on quickly.

Bold initiatives by John the Fearless in the summer of 1405, followed by Louis of Orléans's countermoves, brought France to the brink of civil war. In November 1405 academics protested the collection of the *décime,* from which Benedict XIII steadfastly refused to exempt them, by suspending classes. They ended their strike early in 1406, although their hostility to the pope and the duke of Orléans remained as fierce as ever.[447] A few months later, the university, meeting in plenary assembly, solemnly declared that it considered the ordinance of restitution of obedience to be null and void; the withdrawal of obedience of 1398 remained in effect, and subjects of France were not obliged to obey Benedict.[448]

The university, whose spokesmen were now Pierre Plaoul, Jean Petit, and Pierre Cauchon, faced a new period of turmoil. Pierre Plaoul, born in Liège and a near contemporary of Pierre d'Ailly, had been in his youth the right-hand man of chancellor Jean Blanchard. He had earned his doctorate in theology in 1394. In 1406 he was just past fifty and at the height of his powers. For more than ten years his powerful and indefatigable eloquence had made him one of the university's leading spokesmen. He was also a vehement proponent of the *voie de cession* and withdrawal of obedience. He was one of the staunchest supporters of Simon de Cramaud, the duke of Berry's man and obstinate architect of the withdrawal. There is no reason to think that Pierre Plaoul was especially fond of Pierre d'Ailly, the man who twenty years earlier had brought down Jean Blanchard. As for Jean Petit, he was a much younger man, barely forty, and a former student of Pierre Plaoul. He had just begun to distinguish himself as an actor of the first rank in university assemblies.[449] For a long time he had been a protégé of the duke of Burgundy. Between him and Pierre d'Ailly there was not the slightest bond, either of age or of ideas. Pierre Cauchon was even younger than Jean Petit. Born near Rheims in 1371, he was thirty-five and had a master of arts and licentiate in canon law. He was already rector of the university, at the beginning of a brilliant career that was brought to an end by his sudden death on December 18, 1442, when he was bishop of Lisieux and seventy-one years old.[450]

The university at first chose an indirect way of attacking the restitution of obedience. It conceived the idea of going to Parlement to challenge the 1401 letter in which the University of Toulouse had condemned the withdrawal of obedience. On May 27, 1406, a delegation led by Pierre Cauchon submitted to Parlement two letters from Charles VI mandating the court to find in favor of the University of Paris and the royal prosecutor concerning a "certain injurious epistle written and sent by the University of Toulouse at the time of the withdrawal and to the detriment of the honor of the king, his council, his kingdom, and the aforementioned university."[451] That same day Pierre Plaoul delivered a long speech in Latin to the court. Jean Petit spoke after him. The court invited both men to come argue their case a few days later but to do so in French, "because the case is important, substantial, and noteworthy, and it is expedient that everyone hear and understand." It was necessary to speak French "because not all who attend the session to hear the arguments understand Latin."[452] On June 7 Pierre Plaoul therefore resumed his presentation in French, and one of his major concerns was to explain to the king's counselors why obedience to the pope and obedience to the king of France had nothing in common and why disobedience to the pope in no way authorized disobedience to the king: "The king's customary relation to his people [*habitude à son peuple*] is different from that of the pope to his Church. The king is lord of his subjects; the pope is not lord of the Church, but minister. For the Church is confirmed in faith, in which it does not err. The pope, however, may err. . . . Furthermore, the king is not subject to the people, but the pope is subject to the Church, for he is pope by election and not by succession."[453]

Jean Petit spoke next with his customary familiarity, not to say vulgarity. He began by excusing himself for his youth. He was "summoned to speak between Master Plaoul, doctor of theology, and Master J. Jouvenel, *advocat du roy,* as if he were an ass between two angels, which astounded him, for at a time when he knew nothing and was still wet behind the ears, Plaoul was one of the great clerics of Paris and licensed him in arts, and Jouvenel too was already a noteworthy man . . . and [he] said that he was like the bad horse placed in the middle" of the team. At length he came to the substance of the case. There had been a restitution, he argued, only because Benedict, finding himself in dire straits, without resources, and cornered, had made certain promises. The pope had yielded only "when he saw that his fat was in the fire." Now, however, it was obvious that Benedict XIII had not kept his promises.[454]

On September 11, 1406, the usually more deliberate Parlement rendered a judgment favorable to the university.[455] The case of the Toulouse epistle had already receded into the background, however, because in August a new assembly of the Church of France had been called for All Saints' Day. Once again the assembly was to decide whether or not France ought to continue to obey the pope.[456] The air was thick with pressure and violence. Still, the misfortunes that befell Elie de Lestrange in August 1406 were no accident. Elie was then sixty-six. He had succeeded Pierre d'Ailly as bishop of Le Puy and had had some insulting things to say about his predecessor. Though an enemy of Pierre d'Ailly, the irascible sexagenarian was not on good terms with the enemies of the bishop of Cambrai; having been for many years an ardent defender of Benedict XIII, he had incurred the implacable hostility of the duke of Berry. One night in August, some of the duke's men went to the bishop of Le Puy's Paris hôtel for the purpose of spiriting away "a young girl whom people said the bishop was keeping." When the bishop came to the window to see what the men wanted, an arrow was fired at him. The men then broke down the door and entered the hôtel shouting, "Kill everyone!" They threatened the bishop, stuck a bare sword under his chin, extracted from him a promise to pay a thousand écus, and left, taking with them as a token of this pledge "a bible, breviary, belt, and other small items," as well as the girl. The offenders were incarcerated, but the duke of Berry immediately intervened. On September 1, a delegation from Parlement screwed up its courage and appealed to the high council composed of the dukes of Berry, Orléans, Burgundy, and Bourbon; the magistrates pointed out "that [the duke's intervention] was contrary to the rights and honor of the king, who is this very day confined and ill behind locked doors, and that it was an obstruction of justice, even in the city of Paris, where many excesses are committed, and where everyone with impunity carries swords, daggers and knives, and various other arms in broad daylight." The delegation beseeched the dukes "not to obstruct justice," but in vain. The delinquents, provided with letters of remission, had to be released on September 2.[457]

The air was also thick with menacing theories. Everyone denounced the pope's exactions and foresaw the most dire consequences. These exactions, Jean Petit maintained, "support the tyranny of the pope, who extracts from the Church treasure and finance." Since the pope was a "tyrant," the "aforementioned payments and finances must be withdrawn." Another cleric argued that "whenever the pope . . . contravenes the just and reasonable law out of ambition or love of money, he sins mortally," and "in that case there is no need to obey the pope, and those who do obey him in such a case sin mortally."[458]

It was in this stormy atmosphere that the assembly of the Church called in August finally met in November and December 1406 and January 1407. The language of the assembly was French, as was to be expected since the clerics conducted their discussion in the presence of great lay lords.[459] The use of French posed a problem for certain speakers. At one point Pierre d'Ailly stated: "This matter is a high one and cannot be explained in the French tongue." And Pierre Le Roy, the abbot of Mont-Saint-Michel, begged forgiveness for his clumsiness in wielding the French language: "I would much rather have spoken in Latin. I am not accustomed to speaking French."[460] In 1406 Pierre d'Ailly was fifty-five. Pierre Le Roy, who was a doctor of canon law by 1379, was surely no younger.[461] Was this an accident? Or was it, rather, symptomatic, in a period of great progress in the use of the vernacular, that younger clerics expressed no similar scruples or embarrassment? The most remarkable thing about this assembly is that an anonymous auditor recorded not only the speeches but all the other statements, thus preserving an accurate account of the stormy and impassioned sessions. And these notes have survived.

The number of prelates who came to Paris and attended the sessions was never very high, and as usual it decreased with the passage of time.[462] But all the leading orators were present, except Gilles Des Champs, who was in Rome.[463] Simon de Cramaud opened fire on November 27 and spoke frequently thereafter; Guillaume Fillastre spoke on December 3 and again on December 7; Pierre Le Roy spoke on December 6; Pierre d'Ailly spoke on December 11; Pierre Plaoul on December 15 and 16; Jean Petit on December 17; and Jean Jouvenel, *advocat du roi,* spoke last, on December 20.[464]

The debate was a debate of ideas. Simon de Cramaud, Pierre Le Roy, Pierre Plaoul, Jean Petit, and Jean Jouvenel favored withdrawal of obedience. Guillaume Fillastre defended the pope. Pierre d'Ailly approved the *voie de cession* but only after a council had been held under the auspices of Avignon. For the time being, therefore, he refused to go along with a new withdrawal of obedience and defended the interests of Benedict XIII. Although I have not mentioned all the orators in the two camps, the relative strength of each side is accurately represented. Proponents of withdrawal constituted an overwhelming majority. They brought tremendous pressure to bear on their adversaries, all the more so in that they refused to allow adequate time for preparation of speeches.[465]

The shadow cast over the proceedings by the princes further accentuated the imbalance. The king's backing gave particular weight to the words of Jean Jouvenel. Everyone knew that the duke of Berry was behind Simon de Cramaud and that the duke of Burgundy was behind Jean Petit. Over adversaries of withdrawal hung a threat that was not even veiled, as Guillaume Fillastre knew full well. Admittedly he had overstepped his bounds. On December 7 the dean of Rheims began with a eulogy of Benedict XIII. Then, "wishing to establish with proofs drawn from history and law that kings could not strip the pope's authority but that, on the contrary, it was the pope's right to create and depose kings, he cited the example of King Pepin of France,"[466] and as his authority he invoked the *Liber pontificalis,* a history of the popes written in Rome.[467] An enormous outcry followed. The unlucky orator was refuted with citations from the *Chronicles of Saint-Denis,* the authentic history containing what all French subjects were certain was the truth. Four days later, on December 11, Guillaume Fillastre was obliged to concede that the French monarchy was an exception: "Sire, I know well that your seigneury is unlike any other. The Emperor holds his emperorship of the pope, but your kingdom is by inheritance . . . and you hold it of no one." Guillaume was then forced to plead for royal indulgence: "I am a poor man who was brought up in the fields, and by nature I am quite unpolished. I have not lived with kings or lords, whence I know not the manner or style of speaking in their presence." The royal chancellor's threats persisted, however: "My lord dean, the king has heard what you said the other day. When you spoke, my lord of Berry was present, and he was most displeased. He is not present here today. Monday he will be summoned."[468]

The adversaries of withdrawal were threatened not only by the princes but even more openly by the many clerics, mostly academics, who attended the debates. The university was passionately in favor of withdrawal. Adversaries faced a consistently hostile crowd, which the proponents of withdrawal knew how to exploit. On December 7, Guillaume Fillastre, exasperated by the reactions of ill-informed clerics, exploded: "The two thousand people still sitting out there have no idea where things are headed."[469] On December 11 Pierre d'Ailly argued that not the whole university but only the faculty of theology should have been consulted. On December 18 Jean Petit responded with a veritable comedy routine, allegedly parroting the words of his own supporters and appealing to the jealousy that obscure clerics felt toward illustrious doctors of theology: "He said that the faculty of medicine has no business intervening in this affair, which amazes me, and also the faculty of arts. Because first of all the faculty of arts has a thousand masters—someone in back here says two thousand. Well, anyway, there are a good thousand, of whom there are two or three hundred graduates in other sciences, such as bachelors of theology, medicine, and civil and canon law. So there are more graduates. A theologian belongs to the faculty of arts until he wears the cap on his head. And the cap brings him no knowledge. Someone in back here is telling me what to say. He is afraid I might forget. He tells me, and he is right, that there are plenty of mud-spattered priests who are quite adequate and excellent clerics. Knowledge increases in poverty sooner than in wealth."[470]

This astonishing scene suggests the full extent of the conflict between Pierre d'Ailly and Jean Petit. The debate between them was not simply a debate of ideas. Jean Petit's speeches were larded with personal attacks against Pierre d'Ailly, in part because it was in Petit's nature to make such attacks but also because the two men were spokesmen for two generations that clashed through them. In 1406 Simone de Cramaud had just turned sixty; Guillaume Fillastre would soon be sixty; Pierre Le Roy was scarcely younger; Pierre d'Ailly was fifty-five; and Pierre Plaoul was fifty-two. The leading participants in the assembly of 1406 could and did have different ideas. They could and did divide over old rancor and festering animosities. But they had at least one thing in common: they belonged to the same generation. For more than thirty years they had shared the same experiences and the same memories. And all were to one degree or another successful—all, that is, except Jean Petit, who was just forty and still at the beginning of his career and who could still speak for the obscure majority of university graduates. Ultimately Jean Petit could not help admiring Pierre d'Ailly: "I shall follow him so far as my limited abilities allow," he said as he set about refuting him, "as an ox follows a Calabrian courser, as a hen follows a hare. . . . Monseigneur de Cambrai spoke of many things most subtly, as he can do so well." At bottom, Jean Petit's dream was to become the dazzling leader of the university that Pierre d'Ailly had been in the 1380s. At one point he says that he has no desire to insult Monseigneur de Cambrai or anyone else, but that he must say what he has been delegated to say. "I am well aware that I was very young indeed when Monseigneur de Cambrai was already a very great and much appreciated noble cleric, and highly renowned, and owing to his self-confidence he was often delegated to make various propositions before my lords and other princes, things which were *magni ponderis* and quite dangerous to say, but he was obliged to do that which he was given responsibility for, and so now I am quite certain that it will not displease him at all if I say what I have been enjoined and delegated to say."[471] Pierre d'Ailly was a model for Jean Petit, a man whom Jean wished to emulate but whom he also detested. Jean Petit's voice gave vent to the hatred of youth for the older generation, of modest graduates for illustrious doctors, of poor clerics for wealthy prelates, of insignificant men for "great lords."

Pierre d'Ailly, who fifteen or twenty years earlier, when he was the idol of the university, had been so hard on his elders, had lost nothing of his pugnacity. Though "indisposed by a cold," deprived of his "accustomed volubility,"[472] and without sufficient time to prepare, he launched a powerful attack on Simon de Cramaud on December 11. On December 17 he was seen "rising to his feet" several times to respond to his young and vehement antagonist.[473] In Paris, however, the powerful prince of the Empire was now a man with few if any allies. Arrayed against him were the elderly duke of Berry and the youthful duke of Burgundy, along with his customary enemies, now triumphant, such as Pierre Plaoul and Simon de Cramaud. Against him, too, was the university, led by Jean Petit, with a whole generation of new adversaries so vehement that they decided to exclude from the university a man once idolized by a previous generation of academics.[474] In the midst of such deep hostility and tenacious hatred (and the hatred between Pierre d'Ailly and Jean Petit would continue until their dying day),[475] Pierre d'Ailly could count on his side only the duke of Orléans, powerless for the time being, and a few friends such as his faithful disciple Jean Gerson, still chancellor of the university. Gerson attended the assembly's sessions, but in this pitched battle the man of peace and concord never opened his mouth.[476]

Before dissolving in January 1407, the assembly voted. It did not, as Simon de Cramaud and the university wished, approve total withdrawal of obedience as in 1398, nor did it adopt, as Elie de Lestrange and Pierre d'Ailly advocated, a solution favorable to Benedict XIII. By a large majority it voted in favor of a partial withdrawal of obedience, under which the pope's authority would be recognized but the ancient liberties of the Church would also be reinstated. In other words, the pope was denied the right to award benefices and to tax the clergy.[477] This was the most satisfactory solution for clerics whose consciences had found it hard to deal with a headless Church but who were also exasperated by the pope's fiscal policies. It might also appear to be the most satisfactory solution for the papacy, whose authority was recognized. In fact, partial withdrawal of obedience posed a greater threat to the Universal Church than did total withdrawal. Total withdrawal signified nothing more than refusal to recognize the present pope and carried no implication concerning the future, whereas partial withdrawal actually established a national church subject to the remote authority of the pope.[478] The ordinances adopted on February 18, 1407, in accordance with the wishes of the assembly, marked the discreet triumph of Gallicanism.[479]

From the Embassy of 1407 to the Council of Pisa (1409)

Those ordinances, incidentally, were not immediately published, because Innocent VII, the pope of Rome, died on November 6, 1406.[480] His successor, Gregory XII, had promised to abdicate under certain conditions. The French government again conceived the hope that both popes would resign, as both claimed to be willing to do. The ordinances were therefore kept in reserve, and plans were made to send an embassy to Marseilles, where Benedict XIII was staying, and then on to Rome to see Gregory XII, in the hope that this might facilitate the double abdication.

This important embassy involved thirty-six individuals, an unusually large number. Most are by now familiar to us because for years their paths had crossed that of Pierre d'Ailly. Among them, in addition to Pierre d'Ailly himself, were Simon de Cramaud, the patriarch of Alexandria, and Pierre Le Roy, abbot of Mont-Saint-Michel; all three men were counted among those "who surpassed the others in authority" (*qui aliis auctoritate precellebant*). Also present were Gilles Des Champs, Pierre d'Ailly's successor as the king's chaplain, Dominique Petit, Jean Courtecuisse, Jean Gerson, Pierre Plaoul, and Jean Petit, "learned professors of theology renowned for their eloquence." In addition, there were Guillaume Fillastre, doctor of civil and canon law, Pierre Cauchon, licentiate in canon law, and Jacques de Nouvion, bachelor of theology.[481] The only familiar name not represented is that of Elie de Lestrange. Perhaps the reason for this was that he was too outspoken a partisan of Benedict XIII and had yet to recover from the trauma he suffered in August 1406. And then there was his age. Elie de Lestrange would attend the Council of Pisa in 1409 and even the Council of Constance in 1417, when he was seventy-seven, although it appears that he took no part in the work of the council.[482] In 1412 he was referred to as an old man (*vir etate grandevus*).[483] In 1408 he was sixty-eight and would have been the eldest member of the embassy. Simon de Cramaud was then sixty-two, and most of the others were in their fifties. The only members under fifty were Jean Gerson, who was forty-five, and Jean Petit, who was forty-two but who, through open combat, had just earned himself a place among the leading orators of the day, although he was hardly yet in a position to play an important part in this embassy. And let us not forget the two promising youths who would have to be included in any future embassies: Pierre Cauchon, then thirty-seven, and Jacques de Nouvion, approximately thirty-five.

Jacques de Nouvion was born some time between 1372 and 1374 in Nouvion-sur-Meuse in the diocese of Rheims.[484] It was only natural, therefore, that he should attend the College of Navarre, where he was a student of Nicolas de Clamanges. After earning his master of arts in 1392, he served as professor in the faculty of arts until 1403. According to his friends, he was a great teacher, another Plato or Aristotle, who knew and commented admirably well on the work of both the Stagirite and Cicero. In 1403 Jacques de Nouvion quit teaching and became secretary to the duke of Orléans. He and his friends Jean de Montreuil and Nicolas de Clamanges formed an exemplary trio. They were men of three distinct generations, for Jean was born in 1354, Nicolas in 1363, and Jacques ten years later. But

Nicolas and Jacques were bound by the very strong bond that exists between master and disciple, and all three men were associated with the College of Navarre. All were passionately interested in ancient culture, and all were secretaries, Jean of the king of France, Nicolas of the pope, and Jacques of the duke of Orléans. Clearly it was the duke who saw to it that his secretary was included in the embassy. And Jacques de Nouvion's role in that embassy was the one traditionally reserved for promising young men: he kept the diary. Jacques's promise was nipped in the bud, however, because his patron, the duke of Orléans, died a few months later and because he himself died prematurely, in 1411, before he had reached the age of forty. Nicolas de Clamanges mourned his friend, dead too young, in a beautiful elegy:

> Plange, quod hunc juvenem mors immatura peremit
> Rupit et ante diem stamina Parqua ferox.
>
> [Early death carried this young man off,
> and cruel Fate cut the thread before it was time.][485]

The ambassadors left Paris after Easter (which fell on March 27, 1407). They traveled in small groups, which departed on different days.[486] They had clashed too violently only a few months earlier, and antipathies among them were too strong, to have made the prospect of traveling together an appealing one. They all met, however, on April 30, 1407, at Villeneuve-lès-Avignon, and all were received by Benedict XIII in Marseilles on May 9.[487] Agreement among the ambassadors at that time was greater than some may have feared. With the exception of the one outspoken partisan of Benedict XIII, namely, Guillaume Fillastre, who played no role, the other members of the French delegation found that, once removed from Parisian passions, and with the problem of withdrawal of obedience, over which they once had clashed, now behind them, all were fundamentally united by the hope that both popes would agree to resign in order to pave the way for a resolution of the schism. The only difference was that one group, led by Simon de Cramaud, wanted to take a firm line with Benedict XIII, while the other, led by Pierre d'Ailly, counseled patience. All were ready to collaborate in an effort to persuade the two popes, Benedict XIII in Marseilles and Gregory XII in Rome, first to meet and then to resign.

The two popes—both nearing the grave (Benedict XIII was eighty, while Gregory XII was at least seventy and nothing but skin and bones),[488] both pious, and both convinced that the salvation of the Church depended on their firmness, not to say obstinacy—were willing to make promises and raise hopes, but in the end they were prepared to agree about only one thing: their unwillingness to surrender. On May 19, Benedict XIII, secretly informed of the ordinances of withdrawal that the French government had drafted on February 18 but not published, ordered the drafting of a bull in which he excommunicated all who withdrew their obedience; he kept the text of that bull on his person.[489] For months both popes toyed with the embassy, making detailed plans for a meeting that was repeatedly postponed. Faced with such obstinacy, Simon de Cramaud and those such as Gilles Des Champs, Pierre Plaoul, and Jean Petit who shared his ideas were ready to take a firmer line with Benedict XIII and prepared to recommend publication of the ordinances of withdrawal. Pierre d'Ailly, who had suffered so much for his decision to handle the pope with circumspection, found himself in a far more difficult position. On May 21, two days after Benedict XIII had secretly drafted his bull of excommunication, Pierre d'Ailly along with Jean Gerson and Jacques de Nouvion drafted a memorandum recommending that withdrawal of obedience be delayed still further.[490] The embassy supported this view. The more time passed, however, the more fresh difficulties the embassy encountered, until finally its failure was obvious. For Pierre d'Ailly it was a dramatic moment. He became painfully aware that the only way to resolve the schism, as Simon de Cramaud had long insisted, was the *voie de cession,* but that, contrary to what he, Pierre, had long hoped, neither of the two popes would ever agree to surrender. Little by little Pierre d'Ailly resigned himself to disobey. He resigned himself to the necessity of demanding, rather than asking for, the pope's resignation. He first took a firmer line with Gregory XII. In Rome on July 28, 1407, when the Roman pope raised legal objections to the suggestion of resignation, the bishop of Cambrai responded: "In absolute terms such a course may not be in compliance with the law, but the present circumstances are such that this expedient must be used."[491] On January 26, 1408, after months of maneuvering, expectations, and disappointments, Pierre d'Ailly, preparing to leave Genoa yet again, wrote to Benedict XIII. Pierre was now certain that Gregory XII would never resign. "In these circumstances," he wrote, "and in order to avoid the evils that I foresee, there are three useful remedies. The first is a constitution, which would guarantee union in case one of the pretenders should die." (It must have come as a painful surprise to Benedict XIII to find himself placed on the same plane as the pope of Rome.) "The second is a general council, of your obedience, to be convoked as soon as possible." (This was the solution that Pierre d'Ailly, virtually alone, had been advocating for several years.) "As for the third, I shall say nothing about it now, because it cannot be used without the consent of the council."[492] This solution, which Pierre d'Ailly did not even dare mention to Benedict XIII and which he had been rejecting for years, was obviously the deposition of the pope of Avignon—the revolt of the body against the head. This was the last contact between the pope and the bishop. In closing his letter, Pierre d'Ailly once again professed his devotion to Benedict XIII. In his own eyes the change in his position was not yet definitive. His friends as yet suspected nothing. Hated by the university for having taken so long to divorce himself from Benedict XIII, Pierre nevertheless had begun to admit to himself that he might not follow the pontiff all the way to the end of his rope.

Upon returning to France, Pierre d'Ailly found a situation that recent, tragic events had rendered confused and menacing. In Paris in September 1407 John the Fearless and Louis d'Orléans found themselves pitted against each other in the king's council. Benedict XIII was only one of the issues dividing these implacable foes. Their hatred had reached fever pitch, and armed conflict once again seemed possible.[493]

On October 16, 1407, the provost of Paris, Guillaume de Tignonville, ordered the arrest of two clerics, "sons" of the University of Paris, who no one denied were men "of notoriously dissolute and dishonest reputation." Then, defying the privileges of the Church and the university and renewing the challenge of Hugues Aubriot, he had the two men judged, sentenced them to be hanged, and in fact hanged them "publicly and in broad daylight." The crowd that gathered said: "Here is a clear sign that from now on scholars and regulars will be punished the same as seculars."[494] Many were no doubt pleased at the news, but ecclesiastics were outraged at this violation of their privileges.

On November 23, 1407, after several days' apparent reconciliation between the two rival princes, the duke of Burgundy caused the duke of Orléans to be assassinated on the streets of Paris in the early evening. This assassination caused stupefaction and outrage. The historian's first impulse is to treat it as an unprecedented act, but on reflection our initial surprise must necessarily diminish. The year is 1407. Violence was an everyday occurrence. Civil war was smoldering. Worse still, violence was not an innovation of that year or that generation. John, duke of Berry, and Philip the Bold, duke of Burgundy, passed for wise old heads compared with the youths who succeeded them. But in August 1406 John of Berry had at least tacitly approved, if not instigated, the attack on Elie de Lestrange. In early 1398 Philip of Burgundy would have been glad if his agents had killed Pierre d'Ailly. Since the beginning of Charles VI's reign the greatest personages in France had confessed their fear of the king's uncles, and that fear was in the first place fear of physical violence. And the king's uncles were not the only fearsome princes. In 1392 the duke of Brittany had encouraged Pierre de Craon to assassinate Olivier de Clisson, the constable of France. The attempt failed. By contrast, thirty-eight years earlier, on January 8, 1354, Charles and Philippe de Navarre successfully assassinated Olivier de Clisson's predecessor, the constable Charles of Spain. The minute he knew his orders had been successfully carried out, Charles, king of Navarre, "had sent sealed letters to several of the good cities of the kingdom of France, and also to the Great Council of the King, in which he wrote that he had ordered the constable put to death for several high crimes that the constable had committed against him." And on January 11, 1354, Charles de Navarre claimed responsibility for the assassination of the constable and justified it in a letter to the citizens of Rheims: "Know that . . . we have caused the death of this Charles . . . and if perchance my lord the King is at first somewhat troubled by this deed, to which we were compelled by weighty reasons, we are certain that, if he does not receive bad counsel, he will feel great joy when he has thought it over well."[495] In ordering the assassination of the duke of Orléans, then, John the Fearless was hardly an innovator. Nor was he innovating when, shortly thereafter, encouraged by the favor of the populace, he attempted to justify the deed.

Was the assassination of the duke of Orléans an act of hatred? Or was it a consequence of cold calculation? Did the duke of Burgundy see it as the only possible resolution of a difficult political situation? In any case, the political results were greatly to his liking. The duke remained, after a moment of doubt, in control of the court. The Orléans party, and therefore the party of Benedict XIII, was reduced to impotence. On January 12, 1408, the king solemnly announced that if, by next Ascension (May 24), the Church was not governed by a single pope, he would declare himself to be neutral; that is, as far as Benedict XIII was concerned, he would execute the ordinance of withdrawal of January 1407.[496]

Thus by the end of January 1408, when Pierre d'Ailly set out for home, the affairs of the Church were coming to a climax. The assassination of the duke of Orléans, and even more the duke of Burgundy's determination to justify it, deeply troubled many consciences. A bitter civil war between the partisans of the duke of Burgundy and the avengers of the duke of Orléans lay in the offing. It appeared inevitable that the bishop of Liège, John of Bavaria, was headed for a clash with his rebellious subjects; John the Fearless would be obliged to come to the aid of his brother-in-law the bishop. In Paris all talk was of the bitter battle between the provost on one side and the bishop and university on the other. For the time being this was the primary concern of the chancellor, Jean Gerson. The times were so dark that Pierre d'Ailly felt growing anxiety about his diocese. He returned to Cambrai.

Soon thereafter, the storms presaged by so many gathering clouds finally deluged Paris. The year 1408 was a terrible one. On January 2 John the Fearless chose Jean Petit (who must have fumed throughout 1407 over the minor role he had been assigned to play in the embassy) to justify the assassination of the duke of Orléans.[497] On March 8, in the great hall of the hôtel Saint-Paul, before an audience composed of, among others, "royal" princes, "lords of Parlement and others of the king's council," representatives of the university, and Parisian burghers, at ten in the morning, Jean Petit began to speak. He spoke for four hours, elaborating on the proposition "*Radix omnium malorum cupiditas*" (Greed is the root of all evil).[498] He wove his speech around a very simple syllogism. It is legitimate and meritorious to put to death a man who is truly a tyrant, a traitor guilty of lèse-majesté. The duke of Orléans was truly a traitor and a tyrant. Hence the duke of Burgundy had performed a legitimate and meritorious act in ordering that the duke of Orléans be killed.[499]

It is true that many authors, from Aristotle onward, had found it natural that a tyrant, by nature a man of violence, should die by violence. Cicero went further still. Caesar's enemy rejoiced in the tyrant's death. It was not just permissible but also meritorious to kill him.[500] And Cicero had had readers throughout the Middle Ages. His opinion had been echoed in the twelfth century by John of Salisbury in his *Policraticus.* At the turn of the fifteenth century both the *Policraticus* and its translations and Cicero's *De officiis* and its translations were avidly read. In France the tyrant's murder was a fine theme for literature. In Italy at around the same time the murder of Caesar was the subject of a lively debate within the small circle of Florentine humanists. But Jean Petit, who in 1407 traveled only to Rome, was apparently uninfluenced by this debate, and his purely French cultural background was enough to enable him to evoke Caesar's assassination by Brutus, the murder of any number of Jewish kings in the Bible, and Lucifer's demise at the hands of Saint Michael, who could show no greater "sign of love, reverence, subjection, and obedience to the one who had made him, who was his creator, king, and sovereign lord," than by performing this act.[501]

In these terms Jean Petit was able to justify the crime of November 23. But a literary debate is one thing; the justification of a recent murder is another. What is more, Jean Petit was able to make his case only by confounding the death of a tyrant (a question in dispute among authorities) with the murder of a man who was merely a great lord of the kingdom of France. Audacious though he may have been, the orator was not on the firmest ground in the first part of his speech.

In the second part, in which he tried to blacken the reputation of the duke of Orléans, he was more comfortable. Here his task was easier. The duke had had obvious faults. His ambition, his greed, his prodigality, and his lust were known to all. Jean Petit spoke of these defects with indulgence. In a striking contrast, however, this great sinner was also a pious man. He had been particularly devoted to the Celestines, for whom he had built a chapel in the Church of their Paris monastery, where he had been buried after his tragic death.[502] During his lifetime he had frequently visited the monastery to converse with Philippe de Mézières, who had died there in 1405 at the age of nearly eighty. Thus it was not mere political calculation but a religious and cultural bond that had drawn into the duke's camp the devout Celestines, the partisans of Benedict XIII, and the humanists—in short, all those who constituted Pierre d'Ailly's microcosm.[503] In order to blacken the name of Louis d'Orléans, Jean Petit was obliged to tarnish everything that his adversary of 1406 held dear. No doubt he did so without displeasure. Philippe de Mézières was, for Jean Petit, a "false hypocrite." The duke of Orléans "at the Celestines . . . daily listened to five or six masses out of very great devotion, or so it seemed, but it was false hypocrisy and sham. For under cover of this" piety, the duke and Philippe met "in a chapel and conversed, plotted, and planned."[504]

Jean Petit's words surprised, outraged, and scandalized many people. But for the time being no one said a word. The common people of the kingdom supported the duke of Burgundy, and the duke was powerful. No one condemned his crime, and this "seemed very strange to some notable persons and clerics," according to Juvénal des Ursins. "But no one was bold enough to dare state the contrary."[505] Pierre d'Ailly was not in Paris but in Cambrai. On April 28 he was actually in Rheims to attend a council called by the archbishop.[506] All the while he said nothing about a justification for an assassination that must have troubled him to the depths of his soul. Jean Gerson, for his part, was in Paris, but he said nothing either. For the chancellor was wholly occupied with the university's case against Guillaume de Tignonville, in which Gerson was supported by the duke of Burgundy. On April 30 Guillaume was *désappointé* (relieved) of his duties as provost of Paris.[507] A few days later, the bodies of the two scholars were publicly cut down from the gallows more than six months after their execution and taken to the parvis of Notre-Dame to be returned to the bishop of Paris and the rector of the university.[508] In reality, the university was not pleased, for although the two bodies had been cut down, Guillaume de Tignonville had not been condemned as Hugues Aubriot had been.[509] The king even appointed him *maître extraordinaire* in the Chambre des Comptes. On May 14, however, the affair was quickly forgotten, as the university's passions took a new direction.

May 14, 1408, was the day when word of the bull of excommunication that Benedict XIII had ordered to be drafted on May 19, 1407, became known in Paris. For a long time the pope had kept the bull on his person, but now, a few days before Ascension, the deadline specified in the royal letters of January 12, 1408, he judged that the moment had come to communicate its contents to the king of France. The news caused quite a stir. The very next day Parlement published the ordinances of February 18, 1407. On May 21, within the enclosure of the Palace of La Cité, in the open air, in the presence of the king, the dukes, and an enormous crowd, Jean Courtecuisse spoke on behalf of the university and asked that the papal bull be torn to shreds. The king agreed, and the bull was immediately shredded.[510] Then, on May 25, the day after Ascension, a new ordinance proclaimed the neutrality of the king and his people. As long as the schism lasted, France would not obey either of the "contenders."[511] Meanwhile, persecution of Benedict's supporters had already begun. Several prelates who responded to the king's summons were arrested. Pierre d'Ailly, among those summoned, stayed put in Cambrai.[512]

It was probably during this period of prudent retirement that the indefatigable Pierre found the time to write the life of Celestine V that his Celestine friends had requested of him. In it he displayed the ardent desire to reform the Church and the deep love of country he shared with the Celestines. He praised the humility of Celestine V. He vehemently denounced the pride and ambition of Boniface VIII. And he showed signs of his private irritation with Benedict XIII. "Alas, this example of honorable humility [set by Celestine V] should have been imitated by those who, in these times of misery and suffering, have done all they could to attain this supreme honor. Then the Church would not have been riven for thirty years by their horrible discord and disastrous schism."[513] In condemning Boniface VIII and defending the resignation of Celestine V, Pierre was not simply recounting a safely historical event in a manner designed to please the king of France. He was stating what people in his own day had a right to expect from a pope who was truly humble, from a pontiff not driven by pride and ambition. Pierre's criticism of Boniface VIII was harsh, all the more so because he hoped that the blows struck against Boniface might move Benedict XIII, to whom Celestine V, through his biographer's vexed pen, showed the *voie de cession,* the way of surrender.

While Pierre d'Ailly, entrenched in Cambrai, mulled over bitter memories of his failed embassy, his friend Nicolas de Clamanges came under sharp attack. In January 1408 Nicolas, still serving as papal secretary, was with Benedict XIII on the Ligurian coast. He learned of the royal letters on January 12, at the same time as Pierre d'Ailly. Sensing, like Pierre, that the storm was about to break, he left the pope in February and headed for France. He was aware, however, that the climate there was quite hostile toward him, and in early May, foreseeing dark times ahead, he attempted to exchange certain of his French prebends for benefices situated outside the kingdom. He had even mentioned his plans in a letter to friends in Paris. After the dramatic events of the last two weeks of May, Nicolas de Clamanges became the primary target of the Parisian academics' fury. He was charged with having personally written the notorious papal bull of May 19, 1407, or at least with having had knowledge of it; of having compiled a list of academics hostile to Benedict XIII; and of having spread rumors detrimental to Simon de Cramaud, rumors alleging that he aspired to become pope. And to add insult to injury, the letter that Nicolas sent to Parisian friends in May was made public.[514]

In the summer of 1408 Nicolas de Clamanges faced his accusers, but from a distance. He entered France but remained outside of Paris. We find him dispatching letters first from Avignon, then from Langres. Later, out of prudence, he began to write from "a nameless place" (*Datum in loco sine nomine*).[515] Subsequent letters omit any mention of the place of writing. From his remote and unidentified residences Nicolas wrote frequently. He alerted all his friends. He asked them for what any friend has a right to expect, namely, for help against his persecutors and for a port in a storm.[516] He did not hesitate to write to men, such as Jacques de Nouvion, who were younger than himself and whom he had helped, asking that they now help him. In all these letters, moreover, he attempted to justify his actions.[517]No, he had not written the bull of May 19, 1407. His responses to the other charges were, truth to tell, less firm, but he defended himself with the greatest energy against the charge of having written the bull. Why would such a task have been assigned to him? Why would he have accepted it? He was French, born in France (*francus eram, et regni indigena*).[518] He had no wish to injure the majesty of his country, his kingdom, or his king (*patriae, reipublicae, regine majestatis violator*).[519] He had been papal secretary during a time when the king of France had recognized Benedict XIII, but the moment he had learned, in January 1408, of the change in the king's position, he had not wasted an instant in leaving the pope and returning to the kingdom where he had been born and where he wished to live and die, if his enemies permitted it (*sine ulla cunctatione regnum . . . hoc repetere statui, ubi et originem duxi et vivere etiam ac mori, si per emulos licuerit, est animus*).[520] How dare anyone treat in this way the man who had contributed so much to the rebirth of eloquence in France?[521] He had never used that eloquence but for the honor and glory of France.[522] But envy was the order of the day. The Savior had spoken the truth: "*Non est propheta sine honore nisi in patria sua*" (Matt. 13:57: "A prophet is not without honor, save in his own country").[523] Nicolas ardently proclaimed his love of country, all the more ardently no doubt because his benefices lay within the kingdom's boundaries. He was returning to France in part because that was where his fortune lay. Calculation was no doubt mingled with sentiment, yet sentiment was surely present. Nicolas de Clamanges, Jean de Montreuil, Jean Gerson, and Pierre d'Ailly (among others) had many things in common, but one of those things was an ardent love of country. This feeling, which a few years later would unite them against the English, could, now that it was time to choose between country and pope, have only one effect: to estrange them from Benedict XIII. In part the construction of a national church was a matter of important monetary interests. It was also a sign of national feeling. Since it was necessary to choose between pope and king, French clerics, at least those in the northern part of the kingdom, chose the king.

In any event, Nicolas de Clamanges's efforts were not in vain. Time passed. The storm abated. And Nicolas soon recovered his tranquility, first at the charterhouse of Valprofonde, near Sens,[524] then at the Augustinian priory of Fontaine-au-Bois, near Provins, where he found himself as early as October 1408 and would remain until 1417.[525] But the summer of 1408, so painful for Nicolas de Clamanges, was also painful for his friend Pierre d'Ailly. In order to govern the Church of France during the period of neutrality, the kingdom's prelates were summoned to Paris, where they met on August 11.[526] Several did not come, however, and once again Pierre d'Ailly chose to remain in Cambrai. He excused himself "on account of the need to care for the gout and other maladies." Whereupon the king, "at the instigation and behest of some hateful and malevolent people," ordered Waleran of Luxemburg, count of Saint-Pol, to seize and imprison Pierre d'Ailly "wherever [he might] be found . . . except for holy places, whether in our realm or outside it." Waleran of Luxemburg, the power in the region, was a close ally of the duke of Burgundy, so it seems clear who inspired the king's letter. With the duke of Burgundy hatred was hereditary. But Pierre d'Ailly escaped John the Fearless as he had escaped Philip the Bold. Waleran of Luxemburg went to Cambrai to execute the royal letter, but his behavior roused the city, for "this town [was] not in our kingdom and [was] directly subject to the Empire." The bishop, protected by his subjects, evaded Waleran's grasp.[527]

Within a few days, everything had changed. The duke of Burgundy was obliged to head north to rescue his brother-in-law the bishop of Liège. His absence from Paris left the coast clear. Between August 26 and 28, the queen, the dauphin, the duke of Berry, the duchess of Orléans, and all her supporters returned to the capital.[528]

The first consequence of this change was that a solemn assembly met in the Louvre on September 11. Most of those who had heard Jean Petit's justification of assassination on March 8 were in attendance as Thomas, abbot of Cerisy, undertook to present a lengthy refutation. The abbot of Cerisy was a respectable man in his sixties. He spoke eloquently and had no difficulty refuting the first part of Jean Petit's case. Had Jean Petit spoken the truth, it would have been too easy to kill any prince on the grounds that he was a tyrant.[529] It was more difficult to celebrate the victim's virtues. Nevertheless, Thomas stressed one extenuating circumstance that Jean Petit had been careful to omit: the duke of Orléans had been a young man. Of course he had sinned. But in essence he was a good man. God had given him "prudence and intelligence." He was a "good and loyal Christian," and it was easy to prove "the devotion he had to God, even in his youth, for notwithstanding games and amusements, he nevertheless always returned to God and went frequently to confession. Indeed, the Saturday before his death he had confessed most devoutly and had shown several remarkable signs of contrition for his sins, and [he] had said that from now on he would give up gambling and [other] juvenile [activities] and that in every way he would work to serve God and for the good of the realm."[530] It was the abbot of Cerisy's express opinion that Louis d'Orléans had died at thirty-four at last unburdened of his youth. The orator ended with an ample peroration. His eloquence proved persuasive. The audience was convinced that so great a crime must not go unpunished.[531]

The second consequence of the change in the situation that had taken place in August was that on September 21 the king rescinded his order to Waleran of Luxemburg. The bishop of Cambrai came immediately to Paris. There he saw his friends, Jean Gerson no doubt among them. But he missed Nicolas de Clamanges, who did not arrive in the capital until several days later.

Pierre d'Ailly had barely arrived in Paris, however, when he learned of John the Fearless's victory. On September 23, at Othée, the duke of Burgundy had crushed the Liège rebels. The future was all too clear; the pendulum was about to swing the other way. Pierre d'Ailly immediately left Paris. On his way back to Cambrai he wrote to Gerson: "All that I see is painful to me and almost unbearable."[532]

What did he mean? Now fifty-seven, did Pierre d'Ailly head back to Cambrai beaten, discouraged, and finally crushed by ten years of trials and tribulations? Or was he engaging in one of those well-timed and calculated retreats for which he was famous, waiting, his rage held in check, for an opportune moment to return to the fray? By chance we have, to enlighten us, two letters written at roughly the same time in October 1408. Both were addressed to Pierre d'Ailly by younger men who numbered among his closest friends: Jean Gerson and Nicolas de Clamanges. Their purposes in writing were different. Gerson, who wrote to his former master from Paris on October 16, hoped to win Pierre over to the contemplative life to which he himself felt more and more attracted and about which Pierre, a man of action but also a member of the elite, had already exhibited some curiosity. Gerson therefore attempted to divert the bishop of Cambrai's attention from temporal and mortal matters, full of vanity and folly (*temporalia atque mortalia, plena undique vanitatibus et inaniis falsis*). He encouraged his teacher to scorn and abandon so far as possible the things of this world (*desere per contemptum quidquid in terrenis libere potes*) and to accept Christ's gentle yoke (*suave jugum Christi*) in order to obtain salvation. Gerson's letter is a brief, classical exhortation to renounce earthly things.[533] At about the same time, Nicolas de Clamanges wrote Pierre d'Ailly from Fontaine-au-Bois for a very different purpose. He had just made a brief visit to Paris, but Pierre d'Ailly had already left. Distraught over the state of the Church and the kingdom and depressed by the attacks on his person, Nicolas de Clamanges turned to his friend for advice and comfort. His letter rings with echoes of fierce recent battle.[534]

The two correspondents wrote with different purposes, but the man to whom they addressed their letters was the same. He was a man consumed by worries about church and state (*zelus domus*

Domini et reipublicae salus comedit te, Jean Gerson wrote; *res ecclesiae regnique nostri,* said Nicolas de Clamanges). He was apparently on the brink of disaster. Yet he was a man who had avoided many traps and overcome many adversities. When his friends saw him in Paris, he seemed in good health (*corpore quidem sospitem*). As for his moral state, Gerson seems to have been struck primarily by Pierre's outbursts of anger: "*Desine ab ira et derelinque furorem; noli aemulari*" (Give up your wrath and furor; do not fight), the student, quoting Psalm 36, advised his former teacher. He added that when children fall down, they become angry (*irascuntur*) and beat their heads against the ground; they do not understand that they are too weak to stand up by themselves. And we, who are but grown children (*grandiusculi pueri*), tend to become indignant in adversity without turning to the only one who can save us from the tempest. If nothing else, Gerson's exhortations at least tell us how Pierre d'Ailly had seemed to him during the latter's brief stay in Paris. What is more, Nicolas de Clamanges, who does not conceal his admiration for the old campaigner, says the same thing in different words. In Paris Pierre d'Ailly had struck his friends as fiery (*alacer*) and intrepid (*intrepidus*). Wise and strong, he was a person to whom one could turn. The marvelous way in which he had always managed to avoid the traps prepared for him was something to admire. "Each time that Pierre d'Ailly's enemies rose to attack him, the attack added still more luster to his virtue. In striving to bring him down and consign him to oblivion, they made him famous and glorious throughout the world."[535]

Thus two men, equally unfit for action, reacted in two different ways to that flamboyant man of action Pierre d'Ailly. Jean Gerson, a man who, when caught between the university of which he was chancellor, his benefactor the duke of Burgundy, and his friends Nicolas de Clamanges and Pierre d'Ailly, managed to survive the tempest in Paris without showing his colors or speaking out, counseled Pierre to turn to God. Nicolas de Clamanges, who for years had lived a life of retirement far from the turmoil and crowds of the capital but who nevertheless found himself alone at the eye of the storm, felt the same admiration for the bishop of Cambrai in 1408 that he had felt in 1394 for the chancellor of the university, who in the meantime had only gained in stature by having had the audacity and luck to triumph over all adversity. It was not a beaten man but an angry one who in late September or early October 1408 wrote to Jean Gerson: "All that I see is painful to me and almost unbearable."

For some days after this exchange of letters events in northern France continued at a breathless pace. Sometime between October 17 and October 27 John the Fearless entrusted Jean Petit with the task of answering the abbot of Cerisy, and Jean began work on his second justification, whose themes were necessarily the same as the first but whose victims now included that venerable sexagenarian, the abbot of Cerisy, whom Jean Petit, in his forty-year-old pride, branded a "stinking old abbot" and a "fat-nosed, glorious old wheezer."[536] In early November the king, the queen, the duke of Berry, and many others hastily exited Paris through the Porte Saint-Jacques. On November 28 John the Fearless returned to the capital.[537] On December 8 Valentina Visconti, the duke of Orléans's "bereaved" widow, died at Blois.[538] The truth, however, is that the hostile princes still hoped that things would not go too far, and in any case they lacked the cash necessary to fight. In 1409, while the fate of the Church was being decided at Pisa, the kingdom therefore lived in delicate balance and endured a precarious peace.[539]

Meanwhile, Benedict XIII had gone to Perpignan and Gregory XII to Siena, when the very hopelessness of the situation gave rise to an extraordinary event. Cardinals of both obediences met, and on June 29, 1408, in Livorno, they declared that they were divorcing themselves from both pontiffs and would attempt to restore the unity of the Church by persuading both popes to resign and then holding a general council.[540] At the end of August 1408 they had the audacity to convene such a council on their own. It was to meet in Pisa on March 25, 1409.[541]

For the past year Pierre d'Ailly had found himself disappointed with Benedict XIII. Hence, as he himself said, the convocation of the council caused his heart to jump for joy.[542] In his haste to leave his Cambrai retreat, to escape from the paltry affairs in which he had recently been involved, and to find a theater worthy of his talents, he set out for Pisa well ahead of time. On January 1, 1409, he was in Aix-en-Provence. And then the man who for so long had championed Benedict XIII, because he could not imagine how the Church could survive without its head, justified the Council of Pisa with an argument that deserves praise for its clarity but that simply repeated propositions council proponents had been making since the beginning of the schism. They had made those assertions, moreover, at the University of Paris: namely, that the pope may appear to be the head of the Church but is in fact only the vicar of Christ; that Christ is the true head of the Church; that it is from Christ, its head, that the mystical body of the Church derives the power and authority to convoke councils; that it was not the pope who had convoked the first ecumenical councils; and that now, too, a valid council could be convoked without the authority of the pope.[543] Pierre d'Ailly submitted these propositions to Jean Gerson in Paris, who read them from his chair of theology and approved them to the enthusiastic applause of his audience.[544] On January 29 Gerson himself began writing a brief treatise, intended to silence the council's adversaries, on the *Unity of the Church*.[545] But Gerson, no doubt detained in Paris by his many duties as professor, chancellor, and curate, did not go to Pisa.[546]

Many others did go, but not all were present for the council's opening session, which took place as scheduled on March 25, 1409. The ambassadors representing the king of France and the delegation from the University of Paris did not arrive until April 24. Simon de Cramaud headed the royal embassy, among whose members was Gilles Des Champs.[547] The university delegation consisted of nine or ten members, among them Pierre Plaoul.[548] The representatives of the king and the university mingled with countless bishops, among them Elie de Lestrange.[549] Pierre d'Ailly did not reach Pisa until May 7.[550] Why was the man who was in such a hurry to leave his diocese so slow to reach Pisa? Pierre hoped that the council would designate a single new pope and thus end the schism. But being a cautious and realistic man, he also hoped that the council would have the assent of all Christians, for otherwise it was likely only to add to the confusion.[551] In fact, however, the council did not have the assent of all Christians, and Pierre d'Ailly may have harbored some doubt about its ultimate success. For whatever reason, he did not arrive in Pisa until two weeks after most of the other French delegates.

Among the five hundred or so priests from all over Christendom who met in Pisa, then, were a number of French clerics, some of whom had been among Benedict XIII's fiercest adversaries and others among his most tenacious supporters. They played different roles. Simon de Cramaud worked behind the scenes with his customary efficiency. He also presided over one of the sessions.[552] The council marked the culmination of this sexagenarian tactician's career. Pierre Plaoul at fifty-five still had not lost his voice. As usual he was a brilliant orator. Elie de Lestrange no doubt felt some compunction at the thought of deposing Benedict XIII, but he was in his seventies and not as strong as he used to be. He was little heard from. Pierre d'Ailly probably was not eager to play a leading role, and in any case the council entrusted him with missions that prevented him from attending several important sessions. Thus the various players had very different roles.

Yet all who had come to Pisa knew what was to be done there and had agreed to it in advance. While some were more enthusiastic and others less, all were in agreement about the essential issue. The business was not drawn out. On June 5 both popes were declared to be heretics and *ipso facto* removed from office. On June 26 an Italian, the cardinal of Milan, was elected pope by the cardinals gathered in conclave. The new pope took the name Alexander V.[553] On July 2 he named Simon de Cramaud archbishop of Rheims.[554] On July 13 Pierre d'Ailly left Pisa.[555]

Pierre d'Ailly at Sixty

Less than a year later Alexander V died, and on May 17, 1410, John XXIII was elected to replace him.[556] Broadly speaking, this was the only noteworthy event to occur in two years. In France the hostile princes continued to eye each other warily, but they would not actually clash until the summer of 1411. In the Church, the election of Pisa, the result of many years' prodigious effort, elicited brief bursts of enthusiasm here and there but in the end only added to the confusion. In Aragon Benedict XIII dug in his heels. Gregory XII clung to life, having sought refuge in southern Italy with Ladislas, the king of Sicily. All over Italy Gregory's supporters clashed in contests that, viewed from France, seemed complex and insignificant. The council's efforts ground to a halt, but slowly. For a time the participants remained uncertain whether they had been the architects of momentous change or the dupes of a sideshow. Both church and state faced a future fraught with unresolved problems. For the time being, however, nothing important was going on. And Pierre d'Ailly, about to turn sixty, had the opportunity, perhaps for want of alternatives, to turn his tireless energies to reading, thinking, and writing.

In doing so he remained true to himself. He had always carefully preserved what he wrote and rarely went anywhere without his archives.[557] Now the old man (*senex*) had the opportunity to reread what the young man (*juvenis*) had written.[558] He distanced himself from the texts by urging the old man to go easy on the youth; he annotated, corrected, and revised.[559] Yet nothing essential had changed. The notion of "probability" remained the key to the old man's philosophy as it had been of the youth's.[560] The old man's thought and action were explained solely by the effervescence of the young man's ideas thirty years earlier at the University of Paris. The old man remained faithful to the great writers of the twelfth and thirteenth centuries such as Saint Bernard, Hugh and Richard of Saint-Victor, William of Auvergne, and Saint Bonaventure, from whom the young man had drawn sustenance.[561]

The old man also continued the young man's fervent veneration of Saint Francis but still repudiated the excesses of certain Franciscans. Even in youth Pierre d'Ailly had opposed absolute poverty for clerics. Although he had favored monks' wearing plain habits, even then he had been wary that behind such behavior might lurk pride, ambition, and hypocrisy. Now that he was bishop of Cambrai and the problem of appearances had become even more urgent, the same suspicions continued to plague him. It was good for monks to dress poorly, but the world had its hierarchy, and that hierarchy must be visible. Natural philosophy held that priests should have more to live on than their parishioners, and that lords should have more than their subjects. As Saint Francis himself had said in his rule, each estate ought to have its own clothing and apparel.[562]

Pomp was therefore justified on principle, and the only question was one of degree. Philippe de Mézières had said: "Who keeps to the middle of the road follows the sure path. . . . In all honors there must be rule and measure. . . . Disorderly habits and sumptuous finery must be made subject to rules."[563] Gerson believed that it was better for prelates to emulate evangelical poverty than to live in ostentatious luxury. But the Church was not governed by saints. Prelates morally too weak to command respect had been obliged in the past, and were still obliged, to display some measure of exterior pomp.[564] Pierre d'Ailly condemned "excessive" and "superfluous" pomp, which manifested pride, and luxury, which especially in these times did little to encourage reverence and outraged many people.[565] Only a moderate level of pomp was justified. In his will Pierre d'Ailly specified that his funeral rites should be celebrated "*sine pompa et sumptibus excessivis*" (without excessive pomp or expenditure).[566] Thus while Pierre d'Ailly and his friends may have differed as to the reasons why a moderate degree of pomp was justified, all agreed that it was necessary. The problem is that the chancellor of the University of Paris and the bishop of Cambrai apparently understood the words "moderate pomp" in different ways.

There is nothing surprising about Pierre d'Ailly's fidelity to his own earlier views and to a great Christian tradition. More noteworthy is the fact that on the brink of sixty the bishop of Cambrai should have begun to develop in new ways, to satisfy new curiosities, and to strike out in bold new directions. Of course Pierre's innovation stemmed not from rejecting the past but from delving further into an assured tradition. His vigorous health permitted a late blooming, a rebirth rooted in continuity.

As his activity diminished, the bishop of Cambrai was able to immerse himself more deeply in the contemplative life, to which he had long been drawn. In two works written in this period, *Speculum considerationis* and *Compendium contemplationis,* he attempted to initiate those who would flee the cares of this world into the philosophy of contemplation.[567] Without denigrating the active life he noted the attractions of the contemplative life.[568] He also noted that a monk turned prelate did not necessarily go from better to worse. It was not necessary to renounce the contemplative life in order to take up the active life. The two must be combined. Although a prelate was obliged to lead an active life, he owed it to himself also to excel in the contemplative.[569] As if proposing a model for himself to follow, Pierre wrote: "A prelate must first toil in the plain of action before climbing the mountain of contemplation, as it is said that Moses did. He must lead both kinds of life. Sometimes he is immersed with Martha in the cares of the active life and in a sense estranged from himself. Sometimes he follows Mary in the contemplative life, and alone with God he recovers the unity of his thoughts and in a sense returns to himself."[570]

When Pierre d'Ailly wrote these brief works, Jean Gerson had already completed his first great spiritual works, powerfully original yet steeped in the sources of the new mysticism.[571] Master and disciple thus followed roughly parallel paths, yet neither exerted much influence on the other. For the disciple, Jean Gerson, was truly a master of spirituality, whereas the master, Pierre d'Ailly, did little more than draw on ancient and traditional sources to produce brief and highly classical compilations.[572] When the claims of the active life loosened their grip, the bishop of Cambrai climbed a little way up the mountain of contemplation. But his was not a nature suited to discovering itself in solitude with God. Pierre shared with his friend Jean Gerson a certain need for the spiritual life, but he was no mystic.

Nor was Pierre d'Ailly a humanist, yet he shared with his friends Jean de Montreuil and Nicolas de Clamanges a great interest in Antiquity. The leisure he enjoyed in his sixties provided him with an opportunity to satisfy that interest. He widened his reading in the classics. His knowledge of ancient culture grew more solid.[573] And his increased familiarity with humanism also manifested itself in the most concrete of ways, in his writing.

In this time before the printing press, when culture was based entirely on manuscripts, there was not a single intellectual who did not spend long hours writing. Like many others Pierre d'Ailly was a tireless copyist, and in this activity he employed the cursive script then current in France. But this was a time when reading aloud, either individually or collectively, was in the process of being supplanted by silent reading,[574] and scribes were interested in developing a more legible script that might be more accessible to large numbers of readers.[575] Calligraphy was one of the major concerns of such professional writers as chancellery clerks. Among the various attempts to develop a new handwriting, the most successful was that of an Italian humanist, Poggio Bracciolini. Early in the fifteenth century Poggio perfected a handwriting that borrowed in essential respects from the beautiful *minuscule* of the Carolingian renaissance. To contrast the new script with Gothic cursive, Poggio's contemporaries referred to it as *littera antiqua,* and it was ideally suited to the needs of silent reading.[576] And so it was that in 1410, with newfound time on his hands, Pierre d'Ailly became passionately interested in calligraphy.[577] Although he was in his sixties, his handwriting remained youthful. He achieved remarkable mastery of the cursive script then in use by French clerics.[578] But he was also quick to pick up new styles of writing, and as early as 1410 he was the first person in France to adopt certain features of the *littera antiqua.*[579]

Nevertheless, calligraphic exercises could no more absorb all Pierre d'Ailly's vitality than could spiritual exercises. The bishop of Cambrai now found himself with the leisure to cultivate certain long-standing curiosities and passions. On August 12, 1410, he finished work on the *Imago mundi.*[580] A description of the world, this work touched on the various interests that had gradually drawn Pierre d'Ailly beyond the traditional boundaries of academic theology. While interests such as his in the nature of space and the world may have been uncommon in a theologian, the books that enabled Pierre to satisfy his curiosity had long been part of Western culture. They included the works of Pliny (first century A.D.), Solinus (third century), Orosius (fifth century), and Isidore of Seville (seventh century).[581] The only more recent author Pierre used was Roger Bacon (although he did not cite him, because while medieval authors readily cited ancient authors, who possessed authority, they did not cite modern sources, which possessed none). But Roger Bacon had died in 1294. Since then, and even more since Isidore of Seville, the world had changed greatly. Its horizons had steadily expanded. The *Imago mundi* reflected not the world in which Pierre d'Ailly lived but a much older world. Yet because this "image of the world" was drawn by Pierre d'Ailly, it was of course clear and precise. The *Imago mundi* gave felicitous expression to outmoded ideas. It was a good and useful manual. Christopher Columbus read and annotated it. Hence Columbus's discovery of the New World ensured that Pierre d'Ailly would survive in the memory of many historians.

Thus Pierre d'Ailly put together an accurate and faithful compilation of ancient sources. He did not altogether hide his desire to surpass them in the description of his beloved France, of Paris, where he had lived for so long, and of the northern regions he had come to know so well as bishop of Cambrai. "It must be said that Orosius and Isidore and other ancient geographers say almost nothing about the kingdom of France, which is situated in the Gauls and which is now the greatest of all the states of Europe. Nor do they say anything about its capital, Paris, which is like the light of the world, the greatest center for the study of the divine sciences and human letters. Nor do they say anything about the other great cities of the kingdom or about adjoining lands such as Lorraine, the Liège region, Hainault, Cambrésis, Brabant and Flanders, in which there are populous and wealthy cities and fortified places. This, I think, is because the ancient authors did not deal with states, which change often, but described unchanging regions. Perhaps, too, those countries were not then populous and famous as they are now. And our Greek and Roman geographers were obliged to praise their own countries more than foreign countries."[582] This last hypothesis seemed quite plausible to Pierre d'Ailly, all the more so in that love of country inspired the same attitude in him: England is all but absent from his world.

In writing his *Imago mundi* Pierre d'Ailly also had another concern. Ancient authors, Aristotle in particular, had related the virtues of peoples and their forms of government to the climate. Pierre d'Ailly wondered if the motion of the sun or some other celestial body might also play a part. Perhaps certain celestial motions were favorable to good government and others to tyranny. This reflection brought him to consider a matter that had always interested him but that had lately become an obsession: "The astronomers assign numerous and varied properties or virtues to these signs of the zodiac." Were they justified? Pierre answered: "In regard to these assertions one must display neither the credulity of superstition nor the contempt of pride. But it is not the purpose of the present treatise to discuss these questions."[583] This simple sentence betrays the most audacious thought that Pierre d'Ailly permitted himself in his old age.

The science of astronomy had made great strides in the fourteenth century. By the end of the previous century the use of planetary tables for determining the location and motion of the planets was already widespread. One such was said to have been prepared at the behest of Alphonso X (the Wise), king of Castille from 1252 to 1284. In 1320 a Parisian astronomer produced a new version of this table, and thereafter so-called Alphonsine tables met with prodigious success.[584] Pierre d'Ailly was well enough versed in astronomy to be familiar with the *Tabulae Alphonsi* and capable of proposing a reform of the calendar aimed at correcting flaws in the Julian calendar and eliminating the discrepancy between the astronomical year and the civil year.[585] Early in 1411 Pierre d'Ailly produced a final version of his calendar reform proposal. It remained one of his pet projects until his death, and he tried in vain to have it discussed by the ecclesiastical authorities, who at the time were preoccupied with other matters.[586]

Progress in the science that dealt with the motion of the stars, or the first part of astronomy, was only slightly in advance of progress in what contemporaries considered to be the "second part" of the subject, what we call astrology. Based on the idea that the motion of the stars influences human destinies, astrology sought to establish "from the constellation of the heavens judgments of things to come."[587] By the 1330s a growing interest in astrology was perceptible in Paris, and soon the subject became the indispensable auxiliary of medicine and politics.[588] Yet even though the first part of astronomy was a "most noble and excellent science, legitimate and approved by the church,"[589] the second part remained suspect in the eyes of theologians, for it was based on a principle that negated the liberty of God and man and it claimed to reveal to man what ought to remain hidden, namely, the future. In the middle of the fourteenth century Nicolas Oresme strongly condemned the growing interest in astrology. On September 19, 1398, the faculty of theology of Paris firmly condemned superstitious practices of all kinds and declared that, among other things, it was false to believe "that our intellectual thoughts and inward wishes are immediately caused by the heavens and that one can gain knowledge of thoughts through a magic cabal."[590] Pierre d'Ailly's best friends, Philippe de Mézières and Jean Gerson, shared Nicolas Oresme's hostility to astrology.[591]

In his youth Pierre d'Ailly had himself condemned astrology.[592] Yet in 1410, when he was nearly sixty, he dared to doubt. He rejected both the credulity of superstition and the contempt of pride. Faced with two extreme opinions, one unduly exalting the potential of astronomy and the other unduly disparaging it, he clung to the middle ground.[593] He believed that astronomical judgments were not in all respects condemnable and that the movements of the stars could help to explain the past and explore the future.[594] Nevertheless, he hastened to add that to accept the influence of the stars was not to believe in fatal necessity. It was not to deny either man's free will or God's omnipotence. God may do whatever he likes. While he sometimes manifests his omnipotence through miracles, usually he chooses to intervene by way of natural causality.[595] Pierre d'Ailly no longer doubted that the conjunctions of the stars could explain the roughly simultaneous occurrence of great events and surprising mutations on earth.[596] To demonstrate that truth, he spoke for the first and last time in his life about history.

Before doing so he undertook no special research in history. Like all theologians, Pierre had little interest in the subject. His historical reading included only those books that all theologians read in the course of their studies. He had read the Bible, Flavius Josephus, Eusebius of Caesarea, Saint Augustine, and Isidore of Seville. He had read and quoted Peter the Eater's twelfth-century *Scholastic History,* which summarized all sacred history.[597] He did not quote but probably had read Vincent of Beauvais's *Historical Mirror* and Martin the Pole's *Chronicle,* thirteenth-century works that were found in those days in all good libraries and that satisfied readers with no particular interest in history. Pierre did not profit by his leisure to widen his reading. He was satisfied with his rudimentary historical background, which was in fact sufficient to enable him to prove his point. In Basel on May 10, 1414, he finished his treatise *De concordia astronomice veritatis et narrationis hystorice,* in which he attempted to establish a relation between the conjunctions of the stars and historical events.[598]

History, according to Pierre d'Ailly, was governed first by the great and rare conjunctions of Saturn, Jupiter, and Mars, second by the conjunction of Saturn and Jupiter, which occurred every 960 years, and finally by the revolution of Saturn, whose period was thirty years. World-historical events occurred with every ten revolutions of Saturn, that is, every 300 years. Pierre does not dwell on primitive times, because the Alphonsine tables were inadequate for determining the precise dates of conjunctions before the flood, and no chronicle or history indicated the precise dates of events.[599] Eventually the sources improve to the point where our author is able to go into greater detail. He comes, for example, to the sixth conjunction of Saturn and Jupiter, which occurred 5,120 years after the creation of the world and approximately 225 years before the birth of Christ.[600] The seventh conjunction took place in 737, and Pierre d'Ailly remarks on the great events that occurred around that time: the plague in Constantinople; the Byzantine emperor's order to remove all images of Christ and the saints; the Saracens' conquests in East and West and subsequent persecutions, followed by their defeat by Charles, Pepin's father, at Poitiers in 732; and Boniface's conversion of the Germans.[601]

The conjunction of Saturn and Jupiter in 737 was the last of which Pierre d'Ailly was able to observe the effects. From that date on he therefore proceeds to a more detailed analysis based on the revolutions of Saturn. He first notes a remarkable coincidence between the revolutions of Saturn and the coming of Mohammed.[602] Add ten revolutions of Saturn, or 300 years, and we come to roughly the year 889, the time of the Hungarian and Norman invasions, schism in the Church, and the end of the Carolingian dynasty.[603] Another ten revolutions of Saturn brings us to 1189 or thereabouts, and Pierre ticks off numerous events that he says are related to that remarkable astronomical date: Christendom's loss of Edessa (to which modern scholarship assigns the date 1144); the glorious reign of Frederick I (Barbarossa, 1152–90); the assassination of Thomas à Becket, archbishop of Canterbury (1170); the composition of the *Scholastic History* by Peter the Eater (prior to 1173); Saladin's capture of the Holy Sepulcher (1187); the pontificate of Innocent III (1198–1216); the capture of Constantinople by crusaders (1204); the Saracens' victory in Spain (Las Navas de Tolosa, 1212); the Lateran Council of 1215; the condemnation of the doctrine of Joachim of Floris, "who lived in Calabria and wrote several useful books" ; the flourishing of the mendicant orders; the conquests of the Tartars (who made their deepest foray into Hungary in 1241).[604] Given these striking coincidences, who could possibly doubt the importance of the revolutions of Saturn and of the remarkable date 1189?

Further effects from this same cause were not due until 1489, however. The misfortunes Pierre d'Ailly had experienced were the result not of the revolutions of Saturn or of the conjunction of Saturn and Jupiter but of the very rare conjunction of Saturn, Jupiter, and Mars that occurred in March 1346. This had resulted in a shortage of water and food and had brought on the plague, as well as a host of other evils that Pierre can do no more than mention: epidemics, disasters, wars, and rebellions—misfortunes not only for states and peoples but also for kings and princes. It also had resulted in the dreadful schism in the Church, which had lasted for thirty-six years and which, without the help of God, who alone controlled the stars, might well presage the coming of the Antichrist.[605]

Beneath all this science and calculation lay a deep anxiety about the present and the future it heralded. In order to penetrate this distressing obscurity—of course without setting any precise dates, because God did not permit men to know the future with certainty—Pierre d'Ailly did more than consult the prophecies that circulated in his time. He did more than scrutinize the Book of Revelation sentence by sentence and word by word.[606] He believed that study of the stars could aid in understanding the Bible. When—

if the world lasted that long, which only God could know—would important upheavals, especially of a religious nature, be likely to occur? This was the subject of Pierre d'Ailly's *De concordia* (1414). In 1418 he clarified his thinking still further in *De Persecutionibus Ecclesiae.*[607] Saturn's revolutions suggested the date 1489. "One may therefore take it as probable [*probabilis haberi potest suspicio*] that a great change in laws and sects will take place within one hundred years, particularly in regard to the subject of the law and the Church of Jesus Christ."[608] Then, in 1693, Saturn and Jupiter would enter their eighth conjunction. After that, a new cycle of ten revolutions of Saturn would culminate in 1789 or thereabouts. For ninety-seven years after 1693 times would be hard. It was a probable conjecture (*probabilis conjectura*), based on astronomical reasoning, that at the end of this period, in 1789, the Antichrist would come.[609] The upshot of all this was that while Pierre d'Ailly would be remembered by some for having predicted the discovery of the New World, he would be remembered by others for having foretold the Reformation and the French Revolution.[610]

The Council of Constance (1414–18)

But let us return to 1411. June 6 of that year was one of the happiest days of Pierre d'Ailly's life. John XXIII appointed a new batch of cardinals, among whom were three Frenchmen: Gilles Des Champs, Guillaume Fillastre, and Pierre d'Ailly.[611] Why did that happiness soon turn sour? In going to Pisa, Pierre d'Ailly had simply given in to a necessity that others had felt long before. Having protected Benedict XIII longer than almost anyone else, he had finally given up on the stubborn old pope. But Benedict XIII still had some fairly staunch supporters who would not forgive their former comrade. Nicolas de Clamanges's reproaches were more discreet. In the *Treatise on the Ruin of the Church* he wrote for the bishop of Cambrai in 1400 or 1401, Nicolas consoled himself for the Church's woes by mentioning two noble souls who remained among its luminiaries: Benedict, the pope, and Pierre, the bishop of Cambrai. Now, in revising his text, Nicolas eliminated this passage.[612] Boniface Ferrer's reaction to Pierre d'Ailly's changing sides was more violent. On January 7, 1411, the general of the Carthusians completed a treatise that contained vehement attacks on all who had always opposed Benedict XIII as well as those who had abandoned the pope over the course of the years. Many people fell under one or the other of these two heads: all the members of the Council of Pisa and nearly all the prelates of France and masters and doctors of the university, including the theologians but most of all the jurists.[613] In other words, Boniface Ferrer's treatise was a violent polemic against everyone in France who possessed learning, eloquence, authority, rank, or power.[614]

A Catalan, Boniface Ferrer reproached these Frenchmen first of all for their inconsistency. Petrarch had already stigmatized the haughty fickleness of the French. These Gauls (*Gallici*) were like the cock (*gallus*): clap your hands and they would sing, and then a moment later they would forget and change their minds. They turned against any pope whom they judged to have acted in a manner inimical to themselves or to the house of France. Previously it was Boniface VIII, even though he had canonized Saint Louis, and now it was Benedict XIII.[615] Worse than their fickleness was their intolerable pride (*intolerabilis superbia*), their insatiable voracity (*vorago insatiabilis*), and their devouring ambition, which compelled them to seek glory, honor, and riches.[616]

When they had acquired these honors and riches and had grown old, what hope was there that they would abandon all they had gained to remain loyal to Benedict XIII? Consider Guy de Malsec. He was seventy years old, if not older, and had been a cardinal since 1375. In France he had revenues of eight to ten thousand francs. At the moment he was bishop of Agde, where he lived in splendor, attended by a large retinue. Who could believe that, to remain loyal to Benedict XIII, he would agree to give up all this wealth and go begging? No, he would rather await damnation in his present condition.[617] And so would many others. Boniface Ferrer (whose benefices, incidentally, lay outside France) was enraged to hear them respond: "If we went to Benedict, we would be stripped of our possessions [which are in France]. We would have to beg. It is easier to preach patience than to practice it. Poverty can be recommended with all one's heart, but it must be borne with a sad face. If there were nothing to serve for luncheon or dinner, imagine the murmuring of the servants against their master, imagine the hubbub and tumult. And if penury is unbearable even for a minute, what about poverty in perpetuity? To have been happy is the greatest of misfortunes."[618]

In these terms Boniface Ferrer lashed out at the cardinals, who were perhaps the pillars of the Church, he said, but pillars "of excrement" (*de stercore*).[619] He lashed out at all the scholars, the famous men, the prelates, the masters who, blinded by pride, marched headlong into darkness.[620] He praised those who demonstrated true wisdom and true piety: simple folk and women, peasants and old ladies.[621] In denigrating the great and exalting the humble, Boniface Ferrer was of course following an old Christian tradition. Like many others before him he cited the Bible: "Knowledge puffeth up" (1 Cor. 8:1);[622] "I thank thee, O Father, Lord of heaven and earth, that thou hast hid these things from the wise and prudent, and hast revealed them unto babes" (Luke 10:21).[623]

When Pierre d'Ailly, for whom respect for hierarchy and authority had always been fundamental and who had only recently been named cardinal, read this text in 1411,[624] he reacted with outrage, all the more so because Boniface Ferrer had not limited himself to venomous generalities. He had named names, and in his personal attacks he had stigmatized the lasciviousness of one man, the duplicity of another, the pride, ambition, and greed of many. Upon all he had heaped calumny and slander. And among his principal victims were his inveterate enemy Simon de Cramaud and his erstwhile friend Pierre d'Ailly. In his own way Boniface told how Pierre d'Ailly had conquered Cambrai and how he had behaved at Pisa, and he urged his readers not to take for Gospel the words of a master of theology who was not yet canonized, who was nothing but worldly appetite avid for honors, glory, and riches.[625]

In response to Boniface Ferrer's pamphlet Pierre d'Ailly sent a long letter to the Carthusians on January 10, 1412.[626] He said he had been dumbstruck in reading the text that Boniface had composed—composed, he cannot prevent himself from remarking, if the word can be applied to a text in which there is no order and a horrible confusion prevails. Pierre's letter, by contrast, is a model of order, restraint, and dignity, which shows what degree of self-control the once fiery youth had achieved by the age of sixty-one. His letter, he announces, will consist of three parts: First he will demonstrate that Boniface's treatise is presumptuous, second that it is injurious, and third that it is seditious.

It is presumptuous because it challenges decisions made at Pisa by an assembly composed of countless prelates, doctors, and ambassadors from any number of states. It is seditious because it advocates a horrible thing: disobedience to one's superiors. And it is injurious because it slanders not only private individuals but persons holding various public offices: jurists, theologians, and prominent prelates. It attacks not only the living but also the dead. It lashes out not just at individuals but at entire nations and kingdoms, especially the most Christian kingdom of France and the Gallican Church. Later, in responding to Boniface Ferrer's charge that he himself was nothing more than an ambitious man avid for honors, glory, and riches, Pierre d'Ailly strikes off a passage that admirably captures the way in which he saw himself: "I am not so perfect that I have altogether curbed my hunger for honors and appetite for riches. But I am not so imperfect as to have attempted to obtain them, as Boniface dares to assert, by dubious stratagems allegedly dictated by ambition."[627] Pierre d'Ailly's ambition was not of the evil kind. Like so many others, he was ambitious only when viewed from outside.

By the time Pierre completed this *Apology* on January 10, 1412, he was no longer in Cambrai. Nor was he still bishop of Cambrai. The new cardinal was in Avignon,[628] en route to Rome to fulfill the duties of his new position and to attend the new council that the Council of Pisa at the conclusion of its sessions had scheduled to meet in 1412 to work on reform of the Church.[629] Along the way Pierre d'Ailly devoted a great deal of thought to the question of reform. Hasty as he had been to leave Cambrai, however, he was in no hurry to arrive in Rome. Indeed, no one was in a hurry to get there. The council began in Rome in April 1412. Guillaume Fillastre did not arrive until June 16, and Pierre d'Ailly did not arrive until December 1. On December 19 he was named cardinal-titular of Saint Chrysogonus, and on December 21 he was given responsibility for the administration of the diocese of Limoges; a little later the diocese of Orange was added to his responsibilities.[630] Simon de Cramaud, now archbishop of Rheims, did not leave that city until the end of 1412 and did not reach Rome until early in 1413.[631] By then the council was drawing to a close. Too few people had participated. The Church was not a step closer to reform when the council ended on March 3, 1413.[632] Still, the journeys of Pierre d'Ailly and Simon de Cramaud had not been useless. On March 18, 1413, the pope named Pierre d'Ailly his legate in Germany.[633] On April 14 he (finally!) made Simon de Cramaud a cardinal.[634]

On May 22, 1413, Pierre d'Ailly therefore left Rome.[635] While he was busy taking up his duties as legate in Germany, elsewhere fate was dealing hard blows to many others. Pierre's one-time friend Gilles Des Champs, from whom life had long since estranged him but who had become cardinal on the same day, had died on March 5, 1413, in his sixties. On June 8, less than three weeks after Pierre d'Ailly's departure, Ladislas, the king of Naples and a staunch supporter of Gregory XII, entered Rome and laid waste the city. Simon de Cramaud was forced to flee so quickly that he left some of his books and baggage behind.[636] But the greatest drama unfolded in Paris. In July 1411 war had broken out between supporters of John the Fearless, the duke of Burgundy, who naturally were called Burgundians, and supporters of the duke of Orléans, who owed their name, Armagnacs, to the fact that one of their most powerful leaders was Count Bernard VII of Armagnac, the father-in-law of the young Duke Charles of Orléans, son of the late Duke Louis. In Paris the years 1411 and 1412 were "quite perilous."[637] Discontent was on the rise, and so was insecurity. Following a series of violent episodes, the butchers of Paris, who had thrown in their lot with the duke of Burgundy, seized control of the city. The first riot occurred on April 28, 1413. A mob led, or at any rate headed, by the leaders of the Burgundian party, namely the butchers and skinners, one of whom was named Caboche, took possession of the streets. Further days of mob violence ensued. News of the rioting surely reached Rome, where Pierre d'Ailly was no doubt all the more pleased that his duty took him to Germany. On the very day he left Rome, May 22, Paris experienced its most violent riot to date. But the "Cabochiens" who controlled the streets were short of cash. In June they decided to demand a compulsory loan not only of the burghers of Paris but also of ecclesiastics and academics. The most violent of the Cabochiens resorted to less than gentle methods of collection. Jean Gerson was already suspected by the Cabochiens of being "one of the instigators of the Armagnac faction."[638] In the first few days of July[639] the chancellor, "who was in the habit of paying his legal debts," said "in company" that "the methods being used were not very honest nor were they in accord with God, and he said this with good love and affection." Nevertheless, "they wanted to arrest him, but he hid in the high vaults of Notre-Dame of Paris."[640] Several fanatics then broke into his house, ransacked it, and carried off his furniture and books.[641]

Always a man of peace, the chancellor found this personal drama hard to bear. When the situation was reversed, when the duke of Burgundy was forced to leave Paris on August 22 and the Cabochien nightmare was over, Gerson continued to preach peace. He also felt obliged to attack the dangerous ideas that Jean Petit had put forward in 1408 and that he, Gerson, now reproached himself for not having vigorously combated at the time. Jean Petit himself had died on July 15, 1411, when he was somewhere between forty-five and fifty.[642] By 1413 many people thought of his apology for tyrannicide as ancient history. Yet the duke of Burgundy at the end of 1413 was still a man whom many people, in a world accustomed to innumerable reversals, had no desire to offend. No one was in a hurry to reopen an old dispute whose protagonist had died. Many felt that it was better to remain silent: "*Esse silendum de ista materia.*"[643] But Jean Gerson no doubt saw the chain of events that led from the assassination of the duke of Orléans to the murders committed by the Cabochiens and the ransacking of his residence as an ineluctable chain of violence. As a victim of that violence, he reproached himself for not having spoken out sooner and louder about the assassination. All these things would not have happened "if some people had braved death to resist the errors that have been the roots of our evils."[644] Still, "better late than never."[645] Gerson belatedly devoted all of his efforts to persuade a reluctant university to condemn the subversive doctrine. Finally, on February 23, 1414, the bishop and inquisitor of Paris issued a judgment condemning Jean Petit's *Justification*.[646]

While a battered Jean Gerson continued to do battle for peace in Paris, in Germany Pierre d'Ailly encouraged the efforts of Sigismund, king of the Romans. Dissatisfied with the results of Pisa, Sigismund believed that his position required him to work for reform of the Church and restoration of peace and to that end to support the convocation of a general council. He of course did not convoke that council himself. That was up to the pope. But he forced the pope's hand. On October 30, 1413, Sigismund announced to Christendom that, as a result of an understanding with the pope, a general council would open in Constance on November 1, 1414. On December 9, 1413, John XXIII resigned himself to issuing a bull convoking the council. Pierre d'Ailly rejoiced: "O happy city of Constance, I share in thy joy, for it is from the midst of the German cities entrusted to me as legate that thou hast been chosen."[647]

On May 15, 1414, John XXIII made Pierre d'Ailly a gift of the house in Avignon that had once belonged to the late cardinal Bertrand de Chanac, together with all its dependencies.[648] On October 28 the pope made solemn entry into Constance. Nine cardinals and an escort of six hundred horsemen accompanied him.[649] On November 5 he opened the council. On November 17, his legate in Germany, Pierre d'Ailly, displaying the moderate pomp he favored, entered Constance with an escort of forty-four horsemen. All the cardinals in the city turned out to greet him.[650] Finally, on December 24, Sigismund made his entry.

The Council of Constance began with trivial matters. Few members were present, almost all Italians. Many did not believe in the council's purpose.[651] Gregory XII still had some supporters, as did Benedict XIII. Others, especially the French, disapproved of the implicit challenge to the work of Pisa. The personality of John XXIII of course cast something of a shadow over the council that gave him his legitimacy. Born in 1369, John XXIII was forty-five. There was nothing ecclesiastical about him. He was a condottiere pope who had succeeded in the Church owing to his diplomatic and military talents; his private life was scandalous. But Simon de Cramaud, who owed his cardinal's hat to John XXIII and was no saint himself, opportunely recalled the canonical doctrine. Did not the just sin seven times daily? Saint Peter, who renounced the Savior, had done worse.[652] The sinful prelate was still a prelate.

The council, which began so badly that its members were on the verge of disbanding in March 1415, nevertheless endured.[653] By the time it concluded its work in March 1418, it had become one of the great milestones in the history of the West. It owed this success, first of all, to the fact that little by little representatives of all Europe assembled there. In this sort of business nothing is more difficult to come by than precise figures. Modern estimates differ sharply. Were there twenty-two or twenty-nine cardinals? Three or eight patriarchs? Twenty or thirty-five archbishops? One hundred thirty-two or one hundred fifty bishops? One hundred or one hundred fifty-two abbots? Three hundred two or five hundred eighteen doctors? Fifty-odd or a hundred-odd dukes and counts? One thousand one hundred seventy-six or two thousand four hundred knights? One hundred sixteen or one hundred ninety-five city representatives?[654] The crucial point is that the numbers in each category were exceptionally large. And each of the council members had his retinue, so that ecclesiastics and their escorts numbered in all some eighteen thousand men. At the height of the council, therefore, some tens of thousands of people were crowded into an ordinary good-sized medieval city whose population was normally between five and six thousand.[655]

Owing to its size, the Council of Constance was relatively well equipped to deal with the issues for which it had been convened, namely, to restore the unity of the Church by designating an uncontested pope and "extirpating" heresy and to reform the Church in its head and members. Through lengthy and eventful negotiations the papal problem was finally resolved. On May 29, 1415, John XXIII was deposed. On July 4 of the same year, Gregory XII abdicated. It was not until July 26, 1417, that Benedict XIII, still obstinate but finally abandoned by his last remaining supporters, was officially deposed as a "schismatic and heretic . . . obstinate violator of the article of faith *Unam sanctam catholicam Ecclesiam.*" On November 11, 1417, a conclave whose members were elected by the fathers of the council unanimously chose a new pope, Ottone Colonna, cardinal-deacon of Saint George-in-Velabrum, who took the name Martin V.[656] On this crucial issue the council had proved a success.

In order to thwart the stratagems and obstinacy of the several pontiffs, however, the fathers of the council, in some cases out of conviction, in other cases compelled by events, were obliged to proclaim that supreme authority within the Church belonged not to the pope but to Christ, that is, to the Church as a whole, which meant in effect to the council that represented it. When John XXIII left Constance and the very existence of the headless council was called into question, this principle was invoked; on March 26, 1415, it was decreed that the pope's departure in no way diminished the authority of the council, which could not be dissolved or transferred without its own consent.[657] This was the turning point. A few days later, on April 6, 1415, the triumph of conciliar ideas was confirmed by declarations of principle embodied in the decree *Haec Sancta* or *Sacrosancta:* "This holy synod of Constance. . . , forming a general council and representing the Catholic Church, holds its power directly from Christ. Every man, whatever his estate or dignity, be it even papal, is obliged to obey it in all matters concerning the faith and the extirpation of the aforementioned schism, as well as the reform of said Church [of God] in its head and in its members."[658] On October 9, 1417, a few days before the election of the new pope, the decree *Frequens* went even further. By looking forward to another council in five years and another seven years after that to be followed by still other councils every ten years, the fathers of Constance made the council a regular organ in the life of the Church, thereby tending to transform the Church into a constitutional monarchy.[659] Thus the fathers who by virtue of age and authority played the leading roles at Constance witnessed, and in some cases contributed to, the triumph of the audacious conciliar ideas that they had absorbed thirty years earlier as youths at the university.

By giving concrete embodiment to conciliar doctrine the Council of Constance definitively changed the Church. Its "extirpation" of heresy also had lasting effects; the fire in which Jan Hus perished in Constance on July 6, 1415, was not yet extinguished. Other consequences of this enormous gathering were not intended by its members. Large numbers of people from all over Europe became familiar with works of which they had previously been ignorant; they exchanged and copied books and later took them home. For several years Constance was the most brilliant center of European culture and, among other things, the "true crucible of European humanism."[660] Thus the unity of the West was strengthened in Constance.

At the same time, however, Italians, Frenchmen, Englishmen, and Germans came into contact in Constance and became aware of their differences. While English and French clerics rubbed elbows in Constance, French and English knights clashed at Agincourt on October 25, 1415. The disaster that the French suffered there had a considerable effect in Constance. Like Agincourt, Constance was a narrow battleground on which national passions were kindled.

At this turning point in Western history, at this great clerical gathering, it is hardly surprising that we should find Pierre d'Ailly and many of the other men whose destinies, mingled with his, we have been following for some time. Not all of those others were represented, however. Jean Petit had died in 1411, before he was fifty. Gilles Des Champs had died in 1413, at approximately sixty. Pierre Plaoul had attended the Council of Pisa but had not played a major role there. On October 2, 1409, Alexander V had made him bishop of Senlis. For this man of fifty-six, that appointment seems to have marked the beginning of his retirement. Little more is heard about him until his death on April 11, 1415, just as the Council of Constance was getting under way. Jean de Montreuil remained in Paris, working in the royal chancellery. Jean Courtecuisse continued to preach and to teach in the faculty of theology. Nicolas de Clamanges remained in his hermitage at Fontaine-au-Bois.

But Elie de Lestrange, bishop of Le Puy, was already in Constance in 1415, and in 1417 he was still there. To be sure, his role was obscure. His name was mentioned for a chairmanship. He served as member of a minor committee. Elie, who turned seventy-five in 1415 and who would die on July 17, 1418, just after the end of the council, was an old man whose best days were obviously over.[661] Simon de Cramaud also came to Constance, but he did not arrive until March 1417. Although he had turned sixty-nine in 1414, his health was excellent, and he had intended to go to Constance in February 1415. But the setbacks suffered by "his" pope, John XXIII, had dissuaded him from going, and he chose to remain in France, where after all there was plenty for him to do. Simon de Cramaud would live for five years after the Council of Constance; he died on January 19, 1423, at the age of nearly seventy-eight. He was "very old and suffered from gravel, which among other things affects the understanding." A few days before his death, he suffered a stroke that left him "dazed in sight and mind."[662]

The three Frenchmen who played leading roles in Constance were three men whom we know well. Cardinal Guillaume Fillastre was sixty-seven in 1414. He played an important role in the first phase of the council. It was he who, on July 26, 1417, read the judgment deposing Benedict XIII. A man with a passionate interest in science and cosmography, he arranged for the works of Ptolemy and Pomponius Mela to be copied in Constance. He also kept a diary for the duration of the council, for which we are in his debt. Jean Gerson, who was fifty-one in 1414, represented both the king and the university at the council. He reached Constance on February 21, 1415.[663] There he played a major role in helping the council define its "conciliar" positions. Subsequently, however, his insistence that the theses of Jean Petit be condemned limited his influence. In the end, the man who carried the most weight for nearly four years was Pierre d'Ailly. He owed his influence to several things. First, his position: he was a cardinal; he was John XXIII's legate in Germany as well as procurator of the king of France. Second, his age: he was sixty-three in 1414 and in full possession of his powers. Third, his tactical skill: he made better use than ever of his presence and absence. Fourth, his oratorical talent: in an assembly that counted among its members the oratorical elite, he was a speaker to whom people listened. In an arena where contradictory opinions, passions, and interests from all over Europe clashed, Pierre d'Ailly had to face some difficult moments. He wore himself down, as did many others. But he wore down less quickly. Often he was able to make himself heard and make his point of view prevail. In the twilight of his life Pierre d'Ailly had found a theater worthy of him.

John XXIII had convoked the Council of Constance to restore unity and reform the Church, but he never believed that his own position might be threatened. On December 2, 1414, however, Pierre d'Ailly delivered a sermon praising Sigismund for his zeal, and he dared to allude to a pope whose ambition had led him to enter the sanctuary through the wrong door, whose behavior was scandalous, and who governed the Church badly. Shortly thereafter, Pierre began to express doubts about the authority of the Council of Pisa. Guillaume Fillastre followed suit.[664] In other words, from the very beginning of the Council of Constance, Pierre d'Ailly and Guillaume Fillastre, two of the cardinals whom John XXIII had named on June 6, 1411, displayed their readiness to sacrifice their pope to the unity of the Church. Boniface Ferrer of course would have said that Pierre d'Ailly's betrayal and ingratitude came as no surprise. His behavior was not without precedent. Yet in a sense the ingratitude of a cardinal was only to be expected. In this time of uncertainty, a pope could count on a prelate's loyalty only as long as that prelate's ambitions were not fully satisfied. But once the pope named a cardinal, he created an independent power within the Church, a power with influence of its own and no longer under his control. The new cardinal might even become an eventual rival and possible successor. Of course Pierre d'Ailly would have indignantly rejected this analysis. And he was certainly convinced that in joining the king of the Romans he had taken the only course his conscience would allow to restore the unity of the Church, namely, the abdication of all three popes.

Pierre followed this course and was a potent adversary of John

XXIII until the beginning of February 1415. At that time the council had for some weeks been under the sway of a movement, favored by Sigismund, that called for organizing the representatives by nations. On February 7, 1415, it was decided that voting would be by nations.[665] This development, which threatened the position of the cardinals, worried Pierre d'Ailly. He was also obliged to take account of the ideas of the French delegation, which had just arrived and was not yet ready to abandon John XXIII.[666] Faced with these two difficulties, Pierre ceased to appear at the council's sessions for several weeks. He did not reappear until March 16, to defend John XXIII. On March 26, in an important session, the council decided that it would continue to meet with or without the pope. Although Pierre d'Ailly was in the chair that day, he announced that for the time being he would continue to obey John XXIII.[667] Pierre's memory of this session was highly disagreeable. While continuing to work behind the scenes, he ceased to appear at council sessions during April and May, citing reasons of health, although everyone knew his health to be excellent. He did not reappear until May 25, 1415, when the deposition of John XXIII was nearly settled and when the position of the cardinals was no longer challenged (they were accorded the right to sit as a distinct body in council sessions).[668] On the whole, the council had taken the decisions that Pierre had wanted it to take. It had sacrificed the pope and saved the cardinals. Satisfied, Pierre was able to play a key role in one of the other missions the council had set itself: the extirpation of heresy.

Bohemia, which had been so prosperous under Charles IV in the middle of the fourteenth century, had since then experienced hard times. Economic problems combined with social as well as ethnic tensions, as hostility between Germans and Czechs heated up. In this charged climate a reform movement had flourished. In part this movement continued an old Bohemian tradition that drew its inspiration from the Bible, but in part it also drew on the writings of John Wycliffe, who had taught at Oxford and died in 1384.[669] One of the best known of the reformers was Jan Hus. Born between 1369 and 1372, Hus had studied at the recently founded University of Prague. He had led a joyous life as a student, chatting all night with his friends over a pitcher of beer. But three things had changed him utterly: he had grown older, he had come to know the Bible, and he had seen sin. "As long as I was young in years and in reason, I was also full of mad gaiety. But when the Good God granted me knowledge of the Bible, I gave up the foolishness of youth."[670] He continued: "In the schools I faithfully listened to my masters, who spoke of humility, poverty, courage, and other virtues. They spoke so well that it seemed no fuller realization of these virtues was possible. Yet in their acts I found not those virtues but pride, avarice, intolerance, and cowardice."[671] The student, disappointed in his teachers, resolved to do battle against sin. "The principal aim that I pursued in my sermons, my teaching, and my writings, and in all my other actions," he said just before his death, "was none other than to turn people away from sin."[672] Jan Hus was a prodigious speaker. He preached to the clergy in Latin and to the people in Czech, and before long he became the university's most celebrated Czech teacher.

There was nothing unorthodox about eloquently denouncing vice in either Latin or Czech. Parisian doctors, Pierre d'Ailly foremost among them, had done or were doing the same thing in Latin and in French. And at first Hus preached with the support of the duke of Bohemia and the archbishop of Prague. Like all his contemporaries, however, Jan Hus asked himself the vexing and crucial question: Is a bishop who sins still a bishop? Hus, who did not conceal his admiration for Wycliffe's writings, answered in the negative. He was accused of many other things, but his one unpardonable heresy lay in this refusal to obey a sinful pastor. For, as everyone knew, nobody lived without sin, so that Hus's position threatened to undermine the hierarchy inherent in any society.[673] Such a refusal to obey, such a challenge to authority, would inevitably lead to the destruction of the Church, outside which there is no salvation. The archbishop of Prague was not deceived. For a time, however, Hus retained, as Wycliffe had done, the sympathy of lay princes who were not displeased by the thought of a Church shorn of its vices and still more of its wealth. The logic of Hus's argument carried him even farther than Wycliffe had gone, however. Ultimately he came to believe, and to proclaim, that the same principle that applied to ecclesiastical society also applied to civil society. Later, the fathers of the Council of Constance were correct in their summation of Hus's belief: "*Nullus est dominus civilis, nullus est episcopus dum est in peccato mortali*" (A lay lord or bishop in a state of mortal sin has no rights).[674]

Summoned to Constance, Jan Hus arrived on November 3, 1414, escorted by thirty horsemen at the end of an almost triumphal march.[675] He was certain that he would be able to justify his beliefs. But little by little he was crushed by the hatred of the Germans, the hostility of the ecclesiastical authorities, and the suspicion of the lay authorities. The struggle between John XXIII and the council delayed his trial for a time, but after John's deposition on May 29, 1415, things moved quickly. Hus found no defenders. Jean Gerson proved an implacable foe. Pierre d'Ailly was the central figure on the committee of inquiry. D'Ailly and Hus often found themselves face to face. At the end of the inquiry the cardinal asked Hus to recant, and he refused. On July 6, 1415, his head was shaved, his priesthood was revoked, and he was turned over to the secular authorities and burned. Jan Hus died for his stubborn certitude. Yet his judges, too, were tranquil in their certitudes. A doctrine that threatened hierarchy and authority, encouraged disobedience, and sowed disorder in society was a heresy, and any heretic who did not recant had to be burned. At one point in the session during which Pierre d'Ailly asked Hus to recant, the cardinal shouted: "For a heretic who persists [*pertinax*], I myself would light the fire under him."[676]

The conciliar fathers took a firm line against Jan Hus, all the more so because they had to prove to others and to themselves that their own revolt against the pope was exceptional, that the change in the seat of authority that events had forced on them in no way shook the principle of obedience in either ecclesiastical society or lay society. And they felt that they had the backing of the princes. It was this support that was lacking when the council examined the theses of Jean Petit. Everything was different. In Jean Gerson's eyes Jean Petit's justification of tyrannicide was a doctrine at least as subversive as the idea of Jan Hus. In Paris the chancellor's zealous efforts against Petit's doctrine had been crowned with success, for on September 16, 1416 Parlement made it illegal to publish, affirm, or teach that tyrannicide was legitimate and prohibited the publication or copying of Petit's *Justification.*[677] In Constance the chancellor had been just as zealous against Hus's ideas, and once again his zeal was successful. But when he turned that zeal to a further attack on the ideas of Jean Petit, the one decision in this regard that was taken by the council went against him. The duke of Burgundy had appealed to the pope the February 23, 1414, judgment against Petit's *Justification* by the bishop and inquisitor of Paris. On January 16, 1416, the three cardinals assigned to consider this appeal found that the bishop and inquisitor of Paris (who in effect had rejected their judges and failed to appear) were in contempt and therefore overturned the judgment and voided the sentence. The cardinals later claimed that they had had no intention of judging the substance of the case and had based their decision solely on questions of procedure. But no one was deceived. The judgment of January 16, 1416, was a major victory for the duke of Burgundy. Despite all Jean Gerson's efforts, the case went no further at Constance. It remained, as the saying went, *in sacco* (in the bag).[678]

The reasons for Jean Gerson's failure were obvious. The ambassadors of John the Fearless, particularly Pierre Cauchon and Martin Porée, a Dominican and bishop of Arras, had been most effective.

Some they had won over with gifts; others they had paralyzed with threats. Pierre d'Ailly in particular would have liked to come to the aid of his friend Gerson, whose ideas he shared. In June 1415 he was elected to the committee delegated by the council to deal with the matter. But Martin Porée immediately rejected him on the grounds of his hostility toward Jean Petit and his close friendship with Gerson. The cardinal of Cambrai withdrew in a state of confusion (*confusus abiit*).[679] Subsequently Martin Porée vigilantly opposed what he called clamor and calumny (*clamores et contumeliae*).[680] Jean Gerson may not have been wrong in blaming the festering hatred that the Dominicans had harbored against Pierre d'Ailly ever since the 1389 dispute over the immaculate conception. He was surely wrong, however, to suggest that the condemnation of Jan Hus's errors had been easy because princes and other laymen had not opposed it, whereas the condemnation of Jean Petit's errors had proved impossible because it had met with hostility from those elements.[681]

The Jean Petit affair cost Pierre d'Ailly and Jean Gerson a considerable part of the support they had enjoyed at the council. Gerson's exasperation, if we are to believe his adversaries, drove him to make ill-advised statements at which Martin Porée invariably took offense. One day Gerson allegedly said that he was so sure of what he was saying that if the pope, the sacred college, and even the general council disagreed, he would not believe them. Worse: "Even if God said the opposite, I would not believe him." Was not Martin Porée right to find such single-minded obstinacy dangerous? Another time, on September 8, 1416, while exalting woman in a sermon on the immaculate conception, Gerson is supposed to have said "that by divine right, and by human right, which cannot be contrary to divine right, women may succeed to the thrones of kingdoms." Was not Martin Porée right to find such an assertion, coming from a loyal subject of the Valois king, quite odd?[682] By the end of 1415 Jean Gerson no longer had the audience he had had on his arrival in Constance in February 1415. As for Pierre d'Ailly, John the Fearless launched a violent attack against him in a letter dated April 28, 1416, to the nations of the council. In it John recalled Pierre d'Ailly's moves against his father Philip the Bold, decried the bishop of Cambrai's unwavering hatred for the house of Burgundy, invoked that hatred to explain Pierre d'Ailly's hostility to Jean Petit, and accordingly refused to allow the cardinal to intervene in his affairs.[683]

In fact, however, the disastrous defeat inflicted on the French by the English at Agincourt on October 25, 1415, had a much greater impact on the course of the Council of Constance than did the Jean Petit affair. When, on July 18, 1415, a few days after the abdication of Gregory XII and the death of Jan Hus, Sigismund, more than ever convinced of his role as "advocate and defender of the Church," left Constance with four thousand horsemen to try to force Benedict XIII to abdicate, his attitude toward the king of France was reasonably favorable.[684] After Agincourt, however, he hastily threw his support to the victor. On August 15, 1416, the Treaty of Canterbury joined Sigismund to King Henry V of England in a defensive and offensive alliance against France. Shortly thereafter, Sigismund and John the Fearless entered into cordial relations.[685] So that when the king of the Romans returned to Constance on January 27, 1417, after a year and a half of absence, the French regarded him as a traitor.[686] For some months already, in the face of an alliance between the king of the Romans, the king of England, and the duke of Burgundy, they had felt singularly isolated.

As early as the end of 1416 the hatred between the English and the French had crystallized around the problem of the nations. Recall that at the beginning of 1415 the council had organized itself into nations and that on February 7, 1415, it had decided to vote by nations. After a decision was approved by each nation individually, it was then taken before the plenary assembly for final approval.[687] At that point the number of nations had not been an issue. That number was four, just as at the University of Paris, but they were not the same four nations as at the university. It was possible to ascribe a symbolic value to each, for they were composed of the peoples of the east (German), south (Italian), west (French), and north (English), which taken together constituted the universal Church.[688] Thus in 1415 the nations of the Council of Constance had a symbolic and geographic significance. But not being based on states or languages, they had no more political significance than did the nations of the university.

For more than a year the "nations" of Constance posed no problem. But when national animosities were stirred and storm clouds began to gather, things changed. In July 1416 the Germans and English attempted to alter the council's rules: for a measure to be adopted, they proposed, it should be enough to win the approval of a majority of the nations rather than of all four nations. The tiny English nation would immediately have acquired the same influence as the enormous French nation. This was absurd, and the French blocked the proposal.[689] The nations issue came up again in October 1416 when the Aragonese, who at last had abandoned Benedict XIII, arrived in Constance and insisted on forming a new nation. The French immediately recognized the danger in the proposal. If Aragon's six representatives formed a nation, the whole national system would become unbalanced. Furthermore, if one now gave a political meaning to the term "nation," the representatives of Castille would want to form a nation of their own. And what about the Hungarians, Bohemians, Poles, and Danes, currently members of the German nation—why wouldn't they want to sit as separate nations? And other members from other nations? The whole national structure of the council would be called into question.[690] In the autumn of 1416 the French therefore very rightly observed: "Sometimes measures are taken because they are thought to be in the general interest, but experience shows that they are in fact harmful."[691] And experience showed that Pierre d'Ailly had indeed been right in 1415 to oppose the organization of the council into nations. It was necessary to distinguish the world of the Church from the world of states. A division by nations and kingdoms was more secular than ecclesiastic.[692] In the autumn of 1416, when the "dangers and difficulties"[693] of the national system as it had functioned at Constance for nearly two years became apparent, Pierre d'Ailly again brought up his previous proposal of a vote organized by ecclesiastical provinces.[694] But he did not linger over the issue. The French did not challenge the principle of organization by nations. Motivated by their hatred of the English, they first allowed the Aragonese to join their ranks[695] and then proposed simply that the English nation—like the Aragonese, too small to sit alone—ought to be combined with the German. This partisan proposal, which threatened to disrupt the status quo, had no chance of succeeding, and in fact it did not succeed. But from early October 1416 to late March 1417 it dominated and paralyzed the council, whose atmosphere remained poisoned for a long time thereafter.[696]

The leading sponsors of this rude national rancor were Jean Gerson,Guillaume Fillastre even more, and Pierre d'Ailly most of all. On June 1, 1416, the king of France named Pierre d'Ailly and Guillaume Fillastre to act at the council as his proxies.[697] The two men dreamed of eliminating the English nation. Through his attacks, stratagems, and absences Pierre d'Ailly called the tune, and he became the focus of English hatred and of Sigismund's hostility. He was indeed the person who seemed to be the "head of the French nation."[698] And the failure of the French proposal was his personal failure.

Alas, Pierre d'Ailly had one last opportunity to defy the council and proclaim his love for his country. On August 1, 1417, Henry V landed once again in Normandy. A few days later, John the Fearless marched on Paris. From Constance, Sigismund followed his allies' progress. On August 19 Pierre d'Ailly mounted the pulpit to celebrate the virtues of Saint Louis of Anjou, whose feast fell on that day. Saint Louis of Anjou was a saint cherished by the French dynasty. He was the son of Charles II of Anjou, the king of Sicily, and the grandson of Charles I of Anjou, himself the brother of Saint Louis, the king of France. Saint Louis of Anjou joined the Franciscans and died prematurely as bishop of Toulouse in 1297, the very year in which his great-uncle was canonized. He himself was canonized in 1317 by John XXII at the behest of the Friars Minor and, above all, the house of Anjou. Since then the French and Angevin dynasties had celebrated the cult of the great-uncle and the grand-nephew with equal fervor. On that dark day in August 1417, however, Pierre d'Ailly was thinking not so much of Saint Louis as of the French royal line and not so much of the French royal line as of France itself. About Saint Louis of Anjou people sang:

> Flos ortus inter lilia
> Quorum radix est Francia.
>
> [Flower born among lilies,
> whose root is France.]

Remembering this, Pierre d'Ailly added:

> France—that is, the France that is the head, the highest and greatest part of Gaul, which I recall having praised another time and which I wish to praise again today, not only to praise this saint more fully but also to confound and heap shame upon Gaul's detractors, the invaders who tarnish her honor and glory and disturb her prosperity and peace. Of all the countries in the world this one is the one on which the scholars of the past bestowed the greatest praise. This noble Gaul, as Lucan called it; which took from the war greater glory than the Romans, Sallust said; whose army was so strong and so fortunate, Claudian noted; which can boast of audacity, boldness, and rich pastures, Horace said; whose men are so handsome and whose culture is so flourishing, Virgil observed; and which, if harmony reigns, can hold off the world, as Caesar said. This rude and warlike Gaul, which, after Hercules, conquered the Alpine peaks, as Justin said. This land made terrifying by its inhabitants, as Florus said. The flower and backbone of the Roman Empire, said Cicero. The mother of sciences, said Julius Celsus [Caesar]. Whose men have such penetrating minds, said Isidore [of Seville]. This fortunate country which has no monster, as Quintilian said and Jerome after him. Which is religion's devoted nurse, said Titus Livy. This Gaul, to sum up in a word, which, as Gregory said, surpasses all other states. Yet the same author bestowed the highest praise of all: Gaul is the splendid torch which, by the radiant clarity of its orthodox faith, shines in the midst of the perfidious obscurity of other peoples. And to be

> sure the faith of that Gaul, the clarity of its faith and its religion, which Gregory exalted thus, still today, in this present general council, has shone brilliantly, and it shines still more brilliantly with each passing day, though some strive in vain to veil its light. These fools will be thwarted, however, for as Sallust says most aptly, futile efforts whose only end is hatred are the work of extremely demented minds.[699]

With these words a Frenchman who shared his country's woes employed all the resources of his erudition in calling upon Gaul to come to the aid of France.

Nevertheless, this troubled Frenchman's final words showed that he was still a prelate concerned about the future of the Church. The controversial representative of the king of France was still a cardinal whose words commanded attention. At the very moment when the English and French nations were clashing violently, on All Saints' Day, November 1, 1416, Pierre d'Ailly presented to the council his *Treatise on the Reform of the Church.*[700] He then went into the pulpit to deliver an important sermon to all the fathers of the council.[701] His premise could not have been more traditional: that there is a parallelism between heaven and earth. In the heavens there is the sun, which presides over the day; the moon, which presides over the night; and the stars. On earth there is a sun, the papacy, which governs spiritual things; a moon, the imperial or royal majesty, which governs temporal things; and stars, namely the various estates of society, which are subject to the authority of the two high dignities and expected to demonstrate "filial obedience." This traditional beginning leads first to something less commonplace, which we know Pierre d'Ailly cared about very deeply, astronomy: "Let astronomy's detractors turn red. They say that it is a contemptible or condemnable science. But has it not searched for and found great and admirable things?" He ends with a series of wishes that sums up his vision of political society:

> O, would to heaven that this sacred council bring together and into harmony the sun and the moon. May they achieve perfect concord, respect each other, and humbly obey. Would to heaven that all strive to respect the fixed order, that the lesser not seek to outstrip the greater, that they not bring down the great nor dare usurp their authority. Would to heaven that all the stars in this celestial college shine far from the darkness of error and vice, that neither conflict nor schism nor scandal obscure them, that neither hypocrisy nor an apparent equality that would in fact be a double injustice cast them into shadow. Would to heaven that here, unlike in the sky, there be not five stars in clouds or nine stars in darkness. And if perchance

> there should be, would to heaven that they not thrust themselves before the bright stars and block their light or tarnish their luster. Far from us, yes, far from us the terrible prediction of Joel: "The sun and the moon shall be dark, and the stars shall withdraw their shining."

The odd phrase "apparent equality that would in fact be a double injustice" was an allusion to the conflict between the French nation and the English nation; injustice, Pierre d'Ailly says, would be the result if the two were treated as equals. The whole passage reflects the difficulties and conflicts the council had faced over the previous two years. Yet Pierre also looked beyond that moment and that time to speak of hierarchy, order (*debitum suum ordinem*), the authority (*auctoritas*) of some, the humble obedience (*humiliter oboediant*) of others, and he says one more time that he has never doubted that this world is the only one possible.

After the dispute between the French nation and the English nation had been settled (March 1417) and Pope Benedict XIII had been deposed (July 26, 1417), it remained to choose a pope. The cardinals naturally claimed the right to make the choice. But the fathers of the council found it difficult to see how they could be denied any role in the process. It was Pierre d'Ailly who came up with a compromise solution: the pope would be elected by a conclave which for this one time would consist not only of cardinals but also of representatives of each nation. At first this proposal met with stiff resistance. Old Elie de Lestrange was against it. Pierre d'Ailly had the support of his friend Guillaume Fillastre and of his old enemy Simon de Cramaud.[702] Gradually Pierre's proposal came to be seen as the only possible solution. After months of negotiations, the cardinals and nations gave it their support one by one, and on November 8, 1417, at four in the afternoon, twenty-three cardinals and thirty delegates of the nations began the conclave.[703]

On November 10 Pierre d'Ailly was one of the three prelates still receiving votes. Did he, for one night, see himself as pope? At sixty-six Pierre d'Ailly was still ambitious, but he also was still clear-headed. He knew very well that everyone thought of him as the "father of all evils" and the "particular enemy" of their king.[704] His election would have promised a new schism. No doubt it came as no surprise when, on November 11, 1417, his name vanished and that of Ottone Colonna came to the fore. Cardinal Ottone Colonna was approximately fifty years old. He was a mild and a good man, discreet, and a stranger to intrigue. He had studied law but, it was said, had retained very little. He rarely spoke. In the council he had never taken sides and had done nothing. Nobody had spoken about him. He was elected "by unanimous consent."[705] Since he was elected on Saint Martin's Day, he took the name Martin V.

The council was essentially over. Its members left Constance one after another. Simon de Cramaud left in January 1418. Close to seventy-three, he returned to his episcopal palace in Poitiers rarely to emerge again until his death in 1423.[706] Nicolas de Clamanges did not attend the council, but when Martin V was elected he made a brief visit to Constance, probably in the hope of resuming his service with the new pope. In February 1418 he was with Pierre d'Ailly. Fifty-five years old, he found his hopes dashed and returned to Fontaine-au-Bois.[707] Guillaume Fillastre, aged seventy, left on April 2, 1418.[708] Martin V sent him to persuade the king of France and the duke of Brittany that they ought to recognize the new pope as quickly as possible.[709] The cardinal would die on November 6, 1428, when he was seventy-nine or eighty. Pierre d'Ailly departed a few days later, in April 1418.[710] Although he was sixty-seven, he had nothing to hope for from the new pope. He returned to his house in Avignon. Jean Gerson departed in May 1418.[711] At age fifty-five, his whole future lay in front of him. But he was obliged to head east. Tragic events prevented him from returning to France.

The Final Years (1418–20)

Throughout the Council of Constance Jean de Montreuil had remained in Paris, where he continued to work as a notary-secretary in the royal chancellery. The events of the period had distressed him, however, and he shared the sentiments of his friend Pierre d'Ailly. Like Pierre, Jean loved France and the French. He had long detested the English.[712] Now he despised Sigismund, and in September 1417 he wrote a vehement pamphlet against the king of the Romans.[713] At about the same time he wrote a long letter in which he had no difficulty embroidering on the commonplace theme, "*Tempora nostra pessima sunt*" (Our times are the worst). Among the misfortunes he cites are Crécy, Poitiers, the English conquest, the Parisian revolution, and the "Jacques" (seditious peasants) who had marred his adolescence (*ab adolescentia nostra*), a scourge that Pierre d'Ailly never mentions but whose violence Jean de Montreuil describes with terror.[714] There were also the woes of his adult life, the afflictions of "his time," about which he resolved not to speak (*nihil de nostra etat dixere*).[715] Throughout this disastrous period, Jean had found satisfaction in only one thing: himself. He had had a brilliant career, frequently serving the king of France as ambassador. In that capacity he had been admitted to familiarity with popes, emperors, kings of the Romans, kings of England, kings of Scotland, queens, and others. There follows an admirable passage in which we glimpse, behind Jean's joy at remaining healthy, his discomfort with retirement:

> But, pious Jesus, in addition to so many spiritual and temporal goods, as people commonly say, you have filled my cup by granting me a very vigorous health. So that (thanks be to your goodness) I have never been confined to bed for so much as a single day by any disease, and my colleagues have never had to count me absent. I have just completed my sixty-third year [the figure has been verified], and I have walked, eaten, drunk, and slept as in the past. I have ridden horses at a fast pace without stopping, and I never sat like an old man. And what will astound you even more, I almost always ran or jumped up and down the stairs of my house when I was alone or with my family. And my hand does not tremble when it guides my quill. . . . My greatest desire is still, more than ever, to continue in the duties of my office and in service to the common cause and the king.[716]

Fate was to spare the vigorous sexagenarian the torments of retirement. On the night of May 28–29, 1418, the Burgundian army entered Paris. On May 29 the dauphin left the city. That same day a frenzied mob attacked anything it believed to be Armagnac. The College of Navarre was one of its first targets: "Among them," Michel Pintoin recounts, "was the cantor of Saint-Denis, who spread their violence to the famous College of Navarre, then headed by the venerable Raoul de Laporte, doctor of theology. They forced their way in, broke down the doors of the students' cells, and pillaged them. They also removed the books from the library and heaped abuse upon the scholars. They would even have murdered some of them if Messire de l'Isle-Adam had not arrived in great haste to calm their fury with gentle words. Nevertheless, they ended as ignominously as the rest, languishing in the king's prisons."[717] Many Armagnacs managed to flee, but a good number of others were cast into prison. A few days later, in mid-June, these Armagnac prisoners were massacred by the hundreds, many in an atrocious manner. Jean de Montreuil had been unwilling to flee.[718] He was one of the victims.

Is it worth mentioning one trivial consequence of this terrible tragedy, the epilogue to the Jean Petit affair? On August 9 the university admonished all who had spoken or written in its name. And on March 27, 1419, the Parlement, slower to change its mind, acceded to royal command and revoked its earlier decisions.[719]

These revocations passed unnoticed. The survivors—Nicolas de Clamanges in Fontaine-au-Bois, Jean Gerson in Bavaria, and Pierre d'Ailly in Avignon—mourned their deceased friends.

Slowly life reasserted its rights. Despite his sadness, Jean Gerson was moved to write yet another poignant song of hope (*Carmen de causa canendi*):

> *Nec prorsus omnes Mors tulit effera:*
> *Petrus superstes, quem Sapiencia*
> *Totum replevit . . .*
> *Qui veritatis exul amore fit*
> *Nostri Clamengis dulce sapit stilus.*
> *Etas novellam progeniem dabit*
> *Pro patribus quos perdidit Atropos*
>
> Cruel death has not taken them all:
> Pierre [d'Ailly] remains, full
> of Wisdom . . .
> The gentle pen of our [Nicolas de] Clamanges
> Whom love of truth made an exile remains, still wise
> With time new children will come
> to replace the fathers whom Fate has lost.[720]

Pierre d'Ailly, in his beautiful residence at Avignon not far from the Celestine monastery there[721] and close to the grave of Peter of Luxemburg, found himself out of action and began once more to read and write. He remained true to himself. He reread the authors he always read, Saint Bernard, Hugh and Richard of Saint-Victor, and Saint Bonaventure. He reread and recopied his devotional pamphlets.[722] In 1418 he wrote a brief treatise entitled *De persecutionibus ecclesiae,* which incorporated themes and even whole passages from *De concordia astronomice veritatis et narrationis hystorice,* which he had completed in Basel on May 10, 1414.[723] In 1419 he recopied his *Imago mundi.*[724]

While Pierre d'Ailly lived in industrious, perhaps temporary retirement, the king of England was completing his conquest of Normandy, John the Fearless steered an unsteady course between Henry V and the dauphin Charles. At last the dauphin and the duke of Burgundy agreed to meet. What thoughts lurked in their minds? They were wary of each other, the duke no less than the dauphin. The meeting took place on the bridge of Montereau on September 10, 1419, but the discussion went badly and ended in "harsh words," after which the dauphin left. Then the duke fell, with several sword wounds in his body.[725] The assassin, the man for whom Jean Petit had composed his apology for tyrannicide, died a victim of assassination.

Some weeks later, probably in November 1419, Pierre d'Ailly received from his friend Jean Gerson, now living in Lyons, a treatise in which Gerson once again strongly condemned the second part of astronomy, that is, astrology. In response, Pierre d'Ailly once again preached a middle course between two extremes. Admittedly there were superstitious astronomers who, contrary to theological truth, placed astrology too high. But there were also superstitious theologians who, contrary to philosophical reason, placed astronomy too low. It was quite possible that the position of the stars exerted some influence on the earth. Was that influence difficult to understand? That was no reason to reject theology or any other science that met with inexplicable difficulties. Were there pseudo-astronomers, whose errors were manifest? That was no reason to condemn astronomy, any more than it was a reason to condemn theology for the errors of pseudo-theologians. Pierre then alluded to the two friends' recent bitter experience, in particular to Gerson's efforts to have Jean Petit's theses condemned. "The experience of the general council has shown you how numerous these pseudo-theologians are," he said in rough paraphrase. "For they did not hide themselves in the shadows. All too often they barked in public. Against those voracious wolves in sheep's clothing the prelates, and above all the sovereign pontiff, ought to have issued constant warning. Alas, as the prophet so aptly said, many were the silent dogs who could not bark (Isa. 56:10). That was the source of all these scandals. The lion in his rage cruelly bit you, you and other courageous defenders of the faith. Several who were barbarously massacred in the Paris uprising might, I think, be rightly added to the list of martyred saints." This recollection of bitter experience is followed, however, by a cry of joy, although the ecclesiastic does not wish to seem unduly triumphant in revenge: "But now the tyrant has suffered the shameful death he deserved. His earthly life is over, but thanks to God not his eternal life."[726]

The indomitable old man felt renewed hope for France and, perhaps, for himself. Soon the dauphin would be coming to Lyons. Pierre d'Ailly prepared to travel there. The dauphin actually entered Lyons on January 22, 1420.[727] Was Pierre d'Ailly there? We do not know. In any case, in the months that followed he was still (or again) in Avignon. Was it then that he wrote the remarkable little dialogue between two knights, one French, the other English? We are not sure, but it would be pleasant if it were so.

Scholars have long been familiar with two dialogues between a French and an English knight, who discuss the disputes between their two countries and the rights of their respective kings to accede to the French throne. There is general agreement that both dialogues date from the 1420s. For a long time they were attributed to Pierre d'Ailly, the date of whose death was then uncertain. When it became known that he actually died in 1420, it seemed clear that the dialogues were not his work.[728] Let us consider the matter more closely, however. It is certain that the second dialogue, which was written at the earliest in 1422, is not by Pierre d'Ailly. And in any case this turgid, ponderous, legalistic work would have dishonored his pen. But the first dialogue is admirable both for the vigor of its ideas and for the vivacity of its style. It could be Pierre d'Ailly's work. And it was written, we are told, two years before the second dialogue. One would like to think that it was the last work of Pierre d'Ailly, written in 1420. And there is no evidence to the contrary.[729]

In this first dialogue two knights meet in Vaucluse (in other words, close to Avignon where Pierre d'Ailly was staying). They immediately inquire of each other where they are from. I am French, says one. I am English, responds the other. Therefore, the Frenchman says, you are my enemy (*Ergo, inquit francus, inimicus*). But, the Englishman says, I have laid down my arms and am now a pilgrim. A dialogue ensues, a brief portion of which follows:

> F(renchman): What are you looking for?
>
> E(nglishman): The salvation of my soul.
>
> F: The times are not propitious.
>
> E: How old are you? [A remarkable, and rare, question. People in this period were still not much concerned with their age. The answer is also worthy of note, for it shows a man much less concerned with the beginning of his earthly life than with the beginning of his life in heaven.]
>
> F: I have no years. But death has spared me for fifty years.
>
> E: And me longer. [Both knights are getting on in years, as the Frenchman observes.]
>
> F: We have reached the supper hour. And the world is drawing to an end. No more time remains. We all must fear the death of our bodies. And the salvation of our souls is doubtful.
>
> E: Why doubtful? I am sure of being saved.
>
> F: Why? [We come to the crux of the matter.]
>
> E: Because, on God's order, we obey our prince, who impels us to make war. And if we die because we obeyed him, we die on God's order. [The dialogue continues, and the Frenchman drops the subject of war in general as well as of the just defensive war, the kind of war in which he is engaged. In canonical fashion he confines his attack to the unjust offensive war being waged by the English.]
>
> F: Your war is unjust, because it originates in the will to dominate [*in libidine dominandi*] and in the tyrannical pleasure of enriching

oneself at the expense of Christians. And whoever knowingly commits a sin goes to hell.

E: Therefore I should disobey my prince? Is it not written that whoever disobeys his prince must die? Will not disobedience make me a wretch, a fool, a coward, a deserter, or worse yet, a traitor, an enemy of the state?

F: One must obey what is just, not what is unjust.

E: Whatever the prince orders with the counsel of his prelates and barons I believe to be just.

F: What good is your own conscience, then, if you brave death because you trust in the conscience of others? . . . You are not bound to obey against God.

E: But who can restrain our king, correct him, or force him to pull back? Certainly not we, who are his subjects.

F: If you are all united, it will be possible for you not to share his opinion. But since you do all share his opinion, you are all guilty.

There are many other things in this astonishing dialogue, but let us leave it here. I am not certain that it is by Pierre d'Ailly, although I hope it is, for then it would indicate, in a long and difficult but necessary and logical evolution, one final stage, one ultimate audacity. A champion of obedience, Pierre d'Ailly had naturally opposed Jean Petit, who claimed to justify tyrannicide. On July 6, 1415, he had looked on with satisfaction when Jan Hus burned for ideas that called obedience into question. And he had always rejected the idea of individual disobedience. But after refusing for a long time to abandon Benedict XIII, circumstances—and the old pontiff's stubbornness—finally forced him to admit that the Church, or the general council that represented it, might be obliged in the common interest to disobey and depose the pope.[730] A few years later, devastated by his country's misfortunes, he held out the prospect of hell to an Englishman who refused to use his own conscience and who justified making war on France on grounds of the obedience due his king. Let me be clear: the last sentence I cite from the dialogue marks the limits of Pierre d'Ailly's ultimate audacity. He does not go so far as to encourage individual disobedience by the English knight. But he does say that the people of the kingdom can, and sometimes must, oppose the king—at least in England.

Pierre d'Ailly's patriotism was to suffer one final blow. The Treaty of Troyes was signed on May 20–21, 1420. Charles the dauphin was disinherited; Henry V married Catherine, the daughter of Charles VI and Isabeau, and thus became the "son" of the king and queen and heir to the throne. France sank into misery that would last for years. Jean Gerson lived to sixty-six, long enough to rejoice in the appearance of Joan of Arc.[731] He gave up his soul to God on July 12, 1429,[732] a few days before the anointment of Charles VII at Rheims on July 17. Nicolas de Clamanges returned to a Paris occupied by the English. After thirty years he had come back to the College of Navarre. In 1426 he was there, and he lived on until 1437, when he died at seventy-four. On April 13, 1436, prior to his death, Charles VII's troops recaptured Paris. Was Nicolas able to rejoice in their victory? Apparently not, for it seems that he had been plunged for some years into the night of senility. For Pierre d'Ailly fate reserved neither Nicolas's night nor Jean's joy. He died a few weeks after the Treaty of Troyes on August 9, 1420.[733] He had just turned sixty-nine. A short while earlier he had still been in full possession of his strength.

Pierre d'Ailly, cardinal-priest of Saint Crysogonus and currently known as cardinal of Cambrai, stipulated in his will that his funeral be celebrated without pomp or unreasonable expense.[734] His body was to be buried in the principal church of the place in which he died. Later his bones were to be transported to the cathedral of Cambrai, where his tomb had long stood ready to receive them. Immediately after his death or as soon as possible three hundred masses were to be celebrated for himself, his relatives, and his benefactors. On the first anniversary of his death solemn obits, with vigils and masses, were to be celebrated in the cathedrals of Paris, Soissons, Noyon, and Cambrai, as well as in the Sainte-Chapelle of the palace in Paris and at the College of Navarre; in all the churches of Compiègne; and in all the churches of Cambrai. Finally, Pierre d'Ailly endowed perpetual obits in the church of Saint-Antoine in Compiègne (where he had been baptized), at the College of Navarre, and in the cathedrals of Paris, Soissons, Noyon, and Le Puy. As for the cathedral of Cambrai, all necessary preparations had long since been made. In addition, Pierre had for a long time been a benefactor of the College of Navarre.

Pierre d'Ailly's will also provided for generous bequests to his servants and relatives and to the poor of Compiègne and Cambrai. Among his relatives his greatest generosity was reserved for the twelve most closely related to him by blood, and especially to the four marriageable girls closest to him, each of whom received one hundred *livres parisis.*

One paragraph of the will was devoted to the books and other works that had been one of his principal concerns during his lifetime: "As for my books, it is my wish and order that none of them be sold. They shall be distributed to my closest blood relatives and to my servants, so long as they are of the Church, according to their needs and to the decisions of my executors. However, regarding those books and treatises of which I myself am the author, it is my wish that steps be taken to permit their publication."

Finally, the will designated eight executors to carry out Pierre d'Ailly's last wishes. Among them were his nephews Raoul and Pierre Le Prestre, both of whom he had made canons of Cambrai,[735] and Michel Le Charon, who in 1394 was curé of Saint-Antoine in Compiègne, so dear to Pierre d'Ailly, and who was now canon of Noyon.

On August 31, 1422, Henry V died. On October 21, 1422, Charles VI died. A few weeks earlier, Pierre d'Ailly's executors had scrupulously carried out the wishes of the deceased. On August 6, 1422, the cardinal's remains were laid to rest in his tomb in Cambrai.[736]

CHAPTER

4

THOMAS BASIN (1412–1490)

An Eyewitness Account in the Making (1471–88)

In January 1471 Thomas Bain settled in Trier. In his flight this marked a new milestone. At that moment, Louix XI, at forty-seven, had been king of France for nearly ten years. Charles, whose subjects called him Charles the Bold (*le Hardi*) but who, after the final disaster, would come to be known as Charles the Foolhardy (*le Téméraire*), was, at thirty-seven, duke of Burgundy. He ruled, in one portion of his territory, the duchy of Burgundy, the Franche-Comté, and the counties of Mâcon, Charolais, and Nevers; and, in another portion of his territory, Flanders, Brabant, Holland, Luxemburg, Hainault, Artois, and the cities of the Somme. This vast domain had been assembled piece by piece over a period of more than a hundred years by Philip the Bold, Charles's great-grandfather, who had received the duchy of Burgundy as an appanage from his father, King Charles V of France, in 1363; next, by John the Fearless, son of Philip the Bold and grandfather of Charles; and after him by Charles's father, Philip the Good, who died in 1467. The territory had its weaknesses. It was a mosaic of lands, each with a tradition of its own. Some were in the kingdom of France, others in the Empire. Above all, the territory was not an undivided whole. It fell into two distinct parts, and in order to go from one to the other, the duke of Burgundy was obliged to pass through either Champagne, a part of France, or Lorraine, a part of the Empire, neither of which belonged to him. Nevertheless, all these possessions, taken together, made the duke of Burgundy a powerful and wealthy prince. France, having at last emerged triumphant from its long war with England and slowly regaining its strength, probably could not have tolerated this great menacing shadow for long, regardless of the personalities of the king of France and the duke of Burgundy. Conflict soon erupted between Louis XI and Charles the Bold. Initially it was rough going for the king of France, who was forced to sign the Treaty of Péronne on October 14, 1468.

The conflict, however, was not a straightforward duel. There was also England to reckon with. And England, defeated and humiliated in its Continental war, had succumbed to civil strife. For fifteen years the red rose of Lancaster had clashed with the white rose of York. But the duke of York, crowned Edward IV, had little by little gained the upper hand over the legitimate Lancaster king, Henry VI. In 1465 Henry was imprisoned in the Tower of London, after which, one by one, his last remaining supporters were subdued. Louis XI was an ally of the house of Lancaster, because Marguerite d'Anjou, the wife of Henry VI and soul of the Lancaster party, was a French princess and a close relative. Charles the Bold, on the other hand, was an ally of Edward IV. In 1468 he married Edward's sister, Margaret of York. Louis XI's problems were therefore compounded by the victory of Edward IV.

After some years on the throne, however, the English king had made numerous enemies. In the final months of 1470, as so often in the War of the Roses, the entire situation changed dramatically. In September Lancastrian troops landed in England. On October 2 Edward IV fled his kingdom to seek refuge in his brother-in-law's territory. On October 6 Henry VI was rescued from prison and replaced on the throne. Louis XI felt that the moment had come. In November he assembled a group of prelates, lords, and officers in Tours, and this assembly declared null and void the commitments the king had made in the Treaty of Péronne. On December 3 the king ordered his lieutenants to seize the ducal cities closest to his royal domain. On December 10 Saint-Quentin was captured.

Thomas Basin was then living in Louvain, in Brabant, which he loved for having studied there and where he felt safely remote from the king of France. After the fall of Saint-Quentin Thomas was gripped by panic. He saw French troops at the gates of the city. Without delay he took to the road and did not stop until he reached Trier. The ancient Roman capital was reduced to a small town of no more than a few thousand inhabitants. But it was a prosperous city, dominated in both spiritual and temporal affairs by its archbishop, one of the most prestigious princes of the Empire. Most important, Trier was adjacent to Burgundian territory but not part of it. Here, far from the din of battle, Thomas Basin hoped to find peace and tranquillity.[1]

With leisure time that he intended to devote to letters, restored to the *otium litterale* he had always loved, Thomas began to write.[2] His life had gotten off to a good start. In 1447, at age thirty-five, he had been named bishop of Lisieux. In 1449, at the time of Charles VII's reconquest of Normandy after a lengthy English occupation, he had played an important role, which had attracted the attention of the king and the court. Before he was forty he was named counselor to the king of France. His future seemed bright. But Charles VII died in 1461 without ever having entrusted Thomas with an important mission. Despite the best efforts of the zealous courtier that Thomas had become, Charles's son Louis XI also passed him over. What is more, in the difficult early years of the new reign, Thomas Basin made numerous errors and bad decisions. The king was a redoubtable adversary. Louis XI's hostility increased as rapidly as Thomas's fear. On January 5, 1466, Thomas deemed it wise to take hasty leave of France and return to Louvain. A few months later he returned, not without misgivings, to France in an attempt to regain favor. The king received him coldly but entrusted him with a distant mission. At first Thomas accepted and went to Roussillon. Very quickly, however, he begged to be recalled to more clement skies. The king refused. Unable to bear any more, Thomas Basin once again took flight. By way of Geneva and Basel he returned to Louvain. He was there at the beginning of 1469. And it was there in December 1470 that fear once again gripped him and drove him to Trier. He was fifty-eight. The once ambitious man, aware of his utter failure, was reduced to bitterness.

And in Trier in 1471 Thomas Basin, pondering his failure and eager to explain it and justify his actions, conceived the idea of writing a history of his times, that is, of the two successive reigns of Charles VII and Louis XI, which he had witnessed and in which he had even played a modest role.[3] So in 1471 and 1472, while in England Edward IV decisively defeated the Lancastrian king and while on the Continent the duel between Louis XI and Charles the Bold continued with intervals of calm between tragedies, Thomas Basin wrote the five books of his *History of Charles VII.*[4] In 1473 he wrote the first two books of his *History of Louis XI,* which continued the story up to 1469, breaking it off just before the recent dramatic events that had compelled him to flee Louvain for Trier.[5]

In the city on the Moselle Thomas Basin was a person of no consequence. The count-bishop of Lisieux was a decorative figure, however, so that when the University of Trier was inaugurated in 1473, he was asked to celebrate the inaugural mass.[6] But when Emperor Frederick III and Charles the Bold met in Trier in October and November of the same year, Thomas Basin stood in the crowd, an attentive witness to the grandiose ceremonies that marked the occasion. He was present when the emperor awarded the duke the investiture of Guelders, which he had just conquered. Subsequently he followed all the preparations for the ceremony in which the emperor was supposed to place upon the duke's head the crown he so ardently desired, which would have given him the prestigious title of king. Like everyone else, Thomas Basin learned of Frederick's precipitous departure on the eve of the ceremony. He was able to bemoan, as was his wont, the fickleness of the human will and the fragility of apparent friendships. Yet for all his efforts he was not part of any princely retinue and served no great personage, so he had no way of knowing what the reasons for the emperor's departure might have been.[7]

After life in Trier returned to normal, our solitary historian did not resume his account of the reign of Louis XI. A more urgent problem now preoccupied him. Thomas was still bishop of the diocese of Lisieux, and for eight years since his departure he had stubbornly refused to step down. But now the situation was becoming untenable, both for himself and for those in Lisieux who defended his interests. He resigned. In March 1474 he set out for Rome to negotiate the surrender of his diocese. Sixtus IV granted him certain financial advantages and the title of archbishop of Caesarea in Palestine.[8] Thus he had the pleasure of becoming the distant successor of the great fourth-century historian, Eusebius, bishop of Caesarea, whose writings had left their mark on Christian historiography for a millennium and, in the eyes of Thomas Basin, still remained of the utmost distinction and utility.[9] Yet upon returning to Trier in July 1474 after two months of travel and a two-month sojourn in Rome, the archbishop of Caesarea did not resume his account of the reign of Louis XI. Perhaps he deemed himself too ill-informed about events that had taken place too recently and at too great a distance from where he was. More likely he had become obsessed with his own story. He wanted to recount his differences with Louis XI in the most minute detail, from their remote origins to his quite recent surrender of the diocese of Lisieux. He therefore wrote his *Apology*, which was completed the following year, in 1475.

In that same year Edward IV, who had landed an army on the Continent to aid his brother-in-law, reached an agreement with Louis XI, with whom he signed the Treaty of Picquigny in August. Left alone, Charles the Bold had no choice but to sign a truce of his own with the king of France. He did so in September at the château de Souleuvres in the duchy of Luxemburg. Without the distraction of the war with France, the duke of Burgundy was free to increase his pressure on the Empire, where he had already made numerous forays north and south of the Rhine valley from the county of Ferrette to the city of Neuss. On November 29, 1475, Charles's troops entered Nancy. So, within the space of a few months, peace had been restored between the king of France and the duke of Burgundy; combat had drawn closer to Trier; and throughout the western reaches of the Empire the climate had turned increasingly hostile to the duke of Burgundy and increasingly favorable to the king of France. No longer was Trier the oasis of peace and tranquillity of which Thomas Basin dreamed. In April or May 1476 he set out once more for his beloved Louvain, by now safe from threat of war and Louis XI.

At the same time our historian had clearly understood that the truce of Souleuvres marked a milestone in the reign of Louis XI. He therefore returned to his *History of Louis XI*. In late 1475 and early 1476 in Trier and then in 1476 in Louvain, he wrote the third and fourth books of that work, which traced events up to the truce of Souleuvres. The historian lagged behind events by little more than a year.

While Thomas was writing, however, the pace of events accelerated. Charles the Bold paid the price of his temerity. He was beaten by the Swiss at Grandson (March 2, 1476) and then at Morat (June 22, 1476). Finally, on January 5, 1477, he was defeated again and killed near Nancy. Immediately Louis XI sent his troops into Burgundy and Picardy. The Burgundian state tottered. Thomas Basin left Louvain. On June 4, 1477, he settled in Utrecht, where he had a brother and where the bishop was an old classmate of Thomas's at Louvain. There, in 1477, far from the war and from the king of France, Thomas Basin completed the fifth book of his *History of Louis XI*, which continued the story up to the battle of Nancy and the death of Charles the Bold.

Now sixty-five, Thomas Basin stopped writing for several years. No doubt he wanted to continue working on his *History of Louis XI*. He went on taking notes. But the pace of events was no longer so breathtaking. In the far north Thomas was ill-informed about what was taking place in France. Probably there was something depressing in the success of his old enemy. In addition, it was Thomas's misfortune that in 1481 the city of Utrecht was shaken by serious disturbances. As a person of no importance in Utrecht, the archbishop of Caesarea was able to observe those disturbances without the least danger to himself. But how could a man anxious for peace and tranquillity go on living for nearly two years in a city where daily life was dangerous and difficult? I do not know. In any case, in May 1483 the situation became unbearable. After bitter fighting, the bishop's enemies seized control of the city. Thomas Basin had witnessed the fighting, not without fear (*non sine metu*).[10]

The bishop of Utrecht had been led away a prisoner. It was difficult to get food, and prices soared.[11] There were rumors that Maximilian, the duke of Austria, who in 1477 had married Charles the Bold's sole heir, Marie of Burgundy, and who was already a widower, had taken pity on the most venerable bishop and was about to lay siege to the city. That was the last straw. In June 1483 Thomas, judging that a perilous siege was imminent, departed just in time (*ad tempus*) for Breda in the duchy of Brabant, "a rather calm and peaceful place for now."[12]

During this period of calm and peaceful retirement Thomas was delighted by two events that came in quick succession. On a Sunday, either August 31 or September 7, 1483, Utrecht surrendered to Maximilian. A short while earlier, on Saturday, August 30, at eight in the evening, Louis XI had departed this world. The time had come for Thomas Basin to finish his *History.* Within a few months he had written the last two books, the sixth and the seventh, which took up the tale in 1477, just after the death of Charles the Bold. A disproportionate amount of space was devoted to the events in Utrecht, which Thomas Basin had experienced at first hand but which had nothing to do with Louis XI. The narrative ends in 1483, and the work concludes with a lengthy portrait of the "tyrant." By the time Thomas Basin left Breda in May 1484 he had finished his *History of Louis XI.*[13]

At this point the elderly exile could have returned to France, where Louis XI's most loyal supporters had fallen on hard times. Instead he returned to Utrecht, from which he had been absent for eleven months. There, to ease his old age, he built a very comfortable house. And he hoped that Utrecht would be the last city he would be obliged to live in on this earth.[14] He spent the next few years rereading and correcting his histories of Charles VII and Louis XI, which he was careful not to sign and which he did not trouble himself to distribute. Thomas Basin had satisfied his hatred of Louis XI by writing three major works, the *History of Charles VII,* the *History of Louis XI,* and the *Apology.* Fear of encountering trouble prevented him from distributing the works in his old age.

In May 1488, at the age of seventy-five, Thomas Basin took one final look back at his past. In the Book of Numbers 33 Moses names all the places where the Jews stopped in the desert on their way to the Promised Land. Saint Jerome had used this chapter to write a brief treatise on "The Forty-Two Stations of the Jewish People in the Desert." Inspired by this short book and convinced that mortals are but pilgrims on this earth en route to heaven, Thomas Basin calculated, without undue embellishment, that he too had passed forty-two stations in the course of his seventy-five years. In a brief summary (*breviloquium*) he attempted to enumerate them, whenever possible specifying exactly how long he had remained in each place and providing additional details.

The elderly fugitive was at this point living in his fine house in Utrecht. There he awaited his final journey to that heavenly country where nothing is unstable or transitory and where there is neither hunger nor pestilence nor fear.[15]

Over a period of eighteen years, between his fifty-eighth and his seventy-sixth year, Thomas Basin wrote four works that combined the history of his times with his own personal history. His life was a failure, but the desire to explain that failure made of the luckless old prelate one of the greatest historians of the fifteenth century.

He was also a historian who occupied a unique position in his own time. There is no history less bookish than that of Thomas Basin. He did use written sources, of course. At one point he made use of Jean Juvénal des Ursins's *History of Charles VI*,[16] at another of an anonymous narrative of events in England in 1471,[17] and at still another of archival documents that by chance happened to come into his possession.[18] But the number of passages in his work based on written sources is, all told, rather small, and it is difficult for modern scholars to identify them, all the more so since Thomas rarely allowed himself the luxury—or, perhaps more accurately, rarely subjected himself to the discipline—of copying or translating these sources word by word. For Thomas Basin was no scholar, and it was surely not his ambition to write a compilation in the manner of the great French tradition of scholarship.[19] He had no wish to become another Bernard Gui.

This mention of Bernard Gui is not gratuitous. Thomas Basin himself suggested it. Bernard Gui defined history as a complete and detailed (*ad plenum per singula*) narrative of events.[20] Thomas Basin repeated these words in order to indicate, discreetly but firmly, his distance from Bernard: his history, he said, was not intended to be a detailed (*per singula*) narrative.[21] Jean Golein, who translated Bernard Gui in 1365, said: "Historiography is detailed writing." A few years later Jean Froissart said much the same thing when he expressed his wish "to follow right along with the history of the subject" (*historier tout au long de la matière*).[22] By repudiating detailed narrative, Thomas Basin gave clear notice that his conception of history was not the same as Bernard Gui's or French historians in general, including Jean Froissart, whose success in the fifteenth century must have caused our bishop some little distress.

Thomas Basin allows us to glimpse a similar irritation with

Georges Chastellain, then the official "indexer and historiographer" of Charles the Bold, and in general he distances himself as much from Burgundian historiography as from French historiography.[23] Our historian definitely does not like descriptions. On occasion he may pause briefly to describe an exceptional ceremony such as the one he witnessed in Trier in 1473,[24] or such as the execution in Paris in 1475 of the count of Saint-Pol, which he obviously did not witness but which left a deep scar.[25] But the truth is that Thomas Basin disliked the endless descriptions in which the Burgundian historical school delighted, and he said so openly. In dealing with the marriage of Charles the Bold to Margaret of York, Thomas sketches in a few words the splendid feasts that accompanied the July 1468 wedding, but he immediately adds: "It is not our purpose to recount all the details of so splendid a feast *singulas splendidissime festivitatis partes*. Let them be told by those who have a taste for such things, and let us continue, in order, with the narrative of events."[26]

For Thomas Basin, as for his predecessors of the previous two or three centuries, history was a chronological narrative with dates.[27] But it was Thomas's conviction that a good narrative had above all to stick to the essential. At the end of his *History of Charles VII* he says: "I did not want to report all the battles, all the sieges, and all the attacks. . . . It would have taken too many thick volumes. I have included in my history only the most important and famous events, those that seemed worthy of being recounted and preserved in memory."[28] A good narrative must also avoid the digressions and "incidentals" cherished by the chroniclers of the past. It must avoid dwelling too long on events that coincide in time with the narrative but have no bearing on the subject.[29]

By contrast, Thomas never hesitates to interrupt his narrative to provide fairly lengthy portraits of his protagonists or to search out the causes of a particular event.[30] Although he sometimes allows the reader the liberty to think what he likes,[31] he also does not hesitate to give his own opinion[32] or to set forth, in lengthy digressions, ideas that he holds dear.[33] So that Thomas Basin's history is much less close to French or Burgundian historiographical tradition than it is reminiscent of the history written by classical Latin authors, a kind of history that the Italian historians of the fourteenth and fifteenth centuries had been attempting to revive.

Thomas's ambition to shun the French and Burgundian historical traditions, which dominated his time and which rarely used any language other than French, is clear from his decision to write in Latin. Critics have often had harsh words for Thomas Basin's Latin, which has been judged inauthentic.[34] I, for one, congratulate him that his concern for style did not drive him to the obscurity that mars the work of so many other humanists. In his handling of Latin words he exhibits remarkable mastery. Make no mistake: Thomas Basin was a good Latin technician, a writer whose often personal thoughts are conveyed in clear sentences in which every word counts.

Thomas's library, insofar as we know its contents, hints at the kind of history he would write in old age. Thomas Basin loved books. He purchased some and had others copied. In all his wanderings his books followed him. He was such an attentive reader that he sometimes added headings, pagination, and notes to the books he read, and occasionally he took the trouble to add tables of contents to his manuscripts.[35] Yet this lover of books owned, so far as we know, few works of history, and nearly all of those were the works of classical Latin authors. He drew primarily on Caesar, Suetonius, and Sallust. Of all the French historical production of the Middle Ages the only sign in Thomas's library is a thirteenth-century compilation of universal history in a manuscript copy made in that century and purchased by the bishop of Lisieux. There is no evidence of interest in, or for that matter the slightest familiarity with, the history of France before his time. Fourteenth- and fifteenth-century French and Burgundian historians are simply absent. The only modern historian present in Thomas Basin's library is the great Tuscan Leonardo Bruni, who died in 1444. Bruni wrote a *History of the Florentine People,* which Thomas Basin did not own. But his library did contain a copy of *De Bello italico adversus Gothos gesto,* which Bruni wrote in 1411, in the first printed edition of 1470, that is, shortly before the bishop of Lisieux himself began to write. Some years later Thomas ordered copies of some of Bruni's other works, in particular *De Militia* (1421), in which the Florentine historian expounded military theories that deeply influenced him. Clearly Thomas Basin had no desire to be a new Bernard Gui, Froissart, or Chastellain. He surely wanted to be a new Sallust. And more precisely, perhaps, he wanted to be a new Bruni.

By thus writing the history of his own times, with a minimum of written documentation and based on news he had heard, oral testimony, and personal memories, and by never shrinking from offering his opinions and developing his ideas, Thomas Basin in 1471 wrote a history, highly personal in tone, in which the man behind the work stands out clearly. With time the work's character has taken on even sharper relief. Thomas Basin stood alone, far from the men who made history, far from the places where its course was decided, far from the archives and libraries in which its memory was preserved. In dealing with increasingly recent events, moreover, he was to an ever greater degree the slave of the news that reached him in his retirement and of the rumors that were in the air. Owing to this scarcity of information and perhaps also to age, he now stuck less closely to his subject and allowed himself more and longer digressions. In 1483 and 1484 he recounted remote events about which he had heard: how the Pazzi had hatched a conspiracy in Florence in 1478 and how the Turks had ravaged Otranto in 1480. Yet he was conscious that these were only "incidental" to his narrative.[36] These episodes are followed immediately by a long account of the grave disturbances that had just shaken Utrecht. Thomas was well aware that those disturbances had little to do with the reign of Louis XI and that he was devoting too much space to them, but he did not feel obliged to pass over in silence events that had taken place in the city where he was then residing.[37] Imperceptibly the history of Louis XI thus became the diary of Thomas Basin. Over eighteen years the elderly historian certainly gave us a history of his times; but since the life of Thomas Basin, seen from one vantage or another, was the avowed subject of the *Apologia* and the *Breviloquium* as well as the incidental subject of the *History of Louis XI,* what he gave us was above all a collection of exceptionally interesting autobiographical fragments.

No doubt these fragments ought to be taken for what they are. Thomas Basin never intended to write a running account of his life. He shed light on his life by recounting the history of his times, detailing his quarrels with Louis XI, and enumerating the forty-two stations of his earthly wanderings. But about whole segments of his life he says nothing. And what he does say he says in order to justify his errors or to explain his failure. All too often one has the impression that Thomas Basin wrote his books not so much to reveal himself as to hide behind.

An elderly prelate who had bungled his life used his full talent to provide us with a partial (in both senses) account of himself and his times. Our task is to exploit this stroke of good fortune without being duped by it. We must try to discover the truth about Thomas Basin with his help yet in spite of what he says and notwithstanding what he conceals.

Childhood (1412–24)

Thomas Basin was born at Caudebec in Normandy in 1412. We have this information directly from him.[38] He does not mention either the month or the day. Perhaps he did not know the precise date of his birth. But information he provides subsequently proves that he knew at least that he was born late in the year 1412.

That was nearly ten years before the death of Charles VI but almost ten years after the birth of the son who would succeed him and whose history Thomas Basin would write. The future Charles VII was in fact born on February 22, 1403. Moreover, Thomas Basin was well aware that Charles VII's reign was incomprehensible without knowledge of the tragic years that preceded it. With remarkable historical insight he clearly understood that the period he wished to describe actually began with the assassination of the duke of Orléans in 1407.[39]

Thomas cared little, and knew next to nothing, about what had happened in ancient times (*antiqua tempora, prisca tempora*)[40] and in the times that preceded his own. He alludes in the most banal way to Clovis, "the first king of the Franks who was Christian."[41] He alludes several times to the lengthy English presence in Aquitaine, which ended, he says, in 1453 after some two hundred forty or two hundred fifty years.[42] In other words, he situates the arrival of the English in the reign of Philip Augustus and in the first few years of the thirteenth century, when in fact it occurred some fifty years earlier, in 1154. He makes no other allusion to the time before his own. He says nothing about his family prior to his birth. He was not a scholar. He was not a historian of the past. His only purpose was to speak of his own time (*aetas nostra,*[43] *nostri evi et temporis res gestas*[44]), which began in the early years of the fifteenth century with the assassination of the duke of Orléans and with his own birth.

Normandy was then a beautiful province, rich and populous. It had been an essential part of the French king's domain since 1204, when Philip Augustus had taken it from John Lackland, the Plantagenet heir and at that time king of England, duke of Normandy, and lord of numerous other French territories. Thus for two centuries Normandy had been part of the royal domain. Yet Normans, like the inhabitants of other French provinces and perhaps more so, thought of themselves as forming a distinct entity. They obeyed not so much the king of France as the duke of Normandy. They were jealous of their prerogatives, their customs, and their legal independence. In a moment of crisis, in 1314, the Capetian king had been obliged to sign a solemn Norman Charter recognizing the customs of the duchy and conceding that cases in the Norman courts could not be removed to the Paris Parlement. Throughout the fourteenth century, successive kings, first Capetian, then Valois, confirmed the Norman

Charter. When the heir to the throne, the future John the Good, became duke of Normandy in 1347, and when his son Charles, the future Charles V, also heir-apparent, became duke of Normandy in 1355, the province saw its uniqueness and eminent place in the kingdom formally recognized. The natural place of the Normans was in the kingdom of France, yet Normans felt themselves to be distinct from the *gens de France* and had no intention of allowing their destiny to be decided in Paris.[45] In the first few years of the century, in the absence of any crisis, in a healthy climate of civil peace, this tension between Rouen and Paris was merely part of the backdrop to normal administrative and legal dealings. And no one, in either Normandy or Paris, doubted that the inhabitants of this beautiful and rich province were loyal subjects of the king of France.

Rouen was the political and economic capital of the entire duchy, but its domination was most strongly felt in its own hinterland. Caudebec lived in its shadow. In a few words Thomas Basin said all that needed to be said about Caudebec. It was "a small fortified city [*oppidulum*] located on the banks of the Seine seven Gallic leagues from Rouen, on the road from Rouen to the ocean."[46] Caudebec was in fact a prosperous parish whose patron was the abbot of the nearby abbey of Saint-Wandrille and whose inhabitants included numerous priests and clerics.[47] It was the principal town of a small viscounty and provided work for several administrators. It was also a small city of the rich and fertile *pays de Caux,* a region with a marked personality of its own within the duchy of Normandy.[48] And it was above all a small port on the right bank of the Seine and a way point, some twenty miles from Rouen, on the road from that city to the most important port on the Seine estuary, Harfleur.[49] In this small but active trading center, a few merchants prospered, among them the Basins.

Already in the mid-fourteenth century there were Basins in Caudebec. In the second half of the fourteenth century and early in the fifteenth century three Basins emerge from the obscurity of the sources: Jean, Thomas, and Michel Basin and their families lived in comfort, generally in the Grande Rue.[50] These people were clearly kin of Thomas Basin, but we do not know precisely what the relation was, because Thomas never speaks of these uncles or cousins. He does mention—just barely—his father and mother (*parentes nostri*).[51] Fortunately, modern scholarship has rescued them from the shadows.

Jean Basin, Thomas's father, was born around 1370. He was an *épicier,* that is, a grocer and dealer in exotic spices, and therefore a wealthy merchant. He owned several houses in Caudebec and Rouen. In 1411 he stated that his age was forty. One of Caudebec's most prominent burghers, he lived in an *hôtel* named *La Fleur de Lys* near the church in the Grande Rue.[52] Around 1400, when he was approximately thirty, he married a girl of about twenty, Colette, who had been born in Rouen around 1380 and lived there until her marriage, when she moved to Caudebec.[53] Jean and Colette had no daughters. Or at any rate no evidence has survived of daughters who might have lived to adulthood, married, and provided Thomas Basin with a nephew. But the couple did have nine sons who lived to adulthood. Michel, the eldest, was born around 1400.[54] We know that our Thomas was born in 1412. Between Michel and Thomas surely Louis was born, perhaps Nicolas, and possibly others sons or daughters who did not survive. Then, after Thomas, in the decade that followed 1412, came Etienne, Guillaume, another Michel, another Nicolas, and another Thomas. (We are not sure of the order.) Their mother, Colette, lived to be ninety.[55] And their father, Jean, who died after 1450, lived more than eighty years.[56] Michel, the eldest son, died in 1477, when he was at least seventy-five.[57] Nicolas the elder was still alive in 1491.[58] Nicolas the younger died on June 26, 1495, at not less than seventy years of age.[59] Michel the younger was also not less than seventy when he died in 1494. And his brothers Etienne, Guillaume, and Thomas the younger, all of whom were more than seventy, were still around to claim his inheritance.[60] In the Basin family, therefore, Thomas's longevity was not unusual. In 1477, when Thomas claimed the inheritance of his elder brother, who had died childless, he was sixty-five and had six living brothers, all of whom would survive him. Thomas Basin's father, mother, and brothers exerted a strong influence on his life, the story of which is also the story of a family.

Thomas was indebted to his family for, among other things, his memory of sad events that occurred around the beginning of his life. Even before he was born, civil war had broken out and upper Normandy had suffered the first consequences. In 1411, the viscount and captain of Caudebec, which was surrounded by territory for the most part controlled by the Burgundians, chose to work for the Armagnacs. They were prevented from doing so. A trial followed. In the subsequent investigation "Jean Basin, burgher of Caudebec, aged forty," was the first to testify against the Armagnac officers.[61] Thomas Basin does not mention this episode, which sheds light on his father's feelings as well as on the early stages of an insecurity that had already begun to ruin Normandy's prosperity.[62]

Worse still, on August 13, 1415, Henry V landed near Harfleur and laid siege to that city, which was "by sea the principal key to all Normandy."[63] While Pierre d'Ailly, in Constance, far away and high above the scene of battle, labored on behalf of France and Christendom, the Basin family was buffeted by the backwash of nearby warfare. On September 22, 1415, Henry V entered Harfleur. At this point he held two important beachheads on the French coast, at Calais and Harfleur. With his army he left Harfleur and attempted to join forces with his troops in Calais. He was not far from his destination when, on October 25, 1415, the day of Saints Crispin and Crispinian, he crushed the French army at Agincourt. In his *History of Charles VII* Thomas Basin gives few dates, and no more than four or five precise ones. In fact, from the beginning of his narrative until 1436 he mentions only seven dates, and only one is precise. Agincourt so impressed itself on French memory that Thomas indicates the very day on which the battle occurred: "The year of the Lord 1415, the day of the martyred saints Crispin and Crispinian."[64]

Yet in his *Breviloquium,* where he tells the story of himself and his family, he does not even mention Agincourt. What disrupted the lives of the Basins was not Agincourt but the fact that Harfleur was now English and that French troops bent on recapturing it now filled Caudebec. The residents were subjected to the insolence and violence of the troops (*militum insolentias, injurias atque violentias*).[65] Late in 1415 or early in 1416 Jean and Colette Basin took their children and most precious belongings and left the city. Thus began four years of harsh, itinerant life as refugees, during which she was continually pregnant and he, the wealthy merchant, found himself obliged to fight for the survival of his wife and children. Throughout France, for more than thirty years, civil and foreign wars forced countless refugees, rich and poor alike, to take to the roads. Seldom are we able to reconstruct these lugubrious odysseys, however. The Basins' fate was a common one. What is unusual is that the memory of those years of exile was kept alive in the Basin family,[66] so that, seventy years later, Thomas Basin himself, deeply scarred by the fears and flights of that refugee period, was able to give an account of the experience.[67]

Thomas was three years old when his parents fled Caudebec and made their first stop Rouen. The choice of Rouen was a natural one. But since English soldiers in Harfleur threatened the entire *pays de Caux* and since French soldiers were pillaging everywhere, many peasants left their farms and, like the Basins, sought refuge behind the walls of Rouen. Famine and plague soon ravaged the city. The Basins, seeking safer refuge, left for Vernon, where they remained for several months. When the plague ended in Rouen, they returned there. In the spring of 1417, however, early in little Thomas's fourth year, the rumor spread that a new English invasion was imminent. Nearly everyone believed that Henry V would land in Harfleur, which was already in his control, and march on Rouen, the capital of Normandy. Jean and Colette Basin therefore did what Thomas, all his life, would find it natural to do. Unwilling to tarry in a place of danger, they did not wait for fighting to break out but sought refuge in a safe place. They moved to the highly fortified city of Falaise.

A few months later, however, in August 1417, the rumor flew that Henry V had landed not, as expected, in Harfleur but in Touques, from which he threatened all of lower Normandy, first of all Caen and then, inevitably, Falaise. The Basins hastily (*cum festinatione*) left Falaise for Brittany. They stopped briefly at Saint-James-de-Beuvron on the border between Normandy and Brittany. Then, as rumors preceded the advancing English troops, they left for Rennes, where they remained for nearly a year (probably from September 1417 to the summer of 1418). This was the scene of one of Thomas Basin's earliest memories, the earliest, at any rate, about which he tells us, but in another work.[68] He was in Rennes, just before or just after his fifth birthday, when Vincent Ferrier came there for several days to preach. Ferrier had set out from Avignon in 1398 to preach the world over. He would die a few years later, in 1419, at Vannes. The holy man's reputation was already so great that Thomas Basin the adult clearly remembered having heard him when he, Thomas, was still only a child.

While the Basins were in Rennes, in September 1417, the city and castle of Caen fell to the English. Henry V then drove out the residents, who took to the roads by the thousands. Little by little all of lower Normandy was conquered. Falaise was indeed, as Jean Basin believed, a "highly fortified place." It held out the longest, until February 1418. On May 29, 1418, the Burgundians entered Paris. Thomas Basin devotes several pages of his *History of Charles VII* to this extremely important event, which ended in wholesale massacre and forced many people to flee the city. Yet in his *Breviloquium* he says nothing about it. He had no reason to talk about it, because it caused Jean Basin little concern in Rennes. Jean was much more worried that the English troops now occupying lower Normandy threatened the security of the Breton border. In Jean Basin's eyes Rennes was too close to that border. He wanted to find a less exposed refuge. In the summer of 1418 he and his family left for Nantes at the mouth of the Loire.

We actually know very little about the many refugees forced to take to the roads in those troubled times. Yet it is difficult to believe that Jean Basin was not a rather unusual refugee. As portrayed by his son Thomas, he was a wise and prudent man who, at the first alert, the first rumor, always had the will and the means to flee quickly and travel far in search of a safer refuge.

Jean Basin was not fleeing the English. He was fleeing war, famine, and plague. In fact, he was so little afraid of the English that, once Rouen had surrendered on January 19, 1419, once the conquest of Normandy was complete and peace was restored to the duchy, the prudent Jean Basin waited a few more months and then, after more than a year in Nantes, left Brittany in the fall of 1419. Meanwhile, on September 10, John the Fearless was assassinated. Soon the Basin family was reestablished in Caudebec in the same house it had left four years earlier. Thomas Basin recalls that he was roughly seven years old at the time.

On the borders of Normandy the war raged on. But for the duchy itself, "the fall" of 1417, "the conquest and surrender" of the country[69] marked the beginning of "thirty-three years" of English rule.[70] In order to consolidate his rule, Henry V moved quickly to give Norman land to English soldiers, Norman houses to English merchants and artisans, and Norman prebends to English clerics.[71]

In this same period a number of Italian clerics carved out positions for themselves in the Norman Church. In October 1418 Pandulfus Malatesta became bishop of Coutances.[72] In April 1420 Paul Capranica became bishop of Evreux.[73] And above all, also in 1420, Branda Castiglioni became bishop of Lisieux. Born in 1350 to an illustrious family in the Pavia region, Castiglioni was an exact contemporary of Pierre d'Ailly. He was a famous jurist and had served as professor of law at the University of Pavia. Then, in 1404, he became bishop of Piacenza. In 1411, the same year as Pierre d'Ailly, he became a cardinal. And like Pierre d'Ailly, he had played an important role at the Council of Constance, where he had been a confidential advisor to Sigismund, had helped work out the rapprochement between the emperor and Henry V, and had played a crucial part in the election of Martin V. The pope and the king of England, both in Branda Castiglioni's debt, agreed that he should be named bishop of Lisieux.[74]

The Italian presence in Normandy was inconsequential and brief. Pandulfus Malatesta actually went to Coutances, but he was transferred to Patras and left Normandy in 1424. Paul Capranica never even went to his Norman diocese before being transferred, in 1472, to Benevento. And Branda Castiglioni never went to Lisieux. He was seventy years old and gave up his diocese in 1424, but in favor of his nephew, Zenone Castiglioni. In addition, his prebendary in Lisieux and canonry in Rouen maintained his ties with Normandy. Hence the Castiglionis, the uncle but especially the nephew, remained a presence in Normandy. They were to leave their mark on Norman cultural history in general and on Thomas Basin in particular.[75]

Henry V's intention was thus to establish his domination of Normandy by encouraging a powerful English presence and a more modest Italian presence. The crucial thing, however, was to win the loyalty of the Normans themselves. In order to do this, the king invoked Norman autonomy and did all he could to persuade the Normans to look back beyond the Capetian kings to the glorious days of the Plantagenet dukes. He pledged to treat his subjects "honestly and justly in accordance with the usages and customs observed in our country in the time of our predecessors." In 1417 or 1418 he established a fiscal court in Caen, which under the Plantagenet dukes had been the center of their financial administration. In July 1419 he revived the office of seneschal, abolished by Philip Augustus in 1204. And he was careful to convoke the Estates of Normandy at least once a year.[76]

Henry won over the Normans in part by appealing to their rather strong sense that the duchy was a "unique and singular country held as an imperial possession"[77] but above all by giving them peace. And during this period of peace, at Caudebec, in his parents' house, far from the devastating events in the kingdom, young Thomas spent the five years from his seventh to his twelfth birthday (1419–24) at his initial studies, for which he demonstrated a marked predilection (*noster affectus . . . ad litteras capessendas*).[78]

Studies (1424–37)

While Thomas Basin was quietly mastering the rudiments of learning in Caudebec, Charles VI, by the Treaty of Troyes (May 20 and 21, 1420) gave Henry V the hand of Charles's daughter Catherine, made Henry heir to the throne, and immediately handed him the government of France. Then, in 1422, Henry V and Charles VI died in quick succession. The infant son of Henry V and Catherine became king of France and England. His father's brother, the "valiant and prudent" duke of Bedford, assumed responsibility for the Continental kingdom.[79] The duke was a good administrator who, Thomas Basin tells us, won the love of his Norman and French subjects.[80] He was also a good soldier, under whose command the English armies continued their victories. Bedford was at the head of the English troops when they once again crushed the French army at Verneuil on August 17, 1424. Thomas Basin gives a lengthy account of the battle, but he cannot give the precise date or even the year.[81] Although the Verneuil disaster left less of an impression on French memory than did the defeat at Agincourt, its consequences were considerable.

Since Henry VI was now king of France and England, the duke of Bedford was less inclined than his brother had been to exalt Norman autonomy. Nevertheless, his success in battle removed the location of combat far from Norman borders and restored normal relations between Rouen and Paris, bestowing on Normandy the blessings of a profound peace. Prosperity returned. Abandoned land was once again planted.[82] Commerce resumed. Peasants and merchants enriched themselves to such a degree that, in 1426, the church of Notre-Dame in Caudebec was found to be too small and dilapidated. Work began to make the nave wider and taller. Gifts flowed in, and their sources were commemorated with inscriptions and mottoes. The English captain of Caudebec donated a window.[83] While Normandy enjoyed these happy years and the Basins of Caudebec and Rouen prospered, young Thomas continued his studies in Paris.

In 1424 Thomas was in his twelfth year. The child (*puer*) was about to mark what the elderly historian would count an important milestone in his life. He stood on the threshold of puberty.[84] He was about to enter the age of reason (*anni discrecionis*),[85] or adolescence. The moment had come for his parents to decide on his future. Twelve years earlier, Michel, the eldest of the Basin sons, had probably received the same primary schooling as Thomas. Did he then study arts at the university, or did he remain with his family in its exodus? The sources are silent. In any case, he soon followed in his father's footsteps and went into business. In 1421 he was a money changer. In 1426 he was a burgher of Rouen. In 1428 he purchased a fief. He was certainly a wealthy man. And no doubt it was in this period that he married Marion Le Roux, thereby joining a family of rich Rouen merchants.[86] And like their father and elder brother, Louis, Nicolas the elder, Etienne, Guillaume, Nicolas the younger, and Thomas the younger (known as Thomassin) all sooner or later went into business as merchants.[87] Thomas and his next younger brother Michel were, as far as we know, the only ones who pursued higher education and entered the Church.[88] Why these two? We do not know what determined Michel's fate, but Thomas himself tells us about his.[89] Because he had shown a taste for study at an early age, and because his parents had no desire to interfere with that taste, they decided in 1424, before he was even twelve, that they would send him to the University of Paris.

This was a natural choice. Paris was not far from Rouen. The two cities were politically similarly aligned. Relations between them were by this point placid and secure. And the faculty of arts of the University of Paris was "very famous."[90] In 1490, at the very end of his life, Thomas offered a somewhat more nuanced judgment of the university. It was only one of the most famous schools, new as well as old, to be found this side of the Alps. And its faculties of art and theology had been remarkable and indeed still were remarkable "though not to the same degree of perfection."[91] Did Thomas mean to say that the decline of the university was already noticeable when he was a student there or simply that it was noticeable now, some sixty years later? In any case, Thomas proved to be a brilliant student of literature in the faculty of arts, where he studied for a little more than five years. In 1430 he received the master of arts, for which, because he was not yet eighteen, he required a special dispensation.[92]

Thomas's memory of important events that took place in or near the city toward the end of his stay there was neither vivid nor particularly accurate. True, he was not yet sixteen when, in April 1429, there "came to Paris a Franciscan named Friar Richart," whose visit is described at length in the *Journal* of the man who, for want of a more precise identification, has traditionally been known as the Bourgeois of Paris. Friar Richart was a disciple of Vincent Ferrier. Drawing, as his master had done, on "Holy Scripture . . . the Apocalypse and the writings of my lord Saint Paul." Richart announced that the Antichrist had been born and that the year 1430 would yield "the greatest wonders the world has ever seen." He urged the men and women of Paris to reform themselves. For roughly two weeks he preached nearly every day. He "began his sermon around five in the morning and continued until ten or eleven o'clock." Richart was a powerful orator. Thousands of people turned out to hear him every day. "And truly ten of his sermons . . . turned more people to religion than all the sermoners who had preached in Paris for a hundred years." At the end of April he was supposed to preach one Sunday morning in Montmartre. Thousands of people came out the previous night "in order to secure a better place . . . and slept in the fields in old shacks and wherever they could," but Friar Richart failed to appear. He had left, no one knew why, on the night of April 30.[93]

The previous night, April 29, Joan of Arc had entered Orléans, which was under siege. The city, which held the key to all of southern France, had been under siege by the English since the end of 1428. Orléans had defended itself ably, but it was at the end of its tether when Joan of Arc arrived with her small army. At once everything changed. On May 8 Orléans was saved. On July 17 Charles VII was anointed in Rheims. On August 26 Joan of Arc came to Saint-Denis, where Charles VII met her on September 7. And on September 8 Joan and her soldiers made ready to scale the walls of Paris.

The Parisians, however, were quite hostile to the "Armagnacs." In August they learned that the Franciscan whose preaching they had, only a few months earlier, so passionately believed "to be true was riding with them [that is, Armagnacs], and as soon as the people of Paris were certain that he truly was with them and that with his language he was turning cities that had sworn oaths to the regent of France or his agents, they cursed him in the name of God and his saints and, worse yet . . . all . . . the games that he had prohibited recommenced in spite of him."[94] On September 8, 1429, Joan was insulted, wounded, and repelled after a long and "cruel" assault.

Thomas Basin mentions that after the anointment at Rheims Charles VII went to Saint-Denis. More than that, he says that Charles's coronation took place there, indeed that he was "crowned there as is customary for new kings."[95] In fact this custom never existed. Charles VII was not crowned in Saint-Denis. What false rumor permanently duped Thomas Basin we do not know. As for Friar Richart, Thomas Basin remembered him quite well, well enough to describe him sixty years later. But this description does not figure in the *History of Charles VII.*[96] For Thomas, Friar Richart was nothing more than a Franciscan who heralded the coming of the Antichrist and the Day of Judgment and whose sermons were held suspect by the faculty of theology. Thomas knows nothing of Richart's connections with Charles VII and Joan of Arc.

Yet in his *History of Charles VII* Thomas Basin gives a lengthy account of the Joan of Arc epic. He knew about it, however, primarily from the annulment trial (1450–56), in which he played a role that enabled him to review the records of the case.[97] Forty years after the fact he speaks of Joan with sympathy. For himself he has no compunction about believing that she was sent by God to awaken the kingdom and people of France. But "concerning her mission and the apparitions and revelations affirmed by her," he leaves the reader free to draw his own conclusions.[98] In other words, Thomas's judgment of the Maid of Orléans is sympathetic and measured. Nevertheless, he does not hesitate to say that the attack on Paris on September 8, 1429, was foolhardy, that the people of Paris defended themselves most vigorously (*viriliter*), and that the assailants' retreat was not without dishonor.[99]

No doubt Thomas was still in Paris when Joan of Arc was captured outside Compiègne on May 23, 1430. The epic had ended after slightly more than a year, but it had changed everything. The war had again moved northward. The masters of Paris and Rouen were grievously short of money. High taxes and insecurity compromised the fragile prosperity of English France in general and Normandy in particular. And the number of what were commonly called "brigands" rose sharply in the occupied territories. The brigands were a mixture of desperate men, ruined by war; criminals seeking to avoid punishment; and people who hated the English. Thomas Basin was well aware that the presence of the English was responsible for these brigands, but he detested this plague, this dangerous pack of scoundrels whose rapacity had ruined vast territories.[100]

Dark times loomed once more. But Thomas Basin had his master of arts and wanted to continue his studies. Was this his own choice or the choice of his parents? He chose civil law, a subject not taught in Paris. To study it, Parisians usually went to Orléans. There was also good teaching in civil law at the University of Angers.[101] But Angers, like Orléans, was in territory controlled by Charles VII. Thomas's parents therefore sent their adolescent son to the recently founded University of Louvain.[102] The city of Louvain was in Brabant, and its economy had been on the decline for some time. In order to halt this decline and train the servants his government needed, Duke John IV persuaded Pope Martin V to establish, in 1425, a university for the teaching of arts, medicine, civil law, and canon law. Courses began in 1426.[103] Duke John IV died in 1427, his brother Philip in 1430. In the latter year, therefore, their cousin Philip the Good became duke of Brabant. And in the very same year Jean Basin made the wise decision to send his son to study civil law in this calm and friendly country.

For a time Thomas Basin studied civil law in Louvain. He was there when a faculty of theology was created in 1432. Soon, however, his parents sent him to continue his studies in civil law at Pavia. The University of Pavia had been founded in the fourteenth century. Initially it had prospered. Then, at the beginning of the fifteenth century, plague and the vagaries of politics had nearly ruined it. In 1412, however, Filippo Maria Visconti restored order in the duchy of Milan. Soon thereafter he forbade his subjects to study anywhere but in Pavia. Once again the university prospered, the more so since the city's economic decline had left many buildings vacant.[104] On September 28, 1430, the eighty-year-old Cardinal Branda

Castiglioni, who had been a professor at Pavia and bishop of Lisieux and who still held many benefices, including several at Normandy, endowed a college at Pavia that was to accept twenty-four poor students. Twelve of these scholarship students were to be relatives of the cardinal, and twelve others were to be designated by the cathedral chapters in the dioceses where the old cardinal held benefices. Hence once scholar was to be designated by the cathedral chapter of Rouen, another by that of Bayeux, and a third by that of Lisieux.[105] Thomas Basin does not say that he received one of these scholarships, but the coincidence is too striking. He was certainly one of the scholars of the new college. And he surely received his scholarship, at the behest of his family, from the cathedral chapter of Rouen. In any case, he went to Pavia, studied there for a time, forged ties to the elderly cardinal and his family, and received his licentiate in civil law.[106]

The young licentiate then returned to his native Caudebec to see his parents. He remained there for several months before leaving again for Louvain, this time to study canon law.[107] In going to Louvain in 1430 and then transferring to Pavia a short while later, Thomas Basin says that he was obeying his parents' wishes (note the plural: his parents, that is, his father and mother, not his father alone). But in returning to Louvain to study canon law he does not mention his parents. By now his adolescence was over. He was a young man, and he made up his own mind. Canon law was taught in Paris, but the war had definitely moved too close to that city. Besides, Thomas had no especially fond memories of his years in Paris. He seems to have made no lasting friends there. At Louvain, however, he felt at home. All his life he would speak of his dear Louvain, and often he returned with pleasure "to his dear Louvain, which he had known well since adolescence" (*in Lovanio nostro, loco nobis ab ipsis adolescencie annis notissimo*).[108] He therefore returned to Louvain to study canon law. The years he spent there were happy ones. He met, or renewed acquaintance with, numerous friends to whom he remained attached throughout his life, including David, the bastard son of Philip the Good, who served from 1456 to 1494 as bishop of Utrecht, where, late in life, he and Thomas were to renew their friendship.[109] Thomas soon received his licentiate in canon law. He mentions that this was in 1437, during the seventh year of Eugenius IV's pontificate.[110] Eugenius had been elected pope on March 3, 1431, hence the degree was granted after March 3, 1437. By the spring of 1437 Thomas was therefore a master of arts and a licentiate in both civil and canon law. He had turned twenty-four only a few months earlier.

These facts are certain: that Thomas Basin left Paris for Louvain around the middle of 1430; that he spent time in Louvain, then Pavia, then Caudebec, and then again in Louvain; and that he completed his studies with a licentiate *in utroque jure* in the spring of 1437. It is more difficult to assign precise dates to these various periods of residence. Outside sources cannot be relied on. And as for Thomas Basin himself, although he specifies the duration of each of his forty-two earthly stations precisely in years and sometimes even in months, he is oddly imprecise about these student years, of which he was particularly fond and which remained vivid in his memory. His first residence in Louvain lasted "a certain number of years" (*per annos aliquot*). His stay in Pavia lasted "a good while" (*per aliquantum tempus*). He spent "some months" (*paucis mensibus*) in Caudebec. His second residence in Louvain was "for several years" (*per plures annos*).[111] What strange imprecision for a mind otherwise so precise. Since his memory surely was not at fault, what did he have to hide? In my view, his first residence in Louvain, which lasted "a certain number of years," cannot have been less than three years. His second residence, of "several years," was certainly no briefer. But then, since he remained in Caudebec for several months, he could not have stayed more than a few months in Pavia. Surely it was about this period that Thomas Basin did not wish to go into detail. It had taken him only a few months in Pavia to obtain a licentiate in civil law. As things went in fifteenth-century universities, this was not unusual, but Thomas did not necessarily feel that it redounded to his glory.

It can therefore be stated, in my view, that Thomas Basin's first residence in Louvain lasted from 1430 to 1433; that he was in Pavia in 1433 and 1434; that he spent a few months in Caudebec in 1434; and that he again resided in Louvain from 1434 to 1437. Thus he was already back in Louvain peacefully pursuing his studies when France entered a crucial period filled with sometimes happy, sometimes tragic events. In August and September 1435 representatives of the kings of France and England and the duke of Burgundy, along with representatives of the pope and of the council then meeting in Basel, assembled in Arras for peace talks. The two kings could not come to an agreement. But the duke of Burgundy, tired of the war, having obtained from Charles VII terms that satisfied his honor and his interests and having been released from his oath to the king of England by the pope's representative, worked out a reconciliation with the king of France on September 21. This was a hard blow for the English, all the more so because the duke of Bedford had died a few days earlier, on September 14, 1435. Events followed one another in rapid succession. On October 28 a small army of French soldiers attacked Dieppe and captured it for Charles VII. In November a rebellion in the pays de Caux cost the English Harfleur. Shortly thereafter the English cavalry slaughtered the rebel peasants outside the walls of Caudebec, but Harfleur and Dieppe would remain for a time in French hands. And while the English armies were tied up in Normandy, Charles VII's troops resumed the offensive in Ile-de-France. Cities in the Oise, Marne, and Seine valleys fell one after another. On April 13, 1436, French troops recaptured Paris.

The importance of the events of 1435 and 1436 did not escape Thomas's notice. The Treaty of Arras and the revolt in the pays de Caux were for him major occurrences.[112] There are, moreover, only four exact dates in the entire *History of Charles VII*. The first is that of Agincourt, the second that of the royal troops' return to Paris in 1436—or, rather, that of the royal troops' arrival at the walls of Paris several days earlier: "in the week of Easter, during the celebration of the resurrection of the Lord, in the year 1436."[113] Inevitably Thomas, and no doubt many other Frenchmen as well, were struck by the coincidence of the anniversary of the resurrection with the success of the French troops.

Yet if the years 1435 and 1436 held out to the subjects of Charles VII the promise of a resurrection, they were, for the inhabitants of the pays de Caux, hard times with lasting consequences. Rebellion was followed by war, famine, and plague. For more than ten years the region became an unpopulated wasteland. Brambles, thorns, and new-grown trees turned fields into impenetrable forests. Hardly a trace remained of roads and paths. The people of the region were laid low by this dreadful calamity, and for a long time to come. They were further crushed, at least in the circles Thomas describes, by the attitude of the French. For some of the Cauchois, Thomas tells us, had rebelled out of hatred of the English. The English had exterminated them and ruined their country—a sad fate, but sadder still was the attitude of the king of France, who succumbed to the pleasures of the table, of debauchery, and of luxury and languished in idle passivity. And even sadder were the persecutions inflicted by French troops, who occupied fortresses and castles recaptured from the English, and by local nobles who hastened to wring profits from estates previously under English control. Thomas Basin was not present on the scene. He was in Louvain. But his family endured the whole drama, and its bitterness deeply influenced the young man. Thirty-five years later, Thomas Basin ended his narrative with a quote from Psalm 146:3, a passage which life provided him with all too many occasions to repeat: "Put not your trust in princes, nor in the son of man, in whom there is no help."[114]

In Italy (1437–41)

In the spring of 1437, then, the kingdom of France held no attraction whatsoever for Thomas Basin. So when he received his licentiate in canon law, in May 1437 at the latest, he left Louvain and headed once again for Italy. This time he went to Bologna.

There were several reasons for his choice. Thomas wanted to continue his education. The old and prestigious University of Bologna, with thousands of students, was famous throughout Europe for its courses in civil and canon law. In the second half of the fourteenth century the university also became a center of humanism. It offered its first course in Greek in 1424.[115] Besides the university, Bologna in 1437 offered the further attraction of the papal court.

After becoming pope on March 3, 1431, Eugenius IV had had to confront a series of difficulties stemming on the one hand from the Italians and on the other from the fathers of the Council of Basel. Martin V, prior to his death, had fulfilled the wishes of many Christians by convoking a council at Basel. Prelates and doctors had been slow to arrive for the meeting. But by the end of 1431 the council had been able to hold its first session, and attendance at subsequent meetings had grown steadily. Some of those present had crossed the Alps to reach Basel. Among them were Giuliano Cesarini, whom Martin V had named, and Eugenius IV later confirmed, as head of the council,[116] and the elderly cardinal Branda Castiglioni, now in his eighties but still "very sound in body."[117] The latter was the man who had awarded Cardinal Cesarini his doctorate *in utroque,* who had taken him into his house, and who held him in the highest regard; the two men were therefore very close.[118] But most of the Basel fathers were Germans and Frenchmen, the latter from both the France of Charles VII and the France of Henry VI.[119]

Facing the pope and council were many arduous tasks: reformation of the Church, restoration of peace among Christians, and suppression of the heresy that had spread in Bohemia after the death of Jan Hus. Furthermore, since John VIII, the Byzantine emperor, in failing health and threatened in his very capital by Turkish troops, was prepared, in order to obtain Western aid, to accept a union of the Orthodox and Latin Churches, pope and council needed to do what was necessary to attain that goal.

Together the pope and council achieved some success. The reconciliation between France and Burgundy worked out at Arras in September 1435 owed much to the work of their representatives. From the outset, however, a gulf had opened up between Eugenius IV and the fathers of Basel. The ailing pope had no intention of crossing the Alps. Anxious to achieve union with the Orthodox Church, he knew that the Greek emperor and patriarch would agree to come to Italy but would go no further. He was also wary of a council in which the French representatives were exerting growing influence and were perpetuating the spirit of Constance.

As the dispute between the council and the pope worsened, it seemed for a time that the council might become the supreme authority in the Church. Gradually, however, the pope reestablished his position. Soon it became necessary to choose one side or the other. In 1435 the Italian prelates began leaving Basel one by one. Before the end of that year, old Cardinal Castiglioni was back with the pope.[120] And the pope, who had consolidated his position in Italy but for whom Rome still was not safe, had established his court in Bologna on April 22, 1436.[121]

When Thomas Basin left Louvain in May 1437, he never for a moment considered linking his fate to the Council of Basel, where the spirit of the University of Paris and the College of Navarre, of Pierre d'Ailly and Jean Gerson, was still influential.[122] He went to Bologna, where there was a famous university, where there were the pope and his court, and where there was also Branda Castiglioni, the elderly and powerful cardinal and friend of the humanists[123] as well as the founder of the college to which Thomas had received a scholarship three of four years earlier.

Thomas Basin stayed in Bologna for seven months. He divided his time between the university, where he studied at the faculty of letters, and the papal court. Cardinal Castiglioni probably had taken him into his house.[124] It was during this stay in Bologna, in September or October of 1437, that Thomas Basin obtained his first benefice. He became rector of the parish church of Saint-Germain de Carville in the diocese of Rouen. This was a small benefice. Carville was quite close to Caudebec in the recently war-ravaged pays de Caux. The parish, which was practically devoid of inhabitants, furnished an income of no more than ten *livres de petits tournois.* In fact, it was so small that Thomas was also granted the right to add other benefices to this one later on.[125] At that time, however, the young cleric had received none of the major orders. And he was in so little haste to receive them that he asked to be dispensed for five years from seeking promotion to holy orders. The dispensation was granted on December 6, 1437, but for only two years.[126] And so it was that in Bologna, in 1437, while continuing his studies, Thomas Basin found a powerful protector at the papal court and, modestly and prudently, took the first step in his ecclesiastical career.

A few days later, in December 1437, Thomas left Bologna and, traveling through Germany in order to avoid Charles VII's realm, reached Rouen, where his parents had again taken refuge, just as they had done twenty years before. They were refugees because Caudebec's minor fortification had been destroyed in 1435 along with the rest of the pays de Caux and the region continued to be cruelly oppressed by the captain appointed by the English king, a plundering Englishman of the most impious and barbaric sort, whose name Thomas Basin still remembered fifty years later: Fulk Eton or Ecton. Thomas himself tells us how overwhelmed he was by what he saw in Rouen. The three scourges of divine justice—war, famine, and plague—had all hit at the same time. Hundreds of the poor died every hour from hunger and pestilence. So cruel a spectacle was too much for Thomas to bear. He wore himself out in constant lamentation. Nothing could console him. After four months Jean Basin, that excellent man, gave his son the best possible advice. In April 1438 the overly sensitive curé of Carville left Rouen for Italy.[127]

War and looters made it still unsafe to travel by way of France, so Thomas first crossed the English Channel. In London he came down with a high fever, which detained him for a good while. Fully recovered after two months, he resumed his journey. After landing in Zeeland he traveled by way of Holland, Germany, and across the Alps. In July 1438 he found himself back in Pisa.[128]

During his absence events in Italy had proceeded apace. By now there was a complete break between the pope, who had ordered the Council of Basel transferred once and for all to Ferrara, and the council, which continued to meet in Basel. Cardinal Giuliano Cesarini, who had previously, and with some difficulty, presided over the council on behalf of the pope, had returned to Italy. In January 1438 the Council of Ferrara began, and Eugenius IV established himself and his court in that city. In March the emperor and patriarch of Byzantium arrived. In June discussions began over Purgatory, whose existence the Latins for several centuries had held to be beyond doubt but in which the Greeks, faithful to the writings of the Church Fathers, refused to believe.[129] Shortly thereafter the plague struck Ferrara. Death was all around. Discussions of the hereafter came to an end.[130] Thomas Basin was obliged to remain in Pavia for three or four months.[131]

With the approach of winter the plague in Ferrara abated. On October 8 council sessions resumed. A few days later Thomas Basin arrived in Ferrara. After some ten months' absence he again took up residence at the papal court. Apparently the young cleric did no more than follow from a distance the council sessions in which Latins and Greeks discussed the points of dogma that divided them. But a *studium generale* had been founded in Ferrara in 1391. Humanists, some of them famous, taught there—and by 1438 had been teaching there for several years.[132] Thomas Basin took advantage of their teaching; he continued his study of letters.[133]

He did not, however, lose sight of his interests. Clerics who followed the papal court enjoyed certain privileges. Among other things, they were more likely than other clerics to see their hopes realized for grants of benefices that were not yet vacant. Thomas had spent two months ill in London and three or four months waiting in Pavia for the plague to subside. He was afraid that this prolonged absence might cause him to lose his turn. He therefore sought, and on December 27, 1438, received, assurance that his six months' absence would be overlooked and he would be treated as though he had been present all that time at court. His prolonged absence would not delay receipt of the hoped-for benefices.[134]

In fact, a few months later, Thomas Basin received, in addition to the benefice he already held, the parish church of Guineville in the diocese of Lisieux and, even more important, the archdeaconry of Auge, whose annual income was estimated at fifty *livres de petits tournois*. Thomas was now twenty-six. He was canon of Lisieux and had two parish churches. His annual income was not inconsiderable. Yet he still had received none of the major orders. On April 27, 1439, he was granted one year to become a subdeacon.[135]

On that date Thomas Basin was no longer in Ferrara. Political, military, and financial difficulties had forced Eugenius IV to transfer the council from Ferrara to Florence. In January 1439 the pope and his court took up residence in Florence. A few days later, in February, the patriarch made his entry, followed by Emperor John VIII.[136] After three months in Ferrara, Thomas followed the papal court to Florence, where he lived for a time in an extraordinary climate.[137]

Florence was an economic center of the first magnitude. Politically it was dominated by its business elite. The city ruled a vast surrounding territory. To all intents and purposes Cosimo de' Medici took control of the city in 1434, but Florentines took pride in their republic, which they liked to think of as a land of liberty capable of holding its own against any tyrant. This land of liberty was also hospitable to arts and letters. Brunelleschi was building his cupola atop the Duomo and Fra Angelico was beginning to paint his frescoes in the Dominican monastery of San Marco while Thomas Basin was in Florence. Was the young Norman cleric susceptible to the extraordinary beauty of these sights, so different from any he had previously seen? In any case he was much more influenced by the city's literary climate.

A *studium generale* had been created in Florence in the fourteenth century. The city was too prosperous and the cost of living was consequently too high to attract large numbers of students. The *studium* was not a large institution, but, modest though it was, humanism thrived there. In 1373 a chair of poetry was endowed for the purpose of encouraging commentary on Dante, and the first person to hold the chair was the illustrious Boccaccio. In 1396 the *studium* offered the first course in Greek anywhere in Europe.[138] But the greatest Florentine humanists did not teach there. They were at the chancellery. Petrarch's student Coluccio Salutati had been succeeded in 1427 by Leonardo Bruni. Several of the cardinals who came to Florence with the pope, including Thomas Basin's protectors Branda Castiglioni and Giuliano Cesarini, were fervent humanists.[139] The papal chancellery employed such great humanists as Poggio Bracciolini, known as il Poggio. And many Greek scholars had come to Florence with the emperor and the patriarch. For all these reasons Florence in the time of the council was an extraordinary literary center.

Thomas Basin took advantage of these literary splendors during the "seven and more months" he spent in Florence. He followed the council's ins and outs only from afar. But by his own admission he continued his study of letters (*litterarum semper studia et curiam frequentantes*).[140] He took courses at the university (*in dicta curia vel in studio generali residendo*).[141] And he met frequently with Poggio.[142]

Meanwhile, talks between the Greeks and Latins progressed. On July 5, 1439, union was solemnly proclaimed at Santa Maria del Fiore. Now the need was to ready an expeditionary force to go to the aid of Byzantium. Giovanni Tagliacozzo, the archbishop of Tarento, who had maintained close ties with Giuliano Cesarini since the Council of Basel, was sent to Hungary as papal legate. Every embassy included one or more promising young clerics, and Thomas Basin was chosen to go with the archbishop. He left Florence in August 1439. The time of study was over, and Thomas's active career had begun.[143]

Thomas Basin spent eight months in Hungary, four of them in Buda and four in various other cities in which the legate had business. Nearly fifty years later Thomas Basin could still cite the names of some of these cities, but there is no evidence that he was otherwise marked by his visit.[144] On March 26, 1440, Giovanni Tagliacozzo arrived back in Florence, and Thomas Basin with him.[145] The archbishop was made a cardinal; Thomas Basin was made canon of Rouen. On May 27, 1440, the young canon still had not obtained the subdeaconry that he was supposed to have obtained by April 27 of that year.[146] A short while later he was ordained subdeacon. We do not know when he was ordained priest. For many priests in this period the date of ordination was a major event. Thomas Basin, who has so much to say about himself and who was so precise in his chronology, has nothing to say on the subject.

Back in Florence, Thomas no doubt carried on with his literary pursuits and his contacts with the humanists. And of course he was waiting for his future to take shape. By this time he was an intimate and frequent dining companion of Cardinal Tagliacozzo.[147] Nevertheless, he still enjoyed the protection of Cardinal Cesarini and of the elderly Cardinal Branda Castiglioni, still healthy in his nineties. It was the old cardinal and his nephew Zenone Castiglioni who were responsible for the decisive turn in Thomas's career.

In April 1441, after more than a year in Florence, Thomas bade Italy farewell and headed back to Rouen, Normandy, and his family.[148] On May 23, 1441, he was received as canon by the cathedral chapter in Rouen.[149] His Italian years had been crucial, and he would always carry a vivid memory of them. But he was now twenty-nine, "in the flower of youth."[150] His native Normandy would be the theater of his youthful ambition.

In English Normandy (1441–49)

In France Thomas Basin discovered two exhausted combatants. In both camps peace claimed growing numbers of partisans. Each camp had its doubts and difficulties, yet each strove, with some success, to organize and carry on the struggle.

Between 1437 and 1441 Charles VII's armies recaptured a number of important strongholds around Paris, including Montereau, Meaux, Montargis, and Creil. Thomas Basin was then in Italy, and in his *History of Charles VII* he mentions this campaign only briefly. He knew nothing of the circumstances or chronology.[151]

In these years the government of Charles VII, with the consent of its subjects, took a number of important measures. In July 1438, while Thomas Basin was on his way back to Pavia, the king, in accordance with the decrees of the Council of Basel and with the advice of the prelates he had assembled in Bourges, had imposed the so-called Pragmatic Sanction, which restored the former rights and liberties of the Gallican Church. In particular, ordinary electors and collators regained their rights. The pope lost the power he had enjoyed for some time of appointing bishops, canons, and curates. Eugenius IV fought hard to delay imposition of the Pragmatic Sanction, but to no avail. It seems highly unlikely that a young cleric who had so fruitfully followed the papal court and who owed all his benefices and prebends to the favor of Eugenius IV and his cardinals would have been a fervent admirer of the Pragmatic Sanction. In any case it did not concern him, since he was of the other obedience.

In November 1439 Charles VII, with the consent of the estates assembled in Bourges, had begun to reorganize his army. But that effort was cut short in 1440 by a revolt against the king, led by a few captains worried about the plans for reform, a few dissatisfied *grands seigneurs,* and Louis, the king's own son, then aged seventeen and gaining his first, ill-omened experience of battle.[152] For a while Charles VII overcame his deplorable lethargy (*otium*). The revolts were put down. But such jolts did little to further the war against the English.

In fact the English slowly withdrew from the Paris region, but Normandy at least remained theirs. The havoc wrought by "brigands" no doubt poisoned the atmosphere in the duchy. The economic situation was dire, with the English trying hard to find money. More and more of them favored peace, yet new troops were constantly landing in Normandy. Harfleur was recaptured in 1440. Driven out of Paris, the masters of the duchy again began courting the Normans by encouraging Norman autonomy and Norman liberties. The powers of the royal council for Normandy, meeting in Rouen, were reinforced. A fiscal court was established at Rouen in 1436 and a customs court in 1439. Last but not least, the University of Caen came into its own.[153]

As early as 1424 the king of England had had the idea of establishing a university in Caen. In January 1432 he did establish a *studium generale,* which was to have offered instruction in civil and canon law. But the hostility of the University of Paris and the indifference of the people of Caen, who were not eager to finance the project, thwarted the king's will. After the loss of Paris, however, things changed. In the summer of 1436 a faculty of arts and a faculty of theology were added to the two faculties of law. Quarters were found. Professors were appointed. The first courses were offered. In May 1437 Eugenius IV, then in Bologna, confirmed the royal foundation and named the bishop of Bayeux chancellor of the university. On March 19, 1438, the faculty of medicine came into being. On May 19, 1439, a second papal bull granted the University of Caen the same privileges as the other French universities and named the bishops of Lisieux and Coutances conservators of those privileges. In 1439 and 1440 the young university began to thrive. Its students, drawn from English families living in Caen and from Norman families living in the city's environs, numbered several dozen.[154]

Thus following the grave crisis of 1435 and 1436, the English to some extent restored their power in Normandy. Their strength lay in the human and cash reserves that continued to pour in from the metropolis; in the English colonists, some of whom had lived in the duchy for nearly a quarter of a century; in the enforced obedience of much of the population; and in the efficacious aid offered by a number of Italian clerics, the most important of whom was none other than Zenone Castiglioni.

Zenone Castiglioni was probably fifteen or twenty years older than Thomas Basin. He had been a student at Parma (1415) and later at Padua (1418). In 1421 he joined the papal chancellery, which was headed by his uncle Branda Castiglioni. In 1424 the latter renounced his diocese in Lisieux in favor of his nephew. Unlike his uncle, Zenone took up residence in Lisieux. In January, 1425, in Rouen, he swore an oath to the king of England. He thus earned the gratitude of the English authorities and thereafter enjoyed the support of both the papal court, where his uncle Branda would continue for a long time to play a leading role, and of the court of England, which knew him well and with which, in addition, his uncle maintained close ties. In 1432 Zenone was transferred from Lisieux to Bayeux; he swore an oath between the hands of Henry VI. In 1434 the bishop of Bayeux, Zenone Castiglioni, and the new bishop of Lisieux, Pierre Cauchon, the judge of Joan of Arc, left for Basel as the king of England's ambassadors to the council. Zenone then followed in the footsteps of many others, including his uncle: he left Basel to join the pope in Bologna in 1437 and in Florence in 1439. In May 1437, when Eugenius IV confirmed the foundation of the University of Caen, he chose to please the royal court by appointing as chancellor of the university the bishop of Bayeux, Zenone Castiglioni.[155]

In 1439–40 Zenone Castiglioni enjoyed more than ever the full confidence of the court of England. More precisely, he gained the confidence of the two men who, since the duke of Bedford's death, dominated the court while opposing each other, Henry Beaufort and Humphrey, duke of Gloucester. Henry V had had a number of brothers, including the duke of Bedford and the duke of Gloucester. But his father John of Gaunt had also produced several sons by his mistress Catherine Swynford, and, legitimated, they too were uncles of Henry VI. Cardinal Henry Beaufort was one of them. The cardinal and the duke were personal rivals and political opponents. The cardinal, of whom Thomas Basin says simply that in his day he was believed to be the richest man in all Christendom, knew that the English had reached an impasse on the Continent and therefore favored peace efforts.[156] Thomas Basin respected the duke, whom he judged to be valiant and prudent like his brothers King Henry V and the duke of Bedford.[157] But Gloucester was more than just valiant and prudent. He was also a sophisticated man of letters and a great collector of books. As head of the war party, he also opposed his half-brother the cardinal by advocating that the conquests of his brother Henry V be held no matter what the cost.[158]

Now, while Zenone Castiglioni was on good terms with the cardinal, his closest ties were to the duke. Like his uncle Branda Castiglioni, like Giuliano Cesarini and so many other Italian prelates, the bishop of Bayeux was a fervent humanist. When Zenone went to Basel, Gloucester commissioned him to buy books and to encourage Italian humanists to send their books to the duke in England.[159] In Basel, Bologna, and Florence Zenone faithfully executed this commission. Relations between the bishop of Bayeux and the duke of Gloucester were close not only in the intellectual realm but also in the political: the bishop favored continuation of the war.

In the struggle between proponents of war and proponents of peace within the English court, the duke of Gloucester was able to take satisfaction in a number of points. A few months after union was proclaimed in Florence, toward the end of 1439, his close ally Zenone Castiglioni left Italy and returned to Normandy.[160] On July 2, 1440, Richard, the young duke of York, a descendant of Edward III on both his father's and his mother's side, was named the king's lieutenant general for the kingdom of France and the duchy of Normandy. This was a triumph for Humphrey of Gloucester, because Richard also favored continuation of the war. Richard of York landed at Harfleur in June 1441. Zenone Castiglioni became one of his most efficient aides. On September 9, 1441, the bishop of Bayeux was named secretary to the king of England. On January 20, 1442, he was appointed to the grand council of Rouen.[161]

The proponents of peace also scored some victories, however. In November 1440, for example, a step was taken over the protests of the duke of Gloucester in the hope of creating an atmosphere more favorable to peace: Charles, the duke of Orléans, the poet who had been taken prisoner at Agincourt, was freed after twenty-five years of captivity.[162]

In these uncertain times, at some point between 1440 and 1442, Zenone Castiglioni wrote the duke of Gloucester a long letter that touched on all the themes of English propaganda and turned them to the war party's advantage. Zenone deplored, for instance, the decline of English power and offered a lengthy lament for the misery of the Norman people, but he did not on that account counsel peace. The English royal house, he said, was mistress of Normandy, it enjoyed *dominium* in Normandy, by hereditary right. King John's notorious inactivity had lost that right, to England's shame, and had earned him the humiliating epithet "Lackland." But Henry V had restored England to glorious sovereignty (*imperii gloriam*). Not to preserve it would be most scandalous. What is more, losing Normandy would not end the war. With Normandy gone, how could Aquitaine be protected from hostile assault?[163]

Zenone Castiglioni did not go to Normandy alone. He was assisted by a group of protégés. Among them were several members of the prolific Castiglioni family, in particular Zenone's first cousin Giovanni Castiglioni, who would become papal collector in England in 1443 and bishop of Coutances in 1444.[164] Another member of the group was the humanist Rolando Talenti, who became Zenone's secretary in Lisieux some time before 1432 and whom Zenone had appointed canon of Bayeux in 1434. He was quite happy to go to Normandy with his master in 1440, all the more so in that he shared Zenone's ideas.[165] With Rolando came his brother, Antonio, who was professor of law at the University of Caen, and his cousin, Marco Corio, who for seven years served as the bishop's secretary and copyist.[166] Thomas Basin was a young protégé of Cardinal Branda Castiglioni. He very likely met the cardinal's nephew Zenone in Bologna or Florence. Humanism probably drew the two men together. In Normandy Thomas Basin could be useful to Zenone Castiglioni, and Zenone Castiglioni could further Thomas's career. So in April 1441 Thomas bade Italy farewell and returned to English Normandy to see his family, which was prospering in Caudebec and Rouen, and to pursue his career under the wing of that great servant of the English, Zenone Castiglioni.

Thomas Basin's ambitious hopes were not disappointed. He lived at first, for six months, in Rouen. He was there in September 1441, when Charles VII's armies captured Pontoise and Evreux, and his account of these battles in the history he would write of Charles's reign was quite lengthy because he had been so close to the scene.[167] Then, in October 1441, he left Rouen for Caen, where the royal council had appointed him professor of canon law at the university.[168] As a titular professor, Thomas could now call himself a doctor in civil and canon law.[169] Clearly the new doctor owed his nomination to Zenone Castiglioni's efficacious favor. Any doubt one might have on this score is dispelled by the fact that no sooner had Thomas arrived in Caen than he was named canon of Bayeux; he was given responsibility for cases to be brought before the ecclesiastical conservators of the privileges of the University of Caen; and he became official and vicar general of the bishop of Bayeux.[170] His influence in the university was so great that on October 1, 1442, he was elected rector.[171] Within a year his irresistible rise fostered hopes that he would soon sit on the archiepiscopal throne of Rouen, and in December 1443 he was indeed one of three candidates for this see.[172]

But he was not chosen. A few months later a very remarkable event took place. So great were the reverses suffered by the English armies at Guyenne in 1442 that even the partisans of war had to resign themselves to peace. In September 1442 Richard of York received from England the mission of negotiating a truce. In October 1442 Zenone Castiglioni was named one of the negotiators.[173] Shortly thereafter Rolando Talenti composed and sent to Charles, duke of Orléans, an eloquent plea for peace.[174] These efforts were crowned with success. On May 28, 1444 (Thomas later believed, mistakenly, that it had been in June), the kings of France and England signed a truce after twenty-eight years of war. In later years Thomas vividly remembered the joy with which the news was greeted. The people of the cities, long shut up in their homes as though confined to prison, turned out in large numbers to look at forests and fields, abandoned though they were, and to contemplate the spectacle of green meadows, cool springs, streams and rivers which they knew to exist but had never seen. And everywhere they visited churches dedicated to God, the Virgin, and the saints. "And all was tranquil everywhere for nearly a whole year."[175]

In 1445, however, Charles VII led an army to attack Metz in Lorraine. Thomas Basin was keenly aware of this, because the duke of York had conceived the plan of marrying his eldest son Edward (the future Edward IV) to a daughter of Charles VII and therefore sent an embassy to Lorraine in June 1445. This embassy was headed, as was customary, by a cleric and a layman. The cleric was "the reverend father in God, the bishop of Bayeux, councillor of my lord the king," that is, Zenone Castiglioni. The layman was an Englishman, "Richard Merbury . . . knight and bailiff of Gisors." Immediately after these two heads of the delegation came "Master Thomas Basin, doctor of canon and civil law."[176]

The embassy failed. The marriage did not take place. And Thomas Basin, who had played only a minor role, no doubt came away from the experience with unpleasant memories, for he does not say a word about it in his *History of Charles VII*. He was also oddly embarrassed by the character of Richard of York, whom he had served but who a short while later would assassinate the duke of Somerset and rebel against Henry VI. In the *History of Charles VII* Thomas usually gives in a few sentences or adjectives a description of the people he discusses. Yet while Richard of York is mentioned several times, Thomas utters not a word of judgment, good or bad.

After this brief and fruitless episode, Thomas returned to his teaching in Caen until, in 1447, a vacancy arose in the episcopal see of Lisieux. Zenone Castiglioni's protégé had no difficulty claiming it. All the canons voted for him. The new pope, Nicholas V, awarded him the bishopric on October 19.[177] Lisieux was a good diocese, and among Thomas's predecessors were Nicolas Oresme, whom he had read and admired;[178] Branda Castiglioni and Zenone Castiglioni, his protectors; and Pierre Cauchon, who died in 1442 and whose tomb was located in the cathedral's Chapel of the Virgin. The moment Thomas received Nicholas V's bull, he left Caen after slightly more than six years in residence. On December 28 he was in Rouen.[179] From there he hastened to England, where on February 3, 1448, he swore the required oath of loyalty to Henry VI personally. On February 23 he was again in Rouen, and a few days after that he reached his new diocese.[180] Forty years later, in his *Breviloquium*, Thomas Basin gave the precise date of that important moment in his life, his accession to the rank of bishop. It took place in the first year of the pontificate of Nicholas V, and the king of England who at that time reigned in Normandy was Henry VI of Lancaster, son of Henry V. And Thomas Basin was thirty-five.[181]

Thomas Basin at Thirty-five

Who was this man now in the prime of life? It is not totally out of the question to imagine what he looked like physically. His coffin in Utrecht has been located and his bones have been examined, and in the choir of the Caudebec church there is still a window portraying him as bishop and probably not altogether unlike its subject. Think of him, then, as a man of around five foot seven, of stout build and, on the evidence of both the window and the skeletal remains, with a protruding chin.[182] That is about as much as we can say.

A much less sketchy moral portrait of Thomas Basin can be constructed, however. In his narratives on a variety of subjects he does not hesitate to give his own personal opinion (*nostra sentencia, nostra estimacio vel opinio*).[183] The historian never pretends to hide the man. Thomas also speaks at length about himself. Nevertheless, in fleshing out this moral portrait we face three difficulties. First, he does not tell all about himself—far from it. Second, when he speaks about himself he is in the twilight of his life; over a quarter of a century he must have changed a great deal. And third, what he says has the character not of a dispassionate deposition but of a brief in his own behalf. If we are to find out what the new bishop of Lisieux was really like, we therefore must listen attentively to what he says, but we must also check up on him and with the help of knowledge gleaned elsewhere correct his tardy, biased, self-indulgent testimony.

In the *History of Charles VII* Thomas quite guilelessly describes himself shortly after his accession to the episcopacy: "The bishop of the city and of the diocese [of Lisieux] was at that time Thomas, born in the diocese of Rouen. He was a man well-versed in divine and human letters and, of even greater note, quite remarkable for his judgment, wisdom, and sincere love of God and of his neighbor. In short, he was in those days one of the most famous bishops of the Gauls."[184] It is hardly an overstatement to say that Thomas was not a modest man. Throughout his work he exhibits a vanity as immense as it is ingenuous. His value, his *virtus*, is something he takes for granted.[185] And the most important quality he recognizes in himself is a moral one: his only motives were love of God and of his neighbor.

In his narrative Thomas often speaks of God, for God "on high sees all and governs all"[186] and everything that happens is determined by the presence or absence of divine providence,[187] grace, aid and protection,[188] goodness, clemency, and mercy.[189] Frequently man can comprehend the reasons for divine intervention. God has come to help the unfortunate;[190] he has punished men for their sins;[191] he has, as Thomas, remembering the words of Psalm 33 : 10, repeats several times, thwarted the plans of men and the designs of princes.[192] Often, however, God for no good reason bestows his grace on undeserving people.[193] His wisdom is unfathomable. His judgments cannot be explained.[194] Therefore man seems to be the plaything of indecipherable fortune.

Thomas Basin often speaks of fortune, *fortuna.* The word came to his pen from Virgil, Seneca, and other ancient pagan writers.[195] He frequently refers to the smile of favorable fortune;[196] to ill fortune;[197] to the caprices of changing fortune.[198] In Thomas's writing, however, this fortune has become wholly Christian. It is merely the earthly consequence of divine will.[199] Contemplating the extraordinarily sudden, complete, and favorable turn in the fortunes (*conversio fortune*) of the French in 1429, Thomas Basin can only repeat the words of the Seventy-seventh Psalm: *Haec mutatio dextere Excelsi* (literally, this change is the work of the right hand of the Most High).[200]

Although the reasons of the Most High may be impenetrable to men, they are always just. This no one can doubt.[201] Hence it is God who permits that with which Thomas Basin is obsessed, the inconstancy and fragility inherent in human affairs. "It will be clearly seen how much human things are built on sand and how easily he who places his hope in them is deceived and deluded," he states in the preface that is common to both the *History of Charles VII* and the *History of Louis XI*.[202] And at the end of the *History of Charles VII* he repeats that the book shows "how much human things are in essence uncertain, fragile, and changeable and how wrong are those who locate happiness in the possession of the things of this world."[203] All his work emphasizes "the ever-changing instability of human things."[204] Nothing is trustworthy but the love that Thomas so sincerely believes he feels for God and, through God, for his fellow man.[205]

Thomas Basin does not doubt God. Nor does he doubt the Church. He does not doubt that the Scriptures in which the Church asks us to believe are not only authentic but divine. Why cast doubt on translations approved by the authority of the Church? They must be believed without reservation. In matters of faith, whosoever doubts is an infidel (*Dubius in fide infidelis est*).[206] A man of strong, untroubled belief, Thomas has no doubts, either, about the virtue of good works. Bequests, alms, and pilgrimages are, he believes, necessary things.[207] Yet they are not sufficient. They are worth nothing unless rooted in charity. From Paul he learned that there is no true virtue or piety without charity, that is, without love of God and of one's neighbor. For "as Saint John the Baptist says in his first epistle, he who does not love the brother that he sees, how can he love God whom he does not see?"[208]

Thomas spoke in this way late in life. And he called "God to witness that neither hope of temporal profit nor desire to further earthly ambition dictated [his] behavior, but only [his] love and sincere affection for his neighbor in Jesus Christ."[209] As a young man, he was probably already convinced that power, honors, and riches were wretched and insane pleasures, fleeting joys incapable of bringing lasting happiness.[210] Yet why should he not have felt, like other clerics in his time, a legitimate concern for his own interests?[211] Why should he not have aspired to rise in a hierarchy against which he raised no protest? Perhaps the young man already possessed the wisdom of the old. But that wisdom by no means stood in the way of legitimate ambition. The problem was that Thomas lacked the means to fulfill that ambition.

In ringing words of self-praise, Thomas Basin depicts himself as a man of wise counsel. Notice, first, what he does not say. He does not say that he was a great orator. No doubt this was a sign of the times. Under Charles VI, when decisions were made in tumultuous assemblies, eloquence was a necessary arrow in ambition's quiver. Portraits of individuals always emphasized their oratorical gifts. Under Charles VII and Louis XI political decisions were reached by other means. Speech counted less than in the past, though it still counted. An embassy, for example, still required voluble orators. In 1447 it was only natural that Thomas Basin had yet to act as spokesman for any of the embassies in which he had participated. He was still too young. He did not play the leading role. But the fact that no one subsequently made use of his oratorical gifts is sufficient proof that Thomas did not impress his contemporaries by way of eloquence. He himself was more or less conscious of his limitations in this regard. When he wants to avoid verbosity in his historical works, he simply repeats some commonplace idea.[212] It is revealing, however, that as a jurist he trusts more in knowledge of the documents than in eloquent pleading. He complains, moreover, of the verbosity of the lawyers, of "that malady, prolixity" (*morbus prolixitatis*).[213] Clearly Thomas did not see himself as an eloquent speaker any more than his contemporaries did.

Nor does Thomas Basin say that he was a man of action. He distinguishes carefully between the realm of words (*verba*) and that of things (*res*),[214] between the realm of speech (*verba*) and that of action (*facta*).[215] He was fascinated by action. Countless times he deplores some captain's indecision or hesitation. But clearly he was an armchair strategist. And when it came to maneuvering on his own chosen field of battle, he was no more successful than the captains he criticized. No doubt he had every intention of administering his diocese well, of defending its temporal possessions, "of instructing the people of God in the doctrine of Christ and leading them to salvation."[216] There is no evidence that he did not do so. But while capable of carrying out his duties as bishop, the prelate nevertheless lacked the virtues necessary to make his mark outside his diocese.

To begin with, he lacked physical stamina. Thomas Basin was healthy enough to take countless long trips by mule and to reach seventy-eight with his mind intact.[217] Yet he was a man anxious about his health, vulnerable to fatigue, and easily upset by hunger, harsh winters, and scorching summers.[218] His robust appearance was misleading.

Also working against him was his incredible naiveté, which his vanity only accentuated. For him, honesty was the essential mortar that held society together. He expected to find it everywhere, and he was constantly disappointed. His narratives are filled with stories of cheating, deception, and perfidy. His pessimism drew on endlessly repeated citations from the Bible and the classics: *"Maledictus homo qui confidit in homine"* (Cursed be the man that trusteth in man—Jeremiah 17:5);[219] *"Non intrat unquam regium limen fides"* (Honesty does not cross the royal threshold—Seneca, *Agamemnon* V, 285);[220] and most of all, *"Nolite confidere in principibus neque in filiis hominum, in quibus non est salus"* (Put not your trust in princes, nor in the son of man, in whom there is no help—Psalms 146:3).[221]

Distrust combined with wisdom to paralyze Thomas Basin, whose wisdom in fact stopped at prudence. And his prudence stopped at fear, with which, on the evidence of all his work, he was obsessed.

Did Thomas Basin at least have friends who might have helped him overcome this fear, friends in whom he might have had confidence and who might have backed his ambition? The question has no easy answer, because Thomas was very discreet on the subject. It seems clear that as an old man he was substantially alone. Yet research has revealed that as a youth he had firm allegiances to certain groups, which for a time offered him effective assistance. He had close ties to his family, to his father and to his many brothers. His ties were especially close to the powerful group that revolved around Zenone Castiglioni. Despite the silences (themselves revealing) of the elderly Thomas Basin, the new bishop of Lisieux was not an isolated individual.

The fact remains that Thomas saw himself not as an orator or man of action but as a man of good counsel. His remarkable intelligence is beyond doubt. But he was essentially a man at home in his study, a man of prayer and meditation, a man given to books and documents. As a Christian or a man of letters, Thomas Basin loved solitude. He liked to meditate. He saw himself as a *"contemplacionis amator."*[222] He found it soothing when he had the leisure to read, to pray, and to meditate (*lectioni, oracioni ac suavissimo ocio contemplacionis . . . vacare*), to devote himself fully to spiritual exercises.[223] And as he would admit a short time after 1447, he also derived infinite pleasure from the leisure to immerse himself in literature (*reversus ad otium litterale, in quo mihi summa voluptas est*).[224]

This taste for study and reading explains the final trait in Thomas's self-portrait. He claims to be "well versed in divine and human letters." His broad culture, acquired in Louvain and in Italy and constantly expanded in subsequent years, was primarily Christian. Thomas Basin was steeped in the Bible, especially the Psalms and the Prophets, which confirmed his pessimism. He also drew heavily on the Fathers, especially Saint Augustine,[225] who convinced him of the arbitrariness of divine grace.[226] He was also learned in the law. Nothing in the Code and the Digest, the Decretum and Decretals, was unfamiliar to him. But this Christian and legal culture was after all the traditional culture that one might expect in a cleric and a doctor *in utroque.*

More remarkable was this cleric and jurist's love of letters, his vast humanist culture. He had read and reread Cicero and Virgil, Sallust and Suetonius, and countless other writers, especially Seneca, whose tragedies he often cites. In his library was a manuscript of a work by Seneca, still extant, a gift from none other than Zenone Castiglioni.[227] This gift is an apt token of all that Thomas's humanism owed to Italy and to the Italian humanists he met there. Throughout his life he accumulated works by Leonardo Bruni, for example. He ordered a copy of Bruni's *De Militia* and procured the first printed edition of his *De Bello italico adversus Gothos.*[228]

Such intimate knowledge of ancient Latin literature as well as of the latest Italian authors may not have been altogether unusual in mid-fifteenth-century France. Jean Lebègue was born in 1368 and had obtained a position as royal notary-secretary in the last decade of the fourteenth century. In 1447 he was almost eighty years old but still a royal notary-secretary in Paris. His library contained several of Leonardo Bruni's works. Only a short while earlier he had even translated, and dedicated to Charles VII, Bruni's *History of the First Punic War.*[229] Thus Thomas Basin's cultural background may not have been extraordinary in his own milieu, but it was unusual, and it explains what was original and disturbing about his ideas for subjects of Charles VII and Louis XI.

The vast majority of French men and women in the mid-fifteenth century loved their king and their country and detested the English. This powerful nationalistic sentiment, as we would call it today, was not the only reason why France would ultimately survive a century of tragedy and disaster, but it was at least part of the explanation. Thomas Basin was well aware of the French love of country and hatred of the English. He was well aware of the "natural love" that "as though by natural impulse" inclined the French toward the kingdom and its king.[230] He also knew that the English were "very ancient and in a sense natural enemies of this land and this people"; that they felt toward the French "an inveterate and in a sense innate hatred"; that the French paid them back in kind; and that with each passing day both sides were consumed a little more by their respective enmities.[231] Thomas is a reliable reporter on the hatred of the French and English for each other and on the French love of king and country. It is a mistake, however, to think that he shared the feelings of either side. Thomas Basin recognized the "national" feelings of Charles VII's and Louis XI's subjects and was aware of their importance, but those feelings were not his own.

As a Christian, Thomas Basin had read Saint John (13:34 and 15:2) and Saint Paul (Rom. 12:10). He therefore tried to love his neighbor, and he always felt an immense compassion, an immense pity for poor peasants, urban paupers, and victims of war and tyranny.[232] As a man of letters, however, he was also a reader of Cicero, and he knew that Cicero used love of one's neighbor to justify love of one's country. All fourteenth- and fifteenth-century humanists knew these two sentences of Cicero: "Our parents, our children, our neighbors, and our friends are dear to us, but our fatherland epitomizes all our affections. What man of honor would shrink from death, if by dying he could be useful to the fatherland?"[233] Obviously Thomas Basin knew these lines, and at one point he alludes to them specifically: "In braving death in order to save the fatherland and alleviate the suffering of those victimized by countless exactions, one demonstrates above all love of one's country and neighbors, and, as truth is my witness, no greater love is there than to lay down one's life for one's friends."[234] Cicero's noble sentiments sound false when repeated by Thomas Basin. Nothing about Thomas's life or writings can be remotely construed as an exhortation to die for anyone or anything. It is quite true, however, that Thomas loved his country and his neighbors—but which country and which neighbors?

Although Thomas Basin did indeed see the French as a people and France as a country, his Norman origins made it impossible for him to forget the diversity of France. France was a country, but within it were various "nations." The king of France was, in Thomas's own words, the "father of the country and of all the nations of [his] kingdom."[235] France was indeed a country (*patria*), but one that consisted of a number of smaller lands (*terra*) and regions (*patria*), among them Normandy.[236] The neighbors that God wanted him to love were therefore, first of all, the poor of Normandy. The country that Cicero wanted him to love was, first of all, Normandy, which was after all his country (*pro ea quam debemus ad patriam caritate permoti*).[237]

Roman citizens, however, had been able to love both the smaller country in which they were born and the larger country of which they were citizens. Fifteenth-century jurists and humanists had long since learned to reconcile love of both "fatherlands." Thomas Basin loved his country, but that love did not prevent him from loving his "larger country," namely, France (*zelo caritatis quam post Deum ad patriam maximam habemus permoti*).[238] Nor did it prevent him from loving the "most Christian" kings of France[239] or the French people.

Thomas Basin's love of the French was not blind, however. In those days the French justified their pride in being French on the grounds that their qualities raised them high above other peoples and made borrowing pointless. Thomas Basin saw his compatriots through unclouded eyes. He deplored their pride. He wished that they would demonstrate greater wisdom and less pomposity in speech.[240] And he recognized the qualities of other peoples. Later he refused to believe that a Swiss garrison was guilty of treason, because "the peoples of this Germany are noted rather for their fidelity and loyalty."[241] He continually expressed admiration for many English leaders. All three brothers of Henry V were "valiant and wise."[242] The duke of Bedford, in particular, was "brave, humane, and just."[243] The earl of Salisbury was "the wisest and bravest" of English captains.[244] Andrew Trollope was "one of the bravest and most energetic of soldiers, remarkable for his skill, his prudence, and his courage."[245] Thomas's list of courageous English captains is longer than his corresponding list of Frenchmen. Moreover, Thomas made so little effort to hide his admiration for Italian jurists in general and for Roman court procedure in particular that one day he scandalized Charles VII's entourage by recommending that French justice be improved by borrowing from beyond the Alps.[246] Thomas Basin certainly did not share the blind passions of many Frenchmen.

In Thomas's mind, too, there was something vulgar and common about those excessive passions. His account of a later event is so revealing that it must be mentioned here. The year is 1471. A few years earlier, at Péronne, Louis XI had returned the cities of the Somme, including Amiens, to Charles the Bold, but had retained sovereignty over them. In other words, Charles was lord of Amiens, but Louis was its sovereign lord—so read the law. But that law ran counter to the feelings of Amiens's inhabitants, the vast majority of whom were royalists. Louis XI waited for the first opportunity to renege on his concession. In 1471 he judged that the circumstances were propitious. On January 31 the king's agents went to the city and asked it to return to his obedience. The city refused on the advice of men who, Thomas Basin emphasizes, were "the wisest and most honorable in the city." Thomas dilates at some length on the reasoning of the Amiens authorities, of whose answer he fully approves:

> They answered, in effect, and quite appropriately, that they recognized the king as their superior lord but that they took the duke of Burgundy to be their immediate lord. They had obeyed the king's orders and had sworn oaths of faith and homage to the duke. They could not abandon him and go over to the king. . . . They could not violate the pledge they had given to the duke. . . . But, that said, they nevertheless still recognized the king as their sovereign lord. So that if the king wished to rule them directly, without submission to another lord and without intermediary, they begged him to intervene with the duke of Burgundy, to whom they had pledged their faith on [the king's] orders, so that the duke would release them from their pledge and oath. After which they would joyfully and willingly give themselves to the king and obey all the orders of his majesty. Otherwise they could not honestly do so without incurring the charges of perjury and perfidy.

Such was the response of the Amiens authorities in their wisdom (*prudenter et consulte*). A few days later, however, the common people, stupid and faithless (*stulta et infida plebs*) opened the city to the king.[247] This admirable passage clearly expresses Thomas Basin's persistent mistrust of popular passions. It also explains very well why Thomas had such mixed feelings about France, its king, and its people. His geographical origin and social status were partly responsible, but the crucial element was Thomas's devotion to law. To his way of thinking, "national" passions might have nobility, but they were still passions. And the world of passions was subordinate to the world of wisdom, which was the world of reason and law.

Now, in the world of law one essential notion was that of sovereignty. A good jurist, Thomas Basin employed an extremely precise political vocabulary. *Imperium* referred to the authority, the sovereignty, of the legitimate prince. *Potestas, dominacio,* and *dicio* indicated de facto power, whether legitimate or not. And *administracio, gubernacio,* and *moderacio* referred to the administrative or governmental functions of officers. In 1418 the Burgundians had seized Paris and afterward exercised power (*dominacio*) there, leaving Charles VI only nominal authority (*Karolo sexto titulatenus dumtaxat imperium retinente*).[248] In 1440 Louis, King Charles's son, had tried to seize the government of the realm (*regni moderacionem atque administracionem*). Nowhere does Thomas say that Louis challenged his father's authority.[249] Much later, at the end of his life, during the troubles in Utrecht, Thomas Basin remarked that the city was no longer under the authority of its legitimate prince (*sub legitimi pastoris et principis sui imperio*) and that it had fallen under a tyrannical power (*sub tyrannicam potestatem*).[250]

Let us return now to the 1440s. Among the peoples of Gaul were those who lived under the authority and power of the king of France (*ceteri populi Galliarum qui sub imperio ac dicione regis Francorum degunt*).[251] But what about the others, who lived in English France? In order fully to understand Thomas's position, it is essential to note the words he uses. Here there is no ambiguity. In Guyenne the English had *imperium.*[252] In Normandy they had *imperium.*[253] In those parts of France that they occupied they had *imperium.* The duke of Bedford had exercised the sovereignty that the king of England possessed in France (*Bethfordie dux, imperium pro Anglorum rege in Francia administrans*).[254] Rouen was the capital of the whole territory over which the English held sovereignty in the kingdom of France (*sedes tocius imperii Anglorum in regno Francorum*).[255] If words have meaning (as they did for the precise Thomas Basin), this means that the elderly exile never recanted the opinions expressed by the young bishop. Thomas Basin believed that the English presence in France was legitimate. It was based on a treaty, the Treaty of Troyes, whose validity Thomas Basin never contested. As a young student in Paris he had sworn, between the hands of the rector of the university, an oath to observe the treaty.[256] Later, as the young bishop of Lisieux, he had gone to Windsor to swear the required oath of loyalty to Henry VI personally. With his legalistic conscience clear, Thomas Basin had not the slightest scruple about serving the legitimate king, that is, the king of France and England.

For Thomas Basin, therefore, the problem was not one of passionate attraction to French sovereignty. His respect for English sovereignty, however, was conditional. Every state must guarantee its people certain supreme goods, namely, peace and tranquility, justice and liberty. "Everyone naturally loves liberty." A great reader of Cicero and of the Florentine humanists, Thomas repeatedly affirmed that "love of liberty is innate in almost everyone."[257] English sovereignty was justified so long as English might guaranteed peace, justice, and liberty to French populations. And as long as English might had respected and guaranteed the liberty, rights, and privileges of its subject populations in Guyenne, Normandy, and elsewhere, Thomas had been untroubled. What made the English presence contestable was not the rights of the king of France or his subjects' love for him but the inability of the English to carry out their state duties.

While Thomas Basin followed the course dictated, as he saw it, by reason and law, other Normans, driven by hatred of the English, had left "their fields and their homes" and "were living like wild animals and wolves in the most inaccessible depths of the forests." Whenever "they could lay hands on an Englishman, they put him to death without mercy." Nineteenth- and twentieth-century French historians have hailed these men as "resistance fighters," but for the English at the time they were "brigands."[258] A fair portion of the French population also called them "brigands" and had no sympathy for their activities. Thomas Basin was one who shared this view. He was well aware that without the English presence there would have been no brigands. Yet not all of them were motivated solely by hatred of the English. Some were simply lazy, greedy, or cruel, while others hoped to avoid just punishment for their crimes. And they did not attack only the English. They kidnapped peasants and held them for ransom. They even robbed priests. Far from being heroes in Thomas Basin's eyes, these "desperate and lost" men were rotten scoundrels (*hujuscemodi pestilencium ferarum genere, illo pestilenti hominum incommodo, illud pestiferum latronum genus*) whose wild rage (*efferata rabies*) was the cause of countless evils and deprived people of needed quiet and tranquillity (*quies*).[259]

Thomas was no more sympathetic to the regular army troops. His concept of war was a strictly legalistic one at odds in every way with the realities of his time. Of course he conceded that wars were inevitable and that armies were quite necessary.[260] Since he admired feudal institutions and had read *De Militia,* in which Leonardo Bruni praises the idea of a national army, his ideal was most likely to limit the military to the "ordinary" and "natural" army constituted by the nobility of the realm.[261] He condemned paid armies, although it was already a long time since any state had done without one.

At the very least Thomas Basin hoped that war, if inevitable, could be fought in conformity with international and natural law.[262] Wars should be fought openly. Hostilities should be declared. Battles should be preceded by ultimatums.[263] So far from admiring the ruses to which the French owed so many of their successes in those difficult years, Thomas Basin had no words harsh enough for such damnable ruses (*insidiae*), treacheries (*fraudes*), deceptions (*dola*), betrayals (*tradimenta, prodiciones*), and machinations (*machinamenta*).[264]

Worse was yet to come. Order and discipline should have been the primary concern of all captains, English and French alike. Yet Thomas found all to many opportunities to condemn armies for their lack of those qualities.[265] Incapable of stopping the brigands, the English captains came to a point where they could no longer control pillaging by their own insolent and undisciplined troops.[266] And the French soldiers, so wicked and cruel that people with good reason called them "skinners" and "butchers," made even French victories a bitter pill for the poor to swallow. In telling of the recapture of Paris and the slow reconquest of the Ile-de-France by Charles VII's armies, Thomas remarks that the unfortunate inhabitants of the region had suffered at the hands of the French while under English sovereignty (*sub imperio Anglorum*) but they were now suffering even more at the hands of the skinners.[267]

Given these looming dangers, the character of Charles VII was not of a sort to reassure the bishop of Lisieux. It would be a long while before Thomas would exalt "King Charles of happy memory," the better to denounce his son.[268] In 1447 Thomas saw the king only once, in the course of the embassy that had taken him two years earlier to the northeastern corner of the kingdom. He hardly knew him except by reputation, and that reputation was not good. Thomas did not deny that Charles VII had one essential quality rarely found in princes. He kept his word. He could be trusted. His good faith, his *fides,* had been manifest even in his youth, and nothing subsequently contradicted it.[269]

But the prince's vices,[270] the corruption of his morals,[271] were also manifest. The young king, "as is customary at that age, indulged night and day . . . in revelry, dancing, and pleasures."[272] He gave himself over "to the pleasures of the table, debauchery, and luxury."[273] With age he moderated his eating and drinking, which preserved his health, but he never renounced the pleasures afforded him by "beautiful Agnes" and "an ample flock of little ladies" (*copiosus grex mulierculárum*) who followed him everywhere.[274]

Thus in 1447 Charles VII was mired in torpor and inertia (*inerti ocio torpens*).[275] When God sent Joan to save the kingdom and the people of France, the king did nothing.[276] When the peasants of Caux, moved by fervent, natural love for the king and his realm, rose in rebellion, he did nothing to protect and defend them.[277] What is more, the king's pleasures cost him dearly. And his monetary needs threatened to undermine the liberties of his peoples. Charles VII, the bishop of Lisieux realized, could do nothing to ensure the calm (*quies*) or liberty (*libertas*) of his subjects. All signs indicated that he might well become a "useless" king, as his father had been,[278] or a "tyrant," as his son would later be.[279]

Thomas Basin loved the kingdom of France and the French people.

But he also loved the Normans. And he did not hate the English. Above all he loved peace, justice, and liberty. And he was terribly wary of the king of France.

The Recovery of Normandy (1449–50)

While Thomas Basin was establishing himself in Lisieux at the end of February or the beginning of March 1448, a crisis in relations between Henry VI and Charles VII had arisen over the city of Le Mans. During the truce of 1444, it had been decided that Henry VI would marry Marguerite of Anjou, the daughter of King René, who was to receive Le Mans in return from his future son-in-law. Three years after the marriage, however, Le Mans was still English. Finally the French lost patience. A crisis ensued, but it ended happily. On March 11, 1448, the truce, which had previously been extended twice, on April 1, 1446, and April 1, 1447, was again extended until April 1, 1450.[280] On March 16, 1448, the English left Le Mans.[281] On leaving they even promised to surrender Mayenne in the county of Maine, of which King René's brother Charles d'Anjou was lord. And a short while later they did as they had promised.[282] Like most people Thomas Basin looked forward to two additional years of fragile peace.

Beyond the boundaries of Normandy, the English ruled only a portion of Le Perche. They no longer even ruled all of Normandy, because the French, prior to the truce of 1444, had reconquered Dieppe, to the north of the Seine, and the cities of Evreux, Louviers, and Neubourg to the south. Still, most of Normandy was English; specifically, the English were masters of a vast territory, "six days long and four days wide," which included "six bishoprics and one noble archbishopric and a hundred cities and castles."[283] In those cities and castles were garrisons, whose size we can roughly estimate. There were perhaps three thousand English soldiers in Rouen,[284] three thousand in Caen,[285] and five hundred in Cherbourg.[286] In the smaller cities and larger castles the number of English soldiers was still estimated at between one hundred and two hundred.[287] The Lisieux garrison, for example, consisted of one hundred sixty to two hundred soldiers. But England no longer had the cash necessary to support all these troops. The garrisons were therefore poorly armed. In particular they lacked artillery. They were badly paid, hence increasingly undisciplined. And some of them had been in place for a long time, so that officers and men had become used to their surroundings. With the periods of truce they grew soft with inactivity.[288]

In 1417 the English had encouraged Norman autonomy. Now that they were unsure of their army's effectiveness and deprived of adequate support from home, they were forced to rely more and more on the resources, loyalty, and competence of the Normans. Of course they were not unaware of the misgivings or outright hostility of some of the population. Nevertheless, they believed they could count on the loyalty and wealth of the burghers of Rouen, among them the father, brothers, and brother-in-law of Thomas Basin; and still more on the loyalty and competence of the high-ranking Norman clergy. For the English, Thomas Basin's predecessor in Lisieux was an excellent example of Norman loyalty. Pasquier de Vaux was a native of Vaux, not far from Evreux. He had been trained as a jurist. In 1435 he occupied a key post in the English administration; he was canon of Paris, Rouen, and Amiens; and he was living in Paris. On September 25, 1435, he was elected bishop of Meaux. When Charles VII's armies entered Paris in 1436, Pasquier fled to Meaux. On August 12, 1439, Charles VII's troops entered Meaux. The following October 9, the loyal Pasquier became bishop of Evreux, but on September 15, 1441, the French army captured the city. Pasquier, who refused to have Charles VII for his king and lord, left. In 1443 Charles VII ordered all his property seized, but Pasquier was by then bishop of Lisieux, councillor to Henry VI, and president of the fiscal court of Rouen. He died on July 11, 1448. It was this devoted servant of the masters of Normandy whom Thomas Basin replaced.[289]

In 1449 all Norman bishops had similar close ties to the masters of their country. The least affected was probably the bishop of Sées, Jean d'Escars (or Des Cars), a Limousin noble about whom little is known.[290] But Raoul Roussel, the archbishop of Rouen, was born in the diocese of Coutances in 1389. In 1416 he was a doctor of canon law. In 1420 he was canon of Rouen. In 1429 he supplemented this Rouen prebend with what had been Jean Gerson's prebend in the chapter of Notre-Dame of Paris. Shortly thereafter he played a not inconsiderable role in the trial of Joan of Arc, and on May 30, 1431, he attended her execution. Before long he became a councillor to the king of France and England and a royal magistrate. In 1444 he became archbishop of Rouen, and in 1449 he was an intimate adviser of the duke of Somerset.[291] Martin Pinard was a native of the Bayeux region. He had been canon of Avranches and dean of Bayeux. In 1444 he became bishop of Avranches. In 1449 he too was an intimate adviser of the duke of Somerset.[292] Recall, moreover, that for a long time Zenone Castiglioni, the bishop of Bayeux, had also been a faithful servant of the English in Normandy, and that since 1444 his cousin and protégé Giovanni Castiglioni had been bishop of Coutances. And the bishop of Lisieux was another protégé of Zenone

Castiglioni, another faithful servant of the masters of Normandy: Thomas Basin.

With the backing of the army and these loyal supporters, the English, by availing themselves of the repeatedly extended truce, might have continued to rule for some time to come. Instead they changed course sharply. The dukes of Brittany had been neutral. Their duchy had enjoyed peace and prosperity. And Fougères, not far from Normandy, was a populous and wealthy city. On the night of March 24–25, 1449, François de Surienne, known as the Aragonese, then an English captain in charge of the garrison at Verneuil, sacked the town. Did he take this action on his own initiative, or did the English government put him up to it? From the outset Charles VII and his advisers were convinced that the English were responsible, and to them it was clear that this indirect attack on a neutral prince constituted a violation of the truce. Nevertheless, "in order to make sure, as always, that God and the law were on his side,"[293] Charles VII reacted slowly and cautiously. He sent an embassy to the duke of Somerset asking him to disavow François de Surienne and to return Fougères to the duke of Brittany. "To which the duke responded that he disavowed those who had taken [the city but stated] how happy he was about the seizure and that he would not intervene to secure its return."[294]

Simultaneously a covert war (*bellum insidiosum*) began.[295] Pont-de-l'Arche was an important citadel on the left bank of the Seine only four Gallic leagues—that is, less than thirteen miles, or two hours—from Rouen.[296] On May 15, 1449, Robert de Flocques, the royal bailiff of Evreux, captured the fortress by a ruse, but his men were careful to shout "Sainct Yves! Bretaigne!"[297] as though the attack were nothing more than a Breton riposte to the capture of Fougères. Robert de Flocques then took Conches, southwest of Evreux, while to the north the French captured Gerberoy, not far from Gournay.

In recounting all these events later on, Thomas Basin, like the official French historians, stressed Charles VII's patience and caution.[298] For once he refrained from denouncing the use of a ruse, in this case to take Pont-de-l'Arche. But he did not hide the duke of Somerset's discomfiture upon hearing the news. The duke assembled a council that included the bishops of Bayeux, Avranches, and Lisieux, namely, Zenone Castiglioni, Martin Pinard, and Thomas Basin. The bishops, Thomas Basin remarks, "finding the prince in a state of consternation, understood that, like a benevolent physician, they arrived at just the right moment to administer a soothing balm and consoling hope for his great sadness." They were wholly successful. "Fortified by their words and cordial exhortations, the duke promised that he would quickly recover the lost citadel."[299]

His ambassadors, for their part, remained intransigent. They even refused to exchange Fougères for Pont-de-l'Arche, Conches, and Gerberoy.[300] Therefore, on July 17, 1449, "the king of France, after mature deliberation with the great lords of the kingdom and with persons well-versed in divine and human law,"[301] decided to declare "open and total war against the English."[302]

The count of Dunois was "appointed [*institué*] and named the king's lieutenant general in his wars."[303] Jean was born in 1402. He was the bastard son of Louis, duke of Orléans, who had been murdered in 1407. Thus he was the half-brother of the duke's legitimate sons, Charles, the poet, and Jean, the count of Angoulême, with whom he had been raised. The bastard Orléans had begun his military career in 1421 at age nineteen in the battle of Beaugé, and since then he had continued to serve Charles VII. In 1429–30 he had fought alongside Joan of Arc. In 1432 he had taken Chartres. In 1440 he had been appointed the king's lieutenant general for the region north of the Seine. In 1444 he became conservator of the Truce of Tours. And when that truce was broken, the king had, in July 1449, chosen to head his troops "the count of Dunois, bastard of Orléans, who in those days was widely renowned for his wisdom, prudence, and good conduct and much beloved by all the men of war, as much as or more than any other lord or captain of the kingdom of France."[304]

The French successes were immediate. On July 19, 1449, Verneuil fell. On August 12 Pont-Audemer fell and was then sacked. A few days later the French army laid siege to Lisieux, which was only seven short leagues from Pont-Audemer.[305] Next followed the most eventful period of Thomas Basin's life. The poorly fortified city of Lisieux, caught between its tiny English garrison and the huge French army, had every reason to be fearful. Like Pont-Audemer it could easily have "been taken by force and then could have been slaughtered, pillaged, sacked, and destroyed."[306] It was saved by its bishop, who, Thomas Basin is quick to point out, could easily have fled. "Fully aware of the dangers that threatened him on all sides if he remained in his post, he could, had he wished to, have avoided them easily. He owned, two leagues from the city, a very well fortified castle in which, had he wished to withdraw there accompanied only by his chaplains, he could without fear have withstood the onslaught of the entire French army. But anxious to attend to the salvation of his flock before thinking of his own, he preferred to expose himself to any number of dangers for the common good rather than save himself alone while leaving his people vulnerable to the rapacity and voraciousness of wolves and brutes."[307]

Thomas Basin turned first to the English. What is odd is that he does not tell us in his *History of Charles VII* what arguments he used with them. But Robert Blondel, who was born into a noble Cotentin family in the late fourteenth century, who left his native region early in the English occupation, whose loyalty to Charles VII had always been fierce, who would become, some years after the events in question, the "schoolmaster" of Charles VII's second son Charles, the younger brother of the dauphin Louis,[308] and who, probably at that time, met, in the king's entourage, the bishop of Lisieux, whose past was so different from his own—this Robert Blondel, in his account of the conquest of Normandy, relates the arguments that Thomas allegedly employed, and they square so well with what we know about the bishop that it is impossible to believe that Blondel did not learn of them from Thomas Basin himself.

In substance Thomas Basin reportedly told the English this: "Your King Henry has forced this city to accept your domination [*vestrae ditioni subegit*]. Its inhabitants, defeated, swore loyalty (*fidem sacramento*) to you, and you promised to defend them. Not a single one of them ever violated his sworn oath [*nunquam fidem juratam civis unus . . . infregit*]. The city has always loyally obeyed [*fideli obsequio*] your prince; it has shown the utmost respect [*summa reverentia*] for the sovereignty of the lord [*supremam sui domini majestatem*] that it owed to its defeat [*haec urbs subacta*]. Now, however, your forces are too weak to protect this city, which, if it resists, will be destroyed. It is therefore no longer obliged to remain loyal to you. Natural law [*naturali jure*] invites it to seek its salvation elsewhere."[309]

These words are actually those of Robert Blondel, not of Thomas Basin. Yet they accurately reflect all the leading principles to which Thomas Basin was unwaveringly loyal and which led him, throughout his narrative, to sing the praises of wise capitulations sanctioned by the laws of war and nature.[310] In war no one is required to persist until death and destruction make resistance impossible. The power of the conqueror is legitimate. The vanquished must respect the oath they have sworn, at least as long as they receive the protection of their vanquishers. Once that protection ends, however, they are no longer required to resist.

Once the English had been convinced to take no action, Thomas Basin turned to the French and their leader, Dunois, whom the bishop of Lisieux met for the first time. Within a few hours he obtained from them the most favorable terms. "All persons present in the aforesaid *ville et cité,* regardless of estate, nation, or condition, shall have their bodies, lives, and belongings spared." Any Englishmen who wished to leave could do so with all their belongings. "If any of them wish to stay in the king's obedience, they shall be allowed to do so and shall have full enjoyment of all their inheritances . . . upon swearing an oath to be good, true, and loyal subjects of the king." "All inhabitants shall retain their exemptions, liberties, and seisins" and shall be "governed in justice in accordance with the custom of the country and of this city, as they were when the English came and before." "All churchmen . . . shall remain undisturbed in possession, seisin, and enjoyment of all [their] prebends, dignities, cures, chapels . . . and other benefices." And the bishop and count of Lisieux "shall remain undisturbed in possession and enjoyment of both the spiritual and all the temporal domain that he possessed on the day of the surrender." Finally, "soldiers shall enter said city of Lisieux by order [and] . . . shall be lodged by the justice of Monseigneur de Lisieux" and shall take "nothing without paying."[311] On August 16, 1449, the bishop of Lisieux then surrendered the city to the French, to the great relief of its inhabitants but much to the vexation of the soldiers thus deprived of their spoils."[312]

This "surrender so gentle and so humane" was not the first in the history of the Anglo-French conflict, but it was the first in this campaign.[313] It set the tone and was followed by many others. The fruit of Thomas Basin's courage and wisdom, it earned him a moment of glory. Robert Blondel dwelt at length on the actions of the man who remained so clear-headed in time of peril (*inter pericula vir consultus*).[314] And the most official French historians bestowed their words of praise. Jean Chartier, for example, wrote that the inhabitants of Lisieux placed the city "in the obedience of the king in the hands of his lieutenant . . . owing to the good advice, counsel, and persuasion of its bishop, who in this action behaved and conducted himself wisely and honorably."[315] The Berry Herald echoes these sentiments: "The people of this city . . . fearful . . . that it might be attacked and therefore massacred, pillaged, and destroyed, placed it in the obedience of the king of France owing to the admonition of their bishop, who behaved nobly and honorably for the public benefit and good."[316] And Thomas Basin himself did not hesitate to remark that on that day the bishop of Lisieux worked with prudence and wisdom (*prudenter et sapienter*) for the salvation of all (*pro communi omnium salute*).

The bishop, however, was not content to be simply a good pastor to his flock. He was quick to join forces with the victors, and the victors hastened to employ his services. Hardly had the city surrendered when the French captains, among them Dunois and Pierre de Brézé (the latter, thanks to Agnès Sorel and her talents, was at that time the king's chamberlain and one of his most trusted advisers), "having recognized the wisdom of the bishop, asked his advice on how to proceed with a campaign so happily begun."[317] Or so Thomas tells us. What is certain is that at around this time Charles VII hired the bishop of Lisieux as adviser at an annual salary of one thousand *livres tournois*.[318] And although the compact of August 16 allowed the bishop one year to swear an oath of loyalty to the king,[319] his "beloved and loyal counselor Thomas, bishop of Lisieux" lost no time and in fact swore to Charles VII at Veneuil on August 28 "the oath of fealty he was required to make because of the temporality of said bishopric."[320] And while the king's army was seizing Mantes, Vernon, Harcourt, and Chambrais (August and September) and the duke of Brittany's army was occupying Coutances, Vire, Saint-Lô, and Carentan (September), Thomas Basin was helping Norman clerics swear loyalty and obedience to the king as well as assisting the most seriously compromised in obtaining pardons.[321] In these months Thomas Basin played so important a role, he tells us, that his modest personage was known and celebrated in nearly all the provinces of the Gauls.[322]

In October 1449 the king's army was at the gates of Rouen. The surrender of the capital of Normandy was a decisive moment in the recovery of the region. Thomas Basin is at pains to say that he played a role in it.[323] It was a modest one, however, and no other account of the event mentions it. But the two groups principally involved were precisely those with which Thomas Basin felt most closely allied, namely, the high Norman clergy and the bourgeoisie of Rouen. Thomas fails to mention Raoul Roussel, the archbishop of Rouen. But both Jean Chartier and the Berry Herald indicate that in this instance Roussel played the role that Thomas Basin had played in Lisieux.[324] Next, the inhabitants of Rouen rebelled. On October 20 the gates of the city were opened. The English, having taken refuge in their citadels, left a short while later. On November 3, Giovanni Castiglioni, the bishop of Coutances, whose cathedral had been liberated a few weeks earlier by the duke of Brittany, swore an oath to the king.[325] A few days later, Raoul Roussel also swore an oath to the king.[326] On November 10 Charles VII made his solemn entry into the city. There he was welcomed by the archbishop, Raoul Roussel; by the bishop of Lisieux, Thomas Basin; by the bishop of Coutances, Giovanni Castiglioni; and even by the bishop of Bayeux, Zenone Castiglioni, whose city was still held by the English.[327] He was also welcomed by the city's burghers, who urged him, though it would soon be winter, to continue his campaign to liberate the Seine estuary, so vital to Rouen's economy, "and offered to aid him with men and horses."[328]

Old Jean Basin and his children were among those whose contributions aided Charles VII. Accordingly, in March 1450, in view of his praiseworthy life, respectable demeanor, loyalty, and other virtues, all duly attested by reliable individuals, and, further, in view of his and his children's selfless assistance in securing the surrender of Rouen and the recovery of Normandy, the father of the new counselor of the king of France, now almost eighty, along with his wife Colette, their children, and their legitimate descendants of both sexes born or to be born, were ennobled by the king.[329] In the spring of 1450 fortune smiled on the family of the bishop of Lisieux, who only two years earlier had so enthusiastically sworn allegiance to Henry VI.

The recovery of Normandy continued apace. Those Norman bishops who had not already sworn an oath of loyalty to Charles VII now did so, one after another, as they were required to do because of their temporal authority. Martin Pinard, the bishop of Avranches and confidant of the duke of Somerset, swore loyalty to the king on February 17, 1450.[330] Jean d'Escars, the bishop of Sées, did the same on March 13.[331] And finally, Zenone Castiglioni, the bishop of Bayeux, who had been at Charles VII's side in Rouen along with his cousin Giovanni and Thomas Basin since November 1449 but whose city was not taken until May 16, 1450, took his oath to the king on May 25.[332]

To the French these oaths and changes of allegiance seemed quite natural. But the perjury of the bishops exasperated the English, and they punished those whose possessions were still within their power. They pillaged the cathedral of Sées[333] and the cathedral and episcopal palace of Bayeux.[334] A devotee of the law and a man who was, and wished to be seen as, one who believed with mystical fervor that promises made ought to be kept, Thomas Basin may have found in the spring of 1450 that his personal triumph and the triumph of his family were to some extent spoiled by the bitter taste of perjury.

In any case the recovery of Normandy was coming to an end. On April 15, 1450, the English were beaten at Formigny. On July 1 Caen fell. On August 12 Cherbourg was the last city to succumb. The French were astonished by the speed of the campaign and by the relatively small cost in men lost and cities ruined. For this they were indebted to the king and to "the princes and other lords . . . who [had] accompanied him in the recovery of said duchy, and primarily, especially, to God, who thus demonstrated his miracles. The time also favored [victory], since this was the year of the great general pardon of Rome known as the Year of the Jubilee."[335]

During the course of this long war, in certain liberated cities such as Montargis after 1427, Orléans after 1429, Paris after 1436, and Dieppe after 1443, it became customary to celebrate the end of English occupation with an annual commemorative feast.[336] In August and September 1450 the king of France wrote to all the archbishops and bishops and to all the good cities of the kingdom ordering that masses be said and processions made immediately "to give thanks to God our creator for the noble victory he had given him." Furthermore, "for the purpose of perpetual praise to our creator and in recognition of the favor he has done us," Charles VII ordered that this celebration be repeated every year on August 12.[337] Thus France began to celebrate its first national holiday.[338]

Twenty years later, when Thomas Basin told the story of the recovery of Normandy in his *History of Charles VII,* he faithfully reported the fervor that had impelled the Normans toward France and its king. The Normans, he said, had lived in fear. But "the moment they saw the way to break the rude servitude of fear and violence, they sought, as if joyously carried along by a natural movement, not only to welcome but also to summon and invoke him who had long been the natural sovereign of French land."[339] With such words Thomas bore witness to the fervor of the Normans. Before and after this sentence, however, he wrote other sentences whose admirably precise diction makes it clear to anyone who cares to comprehend where he really stood.

For the historians who had always followed Charles VII, things were simple. The king of France had always been the "natural lord" of the Normans.[340] Normandy had been "improperly occupied" by the English.[341] The king of England and his subjects had occupied the country "wrongly and without reason."[342] For thirty-three years the Normans had been "constrained by the English."[343] Charles VII had done nothing but "recover and conquer his inheritance."[344]

Thomas's report of the Normans' fervor is preceded by the following passage: "Cicero's very just observation then received striking verification, namely, that no power [*imperium*] based on force [*vis*] and fear [*metus*] can endure for long. The English had conquered Normandy by force [*vis*]. Their sovereignty [*imperium*] had been sustained by fear [*metus*]. And the moment the Normans saw the way. . . ." Discreetly, Thomas lets us know that in his view the occupation of Normandy was not improper. The sovereignty of the English was perfectly legitimate (as indicated by the use of the word *imperium*). To be sure, it had been established by force, by right of conquest. It was maintained by fear. But it was perfectly legitimate. Moreover, the inhabitants of Lisieux had faithfully obeyed the king of England and had respected his sovereignty.

But any power, even legal power, that is based on fear cannot endure for long. Since the English were powerless to ensure peace, tranquillity, and justice in Normandy,[345] since they had broken truces on their own initiative, since they had shown themselves to be "*fedifregi*"[346] while Charles VII had proven his faith, that is to say, his respect for promises given, since he had also demonstrated wisdom and efficacity,[347] and since Charles had kept his army in "such good order,"[348] the Normans had renounced English sovereignty and returned to French sovereignty, which was more ancient and seemingly natural (*naturale et vetustissimum terre Francorum . . . imperium*)[349] and the source of their natural tranquillity (*naturalis quietis locum*). For the historians of Charles VII the recovery of Normandy was the end of an occupation. For Thomas Basin it was the end of a legitimate government, a return to an older sovereignty, a substitution of one form of legitimacy for another.

Having demonstrated the fervor of the Normans, Thomas Basin concluded: "Something else increased their desire still more. Nearly everyone had heard, for it was widely repeated, that the king of France made certain his subjects enjoyed proper justice and liberty and that with a firm hand he prevented his troops from robbing and beating the inhabitants of his provinces. Would to Heaven that it had been as true as people said and as the king's representatives promised." The love the Normans felt for the king of France was therefore not, as Thomas saw it, unconditional. Passion counted, but so did law. In the kingdom of France the Normans' chief hope was just what it had been under English sovereignty, namely, that they would go on being able to enjoy their possessions and to maintain their rights and privileges.

In the role he played during the recovery of Normandy as well as in his account, twenty years later, of the events of those two years, Thomas Basin figured as a faithful representative of Norman sentiments toward France and its king. Yet he clearly stated that English rule was legitimate. Even more important, perhaps, was his insistence on the continuity of Norman history.

Between Charles VII and Normandy (1450–61)

Precisely that continuity was called into question by the events of 1449 and 1450. The compacts signed by the Norman cities stipulated that all residents would retain their exemptions and liberties. Once the reconquest of the region was complete, however, the triumphant king was in no haste to confirm the Norman Charter. All Norman institutions were in jeopardy. The office of seneschal was gone. So were the fiscal court and the customs court. The University of Caen legally ceased to exist. The Exchequer feared for its sovereignty. Charles VII, who naturally needed cash, clearly hoped to extract some from Normandy as he did from the rest of the realm, but before levying taxes he did not bother to obtain the consent of the Norman Estates, whose rights the English had so scrupulously respected. The Normans, of course, hoped to pay as little as possible. More than that, in keeping with customs established during the time of English domination, they had no intention of paying at all without consultation and their express consent (*sine expresso consensu eorum*).[350] Furthermore, in 1429, a few days after his anointment, Charles VII had promised in the Edict of Compiègne to restore the rights and possessions of all who followed him.[351] But the various compacts signed in 1449 and 1450 had stipulated, as in Lisieux, that all laymen would continue to enjoy their inheritances, property, and estates and that all clerics would remain in undisputed possession of their prebends and benefices. Inevitably these contradictory principles came into conflict.

This issue was not the only one contributing to the state of uncertainty in which the Norman Church found itself. Under English sovereignty the conditions under which that church lived had been defined by the concordat signed in 1418 by Pope Martin V and King Henry V, whose application had in fact yielded a harmonious compromise between the two powers. No one could become bishop without both the pope's nomination and the king's consent. Thus in 1449 all Norman bishops owed their thrones to both the pope and the king. By contrast, the Gallican Church, which flourished in the obedience of Charles VII, was governed by the Pragmatic Sanction of 1438, which had restored its liberties, or, to put it another way, which had nullified the powers won by the papacy over the previous two centuries, restored the rights of certain bishops to grant benefices, and granted the canons of the cathedral chapters the right to elect their bishop. Of course the monarchy did not forbid itself to intimate more or less firmly to the canons what exercise they ought to make of their free choice. As a result, the Church of France had experienced some difficult times over the past twelve years. Everywhere competitors clashed. Some sought the favor of bishops, while others secured the backing of the king and still others did not shrink from turning to Rome. Lawsuits abounded in the Parlement of Paris.

By 1450 the situation was so tense, and pontifical protestations were so vehement, that the government of Charles VII hesitated whether to press for continuation of the Pragmatic Sanction or negotiation of a concordat. The Norman church was not merely forsaking one legal framework for another. It was faced with the need of adapting to a system that was itself under challenge.

In such uncertain times Norman leaders were obliged both to find their place within the institutions of the French monarchy and to assert Norman continuity under French sovereignty. In these tasks they worked hard, and prominent among them were Thomas Basin and his relatives.

Even before the recovery of Normandy was complete, in May 1450, Charles VII convoked an assembly of the clergy, which met in Chartres to decide whether or not to replace the Pragmatic Sanction with a concordat. The latter option had numerous supporters in Chartres, and the Pragmatic Sanction might have been defeated had the "Pragmatic Sanction of Saint Louis" not suddenly been produced. This bestowed upon the Pragmatic Sanction of 1438 a prestige that saved it. The assembly concluded without coming to a decision. Two years later, in July and August 1452, a second assembly met in Bourges. Proponents of the status quo once again invoked the Pragmatic Sanction of Saint Louis and this time definitively carried the day. Charles VII permanently gave up all thought of a concordat.[352] The bishop of Lisieux was present in Chartres in 1450 and in Bourges in 1452. No one, not even Thomas Basin, claims that he played the slighest role on either occasion.[353] He was a witness to the events, however. Later he wrote: "I saw the signed and sealed ordinance [of Saint Louis] . . . which was shown and exhibited to the solemn conventions of the Gallican Church that met in Chartres and Bourges upon convocation of" Charles VII.[354]

Today it is beyond doubt that the so-called Pragmatic Sanction dated March 1269, of which no one had ever heard prior to 1450, was a forgery produced in the royal chancellery. In the middle of the fifteenth century, however, no subject of the king of France spoke out against the opportunely discovered document. At the university and elsewhere, however, discreet surprise was expressed at the fact that so important a document was never confirmed or renewed by the saintly king's successors. "For the tranquillity of many people's consciences," they believed that it was a matter "of necessity" to find "the confirmations of this [document] by the successive kings of France since Saint Louis."[355] Thomas Basin discreetly voiced similar scruples, yet he did not doubt that Louis IX had published a Pragmatic Sanction or that it had been confirmed by his successors.

Later, in 1464, he told Louis XI that he "believe[d] that in the registers of your court of Parlement and in the chambers of your Comptes et Trésor in Paris several of them will be found to have been registered, if it pleases you to have a search made."[356]

Thomas Basin did not doubt the Pragmatic Sanction of Saint Louis because he was by this time a fervent proponent of the Pragmatic Sanction of Charles VII. Later, in his *History of Charles VII*, he wrote that the king of France, by restoring the rights of ordinaries, had acted in accordance with reason and thus in a manner manifestly consistent with justice, equity, and the public good. He then recalled the debates he had attended in Chartres in 1450 and in Bourges in 1452. The pope and his emissaries, he went on, had done all they could to obtain abolition of the Pragmatic Sanction and to restore the veto power of the Roman Church, which nullified the ordinaries' right as if by tyrannical power and force [*quadam velud tyrannice potestate ac vi majore*]. The king, however, had scorned the advice of men driven by greed and ambition. He had followed those prelates and clerics who preferred truth, faith, and justice to honors and riches. And he had always enforced this most holy and salutary ordinance. To be sure, he had frequently intervened with the electors on behalf of suitable and worthy candidates, but the decree did not prohibit such intervention. All in all, he had shown himself to be a pious protector of the Gallican Church by protecting its ancient liberties.[357] It was in fact this fundamental concern for the liberties of the Church that made Thomas such a staunch supporter of the Pragmatic Sanction. The bishop of Henry VI and Nicholas V was so devoted to the Pragmatic not because he wanted to please his new king but because he saw it as the best way of preserving the liberties of the Church in France.

Thomas's other concern was to preserve the liberties of the Normans. Later, in his *Breviloquium*, he would write that as bishop of Lisieux he had traveled once to Chartres, once to Vernon, once to Bourges, once to Paris, and frequently to Rouen. There he had been summoned to take part in assemblies convoked to deal with the affairs of the kingdom and the Church. In each of these cities he had remained for one or more months.[358] We know now that it was to take part in ecclesiastical assemblies that he went to Chartres in May 1450 and to Bourges in July-August 1452. When did he go to Vernon? Was it between May 1450 and July 1452, as the order of his enumeration would suggest? In June 1451 there was in fact a meeting between Norman officials and officers of the king in Vernon.[359] But the purpose of that meeting was too limited. It concerned, specifically, the merchants of Rouen and Paris. It is unlikely that the bishop of Lisieux would have been present. At the end of 1452, however, certain ecclesiastical bodies, such as the chapter of Rouen,[360] and municipal bodies, such as the city of Rouen,[361] held lengthy discussions. Since the recovery of their region by the king of France, the Normans had already achieved some results. On April 3, 1451, the office of grand seneschal of Normandy was reinstated. Pierre de Brézé, one of Charles VII's closest advisers, was named to fill the post.[362] On October 30, 1452, Charles VII confirmed the University of Caen with its five faculties and all its privileges.[363] The Normans now wanted confirmation of all the king's past promises.[364] Their efforts resulted in the dispatch of an important delegation, which met with the king at Vernon on Easter Sunday in 1453.[365] There can be no doubt that it was for this occasion that Thomas Basin went to Vernon.

Immediately after that meeting, Charles VII left to begin his reconquest of Guyenne, and the discussions at Vernon yielded no result. A few months later the city of Rouen dispatched another delegation to meet with the king. One of its leaders was an alderman of the city, Jean Le Roux, who was the brother-in-law of Michel Basin.[366] Michel, Thomas's older brother, was married to Le Roux's sister.[367] Thus, Thomas and his relatives were among those Normans who had willingly accepted English sovereignty, who had aided in the French reconquest, and who were now working to restore the momentarily interrupted continuity of Normandy's history as a part of France.

Between his stay in Bourges (July-August 1452) and his trip to Vernon (Easter 1453) Thomas's reputation as an expert in canon law earned him a still more important role. The recovery of Normandy was still not complete when, on February 15, 1450, Charles VII ordered an investigation into the trial that had ended in the condemnation of Joan of Arc.[368] The Church was in no hurry to reopen this case. Too many of the participants were still alive and still powerful. Raoul Roussel, for example, the archbishop of Rouen, had not played a key role in 1431, but he had assiduously attended the trial and had been present on May 30 when Joan was burnt at the stake.[369] Nevertheless, in 1452, Jean Bréhal, a Norman and a Dominican, received from the pope and from Guillaume d'Estouteville, the papal legate in France, the mission of investigating the trial of Joan of Arc. Jean Bréhal went eagerly to work. The ecclesiastical inquiry opened on May 2, 1452. In the months that followed Bréhal first interrogated witnesses and then consulted with a dozen doctors. The longest of the treatises he received about the case was that of Thomas Basin.[370]

Like the other doctors, Thomas sought to prove that Joan had been unjustly condemned and that none of the evidence in the record convicted her of being a schismatic, heretic, or idolater.[371] Before entering into the substance of the case, however, he devoted a preliminary section of his brief, which had no equivalent in the briefs submitted by the other experts, to showing that the trial of 1431 was null and void, or at any rate that it could be nullified. Among the arguments that he gives is a long passage intended to show that the trial could be nullified because the judges had been afraid.[372]

Roman antiquity had admired heroes and martyrs. Ancient literature was full of examples of people who continued to demonstrate courage even though it meant death. Roman law, however, recognized weakness and was determined to protect it. In the sixth century, culminating a long history of efforts to protect the weak, Book II, Title XX of the Code (*De his quae vi metusve causa gestum erit*) and Book IV, Title II of the Digest (*Quod metus causa gestum erit*) laid it down that a judge could nullify an action taken as a result of force or fear. Once the principle had been established, moreover, legislation placed precise limits on its application. The fear in question must concern a clear and present danger, not a vague, future one. It must be the fear not of a fearful man but of an ordinarily stalwart and steady person (*non vani hominis, sed qui merito et in hominem constantissimum cadat*). In any case, fear justified rescinding only actions under private law such as the bestowal of a dowry, the sale of a property, or the contracting of an obligation.

Throughout the Middle Ages, the Church was also concerned with defending weakness and with protecting the weak against actions they might have taken as a result of force or fear. Several canons of the twelfth-century Decretum of Gratian dealt with the issue. But the most important attempt to compensate for the effects of fear is to be found in Book I, Title XL (*De his quae vi metusve causa fiunt*) of the Decretals of Gregory IX (1227–41), which was directly inspired by the Code and the Digest. It started from the same basic principle: no act that is not freely taken is valid. But it applied this principle in a different, and broader, way. A marriage, for example, or an oath could be nullified if proven to have been a product of fear. More than that, the Church did not expect its clerics or even its prelates to be heroes. It was well aware that fear of the king or of other laymen could compel clergymen to take regrettable actions, make regrettable promises, or cast regrettable votes. Repeating the very words of the Digest, the decretal declared that actions taken out of fear by usually steadfast men (*in virum constantem*) could and should be nullified. Through the effect of canon law, fear thus became a more or less natural and common element in relations between church and state.

In a world where violence and fear were everyday experiences, clerics steeped in Roman and canon law slowly learned how to turn avowed fears to their own advantage. Invoking fear enabled them to explain their actions, to rescind their decisions, to renounce their promises, to forget their oaths. In 1378 the cardinals who had elected Urban VI acknowledged that they had been afraid, and since in their eyes avowal of that fear nullified the election, they then elected Clement VII instead. In 1397 the canons of Cambrai had failed to give their bishop a proper welcome. But what else was to be expected? They had succumbed to that fear that can befall even steadfast men (*metus . . . qui cadere potuit in viros constantes*).[373] In a dangerous world—and the West in the fifteenth century was a dangerous place—fear was a common emotion; it was also a commonplace argument.

Force and fear came very early to play an essential role in Thomas Basin's work. "The English conquered Normandy by force [*vis*]. Their sovereignty [*imperium*] was maintained by fear [*metus*]."[374] Here, however, fear serves only to enable Thomas to explain why English sovereignty did not endure. Having fought so hard to restore rights that Normans had enjoyed during the English occupation, the prelate in no way meant to imply that fear ought to nullify everything that had been done during the thirty-three years of English presence. In 1453, however, when it came to investigating the trial of Joan of Arc, no such scruple applied. Thomas drew on all his knowledge of Roman law and canon law, on Sallust and Aristotle, to justify his conclusion that, if it were proven that Joan's judges had been afraid of the English, then their judgment was null and void, or at least that it could be nullified, because one may nullify any judgment handed down in the grip of fear by a normally steadfast man (*sententia lata per metum, dico cadentem in constantem virum*).[375] In another summary of the case Jean Bréhal also justified nullfication of the sentence on the grounds that the judges had been afraid, but his argument coincides with Thomas's only in parts.[376] All the Roman and canon law texts dealing with fear were well known to fifteenth-century jurists, but Thomas Basin was particularly well-versed in these matters. His 1453 brief foreshadows the place that fear would one day occupy in his life.

In the list given in the *Breviloquium* of the places he visited on church or royal business in these years, Thomas Basin mentions that after Chartres, Bourges, and Vernon he stayed "one time in Paris."[377]

This visit must have taken place at the end of 1453 or in the first few months of 1454. By that time Charles VII had completed the reconquest of his kingdom. Since acceding to the throne, the king would later recall, he had recaptured Champagne, the Vermandois, Picardy, and the Ile-de-France. "And after that, by the grace of almighty God, we conquered and returned to our obedience our duchy and province of Normandy and our provinces Le Maine and Le Perche, expelled and by force of arms dismissed our ancient enemies, the English, who had long held and occupied [these regions], and restored the liberties and exemptions of our subjects there."[378] Next he conquered Guyenne. And after that a rebellion by the inhabitants and a final English expedition forced him to reconquer Guyenne. On July 17, 1453, his armies were victorious at Castillon, and the following October 19 he finally recaptured Bordeaux. Then, seeing that "because of these wars and divisions . . . justice in our kingdom has been debased and oppressed . . . [and] considering that kingdoms without good order of justice can have neither duration nor solidity . . . [and] wishing to provide our subjects with good justice," the king assembled in Paris "a number of prelates, archbishops, bishops, barons, and lords of our realm, and the members of our great council, and some of the presidents and other men of our court of parlement, and other judges and magistrates of our kingdom."[379] After "long and mature deliberation," this assembly made recommendations that enabled the king, in April 1454, before Easter (which fell that year on April 21), to issue, at Montils-lès-Tours, the great ordinance which, after many troubled years, reformed justice throughout the kingdom[380] and provided modern France with a veritable code of judicial procedure.[381]

It is beyond doubt that both Pierre de Brézé and Thomas Basin took part in the deliberations that led to the ordinance of April 1454. Since the death of Agnès Sorel and his nomination as grand seneschal of Normandy, Pierre de Brézé had spent little time at court.[382] Nevertheless, there is no question that he participated in the deliberations, because Charles VII, a few days after the publication of the ordinance to reform royal justice, toward the end of April 1454, some time after Easter, in response to "the great complaints of our subjects in our province of Normandy regarding various difficulties and impediments placed in their way," solemnly confirmed "the abolitions, concessions, and grants made by us in the reduction and conquest of our province and duchy of Normandy." The text of this solemn confirmation was appended to that of the ordinance for judicial reform.[383] At the same time the customs court in Rouen was reestablished.[384] Thus the Normans had taken advantage of the occasion to exert pressure on the government. It is beyond doubt that the grand seneschal of Normandy was present in Paris in early 1454.

Nor can there be any doubt about Thomas Basin's presence. He was a member of the King's Council. He was a bishop. He was a Norman. He was a jurist. He therefore had every reason to be in Paris at that time. Moreover, he himself confirms that both he and Pierre de Brézé were in Paris for the occasion, although modern scholars until now have not known how to interpret his words. For somewhat later he wrote to Pierre de Brézé: "We were recently together in Paris [*Cum anterioribus diebus una essemus Parisius*]. We went there to sit on the royal commission charged with judicial reform. And we spoke to each other specifically about justice [*de rebus forensibus, circa quas era commissio regia pro qua illo conveneramus, versato inter nos sermone*]."[385]

What was Thomas's state of mind when he left Paris? The bishop of Lisieux was certainly satisfied with the solemn confirmation of the pact of August 16, 1449, which was his principal claim to fame. But the jurist was bitter. The ideas enshrined in the ordinance of April 1454 were not his. That is what he told Pierre de Brézé when they discussed ways to expedite judicial procedures. Thomas Basin wanted more than a change in procedure; he wanted a thoroughgoing judicial reform. He wanted to do away with the oral arguments that were the bane of the French courts and follow instead the example of the papal tribunal, which relied solely on written proceedings, in his view the only way to achieve a more rapid, less costly, and more reliable administration of justice.[386]

Thomas Basin must have set forth these radical views to a commission that did not know what to make of them. The presentation, one may surmise, fell flat, and after the meeting the grand seneschal of Normandy evidently met with the disappointed jurist for an amiable and consoling conversation. Or perhaps Thomas Basin said nothing in public but simply laid out his views to Pierre de Brézé in the corridor after a meeting. In any case, the grand seneschal told him in substance that he ought to put his ideas in writing. And Thomas Basin promised to do so (*vestra adhoratione et suggestione memini me fuisse magnificentiae vestrae pollicitum litteris mandare quidnam mihi super hoc sequendum optimum videretur*).

Some time after the celebration of Christmas 1454, in the year 1455, Thomas Basin left the tumult of Paris for which he was so ill suited and returned to Lisieux, where he was able to indulge his pleasure in reading and writing and savor those literary pursuits that were always his greatest joy (*reversus ad otium litterale in quo mihi summa voluptas est*). He set about writing the treatise he had promised Pierre de Brézé. A short while later, the grand seneschal of Normandy, who also had abandoned the court and returned to his province, received a treatise from the unheeded jurist to whom he once had offered an understanding ear. In that treatise the bishop of Lisieux set forth his noble but impractical views on judicial procedure.

While Thomas Basin was recommending that court procedures be turned upside down, those in power were cautiously implementing reforms. A similar contrast can be found in other areas. Those in power worked to maintain paid professional armies; Thomas Basin still dreamed of a natural army of noble vassals. Those in power stressed the importance of obedience; Thomas Basin insisted on the rights and liberties of subjects. Thomas's ideas were incompatible with those of the royal government.

His temperament was also incompatible with the government's. To be sure, Thomas Basin would later recognize certain virtues in Charles VII, particularly in comparison with Charles's son. The king was a trustworthy and pious man who had respected the liberties of the Church and a just, clement, and magnanimous prince. But if Charles VII exhibited some of the traits of a good prince, Thomas Basin also reproached him for his undisciplined armies, his excessive taxes, and his depraved morals.[387] And he criticized the royal court. He could not find words harsh enough for the "court dogs" (*canes palatini*) who surrounded the king, attended his pleasures, and prevented his subjects from coming close and who "rarely allowed the truth to reach the prince's ears and still more rarely offered counsel inspired by the public interest."[388]

Jacques Coeur was one of the most illustrious victims of court intrigue. The two chapters on Coeur clearly reveal the sentiments of the bishop of Lisieux. Thomas tells us that Jacques Coeur, though an uncultivated plebeian, was nevertheless an industrious and clever man with an admirable knowledge of worldly affairs. With his advice and cash he had helped in the recovery of Normandy. He had served the king with such zeal and loyalty that he had gained the monarch's familiarity and even, it was generally admitted, his friendship. But Agnès Sorel had died on February 9, 1450. Vile slanderers accused Jacques Coeur of having poisoned her. While the beautiful Agnès was alive, anyone accused of speaking ill of her drew the king's wrath. Now the accusations against Jacques Coeur inflamed the king's hatred, sealing his faithful servant's doom. And so, Thomas Basin concluded, there are men who strive to gain the familiarity of kings and princes and who, having obtained it, believe themselves to be happy. But many times what awaits them is an end like Jacques Coeur's. Examples may be found in ancient annals as well as in the most recent histories.[389]

In writing these bitter lines, Thomas Basin was thinking of Jacques Coeur. Undoubtedly he was also thinking of the bishop of Lisieux, who had also hoped to gain the familiarity of Charles VII and who obviously had failed. Thomas Basin still held the title of king's councillor. But his pension of one thousand *livres tournois* had been reduced to six hundred.[390] The bishop of Lisieux, commendable for his valor, zeal for the public good, and services rendered to the state, had ceased to play a role in Charles VII's kingdom.[391] At age forty-five, after a moment in the sun, Thomas Basin was still what he had been at thirty-five: a good Norman bishop who defended the Church's rights, and a prominent Norman prelate who defended the rights of his province.[392]

Thanks, moreover, to him and many others, Normandy's rights were in fact restored nearly ten years after France's recovery of the region. In April 1458 Charles VII finally confirmed the Norman Charter.[393] By the end of 1457 the Estates of Normandy had resumed meeting on a frequent basis.[394] Thomas Basin played a preponderant role in them.[395] And that, to his misfortune, was how he attracted the attention of Louis the dauphin.

Recall that in 1440 Louis, then aged seventeen, had rebelled against his father. The rebellion had failed. After granting his eldest son a pardon, Charles VII gave him the territory known as the Dauphiné, and there Louis was obliged to go in 1446. He remained there for nearly ten years, governing and plotting, until August 30, 1456, when, the misunderstanding between father and son having grown worse, the dauphin suddenly left the Dauphiné and took refuge with Philip the Good, the duke of Burgundy, in Brabant. During his exile in Brabant, Louis hatched a new plot. Now that Normandy had recovered all its rights, Louis, thirty-five and chafing at the bit, hoped to become governor of the province, as John the Good and Charles V had been before acceding to the throne of France. At an undetermined date between 1458 and 1461 he attempted to force his father's hand. He conceived the idea that the Estates of Normandy, which were now meeting once a year, could send a delegation to the king asking that the dauphin be made governor of the province.

To carry out his plan, "he dispatched to Normandy some of his domestics carrying letters addressed to a number of important personalities in the province." Thomas Basin was one of those who received an emissary from the dauphin, who "proposed that he join [the dauphin's] council with promise of a large and honorable pension." Thomas Basin responded that he could not quit the father's service to join the son's without Charles VII's permission. His conscience was clear. To have acted otherwise would not have been "either just or honest." It might even have been dangerous.

Soon, however, Charles VII learned of his son's intrigues and of the dispatch of the emissaries. He knew that one of them had visited the bishop of Lisieux, and the bishop knew that the king knew. Afraid of incurring the king's wrath and becoming suspect in his eyes, he hastened to send him the letter he had received from the dauphin and to inform him of the response he had made to the messenger. Charles VII accepted these explanations, but the dauphin knew what the bishop of Lisieux had done.[396]

In his *Apologia* Thomas Basin tells this story, so trivial that no one else ever mentioned it, at length. To him, however, it was of great consequence, for it was this incident, he later came to believe, that had "probably" aroused Louis's hatred.

It was "in the year 1461, in the month of July, on the day of Saint Mary Magdalene," that is, July 22, that Charles VII died. Louis the dauphin handsomely rewarded the messenger who brought him the first news. He showed no sorrow. He was king.[397]

Between Louis XI and Normandy (1461–64)

Louis was born on July 3, 1423, when Charles VII was twenty and Marie d'Anjou was nineteen.[398] He was the royal couple's first child. On December 28, 1446, when Louis was forty-two, the queen gave birth to her last son,[399] Charles, upon whom his father immediately bestowed the title duke of Berry.[400] At the end of his life Charles VII detested his eldest son, who had caused him so much trouble for the past twenty years, as much as he loved the child who was then still his youngest. For a time it was rumored that the king planned to disinherit Louis, then in Brabant, and to make Charles heir to the throne.[401] On July 22, 1461, it was not entirely inconceivable that opposition to Louis's accession might materialize. But none did. Charles, whom Thomas describes as "around sixteen" but who was really fifteen, was simply too young. The disastrous consequences of the Treaty of Troyes, which had disinherited the eldest son of Charles VI, were still fresh in people's minds. The principle that the eldest son of the deceased king was his natural and uncontestable heir could no longer be violated.[402] People had every reason to fear the new king, but they could not deny that he was king. A few days after his father's death, Louis entered his kingdom. On August 15, 1461, he was anointed at Rheims. On August 31 he made his solemn entry into Paris. And in Paris as well as Rheims people crowded around him. Even Thomas Basin admits that it is not easy to estimate the number of ambitious men who hastened to the king's side from all the provinces of Gaul.[403]

Five archbishops and some twenty bishops attended the anointment. Among them were four Norman prelates: Guillaume d'Estouteville, archbishop of Rouen, cardinal, and "legate of our holy father in the parts of France"; Richard de Longueil, bishop of Coutances and cardinal; Louis d'Harcourt, bishop of Bayeux and patriarch of Jerusalem, who had officiated at the funeral of Charles VII and who also officiated here;[404] and Thomas Basin.[405] The bishop of Lisieux had hastened to leave his episcopal city for Rheims to "assist in the anointment of the new king." He wanted to see Louis and make his acquaintance. He hoped to offer suggestions and to make requests that might be useful to the kingdom in general and to Normandy in particular. He was buoyed by the hope of influencing a prince who, during his sojourn in the duke of Burgundy's territory, had been in a position to learn some excellent lessons in good government.[406]

On the day after the anointment ceremony, August 16, 1461, Thomas Basin therefore went to the monastery of Saint-Thierry outside Rheims where Louis XI was staying. The crowd there was large, but with some difficulty Thomas obtained a brief audience. He was able to tell the king, in few words, that he needed to reduce taxes and reform the courts. The king thanked Thomas and in a lengthy speech assured him that precisely those two items were his most cherished desires and urged him to offer advice on the best ways of achieving those laudable aims. Reassured and overjoyed by the king's kind words (*suis illecti exhylaritique sermonibus optimis*),[407] the prelate hastened to Paris and there wrote a treatise in Latin followed by a précis in French, in which he recommended, among other things, that the king reduce his expenses, and thus taxes, by reducing the size of the army, which was all the more unnecessary now since he was on the best of terms with the duke of Burgundy.[408] Louis XI attentively read Thomas Basin's little treatise and then paid absolutely no heed.

Thomas Basin found himself in Paris with many other Normans, and with prelates, nobles, and men of all estates, who had come to Paris from their provinces for the king's entry and who, like many of Louis's subjects, complained of the heavy burden of taxation. The king had kind words for all, and many understood him to say that his intention was to abolish a broad range of taxes throughout the kingdom.[409]

Accordingly, when royal officials attempted to collect the *taille* (tallage) and *gabelle* (salt tax) as usual, violent riots broke out. Immediately following the king's entry into Paris, on September 1, Angers was the scene of the so-called Tricoterie. And at the end of September Rheims endured the Miquemaque.[410] These revolts were harshly put down by a king who, for all his kind words, quickly showed his true face.

The new king had no intention of respecting his subjects' liberties, of following his father's moderation, or of continuing his policies. To those who attempted to restrain him, Louis XI took to responding that he was the king and could do what he liked (*dicens se et regem esse et que liberei efficere posse*).[411] These, at any rate, are the words Thomas Basin attributes to him, words that clearly presage the tyrant he would soon become.

Out of hatred for his father and a desire to satisfy his new appetites, Louis soon replaced some of Charles VII's old servants and found suitable pretexts to send others away on various missions. "The famous comte de Dunois, who had distinguished himself in the defense and recovery of the kingdom against the English and Burgundians, was banished on the pretext that he was being made governor of the county of Asti in the Piedmont, and he was compelled to go against his will. Pierre de Brézé, the grand seneschal of Normandy and also a victor over the English there, was several times obliged to flee and to go into hiding. Later he persuaded himself that he was once again in the king's good graces. But that did not prevent him from being stripped of his position as seneschal and of his command of a company of a hundred lancers and then being forced to take to the seas and go to Scotland, allegedly to bring help to Henry, king of England, who, banished from his kingdom, had taken refuge there."[412]

In November 1461 Louis took several important steps that seemed to reverse previous policy. Perhaps it would be more accurate to say that in taking these steps Louis XI hoped to achieve the same ends by different means. On November 27 the king informed the pope by personal letter that it was his intention to abrogate the Pragmatic Sanction. And on March 16, 1462, when Louis took his oath of obedience to the pope, he did just that. Since 1458 the reigning pope had been the great humanist Aenea Sylvio Piccolomini, who had taken the name Pius II. A strong oponent of the Pragmatic Sanction, Pius II rejoiced in Louis's decision, even though Louis had merely chosen to use the pope in an effort to subjugate his clergy.

In November 1461 Louis XI also launched a far-reaching reform of France's system of taxation.[413] The more naive Normans believed that this reform would lead to a reduction of their taxes and would bolster their liberties, all the more so in that the king did not wait to be asked before confirming the Norman Charter on January 4, 1462.[414] Soon, however, the Estates of Normandy realized that although the forms of taxation might change, the amount to be paid would remain the same as before.

Other measures taken in November 1461 continued previous policy. For example, Louis XI confirmed his younger brother Charles's title as duke of Berry and gave him the duchy of Berry as his appanage.[415]

On November 14, 1461, Louis XI rescued Thomas Basin from a serious predicament. When a bishop swore an oath of loyalty to the king governing the temporality of his church, he was obliged to provide royal officials with a detailed inventory of church holdings so that he might enjoy his revenue from them without disturbance. Thomas Basin had done precisely that. He had sworn an oath of loyalty to Charles VII on August 28, 1449, and had provided royal officials with an inventory of his diocese's temporal possessions on October 29, 1452. That inventory had been approved on January 8, 1453.[416] The bishop had enjoyed the income from church properties without disturbance. Therefore he was not required to swear another oath to the new king. Bishops were not "constrained" to swear this oath "more than once in a lifetime." Thomas was rather too zealous in his duties, however, and as Louis XI explains, "because he was present at our anointment and entry into our city of Paris, and although he was not constrained by law to do so, he voluntarily swore this oath to us a second time in the company of several other prelates of our kingdom who were also present at our entry into Paris." Consequently royal officials requested that the bishop provide a new inventory of his temporal possessions, "notwithstanding the fact that he had previously duly submitted and verified [such an inventory] during the lifetime of our late lord and father, which would be, as he says, to the great harm, prejudice, and detriment of his Church." Louis XI ordered his tax officials not to require the bishop to file a new inventory if he had indeed submitted one under the previous reign and had "thus obtained *délivrance et expédicion* for his church's temporality."[417]

Thomas Basin's difficulties with the administration were not over, however. A royal order dated July 20, 1463, required the bishop to "submit a second declaration of his temporality." Thomas protested that he had already, under Charles VII, filed a declaration with the fiscal court, which "remained with the court"; that Louis XI at the beginning of his reign had exempted him from filing another declaration; that it "would now be very difficult and much trouble and burden for him to submit a new" declaration; and, finally, that "he could not at present do better or expand on his previous declaration." But his plea was unavailing. On August 31, 1464, he was granted only a year's delay for submitting "in writing a declaration of the temporality of his diocese."[418] In that year, however, Thomas Basin had many other problems far more serious than these minor administrative ones.

On August 15, 1464, a few days before Thomas Basin received his one-year reprieve, Pope Pius II died. Louis XI, who had not obtained all he had hoped from this stubborn pope, asked himself whether it might not be better to take advantage of the opportunity to reinstate the Pragmatic Sanction. The king therefore asked that staunch defender of the sanction, the bishop of Lisieux, if, despite "the full obedience . . . [he had] shown . . . to our holy father Pope Pius, recently deceased,"[419] he might reinstate the Pragmatic Sanction and, if so, how. Thomas Basin answered the king in the final months of 1464. In his eagerness to see the reinstatement come about, our rigorous jurist attached too little importance to the oath the king had sworn on March 16, 1462.

Thomas Basin was well aware, however, that the oath that he, the bishop of Lisieux, had sworn to the king on August 28, 1449, had been sworn not to Charles VII but to the king that never dies, that is, to the monarchy. He also knew that on March 16, 1462, Louis XI had sworn an oath not to Pius II but to the papacy. Nevertheless, in order to liberate his king's conscience, Thomas in late 1464 did not hesitate to write that the pope's recent death freed the king from his obligations: "The form of obedience made by you to our holy father Pope Pius, deceased," cannot prevent the king from reestablishing the Pragmatic Sanction "because that obedience was made by you to Pius personally. Thus, since God has taken him from this world, said obedience in no way binds you with respect to his successor."[420]

Louis XI carefully read the "Advice of Monseigneur de Lisieux."[421] He paid no attention to it. He did not reestablish the Pragmatic Sanction. He chose instead to work toward a definitive agreement with the papacy, a concordat whose signing was delayed only by the War of the Public Weal.[422]

The War of the Public Weal (1464–66)

Around the middle of December 1464 Louis XI openly congratulated himself on the wonderful calm and tranquillity that reigned throughout the kingdom.[423] A few days later the drama that would ultimately destroy Thomas Basin, and whose precise details would remain forever branded in his memory, began to take shape with the inception of the so-called League of the Public Weal.[424]

In late December 1464 a group of conspirators led by the duke of Bourbon met in Paris for the purpose of hatching a plot against the king "in the guise of the public weal."[425] Soon the league included some twenty powerful lords.[426] The three principal conspirators by themselves constituted a serious threat to the king. Central France was the bastion of John II, the duke of Bourbon, master of the Bourbonnais and of docile Auvergne. The east and north were the strongholds of Charles, count of Charolais and soon to be duke of Burgundy but already, owing to the advanced age of his father, Philip the Good, master of the rich Burgundian territories. And in the west the powerful Duke Francis II governed a prosperous and loyal Brittany.[427]

Thomas Basin could not help approving the ideas expressed by the conspirators. They reproached Louis XI for his diseased ambition (*pestifera ambicio*) and frenzied lust for power (*dominandi effrena cupiditas*), which made him a tyrant.[428] A free people enjoyed a natural right to oppose force with force (*vim vi repellere*), to defend itself against tyranny, to refuse servitude, to fight for peace, justice, and liberty, to insist on respect for custom and on lower taxes, and to work, for the sake of all, toward improvement of the kingdom's government (*rempublicam regni reformari in melius*) and reform of the "state of the republic" (*reformari in melius reipublice statum*).[429]

Charles de Berry, Louis XI's younger brother, was eighteen years old. Thomas Basin describes him as an "excellent young prince . . . naturally gifted, impeccable in morals and education."[430] But he was also, at the very least, a young prince, sickly, indecisive, and inexperienced, an ideal instrument for the conspirators to use against his older brother. They had no difficulty winning him over. On March 4, 1465, Charles de Berry slipped away from Louis XI's custody. He left Poitiers and went to Brittany. A few days later, the princes entered into a compact among themselves. They exchanged letters and oaths. "Then, in the name of illustrious Prince Charles, they called all their subjects to arms."[431] So began the War of the Public Weal.

For several months its outcome remained uncertain. From March until June 1465 none of the parties achieved decisive results. On July 16 at Montlhéry the king's troops clashed with troops of the count of Charolais; neither side scored a true victory. In August the princes' armies were able to lay siege to Paris but were unable to take the city. By mid-September fate was still hesitating between the king and the princes.

Fate dithered because the princely conspirators were in no haste to help one another; the nobles were in no rush to follow their princes; and the clergy was content to pray and stage processions intended to persuade God "to bring harmony between the king and lords of France."[432] As for the people, no doubt they were wary of the princes, and certainly they were paralyzed by fear of the king's majesty (*territi cives nomine regio*).[433] They did nothing. Paris, in particular, did not open its gates to the princes. In mid-September Louis XI still nursed hopes of victory. He could count on his subjects.

On September 21, 1465, the princes captured Pontoise. On September 28 they took Rouen. "The surrender of Rouen, metropolis and so to speak mother of the whole province, was followed by the surrender of several other citadels and cities in the region, including Dieppe, Harfleur, Caudebec, Honfleur, Lisieux, and Caen, and by the defection of nearly all the citadels and cities of Lower Normandy." This wave of defections occurred within the space of a few days. Pont-Audemer went over to the princes of September 30, and Lisieux, Thomas's city, changed sides on October 8.[434] Since March, the War of the Public Weal had been bogged down, but within a few days the Norman rebellion dramatically changed the picture. The king could have held off the princes but not the princes and the Normans combined. Stripped of his richest province, Louis XI was compelled to surrender immediately.

What accounts for this sudden, triumphant Norman conflagration? The powderkeg was ignited by a few determined men working in close cooperation. The story begins with Jean, count of Dunois and bastard of Orléans. Recall that he was born in 1402, loyally served Charles VII, and played a key role in the recovery of Normandy. A brilliant and beloved military leader, Dunois, despite his family ties, remained loyal to the victorious Charles VII until his death. In 1455–56 a remarkable episode occurred. John II, duke of Alençon, had been born in 1409. He was a powerful lord, whose duchy, stretching from Alençon to Trun and from Domfront to Verneuil, comprised some 560 parishes and occupied roughly one-seventh of what was traditionally considered Normandy.[435] John was also the son-in-law of Charles d'Orléans, son of the duke assassinated in 1407, prisoner of Agincourt, and poet. Thus he was, by marriage, nephew of the bastard of Orléans, Dunois. John of Alençon was also rather "simple," and in 1455 his "simplicity," according to his defenders, or his "wicked malice," according to his detractors,[436] led him to encourage the English to make yet another foray into Normandy. He would then surrender the province to them. In April 1456 John had sent another messenger to Calais, at that time a hotbed of English intrigue and espionage. On passing through Lisieux, however, the messenger, suspecting the duke of treasonous designs, revealed all to a nobleman of his acquaintance. The king quickly learned of the duke's treason, and on May 27, 1456, Dunois himself made his nephew a "prisoner of the king."[437] In a celebrated trial in 1458, the duke of Alençon was sentenced to death. The judgment had not yet been carried out, however, when Charles VII died. On October 11, 1461, the new king pardoned Alençon even as he was sending Dunois away from France.[438] Thus Dunois was one of the most powerful of Charles VII's old servants whom Louis XI had disappointed. Very early in 1465 he joined forces with the princes of the League.[439] Now sixty-three and so gout-ridden[440] that he was unable to ride a horse and had to be carried in a litter,[441] Dunois thus became the political and military leader of the League of the Public Weal. The man who had recovered Normandy and held it for Charles VII was one of those who wished to take it away from Louis XI.

Dunois was very close to Pierre de Brézé, the grand seneschal of Normandy and former favorite of Agnès Sorel and Charles VII. The two men had fought together during the recovery of Normandy. In 1456 the grand seneschal had offered powerful assistance in unmasking the duke of Alençon.[442] And in 1461 he, too, had been sent away by Louis XI. Reconciled with the king, however, Pierre de Brézé had fought beside him at Montlhéry and died in the battle. But in the hours before his death he had behaved so irresolutely that Louis XI suspected the grand seneschal of having betrayed him.[443] And Pierre's widow, Jeanne du Bec-Crespin, was convinced that her husband had been killed by the king's soldiers and that his death could not have occurred without the king's knowledge or orders. She wished to avenge the insult. Left in charge of the château de Rouen since the death of the seneschal, she surrendered it to the duke of Bourbon during the night of September 27–28, 1465.[444]

Louis d'Harcourt, the man who put the tearful widow up to betraying the king, was an old friend of Pierre de Brézé and Jeanne du Bec-Crespin as well as a relative and friend of Dunois. The Harcourt family was one of the oldest and most illustrious in Normandy.[445] Were the Harcourts truly descendants of a Dane who came to Normandy with Rollo? They could, in any case, trace their history back as far as Robert, the first to bear the name, who some time around 1100 built and lived in Harcourt castle west of Evreux. Since then the Harcourts had made rich marriages, acquired handsome estates, produced many children both legitimate and illegitimate, given the church several bishops and numerous canons, and faithfully served many kings. In 1257 Jean d'Harcourt, the first to bear that name, had founded, near his château d'Harcourt, the priory Notre-Dame-du-

Parc, which belonged to the order of canons regular of Saint Augustine. Jean was buried there when he died, at age seventy-seven, in 1275. And all the lords of Harcourt after him were also buried there. In the fourteenth century the Harcourts were loyal servants of the king and did not challenge the claim that he was their "natural lord." But they also invoked the Norman Charter to justify their ardent defense of Norman liberties against royal pretensions.[446] Meanwhile, the Harcourts continued to rise. In 1328 Jean d'Harcourt, the fourth of that name, took part in the battle of Cassel. In 1338 Philip VI's eldest son, the future John the Good, then duke of Normandy, rewarded Jean d'Harcourt by making the Harcourt estate a county. In 1346 the first count of Harcourt was killed at Crécy, and his body was taken to the priory in the park. The Harcourts' ascent reached its pinnacle with Jean IV's grandson Jean VI, who was born on December 1, 1342. On October 14, 1359, he married Catherine de Bourbon, the sister of Jeanne de Bourbon, who had married Charles V. Jean VI thus became the "very dear brother" of Charles V and the uncle of Charles VI.[447] Jean VI's eldest son, Jean VII d'Harcourt, born in 1370, was the nephew of Louis II, duke of Bourbon, the "very dear and most beloved cousin" of Charles VI. He did not die until 1452, at the age of eighty-two. Jean VII's eldest son, Jean VIII d'Harcourt, born April 9, 1396, died at Verneuil on August 17, 1424, "for the defense of the state and the service of his prince."[448] He left no legitimate son. When Jean VII died in 1452, the eldest branch of the Harcourts therefore became extinct.

The Harcourt family, however, continued to prosper. Jean VI and Catherine de Bourbon had produced, in addition to Jean VII, another son, Louis, who died archbishop of Rouen in 1422, and seven daughters, three of whom became nuns and four others who married. One of the latter, Marguerite, born in 1378, married a member of an equally ancient and illustrious Norman family, Jean II d'Estouteville. Among other children Jean II and Marguerite produced a son, Guillaume, who was born around 1412 and who became a cardinal at the age of twenty-seven in 1439. Cardinal Guillaume d'Estouteville was the pope's legate in France in 1451, and in 1453 he also became archbishop of Rouen. Until the death of Charles VII he played a major role in France. He was present at Louis XI's coronation in 1461. He would die in his seventies, in Rome, on December 24, 1483.[449]

In addition to Jean VIII, who was killed at Verneuil, Jean VII d'Harcourt had had a daughter, Marie, born in 1398, who in 1417 made a very fine marriage. She wed Antoine de Lorraine, count of Vaudémont and Guise and lord of Joinville. The couple had four sons and four daughters. In 1447 the eldest son, Ferry, succeeded his father as count of Vaudémont and Guise. The second son, Henri, born in 1425, died as bishop of Metz in 1505 at the age of eighty. The third son, Philippe, died young. And the fourth, Jean, experienced a Norman fate. In 1449, while still quite young, he fought in the army that recovered Normandy. In 1452, on the death of his grandfather Jean VII, he became count of Harcourt. In 1465, at roughly thirty-five, he was known as Jean de Lorraine, count of Harcourt.[450]

Let us return now to Jean VI d'Harcourt, the "brother" of Charles V. Jean VI himself had a brother, Jacques, born in 1350, who became lord of Montgommeri and had three sons: Jacques II, knight, lord of Montgommeri, and King Charles's lieutenant general in Picardy, who died in 1423;[451] Christophe, "beloved and loyal cousin" of Charles VII, who also served the king as councillor and chamberlain;[452] and Jean, who became bishop of Amiens and Tournai and then archbishop of Narbonne from 1436 until his death in 1452.[453] In 1417 Jacques II married Marguerite de Melun, the only daughter of the lord of Tancarville, and before his death in 1423 he had time to produce two children, a son, Guillaume, and a daughter, Marie.[454] In 1465 Guillaume was approximately forty-five and count of Tancarville. He would live until 1487. As for his sister Marie, she, like so many Harcourt daughters, had made a very fine marriage. She had wed Jean, bastard of Orléans and count of Dunois.

Within this constellation of Harcourts we have yet to situate Louis. Jean VIII, the last of the elder branch of the Harcourt clan, had died at Verneuil without legitimate children, but he was survived by a bastard infant, Louis. Young Louis was legitimated by royal letters in April 1441, not so that he could inherit the property of his grandfather Jean VII, which passed to his cousin Jean de Lorraine, but so that he might enter the Church. And in the Church Louis enjoyed a brilliant career. He began in the shadow of his cousin Jean, the archbishop of Narbonne, whom he succeeded in that post in 1452. He spent little time in southern France, however. He soon became a personage to reckon with as adviser to the king and as a leader in Normandy. In 1456 it was he who informed Charles VII of the duke of Alençon's conspiracy. In 1460 he succeeded Zenone Castiglioni as bishop of Bayeux. He also became patriarch of Jerusalem. In 1461, at Charles VII's burial, he officiated at both Notre-Dame in Paris and Saint-Denis. And he also officiated at the coronation of Louis XI in Rheims. A powerful man, he was also wealthy. He had purchased several estates from his friend Jeanne du Bec-Crespin, the wife of Pierre de Brézé.[455]

The reader, I hope, will excuse this rather austere digression.

Without it there would be no way to grasp the bonds of kinship and friendship that linked the principal actors in the Norman rebellion of 1465. In that year, Louis d'Harcourt, bishop of Bayeux and patriarch of Jerusalem, was just over forty years old. His first cousin, Jean de Lorraine, count of Harcourt, was about thirty-five. The prestigious Guillaume d'Estouteville, aged forty-two, was a more distant cousin, and besides, in 1465 he was at the curia in Rome and played no role in Normandy. But Louis d'Harcourt had still other cousins, more distantly related, perhaps, but to whom he felt closer, and they did play a major role. One was Guillaume d'Harcourt, the lord of Tancarville, who in 1465 was approximately forty-five. Even more important was the count of Dunois, Marie d'Harcourt's husband, who dominated the family by dint of his illustrious birth, his age, and his glorious past. The count of Dunois was one of the leaders of the League of the Public Weal. With the aid of his relatives the Harcourts, he gave the league a badly needed second wind. The Harcourts had always been loyal servants of the king of France and Normandy. They had never wavered in their support for Charles VII. Yet it was they who sparked the Norman rebellion against Louis XI.

The conflagration touched off in Rouen on September 28, 1465, by Louis d'Harcourt and Jeanne du Bec-Crespin could not have engulfed all Normandy in a few days, however, if the conspirators had not fulfilled the wishes of the Normans. Elsewhere the league of princes had met with a lukewarm response from the populace. In Normandy it aroused fervor. Within a few days the canons of Rouen and the burghers of Rouen and other cities had joined the conspirators.[456] Michel Basin, for example, who was then, at sixty-five, a "burgher residing in [the] city of Caudebec" but who happened to be in Rouen "when . . . the duke of Bourbon entered . . . the castle and city . . . of Rouen," played an active role in persuading first Caudebec and then, a few days later, Lisieux, to rally behind the duke.[457]

Philippe de Commynes is clear about the Normans' motives. They wanted a duke of their own. They hoped to use the league to force the king to give them his brother Charles as duke. The burghers of Rouen, Commynes says, joined "madame la grant senechalle de Normandie" (that is, Jeanne du Bec-Crespin) "because they only too desperately wanted a prince who would reside in the province of Normandy. Most if not all the cities and citadels did the same. And it always seemed to the Normans, and still does, that so great a duchy as theirs definitely requires a duke."[458] For the Normans in 1465 the crucial issue was still the continuity of Norman tradition and the defense of Norman liberties. A few decades earlier, many of them had been willing to accept English sovereignty as long as the English respected those liberties and maintained peace. Others, however, had refused the peace the English offered. After the recovery of Normandy by Charles VII's armies, both groups joined together, united by their dual loyalty to the king of France and to their own province. All were now loyal subjects of the king of France. The kingdom, in their view, was the natural setting in which Normandy should flourish. But out of love for their province they had sought since 1450 to persuade the victorious king to recognize Norman liberties and reestablish Norman institutions. Little by little they had achieved their goal. Shortly before his death Charles VII had confirmed the Norman Charter. Now, they believed, the time had come to force Louis XI to give them a duke. The Norman revolt was not intended to repudiate either the king or the kingdom. Its purpose was to use the league to force the king to name his brother duke. In the fourteenth century the duke of Normandy had been the king's brother. Now the Normans joined with the present king's brother to restore that condition. In doing so they hoped to reconcile their Norman patriotism with their loyalty to the crown. The Norman revolt of 1465 was simply the final act in a drama that had lasted fifteen years, a drama in which the Normans sought to restore Normandy to its place as a province of the kingdom of France.

In truth, the Normans did not choose this course. Pierre de Brézé's own son "did not want to take the oath; he defied his mother and returned to the king."[459] Michel Basin's brother-in-law Jean Le Roux, with whom Michel was staying in Rouen, remained loyal to the king.[460] Families were torn apart. When the moment of choice came, a minority of Normans refused to believe that rebellion was the best way to further their patriotism. The majority, however, believed that it was, and Thomas Basin was drawn to that majority in every way. From the first, the bishop of Lisieux had been sympathetic to the princes' expressed desire to reform the kingdom and to defend liberties against tyranny. When Normandy rebelled, Thomas, a man little inclined toward unconditional obedience and firmly devoted to the liberties of his province, was naturally drawn toward the princes. That attraction was only strengthened by the admiration he had felt for the past fifteen years for Dunois, an admiration that naturally drew him also toward the Harcourt family and Louis d'Harcourt, the bishop of nearby Bayeux. It was also strengthened by the decision of his brother Michel and probably of his older brothers to join the rebellion.

What is more, Louis XI and his council had immediately retreated in the face of the rebellion in upper Normandy and the occupation of western Normandy by Breton armies aiding the rebels. On September 29 king and council had decided to award Normandy to Charles, and word of this decision soon spread through Paris. A number of Normans who had been in Paris had reported the news to Thomas Basin. Later, in his defense, Thomas insisted that on October 8 he had been "absolutely certain that the king had already given the duchy to his brother." Among the reasons for his certainty was the fact that the valiant knight Guillaume de Trousseauville, upon his return from Paris, had stated under oath that the king, in issuing his departure orders, had told him: "Go home to Normandy. Welcome my brother as duke and do not fail to obey him and serve him loyally as your prince and duke."[461] For a citizen of Rouen to have joined the duke of Bourbon on September 28 might have posed a problem of conscience. But for a citizen of Lisieux to have backed Charles on October 8, after it had been declared that Louis XI had made Charles duke of Normandy, posed no such problem. In pledging itself to Charles, Lisieux was not disobeying Louis. The king had no reason to find fault—except perhaps with the bishop's hasty embrace of all the rumors.

To explain that haste, Thomas Basin later came up with another argument. However the citizens might have felt, the city of Lisieux found itself on October 8, 1465, in the same difficult situation as in August 1449. The Breton army "was on the march everywhere in the province. It laid siege to the episcopal city, which no royal garrison defended from its attackers."[462] As in 1449, the bishop's duty was to protect the city from soldiers, even friendly soldiers, and spare it the horrors of a siege. The "clergy, nobles, burghers, laborers, and inhabitants of the city of Lisieux" therefore bowed to Duke Charles, obtained from him the same compact just concluded "with the clergy, nobles, burghers, laborers, and inhabitants of the *ville et cité* of Rouen," secured confirmation of all rights "accorded by the late King Charles the Seventh when with God's help he won the obedience of the city of Lisieux," and gained assurance that all persons presently holding office would remain in their positions.[463] They then surrendered the city, which, Thomas was at pains to point out, no soldier entered.[464] The surrender of 1465 was in every detail a repeat of the surrender of 1449.

The count of Charolais was paralyzed by the rebellion of Liège. Louis XI had agreed to make his brother duke of Normandy. He was prepared to make other concessions to the confederation of princes. An agreement was rapidly reached. The Treaty of Conflans, on October 5, and that of Saint-Maur, on October 29, concluded the War of the Public Weal. These treaties contained many clauses. Essentially they satisfied both the confederates and the Normans, because on the one hand they made a start on governmental reform and on the other hand they confirmed Charles as duke of Normandy. Thomas Basin's hopes were fulfilled. The bishop of Lisieux was a happy man, all the more so because there would be a role for him in both the reform of the monarchy and the new ducal Normandy.

To begin work on governmental reform, a commission of thirty-six members was to be appointed, including twelve ecclesiastics, twelve nobles, and twelve members of the common and inferior estate. On October 27 thirty-six men were named by common consent of the king and the princes. The first noble was the count of Dunois. Thomas Basin was one of the twelve prelates. Actually, the commission did not meet right away, and when it did finally meet several months later, Thomas Basin was not among its members.[465] He was in exile, and ducal Normandy was in ruins.

Yet things had gotten off to a good start. On October 30, 1465, Charles had sworn faith and homage to the king on behalf of the duchy of Normandy.[466] Political life and governmental business gradually resumed under the new duke. On November 17 Charles called a meeting of the Estates of Normandy for December 8.[467] On November 25 Duke Charles made his entry into Rouen, "escorted by a hundred lancers and an appropriate number of men at arms" under the command of the "very illustrious and most valiant knight Jean [de Lorraine], count of Harcourt."[468] Finally, on December 1, Charles's investiture offered the occasion for a splendid ceremony in the cathedral of Rouen.[469]

At approximately ten o'clock the duke was solemnly received by the dean and chapter, then seated in the choir near the main altar. Next, in the absence of the archbishop, Guillaume d'Estouteville, who was away in Rome, a solemn mass was celebrated by Louis d'Harcourt, patriarch of Jerusalem and bishop of Bayeux. Then the epistle was read, and the duke took the oaths that dukes customarily swore. The ducal ring was then given to Charles by Thomas Basin, the bishop of Lisieux. Next, Guillaume d'Harcourt, count of Tancarville, for whom the hereditary office of constable of Normandy had just been revived,[470] handed Charles the ducal sword. Finally, Jean de Lorraine, count of Harcourt, to whom Duke Charles had just given the hereditary office of marshal of Normandy,[471] handed him the ducal standard, completing "the formalities connected with the duke of Normandy."

The ceremony of December 1, 1465, of course glorified the Harcourts. But it also did far more. It marked the revival of customs long since fallen into disuse. In the fourteenth century the duke of

Normandy had done homage to the king. When Charles, the future Charles V, became duke of Normandy, he immediately did homage to his father, King John the Good.[472] Louis XI's brother Charles had also recently done homage to the king (on October 30, 1465). But this ceremony of investiture could not have been inspired by any thirteenth-, fourteenth-, or fifteenth-century custom. The ducal ring, sword, and standard had not been piously preserved in any ducal treasury. No chronicle describes any such ceremony involving either John, the future John the Good, or Charles, the future Charles V, both of whom had been dukes of Normandy in the fourteenth century.

At the end of the twelfth century, however, on July 20, 1189, Richard the Lionhearted had been given solemn investiture as duke of Normandy in the cathedral of Rouen. And John Lackland had received a similar investiture on April 25, 1199. It may have been in preparation for these ceremonies that a liturgy had been composed for the investiture of the duke of Normandy, an *Officium ad ducem Normannorum constituendum,* the text of which was then copied into an old benedictional in the cathedral. This benedictional was still in the cathedral library in the fifteenth century. No doubt the oaths sworn by the duke in 1465 were taken from it. This old *ordo* most likely inspired the bestowal of the ring and sword—but not the standard, which is never mentioned.

There was, however, a rather rare text, the *Life of Saint Hugh of Avalon,* bishop of Lincoln from 1186 to 1200, written shortly before 1214 by Adam of Eynsham, who, in describing the investiture of John Lackland in 1199, did say that the new duke had received a lance with a standard "by which the dukes of Neustria are accustomed to receive investiture of their honor." Had the cleric who conceived the liturgy of 1465 read the *Life of Saint Hugh?* Or was he inspired by some other text? He was in any case a most learned cleric, who was not content with the *officium* contained in the old benedictional. And his intention was clear. He wished to reach back beyond Capetian Normandy, and by omitting nearly three centuries of history he hoped to link the duchy of 1465 to the Normandy of the Plantagenets—the same Plantagenet Normandy that Henry V had claimed to represent in 1417.[473]

Who was this Norman patriot who wanted to give the new duchy roots in so remote a past? No one knows. But it was not Thomas Basin, who says nothing in either his *History of Louis XI* or his *Apology* about the ceremony of December 1 even though he played an important role in it.

In any case, a few days after the investiture the new duke of Normandy sent a messenger to inform the count of Charolais that "my lord duke has been received in his province and duchy of Normandy and is presently in tranquil enjoyment and possession thereof."[474] A few weeks later, all was lost.

What doomed the Norman venture was the selfishness of the princes. In the October treaties, Commynes said, "the public weal was converted into private goods."[475] Thomas Basin echoed this judgment: "Many sought private advantages rather than reform of the state or the public weal."[476] The count of Charolais was still paralyzed by the revolt in Liège, and the responsibility of the Liégeois for the Norman debacle of 1465, a responsibility of which Thomas was well aware, no doubt explains part of our bishop's persistent hatred of the "stupid Eburons or Liégeois."[477] But the duke of Brittany lacked even that excuse. Cooperation between Francis II, the duke of Brittany, and Charles, the duke of Normandy, had been essential to the success of the Norman rebellion; the support of the Breton troops had been crucial. When it came time to divide the spoils, however, the Bretons displayed such ambition and greed that the Normans were forced to object. In fighting for a duke, they had not intended to invite the Bretons to feast on their province. But then the Bretons showed that they were not only ambitious and greedy but also treacherous. Francis II struck a bargain with Louis XI. The Norman citadels that Francis's captains had only yesterday held in the duke's name they now held in the king's name. Once again Thomas Basin had reason to moan, "*Nolite confidere in principibus* [Do not trust in princes]."[478] And soon he would have yet another reason, for the duke of Bourbon, also won over by Louis XI, simultaneously embarked on a course of treachery and treason against Duke Charles.[479]

Meanwhile, on November 15, 1465, Parlement had registered the gift of Normandy to Charles but with a protest that this treaty "was concluded against its will and by force and coercion." A few weeks later, the tide having turned, Louis XI also wrote in various places "that, in order to avoid the danger to his person, he had been constrained by fear and force to . . . grant [Charles] the duchy of Normandy and to agree to and grant the lords several other things against his will."[480] Once again, claims of "fear," "doubt," and "force" had allowed a prince to renege on his commitments. Meanwhile, the Normans, now aware that their loyalty to the king and their loyalty to the duke were irreconcilable, wavered.

Some Norman cities had been surrendered by Breton captains or the duke of Bourbon, while others submitted to the king on their own initiative. In the weeks that followed the grandiose ceremony of December 1, nearly all went over to the king, first Harfleur and Honfleur, then Evreux, Dieppe next, then Argentan, Falaise, and Caen, then Granville, followed by Lisieux. On December 25 Vernon returned to the king. On December 26 Pont-Audemer, Le Neubourg, and Conches did the same. That night Louis XI in person entered Louviers.[481] Four weeks after his investiture, Charles still held Rouen but practically nothing else.

On December 28, with the situation desperate, a remarkable thing happened. Many of Rouen's citizens had gathered around the duke, the count of Harcourt, and the aldermen of the city. They reaffirmed their loyalty. Assurances were given that the city would be vigorously defended. The aldermen then took from their library a copy of the *Chronicles of Normandy,* a superb folio volume, recently made and embellished with handsome miniatures.[482] The volume was shown to the count of Harcourt, who showed it to the duke. And the duke, in the presence of the entire assembly, ordered a public reading of the passage describing the difficulties that Louis IV d'Outremer had encountered when he tried to take Normandy from the son of William Longsword and detailing the treaty by which the young prince had finally regained tranquil possession of his inheritance.[483]

The events in question had taken place in the tenth century. Normandy in danger looked to the distant past for a ray of hope. But the Harcourts, who boasted of their descent from a companion of Rollo, the Basins, a family with centuries-old roots in the Caux region, and many other participants in the events of 1465 surely knew, as Thomas Basin did, how little the son of William Longsword resembled the brother of Louis XI. Perhaps some of them said that the deeper reason for their failure lay in their having counted on this young duke from Paris. In his *History of Louis XI* Thomas wrote: "In Normandy Duke Charles was like a recently planted tree, not yet attached to the soil by solid roots and easily uprooted and moved."[484] He liked this image so much that he used it again in his *Apology:* "The duke of Normandy was like a newly planted tree. He had not had time to grow deep roots. His mooring in the soil was weak. He had neither the space nor the time needed to establish order in the province and to organize resistance."[485] Thomas says nothing about the December 1 ceremony. No doubt he found it artificial. His tree metaphor makes us aware that for him there was something artificial about the whole 1465 venture. The duchy of Normandy was doomed because the duke was not Normandy's natural prince.

In January 1466 Louis XI reentered Rouen. Some of the duke's officers were arrested and beheaded or drowned. Jean de Lorraine, count of Harcourt, was arrested before he could reach Picardy. Pierre de Brézé's widow and Louis d'Harcourt successfully escaped. In February 1466 Duke Charles reached Brittany.[486]

As for Thomas Basin, he had no need to flee. In December 1465 Charles had sent four successive ambassadors to the duke of Burgundy and the count of Charolais to ask for help. Thomas Basin was the third of these ambassadors. He met the count of Charolais at Saint-Trond before December 22. From there he went to see the duke of Burgundy in Brussels.[487] There he heard the news from Normandy and decided to avoid the king's wrath by finding a secure refuge. He went to Louvain, where he had once studied civil and canon law. Years later he would recall that he had taken up residence there on January 5, 1466. Around that time, either shortly before or shortly after, the king's soldiers sacked his episcopal palace in Lisieux.[488] The king took possession of the diocese's temporality.[489] All that Thomas managed to salvage was a few books. He would never see his diocese again.

A Bishop Far from His Diocese (1466–74)

After a period of repression, the king's rancor against most of his adversaries subsided. Cities and individuals easily obtained letters of remission. In January 1466 Michel Basin, Thomas's own brother, received remission thanks to his brother-in-law Jean Le Roux.[490] On January 26, 1466, only six persons remained to whom Louis XI refused his pardon, among them Louis d'Harcourt, bishop of Bayeux, and Jean de Lorraine, count of Harcourt. In February, however, Jean de Lorraine was pardoned at the request of Francis II, duke of Brittany. And a short while later Louis d'Harcourt was also pardoned.[491]

The conspirators were not merely pardoned. The count of Dunois died in 1468 at age sixty-six, at which time he was the recipient of a handsome pension of six thousand *livres*. Louis d'Harcourt, soon back in the king's good graces, died in 1479 as bishop of Bayeux and patriarch of Jerusalem; he was about sixty years old. Guillaume d'Harcourt, count of Tancarville, was around sixty-five when he died in 1487 as sovereign master of France's rivers and forests. For most of the conspirators, the League of the Public Weal and the Norman adventure were no more than an interlude, after which they returned to the service of the king of France. Thomas Basin's fate was different. And we would know little or nothing about it had not Thomas himself left us, in his *Apology*, a remarkable account of his obscure disappointments.

In January 1466 Thomas Basin thus found himself in Louvain,

determined to remain there until the royal wrath (*furor*) had subsided.[492] On January 26 Louis XI quashed all charges against supporters of the duke of Normandy. Only six individuals (including Louis d'Harcourt and Jean de Lorraine) were excluded by name from this blanket pardon, which therefore included the bishop of Lisieux.[493] Thomas Basin was informed of the pardon by "numerous relatives and friends," who advised him to return. But Thomas would not trust the word of a prince who had so often reneged on his promises. He displayed extreme—many thought excessive—caution and remained in Louvain.

Louis XI granted a second pardon at Montargis in August 1466.[494] This time, however prudent and fearful he may have been, Thomas could not refuse to return. In September 1466, after "roughly eight months" in "hiding" in Louvain,[495] and not without deep misgivings (*non sine magna animi titubacione*), he abandoned his refuge, taking with him his remaining books and baggage.[496] Shortly thereafter he crossed the border into his native province and thus into territory under the king's jurisdiction and headed for Rouen. Before long he regretted the "inconsiderate confidence" he had placed in Louis XI.[497]

All that Thomas Basin wanted was to return to Lisieux and resume his ministry. But when he arrived in Rouen, where he had a splendid residence and several other houses, he was not allowed to stop but only to pass through the city, which he entered "like an owl, at nightfall" and left the following morning at dawn. He had been told that he must appear immediately before the king, who had been in Orléans since October 4. Thomas Basin went there, but he was not allowed to travel the normal routes. Instead he was obliged to go by way of forests and other unpopulated and inaccessible places.[498]

Upon arriving in Orléans Thomas Basin went to the king. Their interview was brief: "I made as if to speak to him, but he gazed at me with a menacing eye, uttered but a single word of welcome in passing, and refused any more extensive conversation." Thomas then had the clever idea of using the good offices of Jean Balue, who for the time being enjoyed the king's favor. The bishop of Lisieux passed word to the king that his only desire was "to reside in his diocese and serve the king by serving Christ."[499] Soon, however, the cardinal informed Thomas of the terrible news: "The king's will was that I should go to Perpignan and serve him in that region, which lies outside the kingdom's borders."[500]

Early in his reign, Louis XI had aided Juan II, king of Aragon, in his struggles with Catalonian rebels. In reward for this assistance,

Louis had received Roussillon and Cerdagne in May 1462. In November 1462 the region rebelled against the occupying French troops. The king of France was forced to reconquer it. That reconquest was not completed until June 1463.[501] Three years later, it was to this remote and insecure region that Louis XI wished to send the once-rebellious bishop to serve "as chancellor of the counties of Roussillon and Cerdagne."[502] Promotion to a position in a faraway locale was one of Louis XI's standard ways of testing his underlings. Early in his reign he had used the same procedure with the bastard of Orléans and Pierre de Brézé. But the king's decision devastated Thomas Basin.

Was it possible? Catalonia! A torrid region three hundred leagues from Caudebec where he was born and Lisieux where he was bishop! A place where he had no home and knew no one![503] If exile to a remote and dreadful place was unavoidable, our Norman bishop hoped that he might at least he sent somewhere less sweltering. He offered to go "live for example among the steep slopes and rocky peaks of Auvergne and Dauphiné"—in vain. The king's will was confirmed. "The king had recently established in Perpignan a parlement as court of last resort in cases concerning the counties of Roussillon and Cerdagne. He needed a chancellor on the spot to take charge of this court and of the administration of ordinary justice in the region." Thomas Basin was chosen to fill the post.[504]

Thomas, scaling down his ambitions, then tried to obtain better financial conditions. He asked that the king grant him "a decent pension, since he has decided to use my services."[505] The pension was promised but not paid, not even an advance. Thomas then did all he could to drag things out in the hope that ultimately he might receive the pension. At the same time he prudently allowed the winter months, which made long voyages so arduous, to pass. He did not wish to start out until spring had returned.

Months passed while Thomas tried to negotiate. He dogged the king's steps in the hope of obtaining an interview. But the king never showed him the slightest sign of favor: "Either he turned his back on me and looked off in another direction, or he changed the subject and dismissed me without answering."[506] The wounded courtier thus spent two months in Orléans in the greatest vexation.[507]

At the end of December 1466 the king left Orléans for Bourges. Then, at the end of February or the beginning of March 1467, he went to Montils-lès-Tours.[508] The court and council had followed the king from Orléans to Bourges and then had settled in Tours by mid-March 1467. Thomas Basin had followed the court and council. He had remained in Bourges "a little less than three months."[509]

Then he too went to Tours. Immediately he paid a call on the chancellor. No sooner had he descended from his mule, however, than the chancellor (at that time Guillaume Jouvenal des Ursins) showed him a letter from the king, who was in a rage because Thomas Basin had not yet left for Perpignan. The chancellor, "unable to restrain the tears I saw flowing from his eyes," overwhelmed Thomas with kind words and advised him "to give in immediately to the royal wrath, without further discussion of the pension" that had been promised. "That very day, resigned to this injustice, [he] quickly set out for Perpignan." The journey took nearly a month. Finally, in April 1467, Thomas Basin reached Perpignan.[510]

Thomas Basin's administration was careful and honest, or so he tells us. "I never accepted a denarius from anyone, despite the total absence of any subvention or pension from the king or emolument from the chancellery or any other source of income." And Thomas Basin enjoyed remarkable success in his position, again on his own telling: "I daresay that no one appointed to this post by the king earned more gratitude from the inhabitants of the region."[511] In fact, when the bishop of Elne died on September 11, 1467, many hoped that Thomas would give up the diocese of Lisieux and accept that of Elne, "whose revenues were no smaller than those of Lisieux."[512] But Thomas Basin wanted only one thing: for the king to allow him to return to the cool air of his native Normandy. The king refused.

Instead of acceding to Thomas's wishes, Louis XI sent him to Barcelona. The mission was of no interest; "no mention was made of the expenses and costs of travel"; and "the route to be traveled was most dangerous owing to war and brigands."[513] Nevertheless, Thomas Basin set out. He found it difficult to find lodging. Supplies were so short that some of the animals in the train nearly died of hunger, as did Thomas himself. He returned a few weeks later. The arduous and vexing journey had exhausted him and ruined his health, but he hoped at least to have found grace in the king's eyes in reward for his submissive attitude and industrious activity.[514]

Upon his return, however, he learned that a letter from the king would soon arrive with orders that he never again leave Roussillon. Devastated, Thomas Basin took stock of his situation. For fourteen months he had served the king in that region without receiving the slightest reward or compensation. Before his departure the king had promised him a suitable pension. He had failed to keep his promise. It was an intolerable burden to serve the king for so long, and at one's own expense, in a region so far from home. The summer heat in Roussillon was also intolerable. Thomas felt as though he were caught in a circle of fire in a burning, desiccated land. He was suffering the tortures of the damned. And now he was to be condemned to perpetual exile and imprisonment in these parts. Apparently the king wished to grind him down, ruin his health, and drive him to his grave.[515] He had survived one summer, not without difficulty. He had suffered fevers, stomach troubles, and digestive disorders.[516] To endure such torment again was out of the question. He quickly came to a decision.

In June 1468, one year and two months after his arrival, with the sun in this torrid region already scorchingly hot and even before the royal messenger arrived, Thomas Basin left Perpignan. As quickly as possible he crossed Languedoc, Dauphiné, and Savoy. He did not stop until he reached Geneva, where his books and baggage soon caught up with him. By fleeing he had escaped the impious hands of the tyrant. He had ensured his salvation and his liberty. His life was saved.[517]

But slander further exacerbated Louis XI's hatred toward him, and the influence of the king of France was not limited to his kingdom alone. In August 1469, after a three months' stay, Thomas Basin was obliged to leave Geneva. He went to Basel, where he remained for six months. In October 1468, however, the king of France and the duke of Burgundy had concluded a treaty at Péronne, a treaty that Thomas Basin thought durable. He therefore judged it prudent to head for Burgundian territory in the hope that Charles the Bold would help him to obtain a pardon from Louis XI. At the beginning of 1469 Thomas therefore settled once more in his beloved city of Louvain, where we found him at the beginning of our narrative.[518]

In the years that followed it was not Thomas's sole concern to write a work of self-justification. His greatest need was to extricate himself from the difficulties of his situation. In January 1466 the temporality of his diocese had been placed in the king's hands.[519] When he left Perpignan in the summer of 1468, he was stripped of his ecclesiastical and patrimonial revenues and of all his moveable property. Thomas had long ago appointed his older brother Louis and his younger brother Thomas (the younger) to administer his diocesan and personal property. When that property was confiscated, the two brothers were thrown into prison. They "were snatched from their native soil, their homes, and their wives. . . . They were imprisoned at Tours for a year and a half, during which time they suffered anxiety, fear, and anguish."[520] In the same year, 1468, another of Thomas's brothers, Nicolas, made a decision possibly motivated by the persecution of his family. He and his wife left Rouen and moved first to Bruges, then to Utrecht.[521]

Louis and Thomas were freed early in 1470. Several years passed, during which the bishop of Lisieux's only wish was to return to his diocese. His friends continued to implore the king on his behalf. The duke of Burgundy pleaded for him. The king's brother, Charles, the man responsible for Thomas's misfortune, who had become duke of Guyenne and who was for a time reconciled with the king, also pleaded for him. But Thomas's enemies continued to stir up the king's hatred. And the one thing the king was unwilling to permit was for Thomas to return to his diocese. When the duke of Guyenne praised the merits of the bishop of Lisieux "far beyond what they really were," Thomas modestly adds, Louis XI answered: "Since this is a man of such great merit, let him ask for any diocese that may become vacant in the Oc region [that is, in southern France], even if the diocese in question has revenues equivalent or superior to those of Lisieux. I promise to see that he gets it. But as for the bishopric of Lisieux, I shall never suffer him to keep it or to reside there."[522]

Things had reached an impasse. In 1473 the situation became intolerable. At that time Thomas Basin was in Trier. He was still receiving the spiritual revenues of his diocese, which the king could not touch. Norman merchants sent money to him either directly or by way of the Antwerp fairs. For exporting cash they endured prison, fines, and confiscations. Among the victims were Louis and Thomas Basin, the bishop's two brothers who had previously been imprisoned at Tours in 1468; Michel, an older brother, who was more than seventy; and Jean Le Roux, Michel Basin's brother-in-law. Jean Le Roux avoided prison by paying "a great quantity of gold." But the three Basin brothers were once again expelled from their native land (*patria pulsos*) and this time deported to Paris (*in exilium Parisius expulerunt; Parisius confinatos*), interrogated at the Châtelet, and threatened with imprisonment and expropriation.[523]

Thomas Basin is nearly at the end of his tale. There was only one possible solution: that he abdicate his diocese in favor of a man acceptable to the king. Thomas's brothers received authorization from the king to go to Trier to settle the matter. Early in 1474 Thomas learned from them the misfortunes that had befallen his church, his brothers, and many of his dear friends. Wailing and crying, his brothers told him of the critical situation in which they found themselves and spoke of their daily fears (*metus*) and terrors (*pavores*). For all these perils there was only one remedy. Thomas would have to resign his position in favor of someone acceptable to the king.[524] Thomas Basin surrendered. In March 1474 he left for Rome. After a month of travel he arrived there, and after several more weeks he renounced his diocese.

In one respect this resignation was certainly, as Thomas Basin's account would have us believe, the painful conclusion of dramatic tribulations. But it was also the happy outcome of shrewd negotiation. Thomas Basin renounced his diocese but under conditions which, though he says little about them, were quite favorable.

The first thing to understand is the climate in which the negotiations in Rome were conducted. Pope Paul II had died on July 26, 1471. On August 9 the Genoan Francesco della Rovere, general of the Franciscans, was elected pope. He took the name Sixtus IV and from the first gave evidence of his desire "to live on good terms with everybody."[525] On November 4, 1471, Louis XI sent an embassy to Rome, one of the two leaders of which was Antoine Raguier.[526] The embassy arrived on December 30.[527] One of its purposes was to promise the pope that the king would never revert to the Pragmatic Sanction. Negotiations continued after the embassy was complete, and in the summer of 1472 a concordat was signed. Among the terms of the concordat was a provision that French bishops would be named by the pope but not without the consent of the king. Before appointing anyone, the pope was supposed to await the king's letters in order to be sure of choosing someone acceptable to the king.[528] The canons of the cathedral chapter, who were the ordinary electors, no longer had any role to play in the designation of bishops. Everything depended on the pope and the king. Thomas Basin, who had been an ardent champion of the Pragmatic Sanction from 1450 to 1466, was quite comfortable conducting his negotiations in Rome under new conditions, no longer those that had obtained in his youth. The consent of both pope and king was still fundamental, but now the cardinals had no influence, and the resignation of the current bishop was, as we shall see, essential.

The first compensation that Thomas Basin received for his resignation was his appointment on May 26, 1474, as archbishop of Caesarea. Sixtus IV, he tells us, wished to confer on him the honorific title of patriarch. Thomas Basin contented himself with a more modest title and accepted that of archbishop of Caesarea with pleasure, all the more so in that he had always honored the memory of the venerable Eusebius, bishop of Caesarea, whose labors had enriched the church of Christ with the most useful and remarkable books.[529]

That is all Thomas Basin tells us. But we know from other sources that he received another, not inconsiderable compensation of a material sort: an annual pension of 876 *livres* was assigned to him out of the revenues of the church of Lisieux.[530]

It is certain that Thomas Basin obtained even more, which until now has gone unnoticed. Before saying what, however, we must first introduce the Raguier family, of which we have thus far caught only a brief glimpse of one member. Hémon Raguier was a financier who came to France from Bavaria in 1386 with Queen Isabeau.[531] At first he had served as the queen's treasurer. Then he became royal treasurer for war and master of the Chambre des Comptes in Paris.[532] In 1433 we lose track of him. This fortunate financier had a number of offspring who turn up in Charles VII's France at the Chambre des Comptes and several other financial institutions as well as in Parlement and the chancellery. Here I shall mention only two of Hémon's sons, Antoine and Louis Raguier. Louis became clerk councillor of Parlement in 1438. In 1450 he was named bishop of Troyes, In 1474, while still bishop, he also served as president of the Cour des Aides.[533] Antoine Raguier had succeeded his father Hémon as Charles VII's treasurer for war. On August 5, 1441, he married Jacquette Budé, daughter of the royal notary-secretary Dreux Budé.[534] The couple had several children, four of whom are of interest here: Jean, Antoine, Louis, and Jacques. Jean was born in 1445. He was so close to Louis XI that the king later said: "I fed him."[535] And Louis added: "He served me a long time, and so did his predecessors." In fact, Jean Raguier was a collector of the salt tax at Laon in 1463, at age eighteen. When his father Antoine died in May 1468, Jean succeeded him as treasurer for war and at the same time became *receveur général des finances* in Normandy. In 1474 Jean Raguier was not yet thirty, but he was a powerful personage, serving simultaneously as royal notary-secretary in charge of paying the king's troups and as chief tax collector for Normandy. At the same time his brother Antoine was also serving as a royal notary-secretary (and as Louis XI's envoy to Rome in 1471). Their brother Louis, canon of Troyes since 1460 thanks to his uncle the bishop, had also been archdeacon of Sézanne since 1471.[536] Finally, Jacques, although he may have held no prominent position in 1474, would soon be a doctor of law and canon of Paris; in 1483 his uncle Louis would abdicate in his favor as bishop of Troyes.[537] In 1474, then, the Raguiers were a powerful family, close to the king, connected by marriage to the cream of Parisian political society and by friendship to some of the most powerful men in the kingdom. Jean, bastard of Orléans and count of Dunois, died on November 24, 1468, at a château in L'Hay near Bourg-la-Reine that belonged to his friend Antoine Raguier, treasurer for war, who had died himself only a few months earlier.[538]

On June 6, 1474, Thomas Basin was still in Rome when Sixtus IV named as bishop of Lisieux Louis Raguier, the younger, archdeacon of Sézanne, who could not have been much more than thirty and may have been even younger.[539] On June 24 Thomas Basin, "by divine permission archbishop of Caesarea, erstwhile bishop of Lisieux," was no doubt still in Rome when he acknowledged "having had and received from Jean Raguier, councillor and receiver general of our sire the king in Normandy, the sum of three thousand seven hundred *livres tournois.*" To be sure, Thomas Basin's receipt explained that these 3,700 livres were merely reimbursement of a sum entrusted "by way of loan" to Jean Raguier by officers of the bishopric of Lisieux and by Thomas Basin's brothers "for certain affairs" of the king "and also for the passage of the count of Oxenford to England." (The count of Oxford, a Lancastrian refugee in France, had made this crossing in 1473.)[540] Medieval history is so full of fictitious reimbursements that it is difficult not to suspect this one as well, for after all it was made to Thomas Basin by Jean Raguier in Rome a few days after Thomas Basin resigned his bishopric and Jean's brother Louis was named to replace him.

Further information changes our suspicion to certainty. Old Louis Raguier, bishop of Troyes, afflicted by age, resigned his bishopric in 1483 in favor of his nephew Jacques Raguier. Two years later, in 1485, he drew up a will, in which he bequeathed to his nephews Jacques, the new bishop of Troyes, and Jean the sum owed him by his nephew Louis, their brother, bishop elect of Lisieux, which amounted to 1,500 gold *écus.*[541]

Now everything is clear. Early in 1474 Thomas Basin's brothers came to Trier to ask him to resign in favor of a person acceptable to the king, as Thomas himself admits. There is no doubt that his brothers at that time asked him to resign in favor of Louis Raguier. The brothers' trip to Trier was obviously a mission in which they served as intermediaries between the king and his receiver-general for Normandy on the one hand and Thomas Basin on the other. In March 1474 Thomas Basin left Trier for Rome. After several weeks of negotiation, he resigned his bishopric in favor of Louis Raguier. On May 26 he was named archibishop of Caesarea. On June 6 Sixtus IV named Louis Raguier bishop of Lisieux. On June 24 Thomas Basin received the reward for his resignation, the sum of several thousand livres lent to the new bishop by his uncle Louis, bishop of Troyes, and his brother Jean, receiver-general for Normandy, and perhaps by his brother Antoine, the royal notary-secretary. For the Raguiers, Louis's nomination as bishop of Lisieux was the fruit of a shrewd family strategy, a smart deal. The tyrants' victims had been able to strike a bargain with his friends. During the course of the negotiations it is easy to imagine men on both sides speaking warmly of the late Jean, bastard of Orléans, count of Dunois, who had been a dear friend of the Raguiers and whom Thomas Basin not only admired but praised lavishly in his books.

The Raguiers smart deal was very quickly compromised. A few weeks after his nomination, before he had even been consecrated bishop, Louis Raguier died suddenly. It was rumored that he had committed suicide by jumping into a well.[542] In any case, he died on September 29, 1474.[543] In the late fifteenth century venal resignation of benefices and offices was a game of chance. With the Raguiers on the verge of losing their bet, royal favor enabled them to parry fate's cruel blow. On November 1, 1474, Sixtus IV named as bishop of Lisieux Antoine Raguier, the royal notary-secretary and brother of Jean, Louis, and Jacques.[544] The bishopric remained in the family. But not for long, because on Monday, June 10, 1482, between ten and eleven in the morning, Antoine Raguier died at the monastery of Préaux in his diocese of a new disease unknown to physicians. What was it? It was not sweating sickness (miliary fever), which first appeared in England and not before 1485.[545] At the time, however, the death was seen as shameful.[546] Two premature and suspect deaths had stricken the successors of Thomas Basin. But Thomas, who had recounted with ferocious joy the sad fate and tragic death of all the members of the Maunoury family to whom Louis XI had entrusted administration of his bishopric's temporality after its confiscation, says nothing about the premature deaths of Louis and Antoine Raguier even though he was well aware that they had occurred.[547] More clearly than anything else, perhaps, this silence reveals the ambiguous nature of the relations between the Raguiers and Thomas Basin.

We must be careful, therefore, not to be misled by the dramatic narrative of Thomas Basin's *Apology.* All in all, his fate was not that tragic. The bishop of Lisieux was not the only French prelate to have his differences with Louis XI. Nor was he the one who suffered most at the hands of the "tyrant."[548] He knew when to compromise, even if he does not boast about it. But when the new archbishop of Caesarea, now sixty-one, returned to Trier in July 1474, pleasure in the bargain he had just struck was not uppermost in his mind. What dominated his thoughts was bitterness over so many hopes ruined, so many dreams destroyed.

Thomas Basin at Sixty

Failure made Thomas Basin a profound pessimist. For him, the world was wicked. To be sure, Thomas was not the first Christian to find the world a wicked place. And neither Gilles Le Muisit nor many other clerics who lived under Charles VI believed that the world was good. But the age of Louis XI was very different from the age of Charles VI. And Thomas Basin also had his own personal vision and experiences. Hence the wicked world as Thomas Basin saw it did not in every way resemble the wicked world that Gilles Le Muisit had known.

The seven deadly sins, which in the eyes of many had once explained the world's wickedness, no longer explained anything for Thomas Basin. Nevertheless, he still strongly denounced the two sins that the thirteenth and fourteenth centuries had placed above all others, pride and avarice. Pride is a universal evil, which drives people, potentates, and princes. It causes loss of all proportion. It turns men away from wisdom. It makes them presumptuous and reckless. Recklessly, peoples rebel, princes' servants disobey, and princes themselves, fearful of no one, act intemperately. According to Suetonius, Augustus said that a leader must avoid temerity above all else, on which point Thomas Basin quoted Suetonius.[549] In short, pride provokes temerity, and temerity leads to disaster.

Thomas frequently stresses the point that such disastrous pride stems from prosperity. The people of Ghent rebelled in 1452; their reckless pride came from their very good fortune (*ex rebus secundis*).[550] When the people of Liège rebelled in 1465, they displayed that great pride that is the usual consequence of prosperity (*magna superbia . . . que ex rebus secundis oriri* [*solet*]).[551] In 1473 the duke of Burgundy, swollen with pride in his successes (*rebus elatus secundis*), aspired to a royal throne.[552] In the *Aeneid,* which Thomas Basin cites twice, Virgil said: "*Nescia mens hominum fati sortisque future / Nec servare modum, rebus sublata secundis*" (man does not know what fate holds in store, and, swollen by success or good fortune or prosperity, he loses all sense of proportion).[553] When that happens, he rushes headlong toward ruin. A pessimist, Thomas Basin believed that an infernal cycle ruled the world. The fortunate man becomes proud; pride brings on temerity; temerity leads to disaster. Good fortune thus leads to misfortune.

This infernal cycle, moreover, was only the first phase of a cyclical movement well known to the men of the fifteenth century and proverbial since the childhood of Thomas Basin. In 1431 Georges Chastellain described it thus:

> De paix naist richesse sur terre
> De richesse orgueil, d'orgueil guerre,
> De guerre vient povreté,
> De povreté humilité.
> Mais d'humilité revient paix.

[From peace wealth is born on earth.
From wealth, pride; from pride, war.
From war comes poverty;
from poverty, humility.
But from humility peace returns.]

In 1451 Antoine de la Sale gave his own prose version: "From peace comes wealth; from wealth comes pride; from pride comes war; from war comes poverty; from poverty comes peace once more."[554]

"The wicked root of ambition and avarice," "the false and wicked root of ambition and covetousness *que est radix omnium malorum* as the Apostle says,"[555] is, like pride, the source of man's misfortune. For Thomas Basin, ambition, avarice, and covetousness are all one. Ambition, avarice, and greed drive men to seek money, honors, and authority.[556] Misery therefore makes men ambitious, but paradoxically abundance is an even more potent source of insatiable, infinite ambition, which impels man to strive ever higher (*ad altiora ambire*) and to want ever more (*ad ampliora inhians*).[557] Ambition is not so much the sin of the humble as the sin of the prominent. It drives clerics toward benefices and prelatures,[558] laymen toward offices,[559] and princes toward tyranny. Princes ruled by diseased ambition and a frantic desire to rule (*pestifera ambicio et dominandi effrenis cupiditas*), by blind and senseless ambition to dominate all (*ceca et stulta nimium ambicio et cupiditas dominandi*), and by a pernicious instinct of domination (*perniciosissima dominandi cupiditas*) reject all fear of God, cease to heed the voice of reason, neglect justice, respect neither the rights nor the property of their subjects, and reduce those subjects to servitude.[560]

In describing ambition as blind and senseless, Thomas Basin used the very same words as Matthew 23:17 (*stulti et caeci*), and Ecclesiastes 1:15 could only have confirmed his conviction that the senseless were too numerous to count. Since pride and ambition, which turn men away from reason and wisdom and cause them to lose all proportion, were so widespread, how could Thomas's world have been anything other than populated by fools, idiots, and madmen? *Stultus, stolidus, fatuus, insanus, vesanus, demens, furiosus, freneticus; ebetudo, insipientia, stulitia, stoliditas, fatuitas, insania, vesania, dementia, rabies, saevitia.* Thomas Basin's vocabulary was remarkably abundant when it came to describing the legions of those who, ranging from the most doltish to the most frenzied, suffered alike from want of wisdom. In old age Thomas Basin's obsessions were stupidity and madness.

Hatred (*odium*) is also ubiquitous in Thomas's writings. Many events would have been incomprehensible to him had it not been for baseless hatred,[561] ancient hatred,[562] old hatred,[563] inveterate hatred,[564] innate, hereditary, and natural hatred,[565] implacable hatred,[566] or reciprocal hatred.[567] For him such hatreds are the primary data of history; hatred between princes, as between John the Fearless and Louis d'Orléans; hatred between factions, such as the Armagnacs and Burgundians; hatred between a prince and his subjects, like the hatred that drove the inhabitants of Cologne, Liège, and Utrecht to rebel against their bishops; hatred of a people for a neighboring prince or people. There was hatred between the English and the Scots,[568] and between the Liégeois and the Burgundians.[569] And of course there was hatred between the French and English. In the middle of the century the English "were the very ancient and somehow natural enemies of this land and this people." They felt "an inveterate and somehow innate hatred" of the French. The French paid them back in kind. And this mutual hatred grew fiercer every day.[570]

Finally, ambition, stupidity, madness, and hatred drove man to his worst acts: bad faith, perjury, treachery, treason. For Thomas Basin good faith (*fides*) was essential. Thomas quotes Cicero to the effect that loyalty is the foundation of friendship. It alone guarantees stability.[571] But Cicero also said, and Thomas Basin repeats, that loyalty is the foundation of justice.[572] It alone guarantees peace and tranquillity in a state.[573] So great is Thomas's hatred of fraud and deception that he will not allow them under any circumstances. Not even the justest of causes justifies deception, fraud, or perjury. Recall how severely Thomas judged the French use of deception to gain the advantage over the English. In keeping with these principles, he condemns the count of Armagnac, who "by ruse and deception" recaptured the city of Lectoure in 1472, even though Thomas knows perfectly well that the city "belonged to him by law."[574] Shortly thereafter, moreover, the same count of Armagnac was killed in violation of a solemn promise. The murder put an end to the count's crimes and oppression. Thomas continues: "It is quite true that no punishment would have been too harsh for the many enormous crimes he committed, but that he should have been executed (no matter how justly) by means of such treachery and perfidy no decent and upright man can hear without horror. Indeed, it is not enough to desire and observe what is good and just; it must be accomplished by just means, exempt from crimes and shameful acts. On that all the sages and philosophers are in accord with the Bible, which says, 'What is just shalt thou do justly'."[575] For Thomas Basin, the end never justifies the means.

Thomas was therefore devastated by the treachery of peoples: of the "very ambitious, very greedy, and most perfidious" Bretons, whose "treason" played a large part in the Norman disaster of 1465,[576] and of the English, "that perfidious people, more changeable than the waves of the unbridled sea,"[577] who so often betrayed their kings. Above all, however, Thomas was devastated by the treachery of princes. He repeated the words of Psalm 146:2, "*Nolite confidere in principibus*" (Put not your trust in princes), each time events confirmed his pessimism.[578] Immense was his morose pleasure whenever he was able to show treacherous princes betrayed by still more treacherous ones. According to a saying common among jurists at the time, "*Nil Judeus Judeo, nil dolosus doloso*" (A Jew cannot be the Jew of another Jew; there is no deceit among deceivers).[579]

And in this deceitful world, Louis XI was the most deceitful of all. Greedy and ambitious, cruel and demented, this tyrant was considered remarkably treacherous and volatile by nearly all princes and peoples.[580] In his own eyes Thomas's failure therefore had a remarkably simple explanation: good faith had been overcome by bad.

Was it that simple? After all, by Thomas Basin's own admission, Louis XI had reasons for his grudge against him. The bishop of Lisieux had denounced the dauphin's intrigues to Charles VII shortly before the king's death.[581] For Thomas Basin, that denunciation was proof of loyalty, a sign that he was a man whom a king could trust. But Louis XI was not a king willing to forget what had been done to the dauphin.

There was also the brief treatise that Thomas had sent Louis XI shortly after his coronation, urgently recommending that the new king reduce the size of his army.[582] Faithful to his unwavering principles, Thomas had merely repeated what he had always said: that a king concerned about his subjects' rights and possessions ought to reduce the size of his army. But when Louis XI was obliged four years later to do battle with the princes of the league, he remembered Thomas Basin's advice and found it highly irritating. Indignant at that irritation, Thomas pleaded good faith. He had advised the king to reduce the size of his army in 1461, not in 1465. Yet Louis XI resented that counsel "as if, when at his request I offered him my advice, that is, when, after receiving holy unction at Rheims, he entered his royal city of Paris for the first time, I had any way of knowing that civil war would erupt against him."[583] Thomas Basin saw himself as a man of good faith. But Louis XI, who placed little credence in good faith, surely saw him as frightfully naive, if not treacherous, as Thomas's attitude in 1465 seemed to confirm.

Of course Louis XI was also betrayed by many other subjects, whom he later pardoned and who to their own benefit served him well. Why, then, did the king never make amends with "a man of such great merit"?[584] Thomas Basin was a good administrator. His *Apology* shows him exhibiting the greatest concern for his own financial interests. All his work reflects a man of integrity, a careful bookkeeper concerned to keep precise accounts. As bishop of Lisieux and chancellor in Perpignan he demonstrated his administrative abilities. In Lisieux in 1449 and in 1465 he proved to be a shrewd negotiator. The manner of his resignation as bishop proves that he could even be a tenacious negotiator. And this man of talent was not an isolated individual. Although Thomas is very discreet about his associates, it is clear that there were many people on whom he could count both in Normandy and at court. In Normandy his brothers never failed him. And Charles, after becoming duke of Guyenne, intervened on Thomas's behalf with his brother the king. Louis XI could have made good use of Thomas as he did of so many others. In fact he did make good use of him, by sending him to Perpignan. To explain Thomas Basin's failure, then, we must consider not so much Louis XI as Thomas Basin himself. In any case, the problem is not to explain how a good servant of Charles VII came to grief under Louis XI. We know that Thomas's role under Charles VII was minimal. Thomas Basin's fate was implicit in his personality.

Thomas Basin was unsuited to serve the king because he was an incurable naïf, a man of good faith inevitably undone by bad faith and constantly surprised by the changing winds of political life. What is more, this naïf was not prepared to make the slightest concession. He truly wished to serve the king. But he did not wish to renounce his ideas. And his ideas, to put it mildly, were not in accord with the times.

Thomas Basin loved his country; he was not prepared to die for it. Thomas Basin wished to obey his king; he did not have that mystical faith in obedience that lay at the source of so many brilliant careers, past and present, in church and state. Above king and country, Thomas Basin placed the law. And his devotion to the law fostered a wariness of princes, invariably propelled toward tyranny by their desire to dominate. His chief concern was to defend the rights and liberties of the people against princes—the French people for one, which he loved and yet, owing to the exigencies of meter, described as a "fine flock oppressed by treachery" (*Perfidia insignis . . . / Formosi oppressor pecoris nequissimus*).[585] But above all he defended the Norman people, to whom he returned in 1441, whom he protected by every means available to him in 1449, and for whom he dreamed of a duchy in 1465. The deep reason for Thomas Basin's failure was that his ideas were ill adapted to the forces that dominated his time.

There was also a humbler reason for his failure. In 1467, when Louis XI as was his wont sent Thomas Basin away to test his mettle, the bishop of Lisieux was fifty-five years old. He tired easily. He no longer felt fit for long trips. He was afraid of illness and fevers. To this Norman bishop, a summer in Perpignan seemed like a season in hell. It was his refusal to endure a second such summer that was the immediate cause of his final disaster. But was it an accident that, even after Thomas returned to a more temperate clime, he still remarked frequently on the weather, something he had never done before? The summer of 1473 was "particularly hot and dry up to the month of October."[586] The winter of 1474 was "a very harsh winter that lacked neither rain nor ice nor snow."[587] And the winter of 1479 "was particularly hard and painful."[588] Thomas Basin was never a man of action. But if Louis XI did not make more of an effort to use his services, perhaps the reason was that Thomas was now too old to be a useful servant.

One might imagine other causes of Thomas Basin's difficulties. But why not listen to Thomas himself? Why think that the basic cause was other than what Thomas repeatedly says it was, and that all his work seeks to justify? The reason why he was so slow to return to France in 1466 was that he was afraid. The reason why he fled so hastily two years later, when he left France for the last time in 1468, was that he was afraid. The whole story can be summed up in two sentences. Thomas Basin wrote in order to justify his flight. And he justified his flight by proclaiming his fear.

Our astonishment is excusable, and in order to dispel it we must first understand that fear in the Middle Ages was not always the contemptible emotion it is considered today, when few people will admit to having experienced it. There were several Latin words for fear, including *metus, timor,* and *pavor.* These words were often exact synonyms and could be used interchangeably. But each was also used to convey its own specific sense and in its own specific context. *Pavor* refers specifically to terror or dread, to that immediate, irrational, and disastrous fear that no one would ever boast of having felt. From *pavor* came the Old French *paour* and the modern French *peur,* fear. In medieval Latin, however, it was not a common word. It was used much less frequently than the two words classically used to express fear in both antiquity and the Middle Ages, namely, *metus* and *timor.*

The Vulgate uses *metus* on occasion but *timor* far more commonly to denote fear. And the fear mentioned in the Bible is a noble emotion. From the Bible Christians learned to see fear or dread as a virtue. "*Beatus homo qui semper est pavidus* [Blessed is the man who fears the Lord always]," according to Proverbs 28:14. And Ecclesiasticus 18:27 says "*Homo sapiens in omnibus metuet* [The wise man is always afraid]." Above all he is always afraid of God. To be sure, it is better to love God than to fear him. "There is no fear in love, but perfect love casts out fear" (1 John 4:18). Until that far-off day when perfection triumphs, however, wisdom begins with fear of God: "*Initium sapientiae timor Domini.*"[589] The just man fears God. He is *timoratus,* as it was expressed in Latin throughout the Middle Ages[590] and repeated by Thomas Basin.[591] He is *timoré,* as it was said in French, at least in the sixteenth century.

As Paul said in Romans 13:1–7, all power comes from God; the prince is God's minister. Because he is God's minister tribute must be paid to him, and for the same reason he must be feared.

> Reddite omnibus debita
> Cui tributum tributum
> Cui vectigal vectigal
> Cui timorem timorem
> Cui honorem honorem.

[Render therefore to all their dues; tribute to whom tribute is due; custom to whom custom; fear to whom fear; honor to whom honor.]

And in Ephesians 6:5 Paul also says: "*Servi oboedite dominis carnalibus cum timore et tremore* [Servants, be obedient to them that are your masters according to the flesh, with fear and trembling]." Thus *timor* is fear in general, but it is also, in particular, *timor Dei* and *timor principis,* fear of God and fear of the prince, the surest path to wisdom, the best encouragement to obedience, the best cement for political society. For the just and wise man there is no abasement (*minoratio*) in such fear; it ought to be his pride (*gloriatio*).[592]

Such was the good fear (*timor*) that the Bible encouraged in the Middle Ages. As a Christian, Thomas Basin was heir to this long tradition. He knew the beneficial effects of fear. He was proud of being *timoratus.* But Thomas Basin was also a jurist. Roman and canon law also dealt with fear, for which in this context the word was *metus.* The law's laudable aim was to protect the weak, to which end it laid down the principle that anything done as a result of force or fear (*vi metuve*) could be annulled by a judge. It could be annulled, that is, provided that the fear was real and not "vain," and provided that it afflicted not a "timid" or fearful man but one who was steadfast and firm (*in hominem constantissimum; in virum constantem*). To jurists, then, fear was a perfectly admissible, legitimate, and justifiable emotion, the consequences of which it was up to the courts to negate. Now, in the violent circumstances of the Middle Ages, not only was this principle ever more broadly applied, but also the need for a judge's decision to nullify its effects diminished steadily. Increasingly, whatever was done as a result of force or fear was seen as having no value for that very reason. As a jurist, Thomas Basin was well aware of what Roman and canon law said on the subject of fear. He was thoroughly familiar with the practice of his day. And in 1453 he had used his knowledge of both law and practice to make his case for nullification of the judgment against Joan of Arc.[593]

For Thomas Basin, however, fear was not simply a legal argument. As a man steeped in Roman law, canon law, and the Bible and as a witness to so many tragedies and to so much violence, he knew that fear was a basic emotion experienced by all men, even, perhaps especially, the wise. The wise man properly felt fear (*timor*) of God and of his prince. In the face of a tyrant,[594] enemy,[595] or unruly mob he felt legitimate fear (*metus*). It was normal for the wise man to fear the wrath of the tyrant or the frenzy of the mob and only natural for him to admit his fear. In recounting, several years after the fact, the disturbances he had witnessed in Utrecht, Thomas wrote this noteworthy sentence: "*Eramus ipsi tunc in civitate, non sine metu* [I was in the city then, not without fear]."[596] In many cases it was permissible for the wise man to feel fear; indeed, it would be folly not to.[597]

Thus anyone might be afraid. The distinguishing mark of the wise man was that, though afraid, he acted wisely. The first thing to do was to keep quiet. During the troubles in Utrecht (1481–83), the unfortunate city was in the power of most cruel tyrants (*erat misera civitas sub sevissimorum tyrannorum potestatem redacta*). Decent men kept silent. Fear (*metus*) and threats shut their mouths.[598] Once, when Louis XI, dealing with some important issue, received an embassy from a province of the kingdom, his attitude was so threatening and his words were so dreadful that the petitioners, "stricken with terror, chose most often to keep quiet rather than say what they had in mind."[599]

First keep quiet, then give in. Thomas Basin consistently argued that for a city incapable of resisting or an army threatened with defeat it was better to surrender than to risk destruction. He prided himself on twice having obtained the best possible terms before surrendering Lisieux. Of course Thomas was bishop. But in July 1450 Caen came under fire from French artillery: "The English captains, . . . wisely [*prudenter*] considering how easily the citadel, though remarkably well defended by moats, walls, towers, and fortins, could be attacked if the other machines similarly smashed walls and towers, averted danger [*periculo obviam euntes*] by asking for . . . a suspension of hostilities."[600] Or consider the cities of the duchy of Guelders, invaded by the duke of Burgundy in 1473. Nijmegen, the most powerful and populous of all, fell. Terrified, the inhabitants of the other cities saw that they were far less capable of mounting serious resistance than the people of Nijmegen and therefore "prudently averted danger [*periculis prudenter obviam euntes*]" by paying what was asked of them.[601]

Another noteworthy example concerns the troubles in Utrecht in 1481–83. Rebels had seized control of the city. The bishop, legitimate lord of the city, imposed an interdict: no divine service was to be celebrated. The canons of the cathedral decided to observe the interdict. Upon learning of this decision, the rebels invaded the cathedral's capitulary hall where all the clergy had assembled. Thomas Basin reports what happened: "Like wild beasts and roaring lions, they issued orders, backed by threats, that the divine service just interrupted be resumed at once and completed in the normal manner, or else they would massacre [the clergy] without mercy and allow the mercenaries, there present and armed and ready, to exterminate the clerics as soon as the order was given, to ransack their homes and property." It was not astonishing (*nec mirum*), Thomas Basin continued, that the canons were gripped by the fear to which even the most steadfast of men can succumb (*metu qui certe merito in quemvis eciam constantissimum virum cadere potuisset*) when confronting a present as opposed to a future danger (*periculum non comminatum in futurum sed presens*). Hence the canons, compelled by force and fear (*talibus vi ac metu urgentibus*) resumed the suspended service "*pro tempore*"[602] In classical Latin *pro tempore* meant "because of circumstances." In Thomas Basin's Latin it probably meant something closer to "for a time." In this case the phrase may have had something of both meanings, since both fit Thomas's argument quite well.

Thomas's narrative is indeed an argument. It is noteworthy for what it says, but still more noteworthy for the words it uses. It cites the exact words of the Digest IV, II, 6 (*Metum . . . qui merito in hominem constantissimum cadat*) and IV, II, 9 (*Metum . . . praesentem*) as well as of the Code II, XX (*vi metusve causa*). In repeating verbatim these texts of Roman law, Thomas Basin's intention was clearly to signal to informed readers that what the canons had been forced to do by violence and fear was null and void. The wise man has every reason to save his life by giving in to violence and fear, all the more so in that what he does in such circumstances is invalid and will be denounced as soon as the violence and fear cease.

Violence can obtain any end, but as Cicero said long ago, nothing obtained by violence can last. By force (*vi*) the English had conquered Normandy, where their sovereignty was legitimate (*Normannie imperium*). The Normans had accepted that sovereignty in the grip of fear (*metu . . . premente*). But the moment they were able to destroy the harsh servitude of fear and violence (*duram metus atque violencie servitutem*), they returned to the old and natural sovereignty of France.[603] Fifteen years later, in 1465, Louis XI was compelled to sign the treaties of Conflans and Saint-Maur *per vim et metum.* He denounced them as soon as he could.[604] Later, Charles the Bold had seized several châteaux from the duke of Lorraine. Instead of leaving garrisons, however, he entrusted these citadels to local people or nobles who swore an oath of loyalty to him. But these Lorrains abandoned him and returned to their duke as soon as they were able to do so. Thomas Basin is not surprised by this behavior. They loved their duke. They took the oath to Charles the Bold reluctantly (*inviti*), compelled to do so by force and fear (*vi ac metu adacti*). Charles the Bold should have known better than to count on or place much hope in such a fragile guarantee.[605] A man had to know how to surrender. Surrender saved lives. It did not foreclose the future. The canons of Utrecht were indeed right to resume divine services because of the circumstances and for a time, *pro tempore.*

Some of the canons, however, adopted a different but equally wise solution. Thomas Basin ends his account with this sentence: "Several of them meanwhile absented themselves, leaving it to lower-ranking members of the clergy to discharge these duties."[606] Thomas frequently mentions such calculated escapes. After a battle soldiers make a necessary escape (*per fugam necessarium*).[607] In 1466 Charles, duke of Normandy, flees to the protection of the duke of Brittany, while others are wrong not to flee in time (*de tempestiva fuga*).[608] In Utrecht in 1483 a prudent (*prudens*) man would have been torn to pieces by the mob had he not absented himself in time (*nisi mature se absentando*) by making a secret getaway (*per occultam fugam*).[609]

To flee danger is an act of prudence according to Ecclesiasticus 9:13: "Keep far from the man who has the power to kill, and you will not be worried by the fear of death [*metum mortis*]." And Thomas Basin repeats it.[610] "When they persecute you in one town, flee to the next," says Matthew 10:23, and Thomas repeats the passage twice.[611] On God's orders Joseph fled to Egypt to avoid the tyrant's cruelty. The apostle Paul was wise enough to flee the governor of Damascus (*per fugam sibi sapienter consuluit*). The apostle Peter, imprisoned in Jerusalem and warned by an angel of his impending torture, manages to flee. And the Gospels often say that Christ fled to avoid persecution since the day and the hour had not yet come when, in accordance with divine plan, he was to face death for man's redemption. Countless saints had taken these precepts to heart and escaped the violence of their persecutors. Athanasius, patriarch of Alexandria, fled the fury of Constantius. Saint Euchier, bishop of Orléans, fled Charles Martel. Saint Thomas, bishop of Canterbury, "not unreasonably fearing the wrath of the king of England (*regis Anglorum adversum se indignacionem non ab re metuens*)," also fled. In truth, to neglect the human means available to us in order to avoid persecution, not to flee in case of danger, would be a form of cowardice (*ignaviter*) and a grave sin; it would be nothing other than to tempt God (*non aliud esset quam temptare Deum*).[612]

And Thomas Basin had not wanted to tempt God. He had experienced that legitimate fear (*non immerito metuentes*)[613] that can befall even a steadfast man (*metus . . . qui cadere debeat vel possit in virum constantem*).[614] He had wished to avoid the tyrant's fury and cruelty.[615] He had fled.

One final objection might be raised against him, however: that while a pastor, he had abandoned his flock. To this charge he answered: "In truth, it is sufficiently proved by the precept of the Lord and by his example, as well as by the examples of many venerable prelates and numerous saints, that it is permissible and not reprehensible to avoid the cruelty of one's persecutors by taking flight and hiding in the three following cases: when the persecution is directed exclusively at the prelate's person; when the faith of the people is not threatened; and when other members of the clergy can fill the role of the absent pastor."[616]

Thus we can see the deeper meaning of Thomas Basin's work. It is written in praise of proper and legitimate fear. It is an apology for escape.

Cicero and Horace had exalted those who died for their country. Following in their footsteps, poets in the twelfth century, theologians in the thirteenth century, and humanists in the fourteenth century had said that a good citizen ought to risk his life for the sake of the state.[617] Those who had died at Crécy, Poitiers, Agincourt, and Verneuil had set an example of supreme sacrifice. If this heroic atmosphere were that of the fifteenth century, Thomas Basin's work would be, in some respects, incomprehensible and scandalous. Instead, however, and upon reflection, it helps us to avoid a misinterpretation of the late Middle Ages. In this dangerous time, when man was daily threatened by nature, disease, and the violence of other men, the atmosphere was not heroic. Man's imperious duty was to survive. Fear was a familiar feeling, and when a man felt afraid, wisdom counseled flight. Once we realize this, we quickly discover that Thomas Basin was hardly the only person who wrote in praise of escape.

At Poitiers in 1356 John the Good had not fled, and the result had been disaster for France. Ten years earlier, however, his father Philip VI had fled at Crécy. And in 1417, in a letter to Nicolas de Clamanges, Jean de Montreuil, patriot and humanist though he was, had called that flight most prudent (*perprudens aufugium*). I call that flight prudent, he stressed, because obviously there was no remedy. Caesar, too, had fled (*fugisse*) a lost battle and thus lived to triumph another day.[618] Some years earlier, Jean de Montreuil's correspondent, Nicolas de Clamanges, though a cleric and humanist, had written a remarkable letter in the aftermath of a plague epidemic that had nearly killed him. In the event of plague, he told his correspondent, the only remedy is to flee the contaminated place in time (*loca infecta tempestive fugere*). Nicolas had an uncle who was the only physician in Châlons-sur-Marne. In 1399, when Nicolas learned that the plague had come to Châlons, he immediately wrote his uncle that he should look to his own safety rather than to that of others and therefore should leave the city at once. To Nicolas's dismay, however, the uncle had perhaps trusted too much in his art. Perhaps, too, he had deemed it unfitting to flee at such a time. He was dead wrong. He had thought he might treat others; in fact he was one of the first to die. *Fuge loca infecta*, Nicolas concluded. "Flee contaminated places."[619]

Later, under Louis XI, many great lords, contemporaries of Thomas Basin's, had told the interrogating judge quite simply that they had been or were still "in great dread [*en grant crainte*]" or "in great fear and great dread [*en grant paour et en grans craintes*]."[620] And being afraid, many had wanted to do what wisdom commanded in such cases. They had wanted to flee. Few, however, had managed to do so. And Philippe de Commynes explains why: "I have seen few men in my life who knew how to flee in time, whether here or elsewhere. Some had no hope of finding welcome and security in neighboring countries; others loved their property, their wives, and their children too much."[621]

The "timely" flight advocated by Philippe de Commynes was precisely the timely (*tempestive*) flight that Nicolas de Clamanges recommended in the event of plague, and it was precisely the *fuga tempestiva,* the flight *ad tempus,* that Thomas Basin recommended in the event of danger.[622] What distinguished Thomas from his contemporaries was not that he had felt fear and not that he had fled. It was that he had been clever enough to flee in time. It was also that he spoke so well, and at such great length, about the then commonplace emotion of fear and about its equally commonplace remedy, flight.

Yet nothing could prevent the happy fugitive, comfortable in exile, from being also a bitter old man disappointed with his life.

The Final Years (1472–90)

Thomas Basin was still in Trier and had just finished his *Apology* when, late in 1475, the sad end of Louis of Luxemburg, count of Saint-Pol and constable of France, confirmed his blackest pessimism. Louis had been born in 1418, the son of Peter of Luxemburg and grandson of John of Luxemburg, himself the brother of the young and saintly cardinal Peter of Luxemburg whom Pierre d'Ailly had known so well. John, the grandfather, died in 1397, survived by several children, including Peter and John II, the man who would capture Joan of Arc and hand her over to the English. Peter, Louis's father, died in 1433. In that year, at the age of fifteen, Louis of Luxemburg therefore became count of Saint-Pol and Ligny and castellan of Lille. In 1435 he married a wealthy heiress who was countess of Marle and Soissons, viscountess of Meaux, and lady of Oisy, Dunkirk, Bourbourg, Gravelines, Bournhen, Alluye, and Montmirail. At seventeen Louis of Luxemburg was a very wealthy lord.

It was a tradition in the house of Luxemburg to serve the house of Burgundy and to derive from that service both honor and profit. Peter, Louis's father, had been a knight of the Golden Fleece. So had John II, Louis's uncle. And James, Louis's brother, would one day become a knight of the Golden Fleece.[623] Louis's ambition was to make his fortune by serving the king of France and the duke of Burgundy. After the peace of Arras, this was not an easy game to play, but it was still possible. Louis of Luxemburg succeeded at it. He was in favor at the court of Charles VII as well as that of Philip the Good.

Louis of Luxemburg believed that he could continue to prosper by alternating his commitments between Louis XI and Charles the Bold and by engaging in discreet deception. In 1465, during the War of the Public Weal, he supported the princes. At the end of the war Louis XI attempted to win his allegiance by naming him constable (October 5, 1465), governor of Champagne, Brie, and Ile-de-France, and captain of Rouen. Since Louis of Luxemburg's first wife had died in 1462, Louis XI arranged for him to marry the queen's sister, Marie of Savoy (July–November 1466) and for the occasion made him a gift of the county of Guise. As a result of this marriage a man who had been only Louis XI's "dear and beloved cousin, the count of Saint Pol" or "handsome cousin of Saint Pol"[624] now became "our beloved and loyal brother and cousin the count of Saint Pol" or "our very dear and most beloved brother and cousin the count of Saint Pol, constable of France" or "handsome brother the constable" or *delictissimum fratrem et consanguineum nostrum comitem Sancti Poli comestabularium.*[625] In April 1469 Louis XI included Louis of Luxemburg in his Order of Saint Michael. In 1471 he rewarded him with the county of Eu.[626] Louis of Luxemburg was a happy man. He was the king's brother. He was immensely rich and immensely powerful. And God had given him seven children by his first wife, two by his second wife, and eight bastards.

But the hopes that Louis XI had placed in Louis of Luxemburg were soon disappointed. In appearance Louis of Luxemburg served the king. On November 9, 1469, he ordered the ducal ring of Normandy to be broken in front of the Exchequer.[627] In fact, however, the constable was playing his own private game and betraying both the king and the duke of Burgundy. And before long, bitterness envenomed the atmosphere between the king, the duke, and the count. The duke detested the count. The count was wary of both the duke and the king. And the king hated the count, particularly after the count insulted him in an unforgettable way in May 1474. At that time, Louis XI, hoping to regain his constable's loyalty, had asked as was his wont for a face-to-face meeting. Louis of Luxemburg agreed. The king and his constable met at Fargniers, not far from Laon.[628] But the constable came with an escort of horsemen as large as the king's. Haunted by the tragic end of other such interviews, moreover, the constable had asked that a barrier be erected between him and his king. Louis XI angrily resented this insult, inflicted on him by a man who may have been his brother but who surely was his subject and servant. He did not forget it.[629]

As long as the king of France and the duke of Burgundy were at odds, the count of Saint-Pol could survive as an independent. In August 1475, however, Louis XI and Edward IV signed the Treaty of Picquigny. A few days later, in September, Louis XI and Charles the Bold signed a truce. At the time Louis of Luxemburg was in his castle at Ham, a fortress surrounded by stout walls and moats. But it was inside France. The constable distrusted the king more than the duke. He asked the duke for safe-conduct, obtained it, and took refuge at Mons in Hainault in the duke's territory, where he believed he was safe.[630] But the duke, who needed Louis XI's neutrality for his campaign in Lorraine, delivered Louis of Luxemburg up to the king's men on November 24 "and furthermore [lent] all the sealed documents and letters he had from the constable to serve in his trial."[631] The trial in Parlement went rapidly, particularly since the constable's treachery and treason were proven by his own admission, by letters signed by him and sealed with his seal, as well as by other irrefutable evidence.[632] On December 19 Louis of Luxemburg was sentenced to death and immediately executed on the place de Grève. Louis XI wanted a spectacular execution to serve as an example. In his remote exile Thomas Basin received a long account of the constable's torture, which he faithfully repeats.[633]

The historian lays great stress on the punishment of the count of Saint-Pol because to him the drama seems exemplary. Of the three double-dealers involved, Louis XI is the one of whom Thomas is, for once, least critical. After all, the king did nothing but prosecute and after due process condemn a servant who had betrayed him. But Louis of Luxemburg, a man of such illustrious origins and said to be the richest man in France, instead of recognizing that he had enough honors and wealth had aspired to still more (*ad ampliora inhians*); he had been blinded by insatiable greed, and he had committed treason. His ambition and treason were properly punished. The most treacherous of all, however, was Charles the Bold, who had delivered up a man to whom he had given his word of honor. That was the most shameful betrayal of all. Until now Thomas Basin has shown nothing but sympathy for the house of Burgundy. Now, however, he denounces Charles the Bold, and he has no doubt that Charles's fall was punishment for his infamous deed. "The count, seeking refuge and protection, had fled to the duke, who had promised him full security. But the duke had betrayed the count. Now, in return, it was as if he wanted for divine protection, which had previously bestowed its benefits in times of great and manifest danger. For him there was to be no more good fortune or success but only misfortune and reverses until he was massacred and his army destroyed."[634]

Charles the Bold was in fact defeated and killed near Nancy on January 5, 1477. Always positive and rational, Thomas Basin notes at the end of his *History of Louis XI* that many people were crazy or foolish enough to doubt that Charles truly had died. That doubt endured for several days, he wrote in 1477. But several years later, in revising his text, he expressed his astonishment at what he had written. Several days! he exclaims. What am I saying? The doubts lingered on for months or even years. Thomas is aghast at such foolish credulity.[635]

On June 4, 1477, Thomas arrived, a refugee, in Utrecht, where he soon passed some anxious days. Louis XI's successes filled him with bitterness. Utrecht's troubles filled him with fear. Early in 1483, however, he experienced a moment of joy. On December 23, 1482, the Treaty of Arras had been signed. Thanks to the Flemish, Louis XI had obtained from Charles the Bold's son-in-law Maximilian of Hapsburg far more than he had hoped. Unfortunately, this triumph came to Louis XI at a time when he "was already very low."[636] At the beginning of 1483 Thomas Basin had just turned seventy. His health, however, was good. He was a robust old man (*senex*). Louis XI was one of those whom Thomas Basin called *senex et satis gradevus, senex et jam grandevus.*[637] He was old. He was about to turn sixty. But he was done in not so much by age as by disease. He was paralyzed on his right side. He spoke with difficulty. He carried his right arm in a sling across his chest. He had only a few months to live. He did not want to be seen in such a state. The sight of a victorious king vanquished by disease might strike us as tragic or pitiful. In 1483 it was the cause of much mirth, particularly in Thomas Basin.

In any case, the Treaty of Arras had been signed on December 23, 1482. The king then had to swear to abide by it. Early in 1483 Flanders sent a formal embassy to receive the king's oath. The ambassadors told an amusing tale of their interview, just the sort of thing to relieve Thomas's morosity, and he faithfully recounts what he was told: "One night the ambassadors were ushered into a small bedroom. The king sat in a corner where he could barely be seen." He greeted his visitors in a ridiculous manner (*ridicula salutacione*). He begged pardon for the fact that he could not get up or remove his hat. These humble words, uttered in such a ridiculous (*ridicule*) fashion, were so ill suited to the majesty of a sovereign that it was difficult not to burst out laughing (*a risu*) on hearing them, and in fact the witnesses of the scene were convulsed with laughter (*cachinando*). The king then had to take the oath. He touched the Bible with his left hand. Then, with effort, he touched it with his right elbow. And his gesture was so ridiculous (*multum ridicule*) that the witnesses could not help laughing (*ita ut videntes a risu temperare non possent*).[638] This was an age afraid of force and violence, but it felt no pity for weakness and old age.

Thomas Basin was even more overjoyed when he heard that Louis XI had died on August 30, 1483. Would he return to France? The death of Louis XI made it possible to do so.[639] But that death had also triggered a period of political unrest. The new king, Louis XI's son Charles VIII, was only thirteen. The king's eldest daughter, Anne, was only twenty-two, but her husband, Pierre de Beaujeu, was forty-three. He was a powerful and experienced lord, schooled by his father-in-law. For a time the Beaujeus were the real heirs of Louis XI. They withstood the reaction unleashed by his death. They held the ambitions of the grandees in check. Their most powerful adversary was Louis, the young duke of Orléans. Louis d'Orléans was twenty-one, the son of the late Duke Charles, the poet, the grandson of Duke Louis, assassinated in 1407, and the great-grandson of Charles V. After Charles VIII he was next in line to inherit the throne (and in fact he did become king in 1498 under the name Louis XII). In 1483 he was also the unhappy husband of Jeanne de France. Born in 1464, Jeanne was the daughter of Louis XI and the sister of Anne de Beaujeu and Charles VIII. In 1476 Louis XI had forced the young duke of Orléans, then fourteen, to marry little Jeanne, then twelve. The young duke thus became the husband of a saintly but incredibly ugly woman. Louis XII later claimed that the marriage was never consummated. For the time being it made the heir apparent the king's "brother," a redoubtable adversary for the Beaujeus.

The situation called for the convocation of the Estates General, which met in Tours from January 5 to March 14, 1484. There was much talk, including talk of reform. But above all there was conflict in a narrow area between the Beaujeus and the duke of Orléans. Before separating, the Estates were obliged to assent to a substantial tax. Thomas Basin was aware of all these events. He knew about the power struggles. He knew about the approval of the *taille.* The taxless, armyless state of which he long had dreamed was still a long way from reality. And the power struggles among the great promised new troubles ahead. Thomas was then seventy-one. Utrecht had been subdued by its legitimate lord, Bishop David, a bastard of Philip the Good. David and Thomas Basin, classmates at Louvain, had been friends for fifty years. Thomas's brother Nicolas was still living in Utrecht. And Thomas had become accustomed to this northern country, whose language he had learned.[640] He had no wish to commit himself once more to the uncertain tides of fortune.[641] In May 1484 he returned to Utrecht, where he had a comfortable house built to shelter him in his old age. He was still living there in 1488 when, at the age of seventy-five, he wrote his *Breviloquium.* And there he hoped that divine mercy would allow him to remain until the time came to enter the promised land—where there was no fear but no life either.[642]

God did allow Thomas Basin to die in Utrecht shortly thereafter. In the few, finally tranquil years left to him, the septuagenarian turned his still alert mind to other problems that excited his contemporaries but that had previously been of little interest to him—and with which he was poorly prepared to deal. Thomas Basin was neither a theologian nor a calendarist nor a mathematician. He had not explored either of the two aspects of astrology: the study of the stars' movements or the deduction of men's destinies. Yet at the end of his life he did not hesitate to enter into the great debates raging among theologians and computists, mathematicians and astrologers.

The fundamental problem was still the one that Pierre d'Ailly had attacked at the end of his life but that the Council of Constance had neglected in favor of more urgent tasks, namely, the problem of the calendar. In 325 the Council of Nicaea had fixed the date of the vernal equinox as March 21. There was, however, a slight discrepancy between the astronomical year and the calendar year. The astronomical year was nearly six hours longer. The addition of a bissextile day every four years was slightly too much of a correction, for it meant that the astronomical year was now shorter than the calendar year by a few minutes, so that every 128 years the astronomical year gained one day on the calendar year. In the time of Dante the vernal equinox fell on March 13. At the end of the fifteenth century it fell on March 11.[643]

This ten-day discrepancy posed no major problem in everyday life. It was, however, a major problem in the life of the Church. The Council of Nicaea had established that Easter would be celebrated on the first Sunday after the full moon occurring on or after the vernal equinox, that is, between March 22 and April 25. Now that there was a discrepancy of ten days between the vernal equinox and March 21, however, it was certain that the resurrection of Christ was not being celebrated on the Sunday prescribed by the Nicaean fathers. This was intolerable.

In the last twenty-five years of the fifteenth century calendar reform therefore became the subject of a great controversy involving theologians, calendarists, and astrologers. This debate revived another controversy that had never really been settled: On what day was Christ crucified? On what day was he resurrected? The debate further swelled—if such a thing can be believed—the pride of the astrologers, who, encouraged by the interests of the powerful and the fervor of the humble, determined the positions of the stars, planned the reform of the calendar, produced innumerable prognostications and almanacs enabling one and all to predict the future, and drafted learned treatises heralding the end of the world.

One of the humblest soldiers in the army of astrologers was a nameless Carthusian from Ruremonde. In 1485 he wrote a brief treatise in which the position of the stars served to prove that the Antichrist had been born in 1472 and that in 1503 the human race would be called to face the final judgment. This Carthusian asked his bishop, the bishop of Utrecht, for permission to publish his treatise. At a loss, the bishop, David, asked the advice of his friend Thomas.

On April 26, 1486, Thomas Basin answered with a letter marked by the same firmness and clarity as the rest of his writing as well as by the solidity of his orthodox faith.[644] The good brother had displayed presumption and temerity. He was obviously stupid, even crazy. Thomas Basin had no doubt that the man had a deranged mind (*cerebro turbatum*).

Every Christian ought to shun the vainglory of publication. On this point Thomas must have been sincere, since he did not publish either his *History of Charles VII* or his *History of Louis XI* and made no mention of himself. And was it not particularly strange to find such vainglory in a monk who had withdrawn from the world and professed contempt for the things in it?

Perhaps the Carthusian had another reason for wanting to publish his treatise. Perhaps he wished to strike fear into the hearts of the faithful so that, thus frightened (*magno et vehementi pavore deterritos fideles*) by the news that the Antichrist had already been born, they might do penance with greater ardor. But the Carthusian was wrong. The apostle said it well. One must not do evil in the hope of doing good. To lie is wrong. And to deceive in matters of faith is the most pernicious of lies.

The Carthusian, moreover, did more than just lie. For as Christ said, no one knows the hour when the son of man will come or when the world will end. Astrology can study the movements of heavenly bodies, but it cannot deduce that which depends solely on man's free choice or God's will. At this point Thomas invoked, not without pride, the authority of the man "who had once been bishop of Lisieux, [his] predecessor, Master Nicolas Oresme."

Thomas then conjured up two memories from his youth. He had been a child in Rennes when Vincent Ferrier had preached there. Friar Vincent, a Dominican, asserted that the Antichrist had been or was about to be born. He was wrong. Yet he had performed so many miracles that Pope Calixtus III (1455–58) made him a saint. Somewhat later, now almost sixty years ago, Thomas Basin had been a student of arts in Paris. Friar Richart, a Franciscan, preached that the Antichrist had been born and that the Day of Judgment was near. He had made many other erroneous statements as well, and the faculty of arts had wanted to prosecute. He fled.

Thomas Basin was a reliable reporter when it came to recounting the baseless terrors that had gripped many people during his youth. Steadfast in his orthodoxy, he himself had always refused to give in to these fears, and in the twilight of his life he still refused. The ardent defender of legitimate fears (*metus*) was ardently scornful of groundless fear (*pavor*). Thomas Basin's vigorous reply spared the good Carthusian the dangers of vainglory and left him to his obscurity.

Somewhat later, Thomas was less successful in confronting a man who would one day be regarded as the prince of astrologers. Paul of Middelburg was born to a modest family in Middelburg on the island of Walcheren in Zeeland, probably in 1446, at roughly the moment when Thomas Basin, then thirty-five, was being elevated to the episcopate. He received his elementary education in Bruges. At Louvain he did brilliant work in philosophy, theology, and medicine and received a medical doctorate. In 1478, while still in his early thirties, he published, as many astrologers did, an astrological prediction for the coming year, the first in a long series. It immediately earned him a great reputation. In 1479 he became professor ordinarius of astronomy at the University of Padua, and in 1480 he was appointed physician and astrologer to the duke of Urbino. A man of the north, he was conquered by Italy. In turn, popes, princes, and scholars were impressed by the scientific gifts and casuistical verve of the man they regarded as the prince of mathematicians and astrologers. In 1494 Paul of Middelburg became bishop of Fossombrone. In 1513 Leo X appointed him to a commission charged with reform of the calendar. In 1534 Paul III called him to Rome and held out the prospect of a cardinal's hat. But by then Paul of Middelburg was eighty-eight. The journey tired him. After a week in Rome he died suddenly while attending mass on December 14, 1534.[645]

In 1484, when Paul was still a young man, highly talented and already famous in Italy, he paid a brief visit to Louvain, where he had been a student. While there, he engaged in a vigorous polemic with the doctors of the university on two related questions: When was Christ crucified, and when should Easter be celebrated? Peter *de Rivo* (we know only his Latin name), born in Flanders in 1428, was a professor of theology at the university. He had been its rector several times, and it was he who acted as spokesman for the university in the controversy with Paul of Middelburg. It was primarily to him, moreover, that Paul addressed himself when, in February 1488, he published his *Epistola Apologetica ad doctores Lovanienses.*

In this highly learned treatise, Paul displayed an astrologer's pride and presumption: "If only I knew the exact moment when the king of the Romans was born," he says at one point, "I could study him closely, and my work might help save thousands of men."[646] As usual, Paul's work was filled with verbal vehemence. He did not hesitate to insult and offend his native land. I was born, he says in substance, at Middelburg on an island in Zeeland. It was a barbarous island surrounded by an icy ocean. It was a *vervecum patria,* meaning both a country of sheep and a country of imbeciles. It was also a *cerdonum regio,* meaning a land of the poor and a land of wretches, where drunkenness was the supreme virtue. Fortunately God permitted me to leave and to go to Italy![647]

A few months later, still in 1488, Peter de Rivo published, in Louvain, a response to Paul of Middelburg entitled *Epistola Apologetica,* which dealt with the question of when Christ was crucified: what year, what day of the year (*dies*), and what day of the week (*feria*).[648] These were problems within his grasp, problems that a theologian could approach through biblical texts.

Paul's letter, though printed in Louvain, was evidently known elsewhere as well.[649] It caused a commotion in Zeeland when it became known there, and in Utrecht, where Thomas Basin was able to read it. He covered the copy someone had lent him with critical observations, and after the book was returned these remarks were communicated to Paul of Middelburg.[650] Paul sent his overly zealous critic a rather heated letter, which a messenger from Zeeland carried to Thomas Basin. In the remaining months of his life, the old man's passion was to write Paul a long letter, a long treatise really, in response to both the *Epistola Apologetica* published in 1488 and the personal letter he received after reading that work.

Thomas Basin was no more competent than Peter de Rivo to confront Paul on matters of mathematics or astrology. Thomas lacked even the theological training that Peter had. Yet like all cultivated clerics he knew the Bible and something of the problems of reckoning time. He also had firm ideas and ardent sentiments, which allowed him to condemn in the harshest of terms Paul of Middelburg, his presumptuous opinions, and his insulting words. How dare this layman attack a priest?[651] A priest who had been consecrated bishop before his attacker was even born and who was now almost eighty years old?[652] How could a Christian be so proud and so presumptuous as to cast doubt on biblical texts declared authentic by the

Church. Or to claim that those texts had been corrupted? Or that our Latin translation of the Old Testament is no longer that of Saint Jerome and no longer agrees with the Greek and Hebrew texts? Paul must renounce the possibility of knowing more than he should. He must cast aside his presumptuous ideas. He must confine himself to the doctrine of the Holy Roman Church and to the opinions of holy Catholic doctors approved by that church. His faith must be obedient. At stake was his salvation.[653]

Pride and temerity had driven Paul of Middelburg to say that his native country was a land of imbeciles and wretches where drunkenness was the primary virtue. In *De officiis* Cicero had rightly said that dear as a man's parents, children, and friends may be, dearer still is his country, for love of country includes all other loves, and a good man does not shrink from death if his country requires it.[654]

Paul of Middelburg had not confined his insults to his native country. In the same letter he had offended all regions north of the Alps, where he said people disliked astrology and scorned the liberal arts.[655] Thomas Basin defended Gaul, Spain, Brittany, and Germany, which in ancient times as well as today (*priscis temporibus atque eciam nostra etate*) did not lack for men eminent by virtue of eloquence or learning in rhetoric, philosophy, civil law, canon law, medicine, and theology. In particular he singles out Gaul, which, as Saint Jerome said, never had monsters and where courageous and eloquent men have always abounded. More specifically, he mentions the University of Paris, where philosophy and theology had always been cultivated with remarkable diligence and continued to be cultivated today, albeit not on so high a level as before.[656] In conclusion, Thomas protests that he does not wish to be long-winded. But, he tells Paul, if you wish to learn more about these things, try to lay hands on the published letters of Nicolas de Clamanges, one of the most learned and eloquent men to have lived in Gaul in modern times, and read in particular the very beautiful letter to Galeotto da Pietramala in which Nicolas shows how wrong Petrarch was to think that orators and poets were to be found only in Italy.[657]

Nicolas de Clamanges's letters were never published in the fifteenth century or, for that matter, in the sixteenth century. Thomas Basin, in retirement far from France, had happened upon them in a manuscript, which taught him a little about the intense love that French humanists had felt for their country in the time of Charles VI. With encouragement from them and from Cicero, the elderly exile came to understand that it was possible to love one's country with a love that is both strong and heroic. He himself admitted to loving France.

The area he defended against Paul's insults was a broader one, however, a region to which he felt attached, comprising all the countries north of the Alps: everything that was not Italy. In his youth Thomas Basin too had admired Italy, its institutions, and its culture. Now, however, in the face of Paul's provocations, he felt Norman, French, and cismontane.

Paul of Middelburg was not embarrassed by Thomas Basin's treatise. He never read it. Historians who have considered Paul's life were unaware of it. Nevertheless, Thomas Basin attached such importance to it that he hoped it would be published.[658] But it was not, either by him or by his heirs.

Thomas Basin died shortly after writing it, just after his seventy-eighth birthday, on December 30, 1490, at four in the afternoon.[659] He was buried in the choir of the cathedral of Utrecht. On his chest was placed a small copper plate and on that plate a small chalice of wax. Engraved on the plate in Latin were the Apostles' Creed, verses 25 and 27 of chapter 19 of Job, which proclaim the resurrection of the body and the justice of God, and then these simple words: *Thomas, servus Jhesu Christi . . . ,* "Thomas, servant of Jesus Christ, formerly bishop of Lisieux in the province of Rouen, born at Caudebec near Rouen on the Seine."[660]

It was not of Caesarea that Thomas thought while dying. His last thoughts were of his brothers, his native city, and his diocese. This elderly man had eight brothers, six of whom were still living. Five had been, or still were, merchants, and quite wealthy: Nicolas the elder; Nicolas the younger, the one who had preceded Thomas to Utrecht and who would be buried near him in the cathedral of Utrecht in 1495;[661] Etienne and Guillaume, both of Rouen; and Thomas the younger.[662] Michel was still canon of Lisieux.[663] The two Nicolases were named executors of Thomas Basin's will. It was they who carried out the last wishes of their deceased brother. Among other things, they gave the church of Lisieux nearly all his books and six hundred *livres tournois* for the celebration of his obit.[664] And to the church of Caudebec they transmitted a bequest large enough to allow major work to be undertaken there in 1491.[665]

Since the birth of Bernard Gui at the glorious height of Saint Louis's reign, two hundred thirty years had passed—the lifetime of four men. And Thomas Basin had not been dead four years when, in the summer of 1494, Charles VIII set out for Naples. A new world had begun.

NOTES

For full references, see bibliography.

Introduction

1. Momigliano, *The Development;* Momigliano, *Problèmes d'historiographie ancienne et moderne,* pp. 104–19; Heinzelmann, "Neue Aspekte der biographischen und hagiographischen Literatur in der lateinischen Welt (1.–6. Jahrhundert)"; Madelénat, *La Biographie.*

2. Georges Duby, *Guillaume le Maréchal.*

3. Gianola, "La raccolta di biografie."

4. Kohl, "Petrarch's Prefaces."

5. D. Lalande, ed., *Le livre des fais du bon messire Jehan le Maingre* (Geneva: Droz, 1985).

6. Christine de Pisan, *Le Livre des fais et bonnes meurs du sage roy Charles V,* ed. S. Solente, vol. 1 (Paris, 1936), 6.

7. Thomas Basin, *Histoire de Charles VII,* ed. and trans. Charles Samaran, vol. 1 (Paris, 1964), 2–4.

8. Madelénat, *La Biographie,* 20.

9. Vercauteren, "La Biographie et l'Histoire," 561; *Problèmes et méthodes,* 192.

10. Momigliano, *The Development,* 3.

11. *Problèmes et méthodes.*

12. Rudyard Kipling, *Puck of Pook's Hill.*

13. Millet, "L'Ordinateur."

14. Bernard Guenée, "Catalogue des gens de justice de Senlis et de leurs familles (1380–1550)," *Comptes rendus et mémoires de la Société d'histoire et d'archéologie de Senlis,* 1979–1980, 20–84; 1981–1982, 3–96. This catalogue was completed in 1963, and I used it in my thesis: *Tribunaux et gens de justice dans le bailliage de Senlis à la fin du Moyen Age (vers 1380–vers 1550)* (Strasbourg, 1963).

15. J. Verger and J. Jolivet, *Bernard-Abélard ou le cloître et l'école* (Paris, 1982); J. Verger, "Un essai de biographies croisées (Saint Bernard/Abélard) et ses enseignements," *Problèmes et Méthodes,* 79–85.

16. Jugie, *Le Cardinal.*

17. Contamine, "Un traité," 163.
18. Philippe de Mézières, *Le Songe,* I, 572.
19. Ibid.
20. Chauney, "Esquisse prosopographique," 681.
21. Forgeot, *Jean Balue,* 68–69.
22. Lettinck, "Comment les historiens," 74, n. 110.
23. Gregory the Great, *Dialogues,* III, 5, ed. A. de Vogüé (Paris, 1979), 275. Gérard de Frachet, Vitae Fratrum, *Monumenta Ordinis Praedicatorum Historica,* I, 1896, 209–10.
24. Battifol, *Jean Jouvenel,* 319.
25. *La Complainte et le Jeu de Pierre de la Broce, chambellan de Philippe le Hardi, qui fut pendu le 30 juin 1278,* ed. A. Jubinal (Paris, 1835), 25.
26. E. Albe, *Autour de Jean XXII: Hugues Géraud, évêque de Cahors. L'affaire des poisons et des envoûtements* (Cahors-Toulouse, 1904), chap. 1; cited by F. Collard, "Recherches sur le poison mortel au Moyen Age," master's thesis, University of Paris I, 1985, 177.
27. J. W. Hassell, Jr., ed., *Middle French Proverbs, Sentences, and Proverbial Phrases* (Toronto, 1982), C 121.
28. See n. 24 above.
29. Contamine, "Un traité," 147.
30. Ibid., 150.
31. Verger, "Tendances actuelles," 16.
32. Guenée, *Politique et histoire,* 198.
33. Chevalier, *Tours,* 206.
34. Bulst, "Studium und Karriere," 385.
35. Favier, *François Villon,* 85.
36. Quicherat, *Histoire,* IV, 13.
37. Lapeyre and Scheurer, *Les notaires,* I, 75.
38. Ibid.; Bulst, "Studium und Karriere," 392.
39. Chevalier, *Tours,* 206.
40. Guenée, *Politique et histoire,* 198.
41. Mollat, "L'oeuvre oratoire," 271.
42. Batiffol, *Jean Jouvenel,* 319.
43. Demotz, "Le comté de Savoie," 713.
44. Autrand, *Charles VI,* 192.
45. Guenée, *Politique et histoire,* 198.
46. Jean Juvénal des Ursins, *Ecrits politiques,* I, 312.
47. Jehan Masselin, *Journal,* 175.
48. Paul, *Titus,* 2:9.
49. Paul, *Col.* 3:18.
50. 1 Pet., 5:5.
51. Vincent de Beauvais, *Speculum doctrinale,* 1.IV, chap. XL, *De Obedientia.*
52. Cicero, *De officiis,* 20.
53. Jean Buridan, *Quaestiones in octo libros politicorum Aristotelis,* 1640, 400.
54. Cazelles, *Etienne Marcel,* 284.

55. Robert Gervais, *Speculum morale regium* (1384), Bibl. Mazarine, 3524, fol. 61 v. 63 r.
56. Ibid.
57. Nicolas Oresme, *Le Livre de Politiques*, 153.
58. Buridan, *Quaestiones*, p. 401.
59. See n. 55 above.
60. Jean Gerson, *Oeuvres* VII(2), 1114.
61. Louis XI, *Lettres*, V, 386.
62. Forgeot, *Jean Balue*, 11, n. 4.
63. See n. 60 above.
64. *Chronique des quatre premiers Valois*, 333.
65. Bibliothèque nationale 6020, fol. 71 v.
66. *Jean Juvénal des Ursins*, 112.
67. G. Du Fresne de Beaucourt, *Histoire de Charles VII*, vol. 6: *La fin du règne* (Paris, 1891), 192.
68. Jehan Masselin, *Journal*, 36–37, 167.
69. Louis XI, *Lettres*, III, 35; IX, 103; etc.
70. Jehan Masselin, *Journal*, 42.
71. Contamine, "Un traité," 150, 158.
72. Jehan Masselin, *Journal*, 175.
73. Coville, *Le traité*, 40.
74. Code, IV, II, 6. Digest, L, XVII, 184.
75. Eichelaub, "Le 'Tractatus.'"
76. Delumeau, *Le Péché et la peur.*
77. Decretals of Gregory IX, book I, title XL, canons 4 and 6.
78. Paravicini, "Peur," 187.
79. Thomas Basin, *Histoire de Louis XI*, III, 216.
80. Autrand, *Charles VI*, 559.
81. Basin, *Histoire de Louis XI*, III, 266.
82. *Chroniques de Jean Froissart*, ed. S. Luce, vol. 6 (Paris, 1876), 59.
83. See below, chap. 4, nn. 598–99.
84. Kantorowicz, *Mourir*, 105–41.
85. Préaud, *Les astrologues*, 75–77.
86. Guenée, "L'âge."
87. Grmek, *On Ageing and Old Age*, 32; Herlihy, *Vieillir*, 1350.
88. Herlihy, "Vieillir," 1352.
89. Higounet-Nadal, *Périgueux*, 299.
90. Herlihy-Klapisch, *Les Toscans*, 353–54.
91. R. Favreau, *La Commanderie du Breuil-du-Pas et la guerre de Cent Ans dans la Saintonge méridionale* (Jonzac, 1986), 87.
92. Sprandel, *Altersschicksal*, 78, 86–89.
93. Philippe de Mézières, *Le Songe*, I, 205.
94. Gen. 5:9–29; Paravicini Bagliani, "Rajeunir," 10–11.
95. Autrand, *La force de l'âge*, 207–11.
96. Duby, *Guillaume le Maréchal*, 87.
97. Ouy, "Simon de Plumetot," 359.
98. Autrand, *La force de l'âge*, 209.

99. Guenée, "L'âge," nn. 29, 30.
100. Ouy, "Simon de Plumetot," 359.
101. Sprandel, *Altersschicksal*, 89.
102. Higounet-Nadal, *Périgueux*, 328–29.
103. Desportes, "La population," 497–99.
104. Contamine, *La vie quotidienne pendant la guerre de Cent Ans. France et Angleterre (XIVe siècle)* (Paris, 1976), p. 191; Herlihy-Klapisch, *Les Toscans*, 370ff.
105. Guenée, "L'âge," n. 16.
106. Langlois, *La vie en France d'après les moralistes*, 204–40.
107. Cicero, *De senectute*, 17.
108. Gilson, "Sur l'âge," 152.
109. Herlihy, "Vieillir," 1339.
110. Cicero, *De senectute*, 13.
111. Gilson, "Sur l'âge"; Sprandel, *Altersschicksal*, 123.
112. Kings 10:8; Grandsen, "Childhood," 10.
113. Cicero, *De senectute*, 6.
114. Gransden, "Childhood," 16.
115. Cazelles, *Etienne Marcel*, 146.
116. Jacobus da Voragine, *The Golden Legend* (Saint Agnes).
117. See n. 37 above.
118. Autrand, "La force de l'âge," 213–14.
119. Grmek, *On Ageing*, 24–25; Herlihy, "Vieillir," 1351; Sprandel, *Altersschicksal*, 98, 165.
120. Psalm 89:10; Sprandel, *Altersschicksal*, 85–90.
121. Moranvillé, *Jean Le Mercier*, 362–63.
122. Guenée, "L'âge," n. 73.
123. Autrand, "La force de l'âge," 218.
124. Guenée, "L'âge," n. 94.
125. Coulet, *Le "De senectute"*.
126. Guenée, "L'âge."
127. *Les Faictz et Dictz de Jean Molinet*, ed. N. Dupire, vol. 1 (Paris, 1936), lines 337–40.
128. Kerhervé, "Jean Mauléon," 175.
129. Contamine, "Un traité," 163.
130. Anatole France, *La vie littéraire*, vol. 2, 122–24 ("Les torts de l'histoire").

Chapter 1: Bernard Gui

1. Dossat, "Les origines," 321.
2. A. Erlande-Brandenburg, *Le roi est mort. Etude sur les funérailles, les sépultures et les tombeaux des rois de France jusqu'à la fin du XIIIe siècle* (Paris, 1975), 81–83.
3. *Archivum Franciscanum Historicum* 32 (1939): 240.
4. Delisle, "Notice," 175.
5. *Bernard Gui et son monde*, 66.

6. Douais, *Essai,* 60.
7. Ibid., 27, 75.
8. *Bernard Gui et son monde,* 74.
9. Bernardus Guidonis, *De fundatione.*
10. Humbert of Romans, *De Vita Regulari,* 4.
11. Bernardus Guidonis, *De fundatione,* 66.
12. Ibid., 65
13. Ibid., 187.
14. Ibid., VI.
15. Becquet, "Le préchantre Hélie," 94, 97.
16. Stephanus de Salaniaco and Bernardus Guidonis, *De quatuor,* 163.
17. Ibid., 184.
18. Bernardus Guidonus, *De fundatione,* 62, 61.
19. Delisle, "Notice," 443.
20. Ibid., 329; Bernardus Guidonis, *De fundatione,* VII.
21. Delisle, "Notice," 377.
22. Bernardus Guidonis, *De fundatione,* 103.
23. Ibid., 67. *Bernard Gui et son monde,* 96.
24. Douais, *Essai,* 39. Bernardus Guidonis, *De fundatione,* 55, 67. Guenée, *Histoire,* 106.
25. Bernardus Guidonis, *De fundatione,* 67. Thomas, *Bernard Gui,* 145.
26. Douais, *Documents,* I, CCIV. Delisle, "Notice," 180. Thomas, "Bernard Gui," 145, n. 3. Bernardus Guidonis, *De fundatione,* VIII–IX.
27. Delisle, "Notice," 180, 385. Thomas, *Bernard Gui,* 145, n. 3.
28. Bernard Gui, *Manuel,* II, 66–68.
29. Bernard Gui, *Manuel,* II, 66–119, especially 98, 118. Delisle, "Notice," 357.
30. Delisle, "Notice," 397.
31. Stephanus de Salaniaco and Bernardus Guidonis, *De quatuor,* vi–xxi, xxxii–xxxiii.
32. Delisle, "Notice," 397.
33. Valois, "Jacques Duèse," 406.
34. Herde, *Colestin V (1274). Année charnière,* 228.
35. Ibid., 223–29.
36. Herde, *Colestin V,* 4.
37. Mandonnet, "La canonisation," 3.
38. Quillet, *La philosophie politique,* 204.
39. *Historie littéraire de la France,* vol. XXXVI, pp. 190–203.
40. Guillaume de Pierre Godin, *Tractatus,* 7–9.
41. Mandonnet, "La canonisation," 7.
42. Ibid., 8, 20–33.
43. Thomas, "Bernard Gui," 146ff.
44. Martin-Chabot, *Un témoignage.*
45. Delisle, *Notice,* 301–303, 401. Thomas, *Bernard Gui,* 149–150.
46. Thomas, "Bernard Gui," 153, n. 1.
47. Ibid., 151–52.
48. Mandonnet, "La canonisation," 35–44.

49. Mandonnet, *Des écrits,* 63–64.
50. Douais, *Documents,* I, ccv.
51. Delisle, "Notice," 259.
52. Ibid., 184, n. 2.
53. Schneider, "Recherches," 182.
54. Delisle, "Notice," 260–261. Thomas, "Bernard Gui," 219.
55. Humbert of Romans, *De vita regulari,* 4, 7, 9, 533.
56. 1 Peter 5:1–4; *Recueil des historiens des Gaules et de la France,* vol. XXI (Paris, 1855), p. 714.
57. Text: Delisle, "Notice," 429; or *Bernard Gui et son monde,* 31–32. Translation: *Année dominicaine,* 747.
58. Delisle, "Notice," 377.
59. Ibid., 423.
60. *Recueil des historiens des Gaules et de la France,* vol. XXI (Paris, 1855), pp. 710–14.
61. Delisle, "Notice," 396.
62. Ibid., 420–21.
63. Text: Delisle, "Notice," 428; or *Bernard Gui et son monde,* 31. Translation: *Année dominicaine,* 746.
64. Delisle, "Notice," 388–89.
65. Bernard Gui, *Manuel,* I, 36–39.
66. Ibid., I, 100–101.
67. Ibid., II, 68–69.
68. Ibid., I, 43.
69. Douais, *Documents,* I, CCIV.
70. Guenée, *Histoire,* 133–49.
71. Delisle, "Notice,"392, 426.
72. Ibid., 392.
73. Stephanus de Salaniaco and Bernardus Guidonis, *De quatuor,* 41.
74. Delisle, "Notice," 392.
75. Ibid., 262–63.
76. Ibid., 379.
77. *Recueil des historiens des Gaules et de la France,* vol. XXI (Paris, 1855), p. 713, n. 3.
78. Delisle, "Notice," 375.
79. Ibid., 381.
80. Ibid., 302.
81. Baluze, *Vitae Paparum,* II, 241–45. Guillemain, *La Cour pontificale,* s.v.
82. Baluze, *Vitae Paparum,* II, 262–65. Guillemain, *La Cour pontificale,* s.v.
83. Mandonnet, *Des écrits,* 65, 73.
84. Delisle, "Notice," 283.
85. John XXII, *Lettres communes,* nos. 8434, 20665. Thomas, "Bernard Gui," 141–42.
86. John XXII, *Lettres communes,* nos. 8436, 19558, 19559. Thomas, "Bernard Gui," 141–42.

87. Delisle, "Notice," 173–74, 276. *Bernard Gui et son monde,* 108–9.
88. Thomas, "Bernard Gui," 142.
89. *Recueil des historiens des Gaules et de la France,* vol. XXI (Paris, 1855), pp. 730–31. Baluze, *Vitae Paparum,* I, 161–63.
90. Manselli, *Spirituali,* passim and 314.
91. *Bernard Gui et son monde,* 334.
92. Ibid., 334, 336.
93. Ibid., 333–34.
94. *Recueil des historiens des Gaules et de la France,* vol. XXI (Paris, 1855), pp. 732–734. Baluze, *Vitae Paparum,* 165–68. Delisle, "Notice," 216, 250. *Bernard Gui et son monde,* 344.
95. Baluze, *Vitae Paparum,* 167–68.
96. Text: Delisle, "Notice," 429, or *Bernard Gui et son monde,* 32. Translation: *Année dominicaine,* 747–48.
97. Text: Delisle, "Notice," 429–31, or *Bernard Gui et son monde,* 32–33. Translation: *Année dominicaine,* 748–49.
98. Text: Delisle, "Notice," 431, or *Bernard Gui et son monde,* 33. Translation: *Année dominicaine,* 749.

Chapter 2: Gilles Le Muisit

1. Petit-Dutaillis, *Les communes,* 53, 191.
2. Pirenne, *Histoire,* I, 216.
3. Petit-Dutaillis, *Les communes,* 26.
4. Pirenne, *Histoire,* I, 201.
5. Petit-Dutaillis, *Les communes,* 191.
6. Pirenne, *Histoire,* I, 87.
7. Berlière, Monasticon, I, 273ff.
8. D'Haenens, *La crise,* 76.
9. D'Haenens, *L'abbaye,* 27–30; Despy, *RBPH* 41(1963):1281.
10. Coville, "Gilles Li Muisis, 252.
11. *Chronique,* III.
12. Coville, "Gilles Li Muisis," 256.
13. *Chronique,* 3.
14. *Poésies,* II, 204.
15. Coville, "Gilles Li Muisis," 283.
16. Guenée, *Histoire,* 181.
17. Frédéricq, *Corpus,* III, 21. *Grandes Chroniques de France,* IX, 324.
18. *Chronique,* 241–42.
19. *Recueil,* II, 306. *Chronique,* 212.
20. *Recueil,* II, 338ff.
21. *Recueil,* II, 340. *Chronique,* 212.
22. *Poésies,* I, 299.
23. *Recueil,* II, 339.
24. Coville, "Gilles Li Muisis," 283.
25. Ibid., 281–82.
26. R. Bossuat, *Le Moyen Age* (Paris, 1955), p. 201.

27. *Chronique,* 8, 10.
28. Coville, "Gilles Li Muisis," 282–283.
29. *Poésies,* I, 89.
30. Ibid., I, 88.
31. Ibid., I, 87, 356.
32. Ibid., I, 355.
33. Ibid., I, 128.
34. Ibid., I, 104. Coville, "Gilles Li Muisis," 262.
35. D'Haenens, *Gilles Li Muisis historien,* 272.
36. D'Haenens, "Une oeuvre."
37. *Chronique,* 306. Coville, "Gilles Li Muisis," 274–75.
38. *Poésies,* I, 13.
39. Ibid., I, 94.
40. Ibid., I, 13.
41. Ibid., II, 234.
42. Ibid., II, 257.
43. Ibid., I, 24.
44. Ibid., II, 232.
45. Ibid., I, 14.
46. Ibid., II, 234, 236, 273.
47. Ibid., 232.
48. *Recueil,* II, 249–52.
49. *Poésies,* II, 234.
50. Ibid., II, 261.
51. Ibid., II, 259, 262, 263, 264, 268. *Chronique,* 306.
52. *Recueil,* II, 112. *Poésies,* I, 104. *Chronique,* 306.
53. *Poésies,* II, 267.
54. Ibid., II, 226.
55. Ibid., II, 267.
56. Ibid., II, 126, 157, 198, 242, etc.
57. *Poésies,* I, 369; *Poésies,* II, 127, 242, 245, 248, etc.
58. *Poésies,* II, 245, 252. *Chronique,* 56, etc.
59. *Poésies,* II, 245. *Chronique,* 56, etc.
60. Regularium et secularium, *Chronique,* 56. Ecclesiasticorum et mundanorum, *Chronique,* 228.
61. *Chronique,* 56, 293, 300.
62. *Poésies,* II, 7, 245.
63. *Poésies,* I, 310; *Poésies,* II, 242, 275.
64. *Poésies,* I, 188; *Poésies,* II, 248.
65. *Poésies,* II, 343.
66. Ibid., II, 337.
67. Ibid., II, 245.
68. *Poésies,* I, 310; *Poésies,* II, 242, 275.
69. *Poésies,* I, 311, 320; *Poésies,* II, 48, 214.
70. *Poésies,* II, 334.
71. Ibid., II, 245.
72. *Poésies,* I, 288; *Poésies,* II, 153, 248.

73. *Poésies,* I, 292, 349, 367; *Poésies,* II, 252. *Chronique,* 300, etc.
74. *Poésies,* II, 57–59.
75. *Poésies,* II, 127, 153, 252. *Chronique,* 222, 258.
76. *Poésies,* II, 245, 248. *Chronique,* 257.
77. *Chronique,* 190.
78. "Persona auctoritatis," *Chronique,* 254. Compare *Chronique,* 230.
79. For example, the great historian Mathieu Paris in 1250 in his *Historia Anglorum,* ed. F. Madden, vol. 1 (Londong, 1866), p. 4.
80. *Poésies,* I, 106, 325; *Poésies,* II, 149.
81. *Poésies,* I, 106. *Recueil,* II, 325.
82. *Poésies,* I, 258.
83. Ibid., II, 158.
84. Ibid., I, 110.
85. Ibid., I, 262–63.
86. *Chronique,* 23–24.
87. *Poésies,* I, 320.
88. Ibid., I, 326–27.
89. *Recueil,* II, 308.
90. *Poésies,* I, 106, 278; *Poésies,* II, 149.
91. *Poésies,* I, 278.
92. "Multi alii sane mentis et divites," *Chronique,* 209. "Homines sane mentis et periti," *Chronique,* 239. "Multi sapientes et discreti," *Chronique,* 272. "Plurimi autem sapientes et sane mentis," *Chronique,* 298. "Multi sapientes et sane mentis," *Chronique,* 305.
93. *Chronique,* 190. *Recueil,* II, 320.
94. *Chronique,* 98, etc.
95. Ibid., 272, 298, 305.
96. *Poésies,* I, 261; *Poésies,* II, 53. *Chronique,* 214. *Recueil,* II, 324.
97. *Poésies,* II, 252.
98. "To obey suits us as men, possessed of reason." *Poésies,* II, 202.
99. *Poésies,* I, 142. *Recueil,* II, 111.
100. *Poésies,* II, 250, 252.
101. Ibid., II, 247. See also 253.
102. *Poésies,* I, 127, 262, 288; *Poésies,* II, 27, 275. *Chronique,* 38.
103. *Poésies,* I, 104; *Poésies,* II, 180.
104. *Chronique,* 228–30.
105. *Poésies,* II, 308, etc.
106. Ibid., II, 51, 226, etc.
107. Ibid., II, 10.
108. Ibid., II, 22.
109. Ibid., II, 197.
110. Ibid., I, 113, 115, 274.
111. *Poésies,* I, 115; *Poésies,* II, 15, 32, 50, 239, 274.
112. *Chronique,* 224, 259, 265.
113. Ibid., 150.
114. Ibid., 56–57.
115. Ibid., 265.

116. Ibid., 224.
117. *Recueil,* II, 330.
118. *Chronique,* 185.
119. *Recueil,* II, 333.
120. *Chronique,* 213. *Recueil,* II, 340. Coville, "Gilles Li Muisis," 307.
121. All references are in D'Haenens, "La date."
122. *Chronique,* 24.
123. Ibid., 10.
124. *Poésies,* I, 299, 301.
125. D'Haenens, "Une oeuvre."
126. *Poésies,* I, 128–29.
127. *Chronique,* 21.
128. *Poésies,* I, 302–3.
129. Ibid., I, 288–89.
130. *Recueil,* II, 170. Pirenne, *Histoire,* I, 378.
131. *Chronique,* 35, 38.
132. *Poésies,* I, 289.
133. Ibid., I, 137.
134. *Poésies,* I, 136–40. *Recueil,* II, 457.
135. *Recueil,* II, 115.
136. *Poésies,* I, 138.
137. Ibid., II, 49, 153.
138. Ibid., II, 210, 248–49.
139. Ibid., I, 369.
140. *Poésies,* I, 17, 369; *Poésies,* II, 1, 12, 110, 113, 190. *Chronique,* 104, 148.
141. *Poésies,* I, 22. *Recueil,* II, 368.
142. *Poésies,* II, 123.
143. *Poésies,* I, 66, 288; *Poésies,* II, 303. *Chronique,* 27.
144. *Recueil,* II, 337.
145. *Poésies,* II, 245.
146. Ibid., I, 331.
147. Lorcin, "Vieillesse."
148. D'Haenens, *L'abbaye,* 208–11.
149. *Poésies,* I, 32–35; *Poésies,* II, 51. *Recueil,* II, 348.
150. *Poésies,* II, 78–86, 113, 210, etc.
151. Ibid., II, 7.
152. *Poésies,* I, 298; *Poésies,* II, 22.
153. *Poésies,* II, 242.
154. Ibid., II, 246.
155. Ibid., I, 111, 112.
156. Ibid., I, 258, 259, 265.
157. *Chronique,* 23. *Recueil,* II, 118, etc.
158. *Poésies,* I, 324–25; *Poésies,* II, 68–69.
159. *Poésies,* I, 107; *Poésies,* II, 270.
160. *Poésies,* I, 278.
161. *Chronique,* 22.

162. *Poésies*, I, 176; *Poésies*, II, 247.
163. *Chronique*, 91.
164. *Poésies*, II, 232.
165. Ibid., I, 107, 263.
166. *Poésies*, I, 110; *Poésies*, II, 8, 141, 164, etc.
167. *Poésies*, II, 271.
168. Ibid., II, 126.
169. *Poésies*, I, 292, 349; *Poésies*, II, 126–27, 165, etc.
170. *Poésies*, I, 349.
171. Ibid., II, 127.
172. *Recueil*, II, 433.
173. *Poésies*, II, 242.
174. Ibid., I, 261.
175. *Chronique*, 103.
176. *Recueil*, II, 337–38.
177. *Chronique*, 253–54.
178. Ibid., 254–57.
179. *Recueil*, II, 374–77.
180. *Chronique*, 257–58.
181. *Recueil*, II, 344–45.
182. *Chronique*, 230. *Recueil*, II, 348.
183. *Chronique*, 222. *Recueil*, II, 339, 341.
184. *Chronique*, 222–27.
185. *Recueil*, II, 226. Berlière, "Trois traités," 340.
186. Baluze, *Vitae Paparum*, I, 306. Frédéricq, *Corpus*, III, 20.
187. Frédéricq, *Corpus*, III, 17.
188. Berlière, "Trois traités."
189. *Chronique*, 231–32.
190. Froissart, *Oeuvres*, ed. Kervyn de Lettenhove, vol. 18 (Brussels, 1874), pp. 310–11. *Chronique*, 233.
191. *Poésies*, I, 13; *Poésies*, II, 248.
192. *Chronique*, 237, 239, 240, 245.
193. Frédéricq, "Deux sermons."
194. *Recueil*, III, 123–26.
195. Frédéricq, *Corpus*, II, 113.
196. *Chronique*, 258.
197. Frédéricq, *Corpus*, II, 116–17.
198. *Chronique*, 251–52.
199. Berlière, "Trois traités," 341.
200. Frédéricq, "Deux sermons," 708.
201. *Recueil*, III, 25–26.
202. Frédéricq, *Corpus*, II, 116–17.
203. *Grandes Chroniques de France*, IX, 323–24. *Chronique latine de Guillaume de Nangis de 1113 à 1300*, ed. H. Géraud, vol. 2 (Paris, 1843), pp. 216–218. *Recueil*, I, 227. Baluze, *Vitae Paparum*, I, 306. *Chroniques de J. Froissart*, ed. S. Luce, vol. 4: *1346–56* (Paris, 1873), p. 331. Frédéricq, *Corpus*, I, 198; *Corpus*, III, 20–21.

204. *Chronique,* 228.
205. *Chronique,* XI, 306–7. Coville, "Gilles Li Muisis," 276, 280.

Chapter 3: Pierre d'Ailly

1. Pierre d'Ailly, *De concordia,* chap. 57. Tschackert, *Peter von Ailli,* 8.
2. Salembier, *Le Cardinal,* 10–15. *Lexikon des Mittelalters,* III, 101–2.
3. Salembier, *Petrus,* 357–62.
4. Ibid., 357.
5. Ibid., 112.
6. L. Perouas et al., *Léonard, Marie, Jean et les autres. Les prénoms en Limousin depuis un millénaire* (Paris, 1984), pp. 64ff.
7. Salembier, *Le Cardinal,* 16–17.
8. Ornato, *Jean Muret,* 30.
9. Nicolas de Clamanges, *Epistolae,* 10.
10. *Dictionnaire de biographie française,* vol. 1, col. 946. Salembier, *Le Cardinal,* 23.
11. Pierre d'Ailly, *Imago mundi,* I, 332–35.
12. S. Guenée, *Les universités,* 11ff.
13. Salembier, *Le Cardinal,* 25.
14. Ibid., 24.
15. Jean Gerson, *Oeuvres,* VII, 530, 978, 1145.
16. Ibid., 599.
17. Ouy, "La plus ancienne," 473.
18. "Mundi lucerna," Pierre d'Ailly, *Imago mundi,* I, 331–35. "Orbis luminare," Ouy, "La plus ancienne," 472.
19. Jean Gerson, *Oeuvres,* VII, 763, 978.
20. Ibid., 1138.
21. Ibid., 1138.
22. Ibid., 599.
23. Jean Gerson, *Oeuvres,* VII, 763, 978.
24. Ibid., 1146.
25. Salembier, *Le Cardinal,* 25.
26. Ouy, "La plus ancienne," 475.
27. Glorieux, "Deux éloges," 121.
28. Jean Gerson, *Oeuvres,* VII, 530.
29. Ouy, "La plus ancienne," 491.
30. Saenger, "Silent Reading," 385–408. Ouy, "La ponctuation," 426ff.
31. Ouy, "La ponctuation," 60.
32. Ouy, "La plus ancienne," 479.
33. Ouy, "Paris," 83.
34. Gilson, *La philosophie,* 415.
35. Ibid., 528–29, 589, 638–39.
36. Ibid., 642, 712.
37. S. Guenée, *Les universités,* 26.
38. Gilson, *La philosophie,* 639.
39. Ibid., 640–55.

40. Ibid., 657.
41. Glorieux, "Pierre d'Ailly," 50.
42. Gilson, *La philosophie,* 712.
43. Ouy, "La dialectique," 138.
44. Gilson, *La philosophie,* 682. Nicolas Oresme, *Le livre des politiques,* 13–22.
45. Chiavassa-Gouron, "Les lectures," 31, 50, 53, 70, 94.
46. Salembier, *Les oeuvres françaises,* 72.
47. Salembier, *Le Cardinal,* 33.
48. Glorieux, "L'oeuvre littéraire," 62.
49. S. Guenée, *Les universités,* 18.
50. Chiavassa-Gouron, "Les lectures," 31.
51. S. Guenée, *Les universités,* 15. Verger, *Les universités,* 26.
52. Glorieux, "L'oeuvre littéraire," 66.
53. Glorieux, "Deux éloges," 113–14.
54. Glorieux, "L'oeuvre littéraire," 62.
55. Salembier, *Petrus,* 12.
56. Tschackert, *Peter von Ailli,* 12. Salembier, *Petrus,* 14. Salembier, *Le Cardinal,* 368.
57. Guillemain, *La cour pontificale,* 249–51. Logoz, *Clément VII,* 9.
58. Baluze, *Vitae Paparum,* I, 518.
59. C.-H. Lerch, "Le cardinal Jean de la Grange, sa vie et son rôle politique jusqu'à la mort de Charles V (1350–1380)," *PTEC,* 1955, pp. 59–62. A. McG. Morganstern, "The La Grange Tomb and Choir: A Monument of the Great Schism of the West," *Speculum* 48(1973):52–69. Valois, *La France, s.v.,* especially III, 333.
60. N. Jorga, *Philippe de Mézières. Philippe de Mézières's Campaign for the Feast of Mary's Presentation: Edited from Bibliothèque Nationale MSS. Latin 17330 and 1454,* ed. W. E. Coleman (Toronto, 1981). O. Caudron, "La spiritualité d'un chrétien du XIVe siècle: Philippe de Mézières (1327?–1405)," *PTEC,* 1983, pp. 35–45.
61.Tschackert, *Peter von Ailli,* (8).
62. Ibid., 12. Salembier, *Le Cardinal,* 368.
63. Salembier, *Petrus,* 14.
64. Tschackert, *Peter von Ailli,* 12, (3)–(4).
65. Glorieux, "Deux éloges," 118. Bègne, "Exégèse et astrologie," 501–2. Salembier, *Petrus,* 288. Salembier, *Le Cardinal,* 313.
66. Gandillac, "De l'usage."
67. Gilson, *La Philosophie,* 476–82. Salembier, *Petrus,* 305–6. Salembier, *Le Cardinal,* 298ff.
68. Salembier, *Petrus,* 307.
69. Tschackert, *Peter von Ailli,* (7)–(12). Salembier, *Petrus,* 304–9.
70. Glorieux, "Deux éloges," 113, 121–22, 127.
71. Y. Renouard, *La papauté à Avignon* (Paris, 1954).
72. Bernstein, *Pierre d'Ailly,* 34.
73. Valois, *La France,* I, 324–27.
74. Tschackert, *Peter von Ailli,* 14.

75. Valois, *La France,* I, 327.
76. Déprez, *Hugo Aubriot,* 90–102.
77. Ibid., 111.
78. *Chronique des quatre premiers Valois (1327–1393),* ed. S. Luce (Paris, 1862), pp. 294–295.
79. Déprez, *Hugo Aubriot,* 102, 115, 117.
80. Bernstein, *Pierre d'Ailly,* 64.
81. Déprez, *Hugo Aubriot,* 112–13.
82. Ibid., 108.
83. Coville, *Jean Petit,* 137.
84. Salembier, *Le Cardinal,* 32.
85. Déprez, *Hugo Aubriot,* 109.
86. Ibid.
87. Glorieux, "L'oeuvre littéraire," 65.
88. Glorieux, "Deux éloges," 122.
89. Tschackert, *Peter von Ailli,* (15)–(21). Raymond, "D'Ailly's."
90. Déprez, *Hugo Aubriot,* 119–20.
91. Ibid.
92. Valois, *La France,* I, 339.
93. Ibid., I, 340–41.
94. Déprez, *Hugo Aubriot,* 119, n. 2.
95. Valois, *La France,* I, 342.
96. Ibid., 343. Bernstein, *Pierre d'Ailly,* 39.
97. Valois, *La France,* I, 345.
98. Bernstein, *Pierre d'Ailly,* 40.
99. Ibid., 40–44.
100. Valois, *La France,* I, 344.
101. Ibid., 358. Bernstein, *Pierre d'Ailly,* 46, 64.
102. Tschackert, *Peter von Ailli,* 66.
103. Bresc, "Les partis," 45.
104. Kaminsky, *Simon de Cramaud.*
105. J.-B. de Vaivre, "Notes d'héraldique et d'emblématique à propos de la tapisserie de l'Apcalypse d'Angers," *CRAIBL,* 1983, pp. 95–134, especially p. 96.
106. Pierre d'Ailly, *Tractatus et sermones,* "De Adventu Domini, sermo tertius," cols. 10–11.
107. Ibid., col. 14. Salembier, *Petrus,* 290.
108. Salembier, *Petrus,* 290–91. B. Guenée, *L'Occident,* 109–10.
109. Pierre d'Ailly, *Tractatus et sermones,* "De Adventu Domini, sermo tertius," col. 11.
110. Salembier, *Le Cardinal,* 368.
111. Pierre d'Ailly, *Tractatus et sermones,* "De Adventu Domini, sermo tertius," col. 11.
112. Ibid., col. 7.
113. Ibid., col. 14.
114. Ibid., col. 14.
115. Ibid., col. 6.

116. Ibid., col. 8.

117. Ibid., cols. 17–18. Translation: Bègne, "Exégèse et astrologie," 453–54.

118. Jean Courtecuisse, *L'Oeuvre oratoire,* 199–200.

119. Bloomfield, *The Seven,* 57–59.

120. Ibid., 83. B. Guenée, *Histoire,* 209.

121. Bloomfield, *The Seven,* 85–86.

122. Lester K. Little, "Pride Goes before Avarice: Social Change and the Vices in Latin Christendom," *American Historical Review* 76(1971): 16–49.

123. Salembier, *Le Cardinal,* 188.

124. M. Vincent-Cassy, "L'envie au Moyen Age," *Annales* 1980, 253–71, especially p. 257.

125. Pierre d'Ailly, *Tractatus et sermones,* "De sancto Dominico, sermo," col. 2.

126. Jean Courtecuisse, *L'Oeuvre oratoire,* 195.

127. Ibid., 197.

128. *Joannis Gersonii . . . Opera Omnia,* IV, col. 847.

129. Brayer, "Notice," 201.

130. Ibid., 341.

131. Jean Courtecuisse, *L'Oeuvre oratoire,* 196.

132. Ibid., 197.

133. Philippe de Mézières, *Le Songe,* I, 321.

134. Combes, "Sur les 'Lettres de consolation,' *KC-4*" 374.

135. Boniface Ferrer, "Tractatus," cols. 1459–60.

136. Ibid., col. 1456.

137. Brayer, "Notice," 307–8.

138. Boniface Ferrer, "Tractatus," cols. 1454, 1464–65.

139. Philippe de Mézières, *Le Songe,* I, 321–22.

140. *Mittellateinisches Wörterbuch,* vol. 1 (Munich, 1967), s.v. "ambitio." Boniface Ferrer, "Tractatus," col. 1501.

141. Pierre Bersuire, cited by Emile Littré, *Dictionnaire de la langue française,* vol. 1 (Paris, 1885), p. 125, s.v. "ambition."

142. Boniface Ferrer, "Tractatus," cols. 1454, 1464–65.

143. Brayer, "Notice," 308.

144. Jean Courtecuisse, *L'Oeuvre oratoire,* 284.

145. Cicero, "On Old Age," "On Friendship," "On Duties," 190, 222, 236.

146. Ornato, *Jean Muret,* 78.

147. Combes, "L'authenticité," 329–30.

148. Boniface Ferrer, "Tractatus," passim.

149. Salembier, *Petrus,* 372.

150. Ornato, *Jean Muret,* 20, 24.

151. Salembier, *Les oeuvres françaises,* 96.

152. Schreiner, "Laienbildung," 264–65.

153. Boniface Ferrer, "Tractatus," cols. 1501, 1502, 1514.

154. Jean Gerson, *Oeuvres,* VII, 1158.

155. Ouy, "Le thème," 24–26.

156. Tschackert, *Peter von Ailli,* (6).
157. Salembier, *Petrus,* 326.
158. Brayer, "Notice," 265.
159. Salembier, *Petrus,* 124. Ouy, "La plus ancienne," 459. Oakley, *The Political Thought,* 153–54.
160. Tschackert, *Peter von Ailli,* 340.
161. Chiavassa-Gouron, "Les lectures," 113.
162. Nicolas de Clamanges, *Epistolae,* 20 (= 19).
163. Chiavassa-Gouron, "Les lectures," 113.
164. Ouy, "Jean de Montreuil," 51.
165. Ouy, "Le collège," 282–83.
166. Tschackert, *Peter von Ailli,* 340.
167. Ouy, "Le recueil," 24.
168. Salembier, *Les oeuvres françaises,* 75.
169. Bernstein, *Pierre d'Ailly,* 78.
170. Salembier, *Les oeuvres françaises,* 72.
171. Ouy, "La réponse," 354.
172. Ouy, "Le recueil," 10, 16.
173. Tschackert, *Peter von Ailli,* (13). Pierre d'Ailly, "Tractatus et sermones, De sancto Ludovico, sermo primus," col. 10.
174. Saenger, "Silent Reading," 387.
175. Tschackert, *Peter von Ailli,* 345.
176. Gilson, *La philosophie,* 751.
177. Coville, *Jean Petit,* 50.
178. Cicero, "On Old Age," 27.
179. Brayer, "Notice," 165.
180. Tschackert, *Peter von Ailli,* (31).
181. Ibid.
182. Brayer, "Notice," 263–69.
183. Gilson, *La philosophie,* 750. Ouy, "La plus ancienne," 468.
184. Glorieux, "Deux éloges," 124.
185. Ibid., 115–16.
186. Ibid., 126.
187. Salembier, *Les oeuvres françaises,* 89.
188. Brayer, "Notice," 280–81.
189. Ouy, "La plus ancienne," 479.
190. Tschackert, *Peter von Ailli,* 178–79, 196, 273. Oakley, *The Political Thought,* 352–53. Pascoe, "Pierre d'Ailly," 616–18.
191. Brayer, "Notice," 276.
192. Salembier, *Le Cardinal,* 280.
193. Tschackert, *Peter von Ailli,* 109–10.
194. Brayer, "Notice," 278.
195. Lieberman, "Chronologie," VIII, 90. Grenier, "Pierre d'Ailly," 914.
196. Tschackert, *Peter von Ailli,* 107.
197. Jean Gerson, *Oeuvres,* II, 106.
198. Lefebvre, "Documents," 157.
199. Ibid., 151.

200. Jean de Montreuil, *Opera,* I, 250.

201. Ornato, *Jean Muret,* 72.

202. Cicero, *De amicitia,* p. xii.

203. Ornato, *Jean Muret,* s.v.

204. Aristotle, *Ethics,* VIII, 1.

205. Ibid.

206. Bibl. Mazarine, Incunabula 486, Paris, Vérard, 8 Sept. 1488, fol. 166v.

207. Aristotle, *Ethics,* VIII, 1. Bibl. Mazarine, 486, fol. 169.

208. Ibid., fols. 169v., 190 (*sic*).

209. Ibid., fol. 194.

210. Sustrac, *Les Célestins. Lexikon des Mittelalters,* III, 9–12. R. Cazelles, *Etienne Marcel, champion de l'unité française* (Paris, 1984), p. 103.

211. Lapeyre and Scheurer, *Les notaires,* XIII.

212. Ouy, "Gerson, émule," 206.

213. Ibid., 106, 207, 219.

214. Salembier, *Les oeuvres françaises,* 76. Ouy, "La plus ancienne," 450, 475.

215. Lenoble, "Pierre de Luxembourg."

216. Salembier, *Le Cardinal,* 84ff.

217. *Acta Sanctorum Julii tomus primus* (Paris, 1867), p. 476, sec. 100. Lenoble, "Pierre de Luxembourg," 75.

218. *Acta Sanctorum Julii tomus primus* (Paris, 1867), pp. 482–83, sec. 138. Lenoble, "Pierre de Luxembourg," 90.

219. *Acta Sanctorum Julii tomus primus* (Paris, 1867), p. 476, sec. 100. Lenoble, "Pierre de Luxembourg," 75.

220. *Acta Sanctorum Julii tomus primus* (Paris, 1867), pp. 470–82. Lenoble, "Pierre de Luxembourg," 76–81.

221. *Acta Sanctorum Julii tomus primus* (Paris, 1867), p. 477, sec. 107. Lenoble, "Pierre de Luxembourg," 88.

222. Jean Froissart, *Chroniques,* XIV, 183–84.

223. *Acta Sanctorum Julii tomus primus* (Paris, 1867), pp. 470–82. Lenoble, "Pierre de Luxembourg," 76–81.

224. Coville, "Recherches sur Jean Courtecuisse." Jean Courtecuisse, *L'oeuvre oratoire.*

225. Ouy, "Le catalogue," vi.

226. Jean de Montreuil, *Opera,* I, 195.

227. Bernstein, *Pierre d'Ailly,* 109.

228. Chiavassa-Gouron, "Les lectures," 112.

229. Bernstein, *Pierre d'Ailly,* 109–10. Valois, *La France,* IV, 190.

230. Salembier, *Le Cardinal,* 32.

231. Coville, *Jean Petit,* 137. Valois, *La France,* s.v.

232. Jean Gerson, *Oeuvres,* II, no. 36, pp. 167–69.

233. A. Thomas, *De Joannis.* Jean de Montreuil, *Opera* (Turin-Paris, 1963–81). Ornato, *Jean Muret.* Chiavassa-Gouron, "Les lectures." In particular, on this point: Jean de Montreuil, *Opera,* I, 334.

234. Ouy, "Jean de Montreuil," 591–93.

235. Ouy, "La dialectique," 141. Ouy, "Jean de Montreuil," 592.
236. In particular, Jean de Montreuil, *Opera,* I, 36–38.
237. Ouy, "Humanisme et propagande," 13.
238. Ouy, "La réponse,"
239. A. Thomas, *De Joannis,* 11. Gilson, *La philosophie,* 752–53.
240. Nicolas de Clamanges, *Epistolae.* Coville, *Le traité.* Coville, *Gontier et Pierre Col.* Coville, *Recherches sur quelques écrivains.* Glorieux, "Notations." Ornato, *Jean Muret.*
241. Denifle et Chatelain, *Chartularium,* III, 282. Glorieux, "Notations," 293.
242. Glorieux, "Notations," 293.
243. Denifle et Chatelain, *Chartularium,* III, 454, n. 10.
244. Glorieux, "Notations," 295.
245. Jean Gerson, *Oeuvres.* Glorieux, "La vie et les oeuvres."
246. Jean Gerson, *Oeuvres,* II, 8.
247. Ouy, "Gerson, émule," 180.
248. For example, Coville, *Le traité,* chap. xviii, p. 126; chap. xxvi, p. 132.
249. Oakley, *The Political Thought,* 209.
250. Glorieux, "Deux éloges," 119.
251. Oakley, *The Political Thought,* 163, n. 3.
252. Tschackert, *Peter von Ailli,* 10. Glorieux, "Deux éloges," 119.
253. Oakley, *The Political Thought,* 163, n. 3.
254. Gandillac, "De l'usage," 47, n. 1. Oakley, *The Political Thought,* 26, n. 45.
255. Tschackert, *Peter von Ailli,* 268.
256. Salembier, *Petrus,* 124.
257. Valois, *La France,* III, 460, 466.
258. Kaminsky, *Simon de Cramaud.*
259. Ibid., 74.
260. Simon de Cramaud, *De Substraccione.*
261. Kaminsky, *Simon de Cramaud,* 322–23.
262. Ibid., 76–77.
263. Ibid., 102.
264. Ibid., 318.
265. Pierre Ameilh, *La correspondance,* xl.
266. Bernstein, *Pierre d'Ailly,* 76.
267. Ibid., 99.
268. Ibid., 109–10.
269. Ibid., 118–19.
270. Ibid., 69.
271. Ibid., 68–69. But especially Denifle and Chatelain, *Chartularium,* III, no. 1499, p. 338.
272. Bernstein, *Pierre d'Ailly,* 76.
273. Ibid., 81.
274. Ouy, "La plus ancienne," 476–77.
275. Le Bachelet, "Immaculée conception."

276. Ibid., col. 1084.
277. Glorieux, "Pierre d'Ailly," 46.
278. Le Bachelet, "Immaculée conception," col. 1085.
279. Salembier, *Le Cardinal,* 312.
280. Ibid., 79, 370.
281. Ouy, "La plus ancienne," 478, 488. Glorieux, "Pierre d'Ailly," 45–47.
282. See n. 261.
283. Denifle and Chatelain, *Chartularium,* II, 595; III, 128, 340, 446.
284. Ouy, "La plus ancienne," 490–492. Glorieux, "Pierre d'Ailly," 47.
285. Ouy, "La plus ancienne," 492.
286. Le Bachelet, "Immaculée conception," col. 1085.
287. Doncoeur, "La condamnation," 180.
288. Glorieux, "Pierre d'Ailly," 47.
289. Doncoeur, "La condamnation," 182.
290. Salembier, *Le Cardinal,* 72–73.
291. Tschackert, *Peter von Ailli,* 71ff.
292. Coville, *Jean Petit,* 12.
293. Ibid., 1–9.
294. Ibid., 12, 13, 20.
295. Ouy, "Simon de Plumetot," 359–64.
296. Santoni, "Jean de Rouvroy," 22–23.
297. Salembier, *Le Cardinal,* 73.
298. Philippe de Mézières, *Le Songe,* I, 315, 595, 599.
299. *Chronique du Religieux de Saint-Denys,* I, 516. Salembier, *Petrus,* 32.
300. Salembier, *Petrus,* 262–63. Salembier, *Le Cardinal,* 74–75.
301. Tschackert, *Peter von Ailli,* 75. Salembier, *Le Cardinal,* 74.
302. Pierre d'Ailly, *Tractatus et sermones,* "Sermo de Septuagesima," col. 5. Tschackert, *Peter von Ailli,* 85.
303. Tschackert, *Peter von Ailli,* 75.
304. Salembier, *Le Cardinal,* 75–76.
305. Tschackert, *Peter von Ailli,* 76–77. Salembier, *Le Cardinal,* 82–83.
306. Mollat, "L'aumônier du roi."
307. Tschackert, *Peter von Ailli,* 77.
308. Salembier, *Le Cardinal,* 87. Ouy, "La plus ancienne," 450–51.
309. Salembier, *Le Cardinal,* 90.
310. Lavisse, *Histoire de France,* IV, 1, 304. B. Guenée, *Les entrées royales,* 13.
311. Salembier, *Le Cardinal,* 87.
312. Ibid., 38.
313. Ibid., 62.
314. Ibid., 92.
315. *Chronique du Religieux de Saint-Denys,* II, 13.
316. Ouy, "Gerson, émule," 218.
317. *Chronique du Religieux de Saint-Denys,* II, 15.
318. Ibid., 38–40.

319. Ibid., 98. Valois, *La France,* II, 413.
320. Valois, *La France,* II, 407. Coville, *Jean Petit,* 35.
321. *Chronique du Religieux de Saint-Denys,* II, 152–53.
322. Ouy, "Le recueil."
323. *Chronique du Religieux de Saint-Denys,* II, 100–101.
324. Ibid., 182–83. Valois, *La France,* II, 413.
325. Denifle and Chatelain, *Chartularium,* III, 624.
326. Valois, *La France,* II, 428.
327. Logoz, *Clément VII,* 173.
328. Coville, *Le traité,* 149.
329. Valois, *La France,* III, 3.
330. Ouy, "Gerson, émule," 182–83. Ouy, "Le collège," 284–85.
331. Valois, *La France,* III, 16, n. 4.
332. Philippe de Mézières, *Le songe,* I, 292–93.
333. Valois, *La France,* II, 422; III, 12.
334. Nicolas de Clamanges, *Epistolae,* 10.
335. Ibid., 17.
336. Valois, *La France,* III, 26. Ornato, *Jean Muret,* 27.
337. Kaminsky, *Simon de Cramaud,* 126.
338. Valois, *La France,* III, 26.
339. These three *rotuli* are either mentioned or reproduced in part in Denifle and Chatelain, *Chartularium,* IV, 4–5. The originals are in the Vatican archives: Reg. Suppl. 88 (ancient 83), fol. 31; Reg. Suppl. 84 (ancient 79), fol. 187v.–189r.; Reg. Suppl. 86 (ancient 81), fol. 78v. Olivier Guyotjeannin copied them for me there.
340. Salembier, *Le Cardinal,* 16.
341. Ibid.
342. Salembier, *Petrus,* 359. Chiavassa-Gouron, "Les lectures," 57.
343. B. Guenée, "Catalogue," no. 154.
344. *Chronique du Religieux de Saint-Denys,* II, 220–21.
345. Kaminsky, *Simon de Cramaud,* 134.
346. *Chronique du Religieux de Saint-Denys,* II, 220–23.
347. Kaminsky, *Simon de Cramaud,* 126–27, 127–28, 134.
348. *Chronique du Religieux de Saint-Denys,* II, 236–37.
349. Ornato, *Jean Muret,* 25.
350. Guenée, "L'âge," 262.
351. *Chronique du Religieux de Saint-Denys,* II, 250–51.
352. Jean Juvénal des Ursins, "Histoire," 401.
353. Baluze, *Vitae Paparum,* II, 836–37. Lenoble, *Pierre de Luxembourg,* 167–68.
354. Jean Juvénal des Ursins, "Histoire," 401.
355. Salembier, *Le Cardinal,* 112. Ornato, *Jean Muret,* 21.
356. Glorieux, "La vie et les oeuvres," 156.
357. Boniface Ferrer, "*Tractatus,*" cols. 1447–48, 1464. Salembier, *Le Cardinal,* 255–56.
358. Denifle and Chatelain, *Chartularium,* IV, p. 198, no. 1911.

359. Valois, *La France,* III, 131, n. 1. Salembier, *Le Cardinal,* 116. Kaminsky, *Simon de Cramaud,* 97.

360. *Gallia Christiana,* II, 731.

361. Salembier, *Le Cardinal,* 117.

362. Lefebvre, "Documents," 148.

363. Piétresson de Saint-Aubin, "Documents," 111–12.

364. Tschackert, *Peter von Ailli,* 98.

365. Boniface Ferrer, "*Tractatus,*" col. 1464.

366. Valois, *La France,* III, 131, n. 1. Salembier, *Le Cardinal,* 117. Michel de Creney was the king's confessor in 1389; Salembier, *Le Cardinal,* 83. See also Autrand, *Charles VI* (Paris, 1986), 27; and H. Millet, *L'ordinateur et la biographie,* 118–22 and 126–27.

367. Salembier, *Petrus,* 44. Piétresson de Saint-Aubin, "Documents," 112–13.

368. Valois, *La France,* 131, n. 3. Salembier, *Le Cardinal,* 117.

369. Piétresson de Saint-Aubin, "Documents," 113, n. 3.

370. Ibid., 124.

371. Ibid., 123.

372. Philippe de Mézières, *Le songe,* I, 292–93.

373. Piétresson de Saint-Aubin, "Documents," 123–26.

374. Ibid., 114–15, 128–30.

375. Ibid., 126–28. Ouy and Catach, "De Pierre d'Ailly."

376. Piétresson de Saint-Aubin, "Documents," 116.

377. Tschackert, *Peter von Ailli,* 99.

378. Piétresson de Saint-Aubin, "Documents," 116.

379. Salembier, *Le Cardinal,* 122.

380. Boniface Ferrer, "Tractatus," cols. 1464.

381. Piétresson de Saint-Aubin, "Documents," 116.

382. Salembier, "Petrus," 365–66.

383. Piétresson de Saint-Aubin, "Documents," 117.

384. Salembier, *Petrus,* 363–65.

385. Ibid., 365–366.

386. Boniface Ferrer, "Tractatus," cols. 1464–65.

387. Tschackert, *Peter von Ailli,* 100.

388. Piétresson de Saint-Aubin, "Documents," 119, 135–36.

389. *Chronique du Religieux de Saint-Denys,* II, 564–70.

390. Tschackert, *Peter von Ailli,* 100–101.

391. B. Guenée, "Des limites féodales," 20.

392. Tschackert, *Peter von Ailli,* 102.

393. Salembier, *Petrus,* 48.

394. Lefebvre, "Documents," 141, 149.

395. Salembier, *Les oeuvres françaises,* 76.

396. Valois, *La France,* III, 432–33.

397. Montagnes, "Saint Vincent Ferrier."

398. Coville, *Gontier et Pierre Col,* 83.

399. Ornato, *Jean Muret,* 40–45.

400. Ibid., 49–50.
401. Ibid., 78.
402. Coville, *Le traité,* 40.
403. Ibid., 37–39.
404. Glorieux, "La vie et les oeuvres," 157.
405. Jean Gerson, *Oeuvres,* II, 17–23.
406. Valois, *La France,* III, 132.
407. Ibid., 145, 155.
408. Ibid., 174, n. 6.
409. Salembier, *Le Cardinal,* 169.
410. Coville, "Philippe de Vitry," 521.
411. Poirion, *Le Moyen Age,* 303. Philippe de Vitry, *Les oeuvres,* 140.
412. Salembier, *Les oeuvres françaises,* 46. Salembier, *Petrus,* 349.
413. Salembier, *Les oeuvres françaises,* 47.
414. Boniface Ferrer, "Tractatus," col. 1464.
415. Salembier, *Petrus,* 371. Salembier, *Le Cardinal,* 137.
416. Grenier, "Pierre d'Ailly," 901.
417. Salembier, *Le Cardinal,* 362–63.
418. Vatican, Reg. lat. 1964, fol. 166r.–167r., copied for me by O. Guyot-jeannin. Grenier, "Pierre d'Ailly," 915. Salembier, *Le Cardinal,* 361.
419. Grenier, "Pierre d'Ailly," 914.
420. Salembier, *Les oeuvres françaises,* 7–8, 103.
421. Probably in 1404; Poirion, *Le Moyen Age,* 202.
422. Poirion, *Le Moyen Age,* 102.
423. Hicks, *Le débat,* xxxv.
424. Ibid., xxxviii, lii.
425. Gilson, *La philosophie,* 702.
426. Glorieux, "La vie et les oeuvres," 160–61.
427. Jean Gerson, *Oeuvres,* V, 163. Hicks, *Le débat,* xlviii.
428. Hicks, *Le débat,* 162–63.
429. Jean Gerson, *Oeuvres,* VII, 793–934. Hicks, *Le débat,* l.
430. Jean Gerson, *Oeuvres,* II, 63. Combes, "L'authenticité," 323.
431. Tschackert, *Peter von Ailli,* 115.
432. Badel, "Pierre d'Ailly," 377, 379, 380.
433. Brayer, "Notice."
434. Tschackert, *Peter von Ailli,* 109, n. 1.
435. Genet, "Ecclesiastics," 30.
436. Oakley, *The Political Thought,* 70.
437. Ibid., 80.
438. Brayer, "Notice," 312.
439. Ibid., 313. Salembier, *Petrus,* 338.
440. Brayer, "Notice," 278.
441. Oakley, *The Political Thought,* 248–50.
442. Valois, *La France,* III, 341–43.
443. Salembier, *Le Cardinal,* 76, 179–80.
444. Ornato, *Jean Muret,* 106.
445. Valois, *La France,* III, 346.

446. Ibid., 420–22.
447. Ibid., 426.
448. Ibid., 430–31.
449. Coville, *Jean Petit,* 46.
450. Tisset, *Procès,* II, 388–91.
451. Valois, *La France,* III, 431.
452. Nicolas de Baye, *Journal,* I, 158. Coville, *Jean Petit,* 49.
453. Valois, *La France,* III, 433.
454. Coville, *Jean Petit,* 50–51.
455. Ibid., 63.
456. Valois, *La France,* III, 449.
457. Nicolas de Baye, *Journal,* I, 168–70.
458. Coville, *Jean Petit,* 62, 64.
459. Valois, *La France,* III, 456.
460. Salembier, *Les oeuvres françaises,* 100.
461. Coville, *Jean Petit,* 44.
462. Valois, *La France,* III, 456.
463. Ibid., 484–86.
464. Coville, *Jean Petit,* 73–80.
465. Salembier, *Les oeuvres françaises,* 72. Coville, *Jean Petit,* 73.
466. *Chronique du Religieux de Saint-Denys,* III, 468–69.
467. Valois, *La France,* III, 460, n. 2.
468. Ibid., 460–61. Salembier, *Le Cardinal,* 214.
469. Valois, *La France,* III, 456, n. 4.
470. Coville, *Jean Petit,* 80.
471. Ibid., 75–76.
472. Salembier, *Les oeuvres françaises,* 72.
473. Ibid., 91.
474. Tschackert, *Peter von Ailli,* 129.
475. Coville, *Jean Petit,* 73, n. 133.
476. Glorieux, "La vie et les oeuvres," 170.
477. Valois, *La France,* III, 473.
478. Kaminsky, *Simon de Cramaud,* 230–31, 267–68.
479. Valois, *La France,* III, 495.
480. Ibid., 483.
481. *Chronique du Religieux de Saint-Denys,* III, 512–15. Valois, *La France,* III, 499.
482. Valois, *La France,* IV, 398.
483. Denifle and Chatelain, *Chartularium,* IV, p. 198, no. 1911.
484. Coville, *Recherches sur quelques écrivains,* 175–207. Coville, *Jean Petit,* 348–49.
485. Nicolas de Clamanges, *Epistolae,* 202.
486. Valois, *La France,* III, 507, n. 2.
487. Ibid., 510.
488. Ibid., 486.
489. Ibid., 515.
490. Ibid., 517. Ornato, *Jean Muret,* 178–79.

491. Salembier, *Le Cardinal,* 228.
492. Ibid., 232–33.
493. Lavisse, *Histoire de France,* IV, 1, p. 331.
494. *Chronique du Religieux de Saint-Denys,* III, 722–25. Jean Juvénal des Ursins, "Histoire," 444.
495. *Chronique des règnes de Jean II et de Charles V,* I, 39.
496. Valois, *La France,* III, 597. Salembier, *Le Cardinal,* 232.
497. Coville, *Jean Petit,* 101.
498. Ibid., 109–10.
499. Ibid., 211–12.
500. Ibid., 185.
501. Ibid., 214.
502. Ibid., 88.
503. Ornato, *Jean Muret,* 187.
504. Coville, *Jean Petit,* 301, 306.
505. Ibid., 112.
506. Salembier, *Le Cardinal,* 234.
507. G. Dupont-Ferrier, Gallia Regia ou Etat des officiers royaux des bailliages et des sénéchaussées de 1328 à 1515, vol. 4 (Paris, 1954), no. 16481. Coville, *Jean Petit,* 379.
508. *Chronique du Religieux de Saint-Denys,* III, 728–29.
509. Jean Juvénal des Ursins, "Histoire," 446.
510. Valois, *La France,* III, 608–11.
511. Ibid., 614.
512. Ibid., 612.
513. Salembier, *Petrus,* 324. Salembier, *Le Cardinal,* 318.
514. Valois, *La France,* III, 614. Ornato, *Jean Muret,* 179.
515. Nicolas de Clamanges, *Epistolae,* 139.
516. Ibid., 144.
517. Ibid., 127–54.
518. Ornato, *Jean Muret,* 61.
519. Nicolas de Clamanges, *Epistolae,* 129.
520. Ornato, *Jean Muret,* 62.
521. Nicolas de Clamanges, *Epistolae,* 141.
522. Ibid., 133.
524. Salembier, *Le Cardinal,* 236.
525. Combes, "Sur les 'Lettres de consolation,'" 387. Glorieux, "Notations," 291.
526. *Chronique du Religieux de Saint-Denys,* IV, 30–31.
527. Lefebvre, "Documents," 156–59.
528. Coville, *Jean Petit,* 225–26.
529. Ibid., 240.
530. Ibid., 304.
531. Ibid., 244.
532. Valois, *La France,* IV, 24.
533. Jean Gerson, *Oeuvres,* II, 105–7. Lieberman, "Chronologie," V and VIII.

534. Combes, "Sur les 'Lettres de consolation.'"
535. Ibid., 387.
536. Coville, *Jean Petit,* 229.
537. Ibid., 255.
538. Ibid., 256.
539. Lavisse, *Histoire de France,* IV, 1, p. 335.
540. Valois, *La France,* IV, 14–15. Salembier, *Le Cardinal,* 240–42.
541. Valois, *La France,* IV, 18–20.
542. Valois, *La France,* IV, 85. Salembier, *Le Cardinal,* 243.
543. Oakley, "The 'Propositiones utiles.'"
544. Valois, *La France,* IV, 86.
545. Ibid., 83.
546. Ibid., 82.
547. Ibid., 78, 91.
548. Ibid., 79.
549. Ibid., 92.
550. Ibid., 86.
551. Ibid.
552. Kaminsky, *Simon de Cramaud,* 281.
553. Valois, *La France,* IV, 99, 104.
554. Kaminsky, *Simon de Cramaud,* 285.
555. Salembier, *Le Cardinal,* 253.
556. Kaminsky, *Simon de Cramaud,* 284.
557. Ouy, "Simon de Plumetot," 372.
558. Ouy, *Le recueil épistolaire,* xvi.
559. Ouy, "La réponse," 356–57. Glorieux, "L'oeuvre littéraire," 66.
560. 1412: Tschackert, *Peter von Ailli* (32), (38). 1418: Valois, "Un ouvrage inédit," 574.
561. Ouy, "Une énigme codicologique."
562. Lieberman, "Chronologie," VIII, 82, 85. Ouy, *La ponctuation,* 77.
563. Philippe de Mézières, *Le songe,* II, 343. Macary, *Une pensée,* 122.
564. Jean Gerson, *Oeuvres,* II, 127.
565. Lieberman, *Chronologie,* VIII, 82, 85. Ouy, "La ponctuation," 77.
566. Grenier, "Pierre d'Ailly," 914.
567. Pierre d'Ailly, *Tractatus et sermones,* "Speculum considerationis," col. 2, and "Compendium contemplations," col. 1. Lieberman, "Chronologie," VIII, 77.
568. Salembier, *Petrus,* 328.
569. Pierre d'Ailly, *Tractatus et sermones,* "Compendium contemplationis," col. 4.
570. Salembier, *Petrus,* 329.
571. Combes, "L'authenticité," 331.
572. Lieberman, "Chronologie," VIII, 76–80.
573. Ouy, *Le recueil épistolaire,* xxvii.
574. Saenger, "Silent Reading," 410.
575. Ouy, "Enquête," 287.
576. Ouy, "Le collège," 287. Saenger, "Silent Reading," 410.

577. Ouy, "Autographes," 94.

578. Ouy, "La ponctuation," 76.

579. Ouy, *Le recueil épistolaire*, xxvii.

580. Tschackert, *Peter von Ailli*, 333–35. Salembier, *Le Cardinal*, 337–56.

581. B. Guenée, *Histoire*, 169.

582. Pierre d'Ailly, *Imago mundi*, I, 332–35.

583. Ibid., chap. 1, pp. 168-70; chap. 13, pp. 242–44.

584. *Les tables alphonsines avec les canons de Jean de Saxe*, ed. E. Poulle (Paris, 1984).

585. Pierre d'Ailly, "De concordia," fol. 3.

586. Tschackert, *Peter von Ailli*, 331–33. Salembier, *Petrus*, 191–92. Salembier, *Le Cardinal*, 262, 372.

587. Philippe de Mézières, *Le songe*, I, 604.

588. Préaud, *Les astrologues*, 54.

589. Philippe de Mézières, *Le songe*, I, 604.

590. Préaud, *Les astrologues*, 196–98.

591. Philippe de Mézières, *Le songe*, I, 618.

592. Glorieux, "Deux éloges," 118.

593.Tschackert, *Peter von Ailli* (44).

594. Bègne, "Exégèse et astrologie," 502.

595. Pierre d'Ailly, "De concordia," fol. 3.

596. Ibid., fol. 1v.

597. Ibid., fol. 3; chap. 9, fol. 5.

598. Ibid., fol. 19.

599. Ibid., chap. 2, fol. 3.

600. Ibid., fol. 9.

601. Ibid., chap. 54, fol. 15v., 16.

602. Ibid., chap. 53, fol. 15v.

603. Ibid., chap. 55, fol. 16.

604. Ibid., chap. 56, fol. 16–16v.

605. Ibid., chap. 57, fol. 16v.–17; chap. 59, fol. 17.

606. Pascoe, "Pierre d'Ailly."

607. Valois, "Un ouvrage inédit."

608. Ibid., 566.

609. Pierre d'Ailly, "De concordia," chap. 61, fol. 17v. Valois, "Un ouvrage inédit," 574.

610. Bègne, "Exégèse et astrologie," 506–8. Salembier, *Le Cardinal*, 357–59.

611. Valois, *La France*, IV, 190. Salembier, *Le Cardinal*, 261.

612. Coville, *Le traité*, 39, 45.

613. Boniface Ferrer, "Tractatus," chap. 36, col. 1457; chap. 94, col. 1499; chap. 96, col. 1501.

614. Ibid., chap. 98, cols. 1503–4.

615. Ibid., chaps. 23–27, cols. 1448–50; chap. 42, col. 1463.

616. Ibid., chap. 26, col. 1450; chap. 35, col. 1456.

617. Ibid., chap. 39, col. 1460.

618. Ibid., chap. 75, col. 1487.
619. Ibid.
620. Ibid., chap. 95, col. 1500; chap. 97, col. 1502.
621. Ibid., chap. 95, col. 1500; chap. 96, col. 1501.
622. 1 Cor. 8:1; Boniface Ferrer, "Tractatus," chap. 96, col. 1501.
623. Luke 10:21; Boniface Ferrer, "Tractatus," chap. 95, col. 1500.
624. Salembier, *Le Cardinal,* 257.
625. Boniface Ferrer, "Tractatus," chap. 43, col. 1464.
626. Tschackert, *Peter von Ailli,* (31)–(41).
627. Ibid., (35)–(36).
628. Ibid., 171 (41).
629. Salembier, *Le Cardinal,* 261.
630. Ibid.
631. Valois, *La France,* IV, 205. Kaminsky, *Simon de Cramaud,* 300.
632. Kaminsky, *Simon de Cramaud,* 300.
633. Salembier, *Le Cardinal,* 263.
634. Kaminsky, *Simon de Cramaud,* 300.
635. Salembier, *Le Cardinal,* 263.
636. Kaminsky, *Simon de Cramaud,* 300.
637. Lavisse, *Histoire de France,* IV, 1, p. 339.
638. *Chronique du Religieux de Saint-Denys,* V, 62–63.
639. Lavisse, *Histoire de France,* IV, 1, p. 349.
640. Jean Juvénal des Ursins, "Histoire," 484.
641. *Chronique du Religieux de Saint-Denys,* V, 62–63. Chiavassa-Gouron, "Les lectures," 109.
642. Coville, *Jean Petit,* 400–401.
643. Ibid., 472.
644. Ibid., 445.
645. Ibid.
646. Ibid., 498.
647. Salembier, *Le Cardinal,* 264–65.
648. Bègne, *Exégèse et astrologie,* 447.
649. Gill, *Constance,* 41.
650. Valois, *La France,* IV, 262–63. Salembier, *Le Cardinal,* 265.
651. Valois, *La France,* 265.
652. Tschackert, *Peter von Ailli,* 183–84.
653. Valois, *La France,* 251.
654. Gill, *Constance,* 47.
655. Ibid., 41. H. Thomas, *Deutsche Geschichte,* 388.
656. Gill, *Constance,* 54, 56, 63, 67–68.
657. Ibid., 48–49.
658. Ibid., 308.
659. Ibid., 328–29.
660. Ornato, *Jean Muret,* xiv. Ouy, *Le recueil épistolaire,* xv. Ouy, *Le catalogue,* v–vi. B. Guenée, *Histoire,* 293.
661. Valois, *La France,* IV, 382, 398.
662. Kaminsky, *Simon de Cramaud,* 302, 318.

663. Coville, *Jean Petit,* 512.
664. Valois, *La France,* IV, 263, 267, 268.
665. Gill, *Constance,* 46.
666. Valois, *La France,* IV, 281.
667. Ibid., 292.
668. Ibid., 297. Tschackert, *Peter von Ailli,* 223–25.
669. Macek, *Jean Hus.* Smahel, *La révolution hussite.*
670. Macek, *Jean Hus,* 55.
671. Ibid., 58.
672. Ibid., 75.
673. Tschackert, *Peter von Ailli,* 233.
674. Macek, *Jean Hus,* 77.
675. Gill, *Constance,* 75.
676. Tschackert, *Peter von Ailli,* 230.
677. Coville, *Jean Petit,* 551.
678. Ibid., 535, 546.
679. Ibid., 519–20.
680. Ibid., 545.
681. Ibid., 533–34, 549.
682. Ibid., 545.
683. Tschackert, *Peter von Ailli,* 245–46.
684. Valois, *La France,* IV, 332–33. Gill, *Constance,* 57.
685. Valois, *La France,* IV, 364–66.
686. Tschackert, *Peter von Ailli,* 283.
687. Gill, *Constance,* 46.
688. Finke, "Die Nation," 367.
689. Valois, *La France,* IV, 368. Finke, "Die Nation," 360.
690. Finke, "Die Nation," 367.
691. Ibid., 360.
692. Oakley, *The Political Thought,* 152, 348.
693. Finke, "Die Nation," 360.
694. Valois, *La France,* IV, 369.
695. Ibid., 370.
696. Ibid., 377. Finke, "Die Nation," 364.
697. Tschackert, *Peter von Ailli,* 246. Valois, *La France,* IV, 368.
698. Tschackert, *Peter von Ailli,* 283.
699. Pierre d'Ailly, *Tractatus et sermones,* "De sancto Ludovico, sermo primus," cols. 6–7. Salembier, *Petrus,* 296–97.
700. Salembier, *Petrus,* 119–25. Salembier, *Le Cardinal,* 374.
701. Tschackert, *Peter von Ailli,* (41)–(50). Salembier, *Petrus,* 294–95.
702. Valois, *La France,* IV, 397–98.
703. Ibid., 402.
704. Tschackert, *Peter von Ailli,* 296. Valois, *La France,* IV, 403.
705. Tschackert, *Peter von Ailli,* 295. Valois, *La France,* IV, 404–5.
706. Kaminsky, *Simon de Cramaud,* 302.
707. Glorieux, "Notations," 299.
708. Salembier, *Le Cardinal,* 286.

709. Valois, *La France,* IV, 431.
710. Tschackert, *Peter von Ailli,* 297. Salembier, *Le Cardinal,* 286.
711. Glorieux, "La vie et les oeuvres," 184.
712. Jean de Montreuil, *Opera,* II.
713. Valois, *La France,* IV, 385.
714. Jean de Montreuil, *Opera,* I, 327.
715. Ibid., 326.
716. Ibid., 334.
717. *Chronique du Religieux de Saint-Denys,* VI, 234–35. Ouy, "Le collège," 291.
718. Jean de Montreuil, *Opera,* I, 354–55.
719. Coville, *Jean Petit,* 558–61.
720. Ouy, "La 'Deploratio,'" 758.
721. Salembier, *Les oeuvres françaises,* 11.
722. Paris, Bibl. nat., lat., 3769. According to G. Ouy.
723. Valois, "Un ouvrage inédit."
724. Ouy, "La ponctuation," 77.
725. Lavisse, *Histoire de France,* IV, 1, p. 385.
726. Jean Gerson, *Oeuvres,* II, 218–21.
727. Ibid., 222.
728. A. Molinier, *Les sources de l'histoire de France des origines aux guerres d'Italie (1494),* vol. 4 (Paris, 1904), no. 3589. Tschackert, *Peter von Ailli,* 365. Salembier, *Petrus,* 366–70. Pons, "La propagande," 194.
729. *Joannis Gersonii . . . Opera Omnia,* vol. 4, col. 844–849.
730. Oakley, *The Political Thought,* 161–62.
731. S. Guenée, *Bibliographie,* Paris, nos. 2591, 2624, 2657, 4676.
732. Glorieux, "La vie et les oeuvres," 192.
733. Salembier, *Le Cardinal,* 360.
734. Grenier, *Pierre d'Ailly,* cols. 913–15.
735. Salembier, *Le Cardinal,* 16–17.
736. Salembier, *Petrus,* 139.

Chapter 4: Thomas Basin

1. Thomas Basin, *Histoire des règnes de Charles VII et de Louis XI,* ed. J. Quicherat (Paris, 1855–59), vol. IV, 21. Cited hereafter as Quicherat.
2. Quicherat, IV, 31. *Charles VII,* I, 4.
3. *Charles VII,* I, 4.
4. Ibid., xvi.
5. *Louis XI,* I, x.
6. Quicherat, I, lxxiii.
7. *Louis XI,* II, 182.
8. Quicherat, I, lxxii.
9. *Apologie,* 202.
10. *Louis XI,* III, 206.
11. Ibid., 268.
12. Quicherat, IV, 22–23.

13. *Louis XI*, I, xii.
14. Quicherat, IV, 23.
15. Ibid., 7.
16. Ibid., I, 32.
17. Ibid., II, 255.
18. *Louis XI*, II, 24.
19. B. Guenée, "L'historien et la compilation."
20. B. Guenée, *Politique et histoire*, 288.
21. *Charles VII*, I, 90.
22. B. Guenée, *Politique et histoire*, 288.
21. *Charles VII*, I, 90.
22. B. Guenée, *Politique et histoire*, 289.
23. B. Guenée, *Histoire*, 342–43.
24. *Louis XI*, II, 172–82.
25. Ibid., 266–72.
26. Ibid., I, 294.
27. B. Guenée, "Histoire et chronique," 10–11.
28. *Charles VII*, II, 308.
29. For example: *Charles VII*, I, 114, 246; II, 176.
30. For example: *Charles VII*, I, 88; II, 204. *Louis XI*, III, 62, 64.
31. For example: *Charles VII*, I, 72, 166.
32. *Louis XI*, II, 240.
33. For example: *Charles VII*, II, 46.
34. Quicherat, I, ii. *Charles VII*, xx.
35. Samaran and Vernet, *Les livres.*
36. *Louis XI*, III, 122.
37. Ibid., 124–26, 280.
38. Quicherat, IV, 9.
39. *Charles VII*, I, 10.
40. Ibid., II, 32 and 44.
41. Ibid., I, 24.
42. *Charles VII*, I, 8; II, 160. *Louis XI*, III, 318 and 366.
43. Quicherat, IV, 103.
44. *Charles VII*, I, 4.
45. Allmand, *Lancastrian Normandy*, 121–25.
46. Quicherat, IV, 9.
47. Maurice, *Thomas Basin*, 119–21, 147–54.
48. Bois, *Crise du féodalisme*, 14–15.
49. *Histoire du Havre*, 41.
50. Maurice, *Thomas Basin*, 117–19.
51. Quicherat, IV, 10.
52. Maurice, *Thomas Basin*, 119–21, 147–54.
53. Ibid., 120–22.
54. Quicherat, IV, 146. Maurice, *Thomas Basin*, 129–32.
55. Maurice, *Thomas Basin*, 126.
56. Ibid., 123.
57. Ibid., 131.

58. Quicherat, IV, 271.
59. *Bulletin de la Commission des Antiquités de Seine-Inférieure,* vol. 7 (Rouen, 1886), p. 81.
60. Maurice, *Thomas Basin,* 133–34.
61. Ibid., 29, 120.
62. Bois, *Crise du féodalisme,* 184–285.
63. Coville, *Les premiers Valois,* 366. Allmand, *Lancastrian Normandy,* 3.
64. *Charles VII,* I, 44.
65. Quicherat, IV, 10.
66. Maurice, *Thomas Basin,* 121.
67. Quicherat, IV, 10–12.
68. Ibid., 103.
69. Ibid., 165, 169.
70. *Charles VII,* II, 128, 136. *Louis XI,* III, 374.
71. Allmand, *Lancastrian Normandy,* 50–105.
72. *Gallia Christiana,* XI, col. 890.
73. Ibid., col. 601.
74. Ibid., col. 791. Foffano, "Umanisti italiani," 5–6. Groër, "La formation," 272–73, 278.
75. Foffano, "Umanisti italiani."
76. Allmand, *Lancastrian Normandy,* 123, n. 5; 124–25; 173ff.
77. Ibid., 123, n. 6.
78. Quicherat, IV, 13.
79. *Charles VII,* I, 35, 89.
80. Ibid.
81. Ibid., 91–101.
82. Bois, *Crise du féodalisme,* 291.
83. Maurice, *Thomas Basin,* 36, 44, 123.
84. *Charles VII,* I, 56, 126; II, 238.
85. *Louis XI,* III, 236.
86. Quicherat, IV, 145–46. Maurice, *Thomas Basin,* 118, 129–30. M. Mollat, *Le commerce maritime normand à la fin du Moyen Age* (Paris, 1952), s.v.
87. Maurice, *Thomas Basin,* 129–36.
88. Quicherat, IV, 273.
89. Ibid., 13.
90. Ibid.
91. Bibl. nat., Lat. 3658, fol. 29–29v.
92. Quicherat, IV, 13.
93. *Journal d'un Bourgeois de Paris,* 233–37.
94. Ibid., 242–43.
95. *Charles VII,* I, 144.
96. Quicherat, IV, 103–4.
97. *Charles VII,* I, 162.
98. Ibid., 164–66.
99. Ibid., 146.

100. Ibid., 104–14.
101. S. Guenée, *Les universités,* 59–60.
102. Quicherat, IV, 13. *Apologie,* 66.
103. H. Rashdall, *The Universities,* II, 264–65.
104. Ibid., 51–53.
105. *Gallia Christiana,* XI, col. 791. Foffano, "Umanisti italiani," 14. Groër, "La formation," 272–73.
106. Quicherat, IV, 13. Groër, "La formation," 273.
107. Quicherat, IV, 13–14.
108. *Apologie,* 66.
109. Groër, "La formation," 272.
110. Quicherat, IV, 14.
111. Ibid., 13–14.
112. *Charles VII,* I, 197, 225; II, 128.
113. Ibid., I, 230.
114. Ibid., I, 220.
115. S. d'Irsay, *Histoire des universités françaises et étrangères des origines à nos jours,* vol. 1: *Moyen Age et Renaissance* (Paris, 1933), p. 237.
116. Gill, *Constance,* 130.
117. Groër, "La formation," 278.
118. Ibid., 273.
119. *Apologie,* 244. Muller, "Lyon," 35.
120. Gill, *Constance,* 156.
121. Ibid., 163.
122. Muller, "Lyon," 35. Santoni, "Jean de Rouvroy."
123. Groër, "La formation," 278.
124. Quicherat, IV, 14. Groër, "La formation," 274.
125. Samaran, "Documents inédits," 51–52. Groër, "La formation," 274.
126. Samaran, "Documents inédits," 48, n. 4.
127. Quicherat, IV, 14–15. Samaran, "Documents inédits," 53. Groër, "La formation," 275.
128. Quicherat, IV, 15.
129. J. Le Goff, *La Naissance du Purgatoire* (Paris, 1981).
130. Gill, *Constance,* 214, 215, 222.
131. Quicherat, IV, 15.
132. Rashdall, *The Universities,* II, 54.
133. Quicherat, IV, 15.
134. Samaran, "Documents inédits," 52–53.
135. Ibid., 53–55.
136. Gill, *Constance,* 232.
137. Quicherat, IV, 15–16.
138. Rashdall, *The Universities,* II, 47–50.
139. Groër, "La formation," 278.
140. Quicherat, IV, 16.
141. Samaran, "Documents inédits," 55. Groër, "La formation," 277.
142. Quicherat, IV, 118.
143. Ibid., 16. Groër, "La formation," 279–80.

144. Quicherat, IV, 16.
145. Groër, "La formation," 281.
146. Samaran, "Documents inédits," 55.
147. Ibid.
148. Quicherat, IV, 16.
149. Ibid., 147.
150. *Apologie,* 146.
151. *Charles VII,* I, 260–62.
152. Ibid., 256–58.
153. Allmand, *Lancastrian Normandy,* 144–45.
154. Boüard, "Quelques données nouvelles." S. Guenée, *Les universités,* 70. Allmand, *Lancastrian Normandy,* 105–13.
155. Denifle, *La désolation,* I, 525. Foffano, "Umanisti italiani," 4–12.
156. *Charles VII,* II, 66.
157. Ibid., I, 34.
158. Allmand, *Lancastrian Normandy,* 257–59.
159. Foffano, "Umanisti italiani," 11.
160. *DHGE,* vol. 11, col. 1448.
161. Foffano, "Umanisti italiani," 16. Groër, "La formation," 283.
162. Allmand, *Lancastrian Normandy,* 277.
163. Denifle, *La désolation,* 520–26.
164. Foffano, "Umanisti italiani," 13–14, 31.
165. Denifle, *La désolation,* 526–32. Foffano, "Umanisti italiani," 8–9.
166. Foffano, "Umanisti italiani," 14–15.
167. *Charles VII,* I, 262–278.
168. Quicherat, IV, 17.
169. Ibid., 150. Samaran, "Documents inédits," 57.
170. Quicherat, I, xiii; IV, 17. Samaran, "Documents inédits," 56.
171. Quicherat, IV, 150.
172. Maurice, *Thomas Basin,* 66. Groër, "La formation," 284.
173. Foffano, "Umanisti italiani," 16.
174. Denifle, "*La désolation,*" 532–35.
175. *Charles VII,* I, 300; II, 8–10.
176. Quicherat, IV, 151–52.
177. Ibid., 17. Groër, "La formation," 284.
178. Quicherat, IV, 104.
179. Ibid., 153.
180. Ibid., 158–60.
181. Ibid., 17.
182. Maurice, *Thomas Basin,* 22, 25, 115, 143–44.
183. *Charles VII,* II, 36. *Louis XI,* II, 240.
184. *Charles VII,* II, 96. Groër, "La formation," 271.
185. *Apologie,* 90.
186. *Charles VII,* II, 136, 242.
187. Ibid., 150, 196, etc.
188. *Charles VII,* I, 124. *Louis XI,* I, 332; II, 98.
189. *Charles VII,* II, 98. *Louis XI,* II, 98, 324; III, 62, 64, 118.

190. *Charles VII*, II, 254.
191. Ibid., II, 244.
192. Ibid., I, 268. *Louis XI*, II, 48, 196.
193. *Charles VII*, I, 166.
194. *Louis XI*, I, 94.
195. *Charles VII*, II, 310. *Louis XI*, II, 70.
196. *Charles VII*, I, 140; II, 110. *Louis XI*, II, 172.
197. *Louis XI*, III, 178.
198. *Charles VII*, I, 78, 298. *Louis XI*, III, 66, 74.
199. *Louis XI*, II, 220.
200. *Charles VII*, I, 142.
201. Ibid., 166. *Louis XI*, II, 94.
202. *Charles VII*, I, 4.
203. Ibid., II, 308.
204. Ibid., 10–12.
205. *Charles VII*, II, 96. *Apologie*, 38.
206. Bibl. nat., Lat. 3658, fol. 66v., 70v.
207. *Louis XI*, III, 338–42.
208. Ibid., 342.
209. *Apologie*, 38.
210. *Charles VII*, I, 298–300.
211. *Apologie*, 38.
212. *Charles VII*, II, 268.
213. Quicherat, IV, 36, 37, 39.
214. *Louis XI*, II, 14.
216. *Apologie*, 242.
217. Ibid., 90.
218. Ibid., 96, 106, 112.
219. *Charles VII*, I, 220. *Louis XI*, I, 242; III, 208.
220. *Louis XI*, I, 258. *Apologie*, 114.
221. *Charles VII*, I, 220. *Louis XI*, I, 240–42; II, 280; III, 208.
222. *Apologie*, 242.
223. Ibid., 264.
224. Quicherat, IV, 31. *Charles VII*, I, 4.
225. Samaran and Vernet, *Les livres*, 328–29.
226. *Charles VII*, I, 166.
227. Samaran and Vernet, *Les livres*, 334–39. Groër, "La formation," 283.
228. Samaran and Vernet, *Les livres*, 329—32.
229. Ouy, "Le songe," 368–75.
230. *Charles VII*, I, 220; II, 106.
231. Ibid., I, 206–8.
232. *Louis XI*, II, 156; III, 236, 306, 320, 334, etc.
233. Cicero, *De officiis*, I, 17.
234. *Apologie*, 180.
235. Quicherat, IV, 73.
236. *Charles VII*, I, 220, 224. *Louis XI*, I, 264.

237. *Apologie,* 58.
238. Ibid., 180.
239. *Charles VII,* I, 142.
240. Quicherat, IV, 49–50.
241. *Louis XI,* III, 90.
242. *Charles VII,* I, 34.
243. Ibid., 88.
244. Ibid., 120.
245. Ibid., II, 254.
246. Quicherat, IV, 31–65.
247. *Louis XI,* II, 56–58.
248. *Charles VII,* I, 54.
249. Ibid., 256.
250. *Louis XI,* III, 152.
251. *Charles VII,* II, 228.
252. Ibid., 178.
253. Ibid., I, 204; II, 106.
254. Ibid., I, 90.
255. Ibid., 214.
256. Ibid., 68.
257. Ibid., 198; II, 164.
258. Jouet, *La résistance.*
259. *Charles VII,* I, 104–14.
260. Ibid., II, 32.
261. Ibid., 32–46.
262. *Louis XI,* II, 54.
263. Ibid., 54; III, 76.
264. *Charles VII,* I, 114. *Louis XI,* II, 52–54.
265. *Charles VII,* II, 12.
266. Ibid., I, 198.
267. Ibid., 236.
268. *Louis XI,* II, 113.
269. *Charles VII,* I, 194; II, 300. *Louis XI,* I, 2; III, 364.
270. *Charles VII,* II, 307.
271. Ibid., I, 166.
272. Ibid., 103.
273. Ibid., 220.
274. Ibid., II, 280.
275. Ibid., I, 220.
276. Ibid., 164.
277. Ibid., 220.
278. Ibid., 10–18.
279. Ibid., II, 12, 26–28.
280. Ibid., 58–59.
281. Ibid., 61.
282. Ibid., 58. Gilles le Bouvier, *Les chroniques,* 288.
283. Gilles le Bouvier, *Les chroniques,* 353.

284. *Charles VII*, II, 122.

285. F. Lot, *L'art militaire et les armées au Moyen Age*, vol. 2 (Paris, 1946), p. 84.

286. Gilles le Bouvier, *Les chroniques*, 340.

287. Martène and Durand, *Thesaurus*, I, 1816–17. Gilles le Bouvier, *Les chroniques*, 300–305.

288. Allmand, *Lancastrian Normandy*, 209–10.

289. *Gallia Christiana*, VIII, cols. 1639–40; vol. XI, cols. 603 and 794.

290. Ibid., XI, col. 699.

291. Quicherat, IV, 338–41. *Procès de condamnation de Jeanne d'Arc*, II, 422.

292. Quicherat, IV, 338–41. *Gallia Christiana*, XI, col. 493.

293. Martène and Durand, *Thesaurus*, I, 1813. Jean Chartier, *Chronique*, II, 62.

294. Gilles le Bouvier, *Les chroniques*, 289.

295. Robert Blondel, *Oeuvres*, II, 7.

296. *Charles VII*, II, 82.

297. Jean Chartier, *Chronique*, II, 71. Gilles le Bouvier, *Les chroniques*, 292.

298. *Charles VII*, II, 76–78.

299. Ibid., 82–84.

300. Gilles le Bouvier, *Les chroniques*, 293.

301. *Charles VII*, II, 90–92.

302. Jean Chartier, *Chronique*, II, 73–74.

303. Ibid., 82. Gilles le Bouvier, *Les chroniques*, 296.

304. Mathieu d'Escouchy, *Chronique*, I, 186.

305. *Charles VII*, II, 96–98.

306. Jean Chartier, *Chronique*, II, 94.

307. *Charles VII*, II, 98.

308. Robert Blondel, *Oeuvres*, I, x–xiii.

309. Quicherat, IV, 126–27. Robert Blondel, *Oeuvres*, II, 76–78.

310. *Charles VII*, I, 64; II, 132. *Louis XI*, I, 260; III, 92, 162.

311. Quicherat, IV, 174–81.

312. *Charles VII*, II, 96–104.

313. Allmand, *Lancastrian Normandy*, 287.

314. Robert Blondel, *Oeuvres*, II, 76.

315. Jean Chartier, *Chronique*, II, 94.

316. Gilles le Bouvier, *Les chroniques*, 299.

317. *Charles VII*, II, 104–6.

318. Quicherat, IV, 191.

319. Ibid., 177.

320. Ibid., 181–82.

321. Ibid., 183–87.

322. *Apologie*, 12.

323. *Charles VII*, II, 124.

324. Jean Chartier, *Chronique*, II, 146. Gilles le Bouvier, *Les chroniques*, 317.

325. *Gallia Christiana,* XI, col. 892; *DHGE,* XI, 1446–47.
326. Ibid., col. 89–90.
327. Jean Chartier, *Chronique,* II, 167.
328. Gilles le Bouvier, *Les chroniques,* 328. Allmand, *Lancastrian Normandy,* 151.
329. Quicherat, IV, 188–90.
330. *Gallia Christiana,* XI, col. 493.
331. Ibid., 699.
332. Ibid., 379–81.
333. Ibid., 699.
334. Ibid., 379–81. Foffano, "Umanisti italiani," 17, 21.
335. Gilles le Bouvier, *Les chroniques,* 352–53.
336. Allmand, *Lancastrian Normandy,* 305–6.
337. Jean Chartier, *Chronique,* III, 331–32. Gilles le Bouvier, *Les chroniques,* 352–53. Mathieu d'Escouchy, *Chronique,* III, 372. Thomas Basin, *Charles VII,* II, 156.
338. Beaune, *Naissance,* 185.
339. *Charles VII,* II, 106.
340. Gilles le Bouvier, *Les chroniques,* 326.
341. Martène and Durand, *Thesaurus,* I, 1814.
342. Gilles le Bouvier, *Les chroniques,* 357.
343. Mathieu d'Escouchy, *Chronique,* I, 233.
344. Ibid., III, 372.
345. *Charles VII,* II, 52–54. Denifle, *La désolation,* I, 519.
346. Denifle, *La désolation,* I, 529.
347. *Charles VII,* II, 76, 88, 158.
348. Gilles le Bouvier, *Les chroniques,* 354.
349. *Charles VII,* II, 106.
350. Allmand, "Local Reaction," 149.
351. Allmand, *Lancastrian Normandy,* 234.
352. Valois, *Histoire,* clvi–clxxxiv.
353. *Charles VII,* II, 292.
354. Quicherat, IV, 83.
355. Valois, *Histoire,* clxxii.
356. Quicherat, IV, 84.
357. *Charles VII,* II, 290–96.
358. Quicherat, IV, 17–18.
359. Prentout, *Les Etats provinciaux,* I, 193, 195. Allmand, *Lancastrian Normandy,* 301.
360. Allmand, "Local Reaction," 155–57.
361. Prentout, *Les Etats provinciaux,* I, 165.
362. Ibid., 160.
363. Ibid., 165.
364. Ibid., III, 24.
365. Ibid., I, 165.
366. Ibid., 166.
367. Quicherat, IV, 252–55.

368. Pernoud, *Vie et mort,* 13–14.
369. *Procès de condamnation,* II, 422.
370. Pernoud, *Vie et mort,* 56. *Procès en nullité,* II, 157–219.
371. *Procès en nullité,* II, 158.
372. Ibid., 162–64.
373. See chap. 3, n. 382.
374. *Charles VII,* II, 106.
375. *Procès en nullité,* II, 162.
376. Ibid., 543–44.
377. Quicherat, IV, 18.
378. *Ordonnances des Rois de France de la troisième race,* XIV (Paris, 1790), p. 285.
379. Ibid.
380. Ibid., 284–314.
381. Valet de Viriville, *Histoire de Charles VII, roi de France et de son époque (1403–1461),* vol. 3: *1444–1461* (Paris, 1865), p. 320.
382. Bernus, "Le rôle politique," 320.
383. *Ordonnances des Rois de France,* XIV, 314.
384. Allmand, *Lancastrian Normandy,* 301.
385. Quicherat, IV, 31.
386. Ibid., 31–65.
387. *Charles VII,* II, 302–4.
388. Ibid., 306.
389. Ibid., 150–54, 282–86.
390. Quicherat, IV, 222–23.
391. *Apologie,* 90.
392. Quicherat, IV, 222–23.
393. Prentout, *Les Etats provinciaux,* I, 170.
394. Ibid., III, 25–26.
395. Ibid., I, 180.
396. *Apologie,* 10–16. Prentout, *Les Etats provinciaux,* I, 175–81.
397. *Charles VII,* II, 276–78.
398. Gaussin, *Louis XI,* 25.
399. Stein, *Charles de France,* 1.
400. Ibid., 25.
401. *Louis XI,* I, 4.
402. Krynen, "'Le mort saisit le vif.'"
403. *Louis XI,* I, 12.
404. La Chenaye-Desbois, *Dictionnaire de la noblesse,* X, 298.
405. Quicherat, IV, 226.
406. *Apologie,* 18.
407. Ibid., 26.
408. Ibid., 38–40.
409. *Louis XI,* I, 50–52.
410. Ibid., 66–70. Leguai, *Emeutes et troubles,* 447–60.
411. *Louis XI,* I, 42.
412. Ibid., 44–45.

413. Prentout, *Les Etats provinciaux,* I, 181–87.
414. *Louis XI,* I, 52–53.
415. Stein, *Charles de France,* 25–27.
416. Quicherat, IV, 141.
417. Ibid., 229–31.
418. Ibid., 241–44.
419. Ibid., 73, 87.
420. Ibid., 84.
421. Ibid., 73. *Charles VII,* I, xiii.
422. Ourliac, "Le concordat."
423. Stein, *Charles de France,* 45.
424. *Louis XI,* I, 166.
425. Gaussin, *Louis XI,* 226–27.
426. Petit-Dutaillis, *Charles VII, Louis XI,* 345.
427. Stein, *Charles de France,* 48–49.
428. *Louis XI,* I, 150–58.
429. Ibid., 164–84.
430. Ibid., 4, 232.
431. Ibid., 166.
432. Petit-Dutaillis, *Charles VII, Louis XI,* 346.
433. *Louis XI,* I, 188.
434. Ibid., 212–13.
435. Vallez, "La construction," 44.
436. Du Fresne de Beaucourt, *Histoire,* VI, 190–91.
437. Ibid., 59–61.
438. Ibid., 198.
439. Stein, *Charles de France,* 53.
440. *Louis XI,* I, 164.
441. Philippe de Commynes, *Mémoires,* I, 45.
442. Du Fresne de Beaucourt, *Histoire,* VI, 59–60.
443. Philippe de Commynes, *Mémoires,* I, 21–22.
444. *Louis XI,* I, 206–10.
445. La Chenaye-Desbois, *Dictionnaire de la noblesse,* X, 282–300.
446. A. Coville, *Les Etats de Normandie. Leurs origines et leur développement au XIVe siècle* (Paris, 1894), 77–78 and 180.
447. Le Noir, *Preuves,* XIII, 82, 87.
448. La Chenaye-Desbois, *Dictionnaire de la noblesse,* X, 297.
449. Ibid., VII, 563–64. Valois, *Histoire,* clxxvii.
450. La Chenaye-Desbois, *Dictionnaire de la noblesse,* XII, 393–94.
451. Le Noir, *Preuves,* 158.
452. Ibid., 164.
453. *Gallia Christiana,* VI, col. 103.
454. Le Noir, *Preuves,* 153–55, 159.
455. Gilles le Bouvier, *Les chroniques,* 417. *Gallia Christiana,* VI, col. 103. La Chenaye-Desbois, *Dictionnaire de la noblesse,* X, 297–98.
456. Gaussin, *Louis XI,* 312.
457. Quicherat, IV, 252–55.

458. Philippe de Commynes, *Mémoires,* I, 80.
459. Ibid., 81.
460. Quicherat, IV, 252–55.
461. *Apologie,* 42–44.
462. Ibid.
463. Stein, *Charles de France,* 548.
464. *Apologie,* 42–44.
465. Quicherat, IV, 245. *Louis XI,* I, 224.
466. Stein, *Charles de France,* 129.
467. Prentout, *Les Etats provinciaux,* I, 190–91.
468. *Louis XI,* I, 238.
469. Quicherat, IV, 246–48.
470. *Gallia Regia,* no. 16277 bis.
471. *Gallia Regia,* no. 16273.
472. R. Delachenal, *Histoire de Charles V,* vol. 1 (Paris, 1927), p. 119.
473. *Officium ad ducem Normannorum constituendum,* in E. Martène, *De antiquis ecclesiae ritibus,* 2d ed., vol. 2 (Antwerp, 1736), cols. 853–56. P. E. Schramm, *Geschichte des englischen Königtums im Lichte der Krönung* (Weimar, 1937), p. 47. M. Bloch, *Les rois thaumaturges* (Paris, 1961), pp. 194 and 497. A. Gransden, *Historial Writing in England, c. 550 to c. 1307* (London, 1974), pp. 312–17.
474. Stein, *Charles de France,* 561.
475. Philippe de Commynes, *Mémoires,* I, 76.
476. *Louis XI,* I, 226.
477. Ibid., 220.
478. Ibid., 240–42.
479. Ibid., 248–52.
480. Stein, *Charles de France,* 127, 593.
481. *Louis XI,* I, 253. Stein, *Charles de France,* 151–57.
482. This manuscript still exists: Paris, Bibl. nat., Fr. 2623.
483. Stein, *Charles de France,* 159.
484. *Louis XI,* I, 246.
485. *Apologie,* 58.
486. Stein, *Charles de France,* 168–81.
487. *Louis XI,* I, 254–56. *Apologie,* 60–62.
488. *Apologie,* 74–76.
489. Quicherat, IV, 248–51.
490. Ibid., 252–55.
491. *Apologie,* 67–69. Stein, *Charles de France,* 174.
492. Quicherat, IV, 18.
493. *Apologie,* 66.
494. Ibid., 69.
495. Quicherat, IV, 18.
496. *Apologie,* 72–74.
497. Ibid., 76.
498. Ibid., 78.
499. Ibid., 80.

500. Ibid., 82.
501. Gaussin, *Louis XI*, 279–80.
502. *Apologie*, 92.
503. Ibid., 84.
504. Ibid.
505. Ibid., 86.
506. Ibid., 88.
507. Quicherat, IV, 19.
508. *Apologie*, 77, 88.
509. Quicherat, IV, 19.
510. *Apologie*, 90–92.
511. Ibid., 94.
512. Ibid., 96.
513. Ibid., 104.
514. Ibid., 106.
515. Ibid., 108–12.
516. Ibid., 96.
517. *Apologie*, 120, 124. Quicherat, IV, 20.
518. Quicherat, IV, 21.
519. *Apologie*, 116.
520. Ibid., 130.
521. Ibid., 191.
522. Ibid., 144–46.
523. Ibid., 190–96.
524. Ibid., 196–200.
525. Ourliac, "Le concordat," 402.
526. Lapeyre and Scheurer, *Les notaires*, I, 272.
527. Ourliac, "Le concordat," 403.
528. Ibid., 405.
529. *Apologie*, 202.
530. Quicherat, I, lxxii.
531. *Gallia Christiana*, XII, cols. 515–16. La Chenaye-Desbois, *Dictionnaire de la noblesse*, XII, col. 713–14.
532. B.-A. Pocquet du Haut-Jussé, *La France gouvernée par Jean sans Peur. Les dépenses du receveur général du royaume* (Paris, 1959), p. 219.
533. *Gallia Christiana*, XII, cols. 515–16. G. Dupont-Ferrier, *Etudes sur les institutions financières de la France à la fin du Moyen Age*, vol. 2: *Les finances extraordinaires et leur mécanisme* (Paris, 1932), p. 273. F. Autrand, *Naissance d'un grand corps de l'Etat. Les gens du Parlement de Paris, 1345–1454* (Paris, 1981), p. 78. Gaussin, *Louis XI*, 158.
534. Lapeyre and Scheurer, *Les notaires*, I, 272.
535. Louis XI, *Lettres*, IX, cols. 203–4.
536. *Gallia Christiana*, XI, col. 797.
537. Ibid., XII, col. 516. Lapeyre and Scheurer, *Les notaires*, I, 272.
538. *Dictionnaire de Biographie française*, XII, 282.
539. *Gallia Christiana*, XI, col. 797.
540. Quicherat, IV, 266–67.

541. Ibid., 142.
542. Ibid., 137–38.
543. *Gallia Christiana,* XI, col. 797.
544. Ibid., 798.
545. I owe this certainty to M. D. Grmek.
546. Quicherat, IV, 138.
547. *Apologie,* 146–50.
548. Quicherat, IV, 395–403.
549. *Louis XI,* II, 356.
550. *Charles VII,* II, 220.
551. *Louis XI,* I, 218.
552. Ibid., II, 172.
553. Ibid., 356; III, 162.
554. Hassell, *Middle French Proverbs,* 21.
555. Quicherat, IV, 76, 78.
556. *Louis XI,* I, 14.
557. Ibid., II, 114, 274.
558. Quicherat, IV, 75–89. *Apologie,* 112.
559. *Louis XI,* I, 12.
560. Ibid., 152–54; II, 132.
561. Ibid., III, 180.
562. *Charles VII,* II, 246. *Louis XI,* II, 308.
563. *Louis XI,* I, 258; III, 144.
564. *Charles VII,* I, 42. *Louis XI,* I, 214; II, 308.
565. *Louis XI,* II, 150; III, 188.
566. Ibid., I, 100; III, 126, 128, 256, 280.
567. *Charles VII,* I, 212. *Louis XI,* II, 286; III, 188.
568. *Charles VII,* I, 98.
569. Ibid., II, 246. *Louis XI,* I, 214.
570. *Charles VII,* I, 206–8.
571. *Louis XI,* I, 290–92.
572. Ibid., III, 310.
573. Ibid., I, 330.
574. Ibid., II, 140.
575. Ibid., 144.
576. Ibid., I, 242.
577. Ibid., II, 14.
578. *Charles VII,* I, 220. *Louis XI,* I, 240–42; II, 180; III, 208.
579. *Louis XI,* II, 96.
580. Ibid., III, 294, 300.
581. See n. 396.
582. See n. 408.
583. *Apologie,* 40.
584. Ibid., 144.
585. *Louis XI,* III, 386.
586. Ibid., II, 172.
587. Ibid., 208.

588. *Louis XI,* III, 104–6.

589. Psalms 110:10; Proverbs 9:10; Ecclesiasticus 1:16.

590. Luke 2:25. *Sancti Bernardi Opera,* ed. J. Leclercq and H. M. Rochais, vol. 3, pp. 330 and 358; vol. 4, p. 15.

591. *Louis XI,* III, 182.

592. Ecclesiasticus 9:22 and 40:27.

593. See nn. 370–376 above.

594. *Charles VII,* II, 26. *Louis XI,* III, 152, 164.

595. *Charles VII,* II, 34, 106.

596. *Louis XI,* III, 266.

597. Ibid., I, 218–20.

598. Ibid., III, 164.

599. Ibid., 302.

600. *Charles VII,* II, 146–48.

601. *Louis XI,* II, 170.

602. Ibid., III, 216.

603. *Charles VII,* II, 106.

604. *Louis XI,* I, 254.

605. Ibid., II, 308.

606. Ibid., III, 216.

607. *Charles VII,* I, 74.

608. *Apologie,* 64.

609. *Louis XI,* III, 240.

610. *Apologie,* 160.

611. Ibid., 166, 176.

612. Ibid., 6, 164–68.

613. Ibid., 182.

614. Ibid., 154–56.

615. Ibid., 126.

616. Ibid., 184–86.

617. E. H. Kantorowicz, *The King's Two Bodies. A Study in Medieval Political Theology* (Princeton, 1957), pp. 232–72. E. H. Kantorowicz, *Mourir pour la patrie et autres textes* (Paris, 1984), pp. 105–41.

618. Jean de Montreuil, *Opera,* I, 327.

619. Nicolas de Clamanges, *Epistolae,* 98–99. Ornato, *Jean Muret,* p. 53, n. 22.

620. Paravicini, "Peur," 186–87.

621. Ibid., 189.

622. Quicherat, IV, 22. *Apologie,* 64.

623. P. Anselme, *Histoire généalogique et chronologique de la Maison Royale de France,* vol. 1 (Paris, 1712), p. 333. P. Anselme, *Histoire généalogique et chronologique de la Maison de France,* vol. 3 (Paris, 1728), pp. 722ff. Cagé, "Louis de Luxembourg," 29–41.

624. 22 January and 10 May 1465; Louis XI, *Lettres,* II, 227 and 290.

625. 17 August 1466–21 August 1469; Louis XI, *Lettres,* III, 77, 107, 229; IV, 28.

626. Gaussin, *Louis XI,* 124.

627. Cagé, "Louis de Luxembourg," 37.
628. Ibid., 38. Gaussin, *Louis XI,* 124.
629. *Louis XI,* II, 248.
630. Ibid., 254.
631. Philippe de Commynes, *Mémoires,* II, 139.
632. *Louis XI,* II, 266.
633. Ibid., 266–72.
634. Ibid., 258.
635. Ibid., 342.
636. Philippe de Commynes, *Mémoires,* II, 302.
637. *Charles VII,* II, 62. *Louis XI,* I, 220, 268.
638. *Louis XI,* III, 308.
639. Quicherat, IV, 138.
640. *Louis XI,* III, 254.
641. Quicherat, IV, 138.
642. Ibid., 7, 23.
643. Marzi, *La questione,* 1–2, 8, 61.
644. Quicherat, IV, 101–5. Paris, Bibl. nat., Lat. 5970 A, fol. 63–66.
645. Marzi, *La questione,* 12, 39ff. Thorndike, *A History,* IV, 560–61.
646. Quicherat, IV, 118–19.
647. Marzi, *La questione,* 42.
648. Ibid., 16.
649. Ibid., 12.
650. *Charles VII,* I, xv.
651. Quicherat, IV, 119.
652. Ibid., 114.
653. Ibid., 115, 120, 122.
654. Paris, Bibl. nat., Lat. 3658, fol. 28.
655. Ibid., fol. 29.
656. Ibid., fol. 29v.
657. Ibid., fol. 29v.–30.
658. Quicherat, IV, 106.
659. Samaran and Vernet, *Les livres,* 335.
660. Maurice, *Thomas Basin,* 113–15.
661. Ibid., 111–12.
662. Quicherat, IV, 272.
663. Ibid., 273.
664. Ibid., 272.
665. Maurice, *Thomas Basin,* 143, n. 8.

BIBLIOGRAPHY

Introduction

Primary

Basin, Thomas. *Histoire de Louis XI,* ed. and trans. C. Samaran, 3 vols. Paris, 1963–72.

———. *Histoire des règnes de Charles VII et de Louis XI,* ed. J. Quicherat. 4 vols. Paris, 1855–59.

Chronique des quatre premiers Valois (1327–1393), ed. S. Luce. Paris, 1862.

Gerson, Jean. *Oeuvres complètes,* ed. P. Glorieux. 8 vols. Paris, Tournai, Rome, 1960–72.

Louis XI, *Lettres,* ed. J. Vaesen and E. Charavay. 11 vols. Paris, 1885–1909.

Masselin, Jehan. *Journal des états généraux de France tenus à Tours sous le règne de Charles VIII,* ed. A. Bernier. Paris, 1835.

Oresme, Nicole. *Le Livre de Politiques d'Aristote,* ed. A. D. Menut. Philadelphia, 1970.

Ursins, Jean Juvénal des. *Ecrits politiques,* ed. P. S. Lewis. 2 vols. Paris, 1978–85.

Secondary

Autrand, F. *Charles VI. La folie du roi.* Paris, 1986.

———. "La force de l'âge: jeunesse et vieillesse au service de l'Etat en France aux XIV et XV siècles." *CRAIBL,* 1985, pp. 206–23.

Battifol, L. *Jean Jouvenel, prévôt des marchands de la ville de Paris (1360–1431).* Paris, 1894.

Bulst, N. "Studium und Karriere im königlichen Dienst in Frankreich im 15. Jahrhundert." *Schulen und Studium im sozialen Wandel des hohen und späten Mittelalters,* ed. J. Fried. Sigmaringen, 1986, pp. 375–405.

Cazelles, R. *Etienne Marcel, champion de l'unité française.* Paris, 1984.

Chauney, M. "Esquisse prosopographique de l'épiscopat bourguignon suffragant de l'archevêché de Lyon aux XIIIe–XVe siècles." *Comité des Travaux historiques et scientifiques. 109e Congrès national des Sociétés savantes, Dijon, 1984. Histoire médiévale et Philologie,* vol. 1: *L'encadrement religieux des fidèles au Moyen Age et jusqu'au Concile de Trente.* Paris, 1985, pp. 677–86.

Chevalier, B. *Tours, ville royale (1356–1520). Origine et développement d'une capitale à la fin du Moyen Age.* Louvain-Paris, 1975.

Contamine, P. "Un traité politique inédit de la fin du XVe siècle." *Annuaire-Bulletin de la Société de l'histoire de France,* 1983–84, pp. 139–71.

Coulet, N. "De senectute," by a fifteenth-century Provençal Augustin. Forthcoming.

Coville, A. *Le traité de la ruine de l'église de Nicolas de Clamanges et la traduction française de 1564.* Paris, 1936.

Delumeau, Jean. *Le péché et la peur. La culpabilisation en Occident (XIIIe–XVIIIe siècles).* Paris, 1983.

Demotz, B. "Le comté de Savoie du début du XIIIe au début du XVe siècle. Etude du pouvoir dans une principauté réussie." Thesis. Lyons, 1985.

Desportes, P. "La population de Reims au XVe siècle d'après un dénombrement de 1422." *Le Moyen Age,* 1966, pp. 463–509.

Duby. Georges. *Guillaume Le Maréchal ou le meilleur chevalier du monde.* Paris, 1984.

Eichenlaub, J.-L. "Le '*Tractatus de diversis materiis predicabilibus*' d'Etienne de Bourbon. Première partie: '*De dono timoris.*' Edition et étude." *PTEC,* 1984, pp. 37–40.

Favier, J. *François Villon.* Paris, 1982.

Forgeot, H. *Jean Balue, cardinal d'Angers (1421?–1491).* Paris, 1895.

Gianola, G. M. "La raccolta di biografie come problema storiografico nel *De viris* di Giovanni Colonna." *Bulletino dell'Istituto Storico Italiano per il Medio Evo e Archivio Muratoriano* 89 (1980–81): 509–40.

Gilson, E. "Sur l'âge de la maturité philosophique selon saint Thomas d'Aquin." *L'homme devant Dieu. Mélanges offerts au Père Henri de Lubac,* II: *Du Moyen Age au siècle des Lumières.* Paris, 1963, pp. 151–67.

Gransden, A. "Childhood and Youth in Medieval England." *Nottingham Mediaeval Studies* 16 (1972): 3–19.

Grmek, M. D. *On Ageing and Old Age. Basic Problems and Historic Aspects of Gerontology and Geriatrics.* The Hague, 1958.

Guenée, Barnard. *Politique et histoire au Moyen Age. Recueil d'articles sur l'histoire politique et l'historiographie médiévales (1956–1981).* Paris, 1981.

———. "L'âge des personnes authentiques; ceux qui comptent dans la société médiévale sont-ils jeunes ou vieux?" *Prosopographie et genèse de l'état moderne,* ed. F. Autrand. Paris, 1986, pp. 249–279.

Heinzelmann, M. "Neue Aspekte der biographischen und hagiographischen Literatur in der lateinischen Welt (1.–6. Jahrhundert)." *Francia* 1 (1973): 27–44.

Herlihy, David. "Vieillir à Florence au Quattrocento." *Annales,* 1969, pp. 1338–52.

Higounet-Nidal, A. *Périgueux aux XIVe et XVe siècles. Etude de démographie historique.* Bordeaux, 1978.

Jugie, P. "Le Cardinal Gui de Boulogne (1316–1373). Biographie et étude d'une 'familia' cardinalice." *PTEC,* 1986, pp. 83–92.

Kantorowicz, E. H. *Mourir pour la patrie et autres textes.* Paris, 1984.

Kerhervé, J. "Jean Mauléon, trésorier de l'épargne. Une carrière au service de l'état Breton." *Comité des Travaux historiques et scientifiques. Actes du 107e Congrès national des Sociétés savantes, Brest, 1982. Section de philologie et d'histoire jusqu'à 1610,* vol. 2: *Questions d'histoire de Bretagne.* Paris, 1984, pp. 161–84.

Kohl, B. G. "Petrarch's Prefaces to 'De Viris Illustribus,'" *History and Theory* 13 (1974): 132–44.

Langlois, C.-V. *La vie en France au Moyen Age de la fin du XIIe au milieu du XIVe siècle d'après des moralistes du temps.* Paris, 1925.

Lapeyre, A., and R. Scheurer. *Les notaires et secrétaires du roi sous les règnes de Louis XI, Charles VIII et Louis XII (1461–1515). Notices personnelles et généalogies.* 2 vols. Paris, 1978.

Lettinck, N. "Comment les historiens de la première moitié du XIIe siècle jugeaient-ils leur temps?" *Journal des savants,* 1984, pp. 51–77.

Lewis, P. S. "Jean Juvenal des Ursins and the Common Literary Attitude Towards Tyranny in Fifteenth-Century France." *Medium Aevum* 34 (1965): 103–21.

Madelénat, D. *La biographie.* Paris, 1984.

Millet, H. "L'ordinateur et la biographie ou la recherche du singulier." *Problèmes et méthodes de la biographie. Actes du Colloque Sorbonne, 3–4 mai 1985.* Paris, 1985, pp. 115–27.

Mollat, G. "L'oeuvre oratoire de Clément VI." *Archives d'histoire doctrinale et littéraire du Moyen Age* 3 (1928): 239–74.

Momigliano, Arnaldo. *The Development of Greek Biography.* Cambridge, Mass., 1971.

———. *Problèmes d'historiographie ancienne et moderne.* Paris, 1983.

Moranvillé, H. *Etude sur la vie de Jean Le Mercier, 13 . . .–1397.* Paris, 1888.

Ouy, G. "L'humanisme et les mutations politiques et sociales en France aux XIVe et XVe siècles." *L'humanisme français au début de la Renaissance.* Paris, 1973, pp. 27–44.

———. "Simon de Plumetot (1371–1443) et sa bibliothèque." *Miscellanea codicologica F. Masai dicata.* Ghent, 1979, pp. 353–81.

Paravicini, W. "Peur, pratiques, intelligences. Formes de l'opposition aristocratique à Louis XI d'après les interrogatoires du connétable de Saint-Pol." *La France de la fin du XVe siècle. Renouveau et apogée,* ed. B. Chevalier et P. Contamine. Paris, 1985, pp. 183–96.

Paravicini Bagliani, A. "Rajeunir au Moyen Age. Roger Bacon et le mythe de la prolongation de la vie." *Revue médicale de la Suisse romande* 106 (1986): 9–23.

Préaud, M. *Les astrologues à la fin du Moyen Age.* Paris, 1984.

Problèmes et méthodes de la biographie. Actes du Colloque Sorbonne, 3–4 mai 1985. Paris, 1985.

Sprandel, R. *Altersschicksal und Altersmoral. Die Geschichte der Einstellungen zum Altern nach der Pariser Bibelexegese des 12.–16. Jahrhunderts*. Stuttgart, 1981.

Vercauteren, F. "La biographie et l'histoire." *Bulletin de l'Académie royale de Belgique* 52 (1966): 554–65.

Verger, J. "Tendances actuelles de la recherche sur l'histoire de l'éducation en France au Moyen Age (XIIe–XVe siècles)." *Histoire de l'Education* 6 (1980): 9–33.

Chapter 1: Bernard Gui

Année dominicaine. New edition. December 11, Lyons, 1909, pp. 745–52.

Baluze, E. *Vitae Paparum Avenionensium*. New edition, ed. G. Mollat, 4 vols. Paris, 1914–27.

Becquet, J. "Le préchantre Hélie et les chroniques de la cathédrale de Limoges au XIIIe siècle." *Bulletin de la Société archéologique et historique du Limousin* 110 (1983): 89–101.

Benedict XII, *Lettres communes*, ed. J.-M. Vidal. 3 vols. Paris, 1903–11.

Bernardus Guidonis. *De fundatione et prioribus conventium provinciarum Tolosanae et Provinciae Ordinis Praedicatorum*, ed. P.-A. Amargier. Rome, 1961.

———. *Practica Inquisitionis Heretice Pravitatis*, ed. C. Douais. Paris, 1886.

Bernard Gui, *Manuel de l'inquisiteur*, ed. and trans. G. Mollat. 2 vols. 2d printing. Paris, 1964.

Bernard Gui et son monde. Toulouse, 1981 (Cahiers de Fanjeaux, 16).

Campagne, P. "Acquisition d'un recueil manuscrit de Bernard Gui (XIVe siècle) par la Bibliothèque municipale de Limoges." *Bulletin de la Société archéologique et historique de Limousin* 110 (1983): 102–19.

Delisle, L. "Notice sur les manuscrits de Bernard Gui." *Notices et extraits des manuscrits de la Bibliothèque nationale et autres bibliothèques*, vol. 27. Paris, 1879, pp. 169–455.

Dossat, Y. "Les origines de la querelle entre Prêcheurs et Mineurs provençaux: Bernard Délicieux." *Franciscains d'Oc. Les Spirituels, ca. 1280–1324* (Cahiers de Fanjeaux, 10). Toulouse, 1975, pp. 315–54.

Douais, C. *Documents pour servir à l'histoire de l'Inquisition dans le Languedoc*. 2 vols. Paris, 1900.

———. *Essai sur l'organisation des études dans l'ordre des Frères Prêcheurs au treizième siècle (1216–1342), Première province de Provence. Province de Toulouse. . . .* Paris-Toulouse, 1884.

Favier, J. *Philippe le Bel*. Paris, 1978.

Guenée, Bernard, *Histoire et culture historique dans l'Occident médiéval*. Paris. 1980.

Guillaume de Pierre Godin. *Tractatus de causa immediata ecclesiastice potestatis*, ed. W. D. McCready. Toronto, 1982.

Guillemain, B. *La cour pontificale d'Avignon, 1309–1376. Etude d'une société.* Reprint. Paris, 1966.
Herde, P. *Cölestin V. (1294) (Peter vom Morrone). Der Engelpapst.* Stuttgart, 1981.
B. Humberti de Romanis Opera. De vita regulari, ed. J.-J. Berthier. 2 vols. Rome, 1888.
John XXII. *Lettres communes,* ed. G. Mollat. 16 vols. Paris, 1904–46.
Mandonnet, P. "La canonisation de saint Thomas d'Aquin (18 juillet 1323." *Mélanges thomistes publiés à l'occasion du VIe centenaire.* Saint-Maximin, 1923, pp. 1–48.
———. *Des écrits authentiques de s. Thomas d'Aquin.* 2d edition. Freiburg, 1910.
Manselli, R. *Spirituali e Beghini in Provenza.* Rome, 1959.
Martin-Chabot, E. "Un témoignage de séjour à Pise de Bernard Gui et de Bertrand de la Tour durant leur mission en Italie (27 janvier 1318)." *Bull. philologique et historique (jusqu'en 1715) du Comité des travaux historiques et scientifiques, année 1921.* Paris, 1923, pp. 137–41.
Mollat, G. *Les papes d'Avignon (1305–1378).* 10th edition. Paris, 1965.
Quillet, J. *La philosophie politique de Marsile de Padoue.* Paris, 1970.
Schneider, J. "Recherches sur une encyclopédie du XIIIe siècle: le *Speculum Majus* de Vincent de Beauvais." *Comptes rendus de l'Académie des Inscriptions et Belles-Lettres,* 1976, pp. 174–89.
Stephanus de Salaniaco and Bernardus Guidonis. *De quatuor in quibus Deus Praedicatorum ordinem insignivit,* ed. T. Kaeppeli. Rome, 1949.
Thomas, A. "Bernard Gui, frère prêcheur." *Histoire littéraire de la France,* vol. 35. Paris, 1921, pp. 139–232.
1274. Année charnière. Mutations et continuités. Lyon-Paris, 30 septembre–5 octobre 1974. Paris, 1977 (Colloques internationaux du Centre national de la recherche scientifique, no. 558).
Valois, N. "Jacques Duèse, pape sous le nom de Jean XXII." *Histoire littéraire de la France,* vol. 34. Paris, 1915, pp. 391–630.

Chapter 2: Gilles le Muisit

Primary

Chronique et Annales de Gilles Le Muisit, abbé de Saint-Martin de Tournai (1272–1352), ed. H. Lemaître. Paris, 1906.
Poésies de Gilles Li Muisis, ed. Kervyn de Lettenhove. 2 vols. Louvain, 1882.

Secondary

Baluze, E. *Vitae Paparum Avenionensium.* New edition. Ed. G. Mollat. 5 vols. Paris, 1914–27.
Berlière, U. *Monasticon Belge,* vol. 1. Maredsous, 1890.

———. "Trois traités inédits sur les Flagellants de 1349." *Revue bénédictine* 25 (1908): 334–57.

Coville, A. "Gilles Li Muisis, abbé de Saint-Martin de Tournai, chroniqueur et moraliste." *Histoire littéraire de la France*, vol. 37. Paris, 1938, pp. 250–324.

D'Haenens, A. *L'abbaye Saint-Martin de Tournai de 1290 à 1350. Origines, évolution et dénouement d'une crise.* Louvain, 1961. Reviewed by G. Despy, *Revue belge de philologie et d'histoire* 41 (1963): 1281–87.

———. "La crise des abbayes bénédictines au Bas Moyen Age: Saint-Martin de Tournai de 1290 à 1350." *Le Moyen Age* 65 (1959): 75–95.

———. "La date exacte de la naissance de Gilles Li Muisis (janvier 1272)." *Revue bénédictine* 68 (1958): 180–284.

———. "Gilles Li Muisis ou Le Muisit." *Biographie nationale de Belgique*, vol. 32. Brussels, 1964, cols. 528–40.

———. "Une oeuvre à restituer à Gilles Li Muisis: la chronique dite de Jacques Muevin." *Bulletin de la Commission royale d'histoire* 127 (1961): 1–32.

Frédéricq, P. *Corpus Documentorum Inquisitionis Haereticae Pravitatis Neerlandicae.* 3 vols. The Hague, 1889, 1896, 1906.

———. "Deux sermons inédits de Jean Du Fayt sur les Flagellants (5 octobre 1349) et sur le Grand Schisme d'Occident (1378)." *Bulletin de l'Académie royale de Belgique*, 1903, pp. 688–718.

Grandes Chroniques de France (Les), ed. J. Viard. 10 vols. Paris, 1920–53.

Guenée, Bernard. *Histoire et culture historique dans l'Occident médiéval.* Paris, 1980.

Langlois, Charles. *La vie en France au Moyen Age de la fin du XIIe au milieu du XIVe siècle d'après des moralistes du temps.* Paris, 1925.

Lorcin, M.-T. "Vieillesse et vieillissement vus par les médecins du Moyen Age." *Bulletin du Centre d'histoire économique et sociale de la région lyonnaise* 4 (1983): 5–22.

Petit-Dutaillis, Charles. *Les communes françaises. Caractère et évolution des origines au XVIIIe siècle.* Paris, 1947.

Pirenne, Henri. *Histoire de Belgique.* Vol. 1: *Des origines au commencement du XIVe siècle.* 3d edition. Brussels, 1909.

Recueil des chroniques de Flandre, ed. J.-J. De Smet. 4 vols. Brussels, 1837–65.

Chapter 3: Pierre d'Ailly

Primary

Aristotle. *Ethique à Nicomaque*, introduction, translation, and commentary by R.-A. Gauthier and J. Y. Jolif, vol. 1: *Introduction et traduction.* Louvain-Paris, 1958.

Boniface Ferrer. "Tractatus pro defensione Benedicti XIII." In E. Martène and U. Durand, *Thesaurus novus Anecdotorum*, vol. 2. Paris, 1717, cols. 1435–1529.

Chronique des règnes de Jean II et de Charles V, ed. R. Delachenal. 4 vols. Paris, 1910–20.

Chronique du Religieux de Saint-Denys, ed. L. Bellaguet. 6 vols. Paris, 1839–52.

Cicero. "On Old Age." "On Friendship." "On Moral Duties."

———. *De amicitia*, ed. and trans. L. Laurand. Paris, 1957.

Courtecuisse, Jean. *L'oeuvre oratoire française*, ed. G. Di Stefano. Turin, 1969.

Froissart, Jean. *Chroniques*. Vol. 14, *1386 (1325)–1388*, ed. A. Mirot. Paris, 1966.

Joannis Gersonii . . . Opera Omnia, ed. L. Ellies Du Pin, vol. 4. Antwerp, 1706.

Gerson, Jean. *Oeuvres complètes*, ed. P. Glorieux. 8 vols. Paris-Tournai-Rome, 1960–72.

Jean Juvénal des Ursins. "Histoire de Charles VI, roi de France." In Michaud and Poujoulat, *Nouvelle Collection des mémoires pour servir à l'histoire de France*, vol. 2. Paris, 1836, pp. 333–569.

Jean de Montreuil. *Opera*, ed. E. Ornato, N. Grévy-Pons, and G. Ouy. 3 vols. Turin, 1963–75, and Paris, 1981.

Nicolas de Baye, *Journal de Nicolas de Baye, greffier du Parlement de Paris, 1400–1417*, ed. A. Tuetey. 2 vols. Paris, 1885–88.

Nicolas de Clamanges, *Epistolae*, ed. J. Lydius. Leyden, 1613.

Nicole Oresme. *Le livre de Politiques d'Aristote*, ed. A. D. Menut. Philadelphia, 1970.

Philippe de Mézières, *Le songe du vieil Pelerin*, ed. G. W. Coopland. 2 vols. Cambridge, 1969.

Philippe de Vitry. *Les oeuvres*, ed. P. Tarbé. Rheims, 1850.

Petrus de Ailliaco (Pierre d'Ailly), *Tractatus et sermones*. Strasbourg, 1490; reproduced Frankfurt, 1971.

Pierre d'Ailly, "De concordia astronomice veritatis et narrationis hystorice." In Pierre d'Ailly, *Imago mundi*. Bibl. nat., Rés. G 346.

Pierre d'Ailly, *Imago mundi*, ed. E. Buron. 3 vols. Paris, 1930.

Pierre Ameilh. *La correspondance de Pierre Ameilh, archevêque de Naples puis d'Embrun (1363–1369)*, ed. H. Bresc. Paris, 1972.

Simon de Cramaud. *De Substraccione Obedience*, ed. H. Kaminsky. Cambridge, Mass., 1984.

Secondary

Badel, P.-Y. "Pierre d'Ailly, auteur du 'Jardin amoureux.'" *Romania* 97 (1976): 369–81.

Baluze, E. *Vitae Paparum Avenionensium*. New edition, ed. G. Mollat. 4 vols. Paris, 1914–27.

Bègne, J.-P. "Exégèse et astrologie. A propos d'un ouvrage inédit de Pierre d'Ailly." *Revue des sciences ecclésiastiques* 92 (1905): 445–60, 494–508.

Bernstein, A. E. *Pierre d'Ailly and the Blanchard Affair. University and*

Chancellor of Paris at the Beginning of the Great Schism. Leyden, 1978.

Bloomfield, M. W. *The Seven Deadly Sins. An Introduction to the History of a Religious Concept, with Special Reference to Medieval English Literature.* Michigan State College Press, 1952.

Brayer, E. "Notice du manuscrit 574 de la Bibliothèque municipale de Cambrai, suivie d'une édition des sermons français de Pierre d'Ailly." *Notices et extraits des manuscrits de la Bibliothèque nationale et autres bibliothèques,* vol. 43. Paris, 1965, pp. 145–343.

Bresc, H. "Les partis cardinalices et leurs ambitions dynastiques." *Genèse et Débuts* . . . , pp. 45–57.

Chiavassa-Gouron, I. "Les lectures des maîtres et étudians du collège de Navarre: un aspect de la vie intellectuelle à l'université de Paris (1380–1520)." Thesis. Ecoles des Chartes, Paris, 1985.

Combes, A. *Etudes Gersoniennes* I: "L'authenticité gersonienne de l'*Annotatio doctorum aliquorum qui de contemplatione locuti sunt.*" *Archives d'histoire doctrinale et littéraire du Moyen Age* 12 (1939): 291–364.

———. "Sur les 'Lettres de consolation' de Nicolas de Clamanges à Pierre d'Ailly." *Archives d'histoire doctrinale et littéraire du Moyen Age* 13 (1940–42): 359–89.

Coville, A. "Recherches sur Jean Courtecuisse et ses oeuvres oratoires." *BEC* 65 (1904): 469–529.

———. *Jean Petit. La question du tyrannicide au commencement du XVe siècle.* Paris, 1932.

———. "Philippe de Vitry. Notes biographiques." *Romania* 59 (1933): 520 47.

———. *Gontier et Pierre Col et l'humanisme en France au temps de Charles VI.* Paris, 1934.

———. *Recherches sur quelques écrivains du XIVe et du XVe siècle.* Paris, 1935.

———. *Le traité de la ruine de l'Eglise de Nicolas de Clamanges et la traduction française de 1564.* Paris, 1936.

Denifle, H., and E. Chatelain. *Chartularium Universitatis Parisiensis.* 4 vols. Paris, 1889–97.

Déprez. E. *Hugo Aubriot, praepositus parisiensis et urbanus praetor (1367–1381). Quo pacto cum Ecclesia atque Universitate certaverit.* Paris, 1902.

Doncoeur, P. "La condamnation de Jean de Monzon par Pierre d'Orgemont, évêque de Paris, le 23 août 1387." *RQH* 82 (1907): 176–87.

Finke, H. "Die Nation in den spätmittelalterlichen allgemeinen Konzilien." In *Das Konstanzer Konzil,* ed. R. Bäumer. Darmstadt, 1977, pp. 347–68.

Gandillac, M. Patronnier de. "De l'usage et de la valeur des arguments probables dans les questions du cardinal Pierre d'Ailly sur le 'Livre des Sentences,'" *Archives d'histoire doctrinale et littéraire du Moyen Age* 8 (1933): 43–91.

Genèse et Débuts du Grand Schisme d'Occident. Paris, 1980. (Colloques internationaux du C.N.R.S., no. 586, Avignon, 25–28 September 1978).

Genet, J.-P. "Ecclesiastics and Political Theory in Late Medieval England:

The End of a Monopoly." *Church Politics and Patronage,* ed. R. B. Dobson. Gloucester, 1984, pp. 23–44.

Gill, J. *Constance et Bâle-Florence.* Paris, 1965. (Histoire des conciles oecuméniques, 9).

Gilson, Etienne. *La philosophie au Moyen Age.* 2 vols. Paris, 1976.

Glorieux, P. "La vie et les oeuvres de Gerson. Essai chronologique." *Archives d'histoire doctrinale et littéraire du Moyen Age* 25–26 (1950–51): 149–92.

———. "L'oeuvre littéraire de Pierre d'Ailly. Remarques et précisions." *Mélanges de science religieuse* 22 (1965): 61–78.

———. "Pierre d'Ailly et saint Thomas." *Littérature et religion. Mélanges offerts à M. le Chanoine Joseph Coppin . . . , Mélanges de science religieuse* 23 (1966), supplementary volume, pp. 45–54.

———. "Notations bigraphiques sur Nicolas de Clamanges," *Mélanges . . . M.-D. Chenu.* Paris, 1967, pp. 291–310.

———. "Deux éloges de la sainte Ecriture par Pierre d'Ailly." *Mélanges de science religieuse* 29 (1972): 13–129.

Grenier, Dom. "Pierre d'Ailly." *Analecta Juris Pontifici,* series 15 (1876), issue 136, cols. 897–915. O. Guyotjeannin read and checked this article for me at the Vatican Library.

Guenée, Bernard. *Les entrées royales françaises de 1328 à 1515.* Paris, 1968.

———. *Histoire et culture historique dans l'Occident médiéval.* Paris, 1980.

———. "Catalogue des gens de justice de Senlis et de leurs familles (1380–1550)." *Comptes rendus et mémoires de la Société d'histoire et d'archéolgoie de Senlis,* 1979–80, pp. 20–84; 1981–82, pp. 3–96.

———. *L'Occident aux XIV et XVe siècle. Les Etats.* 2d edition. Paris, 1981.

———. "Des limites féodales aux frontières politiques." *Les lieux de mémoire,* ed. P. Nora, vol. 2, *La nation.* Paris, 1986, pp. 11–33.

———. "L'âge des personnes authentiques; ceux qui comptent dans la société médiévale sont-ils jeunes ou vieux?" *Prosopographie et genèse de l'état moderne,* ed. F. Autrand. Paris, 1986, pp. 249–79.

Guenée, S. *Bibliographie de l'histoire des universités françaises des origines à la Révolution.* 2 vols. Paris, 1978–81.

———. *Les universités françaises des origines à la Révolution. Notices historiques. . . .* Paris, 1982.

Hicks, E. ed. "Christine de Pisan, Jean Gerson, Jean de Montreuil, Gontier et Pierre Col." *Le débat sur le Roman de la Rose.* Paris, 1977.

Jorga, N. *Philippe de Mézières, 1327–1405, et la croisade au XIVe siècle.* Paris, 1896.

Kaminsky, H. *Simon de Cramaud and the Great Schism.* New Brunswick, N.J., 1983.

Lapeyre, A., and R. Scheurer. *Les notaires et secrétaires du roi sous les règnes de Louis XI, Charles VIII et Louis XII (1461–1515). Notices personnelles et généalogies. . . .* 2 vols. Paris, 1978.

Lavisse, Ernest. *Histoire de France.* Vol. 4.1: *Les premiers Valois et la guerre de Cent Ans (1328–1422),* by A. Coville. Paris, 1902.

Le Bachelet, X. "Immaculée conception." *Dictionnaire de théologie catholique*, vol. 7. Paris, 1912, cols. 845–1218.

Lefebvre, C.-A., known as Faber. "Documents relatifs à Pierre d'Ailly, évêque de Cambrai." *Revue des sociétés savantes des départements*, series 4, vol. 8 (1868). Paris, 1869, pp. 139–59.

Lenoble, F. "Pierre de Luxembourg. Un saint du XIVe siècle et son image." Master's thesis. Paris, 1983.

Lieberman, M. "Chronologie gersonienne," V and VIII. *Romania* 78 (1957): 433–62; 81 (1960): 44–98.

Macary, M. "Une pensée du XIVe siècle. Recherches sur le 'Songe du vieil Pelerin' de Philippe de Mézières (v. 1327–1405)." Master's thesis. Paris, 1985.

Macek, J. *Jean Hus et les traditions hussites (XVe–XIXe siècle)*. Paris, 1973.

Mollat, G. "L'aumônier du roi de France, du XIIIe au XVe siècle." *CRAIBL*, 1939, pp. 514–25.

Montagnes, B. "Saint Vincent Ferrier devant le Schisme." *Genèse et débuts. . . .*, pp. 607–13.

Oakley, F. "The 'Propositiones utiles' of Pierre d'Ailly: An Epitome of Conciliar Theory." *Church History* 29 (1960): 398–403.

———. *The Political Thought of Pierre d'Ailly. The Voluntarist Tradition.* New Haven, 1964.

Ornato, E. *Jean Muret et ses amis, Nicolas de Clamanges et Jean de Montreuil. Contribution à l'étude des rapports entre les humanistes de Paris et ceux d'Avignon (1394–1420)*. Geneva-Paris, 1969.

Ouy, G. "La plus ancienne oeuvre retrouvée de Jean Gerson: le brouillon inachevé d'un traité contre Juan de Monzon (1389–1390)." *Romania* 83 (1962): 275–301.

———. "Enquête sur les manuscrits autographes du chancelier Gerson et sur les copies faites par son frère le célestin Jean Gerson." *Scriptorium* 16 (1962): 275–301.

———. "La réponse de Jean de Montreuil au chancelier de Florence." *Italia Medioevale e Umanistica* 7 (1964): 351–74.

———. *Le recueil épistolaire autographe de Pierre d'Ailly et les notes d'Italie de Jean de Montreuil.* Amsterdam, 1966.

———. "La 'Deploratio super civitatem aut regionem que gladium evaginavit super se.'" *Divinitas* 11 (1967): 747–84.

———. "Gerson, émule de Pétrarque. Le 'Pastroium Carmen,' poème de jeunesse de Gerson et la renaissance de l'églogue en France à la fin du XIVe siècle." *Romania* 88 (1967): 175–231.

———. "Paris, l'un des principaux foyers de l'humanisme en Europe au début du XVe siècle." *Bulletin de la Société de l'histoire de Paris et de l'Ile-de-France*" (1967–68), pp. 71–98.

———. "Le thème du 'Taedium scriptorum gentilium' chez les humanistes, particulièrement en France au début du XVe siècle." *Cahiers de l'Association internationale des études françaises* 23 (1971): 9–26.

———. "Humanisme et propagande politique en France au début du XVe siècle: Ambrogio Migli et les ambitions impériales de Louis d'Orléans."

Atti del Convegno su: "Culture et politique en France à l'époque de l'Humanisme et de la Renaissance." Turin, 29 March–3 April 1971. Turin, 1974, pp. 13–42.

———. "Le collège de Navarre, berceau de l'humanisme français." *Bulletin philologique et historique du Comité des travaux historiques* (1975), vol. 1, pp. 276–99.

———. "La dialectique des rapports intellectuels franco-italiens et l'Humanisme en France aux XIVe et XVe siècles." *Atti del Colloquio italo-francese sul tema: Rapporti culturali ed economici fra Italia e Francia nei secoli dal XIV al XVI (Roma, 18–20 febbraio 1978).* Rome, 1979, pp. 137–56.

———. "Simon de Plumetot (1371–1443) et sa bibliothèque." *Miscellanea codicologica F. Masai dicata.* Ghent, 1979, pp. 353–81.

———. "La ponctuation des premiers humanistes français." *La Ponctuation: recherches historiques et actuelles.* Paris, 1979, pp. 56–89.

———. "Jean de Montreuil (*alias* de Monthureux-le-Sec), Pétrarque et Salutati." *Mélanges à la mémoire de Franco Simone.* Geneva, 1980, pp. 47–55 and 592–93.

———. "Autographes d'auteurs français des XIVe et XVe siècles: leur utilité pour l'histoire intellectuelle." *Commentationes* 28 (1983): 69–103.

———. (with the cooperation of Mmes. V. Gerz, R. Hubschmid, and C. Regnier). *Le catalogue de la bibliothèque de Saint-Victor de Paris de Claude de Grandrue (1514).* Paris, 1983.

———. "Une énigme codicologique: les signatures des cahiers dans les manuscrits autographes et originaux de Christine de Pisan." *Mélanges offerts à Léon Gilissen.* Brussels.

Ouy, G., and N. Catach. "De Pierre d'Ailly à Jean Antoine de Baïf: un exemple de double orthographe à la fin du XIVe siècle." *Romania* 97 (1976): 218–48.

Pascoe, L. B. "Pierre d'Ailly: Histoire, schisme, et Antéchrist." *Genèse et débuts . . . ,* pp. 615–22.

Piétresson de Saint-Aubin, P. "Documents inédits sur l'installation de Pierre d'Ailly à l'évêché de Cambrai en 1397." *BEC* 113 (1955): 111–39.

Poirion, D. *Le Moyen Age.* Vol. 2: *1300–1480.* Paris, 1971.

Pons, N. "La propagande de guerre française avant l'apparition de Jeanne d'Arc." *Journal des savants,* 1982, pp. 191–214.

Préaud, M. *Les astrologues à la fin du Moyen Age.* Paris, 1984.

Raymond, I. W. "D'Ailly's 'Epistola Diaboli Leviathan.'" *Church History* 22 (1953): 181–91.

Saenger, P. "Silent Reading: Its Impact on the Late Medieval Script and Society." *Viator* 13 (1982): 367–414.

Salembier, L. *Petrus ab Ailliaco.* Lille, 1886.

———. *Les oeuvres françaises du Cardinal Pierre d'Ailly, évêque de Cambrai, 1350–1420.* Arras, 1907.

———. *Le Cardinal Pierre d'Ailly, chancelier de l'Université de Paris, évêque du Puy et de Cambrai, 1350–1420.* Tourcoing, 1932.

Santoni, P. "Jean de Rouvroy, traducteur de Frontin et théologien de l'immaculée conception." *BEC* 137 (1979): 19–58.

Schreiner, K. "Laienbildung als Herausforderung für Kirche und Gesellschaft. Religiöse Vorbehalte und soziale Widerstände gegen die Verbreitung von Wissen im späten Mittelalter und in der Reformation." *Zeitschrift für Historische Forschung* 11 (1984): 257–354.

Smahel, F. *La révolution hussite, une anomalie historique.* Paris, 1985.

Sustrac, C. "Les Célestins de France. Essai sur leur histoire et leurs constitutions (1300–1789)." *PTEC,* 1899, pp. 137–47.

Thomas, A. *De Joannis de Monsterolio vita et operibus.* Paris, 1883.

Thomas, H. *Deutsche Geschichte des Spätmittelalters, 1250–1500.* Stuttgart, 1983.

Tisset, P. *Procès de condamnation de Jeanne d'Arc.* Vol. 2: *Traduction et notes,* by Pierre Tisset. Paris, 1970.

Tschackert, P. *Peter von Ailli (Petrus de Alliaco). Zur Geschichte des grossen abendländischen Schisma und der Reformconcilien von Pisa und Constanz.* Gotha, 1877.

Valois, N. *La France et le Grand Schisme d'Occident.* 4 vols. Paris, 1896–1902.

———. "Un ouvrage inédit de Pierre d'Ailly, le *De Persecutionibus Ecclesiae.*" *BEC* 65 (1904): 557–74.

Verger, J. *Les Universités au Moyen Age.* Paris, 1973.

Chapter 4: Thomas Basin

Primary

Basin, Thomas. *Apologie ou plaidoyer pour moi-même,* ed. and trans. C. Samaran and G. de Groër. Paris, 1974.

———. *Histoire de Charles VII,* ed. and trans. C. Samaran. 2 vols. Paris, 1933–44.

———. *Histoire de Louis XI,* ed. and trans. C. Samaran. 3 vols. Paris, 1963–72.

———. *Histoire des règnes de Charles VII et de Louis XI,* ed. J. Quicherat. 4 vols. Paris, 1855–59.

Blondel, Robert. *Oeuvres,* ed. A. Héron. 2 vols. Rouen, 1891–93.

Bouvier, Gilles le, known as the Berry Herald. *Les chroniques du roi Charles VII,* ed. H. Courteault, L. Celier, and M.-H. Jullien de Pommerol. Paris, 1979.

Chartier, Jean. *Chronique de Charles VII, roi de France,* ed. Vallet de Viriville. 3 vols. Paris, 1958.

Cicero. "On Old Age," "On Friendship," "On Duties."

Clamanges, Nicolas de. *Epistolae,* ed. J. Lydius. Leyden, 1613.

Commynes, Philippe de. *Mémoires,* ed. J. Calmette. 3 vols. Paris, 1924–25.

Escouchy, Mathieu d'. *Chronique,* ed. G. Du Fresne de Beaucourt. 3 vols. Paris, 1863–64.

Journal d'un Bourgeois de Paris, 1405–1449, ed. A. Tuetey. Paris, 1881.

Louis XI. *Lettres*, ed. J. Vaesen and E. Charavay. 11 vols. Paris, 1885–1909.

Montreuil, Jean de. *Opera*, ed. E. Ornato, N. Grévy-Pons, G. Ouy. 4 vols. Turin, 1963–75 and Paris, 1981–86.

Secondary

Allmand, C. T. "Local Reaction to the French Reconquest of Normandy: the Case of Rouen." *The Crown and Local Communities in England and France in the Fifteenth Century*, ed. J. R. L. Highfield and R. Jeffs. Gloucester, 1981, pp. 146–61.

———. *Lancastrian Normandy, 1415–1450. The History of a Medieval Occupation*. Oxford, 1983.

Beaune, C. *Naissance de la nation France*. Paris, 1985.

Bernus, P. "Le rôle politique de Pierre de Brézé au cours des dix dernières années du règne de Charles VII (1451–1461)." *BEC* 69 (1908): 303–47.

Bois, G. *Crise du féodalisme. Economie rurale et démographie en Normandie orientale du début du XIVe siècle au milieu du XVIe siècle*. Paris, 1976.

Boüard, M. de. "Quelques données nouvelles sur la création de l'université de Caen (1432–1436." *Le Moyen Age* 69 (1963): 727–41.

Cagé, C. "Louis de Luxembourg, comte de Saint-Pol, connétable de France, 1418–1475." *PTEC*, 1885, pp. 29–41.

Coville, A. *Les premiers Valois et la guerre de Cent Ans (1328–1422)*. Paris, 1902. (Vol. 4 of E. Lavisse, *Histoire de France*.)

Denifle, H. *La désolation des églises, monastères, hôpitaux en France vers le milieu du XVe siècle*. Vol. 1. Macon, 1897.

Du Fresne de Beaucourt, G. *Histoire de Charles VII*. 6 vols. Paris, 1881–91.

Foffano, T. "Umanisti italiani in Normandia nel secolo XV." *Rinascimento*, ser. 2, vol. 4 (1964), pp. 3–34.

Gaussin, P.-R. *Louis XI, un roi entre deux mondes*. Paris, 1976.

Gill, J. *Constance et Bâle-Florence*. Paris, 1965 (Histoire des conciles oecuméniques, 9).

Groër, G. de. "La formation de Thomas Basin en Italie et le début de sa carrière." *BEC* 142 (1984): 271–85.

Guenée, B. *Histoire et culture historique dans l'Occident médiéval*. Paris, 1980.

———. *Politique et histoire au Moyen Age. Recueil d'articles sur l'histoire politique et l'historiographie médiévales (1956–1981)*. Paris, 1981.

———. "Histoire et chronique. Nouvelles réflexions sur les genres historiques au Moyen Age," *La chronique et l'histoire au Moyen Age*, ed. D. Poirion. Paris, 1984, pp. 3–12.

———. "L'historien et la compilation au XIIIe siècle." *Journal des savants*, 1985, pp. 119–35.

Guenée, S. *Les universités françaises des origines à la Révolution. Notices historiques*. Paris, 1982.

Hassell, J. W., Jr. *Middle French Proverbs, Sentences and Proverbial Phrases*. Toronto, 1982.

Histoire du Havre et de l'estuaire de la Seine, ed. A. Corvisier. Toulouse, 1983.

Jouet, R. *La résistance à l'occupation anglaise en Basse-Normandie (1418–1450).* Caen, 1969.

Krynen, J. "'Le mort saisit le vif.' Genèse médiévale du principe d'instantanéité de la succession royale française." *Journal des savants,* 1984, pp. 187–221.

La Chenaye-Desbois, F. A. Aubert de, and Badier, *Dictionnaire de la noblesse.* 2d ed. 15 vols. Paris, 1770–86.

Lapeyre, A., and R. Scheurer. *Les notaires et secrétaires du roi sous les règnes de Louis XI, Charles VIII et Louis XII (1461–1515). Notices personnelles et généalogies.* 2. vols. Paris, 1978.

Legaui, A. "Emeutes et troubles d'origine fiscale pendant le règne de Louis XI." *Le Moyen Age* 73 (1967): 447–387.

Le Noir, Dom. *Preuves généalogiques et historiques de la maison de Harcourt.* Paris, 1907.

Martène, E., and U. Durand. *Thesaurus novus anecdotorum.* 5 vols. Paris, 1717.

Marzi, D. *La questione della riforma del calendario nel quinto concilio Lateranense (1512–1517).* Florence, 1896.

Maurice, A. *Un grand patriote. Thomas Basin, évêque de Lisieux, né à Caudebec-en-Caux (Seine-Inf.) (1412–1391).* Dieppe, 1953.

Muller, H. "Lyon et le concile de Bâle (1431–1449). Etudes prosopographiques." *Cahiers d'histoire* 28 (1983): 33–57.

Ornato, E. *Jean Muret et ses amis, Nicolas de Clamanges et Jean de Montreuil. Contribution à l'étude des rapports entre les humanistes de Paris et ceux d'Avignon (1394–1420).* Geneva-Paris, 1969.

Ourliac, P. "Le concordat de 1472. Etude sur les rapports de Louis XI et de Sixte IV." *Etudes d'histoire du droit médiéval.* Vol. 1. Paris, 1979, pp. 399–489.

Ouy, G. "Le songe et les ambitions d'un jeune humaniste parisien vers 1395. (Une épître latine inconnue de Jean Lebègue à Pierre Lorfèvre, chancelier de Louis d'Orléans, lui demandant la main de sa fille Catherine. Ms. Paris, B.N. Lat. 10400, fols. 30–35)," *Miscellanea di Studi e Ricerche sul Quattrocento francese,* ed. F. Simone, 1966, pp. 357–407.

Paravicini, W. "Peur, pratiques, intelligences, Formes de l'opposition aristocratique à Louis XI d'après les interrogatoires du connétable de Saint-Pol." *La France de la fin du XVe siècle. Renouveau et apogée,* ed. B. Chevalier and P. Contamine. Paris, 1985, pp. 183–96.

Pernoud, R. *Vie et mort de Jeanne d'Arc. Les témoignages du procès de réhabilitation, 1450–1456.* Paris, 1953.

Petit-Dutaillis, C. *Charles VII, Louis XI et les premières années de Charles VIII (1422–1492).* Paris, 1902. (Volume 4, part 2 of E. Lavisse, *Histoire de France.*)

Prentout, H. *Les Etats provinciaux de Normandie.* 3 vols. Paris, 1925–27.

Procès de condamnation de Jeanne d'Arc, ed. P. Tisset. 2 vols. Paris, 1960–71.

Procès en nullité de la condamnation de Jeanne d'Arc, ed. P. Duparc. 4 vols. Paris, 1977–86.

Rashdall, H. *The Universities of Europe in the Middle Ages.* New edition, ed. F. M. Powicke and A. D. Emden. 3 vols. Oxford, 1936.

Samaran, C. "Documents inédits sur la jeunesse de Thomas Basin." *BEC* 94 (1935): 46–57.

Santoni, P. "Jean de Rouvroy, traducteur de Frontin et théologien de l'immaculée conception." *BEC* 137 (1979): 19–58.

Stein, H. *Charles de France, frère de Louis XI.* Paris, 1921.

Thorndike, L. *A History of Magic and Experimental Science.* Vol. 4. New York, 1934.

Vallez. A. "La construction du comté d'Alençon (1269–1380). Essai de géographie historique." *Annales de Normandie* 22 (1972): 11–45.

Valois, N. *Histoire de la Pragmatique Sanction de Bourges sous Charles VII.* Paris, 1906.

INDEX